CW01338463

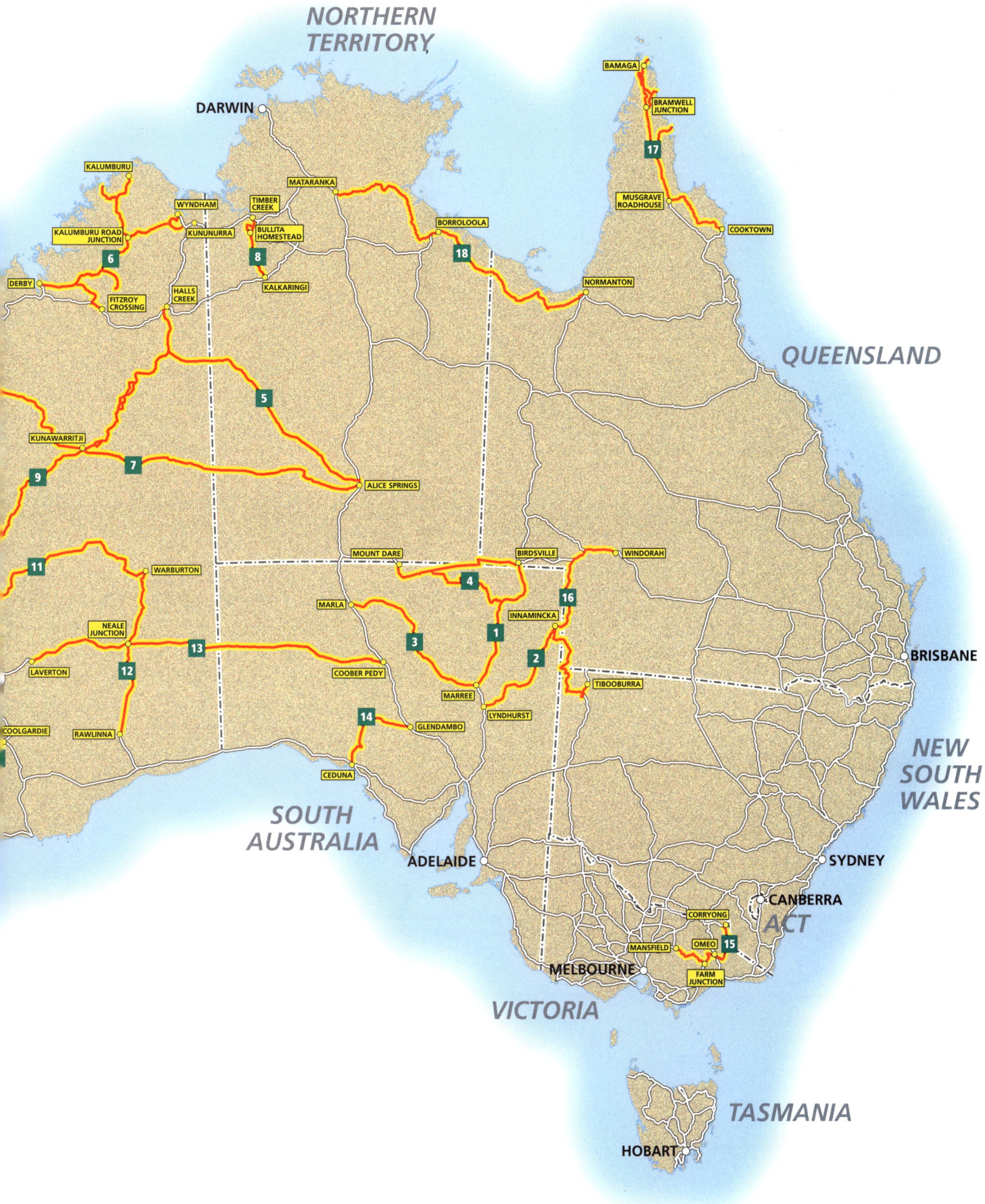
NORTHERN TERRITORY
DARWIN
KALUMBURU
WYNDHAM
TIMBER CREEK
MATARANKA
KALUMBURU ROAD JUNCTION
KUNUNURRA
BULLITA HOMESTEAD
BORROLOOLA
6
8
18
DERBY
KALKARINGI
FITZROY CROSSING
HALLS CREEK
5
KUNAWARRITJI
7
9
ALICE SPRINGS
11
WARBURTON
MOUNT DARE
BIRDSVILLE
WINDORAH
4
16
MARLA
INNAMINCKA
NEALE JUNCTION
3
1
13
2
LAVERTON
12
COOBER PEDY
MARREE
TIBOOBURRA
LYNDHURST
14
GLENDAMBO
COOLGARDIE
RAWLINNA
CEDUNA
SOUTH AUSTRALIA
ADELAIDE
BAMAGA
BRAMWELL JUNCTION
17
MUSGRAVE ROADHOUSE
COOKTOWN
NORMANTON
QUEENSLAND
BRISBANE
NEW SOUTH WALES
SYDNEY
CANBERRA
ACT
CORRYONG
MANSFIELD
OMEO
15
MELBOURNE
FARM JUNCTION
VICTORIA
TASMANIA
HOBART

Explore Australia by 4WD

Adventure Treks

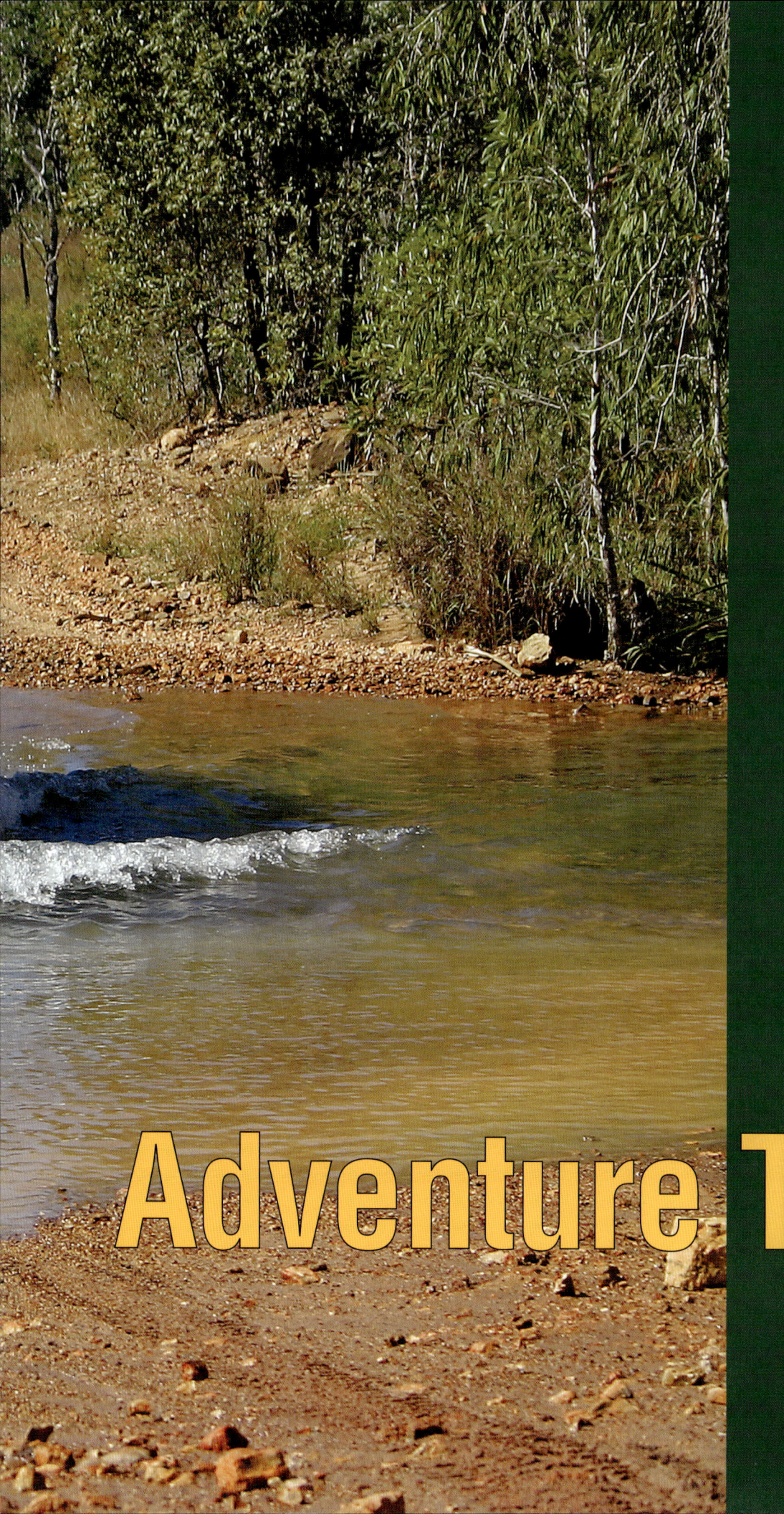

Explore Australia by 4WD

Adventure Treks

Contents

How to Use this Book	viii
Authors' Note	xvi

Adventure Treks — 1

Birdsville Track — 2
Marree to Birdsville — 4

Strzelecki Track — 10
Lyndhurst to Innamincka — 12

Oodnadatta Track — 20
Marree to Marla — 22

Simpson Desert — 30
Mount Dare to Birdsville — 32

Tanami Road — 46
Alice Springs to Halls Creek — 48

Kimberley Grand Tour	56
Kununurra to Kalumburu Road Junction	58
Kalumburu Road Junction to Kalumburu	66
Kalumburu Road Junction to Derby	73
Ocean to Alice	84
Eighty Mile Beach to Kunawarritji	86
Kunawarritji to Alice Springs	90
Gregory National Park	100
Timber Creek to Bullita Homestead	102
Bullita Homestead to Kalkaringi	107
Canning Stock Route	118
Wiluna to Kunawarritji	120
Kunawarritji to Halls Creek	139
Holland Track	156
Hyden to Coolgardie	158

Gunbarrel Highway	166	**Googs Track**	202
Warburton to Wiluna	168	Ceduna to Glendambo	204
Connie Sue Highway	176	**Victoria's High Country**	212
Warburton to Rawlinna	178	Corryong to Omeo	214
Anne Beadell Highway	186	Omeo to Farm Junction	224
Coober Pedy to Neale Junction	188	Farm Junction to Mansfield	230
Neale Junction to Laverton	198	**Corner Country**	240
		Tibooburra to Innamincka	242
		Innamincka to Windorah	254

Cape York Peninsula   262

  Cooktown to Musgrave Roadhouse   264

  Musgrave Roadhouse to Bramwell Junction   275

  Bramwell Junction to Bamaga   286

Across the Gulf   302

  Normanton to Borroloola   304

  Borroloola to Mataranka   314

Making the Most of Your Trip   322

Road Atlas   344

Index   362

Acknowledgements   380

How to Use this Book

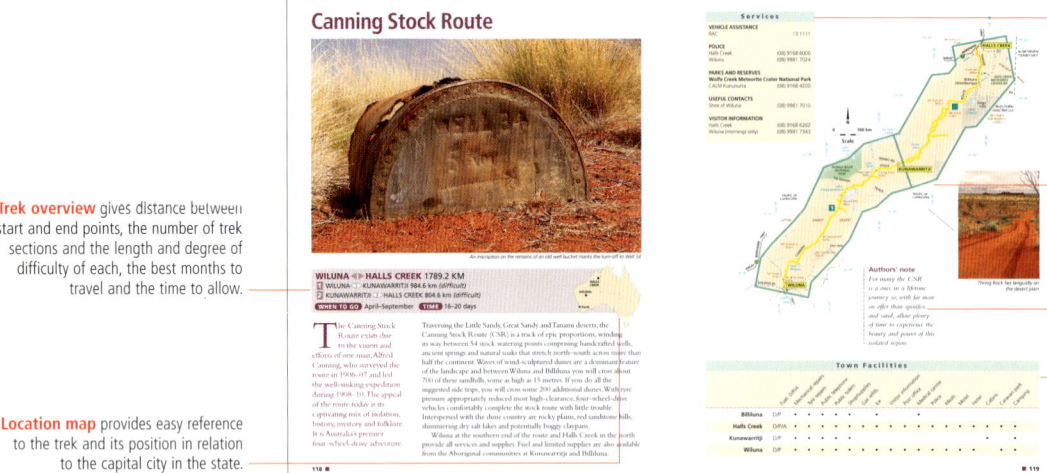

Trek overview gives distance between start and end points, the number of trek sections and the length and degree of difficulty of each, the best months to travel and the time to allow.

Location map provides easy reference to the trek and its position in relation to the capital city in the state.

Services table lists contact numbers for vehicle assistance, police, national park offices and reserves, visitor information centres and other useful organisations – in towns along the route.

Overview map depicts the trek section breakdown and the start and end points of each section.

Authors' note gives advice ranging from tips on what to see and do to specific hints on getting the best out of the trek.

Town Facilities table indicates services available in each town along the route, from fuel and vehicle repairs to shops, medical facilities and the range of accommodation.

Heading gives start and end points of the trek section and kilometre distance between the start and end points (excluding any optional or alternative routes).

Road atlas reference refers you to the trek start point location in the comprehensive road map section in the back of the book.

Total distance includes route-directed side trips but excludes any optional or alternative routes unless specified.

Longest distance no PD gives the longest kilometre distance between fuelling stops, including all side trips and optional detours in between.

Advice and warnings details local information for safe travel, seasonal road conditions and closures, road condition hotlines and camping restrictions.

Inset map shows the location of the trek section within the state and the position of the capital city.

Description offers advice on terrain and road conditions, trek highlights, leisure activities and places of historic interest.

Other useful information lists roadhouses/shops in remote areas, with contact details, opening hours, fuel and supplies available, and also suggests informative visitor brochures and other publications.

Permits and bookings specifies permits required and contact points for obtaining permits and booking campsites and other accommodation. Pay special attention to the advice as you may need to act on the information well in advance.

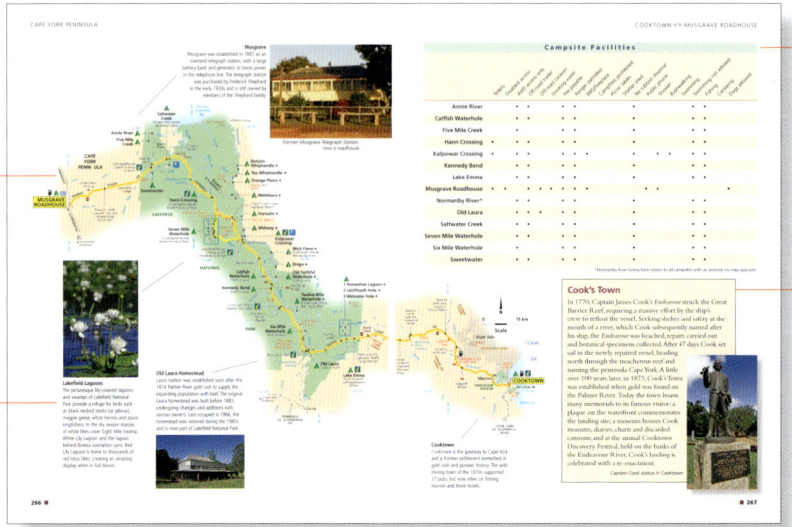

Trek route maps produced from field data provide the latest information available on tracks and roads, give a guide to features en route including fuel stops, campsites, national parks and reserves, scenic highlights, historic monuments and tourist attractions. Map symbols are explained on the cover flaps (softcover edition) and opposite the first page of the book (hardback edition).

Places of interest are illustrated by photographs and informative text.

Campsite Facilities table lists recommended campsites, located on the map and highlighted in the route directions, and indicates the range of facilities available at each site. Generally, campgrounds in towns at the start/end of a trek are not listed, particularly if they are large centres with wide-ranging facilities.

Anecdotes and history boxes describe some of the trials, tragedies and humorous episodes experienced along the track by the authors, and earlier explorers and adventurers.

viii

Cumulative trip meter readings are given in black type (forward directions) and blue type (reverse directions). Abbreviations in the text are explained on the cover flaps (softcover edition) and opposite the first page of the book (hardback edition). Signposted information (preceded by SP:) is given exactly as it appears on the signpost regardless of spelling (for ease of identification when in the field).

Intermediate trip meter readings appears in red type within brackets and is the distance travelled between cumulative readings. Be aware that trip meter readings vary slightly from vehicle to vehicle.

Additional information briefly describes camping areas (highlighted in bold type) listed in the Campsite Facilities table and offers notes on destination of sidetracks and roads, accurate kilometre distances where signposted information is incorrect, historical facts, details on flora and fauna and other points of interest.

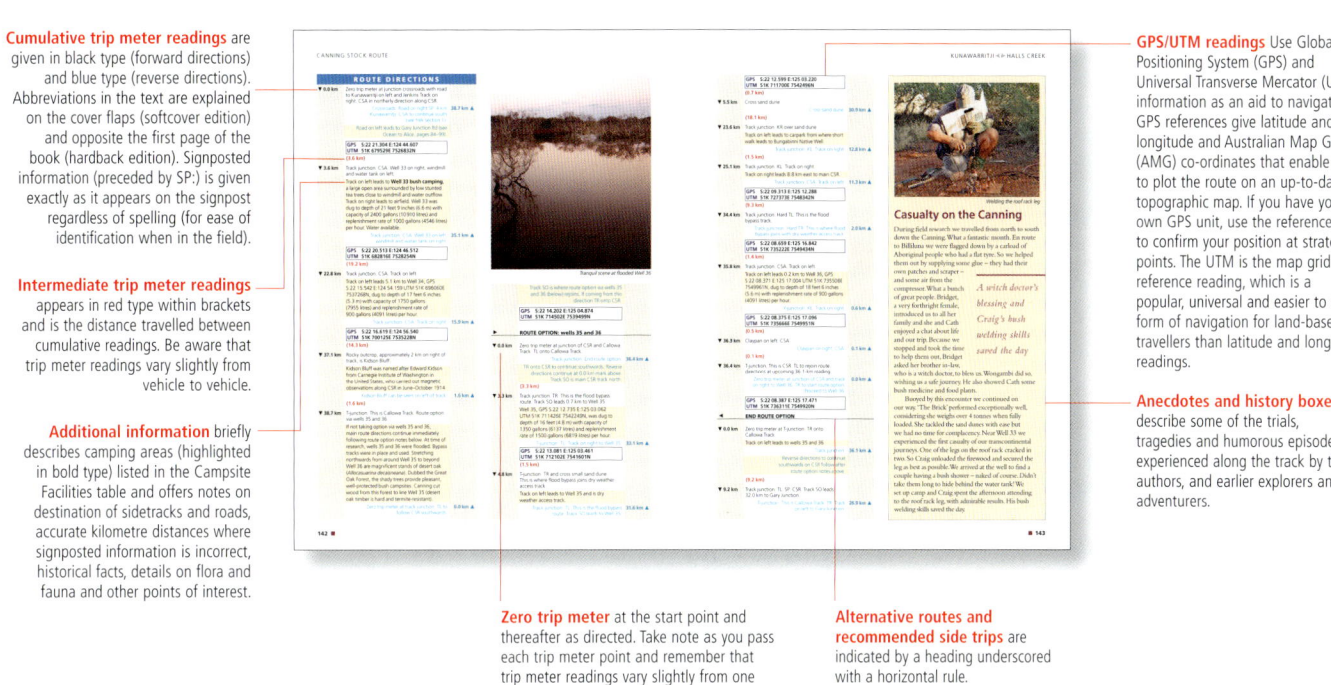

Zero trip meter at the start point and thereafter as directed. Take note as you pass each trip meter point and remember that trip meter readings vary slightly from one vehicle to another.

Alternative routes and recommended side trips are indicated by a heading underscored with a horizontal rule.

GPS/UTM readings Use Global Positioning System (GPS) and Universal Transverse Mercator (UTM) information as an aid to navigation. GPS references give latitude and longitude and Australian Map Grid (AMG) co-ordinates that enable you to plot the route on an up-to-date topographic map. If you have your own GPS unit, use the references to confirm your position at strategic points. The UTM is the map grid reference reading, which is a popular, universal and easier to use form of navigation for land-based travellers than latitude and longitude readings.

Anecdotes and history boxes describe some of the trials, tragedies and humorous episodes experienced along the track by the authors, and earlier explorers and adventurers.

Note: *Use the degree of difficulty rating for each trek as an initial guide but note that track conditions vary depending on the weather, the level of usage and maintenance. Roads can and do change. Four-wheel-drive tracks can alter from time to time, as people diverge to avoid bad patches. Sometimes it may be necessary for authorities to close a track for safety or conservation reasons. Road maintenance and development is ongoing. In some cases the road surface may have been improved or the road realigned since the route directions were compiled.*

Inter-city routes list distances and main route numbers between capital cities.

Trek routes are shown in red and highlighted in yellow in the same style as the trek route maps.

Warning panels offer advice on outback travel.

Contents panel provides a quick guide to the treks that are covered in this map and the relevant page numbers for the corresponding text.

Start/end points locate the start and end point of each trek section.

MAKING THE MOST OF YOUR TRIP
Turn to this section for trip-planning advice, technical know-how, survival hints and general contact details.

INDEX
An extensive index on page 362 includes all town names, camping areas, outback stations and homesteads, national parks and reserves, roadhouses and tracks and roads, which are mentioned in the text.

ix

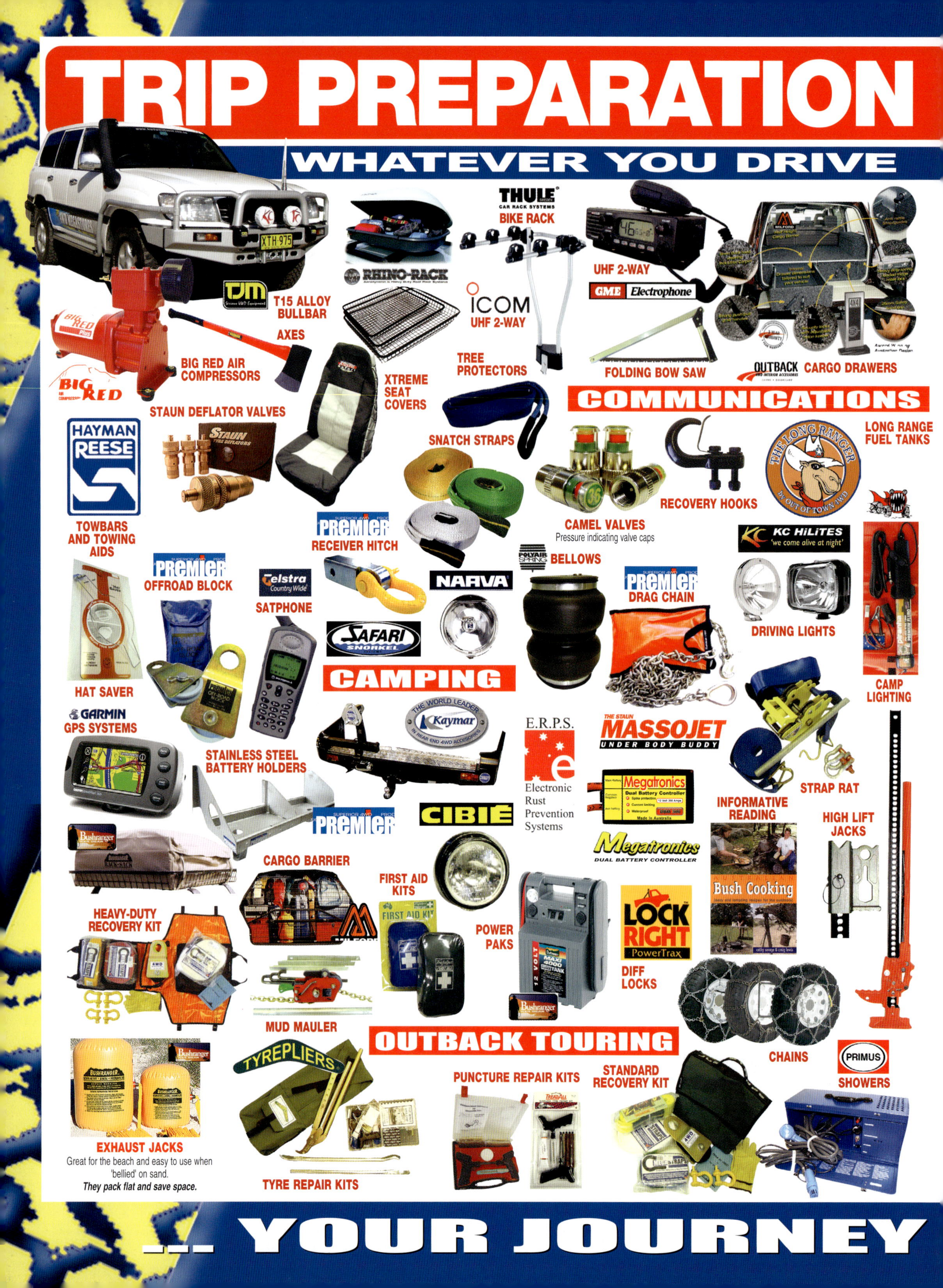

TRIP PREPARATION
WHATEVER YOU DRIVE
TJM
T15 ALLOY BULLBAR
BIG RED AIR COMPRESSORS
BIG RED
AXES
RHINO-RACK
THULE
BIKE RACK
ICOM
UHF 2-WAY
TREE PROTECTORS
UHF 2-WAY
GME Electrophone
FOLDING BOW SAW
OUTBACK
CARGO DRAWERS
XTREME SEAT COVERS
STAUN DEFLATOR VALVES
COMMUNICATIONS
HAYMAN REESE
TOWBARS AND TOWING AIDS
SNATCH STRAPS
CAMEL VALVES
Pressure indicating valve caps
RECOVERY HOOKS
THE LONG RANGER BY OUT OF TOWN 4WD
LONG RANGE FUEL TANKS
PREMIER
RECEIVER HITCH
KC HiLiTES 'we come alive at night'
PREMIER
OFFROAD BLOCK
Telstra Country Wide
SATPHONE
NARVA
POLYAIR SPRINGS
BELLOWS
PREMIER
DRAG CHAIN
DRIVING LIGHTS
SAFARI SNORKEL
CAMPING
CAMP LIGHTING
HAT SAVER
GARMIN
GPS SYSTEMS
Kaymar
E.R.P.S.
Electronic Rust Prevention Systems
THE STAUN MASSOJET UNDER BODY BUDDY
STAINLESS STEEL BATTERY HOLDERS
STRAP RAT
Megatronics
Dual Battery Controller
INFORMATIVE READING
HIGH LIFT JACKS
PREMIER
CIBIE
Megatronics
DUAL BATTERY CONTROLLER
Bush Cooking
Bushranger
CARGO BARRIER
FIRST AID KITS
POWER PAKS
LOCK RIGHT PowerTrax
HEAVY-DUTY RECOVERY KIT
DIFF LOCKS
MUD MAULER
OUTBACK TOURING
CHAINS
PRIMUS
SHOWERS
TYREPLIERS
PUNCTURE REPAIR KITS
STANDARD RECOVERY KIT
EXHAUST JACKS
Great for the beach and easy to use when 'bellied' on sand.
They pack flat and save space.
TYRE REPAIR KITS
... YOUR JOURNEY

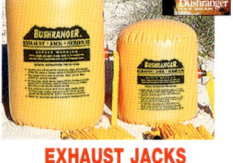

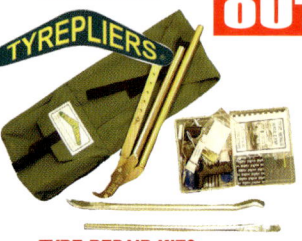

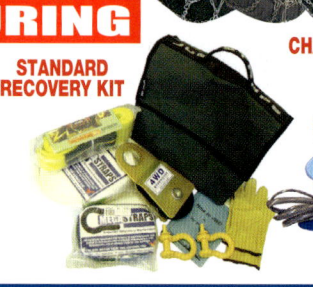

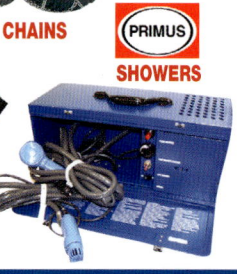

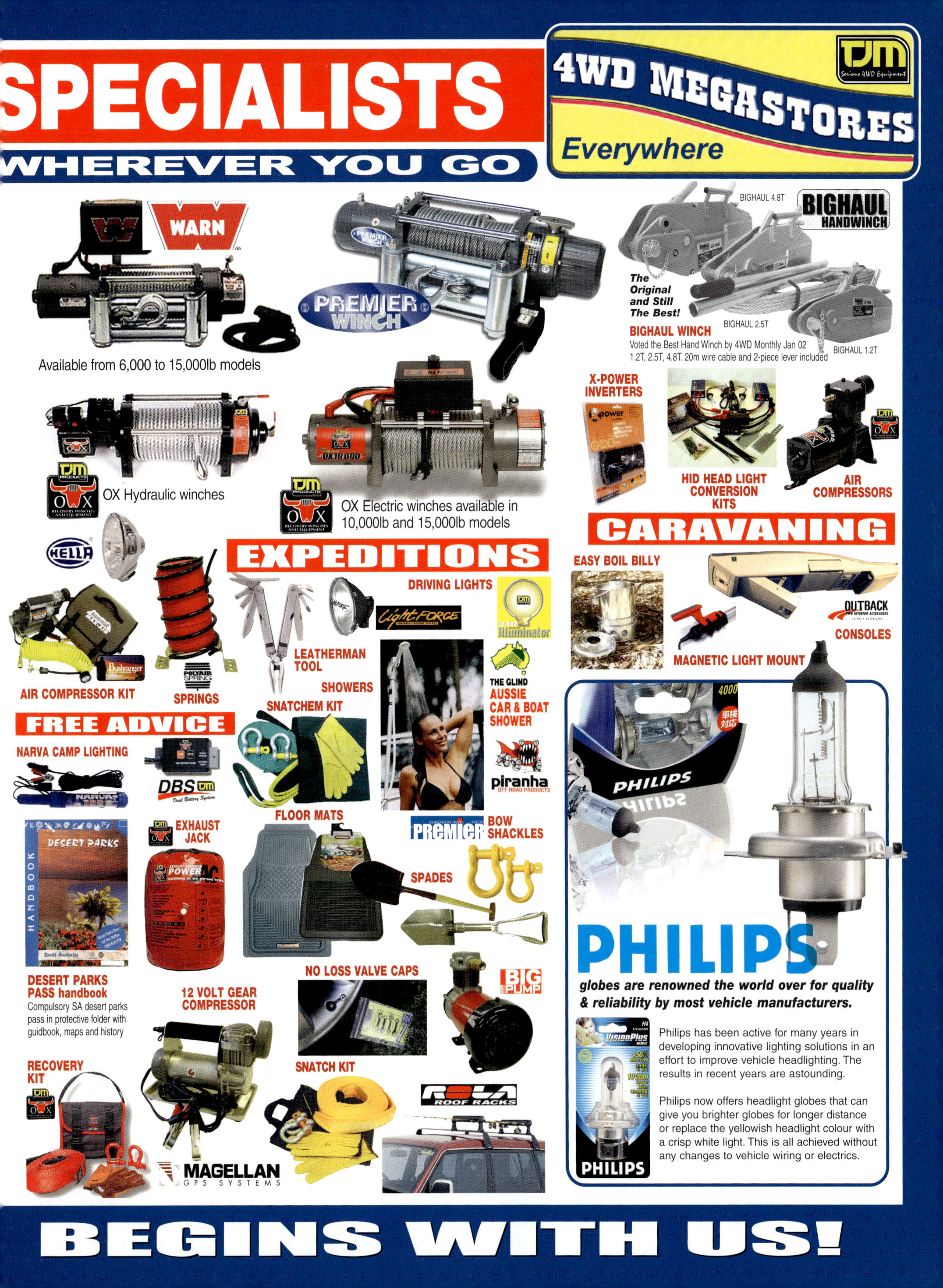

SPECIALISTS
WHEREVER YOU GO
4WD MEGASTORES
Everywhere
TJM Serious 4WD Equipment
WARN
Available from 6,000 to 15,000lb models
PREMIER WINCH
BIGHAUL HANDWINCH
BIGHAUL 4.8T
The Original and Still The Best!
BIGHAUL 2.5T
BIGHAUL WINCH
Voted the Best Hand Winch by 4WD Monthly Jan 02
1.2T, 2.5T, 4.8T. 20m wire cable and 2-piece lever included
BIGHAUL 1.2T
OX Hydraulic winches
OX Electric winches available in 10,000lb and 15,000lb models
X-POWER INVERTERS
HID HEAD LIGHT CONVERSION KITS
AIR COMPRESSORS
CARAVANING
EASY BOIL BILLY
OUTBACK
CONSOLES
MAGNETIC LIGHT MOUNT
HELLA
EXPEDITIONS
DRIVING LIGHTS
Light FORCE
210 Illuminator
AIR COMPRESSOR KIT
SPRINGS
POLYAIR SPRING
LEATHERMAN TOOL
SHOWERS
THE GLIND AUSSIE CAR & BOAT SHOWER
SNATCHEM KIT
FREE ADVICE
NARVA CAMP LIGHTING
DBS TJM Dual Battery System
piranha OFF ROAD PRODUCTS
PHILIPS
FLOOR MATS
EXHAUST JACK
PREMIER
BOW SHACKLES
SPADES
DESERT PARKS
HANDBOOK
DESERT PARKS PASS handbook
Compulsory SA desert parks pass in protective folder with guidbook, maps and history
12 VOLT GEAR COMPRESSOR
NO LOSS VALVE CAPS
BIG PUMP
PHILIPS
globes are renowned the world over for quality & reliability by most vehicle manufacturers.
Philips has been active for many years in developing innovative lighting solutions in an effort to improve vehicle headlighting. The results in recent years are astounding.
Philips now offers headlight globes that can give you brighter globes for longer distance or replace the yellowish headlight colour with a crisp white light. This is all achieved without any changes to vehicle wiring or electrics.
VisionPlus
RECOVERY KIT
SNATCH KIT
RoLA ROOF RACKS
MAGELLAN GPS SYSTEMS
BEGINS WITH US!

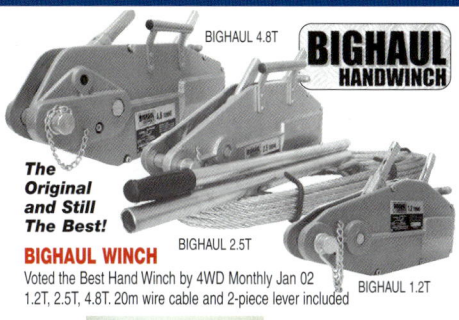

FOR YOUR 4WD
4WD MEGASTORES – where

Hella Australia Pty Ltd

Automotive Lighting and Accessories

Jumbo 320 FF Series

Jumbo 320 FF Driving Lamp
fitted with high-performance H7 65W halogen globe for maximum light output
Part No. 1318

Jumbo 320 FF Fog Lamp
featuring innovative clear glass optic and globe shield for exceptional fog penetration.
Part No. 1118

Jumbo 320 FF Blue Driving Lamp
successfully combines powerful lighting performance with modern 'Cool Blue' design.
Part No. 1318BLUE

Jumbo 320 FF Xenon Driving Lamp
utilising outstanding Xenon Lighting Technology and high-performance LED Position Light.
Part No. 1319
Part No. 1319-24V

 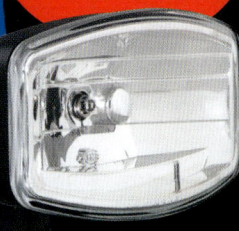  

Clear Protective Covers are available for all models

Available now from all Hella Distributors Australia-wide

Hella Australia Pty Ltd
Hella Customer Service: 1800 061 729
custservice@ha.hella.com.au
www.hella.com.au

Ideas today for the cars of tomorrow

& FOR YOU!
your journey begins!

WAECO
mobile solutions

Mobile Fridge Freezers to suit all application and vehicles

CF-40 AC
NOW WITH 240 VOLTS AC BUILT IN

High Performance, Low Power Consumption

Current draw: 1.0 amp average cycling at 1°C in 32°C ambient. No other product tested ran at lower amps.
Battery protection: 3 stage battery protection earned the title of best model tested for a single-battery set-up.
Weight: 16.8 kg
Capacity: 40 Litres
Dimensions: W360 x H445 x L580 mm (L710 with handles)
Power Source: 12/ 24/240 Volts
Cooling Capacity: 50°C below ambient
Kompressor: German made Danfoss BD-35F

CF-80
FRIDGE/ REEZER/ DAIRY. IT'S ALL IN HERE

Separate refrigerator, freezer and dairy compartments make it easy!

Weight: 23 kg
Capacity: 82 Litres
Dimensions: W503 x H454 x L940 mm (with handles)
Power Source: 12/24 Volts
Cooling Capacity: Up to 50°C below ambient
Insulation: 50mm solid polyurethane foam
Kompressor: German made Danfoss BD-50F

TC-21FL
12 V, 24 V OR 240 V MAINS - YOU CHOOSE

LED read-out and memory function are all award winning features of the TC-FL range. The convenience standards of mobile refrigeration have once again been redefined.
Weight: 6 kg approx.
Capacity: 21 Litres
Dimensions: W303 x H420 x L450 mm
Power Source: 12V DC, 24V DC or 240V AC
Cooling Capacity: Up to 30°C below ambient to 1°C minimum
Warming Capacity: Up to 65°C

TB-08
PERFECT FIT COOLERS FOR YOUR CAR

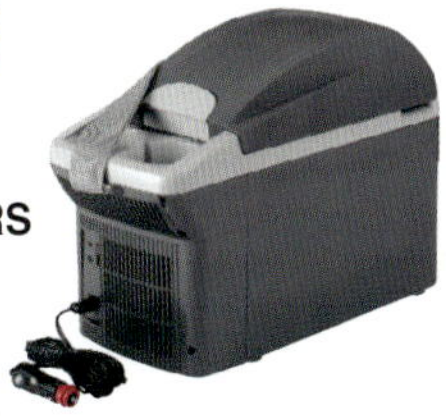

Lightweight simple to carry with astonishing cooling capacity of up to 20°C below the ambient (room) temperature. WAECO's TB-08 is equipped with wear-free and maintenance-free technology and can be used for both cooling and heating.
Weight: 3.2 kg
Capacity: 8 Litres
Dimensions: W200 x H298 x L442 mm
Power Source: 12 Volts
Cooling Capacity: Up to 20°C below ambient Cold/Warm Switch

CoolPower 36
ELIMINATE ALL FRIDGE POWER PROBLEMS

The WAECO CoolPower 36, specifically designed to run fridges, has all the features of a dual battery system normally fitted permanently into 4WD's
Model: RAPS 36
- Heavy duty 12 volt remote power
- 36 amp hours
- Dimensions: W230 x H245 x D227 mm
- Genuine deep cycle AGM battery cells
- Cigarette and hella output sockets
- Digital volts display
- Battery condition LED's/test button
- Secure screw connection charging socket
- 2.4 m charging lead
- Maximum charging current: 14.4A

RAPS-12R-U
UNIVERSAL FAST CHARGE KIT

Heavy duty to suit all WAECO Kompressor Fridge/Freezers.
- Stylish design for internal mounting in the rear of your vehicle
- 6 metres of heavy duty 6 mm cable
- Switchable between constant power for running your portable fridge and on/off with ignition for battery charging
- Flush style rocker switch to reduce risk of accidental operation
- Choice of socket-heavy duty hella style and cigarette type both built in
- Fuse and installation kit

4WD MEGASTORES
Everywhere

Call in and see our friendly staff at a location near you

NEW SOUTH WALES
1/12 Garling Rd, Kings Park BLACKTOWN	02 9622 1000
56 Chard Rd, BROOKVALE	02 9905 5520
2/116, Old Bathurst Rd, EMU PLAINS	02 4735 6691
18 James St, HORNSBY	02 9477 5528
6/3 Yarmouth Pl, NARELLAN	02 4647 1277
37 Peisley St, ORANGE	02 6361 7999
44 Crescent St, TAREE	02 6551 2479

QUEENSLAND
Cnr South Pine & Kremzow Rds, BRENDALE	07 3889 8555
959 Beaudesert Rd, COOPERS PLAINS	07 3277 8255
108 Pickering St, ENOGGERA	07 3855 4444
75 Moss St, SLACKS CREEK	07 3208 7811
221 Scott St, Bungalow CAIRNS	07 4033 7933
95 Gordon St, MACKAY	07 4957 3886
100 Sugar Rd, MAROOCHYDORE	07 5451 1155
17 Simpson St, MOUNT ISA	07 4749 0650
212 Denison St, ROCKHAMPTON	07 4927 6844
55-63 Dalrymple Rd, Garbutt TOWNSVILLE	07 4775 3033

VICTORIA
683 Sydney Rd, COBURG	03 9354 1116
166 Princes Hwy, DANDENONG	03 9792 1116
422 Sutton St, BALLARAT	03 5335 9777
27-29 Baldwin Ave, NORTH GEELONG	03 5277 1444
196 Argyle St, TRARALGON	03 5176 6666

AUSTRALIAN CAPITAL TERRITORY
87 Grimwade St, MITCHELL	02 6241 8161

SOUTH AUSTRALIA
163 Main North Rd, NAILSWORTH	08 8344 6444

WESTERN AUSTRALIA
44-46 Frobisher St, OSBORNE PARK	08 9443 4848

TASMANIA
120 Campbell St, HOBART	03 6238 0380
33 Strahan St, BURNIE	03 6430 2888

NORTHERN TERRITORY
2/498 Stuart Highway, Winnellie DARWIN	08 8984 4926

www.4wdmegastores.com.au

tread lightly! Australia
Respect the Environment with your Recreation

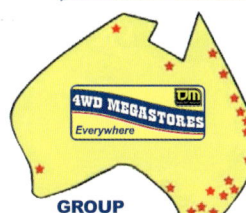

GROUP 4WD MEGASTORE ADMINISTRATION
02 9622 1300

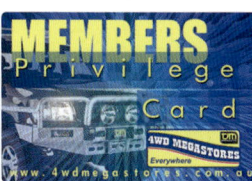

Become a member today and be eligible for "members only" specials and privileges like 5% off Driver Training Courses conducted by Great Divide Tours! It costs nothing to join!
See your local store for details

Tread lightly and look after our 4WD tracks

Can you spot the difference between a good and an outstanding product?

Now you can buy smarter simply by looking out for this seal of approval. Products bearing this seal are proven performers, having been field tested for toughness.

Authors' Note

WHAT AN ADVENTURE! Twenty-five thousand kilometres of four-wheel driving that took in many of the country's classic outback touring destinations. But hey – someone had to do it! And along the way we stumbled across some fantastic characters such as Bruce Farrands of Rabbit Flat, and made some wonderful friends such as the RockVegas crew from Rockhampton. These are the great things about travelling outback Australia: the stunning landscapes, the great people you meet and the wonderful memories you bring away with you.

When we set out in our trusty Land Rover Defender, 'The Brick', we had no idea about the amazing encounters that were to follow. In the course of our travels we experienced two boggings (one in bulldust); an awesome helicopter flight (without doors) over the Kimberley's Mitchell Falls; a swim in the desert; a broken roof rack leg along the Canning Stock Route; an Aboriginal blessing from a medicine man along the Tanami Road; the sight of four naked blokes riding motorbikes on the CSR; millions upon millions of corrugations; a five-day lay-up in a country pub due to rain (unfortunate we hear you say); countless ham sandwiches; the crossing of every Australian desert, including the ascent and descent of 3000 sand dunes; and the odd headache in the morning – must have been something we ate!

All this and more can happen to you, too. Have a read, get inspired, organise some time, prepare your vehicle and follow in our footsteps as we take you on 18 classic four-wheel-drive journeys across the length and breadth of Australia. And to find out more about our travels in 'The Brick', visit the website (www.exploreaustraliaby4wd.com).

Happy travels

Adventure Treks

1	Birdsville Track	2
2	Strzelecki Track	10
3	Oodnadatta Track	20
4	Simpson Desert	30
5	Tanami Road	46
6	Kimberley Grand Tour	56
7	Ocean to Alice	84
8	Gregory National Park	100
9	Canning Stock Route	118
10	Holland Track	156
11	Gunbarrel Highway	166
12	Connie Sue Highway	176
13	Anne Beadell Highway	186
14	Googs Track	202
15	Victoria's High Country	212
16	Corner Country	240
17	Cape York Peninsula	262
18	Across the Gulf	302

Adventure Treks

Birdsville Track

Flat terrain of the Birdsville Track

MARREE ◀▶ BIRDSVILLE 523.6 KM
ONE SECTION ONLY *(easy)*
WHEN TO GO April–October **TIME** 1–2 days

The most famous outback journey in Australia, the legendary Birdsville Track was established in the 1880s as a stock route between south-western Queensland and the railhead at Marree in South Australia, from where cattle could be trucked to the Adelaide markets. During good years as many as 50 000 head walked the track, being watered at a string of waterholes and artesian bores, with some mobs comprising up to 2000 beasts.

These days it takes a day to travel the route that once took drovers and their stock about five weeks, but you are urged to take your time, break up the journey with an overnight camp or two, and absorb some of the history and mystique of this outback adventure. The track cuts through some of Australia's most arid and desolate country, characterised by low rolling sand dunes, meandering outback rivers and creeks, saltbush flats, and vast gibber plains. The road is frequently travelled, and the gravel surface is normally well maintained, but the route can quickly become impassable after rain. The Cooper Creek when in flood – a rare occurrence that cuts the track once every ten to fifteen years – can be crossed by ferry from a bypass track (open only during times of flood) to the east of the Birdsville Track.

Marree, at the southern end of the track, is a tiny settlement with a population of just over a hundred. Surrounded by scraggly saltbush and seemingly in the middle of nowhere, the town nevertheless has a good range of facilities and services for travellers.

Birdsville, the northern destination that gave its name to the stock route, has a population of around 120, which swells to almost 5000 during the annual race meeting in September for which the town is most famous. Most goods and services are available here.

BIRDSVILLE TRACK

Birdsville
Situated on a stony rise above the Diamantina River, the town dates from 1879 when a general store was established for drovers and survey workers. It developed as a customs post to collect a levy on supplies and stock taken over the Queensland–South Australia border. After Federation in 1901 the levy was abolished.

Remains of Royal Hotel (1883)

Services

VEHICLE ASSISTANCE
RAA (SA)/RACQ (Qld)	13 1111
Birdsville Autos*	(07) 4656 3226
*Vehicle recovery service	AH (07) 4656 3254

POLICE
Birdsville	(07) 4656 3220
Marree	(08) 8675 8346

USEFUL CONTACTS
QPWS Birdsville	(07) 4656 3272
SA road report hotline	1300 361 033

VISITOR INFORMATION
Birdsville	(07) 4656 3300
Marree	(08) 8675 8222

Marree
First called Hergott Springs, Marree grew literally overnight when the Ghan railway established its railhead here in 1883. Today, as the start point for travellers along the Oodnadatta and Birdsville tracks, Marree survives on tourism. There are old Ghan engines and information boards on the former railway line.

Authors' note
The once notorious Birdsville Track is a fairly straightforward trip today, but is still one of the country's 'must do' four-wheel-drive touring routes. Synonymous with the outback droving life of the past, it holds a special place in the hearts of Australians.

Town Facilities

	Fuel: D/P/A	Mechanical repairs	Tyre repairs	Public telephone	Public toilets	Shop/supplies	Gas refills	Ice	Visitor information	Post office	Medical centre	Police	Meals	Motel	Hotel	Cabins	Caravan park	Camping
Birdsville	D/P	•	•	•	•	•	•	•	•	•	•	•	•	•	•	•	•	•
Marree	D/P		•	•	•	•	•	•	•	•		•	•	•	•	•	•	•
Mungerannie	D/P		•	•	•	•		•					•		•		•	•

3

MARREE ◀ ▶ BIRDSVILLE 523.6 KM

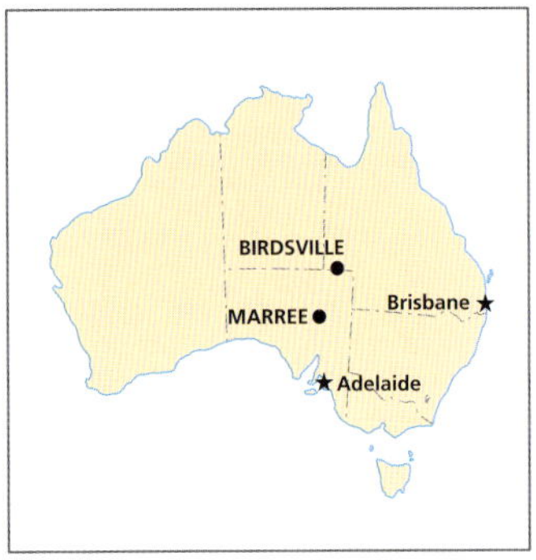

Start point
Marree

Road atlas
348 B1, 353 L3

Total distance
523.6 km

Standard
Easy

Time
1–2 days

Longest distance no PD (includes all options)
319.3 km (Mungerannie to Birdsville)

Topographic maps
Auslig 1:250 000 series: *Marree*; *Kopperanamma*; *Gason*; *Pandie Pandie*; *Cordillo*; *Birdsville*

Other useful information

- Mungerannie Roadhouse open Monday–Saturday 8am–10pm and Sunday 8am–6pm, tel. (08) 8675 8317; accepts cash, EFTPOS and credit cards.
- SA Tourism brochure: *The Kidman Track: The Sidney Kidman Story*.
- SA Tourism booklet: *Discover the Secrets of South Australia: Flinders Ranges & Outback*.
- Local history brochure: *Welcome to Marree: Ghan Town*, available from Marree Tele Centre.
- Kristin Weidenbach's *Mailman of the Birdsville Track: The Story of Tom Kruse* is a delightful and informative read.

Description

For many the remote Birdsville Track is a nostalgic journey that revisits our pioneering past, a reminder of the drovers, mailmen and Afghan cameleers who rode or trod this way in the 19th and early 20th centuries.

Road conditions are reasonably good – the gravel surface is generally well maintained despite some rough sections – but during and after rain the track can become extremely slippery and difficult to negotiate. It is a harsh environment with habitation limited to scattered and remote homesteads, and not all of them close to the track. Wildlife, apart from the birdlife around the artesian bores, consists of rarely sighted snakes, lizards, dingoes and raptors. The Diamantina and Cooper systems are the habitat of the western taipan, one of the most deadly snakes in the world.

Leaving Marree, the track heads north-east. The first place of interest is Lake Harry ruins, the location of a bold but failed attempt to establish a date farm during the early 1900s. A little further north is the Dog Fence, a 5400-kilometre barrier – the longest of its kind in the world – stretching from the Great Australian Bight to New South Wales and Queensland, and constructed to protect sheep from dingoes (see page 207).

The fence marks the end of sheep country and from here to Birdsville the road passes through cattle stations, some of them among the largest in Australia. Along the track are numerous artesian bores, sunk between the late 1890s and 1920 to supply water for stock. The Cooper Creek crossing, which is generally dry, traverses a flood plain approximately 5 kilometres wide. It is a pleasant shady spot to take a break from driving.

A few kilometres beyond the Cooper you cross the Natterannie Sandhills, no longer the formidable obstacle they presented to vehicles in earlier days. During the 1940s, mailman Tom Kruse would sometimes take a day to negotiate this 20-kilometre stretch in his truck. Once past the hills, it is not far to Mungerannie Roadhouse, the only point along the track that offers fuel.

At Lake Howitt saltpan, steaming artesian water from Mirra Mitta Bore flows from a pipe close to the track.

Campsite Facilities

	Toilets	Disabled access	4WD access only	Off-road trailer	Off-road caravan	Drinking water	Fee payable	Ranger patrolled	BBQ/fireplace	Campfires prohibited	Picnic tables	Shelter shed	No rubbish disposal	Public phone	Shower	Bushwalking	Swimming	Swimming not advised	Fishing	Canoeing	Dogs allowed
Clayton Wetlands	•			•	•		•	•	•				•		•						•
Cooper Creek	•			•	•		•						•								•
Tippipilla Creek				•	•								•								•

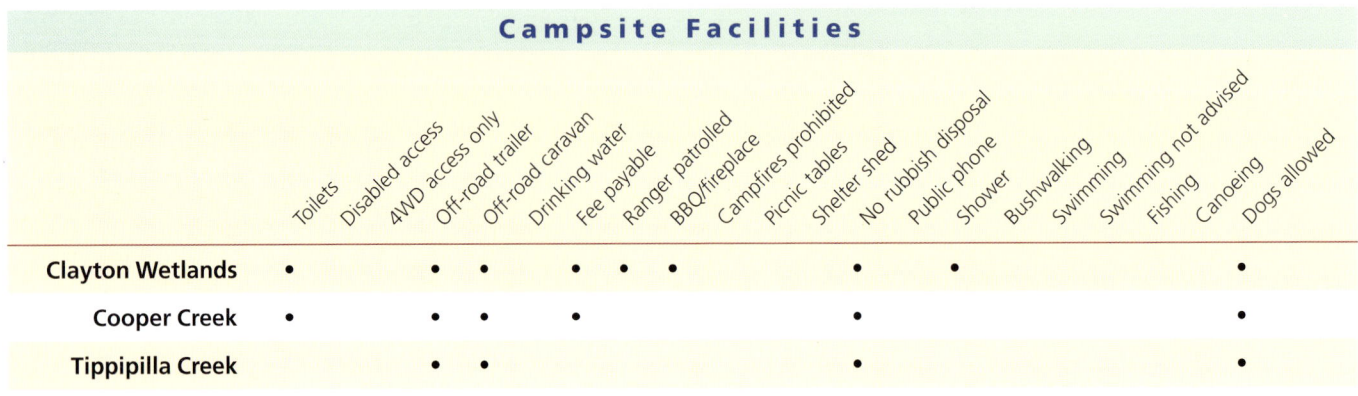

MARREE ◀▶ BIRDSVILLE

Sturt Stony Desert
Characterised by stony plains and immense parallel sand dunes, this desert comprises some of the continent's most desolate country, broken only by a sparse covering of saltbush. This gibber-strewn expanse has claimed the lives of many who attempted to cross its harsh terrain.

Mirra Mitta Bore
Extremely hot artesian water from the bore steadily flows into a depression, creating a fertile wetland in the arid landscape. Brolgas and other birds share the water with cattle from the surrounding pastoral lease.

Cooper Creek
Cooper Creek was forever romanticised for Australians by Banjo Paterson's Clancy of the Overflow, who took off 'down the Cooper where the western drovers go'. The creek traverses Queensland's Channel Country, crosses into South Australia and on rare occasions carries floodwaters as far as Lake Eyre. At the track crossing, the creek is lined with coolibahs and river red gums, habitat of corellas, pink and grey galahs, pelicans and other waterbirds.

Flood plain of Cooper Creek

5

BIRDSVILLE TRACK

Lake Harry ruins

The bore and the artificial wetland it has created attract dingoes, emus and waterbirds such as brolgas.

Just south of Clifton Hills homestead the Yelpawaralina Track heads west into the Simpson Desert, while north of the homestead and just across Tippipilla Creek the Birdsville Inside Track veers off to the north-west, weaving through Goyder Lagoon and on to Birdsville. The lagoon is actually the flood plain of the Diamantina River and this route is often impassable due to floodwaters. The main route, known as the Outside Track, swings to the east. Just to the north-east of Lake Surprise Bore, the Walkers Crossing Track heads south-east to Innamincka, while the Birdsville Outside Track strikes north, skirting across the eastern perimeter of Goyder Lagoon and passing Wiripirie Bore and Pandie Pandie homestead before reaching the South Australia–Queensland border. From here it is a short run to Birdsville and, for most, a visit to Australia's best-known bush pub.

Advice and warnings

- Possible track closures at times of wet weather. Cooper Creek, if closed due to flooding, can be crossed by ferry from the Cooper Creek flood bypass track to the east. Contact South Australian road report hotline, tel. 1300 361 033, to check track conditions.
- Slow down for oncoming road trains and wait for them to pass and for dust to settle before continuing.
- Watch out for roaming stock as much of the track runs through unfenced sheep and cattle stations.
- Standard road tyres are suitable. There are corrugated sections so lower tyre pressure for personal comfort and to limit track damage.
- Towing off-road trailers and off-road caravans is possible. However, note that the Cooper Creek ferry does not take caravans.
- Camping is at designated camping areas and designated bush campsites only (signposted along the route). No bush camping allowed elsewhere.
- Drinking water is not available at any campsites so carry enough for your drinking, cooking and washing needs.
- Rubbish bins are not provided at any campsites so please take your rubbish with you.

Permits and bookings

- No permits required to travel this track.
- Bookings required for accommodation in Birdsville during Gymkhana in June/July and race weekend in September. Contact Birdsville Hotel Motel, tel. (07) 4656 3244, or Birdsville Caravan Park, (07) 4656 3214.
- Bookings recommended for motel accommodation at Birdsville Caravan Park, tel. (07) 4656 3214.
- Mungerannie Roadhouse and Hotel has room and cabin accommodation. Bookings recommended, tel. (08) 8675 8317.
- Fishing licence not required for fishing the Diamantina River, but bag and size limits may apply. Contact Queensland Fisheries, tel. (07) 3225 1843, for details or visit their website (www.dpi.qld.gov.au/fishweb).

ROUTE DIRECTIONS

▼ **0.0 km** — Zero trip meter in Marree at crossroads on Oodnadatta Track, with Marree Post Office on left and road on right SP: Police/Information. Proceed in easterly direction towards Leigh Creek.

Crossroads. Marree. Post office on right and road on left SP: Police/Information. — 53.5 km ▲

GPS S:29 38.739 E:138 03.820
UTM 54J 215733E 6716873N

(1.0 km)

▼ **1.0 km** — Crossroads. TL. SP: Birdsville Track/Mungerannie/Birdsville. Road SO SP: Leigh Creek/Pt Augusta.

Crossroads. TR. SP: Marree/Marla/Oodnadatta Track. — 52.5 km ▲

GPS S:29 39.078 E:138 04.287
UTM 54J 216502E 6716266N

(30.1 km)

▼ **31.1 km** — Road junction. CSA. Track on right.

Track on right leads 0.2 km to Lake Harry ruins, where 2000 date palms were planted in an attempt to create an outback fruit industry. A bore, with tap and shower head, is located near ruins.

Road junction. CSA. Track on left to Lake Harry ruins. — 22.4 km ▲

GPS S:29 26.114 E:138 14.762
UTM 54J 232842E 6740636N

(12.3 km)

▼ 43.4 km	Grid in Dog Fence.		
	Grid in Dog Fence.	10.1 km ▲	
(9.9 km)			
▼ 53.3 km	Cross SP: Clayton River.		
	Cross SP: Clayton River.	0.2 km ▲	
(0.2 km)			
▼ 53.5 km	Road junction.		
	Zero trip meter at road junction. CSA. Track on right SP: Clayton Wetlands Campsite.	0.0 km ▲	

GPS   S:29 16.581 E:138 22.350
UTM   54J 244718E 6758533N

▼ 0.0 km — Zero trip meter at road junction. CSA. Track on left SP: Clayton Wetlands Campsite.

Track on left leads 0.2 km to **Clayton Wetlands Campsite**, a large open area on northern riverbank, with hot artesian spa bath.

Road junction. 112.8 km ▲

(0.5 km)

▼ 0.5 km — Road junction. CSA. Track on right SP: Clayton HS.

Road junction. CSA. Track on left SP: Clayton HS. 112.3 km ▲

(30.3 km)

▼ 30.8 km — Road junction. CSA. Track on right leads to Dulkaninna homestead.

Road junction. CSA. Track on left to Dulkaninna homestead. 82.0 km ▲

(38.7 km)

▼ 69.5 km — Road junction. CSA. Track on right to Etadunna homestead.

Road junction. CSA. Track on left to Etadunna homestead. 43.3 km ▲

(1.2 km)

▼ 70.7 km — Road junction. CSA. Track on right.

Track on right is Cooper Creek flood bypass track, accessible only when Cooper Creek crossing is closed due to flooding.

Road junction. CSA. Track on left. 42.1 km ▲

Track on left is where Cooper Creek flood bypass track rejoins.

GPS   S:28 42.677 E:138 38.382
UTM   54J 269436E 6821719N

(11.5 km)

▼ 82.2 km — MV *Tom Brennan* Memorial on left. CSA.

The restored MV *Tom Brennan* is a steel barge brought here during the 1949 flood to assist with ferrying people, supplies and cattle across the flooded plain.

MV *Tom Brennan* Memorial on right. CSA. 30.6 km ▲

(0.6 km)

▼ 82.8 km — Enter SP: Cooper Creek.

Cooper Creek flood plain stretches for 4.5 km.

End of Cooper Creek flood plain. 30.0 km ▲

GPS   S:28 37.523 E:138 42.591
UTM   54J 276108E 6831373N

(0.1 km)

▼ 82.9 km — Road junction. CSA. Track on left SP: Cooper Creek camping area.

Tom Kruse's mail truck

Early Days on the Track

In about 1880 surveyor E. A. Burt pioneered the route that was to become the Birdsville Track. Taking about five weeks, drovers could overland stock from Queensland via Birdsville to the railhead at Marree in South Australia. The landscape presented many obstacles including the vast gibber plains, the formidable Natterannie Sandhills and, at times, the flooding Cooper Creek. Intense heat, frequent dust storms and lack of water added to the dangers. The last mobs were driven along the track in the 1960s.

Mailman Tom Kruse drove the track for a quarter of a century

Afghan cameleers were a common sight on the track in the late 1800s and several hundred were based in Marree, using their camel teams to transport supplies from the railhead to Birdsville and to outlying stations. With the advent of mechanised transport in the 1920s, camel transport rapidly declined.

The mailmen delivering mail between Marree and Birdsville faced the same problems as drovers. The mail run, operated with a horse-drawn buggy from the 1890s until 1922, when the first vehicle took over, generally took about eight days but could take two weeks or more. One of the best-known mailmen was Tom Kruse, a colourful outback character who drove the track for a quarter of a century, between the 1930s and the 1950s. He featured in a 1952 documentary *Back of Beyond*, which portrayed the hardships of the track and made Kruse a national identity.

BIRDSVILLE TRACK

	Track on left leads short distance to **Cooper Creek camping area**, an open site with some shady trees.	
	Road junction. CSA. Track on right SP: Cooper Creek camping area.	29.9 km ▲
	(4.4 km)	
▼ 87.3 km	End of Cooper Creek flood plain.	
	Enter Cooper Creek.	25.5 km ▲
	Cooper Creek flood plain stretches for 4.5 km.	
	GPS S:28 35.259 E:138 43.120 UTM 54J 276890E 6835572N	
	(0.4 km)	
▼ 87.7 km	Road now passes through SP: Natterannie Sandhills.	
	End of Natterannie Sandhills.	25.1 km ▲
	(5.2 km)	
▼ 92.9 km	Road junction. CSA. Track on right.	
	Track on right is where Cooper Creek flood bypass track rejoins.	
	Road junction. CSA. Track on left.	19.9 km ▲
	Track on left is Cooper Creek flood bypass track, accessible only when Cooper Creek crossing is closed due to flooding.	
	GPS S:28 32.448 E:138 42.511 UTM 54J 275798E 6840745N	
	(11.6 km)	
▼ 104.5 km	End of Natterannie Sandhills.	
	Road now passes through SP: Natterannie Sandhills.	8.3 km ▲
	(8.3 km)	
▼ 112.8 km	Road junction.	
	Zero trip meter at road junction. CSA. Track on right SP: Old Mulka Ruins.	0.0 km ▲
	GPS S:28 22.084 E:138 40.431 UTM 54J 272034E 6859824N	
▼ 0.0 km	Zero trip meter at road junction. CSA. Track on left SP: Old Mulka Ruins.	
	Track on left leads 0.8 km to Old Mulka homestead ruins.	
	Road junction.	39.8 km ▲
	(0.7 km)	
▼ 0.7 km	Road junction. CSA. Track on left SP: 2 Mulka HS.	
	Road junction. CSA. Track on right SP: 2 Mulka HS.	39.1 km ▲
	(12.2 km)	
▼ 12.9 km	Road junction. CSA. Track on left SP: Ooranillanie Ruins.	
	Track on left leads 0.1 km to ruins.	
	Road junction. CSA. Track on right SP: Ooranillanie Ruins.	26.9 km ▲
	(26.7 km)	
▼ 39.6 km	Cross SP: Derwent River.	
	Cross SP: Derwent River.	0.2 km ▲
	(0.2 km)	
▼ 39.8 km	Road junction.	

	Zero trip meter at road junction. CSA. Track on left SP: Mungerannie RH 1 km.	0.0 km ▲
	GPS S:28 01.325 E:138 39.535 UTM 54J 269830E 6898141N	
▼ 0.0 km	Zero trip meter at road junction. CSA. Track on right SP: Mungerannie RH 1 km.	
	Track on right leads 0.6 km to Mungerannie Roadhouse, with diesel, petrol and camping.	
	Road junction.	109.6 km ▲
	(2.3 km)	
▼ 2.3 km	Road junction. CSA. Track on left SP: 63 Kalamurina HS/48 Cowarie HS.	
	Road junction. CSA. Track on right SP: 63 Kalamurina HS/48 Cowarie HS.	107.3 km ▲
	(5.9 km)	
▼ 8.2 km	Mungerannie Gap.	
	Mungerannie Gap.	101.4 km ▲
	GPS S:27 57.162 E:138 39.997 UTM 54J 270440E 6905845N	
	(27.8 km)	
▼ 36.0 km	Mirra Mitta Bore on right. CSA.	
	Mirra Mitta Bore on left. CSA.	73.6 km ▲
	GPS S:27 43.064 E:138 44.296 UTM 54J 277011E 6932017N	
	(28.9 km)	
▼ 64.9 km	Road junction. CSA. Track on right SP: Kilanbar Bore.	
	Track on right leads 0.3 km to Kilanbar Bore.	
	Road junction. CSA. Track on left SP: Kilanbar Bore.	44.7 km ▲
	(29.8 km)	
▼ 94.7 km	SP: Mount Gason Wattle Project, on left. CSA.	
	Mount Gason Wattle Project protects Mount Gason wattle (*Acacia picardii*), a rare plant species found in one other location only (just east of Finke, on western edge of Simpson Desert in Northern Territory).	
	SP: Mount Gason Wattle Project, on right. CSA.	14.9 km ▲
	GPS S:27 13.637 E:138 45.733 UTM 54J 278393E 6986410N	
	(7.4 km)	
▼ 102.1 km	Road junction. CSA. Track on right SP: Bodeys Bore.	
	Road junction. CSA. Track on left SP: Bodeys Bore.	7.5 km ▲
	(7.5 km)	
▼ 109.6 km	Road junction.	
	Zero trip meter at road junction. CSA. Track on right SP: Simpson Desert Regional Reserve via Warburton Crossing (K1).	0.0 km ▲
	GPS S:27 06.496 E:138 49.351 UTM 54J 284137E 6999703N	
▼ 0.0 km	Zero trip meter at road junction. CSA over grid. Track on left SP: Simpson Desert Regional Reserve via Warburton Crossing (K1).	
	Track on left is PAR access to Simpson Desert (see Simpson Desert trek, pages 30–45, and map on page 35 to follow this route west – it joins the Rig Road).	
	Road junction.	84.9 km ▲
	(11.1 km)	

MARREE ◀▶ BIRDSVILLE

▼ 11.1 km Road junction. CSA. SP: 194 Birdsville. Track on left SP: Clifton Hills HS 2.

Road junction. CSA. SP: Marree 323. Track on right SP: Clifton Hills HS 2. **73.8 km** ▲

(11.8 km)

▼ 22.9 km Cross SP: Tippipilla Creek.

Western side of Tippipilla Creek. **62.0 km** ▲

(1.2 km)

▼ 24.1 km Eastern side of Tippipilla Creek.

Tippipilla Creek bush camping is located on eastern edge of creek.

Cross SP: Tippipilla Creek. **60.8 km** ▲

GPS S:26 59.752 E:139 00.950
UTM 54J 303110E 7012475N

(1.0 km)

▼ 25.1 km Road junction. CSA. Track on left.

Track on left is Birdsville Inside Track, favoured by drovers in years past.

Road junction. CSA. Track on right. **59.8 km** ▲

(31.5 km)

▼ 56.6 km Road junction. CSA. Track on right SP: Melon Creek Bore.

Road junction. CSA. Track on left SP: Melon Creek Bore. **28.3 km** ▲

(14.7 km)

▼ 71.3 km Road junction. CSA. Track on right SP: Lake Surprise Bore.

Track on right leads 0.3 km to bore.

Road junction. CSA. Track on left SP: Lake Surprise Bore. **13.6 km** ▲

(13.6 km)

▼ 84.9 km Road junction.

Zero trip meter at road junction. CSA. Track on left is Walkers Crossing Track. **0.0 km** ▲

GPS S:26 52.267 E:139 32.133
UTM 54J 354530E 7026999N

▼ 0.0 km Zero trip meter at road junction. CSA. Track on right is SP: PAR to Innamincka 226 km via Walkers Crossing.

Track on right is Walkers Crossing Track.

Road junction. **123.0 km** ▲

(23.0 km)

▼ 23.0 km Road junction. CSA. Track on left SP: Blue Ute Bore 1.

Road junction. CSA. Track on right SP: Blue Ute Bore 1. **100.0 km** ▲

(24.2 km)

▼ 47.2 km Road junction. CSA. Track on right SP: Moongara 1 & 2 Bores.

Road junction. CSA. Track on left SP: Moongara 1 & 2 Bores. **75.8 km** ▲

(19.7 km)

▼ 66.9 km Road junction. CSA. Track on right SP: Wiripirie Bore.

Road junction. CSA. Track on left SP: Wiripirie Bore. **56.1 km** ▲

(27.4 km)

▼ 94.3 km Road junction. CSA. Road on left SP: Pandie Pandie HS 2.

Front bar at the Birdsville Hotel

Road junction. CSA. Road on right SP: Pandie Pandie HS 2. **28.7 km** ▲

(15.3 km)

▼ 109.6 km Cross SA–QLD border and grid.

Cross QLD–SA border and grid. **13.4 km** ▲

GPS S:25 59.801 E:139 22.588
UTM 54J 337503E 7123674N

(9.2 km)

▼ 118.8 km Road junction. CSA. SP: Birdsville 4. Road on right SP: Betoota 173.

Road junction. CSA. SP: Marree 554. Road on left SP: Betoota 173. **4.2 km** ▲

(1.6 km)

▼ 120.4 km Bridge over Diamantina River.

Bridge over Diamantina River. **2.6 km** ▲

GPS S:25 54.391 E:139 22.487
UTM 54J 337210E 7133660N

(2.6 km)

▼ 123.0 km Birdsville. Birdsville Hotel on right.

Birdsville has several historic buildings including Royal Hotel (1883), Brookland Store (1891), and Birdsville Hotel, built in 1884 but its original structure much ravaged by fire and floods over the years. Large caravan park has good camping facilities right in town centre.

Zero trip meter in Birdsville. Birdsville Hotel on left. Proceed through town towards South Australia. **0.0 km** ▲

GPS S:25 53.950 E:139 21.105
UTM 54J 334892E 7134445N

REVERSE DIRECTIONS START

9

Strzelecki Track

Evening at Cullyamurra Waterhole

LYNDHURST ◄► INNAMINCKA 444.2 KM
ONE SECTION ONLY *(easy)*
WHEN TO GO April–October **TIME** 1 day

Like the Birdsville Track, this route is steeped in tales of tragedy and triumph. Robert O'Hara Burke and William Wills died on the banks of the Cooper in 1861, their companion John King survived with the help of local Aboriginal people, and legendary cattle duffer Harry Redford pioneered the track when he overlanded 1000 head of stolen cattle from central Queensland to South Australia in 1870–71.

Cutting through the Strzelecki Desert of north-eastern South Australia, the Strzelecki Track links Lyndhurst with the Moomba gas fields, Innamincka and south-west Queensland. The route skirts the northern peaks of the Flinders Ranges before heading north.

The main track is well maintained and can be travelled easily in a day. The historic ruins of Blanchewater homestead, where Burke, Wills and King headed in a desperate attempt at survival after returning to their abandoned depot on Cooper Creek, and Montecollina Bore are good places to stop and stretch your legs. The bore is also a popular overnight campsite. In the north, the route follows what is known as the Old Strzelecki Track, which runs parallel to Strzelecki Creek from Merty Merty to Innamincka. There are no services between these two settlements – emergency services only are available at Moomba.

Lyndhurst in the south and Innamincka in the north have fuel, supplies and accommodation. From Innamincka, there is a route-directed side trip across the state border to visit the Dig Tree, where the last stages of the Burke and Wills tragedy started to unfold.

STRZELECKI TRACK

Innamincka
Starting as a customs post to regulate interstate trade prior to Federation, the town boasted a hotel, police lock-up and, in 1928, an Australian Inland Mission (AIM) nursing home. The home closed in 1951, and most other buildings were demolished. The discovery of oil and gas at nearby Gidgealpa in 1963 led to a new hotel and store by the early 1970s, and in 1994 the AIM home was restored and is now the base of National Parks and Wildlife South Australia (NPWSA).

Services

VEHICLE ASSISTANCE
RAA (SA)/RACQ (Qld) 13 1111

POLICE
Leigh Creek (08) 8675 2004

PARKS AND RESERVES
Innamincka Regional Reserve
Strzelecki Regional Reserve
NPWSA Innamincka (08) 8675 9909

VISITOR INFORMATION
Lyndhurst Roadhouse (08) 8675 7782
NPWSA Innamincka (08) 8675 9909

Authors' note
We always pack a fishing line when heading to the Cooper as there's a good chance you'll catch a feed or two of yellowbelly (golden perch). Ask at the Trading Post or hotel for the best spots to fish the creek.

Town Facilities

	Fuel: D/P/A	Mechanical repairs	Tyre repairs	Public telephone	Public toilets	Shop/supplies	Gas refills	Ice	Visitor information	Post office	Medical centre	Police	Meals	Motel	Hotel	Cabins	Caravan park	Camping
Innamincka	D/P	•	•	•	•	•	•	•	•				•	•	•			•
Lyndhurst	D/P/A		•	•	•	•	•	•				•	•	•	•	•	•	•

11

STRZELECKI TRACK

LYNDHURST ◄► INNAMINCKA 444.2 KM

Start point
Lyndhurst

Road atlas
348 B1, 353 L3

Total distance
612.6 km (includes route-directed side trip)

Standard
Easy

Time
1 day

Longest distance no PD (includes all options)
476.9 km (Lyndhurst to Innamincka)

Topographic maps
Auslig 1:250 000 series: *Copley*; *Marree*; *Callabonna*; *Strzelecki*; *Innamincka*; *Durham Downs*

Other useful information
- Lyndhurst Roadhouse and store open seven days 7am–8pm, tel. (08) 8675 7782; accepts cash, EFTPOS and credit cards.
- Innamincka Trading Post store open seven days 8am–6pm, tel. (08) 8675 9900; accepts cash, EFTPOS and credit cards.
- NPWSA park guide: *Innamincka Regional Reserve*.
- SA Tourism brochure: *The Kidman Track: The Sidney Kidman Story*.
- SA Tourism booklet: *Discover the Secrets of South Australia: Flinders Ranges & Outback*.
- Information booklets, brochures and maps enclosed with Desert Parks Pass (see Permits and bookings).

Description

If time permits, visit the Ochre Cliffs before leaving Lyndhurst. The site of an old Aboriginal quarry, it is only a few kilometres north on the Hawker–Marree Road. High-quality ochre used for body decoration and painting was a valuable trade item and a network of Aboriginal trading routes stretched from the Gulf of Carpentaria to the gulfs of South Australia, with shells coming south and ochre going north.

Heading north-east from Lyndhurst, the Strzelecki Track passes the north-western fringes of the Flinders Ranges, their bluish silhouettes contrasting with the featureless plains that stretch away to the west. River red gums line many of the mostly dry watercourses that dissect the plains. Surface water is uncommon in this region, but station bores tap into the Great Artesian Basin to provide water for stock. Montecollina Bore, located north of Blanchewater ruins, is the only bore on the track for the use of drovers moving mobs along the route.

Campsite Facilities

	Toilets	Disabled access	4WD access only	Off-road trailer	Off-road caravan	Drinking water	Fee payable	Ranger patrolled	BBQ/fireplace	Campfires prohibited	Picnic tables	Shelter shed	No rubbish disposal	Public phone	Shower	Bushwalking	Swimming	Swimming not advised	Fishing	Canoeing	Dogs allowed
Burkes Memorial	•		•	•		•	•									•		•			•
Cullyamurra Waterhole	•		•	•		•	•	•								•		•			•
Dig Tree	•		•	•		•	•	•						•	•		•		•		
Innamincka Common	•		•	•		•	•									•			•	•	
Kings Marker	•		•	•		•	•									•			•	•	•
Minkie Waterhole			•	•		•	•									•			•	•	•
Montecollina Bore	•		•	•					•	•	•										•
Policemans Waterhole	•		•	•		•	•									•			•	•	•
Ski Beach	•		•	•		•	•									•			•	•	•
Wills Memorial			•	•		•	•									•			•	•	•

LYNDHURST ◀▶ INNAMINCKA

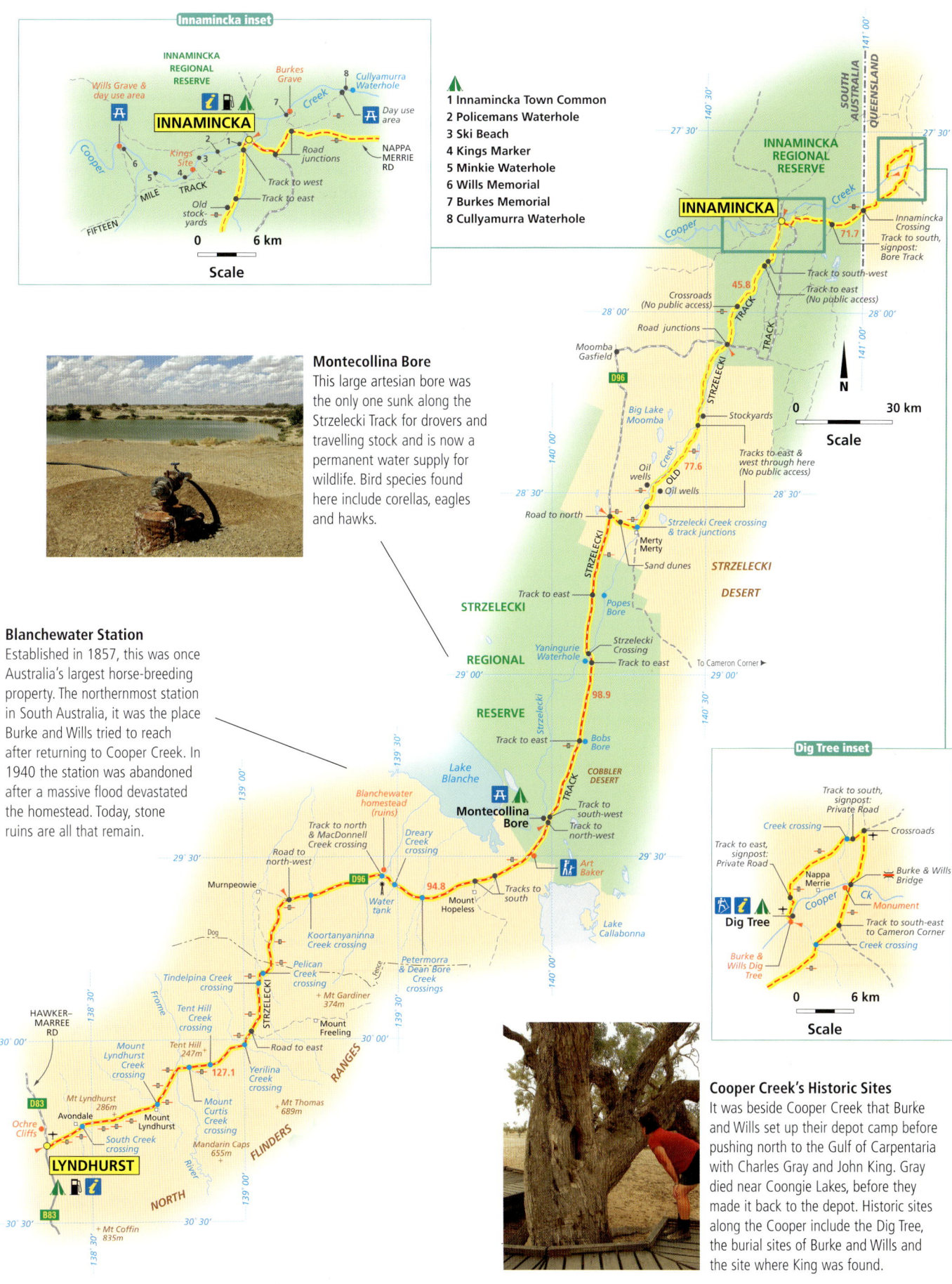

1 Innamincka Town Common
2 Policemans Waterhole
3 Ski Beach
4 Kings Marker
5 Minkie Waterhole
6 Wills Memorial
7 Burkes Memorial
8 Cullyamurra Waterhole

Montecollina Bore
This large artesian bore was the only one sunk along the Strzelecki Track for drovers and travelling stock and is now a permanent water supply for wildlife. Bird species found here include corellas, eagles and hawks.

Blanchewater Station
Established in 1857, this was once Australia's largest horse-breeding property. The northernmost station in South Australia, it was the place Burke and Wills tried to reach after returning to Cooper Creek. In 1940 the station was abandoned after a massive flood devastated the homestead. Today, stone ruins are all that remain.

Cooper Creek's Historic Sites
It was beside Cooper Creek that Burke and Wills set up their depot camp before pushing north to the Gulf of Carpentaria with Charles Gray and John King. Gray died near Coongie Lakes, before they made it back to the depot. Historic sites along the Cooper include the Dig Tree, the burial sites of Burke and Wills and the site where King was found.

13

Ochre Cliffs near Lyndhurst

The bore has created a small wetland that attracts birdlife, which makes it a popular overnight stop.

Montecollina Bore, and Lake Blanche to the west, are within the Strzelecki Regional Reserve. On the eastern side of the track the reserve rims the northern edge of Lake Callabonna, a fossil reserve where the remains of giant megafauna have been found. From here the main track traverses the sandhills of the Cobbler Desert, and on across the Strzelecki Desert, characterised by endless dunes. Some birds, such as the Eyrean grasswren, have adapted to this waterless environment. The main track heads due north towards Moomba, but our route turns east towards Merty Merty homestead, then veers north on the Old Strzelecki Track, meandering across the coolibah-dotted flood plain of Strzelecki Creek to Innamincka. A number of oil wells seen from the track add interest to the landscape, the colourful heads pumping up and down to an almost rhythmic beat as they send the oil via a series of pipelines to the main Moomba complex. In the distance, large blasts of flame shoot into the air from gas fields where gas is being burned off. There is no public access to any of these sites. The Old Strzelecki Track section may cause some problems after rain – definitely dry weather only – but is the only stretch likely to cause any difficulty on an otherwise easy run.

The Innamincka Regional Reserve, established in 1988, originally comprised a number of cattle properties, the first settled in 1873 by pastoralists from Victoria. In 1904 and 1908 Sidney Kidman purchased Coongie and Innamincka stations respectively and they became part of his vast pastoral empire. Today the reserve protects a large area of the Cooper River Basin and Coongie Lakes to the north, where canoeing and fishing are allowed.

A route-directed side trip to the Burke and Wills Dig Tree is included in these pages, and you should visit the memorials at the separate sites where Burke and Wills died beside Cooper Creek. Cullyamurra Waterhole, a 28-metre-deep basin gouged out of the riverbed by a mammoth flood, is a picturesque spot with rocky outcrops and rock-art sites – reminders of a once flourishing Aboriginal community.

There are plenty of bush campsites within the Innamincka Regional Reserve and at the Town Common. Most camping is along Cooper Creek, where tall, majestic river red gums (*Eucalyptus camaldulensis*) rim the banks and flood plains. Accommodation is also available at the Innamincka Hotel, with a popular Sunday night dinner during the peak travel season.

Advice and warnings

- Old Strzelecki Track section can be closed during and after wet weather. During such times, follow the main track to Moomba and on to Innamincka. The Old Strzelecki Track section has a number of bypass tracks, station tracks and tracks used by Santos (the company that owns the lease for the oil and gas fields). Stay on the main track and do not deviate from it. Contact South Australian road report hotline, tel. 1300 361 033, or the NPWSA in Innamincka, tel. (08) 8675 9909, to check road conditions.
- Track has a number of large creek crossings impassable at high water levels.
- Slow down for oncoming road trains and wait for them to pass and for dust to settle before continuing.
- Watch out for roaming stock as much of the track runs through unfenced cattle stations.
- Standard road tyres are suitable.
- Towing off-road trailers and off-road caravans is possible.
- Camping is at designated camping areas and designated bush campsites only.
- Carry plenty of water.
- Rubbish bins are not provided along the track so please take your rubbish with you. There is rubbish disposal at the refuse in Innamincka.
- When camping along Cooper Creek, do not camp directly beneath branches of river red gums as they are prone to falling without warning.

Permits and bookings

- Desert Parks Pass required per vehicle to travel through Innamincka Regional Reserve. This pass covers some other outback parks in South Australia and entitles holder to camp within these parks or at specified locations and to travel on designated park roads. The pass comes in a handy pack with information books and maps.

Contact Desert Parks Hotline, tel. 1800 816 078, to obtain pass or for further details, or NPWSA Innamincka, tel. (08) 8675 9909. Alternatively, a visitor day pass can be purchased. Innamincka Town Common has an honesty box system.
- Advance bookings recommended for Innamincka Hotel Motel, tel. (08) 8675 9901.
- Recreational fishing licence not required for fishing in Cooper Creek (South Australia). Bag and size limits apply. Contact South Australia Fisheries, tel. (08) 8347 6100, or visit their website (www.pir.sa.gov.au/fishing).

ROUTE DIRECTIONS

▼ 0.0 km Zero trip meter in Lyndhurst at junction of Hawker–Marree Rd and SP: Strzelecki Track. Proceed along Strzelecki Track towards SP: Moomba 376/Innamincka 463.
T-junction. This is Hawker–Marree Rd. 127.1 km ▲
TL for Hawker 193 km and Port Augusta 299 km. TR for Marree 80 km.
GPS S:30 17.264 E:138 20.971
UTM 54J 245063E 6646356N
(13.2 km)

▼ 13.2 km Cross SP: South Creek.
Cross SP: South Creek. 113.9 km ▲
(24.2 km)

▼ 37.4 km Road junction. CSA. Road on right SP: Mt Lyndhurst HS 1.
Road junction. CSA. SP: 37 Lyndhurst. 89.7 km ▲
Road on left SP: Mt Lyndhurst HS 1.
(1.3 km)

▼ 38.7 km Cross SP: Mt Lyndhurst Creek.
Cross SP: Mt Lyndhurst Creek. 88.4 km ▲
GPS S:30 10.616 E:138 42.894
UTM 54J 279970E 6659402N
(16.7 km)

▼ 55.4 km Cross SP: Mt Curtis Creek.
Cross SP: Mt Curtis Creek. 71.7 km ▲
(5.9 km)

▼ 61.3 km Cross SP: Tent Hill Creek.
Cross SP: Tent Hill Creek. 65.8 km ▲
(14.0 km)

▼ 75.3 km Cross SP: Yerilina Creek.
Cross SP: Yerilina Creek. 51.8 km ▲
(4.8 km)

▼ 80.1 km Road junction. CSA. SP: Innamincka 380. Road on right SP: Talc Mine 48/Mt Freeling HS 24.
Road junction. CSA. SP: 75 Lyndhurst. Road on left SP: 48 Talc Mine/24 Mt Freeling HS. 47.0 km ▲
GPS S:29 58.688 E:139 01.407
UTM 54J 309305E 6681994N
(15.8 km)

▼ 95.9 km Cross SP: Tindelpina Creek.
Cross SP: Tindelpina Creek. 31.2 km ▲
(4.1 km)

▼ 100.0 km Cross SP: Pelican Creek.
This is a pleasant shaded spot, ideal for a lunch or drink stop.
Cross SP: Pelican Creek. 27.1 km ▲
GPS S:29 49.161 E:139 03.735
UTM 54J 312753E 6699657N
(4.7 km)

▼ 104.7 km Grid in Dog Fence.
The Dog Fence is a 5400-km barrier – the longest of its kind in the world – stretching from the Great Australian Bight to New South Wales and Queensland, and constructed to protect sheep from dingoes.
Grid in Dog Fence. 22.4 km ▲
(22.4 km)

▼ 127.1 km Road junction.
Zero trip meter at road junction. CSA. SP: Lyndhurst 121. Road on right SP: Murnpeowie HS 12. 0.0 km ▲
GPS S:29 37.038 E:139 08.931
UTM 54J 320764E 6722188N

▼ 0.0 km Zero trip meter at road junction. CSA. SP: 333 Innamincka. Road on left SP: 12 Murnpeowie HS.
Road junction. 94.8 km ▲
(7.1 km)

▼ 7.1 km Cross SP: Koortanyaninna Creek.
Cross SP: Koortanyaninna Creek. 87.7 km ▲
(23.6 km)

▼ 30.7 km Track junction. CSA. Track on left.
Track on left leads 0.4 km to Blanchewater ruins.
Track junction. CSA. Track on right. 64.1 km ▲
GPS S:29 33.187 E:139 26.882
UTM 54J 349641E 6729727N
(0.1 km)

▼ 30.8 km Cross SP: MacDonnell Creek.
Cross SP: MacDonnell Creek. 64.0 km ▲
(5.0 km)

Old Strzelecki Track

STRZELECKI TRACK

▼ 35.8 km Cross SP: Dreary Creek.
    Cross SP: Dreary Creek. 59.0 km ▲
(9.2 km)

▼ 45.0 km Cross SP: Petermorra Creek.
    Cross SP: Petermorra Creek. 49.8 km ▲
(1.3 km)

▼ 46.3 km Cross SP: Dean Bore Creek.
    Cross SP: Dean Bore Creek. 48.5 km ▲
(17.3 km)

▼ 63.6 km Road junction. CSA. Track on right to Mount Hopeless station.

Mt Hopeless, a small pointed hill about 10 km south-west of homestead, was named by explorer Edward Eyre after he climbed it to search the horizon for the illusory inland sea.

    Road junction. CSA. Track on left to Mount Hopeless station. 31.2 km ▲
(6.5 km)

▼ 70.1 km Road junction. CSA. SP: Innamincka 264. Road on right SP: Arkaroola 180/Moolawatana HS 54.

    Road junction. CSA. SP: 191 Lyndhurst. Road on left SP: 180 Arkaroola/54 Moolawatana HS. 24.7 km ▲

GPS S:29 33.253 E:139 48.875
UTM 54J 385158E 6730023N

(13.3 km)

▼ 83.4 km SP: Art Baker Lookout, on right. CSA.

Lookout on right has views south to distant Gammon Ranges, located in northern reaches of the Flinders Ranges.

Burke's Tree, carved by a stockman in the early 1900s

16

    SP: Art Baker Lookout, on left. CSA. 11.4 km ▲
(11.4 km)

▼ 94.8 km Road junction.
    Zero trip meter at road junction. CSA. Track on right to Montecollina Bore. 0.0 km ▲

GPS S:29 24.467 E:139 59.277
UTM 54J 401813E 6746408N

▼ 0.0 km Zero trip meter at road junction. CSA. Track on left SP: Montecollina Bore. Now in Strzelecki Regional Reserve.

Track on left leads 0.9 km to **Montecollina Bore** and **camping area**, an open spot among small dune system and short walk from bore.

    Road junction. 98.9 km ▲
(1.5 km)

▼ 1.5 km Road junction. CSA. Track on left to Montecollina Bore.
    Road junction. CSA. Track on right SP: Montecollina Bore. 97.4 km ▲

Track on right leads 0.8 km to Montecollina Bore and camping area.

(26.0 km)

▼ 27.5 km Road junction. CSA. Track on right SP: Bobs Bore.
    Road junction. CSA. Track on left SP: Bobs Bore. 71.4 km ▲
(24.5 km)

▼ 52.0 km Road junction. CSA. Track on right.
    Road junction. CSA. Track on left. 46.9 km ▲
(3.0 km)

▼ 55.0 km Strzelecki Crossing.
    Strzelecki Crossing. 43.9 km ▲

GPS S:28 56.644 E:140 07.190
UTM 54J 414224E 6797892N

(18.9 km)

▼ 73.9 km Road junction. CSA. Track on right SP: Popes Bore.
    Road junction. CSA. Track on left SP: Popes Bore. 25.0 km ▲
(12.0 km)

▼ 85.9 km Grid. Exiting Strzelecki Regional Reserve.
    Grid. Enter SP: Strzelecki Regional Reserve. 13.0 km ▲
(13.0 km)

▼ 98.9 km Road junction.
    Zero trip meter at T-junction. TL. SP: 315 Lyndhurst. Road on right SP: Innamincka 140. 0.0 km ▲

GPS S:28 33.880 E:140 11.195
UTM 54J 420442E 6839974N

▼ 0.0 km Zero trip meter at road junction. TR. SP: Cameron Corner 109. Road SO SP: Innamincka 140.

At times of wet weather, proceed SO here towards Innamincka.

    T-junction. 77.6 km ▲
(9.0 km)

▼ 9.0 km Cross Strzelecki Creek.
    Cross Strzelecki Creek. 68.6 km ▲

GPS S:28 35.610 E:140 16.146
UTM 54J 428533E 6836832N

(0.5 km)

LYNDHURST ◄► INNAMINCKA

▼ 9.5 km   Track junction. CSA. Track on right to Merty Merty homestead.

               Track junction. CSA. Track on left to   68.1 km ▲
                              Merty Merty homestead.

(0.2 km)

▼ 9.7 km   Track junction. TL. SP: Innamincka/Limestone Ck. Track SO SP: Cameron Corner.
            From here numerous tracks to left and right lead to oil wells. No public access. Continue along main track.

             T-junction. TR. SP: Lyndhurst 325. Track   67.9 km ▲
                          on left SP: Cameron Corner.

GPS	S:28 35.761 E:140 16.551
UTM	54J 429194E 6836557N

(12.4 km)

▼ 22.1 km   Oil wells on left and right. CSA.
             No public access to these wells and equipment.

                      Oil wells on left and right. CSA.   55.5 km ▲

(22.7 km)

▼ 44.8 km   Crossroads. CSA. SP: Innamincka. Track on left and right SP: No Public Access.

                         Crossroads. CSA. SP: Lyndhurst.   32.8 km ▲

            From here numerous tracks to left and right lead to oil wells. No public access. Continue along main track.

GPS	S:28 20.594 E:140 27.546
UTM	54J 446986E 6864656N

(3.7 km)

▼ 48.5 km   Cross Strzelecki Creek.

                                Cross Strzelecki Creek.   29.1 km ▲

(3.1 km)

▼ 51.6 km   Track junction. CSA. Track and stockyards on right.

                       Track junction. CSA. Track and   26.0 km ▲
                               stockyards on left.

(19.2 km)

▼ 70.8 km   Track junction. CSA. Track on right.

                           Track junction. CSA. Track on left.   6.8 km ▲

(6.3 km)

▼ 77.1 km   T-junction. TR. Road on left to Lyndhurst via the main road and Moomba.

                     Road junction. TL. SP: Strzelecki Track.   0.5 km ▲
                             This is Old Strzelecki Track.

GPS	S:28 05.360 E:140 33.738
UTM	54J 457000E 6892824N

(0.3 km)

▼ 77.4 km   Grid. Enter SP: Innamincka Regional Reserve.

                     Grid. Exit Innamincka Regional Reserve.   0.2 km ▲

(0.2 km)

▼ 77.6 km   Road junction.

                         Zero trip meter at T-junction. TR.   0.0 km ▲
                         SP: Lyndhurst 413. Track on left.

GPS	S:28 05.377 E:140 34.015
UTM	54J 457453E 6892795N

▼ 0.0 km   Zero trip meter at road junction. TL. This is Old Strzelecki Track.

                                         T-junction.   45.8 km ▲

(13.0 km)

Blanchewater homestead ruins

Captain Starlight

Legendary deeds surround the founding of the Strzelecki Track. In 1870 Harry Redford, a skilled bushman and notorious cattle-duffer, forged a route through the Strzelecki Desert while driving a mob of 1000 stolen cattle from central Queensland to the South Australian markets. Legend has it that Redford's droving exploit was foiled near Blanchewater station where he had offloaded the herd instead of chancing his luck in Adelaide. He was taken back to Roma in Queensland for trial but was acquitted of his crime when the jury, filled with admiration for the daring feat, incredibly found him not guilty despite the irrefutable evidence against him. The episode allegedly prompted writer Rolf Boldrewood to model Captain Starlight, his protagonist in *Robbery Under Arms* (1888), on Redford.

Redford, a skilled bushman and notorious cattle-duffer, forged a route through the Strzelecki Desert

Pastoralists took up land around Innamincka in 1873 and Redford's track was used for about a decade as a droving route to the South Australian markets. However, due to unreliable water and the decline of the Innamincka township in the 1940s and 1950s, it fell into disuse. The discovery of gas and oil in the Cooper Creek Basin in the early 1960s finally created the need for a trafficable route that is today's Strzelecki Track.

STRZELECKI TRACK

Cooper Creek sunset

Craig Crosses Over

Whilst in Innamincka Craig had a real Burke and Wills experience. After spending the night in the Innamincka Hotel learning a few new pool tricks from a local, the next day we visited the memorial to Wills beside the Cooper Creek. It was here that Craig felt just like Wills and wanted to lie down by the creek and die.

I kept telling him how lucky he was to be able to 'connect' to a person who had made such a mark on our country's history, but Craig could not see the funny side of this. In fact, he didn't want to see or do much at all that day! With this being Cath's first visit to Innamincka, and after reading the fantastic book *The Dig Tree* by Sara Murgatroyd, Cath wanted to see everything and dragged Craig and his headache everywhere.

Craig had a real Burke and Wills experience

Memorial to William Wills

▼ 13.0 km — Crossroads. CSA. Track on right and left SP: No Public Access.
    Crossroads. CSA. Track on left and right SP: No Public Access. — 32.8 km ▲
(17.1 km)

▼ 30.1 km — Track junction. CSA. Track on right SP: No Public Access.
    Track junction. CSA. Track on left SP: No Public Access. — 15.7 km ▲
(0.6 km)

▼ 30.7 km — Track junction. CSA. Track on left.
    Y-junction. KL. Track on right. — 15.1 km ▲
(7.3 km)

▼ 38.0 km — Old stockyards on left. CSA.
    Old stockyards on right. CSA. — 7.8 km ▲

GPS S:27 48.679 E:140 43.153
UTM 54J 472345E 6923667N

(1.2 km)

▼ 39.2 km — Track junction. CSA. Track on right.
    Track junction. CSA. Track on left. — 6.6 km ▲
(5.2 km)

▼ 44.4 km — Track junction. CSA. Track on left.

Track on left is Fifteen Mile Track and leads 6.1 km to turn-off to **Kings Marker** and **camping area** and a further 7.0 km to turn-off to **Wills Memorial** and **camping area**. The signposted Kings Site is thought to be the general location of where King was found in September 1861 by Alfred Howitt's search party. The signposted Wills Grave has a cairn marking the place where it is thought Wills died. Howitt's party buried Wills beside the Cooper but his bones were later disinterred and taken to Melbourne for a state funeral. The turn-offs to **Policemans Waterhole**, **Ski Beach** and **Minkie Waterhole camping areas** are also along Fifteen Mile Track, and all areas have widely dispersed bush camping along Cooper Creek with wonderful shade from tall, stately river red gums.

    Track junction. KL. Track on right SP: Fifteen Mile Track/Kings Site 7 km/Wills Grave 19 km. — 1.4 km ▲

GPS S:27 45.431 E:140 43.925
UTM 54J 473599E 6929666N

(0.6 km)

▼ 45.0 km — Track junction. CSA over Strzelecki Creek. Track on left SP: Town Common.

Track on left leads short distance to **Innamincka Town Common camping area**, a large space with shade-giving river red gums stretching along Cooper Creek.

    Track junction. CSA. Track on right SP: Town Common. — 0.8 km ▲
(0.3 km)

▼ 45.3 km — Track junction. CSA. Track on left.

Track on left leads short distance to Town Common bus camping area.

    Track junction. CSA over Strzelecki Creek. Track on right. — 0.5 km ▲
(0.3 km)

LYNDHURST ◀▶ INNAMINCKA

Cooper Creek by a search party led by Alfred Howitt. Burke's remains were later exhumed and taken to Melbourne for a state funeral.) Track on left also leads 8.1 km to **Cullyamurra Waterhole camping area**, with a number of areas, some with secluded sites, beside Cullyamurra Waterhole.

GPS	S:27 44.376 E:140 46.960
UTM	54J 478580E 6931624N

(12.3 km)

▼ 18.7 km   Track junction. CSA. SP: Nappa Merrie. Track on right SP: Bore Track.

(11.1 km)

▼ 29.8 km   Grid. The SA–Qld border. This is Innamincka Crossing.

GPS	S:27 43.165 E:140 59.738
UTM	54J 499570E 6933879N

(4.2 km)

▼ 34.0 km   Creek crossing.

(10.2 km)

▼ 44.2 km   Creek crossing.

(3.2 km)

▼ 47.4 km   T-junction. TL. SP: Dig Tree via Burke & Wills Bridge 25 km/Thargomindah via Jackson Field 308 km. Track on right SP: Cameron Corner via Orientos 256 km/Tibooburra via Warri Gate 253 km.

GPS	S:27 37.772 E:141 07.669
UTM	54J 512610E 6943829N

(4.3 km)

▼ 51.7 km   Burke and Wills Bridge over Cooper Creek.

GPS	S:27 35.525 E:141 08.379
UTM	54J 513782E 6947976N

(6.0 km)

▼ 57.7 km   Crossroads. TL. SP: Burke & Wills Dig Tree/Dig Tree 14 km. Road SO SP: Arrabury 97 km. Road on right SP: Thargomindah via Jackson Oilfield 297 km.

GPS	S:27 32.536 E:141 09.203
UTM	54J 515144E 6953492N

(1.5 km)

▼ 59.2 km   Track junction. CSA. SP: Dig Tree. Track on left SP: Private Road.

(0.6 km)

▼ 59.8 km   Creek crossing.

(9.3 km)

▼ 69.1 km   Track junction. CSA over creek SP: Dig Tree. Track on left SP: Private Road.

(2.3 km)

▼ 71.4 km   Gate. Enter Dig Tree Reserve. Information shelter and self-registration station on right.

(0.3 km)

▼ 71.7 km   Carpark and picnic area. Walk to Dig Tree on right. Track on left to camping area. Return to Innamincka.

Dig Tree camping area is a large open space above Cooper Creek, with some shade.

GPS	S:27 37.404 E:141 04.535
UTM	54J 507457E 6944512N

◀ **END SIDE TRIP**

Camping at Innamincka Town Common

▼ 45.6 km   Track junction. TR. SP: Dillons Hwy/Lyndhurst 471. Track SO SP: Coongie Lakes 106 km.

         T-junction. TL. SP: Kings Site 8 km/Wills Grave 20 km. Track on right SP: Coongie Lakes 106 km.   0.2 km ▲

(0.2 km)

▼ 45.8 km   Innamincka. Innamincka Trading Post and Hotel on left. Side trip to Dig Tree.

         Zero trip meter at Innamincka. Trading Post and Hotel on right. Proceed west to T-junction.   0.0 km ▲

GPS	S:27 44.872 E:140 44.266
UTM	54J 474157E 6930700N

REVERSE DIRECTIONS START

▶   **SIDE TRIP: Dig Tree**

▼ 0.0 km   Zero trip meter at Innamincka with Trading Post and Hotel on left. Proceed in easterly direction towards SP: Dig Tree 69 km/Cullyamurra Waterhole 14 km/Burkes Grave 11 km. This is Strzelecki Track.

GPS	S:27 44.872 E:140 44.266
UTM	54J 474157E 6930700N

(3.4 km)

▼ 3.4 km   Road junction. TL. SP: Dig Tree 66 km/Cullyamurra Waterhole 11 km/Burkes Grave 8 km. Road SO SP: 473 Lyndhurst.

(3.0 km)

▼ 6.4 km   Road junction. CSA. SP: Dig Tree 63 km/Nappamerry. Track on left SP: Cullyamurra Waterhole 8 km/Burkes Grave 5 km.

Track on left leads 4.4 km to carpark and **Burkes Memorial camping area** with scattered bush camping along Cooper Creek. From carpark a walk leads to Burkes Grave. (This spot, generally thought to be the place where Burke died in 1861, does not mark his grave. His body was found and interred near

■ 19

Oodnadatta Track

Oodnadatta Track signpost at Marla

MARREE ◄► MARLA 620.4 KM
ONE SECTION ONLY *(easy)*
WHEN TO GO April–October **TIME** 2–3 days

In 1862 John McDouall Stuart blazed a trail across the continent from Adelaide to Chambers Bay near present-day Darwin. This momentous achievement led to the construction of the Overland Telegraph Line in 1870–72, which followed Stuart's route and led to a string of settlements across the nation's heart. By joining the underwater Java–Darwin cable, the line linked Australia for the first time with the rest of the world.

The route forged by the Overland Telegraph Line was followed when the Great Northern Railway, now known as the Old Ghan, was pushed through in the 1890s, linking Adelaide with Oodnadatta. The telegraph line also created a transport route for Afghan cameleers, who carried supplies from the Oodnadatta railhead to outback homesteads, remote settlements and repeater stations along the line.

The track from Marree to Marla via Oodnadatta, today's Oodnadatta Track, follows a succession of mound springs that provided reliable water along Aboriginal trade routes for thousands of years. The track passes through vast open gibber and sand plains where generally dry creek beds are lined with mallee, gidgee and river red gums. In contrast, mound springs such as the Peake, and Coward Springs where tamarisks and date palms flourish, form oases in an otherwise arid environment.

The track is a historic journey past crumbling telegraph stations, old sidings, water tanks, desalinaters, rail bridges and fettlers' cottages. There are glimpses of Lake Eyre South from vantage points between Marree and William Creek and you can take a scenic flight over the massive expanse of Lake Eyre. All towns along the track supply fuel while Marree, Oodnadatta and Marla have a range of grocery items.

OODNADATTA TRACK

Old Ghan Heritage Trail
A journey along the Oodnadatta Track provides access points to many of the Old Ghan's historic relics such as remote railway sidings, isolated fettlers' cottages and disused railway bridges such as Algebuckina. Information boards describe how life was lived along the line in a bygone era.

Curdimurka Siding at south-western edge of Lake Eyre South

Services

VEHICLE ASSISTANCE
RAA — 13 1111

POLICE
Marla	(08) 8670 7020
Marree	(08) 8675 8346
Oodnadatta	(08) 8670 7805

PARKS AND RESERVES
Lake Eyre National Park
Wabma Kadarbu Mound Springs Conservation Park
NPWSA Port Augusta — 1800 816 078

VISITOR INFORMATION
Marree	(08) 8675 8222
Oodnadatta Pink Roadhouse	(08) 8670 7822 or 1800 802 074

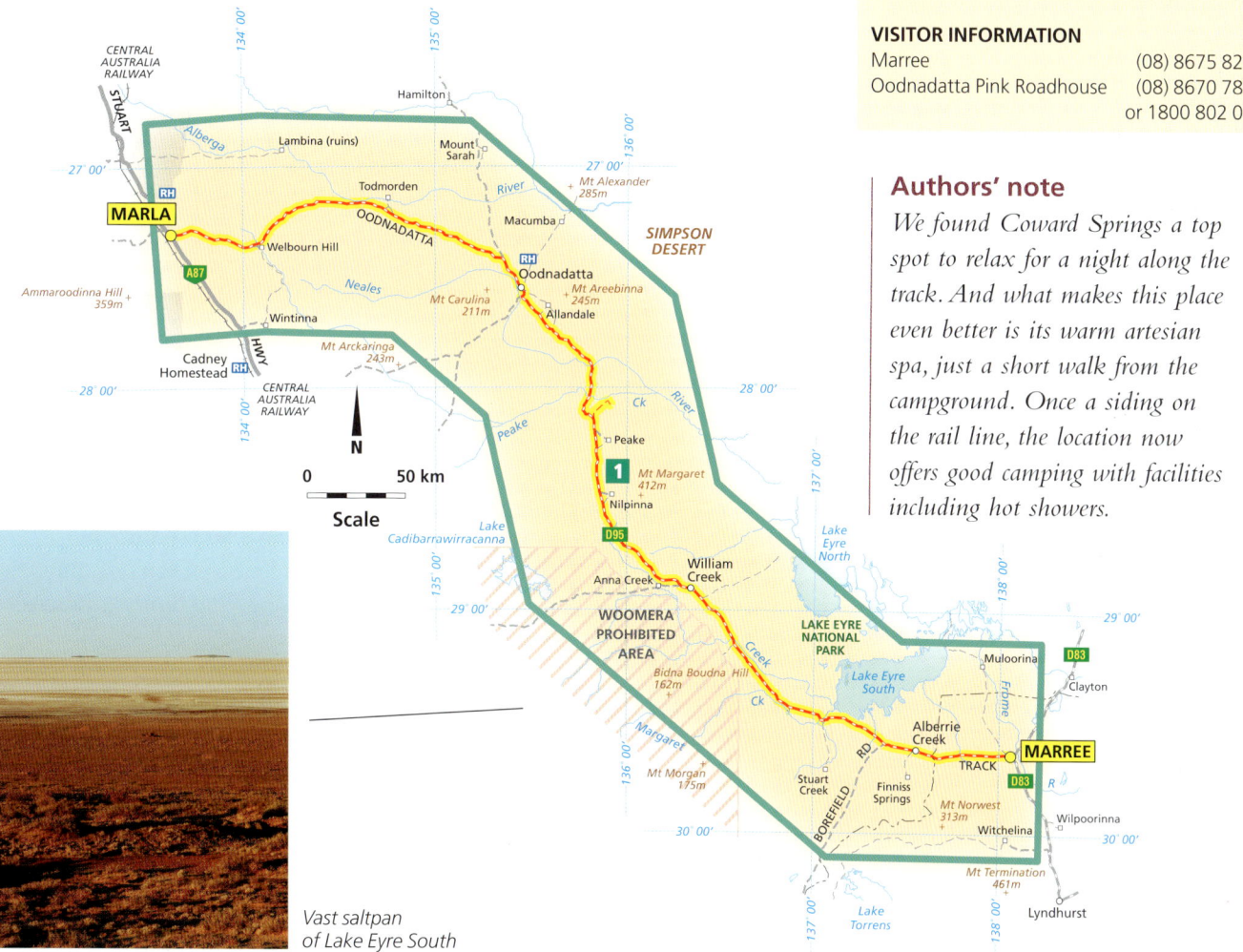

Authors' note
We found Coward Springs a top spot to relax for a night along the track. And what makes this place even better is its warm artesian spa, just a short walk from the campground. Once a siding on the rail line, the location now offers good camping with facilities including hot showers.

Vast saltpan of Lake Eyre South

Town Facilities

Town	Fuel: D/P/A	Mechanical repairs	Tyre repairs	Public telephone	Public toilets	Shop/supplies	Gas refills	Ice	Visitor information	Post office	Medical centre	Police	Meals	Motel	Hotel	Cabins	Caravan park	Camping
Marla	D/P/A	•	•	•	•	•	•			•		•	•	•	•	•	•	•
Marree	D/P		•	•	•	•	•	•	•	•		•	•	•	•		•	•
Oodnadatta	D/P	•	•	•	•	•	•	•	•	•		•	•		•		•	•
William Creek	D/P		•	•	•		•		•				•		•	•	•	•

21

MARREE ◀▶ MARLA 620.4 KM

Start point
Marree

Road atlas
348 B1, 353 L3

Total distance
652.4 km (includes route-directed side trip)

Standard
Easy

Time
2–3 days

Longest distance no PD (includes all options)
242.5 km (William Creek to Oodnadatta)

Topographic maps
Auslig 1:250 000 series: *Marree*; *Curdimurka*; *Billa Kalina*; *Warrina*; *Oodnadatta*; *Wintinna*

Other useful information
- WrightsAir conducts scenic flights over Lake Eyre from William Creek, tel. (08) 8670 7962.
- Local history brochure: *Welcome to Marree: Ghan Town*, available from Marree Tele Centre.
- Mudmap brochure: *Travel the Oodnadatta Track*, available from the Pink Roadhouse at Oodnadatta.
- SA Tourism brochure: *Old Ghan Railway Heritage Trail: Port Augusta to Alice Springs*.
- Information booklets, brochures and maps enclosed with Desert Parks Pass (see Permits and bookings).
- Basil Fuller's *The Ghan: The Story of the Alice Springs Railway* is a great read.
- A bird identification book is helpful in identifying birdlife along the track.

Description
For modern-day travellers the Oodnadatta Track, tracing part of the route of the Old Ghan railway that ran between Adelaide and Alice Springs, is an easy run along a generally well-maintained gravel road, but conditions can vary from season to season depending on the amount of traffic. At peak travel times the route can be dusty and corrugated and, if there is localised rain, some creek crossings may need to be approached with caution due to wash-outs.

The track starts at Marree, once an important rail centre and the base for Afghan cameleers servicing the Birdsville Track (see pages 2–9). As you round the southern shores of Lake Eyre South there are good views over part of this expansive 1300-square-kilometre salt lake from several lookouts beside the road. The huge inland drainage basin of Lake Eyre covers around one-sixth of the Australian continent. When it floods its waters become breeding sites for thousands of waterbirds such as pelicans, silver gulls, banded stilts and gull-billed terns. Fish miraculously appear, carried into the lake by the flooding rivers and streams. A more permanent creature, the Lake Eyre dragon, is a lizard that lives on the edges of the saltpans, having adapted to the arid environment.

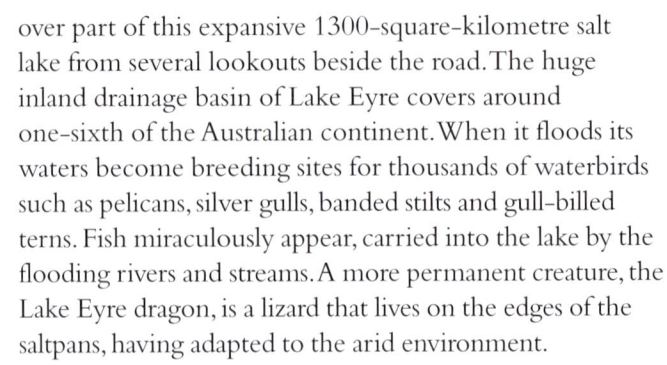

The Bubbler and Blanche Cup mound springs, now protected in Wabma Kadarbu Mound Springs Conservation Park, are located just west of Lake Eyre South and are easily accessible from the track. Formed by a build up of dissolved mineral deposits, many of these springs are associated with Aboriginal mythology. Nearby Coward Springs, once a siding on the rail line, offers camping and the chance to relax in its artesian spa. Old date palms are remnants of an early settlement and now provide a refuge for birds.

The ruins of Beresford and Strangways sidings are further reminders of the Old Ghan as the trek pushes north towards the tiny settlement of William Creek, with its friendly bush pub. This is reputedly Australia's smallest town. From here you can take the track out to Halligan Bay on Lake Eyre North where camping is available.

Between William Creek and Oodnadatta the track passes through a variety of landscapes and vegetation ranging from vast open plains with little ground cover to gibber plains and stands of mallee and gidgee near watercourses. Some of the larger waterways such as Neales River, which offers pleasant campsites amid shady river red gums, are home to a large variety of birds. Historic sites include the impressive Algebuckina Rail Bridge, once traversed by the Old Ghan, and a side trip leads to the remains of the Peake Telegraph Station. In addition to the station ruins there are a number of artesian springs and the remnants of a copper mine.

Oodnadatta, the end of the rail line until 1929, was a thriving town during the early 1900s when goods and supplies were transported by camel teams to remote station properties throughout central Australia. From time to time up to 400 camels and their mostly Afghan handlers camped near town waiting to ship supplies from the railhead. Oodnadatta's importance began to decline after the railway eventually pushed through to Alice Springs in 1929.

The Old Ghan railway closed in 1980 when it was replaced by a new standard gauge all-weather line located to the west of the Stuart Highway. In 2003 a new luxury Ghan ran the long-awaited Adelaide–Darwin line when it opened, burying the Old Ghan forever in the annals of railway history. These days Oodnadatta is a gateway for travellers venturing north to Witjira National Park and Dalhousie Springs and into the Simpson Desert (see pages 30–45).

The 200-kilometre run between Oodnadatta and Marla passes through pastoral country with only the occasional creek crossing to break the landscape. Marla was established as a service centre on the newly aligned Stuart Highway in 1982.

Advice and warnings

- Track conditions can be corrugated and dusty, especially late in the travelling season. Creek crossings and approaches require caution after and during periods of wet weather. Contact South Australian road report hotline, tel. 1300 361 033, to check track conditions.
- There are numerous station access tracks. Do not deviate from main route.
- Watch out for roaming stock as much of the track runs through unfenced cattle stations.
- Standard road tyres are suitable, but lower tyre pressure for personal comfort and to protect tyres and limit track damage.
- Towing off-road trailers and off-road caravans is possible.
- Camping is available at towns along the route and at a number of designated camping areas noted in the route directions. Bush camping is possible, but this is private property so please take your rubbish with you.

Permits and bookings

- No permits required to travel the track.
- Day Entry Fee applies to Lake Eyre National Park and Wabma Kadarbu Mound Springs Conservation Park, payable at onsite self-registration station at Lake Eyre National Park entrance or through National Parks and Wildlife South Australia offices. Alternatively, a current Desert Parks Pass admits you to these parks. Contact NPWSA Port Augusta, tel. 1800 816 078, for details.
- Bookings recommended at William Creek during peak visitor season and when floodwaters fill Lake Eyre. William Creek Hotel has rooms and camping ground, tel. (08) 8670 7880. William Creek Caravan Park has cabins and campsites, tel. (08) 8670 7746.
- Bookings not required for WrightsAir scenic flights over Lake Eyre.

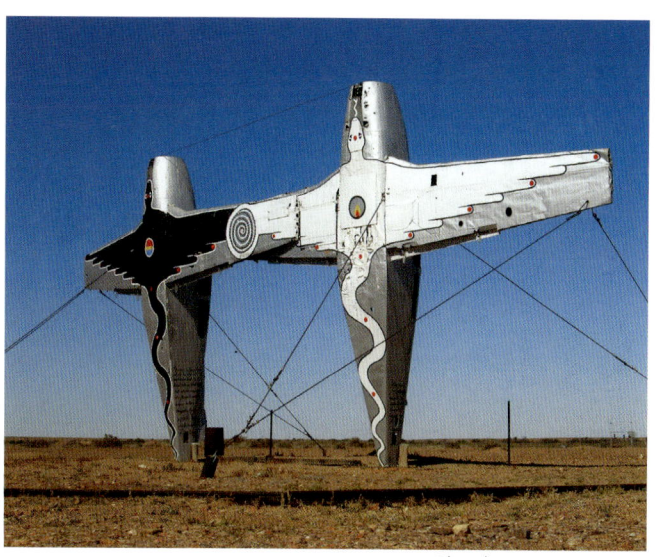

Planehenge near Marree

ROUTE DIRECTIONS

▼ **0.0 km** Zero trip meter in Marree at crossroads on Oodnadatta Track with Marree Post Office on right and road on left SP: Police/Information. Proceed in westerly direction along Oodnadatta Track towards William Creek.

Crossroads. Marree. Post office on left and road on right SP: Police/Information. **101.3 km** ▲

GPS S:29 38.739 E:138 03.820
UTM 54J 215733E 6716873N

(1.6 km)

▼ **1.6 km** Road junction. CSA. SP: William Creek 201. Track on right SP: Muloorina HS. Old Ghan Railway Bridge on left.

Road junction. CSA. SP: 1 Marree. Track on left SP: Muloorina HS. **99.7 km** ▲

(12.6 km)

▼ **14.2 km** Road junction. CSA. Track on left SP: Callanna. Callanna siding ruins on left.

Road junction. CSA. Track on right SP: Callanna. **87.1 km** ▲

(21.3 km)

▼ **35.5 km** Wangianna ruins on left. CSA.

Wangianna ruins on right. CSA. **65.8 km** ▲

(15.9 km)

▼ **51.4 km** SP: Mutonia Sculpture Park on left. CSA. Park is home to Planehenge and other interesting sculptures.

SP: Mutonia Sculpture Park on right. CSA. **49.9 km** ▲

(17.2 km)

▼ **68.6 km** Road junction. CSA. SP: Oodnadatta Track/William Creek 134. Track on left SP: Roxby Downs via Borefield Road 128.

Road junction. CSA. SP: Marree 69/Oodnadatta Track. Track on right SP: Roxby Downs via Borefield Road 128. **32.7 km** ▲

GPS S:29 35.606 E:137 22.842
UTM 53J 730577E 6723898N

(4.8 km)

OODNADATTA TRACK

Romance of the Old Ghan

Construction of the Great Northern Railway began in Port Augusta in 1878, reaching Oodnadatta in 1891. For almost 40 years Oodnadatta was a major railhead from where camel trains transported goods and passengers to remote parts of the outback. In 1929 the line eventually reached Alice Springs via Finke.

When the line became The Ghan is often debated. One of the more popular theories suggests that in 1923 as the train reached Quorn an Afghan passenger, who was late for his sunset prayer, hurriedly disembarked to a spot at the western end of the station, where Muslims prayed. The engine driver, apparently something of a larrikin, commented to those nearby: 'Struth, if that one's going through to Oodnadatta, we should call this the Afghan Express'. The name stuck and was shortened to Ghan Express and then The Ghan.

The train became notorious for running behind schedule. Floods, a frequent occurrence, could turn a three-day journey into a month-long saga. One driver allegedly shot wild goats to feed his stranded passengers. One story relates that a female passenger, who was heavily pregnant, was approached when she alighted at Oodnadatta by the station master, wanting to know why she had undertaken such a long and arduous journey in her present condition. She replied that she had not been in this condition when she boarded the train!

One driver shot wild goats to feed his stranded passengers

Old Ghan locomotive at Marree

Campsite Facilities

	Toilets	Disabled access	4WD access only	Off-road trailer	Off-road caravan	Drinking water	Fee payable	Ranger patrolled	BBQ/fireplace	Campfires prohibited	Picnic tables	Shelter shed	No rubbish disposal	Public phone	Shower	Bushwalking	Swimming	Swimming not advised	Fishing	Canoeing	Dogs allowed
Algebuckina			•							•						•		•	•		
Coward Springs	•	•		•	•	•	•		•			•		•							•
The Peake			•							•											

24

MARREE ◀▶ MARLA

Algebuckina
The 578-metre-long Algebuckina Bridge spans the Neales River and is the longest single-lane bridge in South Australia. It was built in 1889 for the Great Northern Railway and was opened to rail traffic in the early 1890s. Algebuckina was the site of a short-lived gold rush during the early 1880s and also gained notoriety for several murders that were committed during the railway heydays.

The Peake
This place has a varied history. The nearby Freeling Springs supplied water for the original Aboriginal inhabitants, European pastoralists, Overland Telegraph construction workers, Afghan cameleers, Ghan railway fettlers and miners. Ruins in the vicinity include buildings from an 1860s pastoral settlement, old telegraph station and associated structures dating from 1871 and remnants of a copper-mining venture (1900–04).

Curdimurka Siding
At this Old Ghan railway siding are ruins of a desalination plant, overhead water tank, sections of the railway and the fettler's cottage. Desalinators were used to soften the harsh salt-laden and mineralised artesian water for use in steam locomotives.

Mound Springs
The Bubbler and Blanche Cup located within Wabma Kadarbu Mound Springs Conservation Park, with clear fresh water rising from the Great Artesian Basin, are among the more spectacular mound springs along the track. It is fascinating to watch the bubbles spring up from the sandy bottom of The Bubbler.

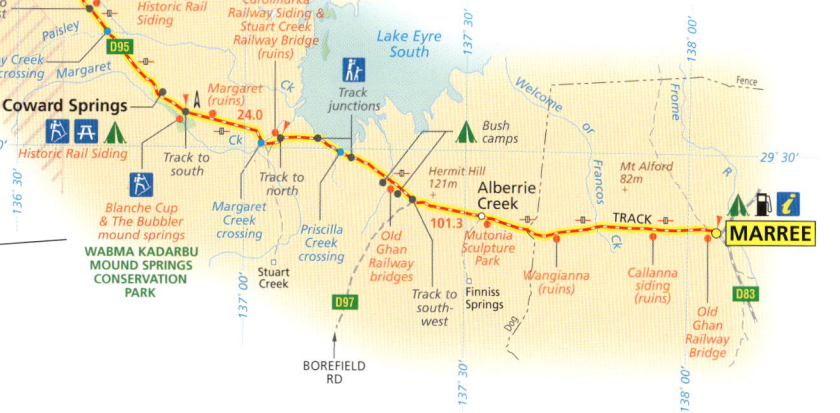

25

OODNADATTA TRACK

Bush campsite near Lake Eyre South

▼ 73.4 km Creek crossing. Old Ghan Railway Bridge on left.
　　　　　　Creek crossing. Old Ghan Railway Bridge on right.　**27.9 km** ▲
(1.0 km)

▼ 74.4 km Creek crossing. Old Ghan Railway Bridge on left.
Track on left prior to creek leads 0.3 km to bush campsites.
　　　　　　Creek crossing.　**26.9 km** ▲
(10.3 km)

▼ 84.7 km Road junction. CSA. Track on right SP: Lake Eyre South.
Track on right leads 0.7 km to lookout area over southern section of Lake Eyre South.
　　　　　　Road junction. CSA. Track on left SP: Lake Eyre South.　**16.6 km** ▲
(3.0 km)

▼ 87.7 km Cross SP: Priscilla Creek.
　　　　　　Cross SP: Priscilla Creek.　**13.6 km** ▲
(5.5 km)

▼ 93.2 km Lake Eyre South Lookout on right. CSA.
　　　　　　Lake Eyre South Lookout on left. CSA.　**8.1 km** ▲
GPS S:29 28.888 E:137 10.194
UTM 53J 710387E 6736709N
(8.1 km)

▼ 101.3 km Road junction.
　　　　　　Zero trip meter at road junction. CSA. Track on left SP: Curdimurka Railway Siding.　**0.0 km** ▲
GPS S:29 28.843 E:137 05.254
UTM 53J 702404E 6736938N

▼ 0.0 km Zero trip meter at road junction. CSA. Track on right SP: Curdimurka Railway Siding.
Track on right leads 0.5 km to Curdimurka Railway Siding and a further 1.0 km to Stuart Creek Railway Bridge.
　　　　　　Road junction.　**24.0 km** ▲
(2.3 km)

▼ 2.3 km Road junction. CSA. Track on left.
　　　　　　Road junction. CSA. Track on right.　**21.7 km** ▲
(3.0 km)

▼ 5.3 km Cross SP: Margaret Creek.
　　　　　　Cross SP: Margaret Creek.　**18.7 km** ▲
(13.0 km)

▼ 18.3 km Margaret ruins on right. CSA.
　　　　　　Margaret ruins on left. CSA.　**5.7 km** ▲
(5.7 km)

▼ 24.0 km Road junction.
　　　　　　Zero trip meter at road junction. CSA. Track on right to Wabma Kadarbu Mound Springs Conservation Park.　**0.0 km** ▲
GPS S:29 26.087 E:136 52.118
UTM 53J 681255E 6742390N

▼ 0.0 km Zero trip meter at road junction. CSA. Track on left.
Track on left leads to Wabma Kadarbu Mound Springs Conservation Park, 4.3 km to Blanche Cup and a further 0.8 km to The Bubbler.
　　　　　　Road junction.　**80.9 km** ▲
(6.6 km)

▼ 6.6 km Road junction. CSA. Track on right SP: Coward Springs Historic Rail Siding.
Track on right leads 0.4 km to **Coward Springs camping area** with a number of well-shaded individual campsites. A short walk leads to Coward Springs spa and old cabin once used by train drivers.
　　　　　　Road junction. CSA. Track on left SP: Coward Springs Historic Rail Siding.　**74.3 km** ▲
GPS S:29 24.235 E:136 48.720
UTM 53J 675813E 6745897N
(18.0 km)

▼ 24.6 km Cross SP: Paisley Creek.
　　　　　　Cross SP: Paisley Creek.　**56.3 km** ▲
(6.1 km)

▼ 30.7 km Road junction. CSA. Track on right SP: 1 Beresford Bore Historic Rail Siding.
Track on right leads 0.6 km to Beresford ruins including fettler's cottage, overhead tank and desalination plant.
　　　　　　Road junction. CSA. Track on left SP: 1 Beresford Bore Historic Rail Siding.　**50.2 km** ▲
GPS S:29 14.549 E:136 39.372
UTM 53J 660948E 6764012N
(12.8 km)

▼ 43.5 km Road junction. CSA. Track on left SP: Strangways Bore Historic Rail Siding.
Track on left leads 2.5 km to carpark and a short walk to historic ruins and mound springs. Ruins include rail siding and remnants of small settlement, graveyard and Overland Telegraph Line repeater station, located here because of reliable water supply.
　　　　　　Road junction. CSA. Track on right SP: Strangways Bore Historic Rail Siding.　**37.4 km** ▲
(2.1 km)

▼ 45.6 km Cross SP: Warriners Creek. Old Ghan Railway Bridge on left.
　　　　　　Cross SP: Warriners Creek. Old Ghan Railway Bridge on right.　**35.3 km** ▲
(14.8 km)

MARREE ◀ ▶ MARLA

▼ 60.4 km   Irrapatana ruins on left. CSA.

                         Irrapatana ruins on right. CSA.   20.5 km ▲

(13.5 km)

▼ 73.9 km   Road junction. CSA. Track on right SP: Lake Eyre National Park/57 Halligan Bay/47 ABC Bay.

Track on right leads short distance to entrance of Lake Eyre National Park and to Halligan Bay and ABC Bay on shores of Lake Eyre.

             Road junction. CSA. Track on left SP: Lake Eyre National Park/57 Halligan Bay/47 ABC Bay.   7.0 km ▲

```
GPS   S:28 56.851 E:136 23.466
UTM   53J 635569E 6797032N
```

(2.0 km)

▼ 75.9 km   Monument to Overland Telegraph Line on right. CSA.

             Monument to Overland Telegraph Line on left. CSA.   5.0 km ▲

(3.2 km)

▼ 79.1 km   Cross SP: Breakfast Time Creek.

This creek also known as William Creek.

             Cross SP: Breakfast Time Creek.   1.8 km ▲

(1.8 km)

▼ 80.9 km   William Creek.

             Zero trip meter in William Creek with hotel on left. Proceed in southerly direction along Oodnadatta Track towards Marree.   0.0 km ▲

```
GPS   S:28 54.400 E:136 20.338
UTM   53J 630539E 6801617N
```

▼ 0.0 km   Zero trip meter in William Creek with hotel on right. Proceed in northerly direction along Oodnadatta Track towards Oodnadatta.

             William Creek.   112.5 km ▲

(5.4 km)

▼ 5.4 km   Road junction. CSA. SP: Oodnadatta Track/Oodnadatta 198/Marla 408. Track on left SP: Coober Pedy 160.

             Road junction. CSA. SP: William Creek 5. Track on right SP: Coober Pedy 160.   107.1 km ▲

```
GPS   S:28 53.646 E:136 17.214
UTM   53J 625477E 6803066N
```

(33.0 km)

Wetland vegetation flourishes around Blanche Cup

▼ 38.4 km   Cross SP: Wilyalallinna Creek.

             Cross SP: Wilyalallinna Creek.   74.1 km ▲

(6.0 km)

▼ 44.4 km   Cross SP: Box Creek.

             Cross SP: Box Creek.   68.1 km ▲

(1.2 km)

▼ 45.6 km   Cross SP: Old Woman Creek.

             Cross SP: Old Woman Creek.   66.9 km ▲

(9.5 km)

▼ 55.1 km   Cross SP: Anna Creek.

             Cross SP: Anna Creek.   57.4 km ▲

(13.8 km)

▼ 68.9 km   Cross SP: Duff Creek.

             Cross SP: Duff Creek.   43.6 km ▲

(0.1 km)

▼ 69.0 km   Road junction. CSA. SP: 136 Oodnadatta. Track on left. Track on right SP: 8 Nilpinna HS.

Track on left leads 0.2 km to Old Ghan Railway Bridge.

             Road junction. CSA. SP: William Creek. Track on left SP: 8 Nilpinna HS. Track on right.   43.5 km ▲

```
GPS   S:28 31.748 E:135 52.479
UTM   53J 585576E 6843869N
```

(6.3 km)

▼ 75.3 km   Road junction. CSA. Track on right leads to Nilpinna homestead.

             Road junction. CSA. Track on left.   37.2 km ▲

(15.7 km)

▼ 91.0 km   Cross SP: Edwards Creek.

             Cross SP: Edwards Creek.   21.5 km ▲

(0.3 km)

▼ 91.3 km   Road junction. CSA. Track on right.

Track on right leads 1.0 km to Old Ghan Railway Bridge and grave sites.

             Road junction. CSA. Track on left.   21.2 km ▲

(0.5 km)

▼ 91.8 km   Edwards Creek ruins on right. CSA.

Note no public access to these ruins.

             Edwards Creek ruins on left. CSA.   20.7 km ▲

```
GPS   S:28 19.850 E:135 50.787
UTM   53J 582971E 6865858N
```

(5.0 km)

▼ 96.8 km   Road junction. CSA. Track on right to Peake homestead.

             Road junction. CSA. Track on left to Peake homestead.   15.7 km ▲

(1.2 km)

▼ 98.0 km   Cross SP: Bungadillina Creek.

             Cross SP: Bungadillina Creek.   14.5 km ▲

(0.2 km)

▼ 98.2 km   Road junction. CSA. Track on right.

Track on right leads 0.6 km to Old Ghan Railway Bridge.

             Road junction. CSA. Track on left.   14.3 km ▲

(8.6 km)

▼ 106.8 km   Cross SP: Warrina Creek. Old Ghan Railway Bridge on right.

27

OODNADATTA TRACK

	Cross SP: Warrina Creek. Old Ghan Railway Bridge on left.	5.7 km ▲

(0.5 km)

▼ 107.3 km Road junction. CSA. Track on left to monument. Warrina ruins on right.

Monument dedicated to Elder Scientific Exploring Expedition led by David Lindsay. Expedition left Adelaide on 2 May 1891 and took 12 months to survey and map 200 000 sq km of country.

	Road junction. CSA. Track on right to monument. Warrina ruins on left.	5.2 km ▲

GPS S:28 11.622 E:135 49.749
UTM 53J 581379E 6881062N

(5.2 km)

▼ 112.5 km Road junction. Side trip to Old Peake Telegraph Station.

Memorial to Ernest Giles on right. Between 1873 and 1876 Giles made numerous forays into central Australia from Adelaide, staying several times at Peake Telegraph Station.

	Zero trip meter at road junction. CSA. Track on left SP: Old Peake Telegraph Stn.	0.0 km ▲

GPS S:28 08.907 E:135 49.399
UTM 53J 580841E 6886079N

▶ **SIDE TRIP: Old Peake Telegraph Station**

▼ 0.0 km Zero trip meter at junction of Oodnadatta Track and track SP: Old Peake Telegraph Stn. Proceed along Old Peake Telegraph Station track past memorial to Ernest Giles.

(0.2 km)

▼ 0.2 km Gate. LAF.

(13.8 km)

▼ 14.0 km Track junction. TR. SP: The Peake OTRS Historic Site.

(1.7 km)

▼ 15.7 km Track junction. CSA. Track on left leads to building ruins.

(0.3 km)

▼ 16.0 km Carpark. Walk from here to ruins of Old Peake Telegraph Station and to old Peake Hill Copper Mine. Return to side trip start.

The Peake bush camping is located to east of carpark along creek line.

GPS S:28 04.608 E:135 54.372
UTM 53J 589039E 6893959N

◀ **END SIDE TRIP**

▼ 0.0 km Zero trip meter at road junction. CSA. Track on right SP: Old Peake Telegraph Stn.

	Road junction. Side trip to Old Peake Telegraph Station.	90.8 km ▲

(17.1 km)

▼ 17.1 km Cross SP: Peake Creek.

	Cross SP: Peake Creek.	73.7 km ▲

(1.2 km)

▼ 18.3 km Road junction. CSA. Track on right.

Track on right leads 0.5 km to stone ruins of old fettler's cottage.

Old Peake Telegraph Station

	Road junction. CSA. Track on left.	72.5 km ▲

(13.2 km)

▼ 31.5 km Road junction. CSA. Track on left.

Track on left leads 0.1 km to Algebuckina ruins.

	Road junction. CSA. Track on right.	59.3 km ▲

(1.1 km)

▼ 32.6 km Crossroads. CSA. Track on left SP: Algebuckina.

Track on left leads 0.4 km to old Algebuckina Bridge and information boards. Track on right leads to **Algebuckina bush camping**, with numerous tracks in the vicinity leading to bush campsites along Neales River.

	Crossroads. CSA. Track on right SP: Algebuckina.	58.2 km ▲

GPS S:27 54.143 E:135 48.739
UTM 53J 579942E 6913346N

(0.2 km)

▼ 32.8 km Cross SP: Neales River.

	Cross SP: Neales River.	58.0 km ▲

(10.5 km)

▼ 43.3 km Cross SP: Ockenden Creek. Old Ghan Railway Bridge on right.

	Cross SP: Ockenden Creek. Old Ghan Railway Bridge on left.	47.5 km ▲

(3.5 km)

▼ 46.8 km Road junction. CSA. Track on right.

Track on right leads 0.8 km to Mount Dutton ruins, including water tank, fettler's cottage and grave site.

	Road junction. CSA. Track on left.	44.0 km ▲

GPS S:27 49.136 E:135 42.886
UTM 53J 570396E 6922650N

(0.6 km)

▼ 47.4 km Road junction. CSA. Track on right.

	Road junction. CSA. Track on left.	43.4 km ▲

Track on left leads 0.8 km to the Mount Dutton ruins.

(3.6 km)

▼ 51.0 km SP: Cadna-owie Lookout on right. CSA.

MARREE ◀ ▶ MARLA

	SP: Cadna-owie Lookout on left. CSA.	39.8 km ▲	

(6.1 km)

▼ 57.1 km Cross SP: Hanns Creek. Old Ghan Railway Bridge some distance to right.

Cross SP: Hanns Creek. Old Ghan Railway Bridge some distance to left. 33.7 km ▲

(4.7 km)

▼ 61.8 km Cross SP: North Creek.

Cross SP: North Creek. 29.0 km ▲

(0.2 km)

▼ 62.0 km Road junction. CSA. Track on right.

Track on right leads short distance to bush campsite near Old Ghan Railway Bridge.

Road junction. CSA. Track on left. 28.8 km ▲

GPS S:27 44.274 E:135 36.234
UTM 53J 559521E 6931685N

(9.7 km)

▼ 71.7 km Road junction. CSA. Track on right SP: 8 Alandale.

Road junction. CSA. Track on left SP: 8 Alandale. 19.1 km ▲

(2.5 km)

▼ 74.2 km Nine Mile Fettlers Quarters ruins on right. CSA.

Walk about 0.8 km to ruins.

Nine Mile Fettlers Quarters ruins on left. CSA. 16.6 km ▲

(11.0 km)

▼ 85.2 km T-junction. TR. SP: Oodnadatta Track/Oodnadatta 6. Track on left SP: Coober Pedy 183.

Road junction. TL. SP: Oodnadatta Track/William Creek 197/Marree 400. Track SO SP: Coober Pedy 183. 5.6 km ▲

GPS S:27 35.433 E:135 27.001
UTM 53J 544413E 6948072N

(5.6 km)

▼ 90.8 km Oodnadatta.

Zero trip meter in Oodnadatta with Pink Roadhouse on right. Proceed south along Oodnadatta Track towards William Creek. 0.0 km ▲

GPS S:27 32.925 E:135 26.906
UTM 53J 544274E 6952703N

▼ 0.0 km Zero trip meter in Oodnadatta with Pink Roadhouse on left. Proceed north along Oodnadatta Track towards Marla.

Oodnadatta. 98.8 km ▲

(7.1 km)

▼ 7.1 km Overland Telegraph monument on right. CSA.

Overland Telegraph monument on left. CSA. 91.7 km ▲

(10.7 km)

▼ 17.8 km Road junction. CSA. SP: Marla 193. Track on right SP: Witjira National Park Simpson Desert/Mt Dare 223.

Road junction. CSA. SP: Oodnadatta 17/Oodnadatta Track. Track on left SP: Witjira National Park Simpson Desert. 81.0 km ▲

GPS S:27 25.243 E:135 21.274
UTM 53J 535047E 6966915N

(15.1 km)

▼ 32.9 km Crossroads. CSA. Track on left SP: Yardinna. Track on right to bore and tank.

Crossroads. CSA. Track on right SP: Yardinna. 65.9 km ▲

(5.4 km)

▼ 38.3 km Road junction. CSA. Track on left SP: Yardinna.

Road junction. CSA. Track on right SP: Yardinna. 60.5 km ▲

(20.8 km)

▼ 59.1 km Cross SP: Woolridge Creek.

Cross SP: Woolridge Creek. 39.7 km ▲

GPS S:27 17.018 E:134 59.089
UTM 53J 498497E 6982149N

(18.3 km)

▼ 77.4 km Grid. Over grid road junction. CSA. Track on right.

Road junction. CSA over grid. Track on left. 21.4 km ▲

(7.2 km)

▼ 84.6 km Cross SP: Kathleen Creek.

Cross SP: Kathleen Creek. 14.2 km ▲

GPS S:27 12.279 E:134 45.244
UTM 53J 475644E 6990874N

(0.1 km)

▼ 84.7 km Road junction. CSA. Track on right SP: Todmorden 8.

Road junction. CSA. Track on left SP: 8 Todmorden. 14.1 km ▲

(14.1 km)

▼ 98.8 km SP: Olarinna Creek.

Zero trip meter after creek crossing. 0.0 km ▲

GPS S:27 09.812 E:134 37.310
UTM 53J 462534E 6995395N

▼ 0.0 km Zero trip meter then proceed across creek. CSA.

Track on right over creek leads 0.4 km to shaded spot, ideal for lunch break.

Cross SP: Olarinna Creek. Track on left prior to crossing. 112.1 km ▲

(26.2 km)

▼ 26.2 km Cross SP: Coongra Creek.

Cross SP: Coongra Creek. 85.9 km ▲

(5.1 km)

▼ 31.3 km Cross SP: Coongra Creek.

Cross SP: Coongra Creek. 80.8 km ▲

GPS S:27 10.660 E:134 19.129
UTM 53J 432522E 6993703N

(80.8 km)

▼ 112.1 km T-junction with bitumen. This is Stuart Hwy at Marla. Marla Roadhouse on right. TL for Coober Pedy. TR for SA–NT border and SP: Alice Springs 453.

Zero trip meter at Marla on Stuart Hwy at junction with SP: Oodnadatta Track. Proceed east along Oodnadatta Track. SP: Oodnadatta 202. 0.0 km ▲

GPS S:27 18.474 E:133 37.512
UTM 53J 363965E 6978712N

REVERSE DIRECTIONS START

■ 29

Simpson Desert

Travelling the French Line

MOUNT DARE ◀▶ BIRDSVILLE 507.4/772.6 KM
Mount Dare ◁▷ Birdsville via French Line/Rig Road 507.4/772.6 km (*difficult*)
WHEN TO GO April–October **TIME** 4–5 days

The arid landscapes of the Simpson Desert sprawl out from Australia's heart into three states. It is the largest parallel dune desert in the world, with spectacularly red sandhills, shimmering salt lakes, impressive claypans, spiky spinifex grassland and stunted gidgee woodland. Covering more than 150 000 square kilometres, there are about 1100 dunes ranging in height from a few metres to a massive 50 metres.

The Simpson is one of Australia's classic four-wheel-drive adventures. It is a roller coaster ride through dunefields culminating, for those who take the west–east northern route, in the largest and most challenging mountain of Simpson Desert sand – Nappanerica Dune or Big Red – before cruising into Birdsville.

There are two route options. The northern route traverses the French Line, constructed during a seismic survey carried out by the French Petroleum Company in 1964. The southern route is the Rig Road, also dating from the 1960s and built to allow fully laden oil-drilling rigs access to the desert. The French Line is the more challenging of the two as it unrelentingly leads across seemingly endless expanses of soft sandhills. The Rig Road has a more varied landscape and the track surface, originally constructed with clay capping over the dunes, makes for an easier drive.

This is remote country. The trek start point, Mount Dare homestead, has limited facilities, as do its closest towns: to the south Oodnadatta (250 kilometres via Eringa ruin); to the north-west Kulgera on the Stuart Highway (252 kilometres). Alice Springs is around 330 kilometres via the Old South Road track or 520 kilometres via Kulgera and the Stuart Highway. At the trek's western end, Birdsville provides all services.

SIMPSON DESERT

Mount Dare

Mount Dare station, acquired by the South Australian government in 1985, subsequently became Witjira National Park. Mount Dare homestead, accessed from the Stuart Highway either from Oodnadatta in South Australia or Kulgera in the Northern Territory, provides basic accommodation, camping, food, fuel and minor repairs.

Desert dweller, the central bearded dragon (Pogona vitticeps)

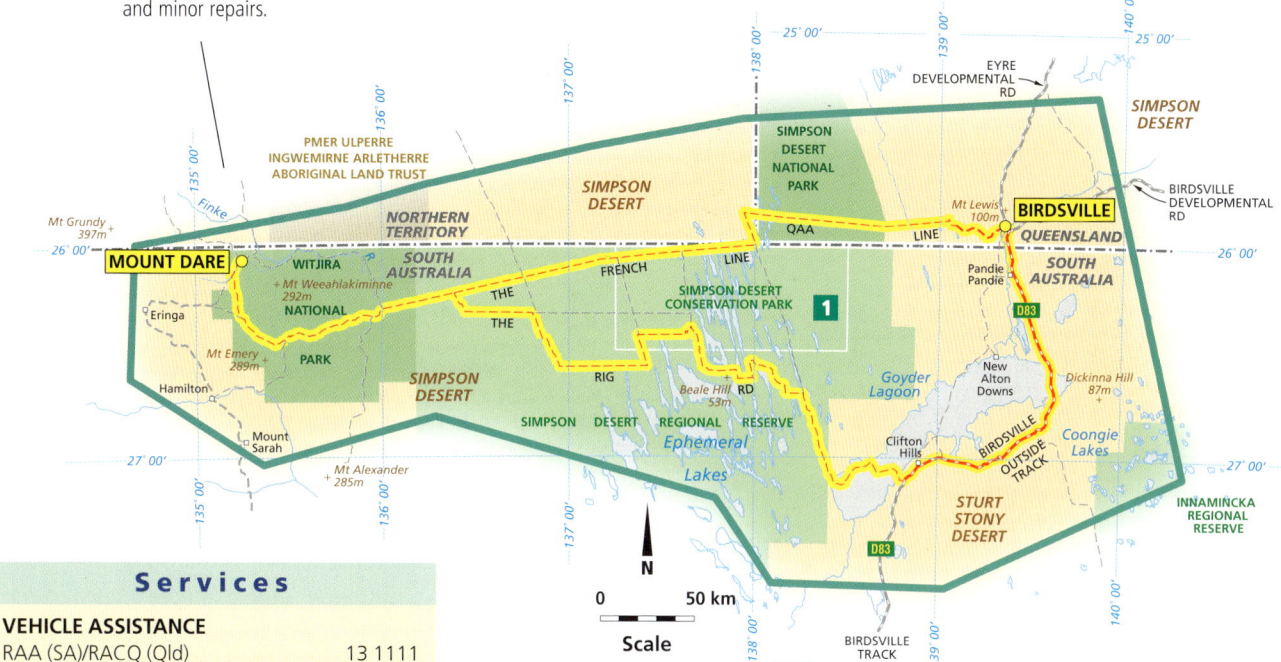

Services

VEHICLE ASSISTANCE
RAA (SA)/RACQ (Qld)	13 1111
Birdsville Autos*	(07) 4656 3226
	AH (07) 4656 3254
Mount Dare*	(08) 8670 7835

*Vehicle recovery service

POLICE
Birdsville (07) 4656 3220

PARKS AND RESERVES
Simpson Desert Conservation Reserve
Simpson Desert Regional Reserve
Witjira National Park
NPWSA Port Augusta 1800 816 078

Simpson Desert National Park
QPWS Birdsville (07) 4656 3272

VISITOR INFORMATION
Birdsville (07) 4656 3300
www.diamantina.qld.gov.au

Authors' note

One crossing of the Simpson is never enough. If you have the chance, either on the same trip or years apart, try both these routes. They traverse vastly different desert landscapes, proving that there is more to the crossing than just conquering sandhills.

Town Facilities

	Fuel: D/P/A	Mechanical repairs	Tyre repairs	Public telephone	Public toilets	Shop/supplies	Gas refills	Ice	Visitor information	Post office	Medical centre	Police	Meals	Motel	Hotel	Cabins	Caravan park	Camping
Birdsville	D/P	•	•	•	•	•	•	•	•	•	•	•	•	•	•	•	•	•
Mount Dare	D/P	•	•	•	•								•					•

31

SIMPSON DESERT

MOUNT DARE ◄►BIRDSVILLE 507.4/772.6 KM

Start point
Mount Dare

Road atlas
355 J8

Total distance
507.4 (via French Line)
772.6 (via Rig Road)

Standard
Difficult

Time
4–5 days

Longest distance no PD (includes all options)
565.0 km (Mount Dare to Birdsville via French Line)
794.4 km (Mount Dare to Birdsville via Rig Road)

Topographic maps
Auslig 1:250 000 series: *Dalhousie*; *Poolowanna*; *Simpson Desert South*; *Birdsville*; *Pandie Pandie*; *Cordillo*; *Gason*

Other useful information
- Mount Dare homestead shop open 8am–9pm with fuel available 9am–8pm, tel. (08) 8670 7835; accepts cash, EFTPOS and credit cards.
- Queensland Parks and Wildlife Service brochures: *Simpson Desert National Park*; *Species List: Mammals and Reptiles of the Simpson Desert National Park*.
- Information booklets, brochures and maps enclosed with Desert Parks Pass (see Permits and bookings).

Junction of the French Line and Rig Road tracks

- Diamantina Shire information pack fact sheets: *Birdsville*; *Burke and Wills Expedition*; *Waddi Trees*; *Buildings of Birdsville and Surrounds*; and town map. All available at Birdsville Visitor Centre.
- Mark Shephard's *The Simpson Desert* is an excellent reference on the natural history, Aboriginal occupation and European exploration of the region.
- Reptile and bird identification guides are helpful in identifying lizards, snakes and birds along the track.

Description
The route directions for the Simpson offer two alternative tracks across the desert. Both start at Mount Dare homestead, lead east to Purnie Bore then after 29 kilometres the French Line spears north-east to Poeppel Corner while the Rig Road winds south-east through the southern reaches of the desert. The two routes conclude at the legendary outback Queensland town of Birdsville on the desert's eastern fringe.

The French Line, the most direct route across the desert, is also the most difficult and demanding as it traverses in excess of 600 large 'active' dunes. The western section of this route is characterised by smaller, closely knit sandhills. The eastern section, particularly on the approaches to Poeppel Corner, has larger, widely spaced dunes with interdunal flats dotted with large claypans and salt lakes. From Poeppel Corner the track veers north for a short distance then swings east, crossing Eyre Creek and Big Red, reputedly the largest of the Simpson dunes and the last before Birdsville. There are now easier route detours around Big Red, and some of the other dunes. A number of the claypans and salt lakes hold water for a considerable time after rain and can become very boggy. Most have detours around them.

The less challenging southern route through the Simpson, the Rig Road, was constructed to provide desert access for drilling rigs and earth-moving equipment. A clay capping was laid over the dune sections of the track, providing a hard surface. Over time the surface has begun to deteriorate, allowing the formation of soft sand drifts across the capping, but the route is still the easier option. After splitting away from the French Line, the Rig Road winds south-eastwards in an almost zigzag fashion. In contrast to the northern route, the landscape here is characterised by low stunted shrubs and spinifex-rimmed dunes. Defying this generality, a single coolibah, the Lone Gum, is located north of Walkandi Junction, standing like a sentinel in the middle of the desert.

From the Knolls Track junction the Rig Road swings south-east, weaving around numerous large salt lakes before joining the Warburton then Yelpawaralina Track, which turns sharply to negotiate the flood plain of Goyder Lagoon via the Warburton Creek Crossing. The route then links up with the Birdsville Track, just south of Clifton Hills homestead. From this point it is a little less than 200 kilometres to Birdsville.

The dominant vegetation in the Simpson is spinifex (*Triodia basedowii*), found between and around the dunes, and sandhill canegrass (*Zygochloa paradoxa*), covering the dune crests and providing a habitat for the elusive Eyrean grasswren. There are also woodlands of Georgina gidgee (*Acacia georginae*), dubbed stinking wattle because of the unpleasant smell it gives off in wet or humid weather. There are some good stands of this species east of Approdinna Attora Knolls. Except for the odd dingo and occasional camel, reptiles in the form of lizards and geckos are the most commonly encountered animals. Other desert dwellers, although rarely seen, are the marsupial mole, mulgara (a mouse-like marsupial), spinifex hopping-mouse and other rodents and bats. Bird species number over 180, with the zebra finch, crested pigeon, black-winged stilt and purple swamphen among those you might see at Purnie Bore.

Whichever route you choose, apart from campgrounds at Mount Dare and Dalhousie Springs and a caravan park at Birdsville, bush camping is the only option.

Advice and warnings
- This is remote country so you should be totally self-sufficient. Carry plenty of food, water and fuel.
- Possible track closures during and after heavy rains, particularly Spring Creek Delta, road from Big Red to Birdsville, Yelpawaralina Track at Warburton Crossing and QAA Line at Eyre Creek. Always check surface of salt lakes and claypans before crossing during and after rain. Drive with caution over wash-outs and corrugations on the Rig Road. Contact South Australian road report hotline, tel. 1300 361 033, or RACQ road reporting service, tel. 1300 130 595, to check track conditions. See also Services table on page 31.
- Watch out for oncoming traffic over sand dunes – mount a high-flying red flag to your vehicle and tune CB/UHF radio to channel 10.
- Watch out for roaming stock at the eastern edge of the Simpson as the track passes through pastoral land. Leave all gates as found and do not disturb cattle or watering points.
- Watch out for wild camels on the track.
- Standard road tyres are suitable. Tyre pressure should be reduced to 20–25 psi for the French Line and marginally reduced for the Rig Road. Carry a tyre-pressure gauge and air compressor.

Camping near Walkandi Junction on the Rig Road

- Towing off-road trailers across the Simpson Desert is not recommended.
- Camping is at designated sites and bush camping is possible throughout the desert within 500 m either side of the track.
- If camping at Dalhousie Springs, collect firewood from signposted firewood collection zone only, near 3 O'Clock Creek.
- Rubbish bins are not provided so please take your rubbish with you.
- Carry sunblock, hats and sunglasses, and bathers for a dip at Dalhousie Springs.

Permits and bookings
- Desert Parks Pass required per vehicle to travel through Witjira National Park, Simpson Desert Conservation Park and Simpson Desert Regional Reserve. This pass covers a range of other outback parks in South Australia and entitles holder to camp within these parks or at specified locations and to travel on designated park roads. Contact Desert Parks Hotline, tel. 1800 816 078, to obtain pass or for further details.
- Camping permit and fee required to camp in Simpson Desert National Park in Queensland. Fees payable to and permits available from Queensland Parks and Wildlife Birdsville office, tel. (07) 4656 3272.
- Bookings not required for camping, but highly recommended for other types of accommodation.
- Mount Dare has homestead accommodation, tel. (08) 8670 7835. Bookings recommended.
- Bookings recommended for Birdsville Caravan Park, especially during Birdsville Races in first weekend in September, tel. (07) 4656 3214.
- Bookings advised at all times for accommodation at Birdsville Hotel, tel. (07) 4656 3244.

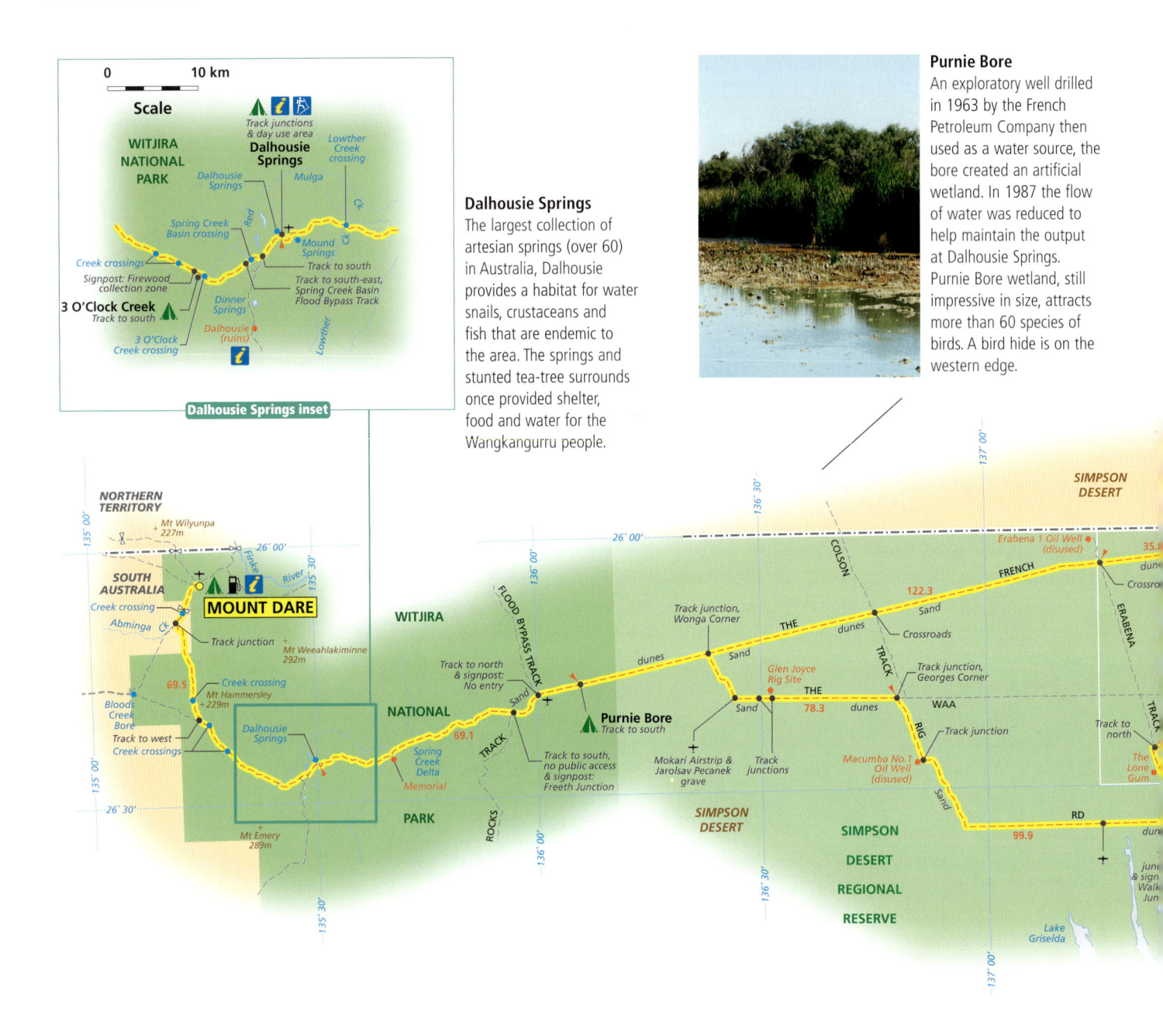

SIMPSON DESERT

Dalhousie Springs
The largest collection of artesian springs (over 60) in Australia, Dalhousie provides a habitat for water snails, crustaceans and fish that are endemic to the area. The springs and stunted tea-tree surrounds once provided shelter, food and water for the Wangkangurru people.

Purnie Bore
An exploratory well drilled in 1963 by the French Petroleum Company then used as a water source, the bore created an artificial wetland. In 1987 the flow of water was reduced to help maintain the output at Dalhousie Springs. Purnie Bore wetland, still impressive in size, attracts more than 60 species of birds. A bird hide is on the western edge.

Campsite Facilities

	Toilets	Disabled access	4WD access only	Off-road trailer	Off-road caravan	Drinking water	Fee payable	Ranger patrolled	BBQ/fireplace	Campfires prohibited	Picnic tables	Shelter shed	No rubbish disposal	Public phone	Shower	Bushwalking	Swimming	Swimming not advised	Fishing	Canoeing	Dogs allowed
3 O'Clock Creek		•	•			•	•				•	•									
Dalhousie Springs	•		•	•		•	•				•	•	•	•	•	•					
Mount Dare	•		•	•	•	•	•						•								
Purnie Bore	•		•	•		•	•					•									
Tippipilla Creek			•	•							•										

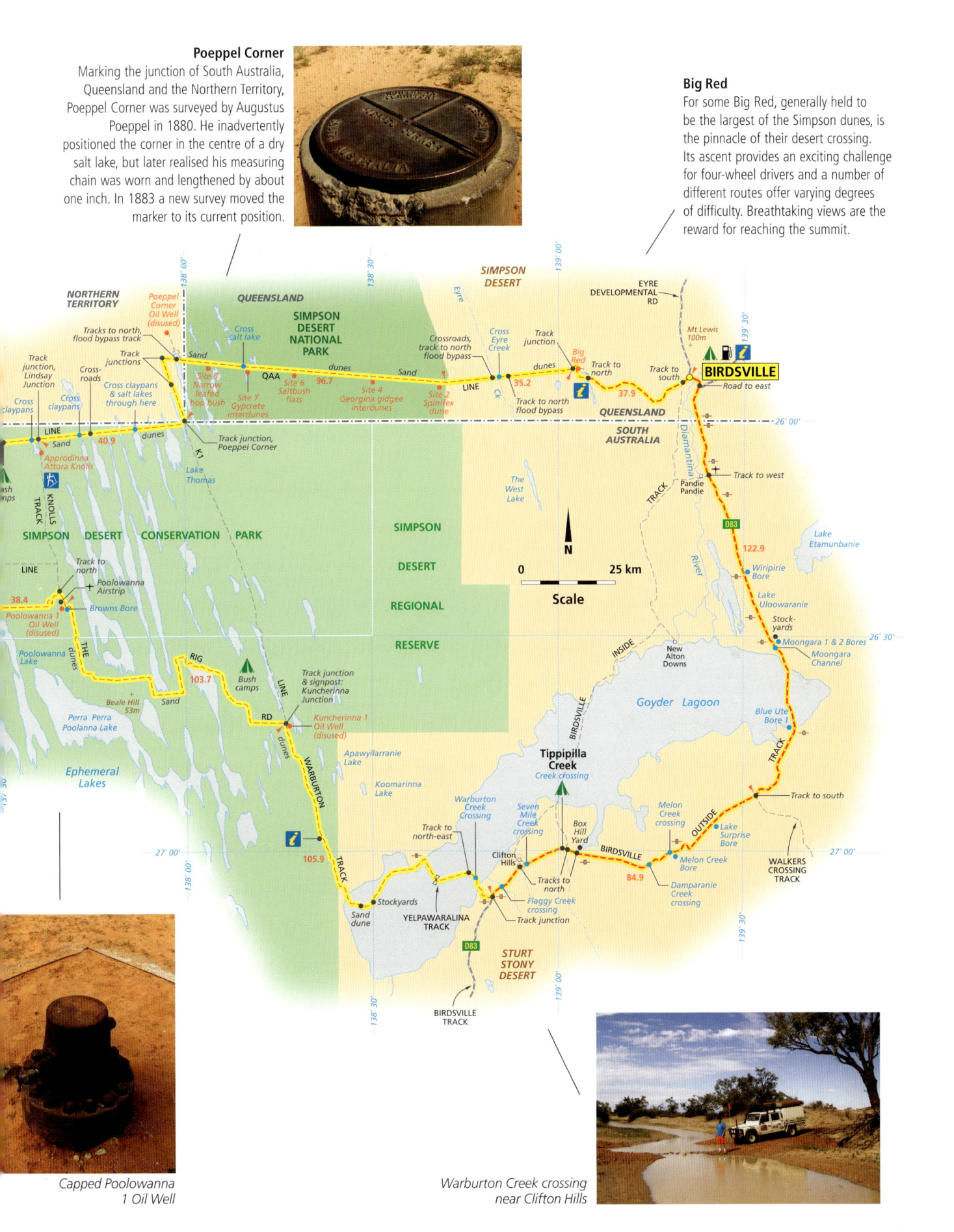

MOUNT DARE ◀▶ BIRDSVILLE

Poeppel Corner
Marking the junction of South Australia, Queensland and the Northern Territory, Poeppel Corner was surveyed by Augustus Poeppel in 1880. He inadvertently positioned the corner in the centre of a dry salt lake, but later realised his measuring chain was worn and lengthened by about one inch. In 1883 a new survey moved the marker to its current position.

Big Red
For some Big Red, generally held to be the largest of the Simpson dunes, is the pinnacle of their desert crossing. Its ascent provides an exciting challenge for four-wheel drivers and a number of different routes offer varying degrees of difficulty. Breathtaking views are the reward for reaching the summit.

Capped Poolowanna 1 Oil Well

Warburton Creek crossing near Clifton Hills

35

SIMPSON DESERT

ROUTE DIRECTIONS

▼ 0.0 km Zero trip meter at Mount Dare homestead with Simpson Desert information boards on left and fuel bowsers on right. Proceed towards SP: Dalhousie Springs 70 km/Kulgera 252.

Mount Dare homestead. Information boards on right and fuel bowsers on left. 69.5 km ▲

GPS S:26 04.226 E:135 14.859
UTM 53J 524769E 7116493N

(0.1 km)

▼ 0.1 km Road junction. CSA. SP: Oodnadatta 250/Dalhousie 70. Road on right SP: Alice Springs 520/Finke 104.

Road junction. CSA. SP: Andado/Mt Dare HS. Road on left SP: Alice Springs 520/Finke 104. 69.4 km ▲

(6.9 km)

▼ 7.0 km Gate. LAF.

Gate. LAF. 62.5 km ▲

(1.0 km)

▼ 8.0 km Creek crossing

Creek crossing. 61.5 km ▲

(2.8 km)

▼ 10.8 km Track junction. TL. SP: 61 Dalhousie. Track SO SP: 241 Oodnadatta.

T-junction. TR. SP: Mt Dare 9. Track on left SP: 241 Oodnadatta. 58.7 km ▲

GPS S:26 08.472 E:135 11.589
UTM 53J 519307E 7108665N

(18.5 km)

▼ 29.3 km Creek crossing.

Creek crossing. 40.2 km ▲

(4.7 km)

▼ 34.0 km Track junction. CSA. SP: Dalhousie Springs 35 km. Track on right SP: Bloods Creek via Federal 15 km.

Federal and Bloods Creek are old station ruins, the latter belonging to Ted Colson, who in 1936 was the first European to complete a west–east trek across the desert.

Track junction. CSA. SP: Mt Dare Homestead 35 km. Track on left SP: Bloods Creek via Federal 15 km. 35.5 km ▲

GPS S:26 19.914 E:135 14.335
UTM 53J 523843E 7087537N

(2.5 km)

▼ 36.5 km Creek crossing.

Creek crossing. 33.0 km ▲

(7.3 km)

▼ 43.8 km Creek crossing.

Creek crossing. 25.7 km ▲

(9.0 km)

▼ 52.8 km Creek crossing.

Good stands of mineritchie or red mulga trees (*Acacia cyperophylla*), named for their brilliant red bark, in this vicinity.

Creek crossing. 16.7 km ▲

(2.3 km)

▼ 55.1 km Creek crossing.

Creek crossing. 14.4 km ▲

(2.0 km)

▼ 57.1 km SP: Firewood collection zone on left. CSA.

SP: Firewood collection zone on right. CSA. 12.4 km ▲

(0.9 km)

▼ 58.0 km Track junction. CSA and cross SP: 3 O'Clock Creek. Track on right.

Track on right leads 0.3 km to **3 O'Clock Creek camping area**, a large open site alongside creek.

Cross 3 O'Clock Creek. Track junction over creek. CSA. Track on left to camping area. 11.5 km ▲

GPS S:26 27.558 E:135 24.696
UTM 53J 541031E 7073384N

(6.5 km)

▼ 64.5 km Cross SP: Spring Creek Basin.

This area can be boggy after rain.

Cross SP: Spring Creek Basin. 5.0 km ▲

(1.7 km)

▼ 66.2 km Track junction. CSA. SP: Dalhousie Springs 3. Track on right SP: Dalhousie Ruins 9.

Track on right leads 8.6 km to Dalhousie ruins and mound spring. Remains of homestead, shed, workmen's quarters and blacksmith's shop, built of local limestone between 1872 and 1885.

Track junction. CSA. SP: Oodnadatta/Mount Dare. Track on left SP: Dalhousie Ruins 9. 3.3 km ▲

GPS S:26 26.627 E:135 28.800
UTM 53J 547856E 7075079N

(3.3 km)

▼ 69.5 km Track junction.

Zero trip meter at T-junction. TL. SP: Oodnadatta/Mount Dare. Track on right to day visitor carpark. 0.0 km ▲

GPS S:26 25.402 E:135 30.099
UTM 53J 550023E 7077332N

▼ 0.0 km Zero trip meter at track junction. TR. SP: Dalhousie Campground 150 m/Purnie Bore/Birdsville. Track SO SP: Day Visitor Car Park 100 m.

Ruins of Dalhousie homestead

MOUNT DARE ◄ ► BIRDSVILLE

Track SO leads short distance to day visitor carpark and walk to Dalhousie Springs, a perfect spot for a refreshing dip.

T-junction. **69.1 km** ▲

(0.1 km)

▼ **0.1 km** Track junction. CSA. Track on left SP: Campground.

Dalhousie Springs camping area is a large open space with a number of individual bays and larger bays for groups. Walking tracks lead from campground to springs and nature walk.

Track junction. CSA. Track on right SP: Campground. **69.0 km** ▲

(0.2 km)

▼ **0.3 km** Track junction. TR. SP: Purnie Bore 70 km. Track SO SP: Ranger Residence/Private Road.

Office and information shelter on left of track.

T-junction. TL. Track on right SP: Ranger Residence. **68.8 km** ▲

(8.7 km)

▼ **9.0 km** Cross SP: Lowther Creek.

Cross SP: Lowther Creek. **60.1 km** ▲

(11.2 km)

▼ **20.2 km** Western side of SP: Spring Creek Delta. CSA over Spring Creek Delta.

Please note this section of track is impassable after rain and remains closed until dry.

Western side of SP: Spring Creek Delta. **48.9 km** ▲

GPS S:26 24.458 E:135 40.168
UTM 53J 566767E 7078999N

(9.7 km)

▼ **29.9 km** Eastern side of SP: Spring Creek Delta. CSA.

Eastern side of SP: Spring Creek Delta. CSA over Spring Creek Delta. **39.2 km** ▲

Please note this section of track is impassable after rain and remains closed until dry.

(21.5 km)

▼ **51.4 km** Track junction. This is SP: Freeth Junction. CSA. SP: Purnie Bore 18 km. Track on right is Rocks Track.

Rocks Track has no public access.

Track junction. This is SP: Freeth Junction. CSA. SP: Dalhousie Springs 50 km. Track on left. **17.7 km** ▲

GPS S:26 20.129 E:135 56.858
UTM 53J 594569E 7086816N

(1.9 km)

▼ **53.3 km** Cross first sand dune.

Cross last sand dune. **15.8 km** ▲

(6.4 km)

▼ **59.7 km** Track junction. CSA. Track on left SP: No Entry.

Track junction. CSA. Track on right SP: No Entry. **9.4 km** ▲

(9.4 km)

▼ **69.1 km** Track junction. SP: Purnie Bore, on right, and track on left. Choose the northern or southern route: route directions for the French Line (Northern Route) follow; those for the Rig Road (Southern Route), see page 41.

Purnie Bore camping area has open campsites on eastern edge of wetland, with bird hide located on western edge.

Delightful Dalhousie Springs

Zero trip meter at track junction. CSA. SP: Purnie Bore, on left, and track on right. **0.0 km** ▲

GPS S:26 17.057 E:136 05.868
UTM 53J 609604E 7092368N

► **NORTHERN ROUTE: The French Line**

▼ **0.0 km** Zero trip meter at track junction. CSA. SP: Purnie Bore, on right.

Track junction. **122.3 km** ▲

(8.2 km)

▼ **8.2 km** Enter SP: Simpson Desert Regional Reserve.

Enter SP: Witjira National Park. **114.1 km** ▲

(21.3 km)

▼ **29.5 km** Track junction. This is known as Wonga Corner. CSA. SP: The French Line/Approdinna Attora Knolls 130 km/Poeppel Corner 170 km/Birdsville 330 km. Track on right SP: The Rig Road.

Track on right is alternative Rig Road route.

Track junction. CSA. Track on left SP: The Rig Road. **92.8 km** ▲

GPS S:26 13.761 E:136 22.980
UTM 53J 638146E 7098180N

(39.1 km)

▼ **68.6 km** Crossroads. CSA. Track on left and right SP: Colson Track.

Crossroads. CSA. Track on left and right SP: Colson Track. **53.7 km** ▲

(53.7 km)

▼ **122.3 km** Crossroads.

Zero trip meter at crossroads. CSA. **0.0 km** ▲

Track on right to Erabena 1 Oil Well. Track on left to WAA Line and Rig Road.

GPS S:26 03.991 E:137 15.456
UTM 53J 725844E 7114994N

▼ **0.0 km** Zero trip meter at crossroads. CSA.

Track on right leads 31 km to WAA Line and 43 km to Rig Road. Track on left leads 7.5 km to disused Erabena 1 Oil Well that was drilled November 1981.

37

SIMPSON DESERT

		Crossroads.	35.8 km ▲
(26.0 km)			
▼ 26.0 km	Bush camping in this vicinity.		
	Well-protected bush campsites on left and right of track among stands of gidgee.		
		Bush camping in this vicinity.	9.8 km ▲
(7.1 km)			
▼ 33.1 km	Cross claypan.		
	Good bush camping from here to Knolls Track among stands of gidgee.		
		Cross claypan.	2.7 km ▲
(0.6 km)			
▼ 33.7 km	Cross claypan.		
		Cross claypan.	2.1 km ▲
(0.6 km)			
▼ 34.3 km	Cross claypan.		
		Cross claypan.	1.5 km ▲
(1.5 km)			
▼ 35.8 km	Track junction. This is Lindsay Junction.		
	Zero trip meter at Lindsay Junction. CSA. Track on left is Knolls Track.		0.0 km ▲
	GPS S:26 02.130 E:137 36.318
UTM 53J 760710E 7117782N		
▼ 0.0 km	Zero trip meter at Lindsay Junction. CSA. Track on right is Knolls Track.		
	Track on right leads 4.1 km to Approdinna Attora Knolls, two low gypsum hills in an otherwise flattish desert landscape. Named by Ted Colson in 1936. Walking track leads to peak of knolls and good views of surrounding desert and salt lakes.		
		Track junction. This is Lindsay Junction.	40.9 km ▲
(11.6 km)			
▼ 11.6 km	Cross claypan.		
		Cross claypan.	29.3 km ▲
(2.9 km)			

Travelling along the Rig Road

▼ 14.5 km	Crossroads. CSA. Faint track on right.		
		Crossroads. CSA.	26.4 km ▲
(3.8 km)			
▼ 18.3 km	Cross claypan.		
		Cross claypan.	22.6 km ▲
(0.6 km)			
▼ 18.9 km	Cross claypan.		
		Cross claypan.	22.0 km ▲
(3.6 km)			
▼ 22.5 km	Cross salt lake.		
		Cross salt lake.	18.4 km ▲
(4.0 km)			
▼ 26.5 km	Cross salt lake.		
		Cross salt lake.	14.4 km ▲
(3.0 km)			
▼ 29.5 km	Cross claypan.		
		Cross claypan.	11.4 km ▲
(1.7 km)			
▼ 31.2 km	Cross claypan.		
		Cross claypan.	9.7 km ▲
(4.1 km)			
▼ 35.3 km	Cross Lake Thomas salt lake.		
		Cross Lake Thomas salt lake.	5.6 km ▲
	GPS S:26 00.503 E:137 56.961
UTM 53J 795224E 7120054N		
(4.4 km)			
▼ 39.7 km	Track junction. Edge of Lake Poeppel salt lake. Proceed on track that runs at 45-degree angle left across salt lake. Track SO leads across lake.		
	Track on immediate left is flood bypass track.		
		Western edge of Lake Poeppel. CSA.	1.2 km ▲
	GPS S:26 00.292 E:137 59.521
UTM 53J 799506E 7120346N		
(1.2 km)			
▼ 40.9 km	Track junction. Poeppel Corner to left of junction. Track on right.		
	Zero trip meter at Poeppel Corner track junction. TR and cross Poeppel Lake. Track SO.		0.0 km ▲
	GPS S:25 59.835 E:137 59.975
UTM 53J 800283E 7121173N		
▼ 0.0 km	Zero trip meter at Poeppel Corner junction. TL and enter SP: Simpson Desert National Park.		
	Park car here and walk 50 metres to Poeppel Corner. Visitor book here.		
		Track junction. Poeppel Corner to right of junction.	96.7 km ▲
(10.7 km)			
▼ 10.7 km	Track junction. CSA. Track on left.		
		Y-junction. KL. Track on right.	86.0 km ▲
(2.7 km)			
▼ 13.4 km	Cross claypan.		
		Cross claypan.	83.3 km ▲
(4.7 km)			
▼ 18.1 km	Track junction. TR. Track on left.		
	Track on left leads to claypan.		

38

Conquering the Simpson Desert

For thousands of years Aboriginal people lived in and criss-crossed the Simpson Desert. They inhabited the mound springs on the edges of the Simpson, making frequent forays into the desert proper in good seasons then retreating to the permanent water sources when dry conditions prevailed. A network of Aboriginal wells and mound springs enabled tribes to traverse the arid terrain. This part of the continent was at the centre of the north–south trade routes, along which pituri from the central regions, ochre from the south and shells from the north were carried and exchanged. The water sources, so crucial for survival, featured in the myths and song cycles of the Simpson Desert people. It is not surprising that Aboriginal desert dwellers guided a number of later European expeditions.

In the 19th century, European explorers tried to conquer the desolate inland expanses of northern South Australia. Charles Sturt was the first to enter the Simpson, venturing into the eastern fringes in 1844–45, before turning back in despair at the prospect of yet more gibber plains, sandhills and salt lakes. Peter Warburton in 1866 and John Lewis in 1874–75 surveyed the southern reaches of the desert north of Lake Eyre. Surveyor Augustus Poeppel was the first to penetrate the dunes when he marked out the junction and adjoining state boundaries of Queensland, Northern Territory and South Australia in 1880. In 1883 Charles Winnecke made a south–north crossing from Cowarie station to Poeppel Corner and on to the Hay River. In 1886 David Lindsay, with Dalhousie station owner Charles Bagot and Aboriginal guide Paddy, followed Aboriginal wells and trekked north-east from Dalhousie to the Queensland border north of Poeppel Corner. The three men returned by the same route, travelling almost 700 kilometres in 19 days. Despite this significant achievement, Lindsay's journey fell short of qualifying as a complete crossing.

In 1929 Cecil Madigan undertook a number of aerial surveys over the desert, financed by industrialist Alfred Simpson. Madigan named the desert after his sponsor. In 1936, inspired by Madigan's efforts, Ted Colson and Peter Ains, an Aboriginal guide, made the first complete west–east crossing of the desert, from Colson's property at Bloods Creek, just south of Mount Dare, to Birdsville. Colson was a remarkable bushman, experienced camel handler and fluent in local Aboriginal dialects, and his achievement was all the more extraordinary because it was carried out by two men who were alone and unassisted.

Ted Colson (centre), his wife Alice and Peter Ains in 1936

Ted Colson and Peter Ains made the first complete east–west crossing

The first vehicle crossing was undertaken in 1962 by Reg Sprigg as part of a survey for a petroleum company. Sprigg, with his wife and two children, drove from near Mount Dare to Birdsville. Three backup teams, starting from points to the north, linked up with the Spriggs near Poeppel Corner, and aerial support made regular safety checks and provided fuel and supplies. As a result, mining companies cut tracks across the Simpson to carry out seismic surveys, searching for oil and natural gas. These tracks evolved into the French Line and the Rig Road, which are the main routes used to cross the desert today.

SIMPSON DESERT

		Track junction. TL. Track SO.	78.6 km ▲
	(3.4 km)		
▼ 21.5 km	Crossroads. CSA and cross salt lake. Track on right SP: K1 Line.		
	Note centre of this salt lake can remain wet and boggy for some time after rain. Check crossing prior to driving over. Track on left leads 3.1 km to flood bypass track, on right, which joins route directions at the 23.3 km reading, and a further 5.0 km to Poeppel Corner Oil Well, drilled in August 1984.		
		Crossroads on western side of salt lake. CSA. Track on left SP: K1 Line.	75.2 km ▲
	GPS S:25 51.228 E:137 58.366 **UTM** 53J 797958E 7137134N		
	(1.8 km)		
▼ 23.3 km	Track junction. CSA. Track on left. Track on left is where flood bypass track joins.		
		Track junction. CSA. Track on right.	73.4 km ▲
		Track on right is flood bypass and joins route notes at 75.2 km reading.	
	(7.7 km)		
▼ 31.0 km	Marker on right. SP: Site 8 Narrow leafed hopbush.		
		Marker on left. SP: Site 8 Narrow leafed hopbush.	65.7 km ▲
	(9.5 km)		
▼ 40.5 km	Cross salt lake. If wet a flood bypass skirts around lake's southern edge.		
		Cross salt lake.	56.2 km ▲
		If wet a flood bypass skirts around lake's southern edge.	
	GPS S: 25 52.323 E:138 09.453 **UTM** 54J 215154E 7135401N		
	(0.8 km)		
▼ 41.3 km	Marker on right. SP: Site 7 Gypcrete Interdunes.		
		Marker on left. SP: Site 7 Gypcrete Interdunes.	55.4 km ▲
	(13.3 km)		
▼ 54.6 km	Marker on right. SP: Site 6 Saltbush flats.		
		Marker on left. SP: Site 6 Saltbush flats.	42.1 km ▲
	(21.9 km)		
▼ 76.5 km	Marker on right. SP: Site 4 Georgina Gidgee Interdunes.		
		Marker on left. SP: Site 4 Georgina Gidgee Interdunes.	20.2 km ▲
	(18.2 km)		
▼ 94.7 km	Marker on right. SP: Site 2 Spinifex dune.		
		Marker on left. SP: Site 2 Spinifex dune.	2.0 km ▲
	(2.0 km)		
▼ 96.7 km	Park boundary.		
		Zero trip meter at park boundary. CSA entering SP: Simpson Desert National Park.	0.0 km ▲
	GPS S:25 54.683 E:138 42.148 **UTM** 54J 269858E 7132113N		
▼ 0.0 km	Zero trip meter at park boundary. CSA. SP: Birdsville. Exiting Simpson Desert National Park and entering SP: Private Property/Adria Downs Station.		

Eyre Creek crossing

		Park boundary.	35.2 km ▲
	(14.9 km)		
▼ 14.9 km	Crossroads. CSA. Track on left is Eyre Creek flood bypass track.		
		Crossroads. CSA.	20.3 km ▲
		Track on right is where Eyre Creek flood bypass track joins.	
	(0.4 km)		
▼ 15.3 km	Cross Eyre Creek.		
		Cross Eyre Creek.	19.9 km ▲
	GPS S:25 53.906 E:138 51.049 **UTM** 54J 284699E 7133800N		
	(0.3 km)		
▼ 15.6 km	Track junction. CSA. Track on left.		
		Track junction. CSA. Track on right.	19.6 km ▲
	(1.0 km)		
▼ 16.6 km	Creek crossing		
		Creek crossing.	18.6 km ▲
	(0.1 km)		
▼ 16.7 km	Track junction. CSA. Track on left and minor track on right. Track on left is where Eyre Creek flood bypass track joins.		
		Track junction. CSA. Track on right and minor track on left.	18.5 km ▲
		Track on right is Eyre Creek flood bypass track.	
	(18.5 km)		
▼ 35.2 km	Track junction.		
		Zero trip meter at track junction. TL. Track on right SP: Big Red.	0.0 km ▲
	GPS S:25 52.838 E:139 02.718 **UTM** 54J 304157E 7136077N		
▼ 0.0 km	Zero trip meter at track junction. TR. SP: Birdsville. Track SO SP: Big Red. Track SO leads 0.2 km to base of impressive and challenging Big Red sand dune.		
		Track junction.	37.9 km ▲
	(3.0 km)		

MOUNT DARE ◀▶ BIDSVILLE

▼ 3.0 km — Cross last sand dune.
    Cross first sand dune. — 34.9 km ▲
(0.9 km)

▼ 3.9 km — Information boards, picnic tables and shelter on right. CSA.
    Information boards, picnic tables and shelter on left. CSA. — 34.0 km ▲

GPS	S:25 54.071 E:139 04.243
UTM	54J 306738E 7133838N

(0.9 km)

▼ 4.8 km — Track junction. CSA. Track on left.
    Track junction. CSA. Track on right. — 33.1 km ▲
(30.8 km)

▼ 35.6 km — Track junction. CSA. Track on right. Track on right is Birdsville Inside Track.
    Track junction. CSA. Track on left. — 2.3 km ▲
(2.3 km)

▼ 37.9 km — Birdsville. Birdsville Hotel on left.
    Zero trip meter in Birdsville with Birdsville Hotel on right. Proceed in westerly direction out of town towards Simpson Desert and Northern Territory. — 0.0 km ▲

GPS	S:25 53.950 E:139 21.105
UTM	54J 334892E 7134445N

FRENCH LINE REVERSE DIRECTIONS START

▶ **SOUTHERN ROUTE: The Rig Road**

▼ 0.0 km — Zero trip meter at track junction. CSA. SP: Purnie Bore, on right.
    Track junction. SP: Purnie Bore, on left. Reverse directions continue on page 37. — 78.3 km ▲
(8.2 km)

▼ 8.2 km — Enter SP: Simpson Desert Regional Reserve.
    Enter SP: Witjira National Park. — 70.1 km ▲
(21.3 km)

▼ 29.5 km — Track junction. This is known as Wonga Corner. TR. SP: The Rig Road/Knolls Track 181 km/K1 Line 283 km/Birdsville Track 388 km. Track SO SP: The French Line. Track SO is French Line route option via Poeppel Corner.
    Track junction. KL. Track on right SP: The French Line. — 48.8 km ▲

GPS	S:26 13.761 E:136 22.980
UTM	53J 638146E 7098180N

(12.6 km)

▼ 42.1 km — Grave site on left. CSA over Mokari Airstrip.
    Cross Mokari Airstrip. Grave site on right over airstrip. — 36.2 km ▲
(5.3 km)

▼ 47.4 km — Track junction. CSA. Track on right.
    Track junction. CSA. Track on left. — 30.9 km ▲
(3.0 km)

▼ 50.4 km — Track junction. CSA. Track on left. Track on left leads 2.0 km to old Glen Joyce Rig Site.
    Track junction. CSA. Track on right. — 27.9 km ▲

GPS	S:26 19.171 E:136 31.501
UTM	53J 652216E 7088033N

(27.9 km)

▼ 78.3 km — Track junction. This is Georges Corner.
    Zero trip meter at Georges Corner. TL. Track on right is WAA Line. — 0.0 km ▲

GPS	S:26 19.395 E:136 48.051
UTM	53J 679747E 7087265N

▼ 0.0 km — Zero trip meter at Georges Corner. TR. SP: The Rig Road/K1 Line 232 km/Birdsville Track 339 km. Track SO is WAA Line.
    T-junction. This is Georges Corner. — 99.9 km ▲
(14.7 km)

▼ 14.7 km — Macumba No 1 Oil Well on right. CSA.
    Macumba No 1 Oil Well on left. CSA. — 85.2 km ▲
(0.3 km)

▼ 15.0 km — Track junction. TL in easterly direction. Track SO.
    Track junction. TR in north-westerly direction. Track on left. — 84.9 km ▲
(67.0 km)

▼ 82.0 km — Track junction. This is SP: Walkandi Junction. KL. SP: Erabena Track/French Line 60 km. Track on right SP: No Access.
    Track junction. This is SP: Walkandi Junction. TR. — 17.9 km ▲

GPS	S:26 34.355 E:137 25.378
UTM	53J 741341E 7058620N

(11.4 km)

▼ 93.4 km — SP: The Lone Gum, on left. CSA.

This coolibah tree is the only one of its species known to exist in the desert, as coolibahs are generally associated with alluvial floodout country. It remains a mystery as to how and why this tree grows at this site.

    SP: The Lone Gum, on right. CSA. — 6.5 km ▲

GPS	S:26 28.563 E:137 23.303
UTM	53J 738094E 7069382N

(6.5 km)

▼ 99.9 km — Track junction.
    Zero trip meter at track junction. CSA. SP: The Rig Road. Track on right is Erabena Track. — 0.0 km ▲

GPS	S:26 25.667 E:137 22.594
UTM	53J 737015E 7074752N

▼ 0.0 km — Zero trip meter at track junction. CSA. SP: The Rig Road/K1 Line 137 km/Birdsville Track 241 km. Track on left.

The Lone Gum

41

SIMPSON DESERT

Cath glumly surveys the scene

Bogged Outside Birdsville

We were looking forward to this trip, the plan being to enjoy a counter meal and drink at the Birdsville Hotel at the end. Once again 'The Brick' handled the sand dunes with ease, just walking over them with the right tyre pressure. We spent four days crossing the desert and arrived at Big Red at sunset on the fourth day. Cruising towards Birdsville we came to a large pool of water across the track. In the night light we saw tracks where other vehicles had made their way to the right of the water. So we followed suit, only to sink deep into mud.

'The Brick' was on a very nice angle to the right and Craig was out of the car in water and mud up to his knees. What to do? Oh, those beers in the pub were getting further and further away. So it was on the Sat phone to Theo at Birdsville Autos – the first time in seven years since we've been writing guide books that we needed outside assistance.

Theo arrived in a blaze of lights around 9pm and pulled us out with a few hefty tugs on a snatch strap. However, the trip into Birdsville was pretty slow due to large sheets of water on the road. We finally pulled into town around 11pm, set up camp in record time in the caravan park and headed straight to the pub. At least we got a couple of sherberts in before closing!

> *What to do? Oh, those beers in the pub were getting further and further away*

	Track on left is Erabena Track and leads 12 km north to WAA Line and 43 km to French Line. Track junction.	**38.4 km** ▲
	(34.1 km)	
▼ 34.1 km	Track junction. CSA. Track on left.	
	Track on left is Knolls Track and leads 35 km to the French Line via Approdinna Attora Knolls. Y-junction. KL. Track on right is Knolls Track.	**4.3 km** ▲
	(4.3 km)	
▼ 38.4 km	Track junction.	
	Zero trip meter at track junction. CSA. Track on left to Poolowanna Oil Well and Browns Bore.	**0.0 km** ▲
	GPS S:26 25.490 E:137 40.421 **UTM** 53J 766665E 7074497N	
▼ 0.0 km	Zero trip meter at track junction. CSA. Track on right.	
	Track on right leads short distance to Poolowanna 1 Oil Well and to Browns Bore. Track junction.	**103.7 km** ▲
	(66.2 km)	
▼ 66.2 km	Northern edge of salt lake system. Track now skirts around eastern shores of lake system. End of salt lake system.	**37.5 km** ▲
	(28.0 km)	
▼ 94.2 km	End of salt lake system.	
	From here to next reading there are good bush campsites amid dunes. Southern edge of salt lake system. Track now skirts around eastern shores of lake system.	**9.5 km** ▲
	(9.5 km)	
▼ 103.7 km	Track junction. This is SP: Kuncherinna Junction.	
	Zero trip meter at Kuncherinna Junction. KL. This is the Rig Road. Track on right SP: Poeppel Corner 86 km.	**0.0 km** ▲
	From here to next reading there are good bush campsites amid dunes.	
	GPS S:26 42.173 E:138 15.966 **UTM** 54J 227984E 7043555N	
▼ 0.0 km	Zero trip meter at Kuncherinna Junction. CSA. SP: Birdsville Track 105 km. Track on left SP: Poeppel Corner 86 km.	
	Y-junction. This is SP: Kuncherinna Junction.	**105.9 km** ▲
	(0.8 km)	
▼ 0.8 km	Kuncherinna 1 Oil Well on left. CSA.	
	Oil well drilled December 1981 and plugged February 1982.	
	Kuncherinna 1 Oil Well on right. CSA.	**105.1 km** ▲
	(31.2 km)	
▼ 32.0 km	Exit Simpson Desert Regional Reserve.	
	Enter SP: Simpson Desert Regional Reserve.	**73.9 km** ▲
	GPS S:26 57.893 E:138 21.702 **UTM** 54J 238104E 7014719N	
	(23.7 km)	
▼ 55.7 km	Cross last sand dune.	

MOUNT DARE ◀▶ BIRDSVILLE

		Cross first sand dune.	50.2 km ▲	▼ 84.9 km	Road junction.	
	(30.1 km)				Zero trip meter at road junction. CSA. Track on left is Walkers Crossing Track.	0.0 km ▲
▼ 85.8 km	Gate. LAF.				GPS S:26 52.267 E:139 32.133 UTM 54J 354530E 7026999N	
		Gate. LAF.	20.1 km ▲			
	(9.1 km)			▼ 0.0 km	Zero trip meter at road junction. CSA. Track on right.	
▼ 94.9 km	Track junction. KR. Track SO.				Track on right is Walkers Crossing Track.	
		Track junction. KL. Track on right.	11.0 km ▲		Road junction.	122.9 km ▲
	(2.3 km)				(45.2 km)	
▼ 97.2 km	Cross Warburton Creek. This is Warburton Crossing.			▼ 45.2 km	Cross SP: Moongara Channel.	
		Cross Warburton Creek.	8.7 km ▲		Cross SP: Moongara Channel.	77.7 km ▲
	GPS S:27 03.763 E:138 46.614 UTM 54J 279525E 7004672N				(1.9 km)	
	(8.7 km)			▼ 47.1 km	SP: Moongara 1&2 Bores, on right. CSA.	
▼ 105.9 km	T-junction. This is Birdsville Track.				SP: Moongara 1&2 Bores, on left. CSA.	75.8 km ▲
	See also Birdsville Track trek, pages 2–9.				(19.7 km)	
		Zero trip meter at road junction. TR. SP: Public Access Route to Simpson Desert Regional Reserve 80 km via Warburton Crossing. This is Yelpawaralina Track.	0.0 km ▲	▼ 66.8 km	SP: Wiripirie Bore, on right. CSA.	
					SP: Wiripirie Bore, on left. CSA.	56.1 km ▲
	GPS S:27 06.496 E:138 49.351 UTM 54J 284137E 6999703N				(27.4 km)	
▼ 0.0 km	Zero trip meter at T-junction with Birdsville Track. TL in northerly direction.			▼ 94.2 km	Road junction. CSA. Road on left SP: Pandie Pandie HS 2.	
	Track on right leads 625 km to Marree.				Road junction. CSA. Road on right SP: Pandie Pandie HS 2.	28.7 km ▲
		Road junction.	84.9 km ▲		(15.2 km)	
	(3.9 km)			▼ 109.4 km	Cross SA–QLD border and grid.	
▼ 3.9 km	Cross SP: Flaggy Creek.				Cross QLD–SA border and grid.	13.5 km ▲
		Cross SP: Flaggy Creek.	81.0 km ▲		GPS S:25 59.801 E:139 22.588 UTM 54J 337503E 7123674N	
	(7.2 km)				(9.2 km)	
▼ 11.1 km	Road junction. CSA. Track on left SP: Clifton Hills HS 2.			▼ 118.6 km	Road junction. CSA. SP: Birdsville 4. Road on right SP: Betoota 173.	
		Road junction. CSA. Track on right SP: Clifton Hills HS 2.	73.8 km ▲		Road junction. CSA. SP: Marree 554. Road on left SP: Betoota 173.	4.3 km ▲
	(2.0 km)				(1.6 km)	
▼ 13.1 km	Cross SP: Seven Mile Creek.			▼ 120.2 km	Bridge over Diamantina River.	
		Cross SP: Seven Mile Creek.	71.8 km ▲		Bridge over Diamantina River.	2.7 km ▲
	(9.8 km)				GPS S:25 54.391 E:139 22.487 UTM 54J 337210E 7133660N	
▼ 22.9 km	Cross SP: Tippipilla Creek.				(2.5 km)	
	Tippipilla Creek bush camping is located on eastern, or Birdsville, side of creek. Bush camping along edge of creek.			▼ 122.7 km	Crossroads. CSA. Road on right SP: Bedourie 192. Road on left to Birdsville Caravan Park.	
		Cross SP: Tippipilla Creek.	62.0 km ▲		Crossroads. CSA. Road on left SP: Bedourie 192. Road on right to Birdsville Caravan Park.	0.2 km ▲
	GPS S:26 59.754 E:139 00.692 UTM 54J 302683E 7012464N				(0.2 km)	
	(2.3 km)			▼ 122.9 km	Birdsville. Birdsville Hotel on right.	
▼ 25.2 km	Road junction. CSA. Track on left.				Zero trip meter in Birdsville with Birdsville Hotel on left. Proceed through town towards South Australia.	0.0 km ▲
	Track on left is Birdsville Inside Track.				GPS S:25 53.950 E:139 21.105 UTM 54J 334892E 7134445N	
		Road junction. CSA. Track on right.	59.7 km ▲			
	(23.1 km)				RIG ROAD REVERSE DIRECTIONS START	
▼ 48.3 km	Cross SP: Damparanie Creek.					
		Cross SP: Damparanie Creek.	36.6 km ▲			
	(6.8 km)					
▼ 55.1 km	Cross SP: Melon Creek.					
		Cross SP: Melon Creek.	29.8 km ▲			
	(29.8 km)					

FOLLOWING PAGES
Wind-sculptured dune

■ 43

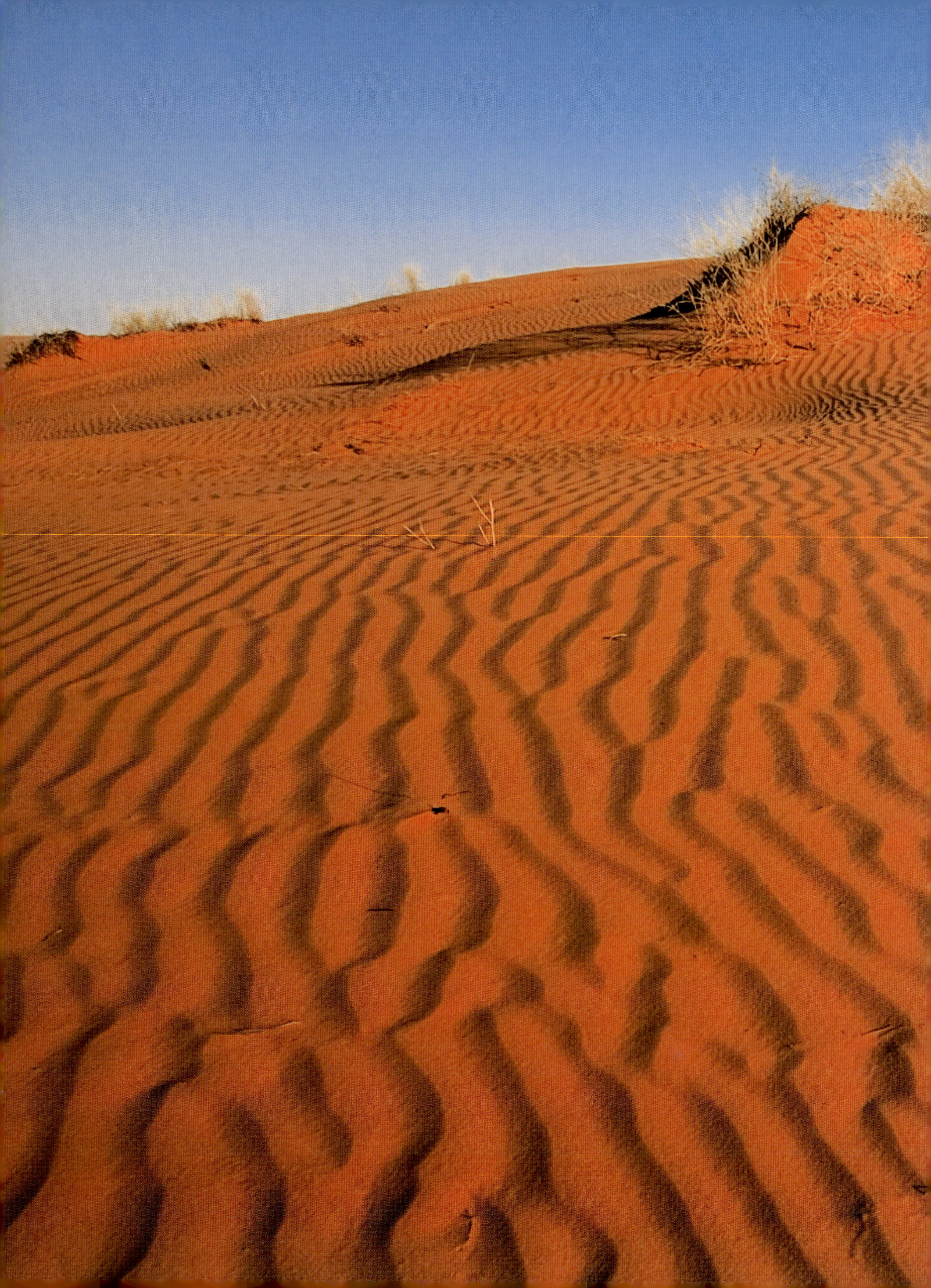

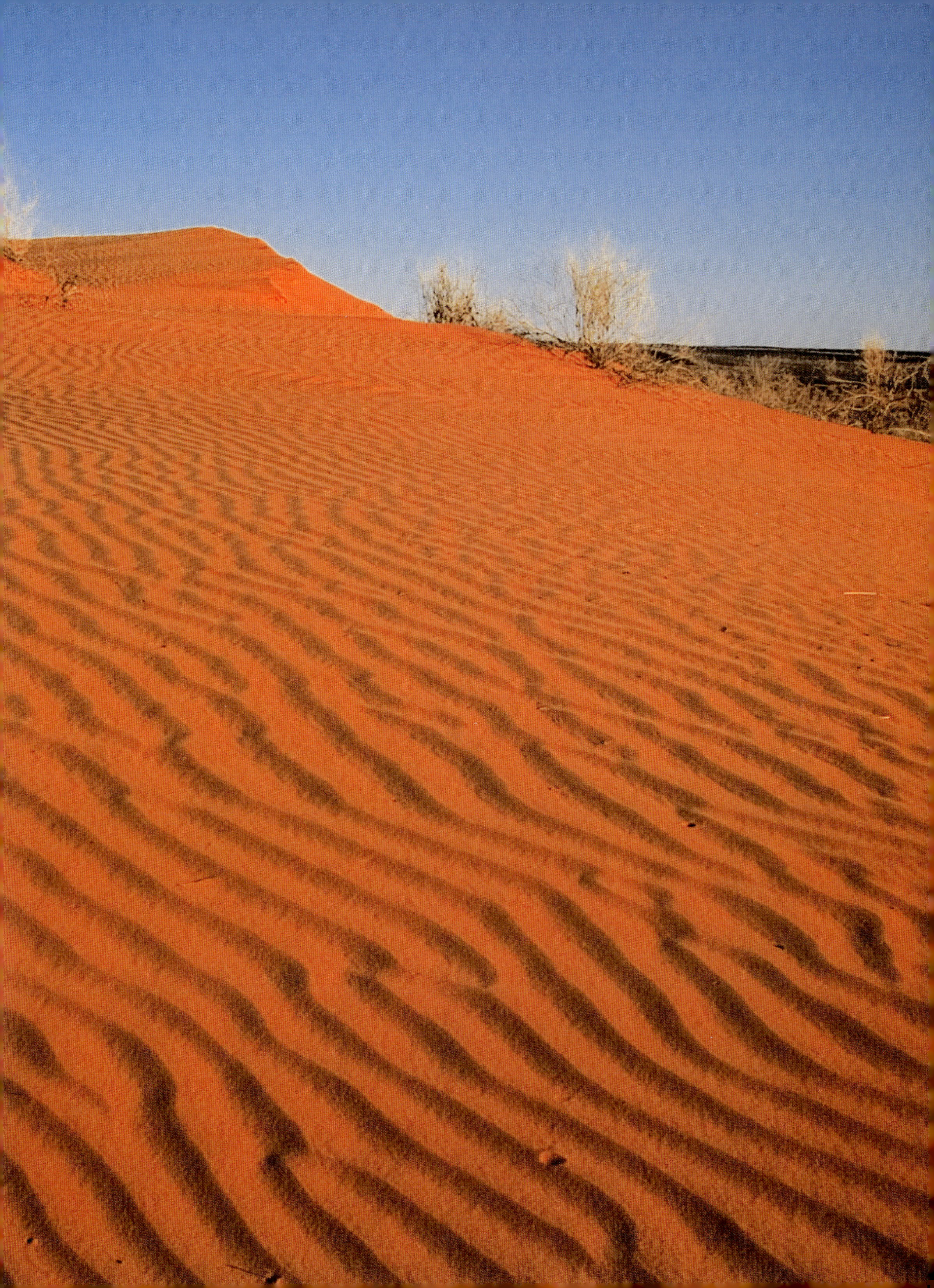

Tanami Road

Albert Edward Range near Ruby Plains station

ALICE SPRINGS ◄► HALLS CREEK 1054.8 KM
ONE SECTION ONLY *(easy)*
WHEN TO GO April–October, but possible all year **TIME** 2–3 days

For those unfamiliar with the harsh desert landscape that makes up much of inland Australia, the Tanami Road will serve as a good introduction. Much of the trek passes through Aboriginal land owned by the Warlpiri people. At some of the community settlements you can view artworks that reveal the fascinating stories of the Dreamtime.

From Alice Springs to Yuendumu the road passes through sections of pastoral lease, where large mobs of cattle graze on vast shimmering plains. North-west of Yuendumu the landscape changes, with granite outcrops close to the road and mineral-laden hills where wolfram was mined in earlier days. Evidence of this mining activity is still visible. On either side of Rabbit Flat Roadhouse, which is 124.4 kilometres east of the Western Australian border, large-scale gold mining operations are conducted at Granites Gold Mine and Tanami Mine but public access is not permitted.

The Tanami Road is a well-traversed track and it would be unusual not to see another vehicle every hour or so during the visitor season from April to October. It is not a particularly difficult drive, but it can be treacherous for the ill-prepared. There are heavily corrugated sections and fine red dust, and you need to watch out for road trains, wandering cattle and straying wildlife.

All facilities and services are available at the start and end of the road, at Alice Springs and at Halls Creek. Along the way fuel and basic supplies can be purchased at several roadhouses and at a number of Aboriginal communities.

TANAMI ROAD

Services

VEHICLE ASSISTANCE
AANT (NT)/RAC (WA)   13 1111

POLICE
Alice Springs	(08) 8951 8888
Halls Creek	(08) 9168 6000
Yuendumu	(08) 8956 4004

PARKS AND RESERVES
Wolfe Creek Meteorite Crater National Park
CALM Kununurra   (08) 9168 4200

VISITOR INFORMATION
Alice Springs	(08) 8952 5800
	or 1800 645 199
Halls Creek	(08) 9168 6262

Authors' note

The Tanami Road is a common short cut from Alice Springs to the Kimberley and yields many hidden delights. Take an extra day to meet the local people and enjoy the desert landscape at a leisurely pace.

Town Facilities

	Fuel: D/P/A	Mechanical repairs	Tyre repairs	Public telephone	Public toilets	Shop/supplies	Gas refills	Ice	Visitor information	Post office	Medical centre	Police	Meals	Motel	Hotel	Cabins	Caravan park	Camping
Alice Springs	D/P/A	•	•	•	•	•	•	•	•	•	•	•	•	•	•	•	•	•
Balgo Hills	D/P				•						•		•					
Billiluna	D/P	•	•	•	•	•		•			•							
Halls Creek	D/P/A	•	•	•	•	•	•	•	•	•	•	•	•	•	•	•	•	•
Rabbit Flat	D/P				•	•								•			•	•
Tilmouth Well	D/P		•	•	•	•					•		•			•	•	•
Yuendumu	D/P			•	•	•	•	•		•	•	•						

47

TANAMI ROAD

ALICE SPRINGS ◄► HALLS CREEK 1054.8 KM

Start point
Alice Springs

Road atlas
355 I6

Total distance
1054.8 km

Standard
Easy

Time
2–3 days

Longest distance no PD (includes all options)
318.3 km (Yuendumu to Rabbit Flat Roadhouse)

Topographic maps
Auslig 1:250 000 series: *Alice Springs*; *Hermannsburg*; *Napperby*; *Mount Doreen*; *Mount Theo*; *Mount Solitaire*; *The Granites*; *Tanami*; *Billiluna*; *Gordon Downs*

Other useful information

- Tilmouth Well Roadhouse open seven days 7am–9pm, tel. (08) 8956 8777; accepts cash, EFTPOS and credit cards.
- Yuendumu has two stores. Community store open Monday–Friday 8.30am–5pm and Saturday–Sunday 9am–1pm, tel. (08) 8956 4006; accepts cash, EFTPOS and credit cards. Mining Co. store open Monday–Friday 9am–2pm and 3–5pm and Saturday–Sunday 1–5pm, tel. (08) 8956 4040; accepts cash only.
- Rabbit Flat Roadhouse open Friday–Monday only, 7am–9pm, tel. (08) 8956 8744; accepts cash, EFTPOS and travellers cheques.
- Balgo Hills offers fuel and supplies from Wirrimanu store, open Monday–Friday 9am–12noon and 2–4pm and Saturday 9am–12noon, tel. (08) 9168 8894; accepts cash and EFTPOS.
- Billiluna has fuel and supplies. Fuel from Billiluna Corporation, open Monday–Friday 7am–12noon and 1–3pm and Saturday 9–11am (other times possible but call-out fee applicable), tel. (08) 9168 8988; accepts cash and EFTPOS. Good range of supplies from Kururrungku store, open Monday–Friday 8–11.30am and 2–4.30pm and Saturday 9–11am, tel. (08) 9168 8076; accepts cash and EFTPOS.
- F. E. Baume's *Tragedy Track: The Story of The Granites* gives early history of search for and discovery of gold in Tanami Desert and life on the goldfields.

Description

Prospectors were the first to forge a rough track across the Tanami Desert from Halls Creek, in 1900, when gold was discovered near Mount Tanami. By World War I the mining had ceased but new discoveries at Chapman Hill in 1932 started another rush, which more clearly defined the western section of the track. Fortune-seekers, often on foot, travelled the 500 kilometres from either Halls Creek or Alice Springs. The route was dubbed the Tragedy Track after those who perished in the harsh environment. Wells were sunk in 1910 following the first gold rush, but many of the bores, windmills, tanks and troughs that you see today were constructed in the 1960s, when a cattle track linked Billiluna station with Alice Springs.

Unlike the desert dune landscapes found elsewhere in Australia, the Tanami is a flat plain, often covered with thick scrub and trees such as bloodwood. The road runs north-west from Alice Springs to the border of Western Australia and onto Halls Creek. The striking purple-red terrain of the MacDonnell Ranges near Alice gives way to vast plains of spinifex and stunted shrubs, broken only by river and creek beds lined with river red gums. Most of the trek is through Aboriginal land.

The flat plains in the trek's southern section are sparsely inhabited by cattle. Beyond Yuendumu large granite outcrops rise from the desert floor and hundreds of termite mounds dot the landscape. Lizard species are common, particularly skinks, dragons and smooth knob-tailed geckos that feed on termites that infest the spinifex. As you approach Halls Creek in the north the country begins to change, with undulating ranges predominating. Wolfe Creek Crater, caused by a meteorite plunging to earth thousands of years ago, is around 130 kilometres south of Halls Creek and is not to be missed.

The road is maintained but there are heavily corrugated sections and deep sandy patches. During the dry season the creek and river crossings generally hold little or no water. In the wet these crossings may cut the road, making it impassable.

Advice and warnings

- Possible road closure at northern end after heavy rains, usually during wet season. Road has sandy stretches, heavily corrugated sections and patches of bitumen. Ring NT road information service, tel. 1800 246 199, and WA road condition report service, tel. 1800 013 314, to check road conditions (both numbers give recorded messages).

ALICE SPRINGS ◄► HALLS CREEK

Tanami landscape north of Yuendumu

- Slow down for oncoming road trains and wait for them to pass and for dust to settle before continuing.
- Watch out for roaming stock as much of the track runs through unfenced cattle stations.
- Standard road tyres are suitable.
- Towing off-road trailers and caravans is possible but be well prepared for heavy corrugations, which can make the trip slow.
- Camping is possible at the roadhouses and at several bush sites. Most bush camping areas are on private property or Aboriginal land so leave environment as found and take your rubbish with you.
- No fresh fruit, vegetables, nuts or honey can be taken into Western Australia from the Northern Territory. Dispose of these items in the quaratine bin at the location noted in the route directions.

Permits and bookings

- No permits required to travel this route.
- Permit required to visit Aboriginal sites and gallery in Balgo Hills. Contact Wirrimanu Corporation office in Balgo Hills, open Monday–Friday 9am–12noon and 2–4pm, tel. (08) 9168 8900. Permit can be pre-arranged or obtained on arrival in the community. Permit not required to visit general store.
- No entry to Newmont Granites Mine, unless an absolute emergency.
- No access to Old Granites Mine.
- Bookings recommended for cabins at Tilmouth Well Roadhouse, tel. (08) 8956 8777.
- Visitors to Yuendumu gallery can ring beforehand to confirm opening hours, tel. (08) 8956 4031.

ROUTE DIRECTIONS

▼ **0.0 km** — Zero trip meter on Stuart Hwy just north of Alice Springs at turn-off to SP: Old Telegraph Stn, and SP: Herbert Heritage Drv, on right.

Alice Springs. SP: Herbert Heritage Drv/Old Telegraph Stn, on left. **123.0 km** ▲

GPS   S:23 40.487 E:133 52.444
UTM   53K 385189E 7381326N

(17.1 km)

▼ **17.1 km** — Road junction. TL. SP: Tanami Road/Yuendumu/Halls Creek. Road SO SP: Tennant Creek.

T-junction. This is the SP: Stuart Highway. TR. SP: Alice Springs. **105.9 km** ▲

(105.9 km)

▼ **123.0 km** — Road junction.

Zero trip meter at road junction. CSA. Road on left SP: Roadside Stop. **0.0 km** ▲

GPS   S:23 16.260 E:132 55.056
UTM   53K 286988E 7424950N

▼ **0.0 km** — Zero trip meter at road junction. CSA. Road on right SP: Roadside Stop.

Roadside stop has shelters, tables, wood barbecues, bins and water tank.

Road junction. **164.8 km** ▲

(12.2 km)

▼ **12.2 km** — Road junction. CSA. SP: 152 Yuendumu. Road on left SP: 380 Kintore/105 Papunya.

Road junction. CSA. SP: Alice Springs 137. Road on right. **152.6 km** ▲

GPS   S:23 11.310 E:132 50.871
UTM   53K 279716E 7433984N

(11.2 km)

▼ **23.4 km** — Gravel road commences.

Bitumen road commences. **141.4 km** ▲

(38.7 km)

▼ **62.1 km** — Road junction. CSA. Road on right SP: Tilmouth Well.

Road on right leads short distance to **Tilmouth Well Roadhouse** and **camping area**, a well-grassed site located behind roadhouse.

Road junction. CSA. Road on left SP: Tilmouth Well. **102.7 km** ▲

GPS   S:22 48.697 E:132 35.913
UTM   53K 253505E 7475330N

(24.5 km)

▼ **86.6 km** — Road junction. CSA. Road on left SP: Mt Wedge Stn/Newhaven Stn.

Road junction. CSA. Road on right. **78.2 km** ▲

(19.2 km)

▼ **105.8 km** — Road junction. CSA. Road on right SP: Purladi.

Road junction. CSA. Road on left. **59.0 km** ▲

(21.6 km)

▼ **127.4 km** — Offset crossroads. CSA. Road on right, SP: Yuelamu 31, and track on left.

Track on left leads 0.1 km to possible bush campsite.

Offset crossroads. CSA. Road on left SP: Yuelamu 31. Track on right to possible bush campsite. **37.4 km** ▲

(37.4 km)

49

TANAMI ROAD

Tanami Gold

The harsh and desolate Tanami Desert was the scene of a short-lived gold rush during the early 1900s, when small amounts of the precious metal were discovered by a prospecting party led by Alan Davidson at an area known as Tanami, about 600 kilometres north-west of Alice Springs. After the rush was over, a few hardy prospectors remained and mined both alluvial and quartz vein gold from Chapman Hill at The Granites, 100 kilometres south-east of Davidson's original find. Discoveries at Bullakitchie and Shoe produced roughly 300 kilograms of gold over the next 20 years.

The area around The Granites was explored by large mining concerns at various times between 1939 and 1970. In 1975 North Flinders Mines was granted an 80-square-kilometre exploration licence at The Granites. After reaching an agreement with the traditional owners, exploration commenced in 1983 and the first gold was produced in mid-1986. Today, the Newmont Tanami Operation employs around 500 people and ore is hauled from a number of mines, such as Dead Bullock Soak, to the mill plant at The Granites. The company also operates Groundrush Mine, which is north-west of Rabbit Flat Roadhouse.

Old mine workings at Chapman Hill

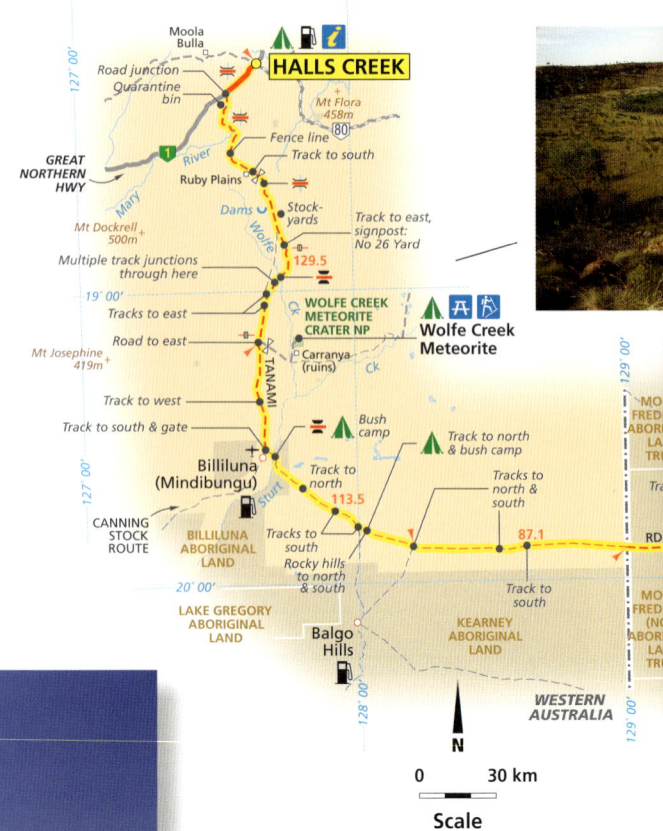

Campsite Facilities

	Toilets	Disabled access	4WD access only	Off-road trailer	Off-road caravan	Drinking water	Fee payable	Ranger patrolled	BBQ/fireplace	Campfires prohibited	Picnic tables	Shelter shed	No rubbish disposal	Public phone	Shower	Bushwalking	Swimming	Swimming not advised	Fishing	Canoeing	Dogs allowed
Rabbit Flat	•			•	•	•		•													•
Renehans Bore			•	•			•		•	•											•
Tilmouth Well	•	•		•	•	•	•	•	•				•	•							•
Wolfe Creek	•			•	•				•	•			•								

ALICE SPRINGS ◀▶ HALLS CREEK

Wolfe Creek Meteorite Crater
This extraordinary feature was caused by a massive meteorite that fell to earth a million years ago. When it hit the ground it was travelling at 15 kilometres per second and was estimated to weigh 50 000 tonnes. The resulting crater measured 850 metres across and 120 metres deep, but over time the rim has eroded and the depth has been reduced by desert sand to 20 metres below the surrounding plain. The crater floor retains more moisture than the desert above, encouraging the growth of wattle and tea-tree species.

Artists of Yuendumu

About 300 kilometres north-west of Alice Springs is the friendly Aboriginal community of Yuendumu, a showcase for Aboriginal art and culture. The people here pioneered Aboriginal community broadcasting with the extremely inventive ABC television series 'Bush Mechanics'.

Yuendumu is also home to the Warlukurlangu Artists Group, which is fast gaining a reputation as one of the most significant Aboriginal art centres in the Northern Territory. The 160 artists are Warlpiri people, whose homelands are the central and western deserts. They have a rich culture of song and dance, which is embodied in their art. Many of the colourful and vibrant paintings are in the desert, or dot, style and tell of the 'Jukurrpa', the many aspects of Warlpiri traditional culture and law, and stories of the Dreamtime and the links between the land and the people.

Visitors to the centre can purchase art and craft, and may be fortunate enough to see some of these talented people at work.

Aboriginal artists at Yuendumu

Renehans Bore
Located almost at the halfway point of the Tanami Road, this old bore and windmill is a convenient spot to break the trip. As such it has become a popular overnight camping place for travellers.

51

TANAMI ROAD

Warning sign on the Tanami Road

▼ 164.8 km — Road junction.
    Zero trip meter at road junction. CSA. SP: 289 Alice Springs. Road on left SP: Yuendumu 3.   0.0 km ▲

GPS	S:22 16.487 E:131 49.027
UTM	52K 790306E 7534051N

▼ 0.0 km — Zero trip meter at road junction. CSA. SP: Rabbit Flat 310. Road on right SP: Yuendumu 3/Pine Hill 154.

Road on right leads 3.0 km to Yuendumu, general store, fuel and Aboriginal art gallery.

    Road junction.   160.2 km ▲

(2.2 km)

▼ 2.2 km — Road junction. CSA. Road on right leads 1.5 km to Yuendumu.
    Road junction. CSA. Road on left leads to Yuendumu.   158.0 km ▲

(0.3 km)

▼ 2.5 km — Road junction. CSA over grid. Road on left SP: 160 Nyrippi.
    Road junction. CSA. Road on right.   157.7 km ▲

(26.0 km)

▼ 28.5 km — Road junction. CSA. Road on left SP: 77 Vaughan Springs.
    Road junction. CSA. Road on right.   131.7 km ▲

(14.4 km)

▼ 42.9 km — Interesting rocky outcrops on left. CSA.

Possible bush camping in this vicinity.

    Interesting rocky outcrops on right. CSA.   117.3 km ▲

GPS	S:22 08.664 E:131 26.235
UTM	52K 751374E 7549174N

(5.8 km)

▼ 48.7 km — Road junction. CSA. Track on left SP: 8 Mile.
    Road junction. CSA. Track on right.   111.5 km ▲

(13.0 km)

▼ 61.7 km — Road junction. CSA. Track on left.
    Road junction. CSA. Track on right.   98.5 km ▲

(29.3 km)

▼ 91.0 km — Cross Floodout Creek.

Possible bush camping on left prior to creek.

    Cross Floodout Creek.   69.2 km ▲

GPS	S:21 48.438 E:131 10.732
UTM	52K 725247E 7586910N

(0.2 km)

▼ 91.2 km — Crossroads. CSA.

Possible bush camping in this vicinity.

    Crossroads. CSA.   69.0 km ▲

(35.3 km)

▼ 126.5 km — Road junction. CSA. Track on right SP: Mt Theo Aboriginal Community Outstation.
    Road junction. CSA. Track on left.   33.7 km ▲

(1.2 km)

▼ 127.7 km — Road junction. CSA. Track on left SP: Chilla Well 2.
    Road junction. CSA. Track on right.   32.5 km ▲

(2.1 km)

▼ 129.8 km — Causeway.
    Causeway.   30.4 km ▲

(30.4 km)

▼ 160.2 km — Road junction.
    Zero trip meter at road junction. CSA. Track on right SP: Renehans Bore.   0.0 km ▲

GPS	S:21 16.691 E:130 50.999
UTM	52K 691933E 7645940N

▼ 0.0 km — Zero trip meter at road junction. CSA. Track on left SP: Renehans Bore.

Track on left leads short distance to Renehans Bore rest area and bush camping. Large open spot on small rise with sheltered bush campsites set back from road. Tables, shelter, wood barbecue and bin.

ALICE SPRINGS ◀▶ HALLS CREEK

	Road junction.	100.0 km ▲

(27.4 km)

▼ 27.4 km Road junction. CSA. Track on right leads to possible bush campsite.

          Road junction. CSA. Track on left to possible bush campsite.   72.6 km ▲

(44.1 km)

▼ 71.5 km Road junction. CSA. Track on left SP: Sangsters Bore.

          Road junction. CSA. Track on right.   28.5 km ▲

(19.5 km)

▼ 91.0 km Road junction. CSA. Track on right.
Track on right leads 0.2 km to possible bush campsite.

          Road junction. CSA. Track on left.   9.0 km ▲

(5.8 km)

▼ 96.8 km Chapman Hill on left. CSA.
Ruins of original Granites Gold Mine on hill can be seen from road. No access to hill or ruins. The Granites is named after a group of large granite outcrops in the vicinity.

          Chapman Hill on right. CSA.   3.2 km ▲

```
GPS   S:20 33.448 E:130 21.655
UTM   52K 641861E 7726236N
```

(3.2 km)

▼ 100.0 km Road junction.

          Zero trip meter at road junction. CSA. Road on right SP: Newmont Australia/Granites Gold Mine – No Entry.   0.0 km ▲

```
GPS   S:20 32.633 E:130 20.025
UTM   52K 639041E 7727763N
```

▼ 0.0 km Zero trip meter at road junction. CSA. Road on left SP: Newmont Australia/Granites Gold Mine – No Entry.
Numerous roads from here to next reading lead to mining operations. Restricted roads and no entry is permitted. Stay on Tanami Road.

          Road junction.   52.3 km ▲

(11.4 km)

▼ 11.4 km Road junction. CSA. Track on left.
Track on left leads 0.3 km to Quartz Ridge, with good views over surrounding area.

          Road junction. CSA. Track on right.   40.9 km ▲

          Track on right leads 0.3 km to Quartz Ridge, with good views over surrounding area. From here to next reading numerous tracks lead to mining operations. Restricted roads and no entry is permitted. Stay on Tanami Road.

(40.9 km)

▼ 52.3 km Road junction.

          Zero trip meter at road junction. CSA. Road on left SP: Rabbit Flat 2 km.   0.0 km ▲

```
GPS   S:20 11.914 E:130 01.239
UTM   52K 606635E 7766217N
```

▼ 0.0 km Zero trip meter at road junction. CSA. Road on right SP: Rabbit Flat 2 km.
Road on right leads 1.8 km to **Rabbit Flat Roadhouse** and **camping area**, a large shaded space only a short distance from roadhouse.

The Farrands of Rabbit Flat

Proprietor of one of Australia's most remote roadhouses, Bruce Farrands has become a legendary personality on the Tanami since he and his wife, Jacquie, established a tiny outpost to serve the travelling public over 30 years ago. Originally from the south-west of Western Australia, Bruce moved to the Tanami area in the 1940s to work as a stockman on Mongrel Downs (now Tanami Downs). When the Tanami Track was pushed through to Halls Creek in the early 1960s, Bruce and his wife set upon the idea of establishing a roadhouse. By the late 1960s the Farrands had purchased five acres of land, sunk a bore that provided good water and swung the doors open for business.

The early days saw a number of coach tour operators listing Rabbit Flat on their itineraries, but as the popularity of the Tanami Track grew so did the number of independent travellers, many using the route as a short cut from Alice Springs to the Kimberley. In those days Rabbit Flat was the only supply point on the long haul from Alice Springs in the Northern Territory to Halls Creek in Western Australia. Later the rising number of miners employed at the nearby goldmines of Granites and Tanami added to the Farrands' clientele. Nowadays Rabbit Flat Roadhouse, nestled amid lush green foliage, is a virtual oasis in the spinifex plains of the surrounding desert and offers a cool place to sit and rest.

We asked Bruce about the origin of the name Rabbit Flat. 'Well, there are rabbits around here, but we named it after a well that was sunk by the old timers a couple of miles further up the old track. If the name Rabbit Flat was good enough for them, well, it was good enough for us.'

Bruce Farrands

■ 53

TANAMI ROAD

	Road junction.	**124.4 km** ▲

(3.3 km)

▼ **3.3 km** Road junction. CSA. Road on left leads to Tanami Downs.

Once called Mongrel Downs, Tanami Downs was bought by local Aboriginal people in 1989. It is a working cattle station. The road and the desert take their name from Tanami Rockhole, located in the vicinity of Tanami Mine.

Road junction. CSA. Road on right. **121.1 km** ▲

(39.5 km)

▼ **42.8 km** Road junction. CSA. Road on right SP: Groundrush/Tanami Mine – No Entry.

Numerous roads from here to next reading lead to mining operations. Restricted roads and no entry is permitted. Stay on Tanami Road.

Road junction. CSA. Road on left SP: Groundrush/Tanami Mine – No Entry. **81.6 km** ▲

GPS S:19 58.813 E:129 42.603
UTM 52K 574286E 7790551N

(2.5 km)

▼ **45.3 km** Road junction. CSA. SP: Halls Creek 406. Road on right SP: Lajamanu 229.

Road junction. CSA. SP: 644 Alice Springs. Road on left SP: Lajamanu 229. **79.1 km** ▲

Numerous roads from here to next reading lead to mining operations. Restricted roads and no entry is permitted. Stay on Tanami Road.

(79.1 km)

▼ **124.4 km** NT–WA border.

Zero trip meter at WA–NT border. CSA. **0.0 km** ▲

GPS S:19 53.862 E:129 01.329
UTM 52K 502318E 7799839N

▼ **0.0 km** Zero trip meter at NT–WA border. CSA.

WA–NT border. **87.1 km** ▲

(87.1 km)

▼ **87.1 km** Road junction.

Zero trip meter at road junction. CSA. Road on right SP: Balgo Hills 31 km. **0.0 km** ▲

GPS S:19 52.823 E:128 12.150
UTM 52K 416512E 7801558N

▼ **0.0 km** Zero trip meter at road junction. CSA. Road on left SP: Balgo Hills 31 km.

Road on left leads 31 km to Balgo Hills, general store, fuel and Aboriginal art gallery. Permit required (see Permits and bookings).

Road junction. **113.5 km** ▲

(19.3 km)

▼ **19.3 km** Road junction. CSA. Track on right to possible bush campsite.

Road junction. CSA. Track on left to possible bush campsite. **94.2 km** ▲

(3.8 km)

▼ **23.1 km** Road junction. CSA. Track on left.

Road junction. CSA. Track on right. **90.4 km** ▲

(44.7 km)

▼ **67.8 km** Concrete causeway over Sturt Creek.

Bush camping in this vicinity.

Concrete causeway over Sturt Creek. **45.7 km** ▲

GPS S:19 33.629 E:127 41.631
UTM 52K 362985E 7836632N

(3.6 km)

▼ **71.4 km** Road junction. CSA. Road on left SP: Billiluna Station/Mindibungu Aboriginal Community.

Billabong on Sturt Creek

Stunted trees cling to the steep sides of Wolfe Creek Meteorite Crater

	Road on left leads 1.9 km to Billiluna store and northern access to Canning Stock Route (see pages 118–55).	
	Road junction. CSA. Road on right SP: Billiluna Station/Mindibungu Aboriginal Community.	42.1 km ▲
	(18.7 km)	
▼ 90.1 km	Road junction. CSA. Track on left.	
	Track on left leads approximately 95.0 km to abandoned oil well.	
	Road junction. CSA. Track on right.	23.4 km ▲
	(23.4 km)	
▼ 113.5 km	Road junction.	
	Zero trip meter at road junction. CSA. Road on left.	0.0 km ▲
	Road on left leads 23.0 km to Wolfe Creek Meteorite Crater National Park.	

GPS	S:19 10.401 E:127 38.941
UTM	52K 357947E 7879441N

▼ 0.0 km Zero trip meter at road junction. CSA over grid. Road on right.

Road on right leads 23.0 km to **Wolfe Creek Meteorite camping area** and carpark. Camping area is open space with individual camping bays. A 200-m walk leads from carpark to crater rim. Access into crater is possible via a steep walking trail but take care as you descend as surface has loose rocks. The crater takes its name from a nearby creek, which was named after Robert Wolfe, an early prospector.

	Road junction.	129.5 km ▲
	(72.8 km)	
▼ 72.8 km	Road junction. CSA. Road on left SP: Ruby Plains Station.	
	Road junction. CSA. Road on right SP: Ruby Plains Station.	56.7 km ▲
	(39.8 km)	

ALICE SPRINGS ◀▶ HALLS CREEK

▼ 112.6 km Quarantine bin on left. CSA.

The quarantine bin is for disposal of all fresh fruit, vegetables, nuts and honey brought into Western Australia from the Northern Territory.

	Quarantine bin on right. CSA.	16.9 km ▲

GPS	S:18 19.646 E:127 33.366
UTM	52K 347417E 7972983N

(0.3 km)

▼ 112.9 km T-junction with bitumen. This is Great Northern Hwy. TR. SP: Halls Creek 18. Road on left SP: 282 Fitzroy Crossing.

	Road junction. TL onto gravel road. SP: Tanami Road/Alice Springs.	16.6 km ▲

GPS	S:18 19.475 E:127 33.281
UTM	52K 347264E 7973297N

(16.6 km)

▼ 129.5 km Halls Creek. Road on right SP: Hall Street.

	Zero trip meter in Halls Creek on Great Northern Hwy at junction with SP: Hall Street, on left. Proceed in southerly direction along highway towards Fitzroy Crossing.	0.0 km ▲

GPS	S:18 13.469 E:127 40.047
UTM	52K 359102E 7984466N

REVERSE DIRECTIONS START

Kimberley Grand Tour

Tier Gorge on El Questro station

KUNUNURRA ◀▶ DERBY 1246.2 KM

1. KUNUNURRA ◀▶ KALUMBURU ROAD JUNCTION 298.0 km *(easy)*
2. KALUMBURU ROAD JUNCTION ◀▶ KALUMBURU 531.0 km return *(easy)*
3. KALUMBURU ROAD JUNCTION ◀▶ DERBY 417.2 km *(easy)*

WHEN TO GO May–September **TIME** 8–11 days

Western Australia's vast Kimberley region lies in the far north of the state, flanked by the towns of Kununurra and Wyndham in the north-east, Broome and Derby in the west and Fitzroy Crossing in the south. Once remote and sparsely populated, the heart of this ancient land is now accessible via the Gibb River Road, built in the 1950s to open up the pastoral country to road transport.

This trek offers several options, including alternative start points and a trek finish at either Derby or Fitzroy Crossing. Along the way you branch off the Gibb River Road and take the Kalumburu Road to the coast, exploring the Drysdale River and Mitchell Plateau areas.

The Gibb River Road has a reasonably well-maintained gravel surface but during the wet season, generally December–April, many of the rivers make it impassable. Travel only during the dry season, preferably as early in the Dry as possible, as towards the end of the season the area becomes progressively parched and brown and ground water is scarce.

The rugged landscape is a combination of sandstone ranges, ancient volcanic rocks, open woodlands, mangrove swamps and lush vegetation around watercourses. Over millennia the limestone hills have eroded to form gorges and caves, where cool streams and crystal-clear pools are fringed by palms and pandanus. The cave walls and rock surfaces of hidden canyons often feature Aboriginal paintings dating back thousands of years. On the coast, isolated beaches at Kalumburu provide some great reef fishing in the tropical waters, while the highly prized barramundi inhabit the Pentecost and King rivers.

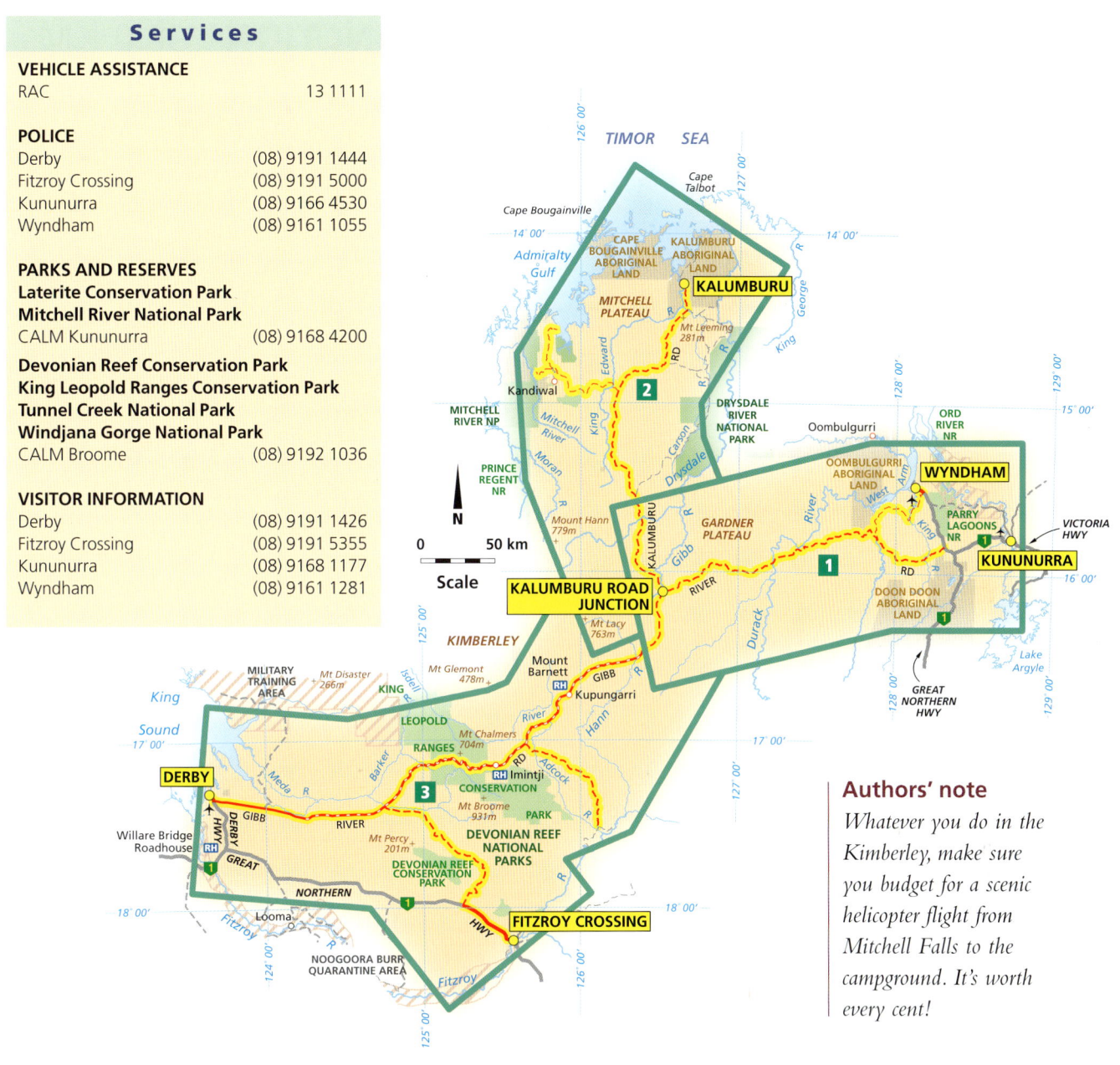

KIMBERLEY GRAND TOUR

Services

VEHICLE ASSISTANCE
RAC   13 1111

POLICE
Derby   (08) 9191 1444
Fitzroy Crossing   (08) 9191 5000
Kununurra   (08) 9166 4530
Wyndham   (08) 9161 1055

PARKS AND RESERVES
Laterite Conservation Park
Mitchell River National Park
CALM Kununurra   (08) 9168 4200

Devonian Reef Conservation Park
King Leopold Ranges Conservation Park
Tunnel Creek National Park
Windjana Gorge National Park
CALM Broome   (08) 9192 1036

VISITOR INFORMATION
Derby   (08) 9191 1426
Fitzroy Crossing   (08) 9191 5355
Kununurra   (08) 9168 1177
Wyndham   (08) 9161 1281

Authors' note

Whatever you do in the Kimberley, make sure you budget for a scenic helicopter flight from Mitchell Falls to the campground. It's worth every cent!

Town Facilities

	Fuel: D/P/A	Mechanical repairs	Tyre repairs	Public telephone	Public toilets	Shop/supplies	Gas refills	Ice	Visitor information	Post office	Medical centre	Police	Meals	Motel	Hotel	Cabins	Caravan park	Camping
Derby	D/P/A	•	•	•	•	•	•	•	•	•	•	•	•	•	•	•	•	•
Fitzroy Crossing	D/P/A	•	•	•	•	•	•	•	•	•	•	•	•		•	•	•	•
Imintji	D	•	•	•	•	•												
Kalumburu*	D/P	•	•	•	•	•	•	•		•			•			•	•	•
Kununurra	D/P/A	•	•	•	•	•	•	•	•	•	•	•	•	•	•	•	•	•
Mount Barnett	D/P	•		•	•	•												
Wyndham	D/P	•	•	•	•	•	•	•	•	•	•	•	•	•	•	•	•	•

*To contact police in Kalumburu, telephone Wyndham police (see Services above).

KIMBERLEY GRAND TOUR

1 KUNUNURRA ◀▶ KALUMBURU RD JUNCTION 298.0 KM

Start point
Kununurra or Wyndham

Road atlas
356 F5, 356 E5

Total distance
298.0 km (Kununurra to Kalumburu Road Junction)
265.5 km (Wyndham to Kalumburu Road Junction)

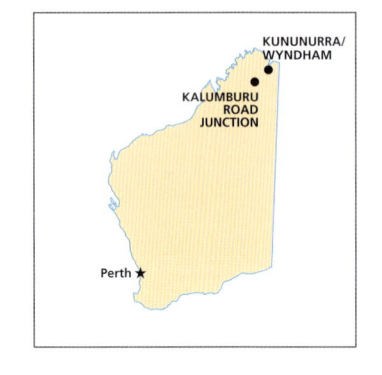

Standard
Easy

Time
1–2 days

Longest distance no PD (includes all options)
301.1 km (El Questro to Drysdale River station in trek section 2)

Topographic maps
Auslig 1:250 000 series: *Cambridge Gulf*; *Lissadell*; *Ashton*; *Mount Elizabeth*

Other useful information
- El Questro Wilderness Park's station township has petrol and diesel, limited supplies and mechanical repairs, tel. (08) 9161 4318; accepts cash, EFTPOS and credit cards.
- Visitor guide: *Travellers Guide to the Gibb River and Kalumburu Roads*.
- Road safety booklet: *Driving The Gibb River Road and Other Roads in the Kimberley*.
- CALM Bush Books: *Common Plants of the Kimberley*; *Geology & Landforms of the Kimberley*; *Common Birds of the Kimberley*.
- *The Riches of Australia* by Josephine Flood is an informative guide to prehistoric Australia and to accessible Aboriginal rock-art sites.

Description
This trek offers two alternative starting points, Kununurra and Wyndham. If departing from Kununurra, there are great views of the southern escarpment of the Cockburn Range and visits to the popular tourist site of El Questro station, which includes Emma Gorge. This drive, the less demanding of the two alternatives, is relatively easy along the regularly maintained Gibb River Road, but the gravel surface can become corrugated after heavy traffic.

The Wyndham option follows the meandering course of the King River for a little over 33 kilometres, before crossing the river near the historic prison tree, a huge boab once used as a lockup. The river crossing is rocky but shallow during the dry season. The Karunjie Track then winds around the northern side of the Cockburn Range, traversing the large flood plain of the Pentecost River and on to the junction of the river and the Gibb River Road. The route has large stretches of bulldust in the Dry and is impassable in the Wet. However, it is the more scenic and diverse route and will hold more appeal to four-wheel drivers. The port town of Wyndham, like Derby at the other end of the trek, is a good place to observe the huge tidal movements unique to the region.

The two routes converge at a rocky crossing of the Pentecost River. From here the trek heads westwards, past Home Valley station, over several small creeks and Gregorys and Rollies jump-ups, before arriving at the Durack River – a pleasant resting spot – named after one of the famous pioneering families of the Kimberley. The terrain from here to Kalumburu Road Junction is unremarkable but stay alert. The drovers of the past have been replaced by large road trains, which cart cattle along the track from the outback stations to the ports of Wyndham and Derby or to the meatworks at Broome. These massive vehicles create clouds of dust so slow down and wait for them to pass.

There are no designated bush campsites on this trek section, but a number of stations have established camping areas for travellers. El Questro station provides numerous shaded sites beside the Pentecost River, Home Valley homestead has a small camping area and Ellenbrae station offers creek-side sites.

At Kalumburu Road Junction, you have the option of tackling the rough and corrugated journey to the Mitchell Plateau and on to the coast at Kalumburu (trek section 2), or continuing south-westwards along the Gibb River Road (trek section 3).

Advice and warnings
- This is a remote area so you need to be totally self-sufficient and your vehicle well equipped. Carry cash; EFTPOS and credit card facilities are rarely available.
- Roads closed and impassable during and after heavy rain. Gibb River Rd has heavily corrugated sections and Karunjie Track has bulldust and rocky stretches. Approach creek and river crossings with caution. Ring WA road condition report service, tel. 1800 013 314, to check road conditions.

KUNUNURRA ◀▶ KALUMBURU ROAD JUNCTION

- Slow down for oncoming road trains and wait for them to pass and for dust to settle before continuing. Exercise caution when overtaking and approaching other vehicles as dust may impede visibility.
- Watch out for roaming stock (and wildlife) as much of the road runs through unfenced cattle stations.
- Gibb River Rd and Karunjie Track run through private land and there are numerous station access tracks. Do not deviate from the main road or track without prior approval from landholders. Leave all gates as found, observe all advisory signs, do not disturb stock and do not damage or pollute stock watering points.
- Standard road tyres or all-terrain tyres are suitable. Tyre pressure can be lowered to assist with travel comfort. Always carry two spare tyres as punctures and tyre damage are common. Tyre repair equipment is a worthy addition to your toolkit.
- Towing off-road trailers and off-road caravans is possible but ensure they are well prepared for corrugations.
- Camping along Gibb River Rd is at designated sites only. There is no bush camping along the Karunjie Track.
- Rubbish bins are not provided along the roads so please take your rubbish with you.
- Saltwater and freshwater crocodiles inhabit the King and Pentecost rivers so do not swim in these waters. Check with locals regarding possible safe swimming in other creeks and rivers.
- Be sure to carry some means of communication such as a satellite phone or HF radio.

Permits and bookings
- No permits required to travel roads on this trek section.
- Wilderness Park permit required to access sites on El Questro station. Contact El Questro Wilderness Park, tel. (08) 9161 4318. Permit valid for seven days.
- El Questro Wilderness Park has a full range of accommodation and a number of tours are available, tel. (08) 9161 4318.
- Bookings not required for camping at stations, but bookings for other types of accommodation highly recommended.
- Diggers Rest offers private room and bunkhouse accommodation, safari huts and camping, along with a variety of tours, tel. (08) 9161 1029.
- Home Valley station offers dinner, bed and breakfast, plus camping, tel. (08) 9161 4322.
- Ellenbrae station has camping facilities, tel. (08) 9161 4325.
- Fishing licence required for freshwater fishing. Bag and size limits apply. Contact Department of Fisheries Western Australia, tel. (08) 9482 7333, or visit their website (www.fish.wa.gov.au).

Kimberley Bulldust

We were travelling along a track in the Kimberley when we happened upon a particularly large bulldust patch. From the number of sizeable logs in the wheel ruts we could tell that other vehicles had obviously been stuck there. However, nothing ventured, nothing gained. One of the logs was sticking up so Craig had to drive skilfully around it to avoid causing damage to the car. But with his clever manoeuvring we lost momentum and the inevitable happened – 'The Brick' sank in. We thought we could dig it out, but the sand was so soft and 'The Brick' so heavy that it was a waste of time, and it was a very hot day. So we just hooked up the trusty Premier winch to the nearest tree and 'The Brick' was out in a jiffy. It all took place so quickly that we were fortunately saved the embarrassment of another vehicle coming along and seeing the so-called 'four-wheel-drive experts' bogged to the axles – with not a splatter of mud in sight! We didn't even have time to take an action photo of our plight.

We were bogged to the axles – with not a splatter of mud in sight!

'The Brick' hits a bulldust patch

Aboriginal Art of the Kimberley

Throughout the Kimberley region are numerous Aboriginal rock-art sites, evidence that the land has been occupied for thousands of years. Four styles of rock art have been identified: irregular infill paintings, the oldest style at 30 000 to 40 000 years old; Gwion (Bradshaw) with a minimum age of 17 000 years old; clawed hand paintings believed to be less than 7000 years old; and Wandjina figures, considered less than 1000 years old.

The infill paintings are simple infilled forms of humans, plants and animals. Gwion, or Bradshaw art, named after pastoralist Joseph Bradshaw who explored the area in 1891, is a more complex style, portraying humans wearing elaborate headdresses, armbands and tassels, often engaged in animated scenes of dancing, hunting and fighting. The figures are typically small and generally painted red. The clawed hand paintings, a term applied by archaeologist and rock-art historian Grahame Walsh, depict figures with clawed hands and feet. Wandjina art features large humanoid figures with halo-like arcs around their heads, and faces with a nose and big eyes but no mouth. These ancestral beings control rain, storm and floods, and are painted in vibrant colours of black, red, yellow and white.

Examples of Bradshaw and Wandjina art can be seen on the Mitchell Plateau – in the overhangs below Little Merten Falls on the walk to Mitchell Falls, and at sites close to King Edward River camping area – and in Chamberlain Gorge on El Questro station.

Aboriginal rock art is protected by state and federal laws. If you are lucky enough to view any of these spectacular and culturally significant sites, do not touch any art works and do not remove any artefacts.

Examples of Aboriginal art on a rock wall

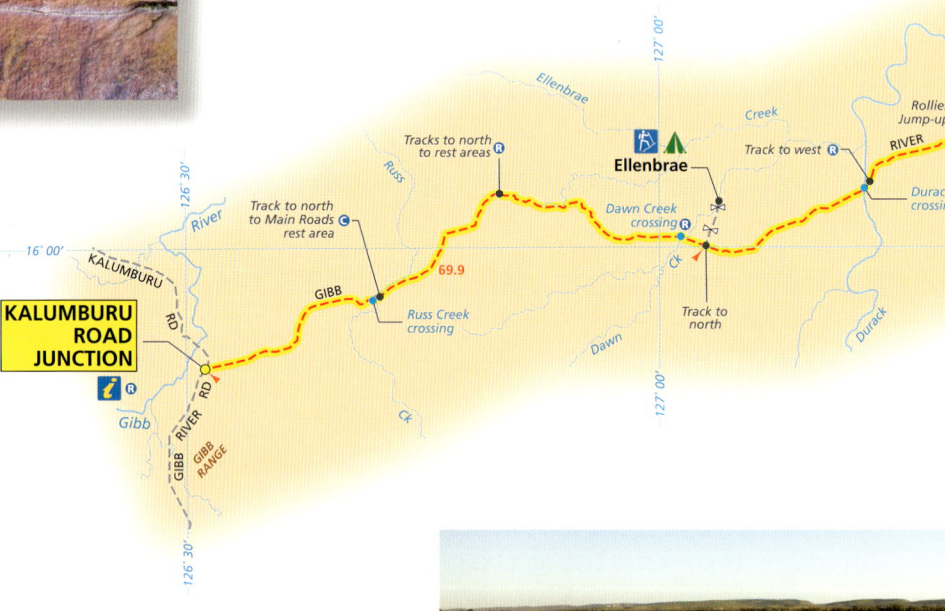

Cockburn Range
The magnificent sandstone escarpment of the Cockburn Range rises some 600 metres above the surrounding plains, dominating the landscape along the Gibb River Road near the Pentecost River. Admire the breathtaking colours from the lookout located 1.6 kilometres west of the Home Valley station turn-off.

Wide expanse of the Pentecost River

KUNUNURRA ◀▶ KALUMBURU ROAD JUNCTION

Pentecost River
The wide causeway crossing the Pentecost River marks where the fresh water of the river meets the salt water of the sea. Downstream there is excellent fishing from the riverbanks but be warned: this is saltwater crocodile territory.

Prison Tree
South of Wyndham on the King River is a large boab prison tree. Police patrols would camp here overnight when travelling to and from Wyndham, comforted by the knowledge that they could safely lock up their prisoners inside the tree.

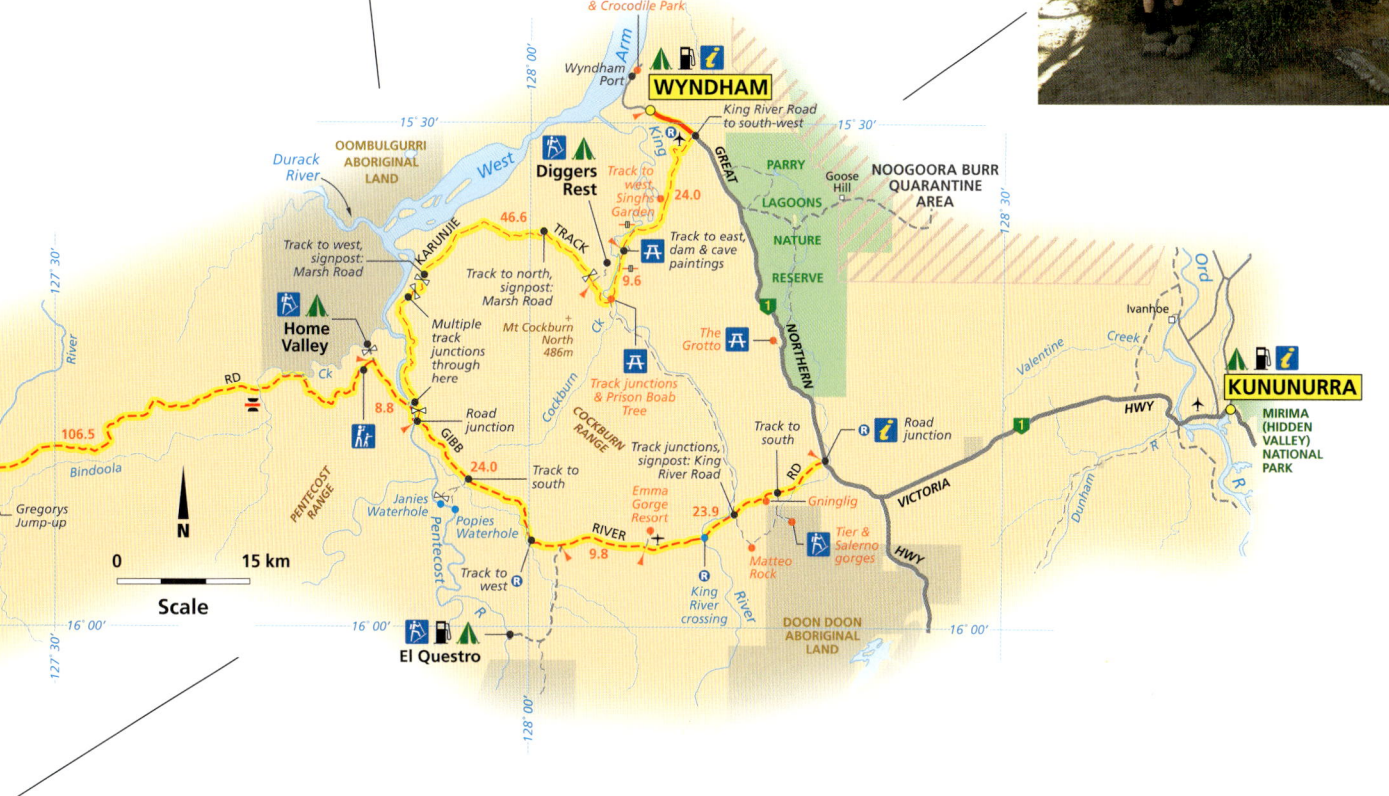

Campsite Facilities

	Toilets	Disabled access	4WD access only	Off-road trailer	Off-road caravan	Drinking water	Fee payable	Ranger patrolled	BBQ/fireplace	Campfires prohibited	Picnic tables	Shelter shed	No rubbish disposal	Public phone	Shower	Bushwalking	Swimming	Swimming not advised	Fishing	Canoeing	Dogs allowed
Diggers Rest	•		•	•	•		•						•	•				•			•
El Questro	•			•	•	•	•				•		•	•	•			•	•	•	
Ellenbrae	•		•	•	•		•						•		•				•		•
Home Valley	•			•	•	•	•						•		•			•	•		•

61

KIMBERLEY GRAND TOUR

ROUTE DIRECTIONS

The notes below detail the route from Kununurra to the Pentecost River crossing. Alternative route from Wyndham to same river crossing then follows. If departing from Kununurra, head west along Victoria Hwy for around 46 km to T-junction with Great Northern Hwy. TR onto highway SP: Wyndham. After approximately 9 km you reach junction of Great Northern Hwy and Gibb River Rd.

▼ 0.0 km — Zero trip meter at junction of Great Northern Hwy and SP: Gibb River Road. Proceed westwards along Gibb River Rd SP: Mt Barnett.

Off Great Northern Hwy, 13.6 km north of this junction, is Grotto Rd, which leads 1.9 km to the Grotto, a popular swimming spot for locals and travellers. One hundred and forty steps lead down to the swimming hole.

T-junction with bitumen. This is SP: Great Northern Highway. TL for SP: Wyndham. TR for SP: Kununurra. — 23.9 km ▲

GPS S:15 50.055 E:128 18.702
UTM 52L 426296E 8249278N

(6.8 km)

▼ 6.8 km — Road junction. CSA. Track on left SP: Tier Gorge/Matteo Rock.

Tier Gorge and Matteo Rock are located on El Questro station. Wilderness Park permit required to visit these sites (see Permits and bookings).

Road junction. CSA. Track on right SP: Tier Gorge/Matteo Rock. — 17.1 km ▲

(1.7 km)

▼ 8.5 km — Road junction. CSA. Track on left.

Track on left leads to rock-art sites at Gninglig located on El Questro station. Wilderness Park permit required to visit.

Road junction. CSA. Track on right. — 15.4 km ▲

(3.9 km)

▼ 12.4 km — Road junction. CSA. Track on right SP: King River Road.

Road junction. CSA. Track on left SP: King River Road. — 11.5 km ▲

GPS S:15 53.195 E:128 13.068
UTM 52L 416262E 8243454N

(4.5 km)

▼ 16.9 km — Road junction. CSA. Track on left.

Track on left leads to small rest area beside King River. No camping but good lunch spot.

Road junction. CSA. Track on right. — 7.0 km ▲

(0.1 km)

▼ 17.0 km — Cross King River.

Cross King River. — 6.9 km ▲

GPS S:15 54.676 E:128 11.076
UTM 52L 412718E 8240709N

(6.9 km)

▼ 23.9 km — Road junction.

Zero trip meter at road junction. CSA. Track on left SP: Emma Gorge. — 0.0 km ▲

GPS S:15 55.292 E:128 07.343
UTM 52L 406063E 8239547N

▼ 0.0 km — Zero trip meter at road junction. CSA. Track on right SP: Emma Gorge.

Track on right leads 1.8 km to Emma Gorge Resort, which is on El Questro station. Wilderness Park permit required to visit gorge. Accommodation includes tented cabins with varying facilities from standard to deluxe.

Road junction. — 9.8 km ▲

(9.8 km)

▼ 9.8 km — Road junction.

Zero trip meter at road junction. CSA. Track on right SP: El Questro Wilderness Park. — 0.0 km ▲

GPS S:15 55.170 E:128 02.077
UTM 52L 396667E 8239730N

▼ 0.0 km — Zero trip meter at road junction. CSA. Track on left SP: El Questro Wilderness Park.

Track on left leads 16.5 km to **El Questro camping area**, with 25 sites beside Pentecost River, stretching from station township to Chamberlain River. The further away from the station store, the more secluded the sites (and bookings are required for these). Wilderness Park permit required.

Road junction. — 24.0 km ▲

(3.7 km)

▼ 3.7 km — Road junction. CSA. Track on left.

Track on left leads 0.3 km to rest area beside a creek; possible lunch spot.

Road junction. CSA. Track on right. — 20.3 km ▲

(11.2 km)

▼ 14.9 km — Road junction. CSA. Track on left SP: Janies and Popies Waterholes.

Janies and Popies waterholes are located on El Questro station. Wilderness Park permit required to visit these sites.

Road junction. CSA. Track on right SP: Janies and Popies Waterholes. — 9.1 km ▲

(9.1 km)

▼ 24.0 km — Road junction. Directions continue after the end of Wyndham start notes, see page 64.

Zero trip meter at road junction over Pentecost River. CSA. Track on left SP: Karunjie Track. — 0.0 km ▲

Track on left is start of alternative end trip to Wyndham.

GPS S:15 47.829 E:127 52.951
UTM 52L 380312E 8253185N

▶ **ALTERNATIVE START: Wyndham**

▼ 0.0 km — Zero trip meter in Wyndham on Great Northern Hwy with statue of large crocodile on left. Proceed south along highway towards Kununurra.

Wyndham. Large crocodile on right. — 24.0 km ▲

GPS S:15 29.259 E:128 07.427
UTM 52L 406014E 8287545N

(5.9 km)

▼ 5.9 km — Road junction. TR. SP: King River Road/Prison Tree 22/Moochalabra Dam. Road SO SP: Kununurra 95.

T-junction with bitumen. TL. SP: 6 Wyndham. — 18.1 km ▲

KUNUNURRA ◀▶ KALUMBURU ROAD JUNCTION

	GPS S:15 30.736 E:128 10.298 UTM 52L 411157E 8284842N		
	(9.6 km)		
▼ 15.5 km	Track junction. CSA. Track on right SP: Singhs Garden.		
	Track on right leads 0.2 km to small clearing beside creek.		
	Track junction. CSA. Track on left SP: Singhs Garden.	8.5 km ▲	
	(8.5 km)		
▼ 24.0 km	Track junction.		
	Zero trip meter at track junction. CSA. Track on right SP: Cave Paintings 0.6 km/Moochalabra Dam 1.2 km.	0.0 km ▲	
	GPS S:15 37.627 E:128 05.842 UTM 52L 403245E 8272105N		
▼ 0.0 km	Zero trip meter at track junction. CSA. SP: Prison Tree 4.4 km. Track on left SP: Cave Paintings 0.6 km/Moochalabra Dam 1.2 km.		
	Track on left leads 0.6 km to small carpark on right of track with short walk to rock overhang with Aboriginal paintings, and 1.2 km to viewing point over Moochalabra Dam. Picnic area below viewing area.		
	Track junction.	9.6 km ▲	
	(5.0 km)		
▼ 5.0 km	Y-junction. KR. SP: Gibb River Rd via Prison Boab Tree.		
	Track junction. CSA. Track on right.	4.6 km ▲	
	(0.7 km)		
▼ 5.7 km	Track junction. CSA. Track on right SP: Prison Boab Tree.		

	Track on right leads to Prison Boab Tree and picnic area.		
	Track junction. CSA. Track on left SP: Prison Boab Tree.	3.9 km ▲	
	GPS S:15 40.528 E:128 05.132 UTM 52L 402000E 8266751N		
	(0.2 km)		
▼ 5.9 km	Track junction. CSA. Track on left is King River Rd.		
	Track junction. CSA SP: Wyndham via Moochalabra Dam. Track on right.	3.7 km ▲	
	(3.7 km)		
▼ 9.6 km	Y-junction.		
	Zero trip meter at gate. LAF. Track junction through gate. CSA. SP: 30 Wyndham via King River. Track on left SP: Diggers Rest.	0.0 km ▲	
	GPS S:15 39.487 E:128 03.918 UTM 52L 399823E 8268661N		
0.0 km	Zero trip meter at Y-junction. KL through gate. LAF. This is Karunjie Track. Track on right SP: Diggers Rest.		
	Track on right leads 3.2 km to **Diggers Rest** and **camping area** with campsites located close to homestead.		
	Gate.	46.6 km ▲	
	(4.0 km)		
▼ 4.0 km	Track junction. CSA. SP: Karunjie Track. Track on right SP: Diggers Rest.		
	Track junction. CSA. SP: Wyndham via Karunjie Rd and King River Rd. Track on left SP: Diggers Rest.	42.6 km ▲	
	(4.3 km)		
▼ 8.3 km	Y-junction. KL. SP: Karunjie Track. Track on right SP: Marsh Road.		

View of False Mount Cockburn from the Karunjie Track

KIMBERLEY GRAND TOUR

| | Track junction. CSA. Track on left SP: Marsh Road. | 38.3 km ▲ |

GPS S:15 36.461 E:128 00.850
UTM 52L 394316E 8274215N

(18.8 km)

▼ 27.1 km — Track junction. CSA and cross creek. Track on right SP: Marsh Road.

| | Track junction. CSA. Track on left SP: Marsh Road. | 19.5 km ▲ |

(0.4 km)

▼ 27.5 km — Gate. LAF. CSA. Track on left to yards.

| | Gate. LAF. | 19.1 km ▲ |

(0.9 km)

▼ 28.4 km — Gate. LAF.

| | Gate. LAF. | 18.2 km ▲ |

(1.2 km)

▼ 29.6 km — Track junction. CSA. Track on right to gate.

| | Track junction. CSA. Track on left to gate. | 17.0 km ▲ |

(2.1 km)

▼ 31.7 km — Y-junction. KL. Track on right.

| | Track junction. CSA. Track on left. | 14.9 km ▲ |

(3.3 km)

▼ 35.0 km — Track junction. CSA. Track on right.

Track on right leads 0.1 km to banks of Pentecost River.

| | Y-junction. KR. Track on left to river. | 11.6 km ▲ |

GPS S:15 42.885 E:127 52.522
UTM 52L 379498E 8262297N

(4.6 km)

▼ 39.6 km — Track junction. CSA. Track and dam on right.

| | Y-junction. KR. Track and dam on left. | 7.0 km ▲ |

(2.3 km)

▼ 41.9 km — Track junction. CSA. Track on right.

| | Track junction. CSA. Track on left. | 4.7 km ▲ |

(0.2 km)

▼ 42.1 km — Crossroads. CSA.

| | Crossroads. CSA. | 4.5 km ▲ |

(2.0 km)

▼ 44.1 km — Track junction. CSA. Track on right.

| | Y-junction. KR. Track on left. | 2.5 km ▲ |

(1.4 km)

▼ 45.5 km — Gate. LAF.

| | Gate. LAF. | 1.1 km ▲ |

(1.1 km)

▼ 46.6 km — T-junction with Gibb River Rd.

This junction is where alternative start option joins main route. Road on left leads to Kununurra.

| | Zero trip meter at road junction on eastern side of Pentecost River. TL. SP: Karunjie Track. | 0.0 km ▲ |
| | Road SO is Kununurra end option. | |

GPS S:15 47.829 E:127 52.951
UTM 52L 380312E 8253185N

◀ **END ALTERNATIVE START**

▼ 0.0 km — Zero trip meter at road junction. CSA over Pentecost River. Track on right SP: Karunjie Track.

Track on right is where alternative start option joins Gibb River Rd. Travellers from this direction turn right onto Gibb River Rd.

| | Road junction on eastern side of Pentecost River. CSA to follow main route directions to Kununurra, see page 62. TL to follow alternative route notes to Wyndham. | 8.8 km ▲ |

(8.8 km)

▼ 8.8 km — Y-junction.

| | Zero trip meter at track junction. CSA. Track on left SP: Home Valley Station 1 km. | 0.0 km ▲ |

GPS S:15 44.268 E:127 50.211
UTM 52L 375384E 8259724N

▼ 0.0 km — Zero trip meter at Y-junction. KL. Road on right SP: Home Valley Station 1 km.

Road on right leads 1.7 km to **Home Valley station camping area**, a large space close to station homestead with some shady trees.

| | Track junction. | 106.6 km ▲ |

(0.2 km)

▼ 0.2 km — Road junction. CSA. Track on right.

| | Y-junction. KR. Track on left SP: Home Valley Station. | 106.4 km ▲ |

Track on left leads 1.7 km to Home Valley station and camping area.

(1.4 km)

▼ 1.6 km — Lookout point on left. CSA.

Excellent views across to Cockburn Range and over Pentecost River.

| | Lookout point on right. CSA. | 105.0 km ▲ |

GPS S:15 44.778 E:127 49.537
UTM 52L 374186E 8258777N

(17.4 km)

▼ 19.0 km — Concrete causeway over Bindoola Creek.

| | Concrete causeway over Bindoola Creek. | 87.6 km ▲ |

(38.9 km)

▼ 57.9 km — Track junction. CSA. Track on right SP: Jacks Waterhole.

| | Track junction. CSA. Track on left SP: Jacks Waterhole. | 48.7 km ▲ |

GPS S:15 50.665 E:127 24.646
UTM 52L 329816E 8247630N

(9.6 km)

▼ 67.5 km — Concrete causeway over Bamboo Creek.

| | Concrete causeway over Bamboo Creek. | 39.1 km ▲ |

(18.0 km)

▼ 85.5 km — Track junction. CSA. Track on right.

Track on right leads short distance to shaded rest area overlooking Durack River.

| | Track junction. CSA. Track on left. | 21.1 km ▲ |

(0.3 km)

▼ 85.8 km — Cross SP: Durack River.

Access to river is possible on right; good picnic or lunch spot.

| | Cross SP: Durack River. | 20.8 km ▲ |

GPS S:15 56.447 E:127 13.174
UTM 52L 309426E 8236801N

(20.8 km)

KUNUNURRA ◀▶ KALUMBURU ROAD JUNCTION

Cracked earth of Pentecost River flood plain

▼ 106.6 km Road junction.

        Zero trip meter at road junction. CSA.   **0.0 km** ▲
        Track on left SP: Ellenbrae Station.

GPS	S:15 59.936 E:127 02.937
UTM	52L 291219E 8230203N

▼ 0.0 km Zero trip meter at road junction. CSA. Track on right SP: Ellenbrae Station.

Track on right leads 4.9 km to **Ellenbrae station** homestead and two **camping areas**, one located close to water.

        Road junction.   **69.9 km** ▲

(3.0 km)

▼ 3.0 km Cross SP: Dawn Creek.

Small rest area on right over creek.

        Cross SP: Dawn Creek.   **66.9 km** ▲

(23.5 km)

▼ 26.5 km Road junction. CSA. Track on right.

Track on right leads 0.2 km to small shady rest area beside river.

        Road junction. CSA. Track on left.   **43.4 km** ▲

(0.1 km)

▼ 26.6 km Road junction. CSA. Track on right.

Track on right leads short distance to large shady rest area.

        Road junction. CSA. Track on left.   **43.3 km** ▲

(19.6 km)

▼ 46.2 km Road junction. CSA. Track on right.

Track on right leads 0.3 km to large shady Main Roads rest area.

        Road junction. CSA. Track on left.   **23.7 km** ▲

GPS	S:16 03.022 E:126 42.192
UTM	52K 254267E 8224131N

(0.4 km)

▼ 46.6 km Cross SP: Russ Creek.

        Cross SP: Russ Creek.   **23.3 km** ▲

(23.3 km)

▼ 69.9 km T-junction. Road on right SP: Kalumburu (start of trek section 2). Road on left SP: Derby (start of trek section 3).

Rest area located opposite junction with information boards on Gibb River and Kalumburu roads.

        Zero trip meter at junction of Gibb River Rd   **0.0 km** ▲
        and Kalumburu Rd. Proceed east
        along Gibb River Rd. SP: Wyndham.

GPS	S:16 07.134 E:126 31.215
UTM	52K 234775E 8216318N

REVERSE DIRECTIONS START

KIMBERLEY GRAND TOUR

2 KALUMBURU RD JUNCTION ◄► KALUMBURU 531.0 KM*

Start point
Kalumburu Road Junction

Road atlas
356 D5

Total distance
798.2 km (includes return trip and route-directed side trips)

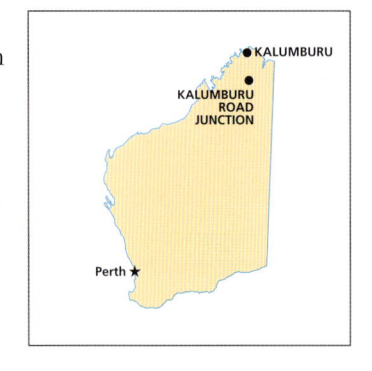

Standard
Easy
Track to Walsh Point (last 8 km difficult)

Time
4–5 days

Longest distance no PD (includes all options)
301.1 km (El Questro in section 1 to Drysdale River station)
482.6 km (Drysdale River station to Kalumburu)

Topographic maps
Auslig 1:250 000 series: *Mount Elizabeth*; *Ashton*; *Drysdale*; *Montague Sound*

Other useful information

- Drysdale River station has petrol, diesel, supplies, meals and mechanical and tyre repairs; open seven days 8am–5pm, tel. (08) 9161 4326; accepts cash, EFTPOS and credit cards. (See also www.drysdaleriver.com.au)
- Kalumburu has fuel and supplies. Mission Fuel Outlet open Monday–Friday 7.15–11.15am and 1.30–4pm, tel. (08) 9161 4333; accepts cash, EFTPOS and credit cards. Kwini store, next to corporation office, has all supplies; open Monday and Saturday 8.30–10.50am, Tuesday–Friday 9.30–10.50am and 1.30–3.50pm, tel. (08) 9161 4336; accepts cash, EFTPOS and credit cards.
- Mitchell Falls camping area has authorised firewood collection zone located on Mitchell Plateau prior to arrival; collection within signposted zone only.
- Heliwork WA operates scenic flights from Mitchell Falls campground over falls and coastline, late March–September, depending on weather and road conditions, tel. (08) 9168 1811.
- Visitor guide: *Travellers Guide to the Gibb River and Kalumburu Roads*.
- Road safety booklet: *Driving The Gibb River Road and Other Roads in the Kimberley*.
- CALM Bush Books: *Common Plants of the Kimberley*; *Geology & Landforms of the Kimberley*; *Common Birds of the Kimberley*.
- CALM brochures: *Ngauwudu–Mitchell Plateau*; *Mitchell Plateau*.
- National park information sheets: *Historical Exploration and Settlement of the Mitchell Plateau*; *Birds of Mitchell Plateau*; *Flora of Mitchell Plateau*; *Animals of Mitchell Plateau*; *Rock Art of Mitchell Plateau*.
- *The Riches of Australia* by Josephine Flood is an informative guide to prehistoric Australia.
- Ranger campfire talks and walks during peak visitor season at Mitchell Falls campground; times and dates signposted onsite.

Description

The Kalumburu Road strikes north from its junction with the Gibb River Road, passing through open farmland and crossing numerous rivers and creeks. Drysdale River station, almost 60 kilometres from the junction, is a large cattle property that caters for travellers, supplying fuel, limited provisions, camping and scenic flights.

Although this part of the route is considered easy, the road beyond the Drysdale River begins to deteriorate, with some sandy patches, and severe corrugations that continue to the King Edward River and on to the Mitchell Falls. This makes the side trip over the Mitchell Plateau fairly slow going in some sections.

The plateau, an elevated laterite-capped plain, has large stands of Mitchell Plateau fan palms (*Livistona eastonii*). In the falls area small patches of rainforest are found on the steep slopes, woodlands of grey box and white gum grow in the valleys and along creek lines, and paperbarks and pandanus line the watercourses. Highlights of the region are numerous: Aboriginal rock-art sites, the multi-tiered Mitchell Falls, good swimming in the river above the falls and a scenic helicopter flight for spectacular 'birds-eye' views. Keen anglers or those with a yen to explore further can continue north on the plateau road, take the side road to Surveyors Pool (a 6-kilometre drive followed by an 8-kilometre-return walk), have a dip in the upper pools, then continue on to Walsh Point at Port Warrender. Drivers are warned that the last 8 kilometres are difficult going and will take about an hour. Once at Walsh Point there is excellent fishing for barramundi and mangrove jack.

Back on the Kalumburu Road, it is an easy drive to the Aboriginal community of historic Kalumburu.

*Total distance of return trip (Kalumburu Road Junction to Kalumburu and return to Kalumburu Road Junction).

Emu bush, as identified by a local Aboriginal guide

The first European settlement of the area was in 1908 by Benedictine monks from New Norcia, 132 kilometres north of Perth. They established a mission at Pago, then moved to Kalumburu in 1927. A visit to the mission church and a tour of the museum are recommended.

From Kalumburu there is good access to the King Edward River and excellent fishing for barramundi and mangrove jack, but crocodiles inhabit these waters so heed the warning signs. Camping at Kalumburu is at the mission campground, as well as at a number of camping areas set up by local families. Those at McGowans Beach, Honeymoon Bay and Pago have access to water and you can launch a tinnie and explore or fish along the coast. Check with locals before swimming.

Advice and warnings

- This is a remote area so you need to be totally self-sufficient and your vehicle well equipped. Carry cash because EFTPOS and credit card facilities are rarely available.
- Roads generally closed and impassable during and after heavy rains. Kalumburu Rd has heavily corrugated sections and sandy patches. Mitchell Plateau Rd is often heavily corrugated – a blade is put over the surface once a year at the beginning of the dry season. Approach creek and river crossings with caution. Ring WA road condition report service, tel. 1800 013 314, to check road conditions.
- Slow down for oncoming road trains and wait for them to pass and for dust to settle before continuing. Exercise caution when overtaking and approaching other vehicles as dust may impede visibility – slow down or stop if necessary.
- Watch out for roaming stock (and wildlife) as much of the track runs through unfenced cattle stations.
- Kalumburu Rd runs through private land and there are numerous station access tracks. Do not deviate from main road without prior approval from landholders.
- Standard road tyres or all-terrain tyres are suitable. Tyre pressure can be lowered to assist with travel comfort and to limit strain on your vehicle – particularly on side trip over Mitchell Plateau. Always carry two spare tyres as punctures and tyre damage are common. Tyre repair equipment is a worthy addition to your toolkit.
- Towing off-road trailers and off-road caravans is possible but ensure they are well prepared for corrugations.
- Camping is at designated sites only. Bush camping is possible at the Gibb River crossing, Plain Creek rest area and Carson River crossing.
- Rubbish bins are not provided along the roads so please take your rubbish with you.
- Saltwater crocodiles inhabit the waterways. Seek local advice prior to swimming.
- Be sure to carry some means of communication such as a satellite phone or HF radio.

Permits and bookings

- No permits required to travel these roads.
- Two permits required to enter Kalumburu. Access permit (no cost) obtainable from Aboriginal Lands Trust, tel. (08) 9235 8000. Allow at least two weeks for processing and posting or faxing. Entry permit (fee payable) obtainable from Kununurra Visitor Centre, Coolibah Dr, open Monday–Saturday 8am–5pm and Sunday 9am–4pm (dry season hours, April–October). If not travelling via Kununurra, permit available from Kalumburu Aboriginal Corporation office (cash only) on arrival; open Monday–Friday 8.30am–12noon and 2–4pm, tel. (08) 9161 4300.
- Bookings not required for camping at station campgrounds but highly recommended for other types of accommodation.
- Drysdale River station has camping and room accommodation, tel. (08) 9161 4326; accepts cash, EFTPOS and credit cards. Bookings recommended for rooms, but not necessary for camping.

KIMBERLEY GRAND TOUR

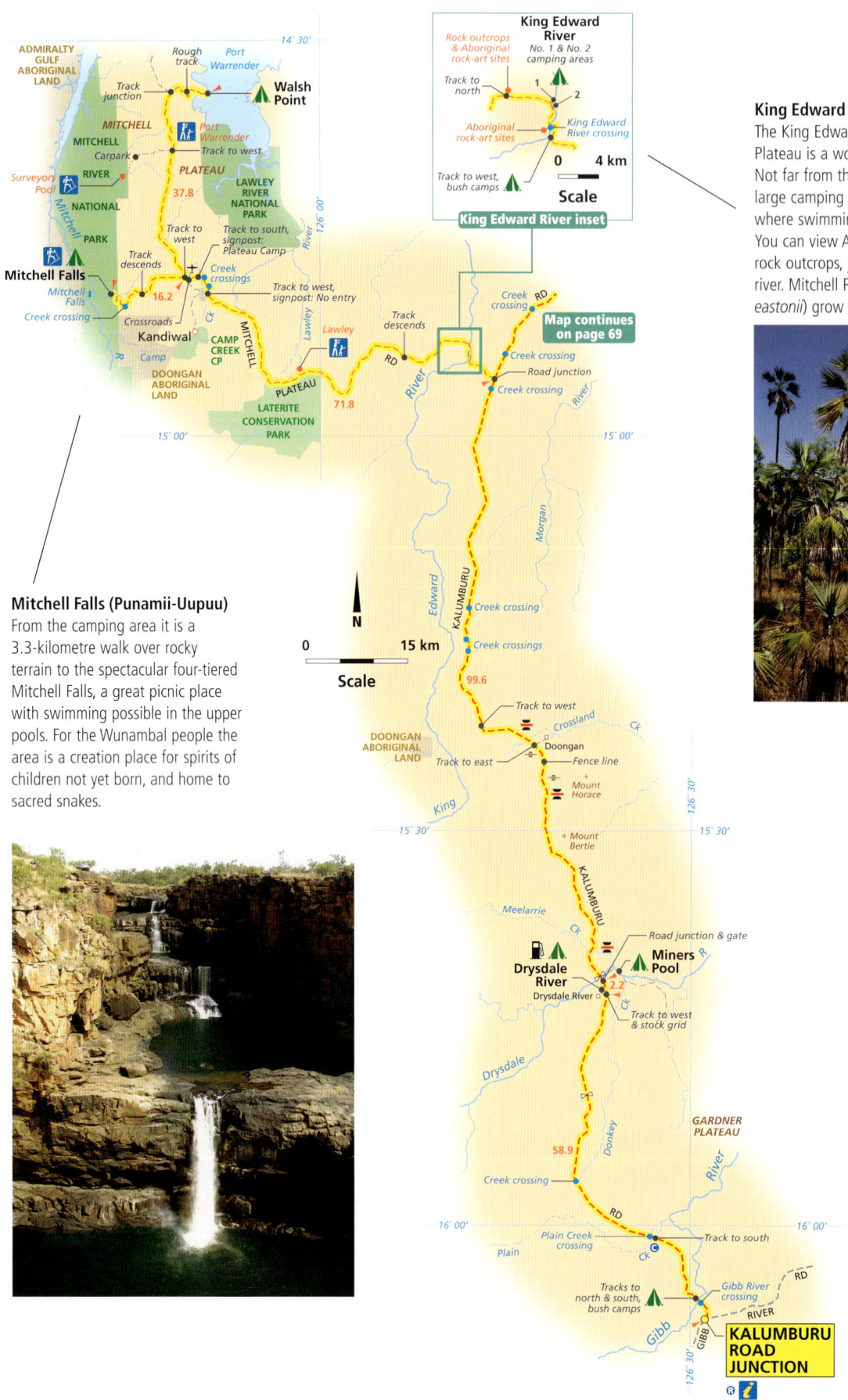

King Edward River
The King Edward River on the Mitchell Plateau is a wonderful place to explore. Not far from the river crossing are two large camping areas beside the river, where swimming and fishing are possible. You can view Aboriginal art on some large rock outcrops, just a short drive from the river. Mitchell Plateau fan palms (*Livistona eastonii*) grow on the plateau.

Mitchell Falls (Punamii-Uupuu)
From the camping area it is a 3.3-kilometre walk over rocky terrain to the spectacular four-tiered Mitchell Falls, a great picnic place with swimming possible in the upper pools. For the Wunambal people the area is a creation place for spirits of children not yet born, and home to sacred snakes.

KALUMBURU ROAD JUNCTION ◀▶ KALUMBURU

Fishing at Honeymoon Bay

Kalumburu Mission
Kalumburu Mission was bombed during World War II and then rebuilt. The mission building is set amid giant mango trees and coconut palms. Visitors can view the quaint church and beautiful St Benedict's Monastery, built of King Leopold sandstone. During the week there is a lecture tour of the fascinating Father Thomas Gil Museum (closed Friday and Sunday).

Kalumburu Mission campground

Campsite Facilities

	Toilets	Disabled access	4WD access only	Off-road trailer	Off-road caravan	Drinking water	Fee payable	Ranger patrolled	BBQ/fireplace	Campfires prohibited	Picnic tables	Shelter shed	No rubbish disposal	Public phone	Shower	Bushwalking	Swimming	Swimming not advised	Fishing	Canoeing	Dogs allowed
Drysdale River	•		•	•	•	•	•	•				•	•							•	
Honeymoon Bay	•		•	•	•		•		•						•	•	•		•		•
Kalumburu Mission	•		•	•	•	•	•							•							
King Edward River	•		•	•			•				•				•		•				
McGowans Beach	•		•	•									•		•	•		•	•		•
Miners Pool	•		•	•											•			•			
Mitchell Falls	•		•	•			•					•				•					
Pago			•	•			•					•							•		•
Walsh Point			•							•							•	•			

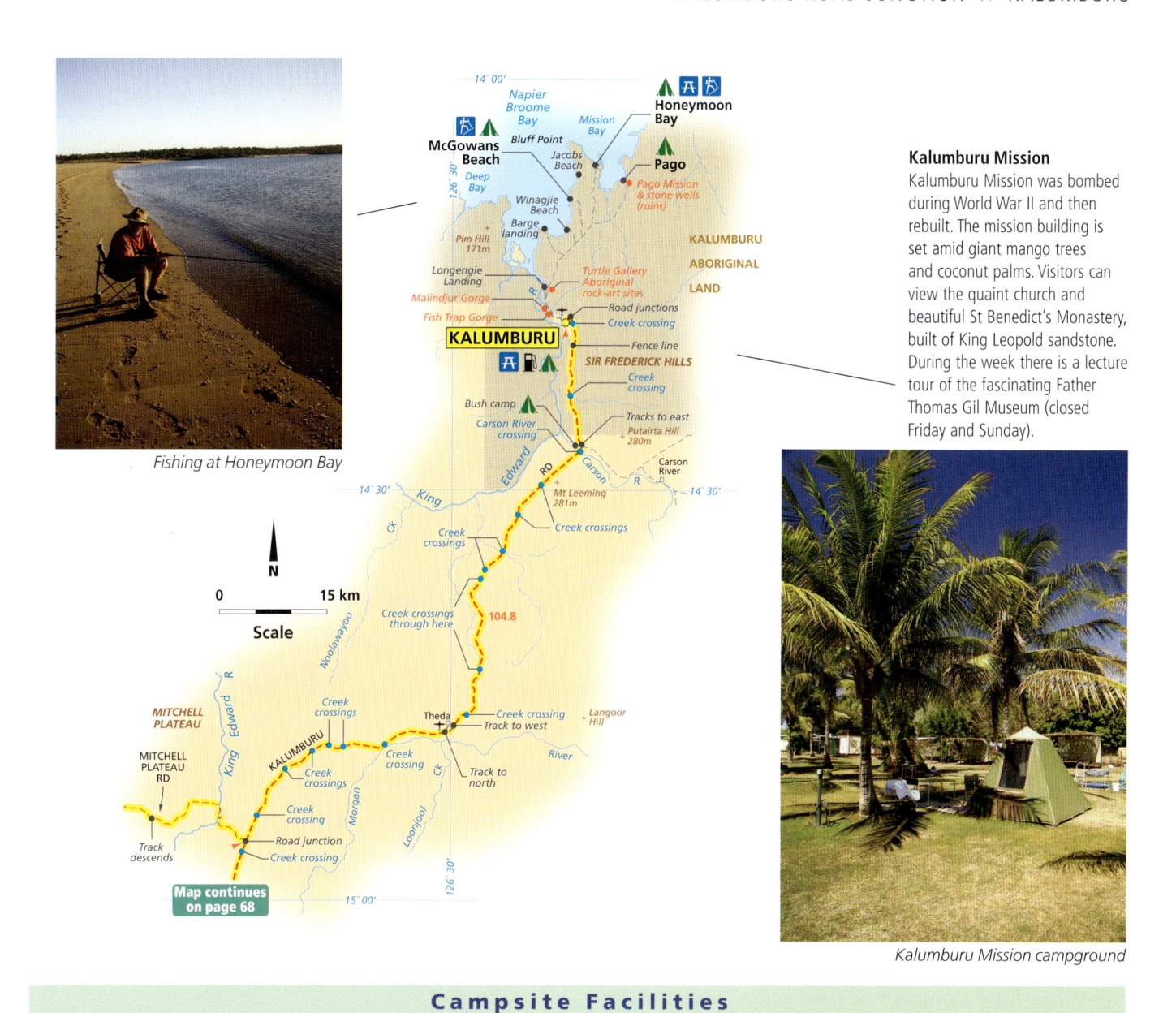

69

KIMBERLEY GRAND TOUR

ROUTE DIRECTIONS

▼ 0.0 km — Zero trip meter at junction of Gibb River Rd and SP: Kalumburu Road. Proceed north along Kalumburu Rd SP: Kalumburu.

Road junction. Road SO SP: Derby (see trek section 3). Road on left SP: Wyndham (see trek section 1). — 58.9 km ▲

GPS   S:16 07.134 E:126 31.215
UTM   52K 234775E 8216318N

(3.1 km)

▼ 3.1 km — Cross Gibb River.

Cross Gibb River. — 55.8 km ▲

GPS   S:16 05.802 E:126 30.726
UTM   52K 233873E 8218765N

(0.1 km)

▼ 3.2 km — Road junction. CSA. Track on left and right.

Track on left and right lead to overnight bush campsites. Delightful shady locations.

Road junction. CSA. Track on left and right. — 55.7 km ▲

(12.7 km)

▼ 15.9 km — Road junction. CSA. Track on left.

Track on left leads to Plain Creek rest area and overnight bush campsite.

Road junction. CSA. Track on right. — 43.0 km ▲

(0.1 km)

▼ 16.0 km — Cross Plain Creek.

Cross Plain Creek. — 42.9 km ▲

GPS   S:16 00.932 E:126 26.997
UTM   52K 227110E 8227670N

(42.9 km)

▼ 58.9 km — Road junction.

Zero trip meter at road junction. CSA. Track on right SP: Drysdale River Station. — 0.0 km ▲

GPS   S:15 42.453 E:126 23.246
UTM   52L 219991E 8261684N

▼ 0.0 km — Zero trip meter at road junction. CSA. Track on left SP: Drysdale River Station.

Track on left leads 1.2 km to **Drysdale River station camping area**, a large open campground located close to homestead, with restaurant and bar.

Road junction. — 2.2 km ▲

(2.2 km)

▼ 2.2 km — Road junction.

Zero trip meter at road junction. CSA. Track on left SP: Miners Pool Camp Area. — 0.0 km ▲

GPS   S:15 41.303 E:126 22.887
UTM   52L 219323E 8263798N

▼ 0.0 km — Zero trip meter at road junction. CSA. Track on right SP: Miners Pool Camp Area.

Track on right leads 3.2 km to **Miners Pool camping area**, a spacious place with scattered tall eucalypts providing shade beside lovely waterhole. Camping fees payable at Drysdale River station.

Road junction. — 99.6 km ▲

(0.4 km)

▼ 0.4 km — Cross SP: Drysdale River.

Cross SP: Drysdale River. — 99.2 km ▲

GPS   S:15 41.114 E:126 22.724
UTM   52L 219027E 8264143N

(37.4 km)

▼ 37.8 km — Road junction. CSA. Track on right SP: Doongan.

Road junction. CSA. Track on left SP: Doongan. — 61.8 km ▲

(9.0 km)

▼ 46.8 km — Road junction. CSA. Track on left SP: Marunbabidi.

Road junction. CSA. Track on right SP: Marunbabidi. — 52.8 km ▲

(52.8 km)

▼ 99.6 km — Road junction. Side trips to Mitchell Plateau and Walsh Point.

Track SO SP: 103 Kalumburu.

Zero trip meter at road junction. CSA: SP:Wyndham 454. Track on right SP: Mitchell Plateau/Port Warrender. — 0.0 km ▲

GPS   S:14 55.742 E:126 14.142
UTM   52L 202619E 8347674N

▶ **SIDE TRIP: Mitchell Plateau**

▼ 0.0 km — Zero trip meter on Kalumburu Rd at track junction. Proceed westwards along track SP: Mitchell Plateau/Port Warrender.

(5.1 km)

▼ 5.1 km — Track junction. CSA. Track on left.

Track on left leads to bush campsites.

(1.3 km)

▼ 6.4 km — Cross King Edward River.

Numerous bush campsites in this vicinity.

GPS   S:14 54.027 E:126 12.102
UTM   52L 198919E 8350793N

(0.2 km)

▼ 6.6 km — Track junction. CSA. Track on left.

Track on left leads 0.6 km to carpark and walk to impressive Aboriginal rock-art sites.

(1.6 km)

▼ 8.2 km — Track junction. CSA. Track on right.

Track on right leads 0.1 km to **King Edward River No. 2 camping area**, a large open space with some shady trees beside the river.

(0.3 km)

▼ 8.5 km — Track junction. CSA. Track on right.

Track on right leads 0.1 km to **King Edward River No. 1 camping area**, a large open space with some shady trees beside the river.

(3.4 km)

▼ 11.9 km — Track junction. CSA. Track on right.

Track on right leads 0.5 km to carpark and walk to Aboriginal rock-art sites.

(8.1 km)

▼ 20.0 km — Track descends into valley.

(22.2 km)

▼ 42.2 km — Lawley Lookout on right. CSA.

Good views north over Lawley River National Park.

KALUMBURU ROAD JUNCTION ◀▶ KALUMBURU

	GPS S:14 55.400 E:125 58.372 **UTM** 51L 819844E 8348015N **(23.5 km)**
▼ 65.7 km	Y-junction. KR. Track on left SP: No Through Road/Private Property. **(3.2 km)**
▼ 68.9 km	Creek crossing. **(0.6 km)**
▼ 69.5 km	Track junction. CSA. Track on left SP: Plateau Camp. Plateau Camp has pre-booked safari-style accommodation only, tel. (08) 9168 2213. **(1.6 km)**
▼ 71.1 km	Crossroads. CSA. SP: Mitchell Falls Camping Area 18 km/Surveyors Pool 27 km/Port Warrender Coastal Access 44 km. Track on left SP: Kimberley Safari Camp. Track on right SP: Mitchell Plateau Airfield. **(0.7 km)**
▼ 71.8 km	Y-junction. **GPS** S:14 47.989 E:125 49.081 **UTM** 51L 803345E 8361908N
▼ 0.0 km	Zero trip meter at Y-junction on Mitchell Plateau Rd. KL. SP: Mitchell Falls. Track on right SP: Port Warrender Coastal Access/Surveyors Pool. Track on right, see Walsh Point side trip. **(8.1 km)**
▼ 8.1 km	Track descends into valley. **(4.2 km)**
▼ 12.3 km	Creek crossing. **(3.9 km)**
▼ 16.2 km	Mitchell Falls camping area. To take side trip to Walsh Point, return 16.2 km to junction, with track to north SP: Port Warrender Coastal Access/Surveyors Pool, or return to Mitchell Plateau side trip start. Mitchell Falls camping area is a large spacious site with many shady trees. Heliwork WA operates helicopter scenic flights from camping area. **GPS** S:14 49.212 E:125 43.104 **UTM** 51L 792587E 8359784N
▶	**SIDE TRIP: Walsh Point**
▼ 0.0 km	Zero trip meter at Y-junction on Mitchell Plateau Rd. KR. SP: Port Warrender Coastal Access/Surveyors Pool. Track on left SP: Mitchell Falls. **(20.4 km)**
▼ 20.4 km	Track junction. CSA. SP: Port Warrender. Track on left SP: 6 km Surveyors Pool. Track on left leads 6.5 km to carpark and start of 4-km (45–60-minute) walking track to scenic Surveyors Pool. Swimming is possible in the upper pools. **GPS** S:14 38.342 E:125 48.134 **UTM** 51L 801866E 8379731N **(3.0 km)**
▼ 23.4 km	Port Warrender Lookout on right. CSA. Excellent views from this point. **(6.5 km)**

Surveyors Pool in Mitchell River National Park

▼ 29.9 km	Track junction. CSA. SP: Port Warrender Coastal Access Track/Walsh Point 8 km/Poor Track Condition. Minor track on left. Track to Walsh Point becomes very rocky and rough. Allow 1 hour to drive remaining 7.9 km. **GPS** S:14 33.907 E:125 48.036 **UTM** 51L 801791E 8387917N **(7.9 km)**
▼ 37.8 km	Walsh Point. Return to Mitchell Plateau side trip start. Walsh Point bush camping area has seven sites on shores of Port Warrender, with some great fishing. Most popular targeted fish species are barramundi and mangrove jack. Fishing is from shore or boat – possible to launch small craft here. Bring insect repellent to ward off sandflies. **GPS** S:14 34.101 E:125 50.896 **UTM** 51L 806927E 8387495N
◀	**END SIDE TRIPS**
▼ 0.0 km	Zero trip meter on Kalumburu Rd at junction with SP: Mitchell Plateau/Port Warrender, on left. CSA. SP: 103 Kalumburu. Road junction. Track SO SP: Wyndham 454. **104.8 km ▲** Track on right SP: Mitchell Plateau/Port Warrender. Track on right. See Mitchell Plateau side trip. **(3.9 km)**

■ 71

KIMBERLEY GRAND TOUR

▼ 3.9 km Creek crossing.

　　　　　　　　　　　　　Creek crossing. 100.9 km ▲

(7.7 km)

▼ 11.6 km Cross SP: Ngoollalah Creek.

　　　　　　　　　Cross SP: Ngoollalah Creek. 93.2 km ▲

GPS	S:14 50.416 E:126 17.184
UTM	52L 207957E 8357569N

(4.6 km)

▼ 16.2 km Creek crossing.

　　　　　　　　　　　　　Creek crossing. 88.6 km ▲

(10.9 km)

▼ 27.1 km Creek crossing.

　　　　　　　　　　　　　Creek crossing. 77.7 km ▲

(9.2 km)

▼ 36.3 km Airstrip on left. CSA.

　　　　　　　　　　　　Airstrip on right. CSA. 68.5 km ▲

(1.3 km)

▼ 37.6 km Road junction. CSA. Track on left SP: Theda Homestead.

　　　　　Road junction. CSA. Track on right SP: Theda Homestead. 67.2 km ▲

(2.6 km)

▼ 40.2 km Cross SP: Station Creek.

　　　　　　　　　　　Cross SP: Station Creek. 64.6 km ▲

GPS	S:14 46.455 E:126 31.210
UTM	52L 233049E 8365169N

(22.6 km)

▼ 62.8 km Creek crossing.

　　　　　　　　　　　　　Creek crossing. 42.0 km ▲

(3.7 km)

▼ 66.5 km Creek crossing.

　　　　　　　　　　　　　Creek crossing. 38.3 km ▲

(18.1 km)

▼ 84.6 km Cross Carson River.

Possible bush camping along rocky banks of river under shady trees. This is crocodile territory so take extreme care.

　　　　　　　　　　　　Cross Carson River. 20.2 km ▲

GPS	S:14 27.168 E:126 39.789
UTM	52L 248082E 8400913N

(0.5 km)

▼ 85.1 km Road junction. CSA. Track on right SP: Carson River.

Track on right is entrance to Carson River station.

　　　　　Road junction. CSA. Track on left SP: Carson River. 19.7 km ▲

(0.5 km)

▼ 85.6 km Road junction. CSA. Track on right.

　　　　　　Road junction. CSA. Track on left. 19.2 km ▲

(7.1 km)

▼ 92.7 km Creek crossing.

　　　　　　　　　　　　　Creek crossing. 12.1 km ▲

(10.9 km)

▼ 103.6 km Creek crossing.

　　　　　　　　　　　　　Creek crossing. 1.2 km ▲

(0.1 km)

▼ 103.7 km Road junction. CSA. Track on right.

　　　　　　Road junction. CSA. Track on left. 1.1 km ▲

(0.4 km)

▼ 104.1 km Road junction. CSA. Track on right.

　　　　　　Road junction. CSA. Track on left. 0.7 km ▲

(0.7 km)

▼ 104.8 km Kalumburu Mission on left. Return to trek section 2 start point to continue on section 3 of Kimberley Grand Tour.

Kalumburu Mission camping area, located on left behind store, is grass-covered and shady. Continue north through Kalumburu for 14.8 km to signposted turn-off to **McGowans Beach camping area**, a small place with some shade at water's edge. A further 2.2 km brings you to signposted turn-off to **Pago camping area**, located a further 8.0 km and offering a choice of camping at water's edge near landholder's homestead or further north at more secluded sites. From Pago turn-off it is a further 8.3 km to signposted access road to **Honeymoon Bay camping area**, which has beach campsites or sites among shady trees closer to landholder's homestead.

　　　　　　　　　Zero trip meter in Kalumburu. 0.0 km ▲
　　　　　　　　　Kalumburu Mission on right.
　　　　　　　　　Proceed south to Gibb River Rd.

GPS	S:14 17.729 E:126 38.605
UTM	52L 245776E 8418303N

REVERSE DIRECTIONS START

Catholic Mission at Kalumburu

72

3 KALUMBURU ROAD JUNCTION ◀▶ DERBY 417.2 KM

Start point
Kalumburu Road Junction

Road atlas
356 D5

Total distance
722.0 km to Derby (includes route-directed side trip and Tunnel Creek)
660.5 km to Fitzroy Crossing (includes route-directed side trip)

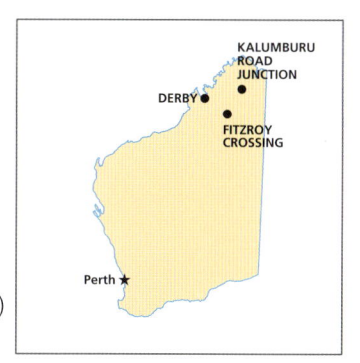

Standard
Easy

Time
3–4 days

Longest distances no PD (includes all options)
243.0 km (Drysdale River station in section 2 to Mount Barnett Roadhouse)
423.4 km (Imintji to Derby)
354.9 km (Imintji to Fitzroy Crossing)

Topographic maps
Auslig 1:250 000 series: *Mount Elizabeth*; *Charnley*; *Lennard River*; *Lansdowne*; *Noonkanbah*; *Derby*

Other useful information
- Mount Barnett Roadhouse has petrol and diesel, a well-stocked store and take-away meals; open seven days (in dry season) 7am–5pm, tel. (08) 9191 7007; accepts cash, EFTPOS and credit cards.
- Imintji store has large range of groceries, diesel only and can arrange mechanical and tyre repairs; open seven days 8am–5pm; accepts cash, EFTPOS and credit cards.
- Visitor guide: *Travellers Guide to the Gibb River and Kalumburu Roads*.
- Road safety booklet: *Driving The Gibb River Road and Other Roads in the Kimberley*.
- CALM Bush Books: *Common Plants of the Kimberley*; *Geology & Landforms of the Kimberley*; *Common Birds of the Kimberley*.
- *The Riches of Australia* by Josephine Flood is an informative guide to prehistoric Australia.

Description
This trek section traverses some of the Kimberley's most productive pastoral country along with scenic landscapes that typify the region. Barnett River Gorge, around 80 kilometres from the trek section start, and Manning Gorge, a further 30 kilometres, are excellent places for swimming and bushwalking. A further 54 kilometres brings you to the start of a side trip to Old Mornington, a one-time pastoral lease and now a huge conservation area protecting rare and endangered bird and animal species. The gorges here are awesome and you can experience the environment by canoe.

Back on the Gibb River Road, you enter King Leopold Ranges Conservation Park. From the top of the ranges there are spectacular views of the surrounding plains, rivers and mountains. On the western side, not far past Napier Downs, is the junction with the Fairfield–Leopold Road. At this point, travellers can continue west to Derby or divert southwards to visit some spectacular parks, or continue south and finish the trek at Fitzroy Crossing. If ending your trip in Derby (the shortest route for those planning to visit Broome), once past the Fairfield–Leopold Road turn-off it is a straightforward run with one of the few highlights a detour to the May River.

The route option via the Fairfield–Leopold Road showcases a number of the region's superb natural attractions. The track takes you into the heart of the Kimberley's ancient coral reefs that were once submerged 350 million years ago during Devonian times by a vast tropical sea. The national parks of Windjana Gorge and, north-east of Fitzroy Crossing, Geikie Gorge were carved deeply by the flooding of two rivers – the Lennard and Fitzroy – while Tunnel Creek, comprising Western Australia's oldest limestone caves, was formed by a creek flowing along a fault line. The five gorges – Bell, Lennard, Windjana, Tunnel Creek and Geikie – all offer something unique. Vegetation along the riverbanks includes paperbarked cadjeputs, river gums, freshwater mangroves, pandanus, native figs and wild passionfruit.

Walking through Tunnel Creek is a 'must do' activity in the Kimberley. Although the walk is short and relatively easy, the varying water level makes it an exciting and fun experience. Exposed cross-sections of the limestone strata reveal ancient marine fossils and open a window on life before the evolution of reptiles or mammals.

Roads in this region include a mix of well-maintained gravel surfaces and stretches of bitumen – a welcome respite from the corrugations and dust – where the road traverses the King Leopold Ranges as well as the last kilometres of the run into Derby. In addition to the listed campsites, there are a number of stations that offer camping and other accommodation options. Bush camping is also possible in places.

KIMBERLEY GRAND TOUR

Advice and warnings

- This is a remote area so you need to be totally self-sufficient and your vehicle well equipped. Carry cash; EFTPOS and credit card facilities are rarely available.
- Roads can be closed and impassable during and after heavy rains. Gibb River Rd has heavily corrugated sections. Approach grids and creek and river crossings with caution. Ring WA road condition report service, tel. 1800 013 314, to check road conditions.
- Slow down for oncoming road trains and wait for them to pass and for dust to settle before continuing. Exercise caution when overtaking and approaching other vehicles as dust may impede visibility.
- Watch out for roaming stock (and wildlife) as much of the track runs through unfenced cattle stations.
- Gibb River Rd runs through private land and there are numerous station access tracks. Do not deviate from main road without prior approval from landholders.
- Standard road tyres or all-terrain tyres are suitable. Tyre pressure can be lowered to assist with travel comfort. Always carry two spare tyres as punctures and tyre damage are common. Tyre repair equipment is a worthy addition to your toolkit.
- Towing off-road trailers and off-road caravans is possible but ensure they are well prepared for corrugations.
- Camping is at designated sites and at a small number of bush campsites that are noted in the route directions.
- Rubbish bins are not provided along the roads so please take your rubbish with you.
- Crocodiles inhabit gorges and river systems so do not swim unless advised to do so. Be crocodile-wise.
- Do not touch or disturb Aboriginal cave and rock paintings at Windjana and Tunnel Creek national parks.
- Be sure to carry some means of communication such as a satellite phone or HF radio.
- Pack a good torch for the Tunnel Creek walk and be prepared to get wet.

Permits and bookings

- No permits required to travel roads on this trek section.
- Permit to camp at Manning Gorge obtainable from Mount Barnett Roadhouse, open seven days (in dry season) 7am–5pm, tel. (08) 9191 7007; accepts cash, EFTPOS and credit cards.
- Bookings not required for camping at stations, but highly recommended for other accommodation.
- Mount Elizabeth station has homestead accommodation as well as camping, tel. (08) 9191 4644; accepts cash and travellers cheques.
- Beverley Springs station has bed and breakfast accommodation as well as camping (plus magnificent gorges for swimming and fishing), tel. (08) 9191 4646; accepts cash and travellers cheques.

Police station ruins at Lillimulura, near Windjana Gorge National Park

- Old Mornington has camping, safari tent accommodation, meals, tours and canoe hire, tel. (08) 9191 7406; accepts cash and credit cards.
- Mount Hart Wilderness Lodge offers dinner, bed and breakfast accommodation. No camping. Bookings essential, tel. (08) 9191 4645, or visit their website (www.mthart.com.au).
- Birdwood Downs station has Savannah Hut accommodation, camping and ecotours, tel. (08) 9191 1275; accepts cash only.

ROUTE DIRECTIONS

▼ **0.0 km** — Zero trip meter at junction of Gibb River Rd and SP: Kalumburu Rd. Proceed south-west on Gibb River Rd SP: Derby.

Road junction. Road SO SP: Kalumburu Rd/ Kalumburu (see trek section 2). Road on right SP: Gibb River Rd/Wyndham (see trek section 1). **70.0 km** ▲

GPS S:16 07.134 E:126 31.215
UTM 52K 234775E 8216318N

(9.6 km)

▼ **9.6 km** — Creek crossing.

Creek crossing. **60.4 km** ▲

(6.7 km)

▼ **16.3 km** — Creek crossing.

Creek crossing. **53.7 km** ▲

(23.7 km)

▼ **40.0 km** — Road junction. CSA. Track on right SP: Gibb River Station 2 km.

Road junction. CSA. Track on left SP: Gibb River Station 2 km. **30.0 km** ▲

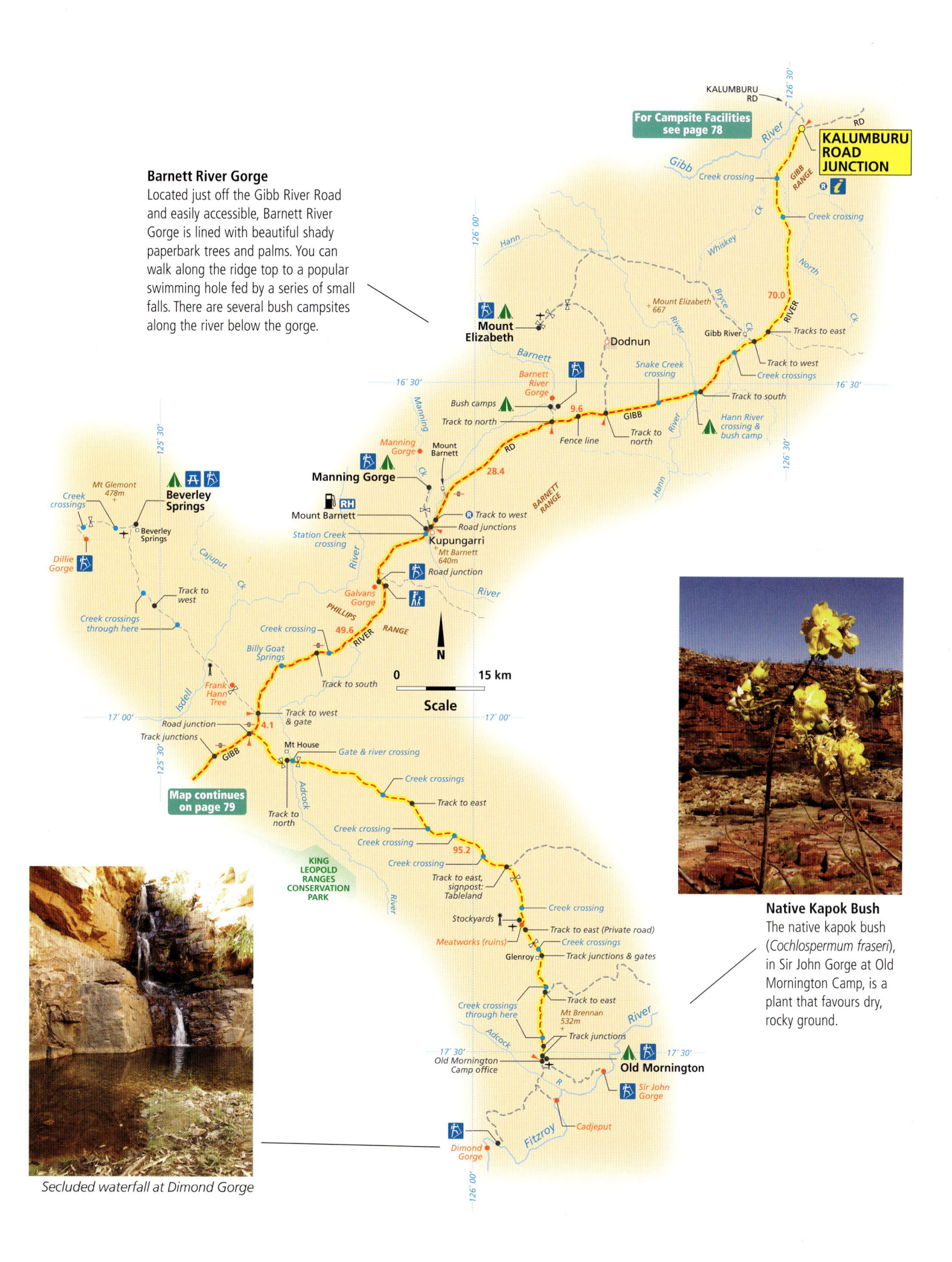

KALUMBURU ROAD JUNCTION ◀▶ DERBY

Barnett River Gorge
Located just off the Gibb River Road and easily accessible, Barnett River Gorge is lined with beautiful shady paperbark trees and palms. You can walk along the ridge top to a popular swimming hole fed by a series of small falls. There are several bush campsites along the river below the gorge.

Native Kapok Bush
The native kapok bush (*Cochlospermum fraseri*), in Sir John Gorge at Old Mornington Camp, is a plant that favours dry, rocky ground.

Secluded waterfall at Dimond Gorge

KIMBERLEY GRAND TOUR

GPS	S:16 26.218 E:126 26.832
UTM	52K 227397E 8181010N

(3.4 km)

▼ 43.4 km Cross SP: Bryce Creek.

    Cross SP: Bryce Creek.   26.6 km ▲

(1.1 km)

▼ 44.5 km Cross SP: Mistake Creek.

    Cross SP: Mistake Creek.   25.5 km ▲

(9.3 km)

▼ 53.8 km Cross SP: Hann River.

Possible bush camping in vicinity. Water generally flows throughout dry season.

    Cross SP: Hann River.   16.2 km ▲

GPS	S:16 30.846 E:126 21.339
UTM	52K 217727E 8172344N

(7.0 km)

▼ 60.8 km Cross SP: Snake Creek.

    Cross SP: Snake Creek.   9.2 km ▲

(9.2 km)

▼ 70.0 km Road junction.

    Zero trip meter at road junction. CSA. Track on left SP: Mount Elizabeth.   0.0 km ▲

GPS	S:16 32.752 E:126 12.565
UTM	52K 202156E 8168616N

▼ 0.0 km Zero trip meter at road junction. CSA. Track on right SP: Mount Elizabeth.

Track on right leads 30.0 km to **Mount Elizabeth station camping area**, a well-shaded site close to homestead.

    Road junction.   9.6 km ▲

(9.6 km)

▼ 9.6 km Road junction.

    Zero trip meter at road junction. CSA. Track on left SP: Barnett River Gorge 3.   0.0 km ▲

GPS	S:16 33.523 E:126 07.383
UTM	52K 192952E 8167063

▼ 0.0 km Zero trip meter at road junction. CSA. Track on right SP: Barnett River Gorge 3.

Track on right leads 2.9 km to a number of possible bush campsites beside Barnett River and 4.2 km to carpark and a walk to gorge with great swimming hole.

    Road junction.   28.4 km ▲

(27.2 km)

▼ 27.2 km Road junction. CSA. Track on right.

Track on right leads 0.2 km to rest area.

    Road junction. CSA. Track on left.   1.2 km ▲

(0.2 km)

▼ 27.4 km Cross SP: Mt Barnett River.

    Cross SP: Mt Barnett River.   1.0 km ▲

(1.0 km)

▼ 28.4 km Road junction.

    Zero trip meter at road junction. CSA. Road on left SP: Mt Barnett.   0.0 km ▲

GPS	S:16 42.969 E:125 55.843
UTM	51K 812535E 8149545N

▼ 0.0 km Zero trip meter at road junction. CSA. Road on right SP: Mt Barnett.

Road on right leads 0.3 km to Mount Barnett Roadhouse and further 7.0 km to **Manning Gorge camping area**, a very large site spread along banks of Manning River with shady trees. Good swimming and bushwalking. Camping permit required and available from roadhouse.

    Road junction.   49.6 km ▲

(0.3 km)

▼ 0.3 km Road junction. CSA. Track on left SP: Kupungarri Community.

    Road junction. CSA. Track on right SP: Kupungarri Community.   49.3 km ▲

(1.1 km)

▼ 1.4 km Cross SP: Station Creek.

    Cross SP: Station Creek.   48.2 km ▲

(12.7 km)

▼ 14.1 km Road junction. CSA. Small carpark on right.

A 1.0-km walking trail leads from carpark to Galvans Gorge. Main pool is lovely swimming spot. Faint rock art depicting Wandjina spirit beings in vicinity.

    Road junction. CSA. Small carpark on left.   35.5 km ▲

GPS	S:16 47.901 E:125 50.898
UTM	51K 803610E 8140570N

(1.1 km)

▼ 15.2 km Lookout point on left. CSA.

    Lookout point on right. CSA.   34.4 km ▲

(24.7 km)

▼ 39.9 km Cross SP: Billy Goat Springs.

    Cross SP: Billy Goat Springs.   9.7 km ▲

(9.7 km)

▼ 49.6 km Road junction.

    Zero trip meter at road junction. CSA. Track on left SP: Beverley Springs 43 km.   0.0 km ▲

GPS	S:16 59.672 E:125 39.432
UTM	51K 782934E 8119131N

▼ 0.0 km Zero trip meter at road junction. CSA. Track on right SP: Beverley Springs 43 km.

Track on right leads 43.0 km to homestead and nearby **Beverley Springs camping area**, a large open space rimmed by shady trees. Several scenic gorges on station are ideal for swimming and marron fishing.

    Road junction.   4.1 km ▲

(4.1 km)

▼ 4.1 km Road junction. Side trip to Old Mornington Camp.

    Zero trip meter at road junction. CSA. Track on right SP: Mount House/Old Mornington Camp.   0.0 km ▲

GPS	S:17 01.521 E:125 38.600
UTM	51K 781410E 8115739N

▶ **SIDE TRIP: Old Mornington Camp**

▼ 0.0 km Zero trip meter on Gibb River Rd at road junction. Proceed south-east on track SP: Mount House/Old Mornington Camp.

(8.7 km)

KALUMBURU ROAD JUNCTION ◀▶ DERBY

▼ 8.7 km	Gate. LAF.	
	(0.7 km)	
▼ 9.4 km	Track junction. CSA. SP: Old Mornington. Track on left.	
	Track on left leads to Mount House homestead. No public access.	
	(0.4 km)	
▼ 9.8 km	Gate. LAF.	
	(0.1 km)	
▼ 9.9 km	River crossing.	
	(0.6 km)	
▼ 10.5 km	Gate. LAF.	
	(17.2 km)	
▼ 27.7 km	Creek crossing.	
	(4.7 km)	
▼ 32.4 km	Track junction. CSA. Track on left.	
	GPS S:17 07.745 E:125 54.108	
	UTM 51K 808775E 8103861N	
	(9.7 km)	
▼ 42.1 km	Creek crossing.	
	(11.5 km)	
▼ 53.6 km	Creek crossing.	
	(4.7 km)	
▼ 58.3 km	Track junction. CSA. SP: Mornington. Track on left SP: Tableland.	
	GPS S:17 13.422 E:126 03.211	
	UTM 52K 186627E 8093310N	
	(2.5 km)	
▼ 60.8 km	Gate. LAF.	
	(7.7 km)	
▼ 68.5 km	Stockyards and windmill on right. CSA.	
	(0.4 km)	
▼ 68.9 km	Ruins of old meatworks on right. CSA.	
	GPS S:17 18.603 E:126 04.664	
	UTM 52K 189349E 8083787N	
	(1.1 km)	
▼ 70.0 km	Track junction. CSA. SP: Old Mornington Camp. Track on left SP: Top Bore.	
	(2.6 km)	
▼ 72.6 km	Gate. LAF.	
	(1.7 km)	
▼ 74.3 km	Creek crossing.	
	(0.8 km)	
▼ 75.1 km	Creek crossing.	
	(0.3 km)	
▼ 75.4 km	Y-junction. KL through gate. LAF. SP: Old Mornington Bush Camp. Track on right SP: Glenroy Homestead.	
	GPS S:17 21.372 E:126 06.607	
	UTM 52K 192871E 8078728N	
	(0.3 km)	
▼ 75.7 km	Gate. LAF.	
	(0.2 km)	
▼ 75.9 km	Gate. LAF.	
	(5.8 km)	

Old Mornington Camp

This one-time 312 000-hectare pastoral lease is now managed by the Australian Wildlife Conservancy to protect the shrinking habitat of a number of rare and endangered birds and animals once common in the Kimberley. Notable endangered bird species that have been identified here are the Gouldian finch and the purple-crowned fairy wren and animals such as the short-eared rock wallaby. Old Mornington is fast gaining a reputation with nature lovers, especially birdwatchers, who come in the hope of observing some of the 180 recorded bird species.

Added attractions of the property are two massive gorges, Sir John and Dimond, carved by the mighty Fitzroy River on its way to the coast at King Sound. Canoes are available for hire to explore Dimond Gorge. Gliding downstream with the towering walls of the gorge rising up from the river provides a breathtaking experience. Water thundering through the gorge during the wet season would be an awesome sight.

Other activities include a number of enjoyable self-drive four-wheel-drive routes to points of interest around the property and at times there are escorted bird-watching tours. Facilities at Old Mornington include a campground with showers, a restaurant and bar as well as accommodation in safari tents (see Permits and bookings).

Fitzroy River at Dimond Gorge

77

KIMBERLEY GRAND TOUR

Tunnel Creek

Tunnel Creek is part of Western Australia's oldest cave system. A walk through to the other side of the range is broken up by a roof collapse – you have to wade through permanent freshwater pools to experience the wonders of the fossil reef. Keep an eye out for small fish and yabbies in the clear waters, and for flying foxes roosting overhead. Aboriginal people decorated the north entrance with paintings, and once made stone axes out of the black dolorite and basalt rocks found at the other end. Tunnel Creek was the final hideout of Jandamarra after a two and a half year battle with the law, during which time he killed a policeman and several stockmen. He was shot dead by an Aboriginal trooper in 1897 at the entrance to Tunnel Creek.

Track into Bell Gorge in King Leopold Ranges

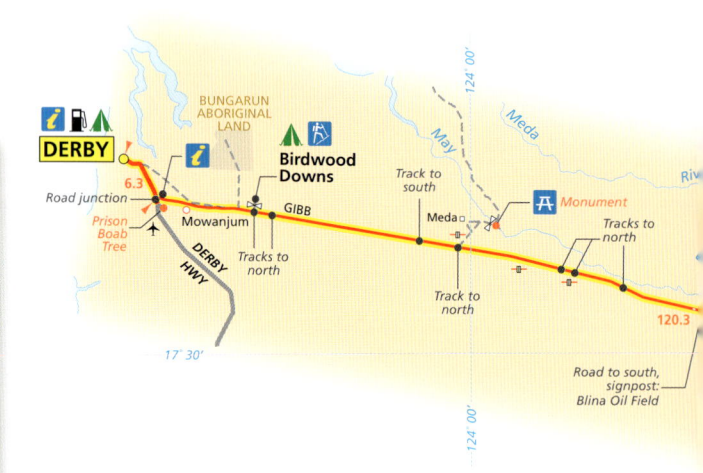

Cavernous entrance to Tunnel Creek

Campsite Facilities

	Toilets	Disabled access	4WD access only	Off-road trailer	Off-road caravan	Drinking water	Fee payable	Ranger patrolled	BBQ/fireplace	Campfires prohibited	Picnic tables	Shelter shed	No rubbish disposal	Public phone	Shower	Bushwalking	Swimming	Swimming not advised	Fishing	Canoeing	Dogs allowed
Bell Creek	•	•				•	•		•						•	•					
Beverley Springs	•		•	•	•	•			•		•				•	•			•		•
Birdwood Downs	•			•	•										•	•					
Manning Gorge	•		•	•	•	•	•								•	•	•		•		
Mount Elizabeth	•												•		•	•				•	
Old Mornington	•	•													•	•		•	•	•	
Silent Grove	•	•	•					•	•					•	•						
Windjana Gorge	•		•	•	•	•			•					•	•	•					

78

KALUMBURU ROAD JUNCTION ◀▶ DERBY

King Leopold Ranges Conservation Park
Lying at the south-western edge of the Kimberley Plateau the ranges were named by explorer Alexander Forrest in 1879 after King Leopold II of Belgium. Spectacular landscapes include Bell Gorge, with swimming holes reached via a short walking track, and Lennard Gorge where a lookout is accessed via a rough 2.2-kilometre track.

Windjana Gorge
The gorge is cut by the Lennard River, which in the dry season becomes a string of pools. These are home to various fish species and freshwater crocodiles, which bask in the sun on the sandy shores. The only way to see most of the gorge is via a 3.5-kilometre trail that winds from the camping area along the water's edge. Marine fossils, evidence of the ancient coral reef, can be seen embedded in the limestone walls of the gorge.

Signpost near Derby

KIMBERLEY GRAND TOUR

▼ 81.7 km Creek crossing.
(0.9 km)

▼ 82.6 km Track junction. CSA. SP: Old Mornington Camp 13 km. Track on left.
GPS S:17 24.655 E:126 06.962
UTM 52K 193591E 8072678N
(3.9 km)

▼ 86.5 km Creek crossing.
(1.7 km)

▼ 88.2 km Creek crossing.
(1.0 km)

▼ 89.2 km Creek crossing.
(3.5 km)

▼ 92.7 km Track junction. CSA. Track on left.
(0.1 km)

▼ 92.8 km Creek crossing.
(1.6 km)

▼ 94.4 km Track junction. CSA. Track on left.
Track on left leads into camping area.
(0.4 km)

▼ 94.8 km Old Mornington camping area. CSA.
Old Mornington camping area, with shady trees, has numerous sites spread along picturesque Annies Creek. The creek and surrounds provide good places for birdwatching. We spotted a purple-crowned fairy wren in the vicinity.
(0.4 km)

▼ 95.2 km Old Mornington Camp office and restaurant on right. Return to side trip start.

GPS S:17 30.799 E:126 06.624
UTM 52K 193164E 8061328N

◄ **END SIDE TRIP**

▼ 0.0 km Zero trip meter at road junction. CSA. Track on left SP: Mount House/Old Mornington Camp.
Road junction. See side trip to Old Mornington Camp.   33.7 km ▲
(20.1 km)

▼ 20.1 km Cross SP: Grave Creek.
Cross SP: Grave Creek.   13.6 km ▲
(4.3 km)

▼ 24.4 km Cross SP: Saddler Springs.
Cross SP: Saddler Springs.   9.3 km ▲
(1.1 km)

▼ 25.5 km Road junction. CSA. Road on left SP: Imintji Store and Community.
Road junction. CSA. Road on right SP: Imintji Store and Community.   8.2 km ▲
(8.2 km)

▼ 33.7 km Road junction.
Zero trip meter at road junction. CSA. Road on left SP: Bell Gorge 29.   0.0 km ▲
GPS S:17 09.024 E:125 23.143
UTM 51K 753801E 8102248N

▼ 0.0 km Zero trip meter at road junction. CSA. Road on right SP: Bell Gorge 29.

Road on right leads 19.3 km to **Silent Grove campground**, a large open area with several shady sites, and further 6.8 km to **Bell Creek camping area** with 10 individual sites along

Swimmers at Bell Gorge

80

KALUMBURU ROAD JUNCTION ◂▸ DERBY

	Bell Creek – these are very popular. Walking trail to Bell Creek Falls leaves from carpark located 3.2 km from Bell Creek camping area.			Track on left leads 4.7 km to carpark and a 2.2-km walk to Lennard Gorge. (It is possible to drive the 2.2 km to gorge, but track quite rough and eroded. It is recommended you park and walk this section.)	
	Road junction.	23.1 km ▲		Road junction.	72.1 km ▲
	(3.5 km)			(6.8 km)	
▼ 3.5 km	Cross SP: Bell Creek.		▼ 6.8 km	Road junction. CSA. Track on right SP: Mount Hart.	
	Cross SP: Bell Creek.	19.6 km ▲		Track on right leads 50.0 km to Mount Hart Wilderness Lodge. Access for those with confirmed bookings only (see Permits and bookings).	
	(0.3 km)				
▼ 3.8 km	Road junction. CSA. Track on right.				
	Track on right leads 0.2 km to possible bush campsite.			Road junction. CSA. Track on left SP: Mount Hart.	65.3 km ▲
	Road junction. CSA. Track on left.	19.3 km ▲		(0.3 km)	
	(0.2 km)		▼ 7.1 km	Cross SP: Apex Creek.	
▼ 4.0 km	Road junction. CSA onto bitumen and climb King Leopold Ranges. Track on left.			Track on right over creek leads to possible bush campsite. Small area only.	
	Track on left leads 0.4 km to bush campsite.			Cross SP: Apex Creek.	65.0 km ▲
	Road junction. CSA onto gravel. Track on right.	19.1 km ▲		GPS S:17 06.470 E:125 10.968 UTM 51K 732258E 8107214N	
	(1.2 km)			(1.2 km)	
▼ 5.2 km	Lookout point on right.		▼ 8.3 km	Lookout point on left. CSA.	
	Lookout point on left.	17.9 km ▲		Lookout point on right. CSA.	63.8 km ▲
	(0.4 km)			(11.3 km)	
▼ 5.6 km	End of bitumen. Top of King Leopold Ranges.		▼ 19.6 km	Cross SP: Boundary Creek.	
	Bitumen begins. Descend ranges.	17.5 km ▲		Cross SP: Boundary Creek.	52.5 km ▲
	(2.6 km)			(2.6 km)	
▼ 8.2 km	Lookout point on left.		▼ 22.2 km	Bridge.	
	Lookout point on right.	14.9 km ▲		Bridge.	49.9 km ▲
	(1.3 km)			(6.1 km)	
▼ 9.5 km	Cross SP: March Fly Glen.		▼ 28.3 km	Cross SP: Fletcher River.	
	Cross SP: March Fly Glen.	13.6 km ▲		Cross SP: Fletcher River.	43.8 km ▲
	(0.2 km)			(4.6 km)	
▼ 9.7 km	Road junction. CSA. Track on right to rest area.		▼ 32.9 km	Cross SP: Yates Creek.	
	Track on right leads short distance to March Fly Glen rest area with tables, toilets and barbecues.			Cross SP: Yates Creek.	39.2 km ▲
				(3.2 km)	
			▼ 36.1 km	Bridge over SP: Mac Creek.	
	Road junction. CSA. Track on left to rest area.	13.4 km ▲		Bridge over SP: Mac Creek.	36.0 km ▲
	GPS S:17 09.827 E:125 18.572 UTM 51K 745675E 8100865N			GPS S:17 09.597 E:124 57.337 UTM 51K 708018E 8101703N	
	(2.5 km)			(3.4 km)	
▼ 12.2 km	Cross SP: Same Creek.		▼ 39.5 km	Cross SP: Donkey Creek.	
	Cross SP: Same Creek.	10.9 km ▲		Cross SP: Donkey Creek.	32.6 km ▲
	(2.9 km)			(11.4 km)	
▼ 15.1 km	Cross SP: Fern Creek.		▼ 50.9 km	Cross SP: Wombarella Creek.	
	Cross SP: Fern Creek.	8.0 km ▲		Cross SP: Wombarella Creek.	21.2 km ▲
	(5.7 km)			(11.1 km)	
▼ 20.8 km	Cross SP: Dog Chain Creek.		▼ 62.0 km	Road junction. CSA and cross SP: Napier Creek. Track on right SP: Napier Downs 1.	
	Cross SP: Dog Chain Creek.	2.3 km ▲		Cross SP: Napier Creek. Road junction over creek. CSA. Track on left SP: Napier Downs 1.	10.1 km ▲
	(2.3 km)				
▼ 23.1 km	Road junction.				
	Zero trip meter at road junction. CSA. Track on right SP: 8 Lennard Gorge.	0.0 km ▲			
	GPS S:17 08.595 E:125 14.113 UTM 51K 737792E 8103230N			(9.7 km)	
▼ 0.0 km	Zero trip meter at road junction. CSA. Track on left SP: 8 Lennard Gorge.		▼ 71.7 km	Bridge over Lennard River.	
				Bridge over Lennard River.	0.4 km ▲

81

KIMBERLEY GRAND TOUR

GPS	S:17 23.541 E:124 45.402
UTM	51K 686620E 8076185N

(0.1 km)

▼ 71.8 km Road junction. CSA. Track on right.

Track on right leads to possible bush campsites.

    Road junction. CSA. Track on left. 0.3 km ▲

(0.3 km)

▼ 72.1 km Road junction. Directions to Derby (CSA. SP: 125 Derby) continue after Fitzroy Crossing finish notes, see page 83. Track on left leads to Fitzroy Crossing and/or possible side trips to Windjana Gorge and Tunnel Creek national parks.

    Zero trip meter at road junction. CSA. SP: Gibb River 249. Road on right SP: Windjana Gorge National Park. 0.0 km ▲

Road on right leads to Windjana Gorge and Tunnel Creek national parks, and Fitzroy Crossing.

GPS	S:17 23.728 E:124 45.264
UTM	51K 686372E 8075842N

▶ **ALTERNATIVE FINISH: Fitzroy Crossing**

▼ 0.0 km Zero trip meter at road junction. TL into road SP: Windjana Gorge National Park 23/167 Fitzroy Crossing. Proceed in south-easterly direction towards Fitzroy Crossing.

    T-junction with Gibb River Rd. Road on left SP: 125 Derby. Road on right SP: Gibb River 249. 20.5 km ▲

Road on left to Derby is alternative start/end of trek. Road on right is continuation of trek reverse directions.

(0.1 km)

▼ 0.1 km Rubbish disposal point on left. CSA.

    Rubbish disposal point on right. CSA. 20.4 km ▲

(4.5 km)

▼ 4.6 km Cross SP: Mt North Creek.

    Cross SP: Mt North Creek. 15.9 km ▲

(15.9 km)

▼ 20.5 km Road junction.

    Zero trip meter at road junction. CSA. SP: Derby 150/Gibb River Rd 21. Track on right SP: Windjana Gorge National Park. 0.0 km ▲

GPS	S:17 25.351 E:124 56.193
UTM	51K 705698E 8072662N

▼ 0.0 km Zero trip meter at road junction. CSA. SP: 154 Fitzroy Crossing/37 Tunnel Creek. Track on left SP: Windjana Gorge National Park.

Track on left leads 1.2 km to **Windjana Gorge camping areas**, two large open places with shady trees scattered around perimeter. Only one area allows use of a generator. Walking track leads from campsites to scenic gorge.

    Road junction. 35.4 km ▲

(3.0 km)

▼ 3.0 km Road junction. CSA. Track on left SP: Historical Site.

A freshwater crocodile suns itself at Windjana Gorge

Track on left leads 0.1 km to Lillimulura Police Station ruins. Site where Aboriginal tracker Jandamarra shot dead Police Constable Richardson on 31 October 1894.

    Road junction. CSA. Track on right SP: Historical Site. 32.4 km ▲

GPS	S:17 25.610 E:124 57.804
UTM	51K 708546E 8072155N

(32.4 km)

▼ 35.4 km Road junction.

    Zero trip meter at road junction. CSA. Track on left SP: Tunnel Creek National Park. 0.0 km ▲

GPS	S:17 36.362 E:125 08.800
UTM	51K 727795E 8052109N

▼ 0.0 km Zero trip meter at road junction. CSA. Track on right SP: Tunnel Creek National Park.

Road on right leads to carpark and short 750-m walk to Tunnel Creek, an adventurous and interesting experience.

    Road junction. 70.1 km ▲

(1.2 km)

▼ 1.2 km Creek crossing.

    Creek crossing. 68.9 km ▲

(13.5 km)

▼ 14.7 km Creek crossing.

Possible bush camping on left prior to creek and on right over creek.

KALUMBURU ROAD JUNCTION ◀▶ DERBY

		Creek crossing.	55.4 km ▲		Gravel road commences.	62.8 km ▲

(11.6 km)

▼ 26.3 km Creek crossing.

GPS S:17 27.362 E:124 14.212
UTM 51K 631342E 8069570N

Creek crossing. 43.8 km ▲

(27.8 km)

(4.0 km)

▼ 85.3 km Road junction. CSA. Road on right SP: May River/Meda 6.

▼ 30.3 km Creek crossing.

Road on right leads 6.3 km to May River and picnic area beside river.

Creek crossing. 39.8 km ▲

Road junction. CSA. Road on left SP: May River/Meda 6. 35.0 km ▲

(28.7 km)

(23.7 km)

▼ 59.0 km Road junction. CSA. Track on left.

▼ 109.0 km Road junction. CSA. Track on right SP: Birdwood Downs.

Y-junction. KL. Track on right. 11.1 km ▲

Track on right leads 1.2 km to **Birdwood Downs camping area**. This impressive property is working to create a sustainable biodiverse ecology in the harsh Kimberley environment.

GPS S:17 54.702 E:125 17.765
UTM 51K 743243E 8018084N

(2.1 km)

Road junction. CSA. Track on left SP: Birdwood Downs. 11.3 km ▲

▼ 61.1 km Road junction. CSA. Track on left.

GPS S:17 21.481 E:123 46.111
UTM 51K 581649E 8080675N

Track on left leads 0.2 km to possible bush campsites between rocky outcrops.

(10.7 km)

Road junction. CSA. Track on right. 9.0 km ▲

▼ 119.7 km Information bay on right. CSA.

(9.0 km)

Information bay on left. CSA. 0.6 km ▲

▼ 70.1 km T-junction with bitumen.

(0.6 km)

Zero trip meter at road junction. TR. SP: Leopold Downs/63 Tunnel Creek/95 Windjana Gorge. 0.0 km ▲

▼ 120.3 km T-junction.

Zero trip meter at road junction. TL. SP: Gibb River Road/Tunnel Creek 178/Windjana Gorge 141. 0.0 km ▲

GPS S:17 59.224 E:125 14.623
UTM 51K 737593E 8009808N

GPS S:17 20.651 E:123 39.886
UTM 51K 570631E 8082247N

▼ 0.0 km Zero trip meter at T-junction. This is Great Northern Hwy. TL. SP: 42 Fitzroy Crossing. Road on right SP: Derby 215.

▼ 0.0 km Zero trip meter at T-junction with SP: Derby Highway. TR. SP: Derby 6. Road on left SP: 211 Broome/Fitzroy Crossing.

Road junction. 43.5 km ▲

Road on left leads 0.6 km to prison boab tree.

(43.5 km)

Road junction. 6.3 km ▲

▼ 43.5 km Fitzroy Crossing. Road junction. Road on left, SP: Town Centre, is Forrest Rd. Visitor Information centre on left in Forrest Rd.

(6.3 km)

▼ 6.3 km Derby. Post office on right.

Zero trip meter in Fitzroy Crossing at junction of Great Northern Hwy and Forrest Rd, SP: Town Centre, on right. Proceed west towards Broome. 0.0 km ▲

Zero trip meter on main street of Derby, Loch St, with post office on left. Proceed southwards out of town towards Broome. 0.0 km ▲

GPS S:17 18.243 E:123 37.858
UTM 51K 567054E 8086699N

GPS S:18 11.882 E:125 34.025
UTM 51K 771527E 7986004N

REVERSE DIRECTIONS START

REVERSE DIRECTIONS ALTERNATIVE START

◀ **END ALTERNATIVE FINISH**

▼ 0.0 km Zero trip meter at road junction. CSA. SP: 125 Derby. Road on left SP: Windjana Gorge National Park 23/167 Fitzroy Crossing.

Road junction. Track on right leads to Fitzroy Crossing and/or possible side trips to Windjana Gorge and Tunnel Creek national parks. See Alternative Finish: Fitzroy Crossing. 120.3 km ▲

(45.6 km)

▼ 45.6 km Road junction. CSA. Road on right SP: Kimberley Downs Station.

Road junction. CSA. Road on left SP: Kimberley Downs Station. 74.7 km ▲

(10.7 km)

▼ 56.3 km Road junction. CSA. Road on left SP: Blina Oil Field.

Road junction. CSA. Road on right SP: Blina Oil Field. 64.0 km ▲

(1.2 km)

▼ 57.5 km Bitumen road commences.

■ 83

Ocean to Alice

Dune crossing on the WAPET Road

EIGHTY MILE BEACH ◀▶ ALICE SPRINGS 1660.2 KM
1. EIGHTY MILE BEACH ◁▷ KUNAWARRITJI 616.8 km *(moderate)*
2. KUNAWARRITJI ◁▷ ALICE SPRINGS 1043.4 km *(easy)*

WHEN TO GO May–September   **TIME** 5–6 days

This lengthy desert trek stretches halfway across the continent, from the white sands and turquoise waters of Eighty Mile Beach on the Western Australian coast to the crimson ranges of Alice Springs in the Red Centre. It is a journey through remote arid landscapes and despite generally well-defined roads it is not a trip that travellers should undertake lightly.

The first trek section traverses the spinifex plains and dune country of the Great Sandy Desert. The second section leads from the Aboriginal community of Kunawarritji into the unforgiving terrain of the Gibson Desert, named after a hapless explorer who perished there in 1874. Once across the border into the Northern Territory the country soon changes dramatically, with the striking colours and shapes of the West MacDonnell Ranges dominating the landscape all the way to Alice Springs. Spectacular gorges and rugged red escarpments are home to rare fauna such as the black-footed wallaby and the long-tailed dunnart.

The route follows roads and tracks put in by several oil exploration companies and outback road builders in the 1960s. It is a longer and more adventurous alternative to the Tanami Road and is a good option for four-wheel-drive travellers either heading to or returning from the Kimberley.

Main towns are few and far between on this trek, but fuel (generally diesel) and food can be purchased at a number of Aboriginal communities. Port Hedland, the only town of reasonable size at the eastern end, is 250 kilometres south of the start point. It has a comprehensive selection of travellers' needs, while Alice Springs has a full range of goods and services.

OCEAN TO ALICE

Eighty Mile Beach
A popular holiday destination located 250 kilometres north of Port Hedland and 365 kilometres south of Broome, the white sands and turquoise waters of this vast beach attract beachcombers and anglers. The catch may include salmon and even small sharks. If you wish to find a quiet spot along the coast, four-wheel-drive vehicles can access the beach from the parking area beside the caravan park.

Services

VEHICLE ASSISTANCE
AANT (NT)/RACV (WA)   13 1111

POLICE
Alice Springs	(08) 8951 8888
Kintore	(08) 8956 8488
Papunya	(08) 8956 8510
Port Hedland*	(08) 9173 1444

PARKS AND RESERVES
West MacDonnell National Park
PWCNT Alice Springs   (08) 8951 8211

VISITOR INFORMATION
Alice Springs   (08) 8952 5800
  or 1800 645 199
Port Hedland*   (08) 9173 1711

*Port Hedland is on the coast, 250 km south of Eighty Mile Beach

Authors' note
After a few days without seeing anyone we met some travellers near Jupiter Well. The man jumped out of the car and said, 'Great, someone else to speak to besides my wife'! As they drove off we were hoping the rest of their trip wasn't too quiet.

Town Facilities

	Fuel: D/P/A	Mechanical repairs	Tyre repairs	Public telephone	Public toilets	Shop/supplies	Gas refills	Ice	Visitor information	Post office	Medical centre	Police	Meals	Motel	Hotel	Cabins	Caravan park	Camping
Alice Springs	D/P/A	•	•	•	•	•	•	•	•	•	•	•	•	•	•	•	•	•
Eighty Mile Beach				•	•	•	•	•								•	•	•
Glen Helen Resort	D/P			•	•			•	•				•	•		•	•	•
Kintore	D/P				•					•	•						•	
Kunawarritji	D/P	•			•											•		•
Papunya	D/P			•		•				•	•							
Port Hedland	D/P/A	•	•	•	•	•	•	•	•	•	•	•	•	•	•	•	•	•
Sandfire Roadhouse	D/P/A	•	•	•								•	•			•	•	

OCEAN TO ALICE

1 EIGHTY MILE BEACH ◀▶ KUNAWARRITJI 616.8 KM

Start point
Eighty Mile Beach Caravan Park

Road atlas
359 E2

Total distance
616.8 km

Standard
Moderate

Time
2–3 days

Longest distance no PD (includes all options)
654.6 km (Sandfire Roadhouse to Kunawarritji)

Topographic maps
Auslig 1:250 000 series: *Mandora*; *Yarrie*; *Anketell*; *Joanna Spring*; *Sahara*; *Tabletop*; *Ural*

Other useful information
Kunawarritji community store has fuel and supplies; open Monday–Friday 8am–5pm (during peak visitor season) and Saturday 9am–12noon (closed Sunday and public holidays), tel. (08) 9176 9040; accepts cash and EFTPOS.

Description
This section of the trek leads along the WAPET Road, constructed by West Australia Petroleum Pty Ltd in the early 1960s to provide desert access for oil exploration parties. The road, also known as the Kidson Track, was built to withstand use by heavy drilling rigs, huge machinery and large supply trucks, and although it now receives only minimal maintenance it is suitable for four-wheel-drive vehicles.

Great Sandy Desert
Extending over an area of 267 350 square kilometres, the Great Sandy Desert covers 3.5 per cent of mainland Australia. First sighted and named the Great Australian Desert in 1856 by Augustus Gregory, the vast expanse of dunes, salt-encrusted lakes and claypans was first crossed from east to west by Peter Egerton Warburton during his 1873 expedition from Alice Springs to Roebourne in Western Australia. The gravel plains, broken by rocky outcrops and shimmering white salt lakes, are the habitat of reptiles, small marsupials and native rodents.

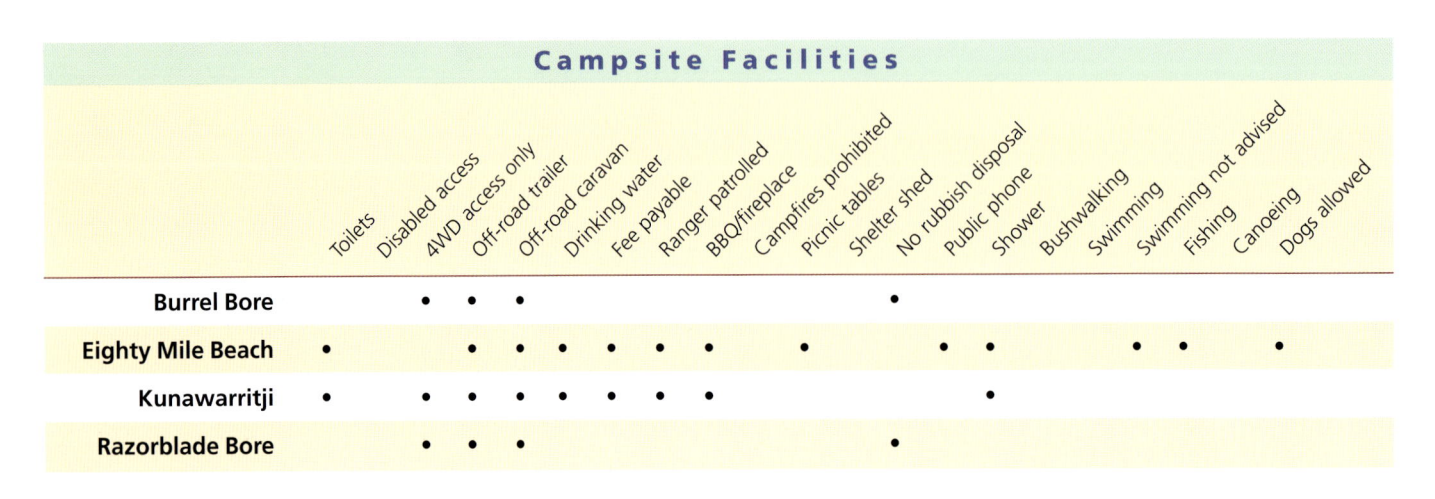

Campsite Facilities

	Toilets	Disabled access	4WD access only	Off-road trailer	Off-road caravan	Drinking water	Fee payable	Ranger patrolled	BBQ/fireplace	Campfires prohibited	Picnic tables	Shelter shed	No rubbish disposal	Public phone	Shower	Bushwalking	Swimming	Swimming not advised	Fishing	Canoeing	Dogs allowed
Burrel Bore		•	•	•							•										
Eighty Mile Beach	•			•	•	•	•		•		•			•	•				•	•	•
Kunawarritji	•		•	•		•						•									
Razorblade Bore		•	•	•							•										

86

EIGHTY MILE BEACH ◀▶ KUNAWARRITJI

Emergency water barrel beside the WAPET Road

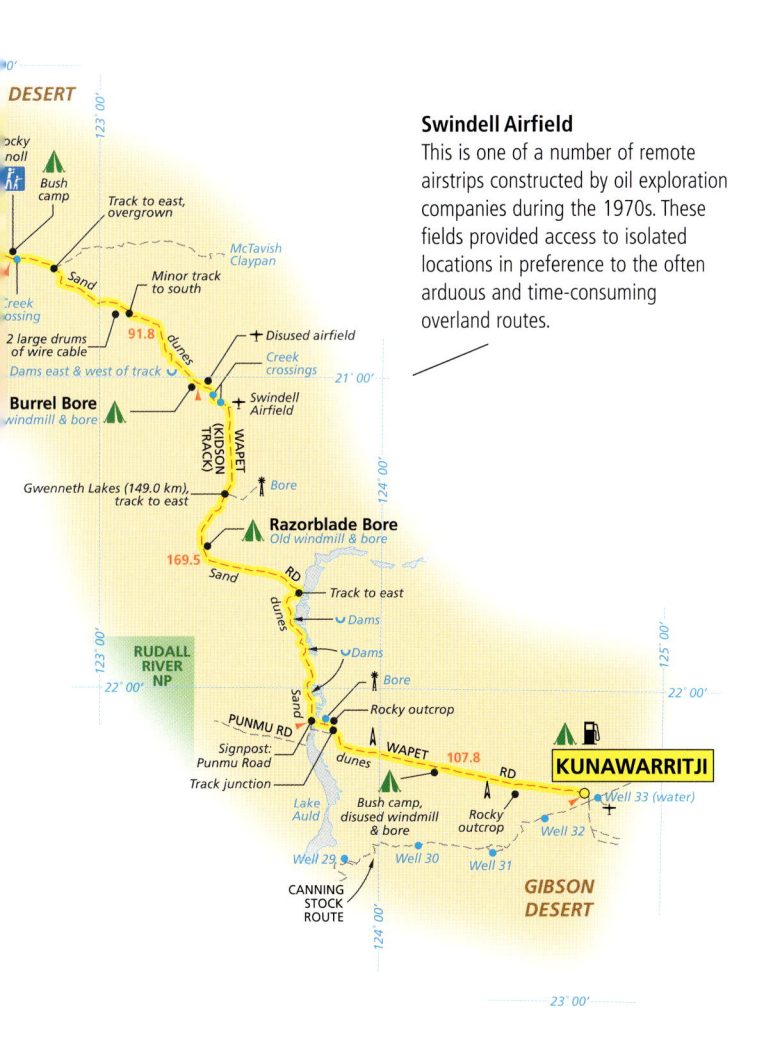

The terrain is relatively flat and most parts of the track are in reasonable condition. The only variety is provided by the crossing of a couple of sand dunes via a well-formed gravel track, several wash-outs and some sections of deep, soft sand. Spinifex plains predominate, broken occasionally by stands of hardy eucalypts – generally in the lower lying areas and in the vicinity of Burrel and Razorblade bores. Except for wild camels, animals are rarely seen.

There are a number of low rocky rises and knolls close to the track, which offer panoramic views of the surrounding landscape. It is worth taking the opportunity to stretch your legs by climbing some of these. There are very few good campsites on this section, but you can make a comfortable overnight stop at a number of clearings beside the track. These places are noted in the route directions. The best camping is at Razorblade Bore.

Advice and warnings

- Few people travel this route so you should be totally self-sufficient. Carry plenty of fuel, water and food. Note that there is no fuel and only limited supplies available at the start point at Eighty Mile Beach. Sandfire Roadhouse, 54.2 km north of the start point, has fuel and limited supplies.
- WAPET Road may be impassable after heavy rain. Some sections have large, deep wash-outs and sandy patches. Contact Kunawarritji community, tel. (08) 9176 9040, to check road conditions.
- Watch out for wild camels on the road.
- Standard road or all-terrain tyres are suitable. Lowered tyre pressure will help with ride comfort and track maintenance.
- Towing off-road trailers and off-road caravans is possible.
- Bush camping only. Water is not available along the track but there are emergency water supplies placed at intervals of 50 to 100 km. These water supplies are not to be used except in an emergency.
- This is remote country so be sure to carry some means of communication such as a satellite phone or HF radio.

Permits and bookings

- No permits required.
- Advance bookings required for Eighty Mile Beach Caravan Park, especially for June–August, tel. (08) 9176 5941.
- Fishing licence required for fishing at Eighty Mile Beach. Contact Department of Fisheries Western Australia, tel. (08) 9482 7333, for regulations and licensing details or visit their website (www.fish.wa.gov.au).

Swindell Airfield
This is one of a number of remote airstrips constructed by oil exploration companies during the 1970s. These fields provided access to isolated locations in preference to the often arduous and time-consuming overland routes.

87

OCEAN TO ALICE

ROUTE DIRECTIONS

▼ 0.0 km — Zero trip meter at entrance to Eighty Mile Beach Caravan Park. Proceed east towards Great Northern Hwy.

Eighty Mile Beach Caravan Park entrance on right. 10.5 km ▲

Eighty Mile Beach Caravan Park has a large, formal camping area, some sites with shade set behind the beach.

GPS	S:19 45.358 E:120 40.263
UTM	51K 255954E 7813846N

(9.1 km)

▼ 9.1 km — T-junction with Great Northern Hwy. TL onto bitumen. Highway on right leads to Port Hedland.

Road junction. TR onto gravel. SP: Eighty Mile Beach 10. 1.4 km ▲

(1.4 km)

▼ 10.5 km — Road junction.

Zero trip meter at T-junction. TL. This is Great Northern Hwy. Highway on right to Sandfire Roadhouse and Broome. 0.0 km ▲

GPS	S:19 50.050 E:120 41.541
UTM	51K 258305E 7805218N

▼ 0.0 km — Zero trip meter at road junction. TR. This is start of WAPET Rd.

Road SO leads 43.7 km to Sandfire Roadhouse where fuel is sold. WAPET Rd is not signposted. Communications tower on left after turn.

T-junction with bitumen. 60.2 km ▲

(11.6 km)

▼ 11.6 km — Track junction. CSA. Track on left.

Track on left leads to communications tower.

Track junction. CSA. Track on right. 48.6 km ▲

(48.6 km)

▼ 60.2 km — Crossroads.

Zero trip meter at crossroads. CSA. Minor track on right and left. 0.0 km ▲

GPS	S:20 05.910 E:121 08.932
UTM	51K 306457E 7776544N

Wire cable left behind by oil exploration teams

▼ 0.0 km — Zero trip meter at crossroads. CSA. Minor track on right and minor track on left.

Tracks on right and left are old telegraph line tracks and are overgrown and largely impassable. Track on right SP: Marble Bar via Callawa Stn.

Crossroads. 177.0 km ▲

(35.9 km)

▼ 35.9 km — Track junction. CSA. Track on right.

Track junction. CSA. Track on left. 141.1 km ▲

(112.9 km)

▼ 148.8 km — Creek crossing.

Creek crossing. 28.2 km ▲

(28.2 km)

▼ 177.0 km — Track junction.

Zero trip meter at track junction. CSA. Track on right. 0.0 km ▲

GPS	S:20.37.184 E:122 41.152
UTM	51K 467270E 7719905N

▼ 0.0 km — Zero trip meter at track junction. CSA. Track on left.

Track on left leads short distance to possible bush campsite and walk up rocky knoll for views of surrounding area.

Track junction. 91.8 km ▲

(17.0 km)

▼ 17.0 km — Track junction. CSA. Minor track on left.

Minor track on left is overgrown and leads approximately 70 km to McTavish Claypan.

Track junction. CSA. Minor track on right. 74.8 km ▲

(4.5 km)

▼ 21.5 km — Cross first sand dune.

Cross last sand dune. 70.3 km ▲

GPS	S:20 41.120 E:122 51.745
UTM	51K 485671E 7712671N

(27.3 km)

▼ 48.8 km — Two large drums of wire cable on right. CSA.

Two large drums of wire cable on left. CSA. 43.0 km ▲

(4.1 km)

▼ 52.9 km — Y-junction. KL. Minor track on right.

Track junction. CSA. Minor track on left. 38.9 km ▲

(38.9 km)

▼ 91.8 km — Track junction.

Zero trip meter at track junction. CSA. Track on left. 0.0 km ▲

GPS	S:21 01.144 E:123 20.482
UTM	51K 535474E 7675704N

▼ 0.0 km — Zero trip meter at track junction. CSA. Track on right.

Track on right leads 0.3 km to **Burrel Bore bush camping area** beside disused bore and windmill.

Track junction. 169.5 km ▲

(0.3 km)

▼ 0.3 km — Track junction. CSA. Track on right to windmill and track on left to disused airfield.

Track junction. CSA. Track on left to windmill. 169.2 km ▲

(15.9 km)

EIGHTY MILE BEACH ◄► KUNAWARRITJI

Late afternoon at Razorblade Bore

▼ **16.2 km** Track junction. CSA. Track on left.

Track on left leads 0.5 km to Swindell Airfield, one of several remote airstrips constructed by oil exploration teams in the 1970s.

Track junction. CSA. Track on right. **153.3 km** ▲

GPS	S:21 06.113 E:123 26.808
UTM	51K 546404E 7666511N

(31.5 km)

▼ **47.7 km** Track junction. CSA. Track on left.

Track on left leads 13.9 km to disused windmill and further 135.0 km to Gwenneth Lakes. This track extremely overgrown, remote and slow going.

Track junction. CSA. Track on right. **121.8 km** ▲

(23.1 km)

▼ **70.8 km** Track junction. CSA. Track on left.

Track on left leads short distance to **Razorblade Bore** and **bush campsites** beside old windmill and water tank.

Track junction. CSA. Track on right. **98.7 km** ▲

GPS	S:21 33.198 E:123 21.666
UTM	51K 537389E 7616572N

(42.5 km)

▼ **113.3 km** Track junction. CSA. Track on left.

Track junction. CSA. Track on right. **56.2 km** ▲

(56.2 km)

▼ **169.5 km** Track junction.

Zero trip meter at track junction. **0.0 km** ▲
CSA. Track on left SP: Punmu/Punmu Rd.

GPS	S:22 06.374 E:123 45.329
UTM	51K 577925E 7555221N

▼ **0.0 km** Zero trip meter at track junction. CSA. Track on right SP: Punmu/Punmu Rd.

Track junction. **107.8 km** ▲

(4.9 km)

▼ **4.9 km** Track junction. CSA. Track on left.

Track on left leads 0.4 km to disused windmill and bore.

Track junction. CSA. Track on right. **102.9 km** ▲

(4.5 km)

▼ **9.4 km** T-junction. TL. Road on right leads to Punmu.

Track junction. TR. **98.4 km** ▲

GPS	S:22 08.188 E:123 50.002
UTM	51K 585940E 7551832N

(5.8 km)

▼ **15.2 km** Cross last sand dune.

Cross first sand dune. **92.6 km** ▲

(36.5 km)

▼ **51.7 km** Track junction. CSA. Track on right.

Track on right leads 1.0 km to disused windmill and possible bush campsites.

Track junction. CSA. Track on left. **56.1 km** ▲

(56.1 km)

▼ **107.8 km** Track junction. Trek section ends.

Track on left leads 0.2 km to Kunawarritji, where fuel and supplies are available. **Kunawarritji camping area**, with well-grassed sites, is located behind the shop and buildings.

Zero trip meter at track junction. **0.0 km** ▲
CSA. Track on right to Kunawarritji.

GPS	S:22 19.882 E:124 43.569
UTM	51K 677777E 7529477N

REVERSE DIRECTIONS START

2 KUNAWARRITJI ◄► ALICE SPRINGS 1043.4 KM

Start point
Kunawarritji

Road atlas
354 C5

Total distance
1052.8 km (includes route-directed side trip)

Standard
Easy

Time
3–4 days

Longest distance no PD (includes all options)
549.7 km (Kunawarritji to Kintore)

Topographic maps
Auslig 1:250 000 series: *Ural*; *Wilson*; *Webb*; *MacDonald*; *Mount Rennie*; *Mount Liebig*; *Hermannsburg*; *Alice Springs*

Other useful information
- Kunawarritji community store open Monday–Friday 8am–5pm (during peak visitor season) and Saturday 9am–12noon (closed Sunday and public holidays), tel. (08) 9176 9040; accepts cash and EFTPOS.
- Kintore general store open Monday–Saturday 8am–12noon and 3–4pm and Sunday 2–3pm (closed public holidays); for fuel supplies call ahead first to arrange time, tel. (08) 8956 8575; accepts cash, EFTPOS and credit cards.
- Papunya general store open Monday–Friday 9am–12.30pm and 2–4pm and Saturday 9–11.30am, tel. (08) 8956 8506; accepts cash and EFTPOS.

Description
This part of the trek, much of it through Aboriginal lands, first takes you along Jenkins Track and Gary Junction Road, both well-formed gravel tracks with occasional corrugations, and a number of large, dry creek crossings, which are mostly sandy. Take care at these crossings as some may be scoured after recent rain. Once past the turn-off to Haasts Bluff, it is 62.6 kilometres to Namatjira Drive. At this point the track changes to a regularly maintained gravel road before hitting the bitumen near Glen Helen Gorge. The bitumen continues to Alice Springs.

After leaving Kunawarritji, the spinifex plains continue as before, broken by some magnificent stands of desert oak. There is an impressive forest of these trees encircling Jupiter Well. At approximately the halfway point of this trek section, you cross into the Northern Territory and the plains soon start to give way to the West MacDonnell Ranges, which are protected within a national park that stretches westwards from Alice Springs for more than 150 kilometres. Keen walkers should explore some of the numerous gorge walks that are an attraction of this area. Highlights are the gorges of Redbank, Glen Helen, Ormiston and Serpentine. The Ochre Pits, once used by the Arrernte people as a source of ochre for body decoration, is a site of geological and cultural significance.

Camping is possible at a number of small cleared areas along the track. When travelling through Aboriginal lands please observe the conditions on the required permits. However, once in West MacDonnell Ranges National Park there is a choice of established campsites with a range of facilities.

Advice and warnings
- Gary Junction Road, which has heavily corrugated and sandy sections, may be closed or impassable after heavy rain. Contact Ngaanyatjarra Council, tel. (08) 8950 1711, to check road conditions.
- Contact Central Land Council, tel. (08) 8951 6320, to check road conditions on the Northern Territory section of the trek.

Famous telephone box (not operational) at WAPET Road–Canning Stock Route junction near Kunawarritji

KUNAWARRITJI ◄► ALICE SPRINGS

Imposing peak of Haasts Bluff

- Standard road or all-terrain tyres are suitable.
- Towing off-road trailers and off-road caravans is possible.
- Bush camping is possible at Jupiter Well and at clearings along the track.
- When travelling through Aboriginal lands please observe the conditions on the required permits.
- You must be self-sufficient so carry plenty of water and food and please take your rubbish with you.
- If travelling east to west, no fresh fruit, vegetables, nuts or honey can be taken into Western Australia from the Northern Territory.
- This is remote country so be sure to carry some means of communication such as a satellite phone or HF radio.

Permits and bookings

- Permit required to travel on Gary Junction Road through Ngaanyatjarra land in Western Australia, obtainable in the Northern Territory from Ngaanyatjarra Council, 58 Head St, Alice Springs 0870, tel. (08) 8950 1711, or in Western Australia from Aboriginal Lands Trust, 197 St Georges Tce, Perth 6000, tel. (08) 9235 8000. Allow up to 4 weeks for delivery.
- Permit required to travel Gary Junction Road through Haasts Bluff Aboriginal Land Trust from Kintore to Papunya, obtainable from Central Land Council, 33 Stuart Hwy, Alice Springs 0870, tel. (08) 8951 6320. Allow up to 4 weeks for delivery.
- Bookings recommended for camping and accommodation at Glen Helen Resort, tel. (08) 8956 7489.

ROUTE DIRECTIONS

▼ **0.0 km** Zero trip meter at junction of WAPET Rd and track to Kunawarritji. CSA in easterly direction towards Alice Springs.

Track junction. **70.2 km** ▲

Track on right leads 0.2 km to Kunawarritji, where there is fuel, supplies and camping. **Kunawarritji camping area**, with well-grassed sites, is located behind shop.

GPS S:22 19.882 E:124 43.569
UTM 51K 677777E 7529477N

(3.6 km)

▼ **3.6 km** Crossroads. CSA. Track on left and right is Canning Stock Route.

Track on left leads 3.7 km to **Well 33**, where there is **bush camping** and good water supply.

Crossroads. CSA. SP: Kunawarritji 4 km. Track on left and right is Canning Stock Route. **66.6 km** ▲

GPS S:22 21.304 E:124 44.607
UTM 51K 679529E 7526832N

(10.5 km)

▼ **14.1 km** Y-junction. KL. This is Jenkins Track. Track on right.

Track on right leads approximately 56 km to Gary Hwy.

Track junction. CSA. Track on left. **56.1 km** ▲

(31.3 km)

▼ **45.4 km** Track junction. KR. Track on left.

Track junction. CSA. Track on right. **24.8 km** ▲

(9.0 km)

▼ **54.4 km** Track junction. CSA. Track on left.

OCEAN TO ALICE

Gary Junction
Gary Junction is the point where Gary Junction Road meets the Gary Highway. The road was built in stages during 1960–63, and the highway was constructed in April–May 1963. At the junction is a marker placed by Len Beadell in May 1963, and a visitor book in which present-day travellers can leave their mark.

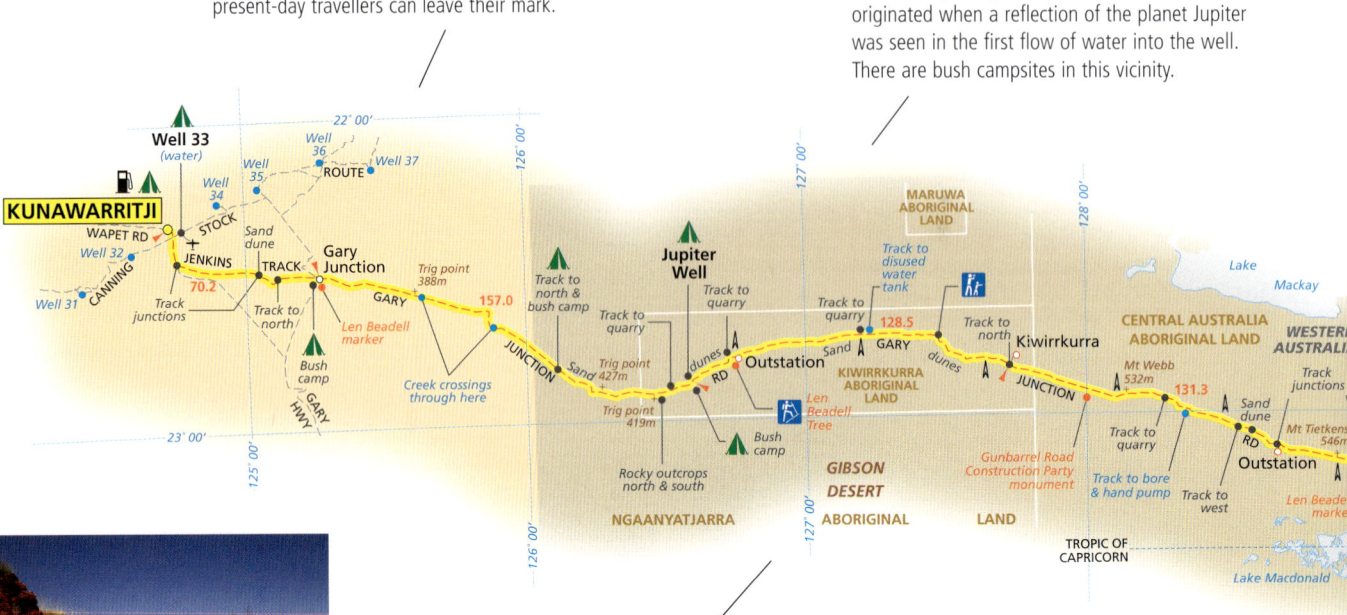

Jupiter Well
Situated within a forest of desert oaks, Jupiter Well, sunk in 1963, provides water, which is extracted by using a hand pump. The well's name originated when a reflection of the planet Jupiter was seen in the first flow of water into the well. There are bush campsites in this vicinity.

Rocky outcrop at the edge of the desert

Gibson Desert
The almost uninhabitable terrain of the Gibson Desert thwarted attempts by early explorers to cross the continent from west to east. Ernest Giles was the first European to discover the area, in 1873. On the same expedition, early in 1874, Giles lost his companion Alfred Gibson, who wandered off the track while riding ahead for help. Giles named the desert after the young stockman, whose remains were never found.

Campsite Facilities

	Toilets	Disabled access	4WD access only	Off-road trailer	Off-road caravan	Drinking water	Fee payable	Ranger patrolled	BBQ/fireplace	Campfires prohibited	Picnic tables	Shelter shed	No rubbish disposal	Public phone	Shower	Bushwalking	Swimming	Swimming not advised	Fishing	Canoeing	Dogs allowed
2 Mile		•	•	•								•			•	•					
Ellery Creek Big Hole	•	•		•	•	•	•		•		•	•				•	•				
Glen Helen Resort	•	•		•	•	•	•	•						•	•	•	•				
Jupiter Well			•	•	•							•									
Kunawarritji	•													•							
Ormiston Gorge	•	•		•	•		•	•	•						•	•					
Ridgetop	•				•		•	•		•		•				•					
Serpentine Chalet							•					•									
Well 33			•	•	•							•									
Woodlands	•			•	•		•	•	•		•		•			•					

92

KUNAWARRITJI ◀▶ ALICE SPRINGS

West MacDonnell National Park
Dominating this park's ancient landscape are high rugged escarpments and spectacular gorges with crimson cliffs that fall away to deep blue rock pools. Walking tracks climb the ridges and lead to hidden waterholes, chasms and lookouts that offer views of majestic ghost gums and remnants of tropical rainforest. The Ochre Pits, pictured, comprise a spectacularly coloured seam of ochre in the banks of a sandy creek.

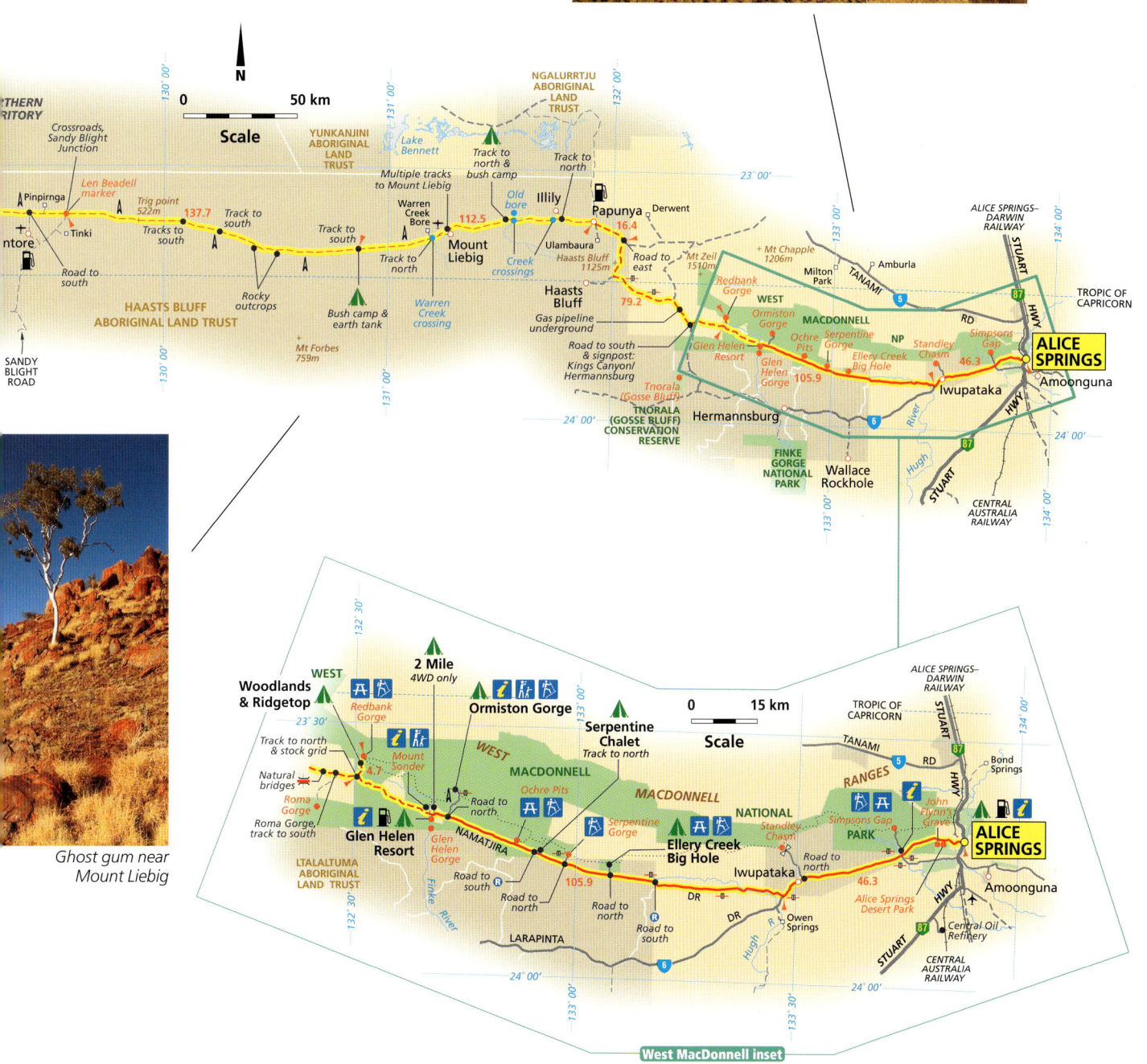

Ghost gum near Mount Liebig

West MacDonnell inset

93

OCEAN TO ALICE

	Track junction. CSA. Track on right.	15.8 km ▲

(15.8 km)

▼ 70.2 km Track junction. This is Gary Junction.

Zero trip meter at Gary Junction. KR. This is Jenkins Track. Track on left is Gary Hwy. — 0.0 km ▲

GPS S:22 30.520 E:125 15.974
UTM 51K 733122E 7509103N

▼ 0.0 km Zero trip meter at Gary Junction. CSA on Gary Junction Rd.

At Gary Junction a Len Beadell marker is on right-hand side of track, placed in May 1963. Track on right is Gary Hwy and leads 0.3 km to possible bush campsite. Minor track on hard left leads to Well 35 on Canning Stock Route.

Y-junction. This is Gary Junction. 157.0 km ▲

(36.0 km)

▼ 36.0 km Trig point on left. CSA.

Trig point on right. CSA. 121.0 km ▲

(65.2 km)

▼ 101.2 km Track junction. CSA. Track on left.

Track on left leads to clearing and bush campsites.

Track junction. CSA. Track on right. 55.8 km ▲

(47.4 km)

▼ 148.6 km Track junction. CSA. Track on left leads to quarry.

Track junction. CSA. Track on right. 8.4 km ▲

(8.4 km)

▼ 157.0 km Track junction.

Zero trip meter at track junction. CSA. Track on right to Jupiter Well. 0.0 km ▲

GPS S:22 52.613 E:126 35.793
UTM 52K 253417E 7468098N

▼ 0.0 km Zero trip meter at track junction. CSA. Track on left to well.

Jupiter Well on left, with hand pump, and **bush camping** and forest of desert oaks in this vicinity.

Track junction. 128.5 km ▲

(18.1 km)

▼ 18.1 km Track junction. CSA. Track on right.

Park car in track on right and walk to Len Beadell Tree (GPS S:22 48.471 E:126 44.227 UTM 52K 267727E 7475972N) beside original road alignment, approximately 500 m due south. If you have a GPS use your GOTO function to find the tree.

Track junction. CSA. Track on left. 110.4 km ▲

GPS S:22 48.221 E:126 44.315
UTM 52K 267870E 7476436N

(0.6 km)

▼ 18.7 km Track junction. CSA. Track on left to quarry.

Track junction. CSA. Track on right to quarry. 109.8 km ▲

(1.8 km)

▼ 20.5 km Track junction. CSA. Track on right to Aboriginal community outstation.

Track junction. CSA. Track on left to Aboriginal community outstation. 108.0 km ▲

(46.6 km)

▼ 67.1 km Track junction. CSA. Track on left to quarry.

Track junction. CSA. Track on right to quarry. 61.4 km ▲

(2.7 km)

▼ 69.8 km Track junction. CSA. Track on left.

Track on left leads 0.2 km to disused water tank.

Track junction. CSA. Track on right. 58.7 km ▲

(58.7 km)

▼ 128.5 km Road junction.

Zero trip meter at road junction. CSA. Track on right SP: Kiwirrkurra Community. 0.0 km ▲

GPS S:22 50.531 E:127 43.483
UTM 52K 369148E 7473385N

▼ 0.0 km Zero trip meter at road junction. CSA. Track on left SP: Kiwirrkurra Community.

Road junction. 131.3 km ▲

(31.2 km)

▼ 31.2 km Monument and plaque on right commemorating the work of the Gunbarrel Road Construction Party. CSA.

Monument and plaque on left commemorating the work of the Gunbarrel Road Construction Party. CSA. 100.1 km ▲

GPS S:22 55.558 E:128 00.579
UTM 52K 398449E 7464334N

(29.5 km)

▼ 60.7 km Road junction. CSA. Track on right.

Desert Oaks at Jupiter Well

KUNAWARRITJI ◀ ▶ ALICE SPRINGS

	Track on right leads 0.5 km to water pump and bore.	
	Road junction. CSA. Track on left.	70.6 km ▲
	(20.0 km)	
▼ 80.7 km	Y-junction. KL.	
	Road junction. CSA. Track on left.	50.6 km ▲
	(16.4 km)	
▼ 97.1 km	Road junction. CSA. Track on right.	
	Track on right leads 1.6 km to Aboriginal community outstation.	
	Road junction. CSA. Track on left.	34.2 km ▲
	(34.2 km)	
▼ 131.3 km	WA–NT border.	
	Zero trip meter at NT–WA border. CSA.	0.0 km ▲
	GPS S:23 09.799 E:129 00.097 UTM 52K 500166E 7438401N	
▼ 0.0 km	Zero trip meter at WA–NT border. CSA.	
	Len Beadell marker on right, placed 12 October 1960.	
	NT–WA border.	58.4 km ▲
	(0.1 km)	
▼ 0.1 km	Road junction. CSA. Minor track on left.	
	Track on left leads to Aboriginal community outstation.	
	Road junction. CSA. Minor track on right.	58.3 km ▲
	(16.5 km)	
▼ 16.6 km	Road junction. CSA. Track on left.	
	Track on left leads to Aboriginal community outstation.	
	Road junction. CSA. Track on right.	41.8 km ▲
	(24.3 km)	
▼ 40.9 km	Road junction. CSA. SP: Papunya 267. Road on right SP: Kintore 9/Airstrip.	
	Road on right leads 9.0 km to Kintore, which has fuel and supplies.	
	Road junction. CSA. SP: 177 Kiwirrkurra. Road on left SP: Kintore 9/Airstrip.	17.5 km ▲
	GPS S:23 11.530 E:129 23.568 UTM 52K 540198E 7435153N	
	(6.9 km)	
▼ 47.8 km	Road junction. CSA. Track on left.	
	Track on left leads 0.1 km to bore.	
	Road junction. CSA. Track on right.	10.6 km ▲
	(10.6 km)	
▼ 58.4 km	Crossroads. This is Sandy Blight Junction.	
	Zero trip meter at Sandy Blight Junction. CSA. SP: 27 Kintore. Road on left SP: Docker River 340/4 Wheel Drive Only.	0.0 km ▲
	GPS S:23 11.743 E:129 33.651 UTM 52K 557394E 7434704N	
▼ 0.0 km	Zero trip meter at Sandy Blight Junction. CSA. SP: Papunya 250. Road on right SP: Docker River 340/4 Wheel Drive Only.	
	Road on left leads short distance to Len Beadell marker, placed 27 August 1960.	
	Crossroads. This is Sandy Blight Junction.	137.7 km ▲
	(54.5 km)	

Remains of the Gunbarrel Road Construction Party's ration truck, moved to Kiwirrkurra in 2004

▼ 54.5 km	Road junction. KL. Track on right.	
	Road junction. CSA. Track on left.	83.2 km ▲
	(1.4 km)	
▼ 55.9 km	Road junction. CSA. Track on right.	
	Road junction. CSA. Track on left.	81.8 km ▲
	(81.8 km)	
▼ 137.7 km	Road junction.	
	Zero trip meter at road junction. CSA. Track on left.	0.0 km ▲
	GPS S:23 19.734 E:130 51.857 UTM 52K 690612E 7418842N	
▼ 0.0 km	Zero trip meter at road junction. CSA. Track on right.	
	Track on right leads 0.2 km to earth tank and possible bush campsites.	
	Road junction.	112.5 km ▲
	(34.1 km)	
▼ 34.1 km	Road junction. CSA. Track on left SP: Warren Creek.	
	Road junction. CSA. Track on right SP: Warren Creek.	78.4 km ▲
	(3.3 km)	
▼ 37.4 km	Y-junction. KL.	
	Road junction. CSA. Track on left.	75.1 km ▲
	(5.0 km)	
▼ 42.4 km	Offset crossroads. CSA. Track on left SP: Airstrip. Track on right leads to Mount Liebig community.	

OCEAN TO ALICE

Late afternoon sunshine on the picturesque Amunurunga Range

	Offset crossroads. CSA.	70.1 km ▲

(1.7 km)

▼ 44.1 km Road junction. CSA. SP: Papunya 67. Road on right SP: Mt Liebig 3.

Road junction. CSA. SP: 207 Kintore. Road on left SP: Mt Liebig 3.   68.4 km ▲

GPS   S:23 14.430 E:131 16.493
UTM   52K 732761E 7428033N

(26.8 km)

▼ 70.9 km Road junction. CSA. Track on left.
Track on left to possible bush campsites.

Road junction. CSA. Track on right.   41.6 km ▲
Track on right to possible bush campsites.

(3.8 km)

▼ 74.7 km Old bore on left. CSA.

Old bore on right. CSA.   37.8 km ▲

(0.1 km)

▼ 74.8 km Creek crossing.

Creek crossing.   37.7 km ▲

(18.0 km)

▼ 92.8 km Creek crossing.

Creek crossing.   19.7 km ▲

(3.9 km)

▼ 96.7 km Road junction. CSA. Road on left SP: Illily Outstation.

Road junction. CSA. Road on right SP: Illily Outstation.   15.8 km ▲

(15.1 km)

▼ 111.8 km Crossroads with bitumen. TL.
Papunya School on corner.

Papunya School on left and crossroads. TR onto gravel.   0.7 km ▲

GPS   S:23 12.164 E:131 54.556
UTM   52K 797788E 7431057N

(0.5 km)

▼ 112.3 km Road junction. TR.

Road junction. TL.   0.2 km ▲

(0.2 km)

▼ 112.5 km Papunya store on right.

Zero trip meter at Papunya, with store on left. CSA.   0.0 km ▲

GPS   S:23 12.152 E:131 54.747
UTM   52K 798114E 7431073N

▼ 0.0 km Zero trip meter at Papunya, with store on right. CSA.

Papunya Store on left.   16.4 km ▲

(16.4 km)

▼ 16.4 km Road junction.

Zero trip meter at T-junction. TL. SP: 16 Papunya/291 Kintore. Road on right SP: Alice Springs 225/To Tanami Track 89.   0.0 km ▲

GPS   S:23 16.575 E:132 02.702
UTM   53K 197697E 7422817N

▼ 0.0 km Zero trip meter at junction. TR. SP: Haasts Bluff 30/Glen Helen 98/Kings Canyon 283. Road SO SP: Alice Springs 225/To Tanami Track 89.

T-junction.   79.2 km ▲

(17.4 km)

▼ 17.4 km Road junction. TL. SP: 81 Glen Helen/266 Kings Canyon. Road SO SP: 14 Haasts Bluff.

T-junction. TR. SP: Papunya 33.   61.8 km ▲

GPS   S:23 25.212 E:132 00.251
UTM   53K 193847E 7406780N

(45.2 km)

▼ 62.6 km T-junction. TL. SP: Glen Helen/Alice Springs. This is Namatjira Dr. Road on right SP: Kings Canyon/Hermannsburg.

Road junction. TR. SP: Haasts Bluff 58/Papunya 78.   16.6 km ▲

GPS   S:23 36.552 E:132 21.144
UTM   53K 229837E 7386538N

(11.4 km)

Some Highlights of the West MacDonnells

The dramatic forms of the West MacDonnell Ranges have been shaped over 800 million years and today comprise one of Central Australia's most popular natural attractions. The ancient hills were named in 1860 by explorer John McDouall Stuart for the then governor of South Australia, Sir Richard MacDonnell.

A vast national park, 1330 square kilometres in size, protects an array of outstandingly beautiful natural features, which include the sheer-sided Standley Chasm, Simpsons Gap (a top spot to see black-footed rock wallabies) and the gorges of Ormiston, Serpentine, Ellery Creek Big Hole, Glen Helen and Redbank.

Located 135 kilometres west of Alice Springs, the awesome Ormiston would have to be our favourite gorge. Its interesting geology and intriguing landforms are enhanced by its near-permanent waterhole, believed to be almost 15 metres deep at the southern end. It would be a delightful place in which to cool off during the warmer months. The pool, framed by towering red sheer-sided cliffs that rise to almost 300 metres, is accessible from the visitor centre and parking area via an easy five-minute stroll (one way) along the Waterhole Walk.

Our visit to the area was in mid-winter and, although the days were beautiful and warm and the water incredibly inviting, it was not really hot enough for a swim. We enjoyed the best part of a day at this picturesque location, taking in the late afternoon glow over the ranges from Ghost Gum Lookout. We also glimpsed a number of rock wallabies basking in the late afternoon sun but they were just a little too far away to photograph.

We glimpsed a number of rock wallabies basking in the late afternoon sun

It is well worth exploring at least one of the walking trails through Ormiston. A marked walking track leads to Ghost Gum Lookout and we can vouch for the great views you get from here. The walk takes about 40 minutes return, going at a leisurely pace, while the Ghost Gum Loop Walk will take you about an hour and a half to complete. There is also the much longer 7-kilometre Ormiston Pound Walk, which leads hikers along a circular route to Ormiston Pound, returning via the pool.

If you are looking to get off the beaten track then head for Redbank Gorge in the far west of the park. There is vehicle-based camping just before the carpark and from here it is a 30-minute walk to the waterhole at the start of the gorge or you may like to tackle the 16-kilometre return walk to Mount Sonder. Apart from this challenging walk, serious hikers visiting the West MacDonnells should check out the Larapinta Trail, a 230-kilometre walk from just north of Alice Springs to Mount Sonder. You can walk individual sections or take several weeks to go the whole distance.

Ormiston Gorge Waterhole

OCEAN TO ALICE

▼ 74.0 km	Creek crossing and track junction. CSA. Track on right SP: Roma Gorge.			Drive. Road on right SP: Glen Helen Resort.	
	Track on right leads 8.5 km to Roma Gorge, a 1-hour drive.			Road on right leads 0.6 km to **Glen Helen Resort caravan and camping area**, where there is fuel, motel and kiosk. Campsites are located beside the resort, with walks to gorge.	
	Creek crossing and track junction. CSA. Track on left SP: Roma Gorge.	5.2 km ▲		Road junction. CSA. SP: Haasts Bluff. Road on left SP: Glen Helen Resort.	85.8 km ▲
	(5.2 km)			**(3.7 km)**	
▼ 79.2 km	Road junction. Side trip to Redbank Gorge.		▼ 23.8 km	Road junction. CSA. SP: 128 Alice Springs. Road on left SP: Ormiston Gorge.	
	Zero trip meter at road junction. CSA. Road on right SP: Redbank Gorge.	0.0 km ▲		Road on left leads 7.2 km to visitor centre, picnic area and **Ormiston Gorge camping area**, a small place situated close to gorge walks and lookouts.	
	GPS S:23 36.606 E:132 30.290 UTM 53K 245400E 7386718N				
▶	**SIDE TRIP: Redbank Gorge**			Road junction. CSA. SP: Glen Helen 4. Road on right SP: Ormiston Gorge.	82.1 km ▲
▼ 0.0 km	Zero trip meter at junction. Proceed north towards SP: Redbank Gorge.			GPS S:23 41.084 E:132 42.569 UTM 53K 266423E 7378801N	
	(2.9 km)			**(17.0 km)**	
▼ 2.9 km	Road junction. CSA. Track on left SP: Woodlands Camping Area.		▼ 40.8 km	Road junction. CSA. Road on left SP: Ochre Pits.	
	Woodlands camping area is large space with 13 individual camping bays.			Road on left leads 0.5 km to carpark and short walk to scenic Ochre Pits.	
	(0.7 km)			Road junction. CSA. Road on right SP: Ochre Pits.	65.1 km ▲
▼ 3.6 km	Road junction. CSA. Track on right SP: Ridgetop Camping Area.			**(4.2 km)**	
	Perched on top of a ridge line, **Ridgetop camping area** has 5 camping sites with commanding views of valley below.		▼ 45.0 km	Road junction. CSA. Road on right SP: Roadside Stop.	
	(1.1 km)			Road on right leads 0.6 km to rest area with picnic facilities and lookout.	
▼ 4.7 km	Redbank Gorge carpark and picnic area. Return to side trip start.			Road junction. CSA. Road on left SP: Roadside Stop.	60.9 km ▲
	Picnic facilities and information shelter. Walks to Redbank Gorge.			**(1.7 km)**	
	GPS S:23 34.649 E:132 31.115 UTM 53K 246741E 7390356N		▼ 46.7 km	Road junction. CSA. Track on left SP: Serpentine Chalet Bush Camping.	
◀	**END SIDE TRIP**			Track on left leads short distance to **Serpentine Chalet bush camping area**, an open spot with 5 cleared sites accessible by conventional vehicle and another 6 sites further on accessible by four-wheel drive.	
▼ 0.0 km	Zero trip meter at road junction. CSA. Road on left SP: Redbank Gorge.				
	Road junction. Road on right SP: Redbank Gorge. See side trip.	105.9 km ▲		Road junction. CSA. Track on right SP: Serpentine Chalet Bush Camping.	59.2 km ▲
	(19.4 km)			GPS S:23 45.229 E:132 55.051 UTM 53K 287756E 7371475N	
▼ 19.4 km	Road junction. CSA. Road on left SP: Mt Sonder Lookout.			**(6.2 km)**	
	Road on left leads 0.2 km to information bay and lookout with views across to Mt Sonder and over Finke River.		▼ 52.9 km	Road junction. CSA. SP: 99 Alice Springs. Road on left SP: Serpentine Gorge.	
	Road junction. CSA. Road on right SP: Mt Sonder Lookout.	86.5 km ▲		Road on left leads 1.7 km to carpark and 1.3-km walk to Serpentine Gorge.	
	(0.5 km)			Road junction. CSA. SP: Glen Helen 33. Road on right SP: Serpentine Gorge.	53.0 km ▲
▼ 19.9 km	Road junction. CSA. Track on left.			**(10.9 km)**	
	Track on left leads 0.1 km to start of four-wheel-drive access to **2 Mile bush camping area**, which has good campsites under shady gums for 3.0 km along eastern bank of Finke River.		▼ 63.8 km	Road junction. CSA. SP: 88 Alice Springs. Road on left SP: Ellery Creek Big Hole.	
				Road on left leads 1.7 km to **Ellery Creek Big Hole camping area**, a small camping place surrounded by high red cliffs and situated a short walk from permanent waterhole. Picnic area and walking tracks.	
	Road junction. CSA. Track on right leads to 2 Mile bush camping area.	86.0 km ▲			
	GPS S:23 40.839 E:132 40.405 UTM 53K 262736E 7379194N			Road junction. CSA. SP: Glen Helen 44. Road on right SP: Ellery Creek Big Hole.	42.1 km ▲
	(0.2 km)				
▼ 20.1 km	Road junction. CSA. SP: Alice Springs/Namatjira				

KUNAWARRITJI ◀▶ ALICE SPRINGS

Finke River from the access track to 2 Mile bush camping area

GPS	S:23 47.593 E:133 04.551
UTM	53K 303956E 7367339N

(10.5 km)

▼ **74.3 km** Road junction. CSA. Road on right SP: Roadside Stop.

Road on right leads 0.1 km to rest area with tables and shelter.

Road junction. CSA. Road on left SP: Roadside Stop. **31.6 km** ▲

(31.6 km)

▼ **105.9 km** T-junction.

Zero trip meter at road junction. TR. SP: Namatjira Dr/Glen Helen. Road SO SP: Hermannsburg. **0.0 km** ▲

GPS	S:23 49.342 E:133 28.417
UTM	53K 344525E 7364603N

▼ **0.0 km** Zero trip meter at T-junction. TL. SP: Larapinta Dr/Alice Springs. Road on right SP: Hermannsburg.

Road junction. **46.3 km** ▲

(6.3 km)

▼ **6.3 km** Road junction. CSA. SP: 41 Alice Springs. Road on left SP: Standley Chasm.

Road on left leads 9.0 km to Standley Chasm, a privately owned natural attraction, open 8am–5pm; tel. (08) 8956 7440, for further details. Entrance fee applies.

Road junction. CSA. SP: Hermannsburg 88. Road on right SP: Standley Chasm. **40.0 km** ▲

(24.0 km)

▼ **30.3 km** Crossroads. CSA. SP: Alice Springs. Road on right SP: Bullen Rd. Road on left SP: Simpsons Gap.

Road on left leads 1.1 km to visitor centre and 6.9 km to carpark and walk to Simpsons Gap. Park is open 5am–8pm.

Crossroads. CSA. SP: Hermannsburg. Road on right SP: Simpsons Gap. Road on left SP: Bullen Rd. **16.0 km** ▲

GPS	S:23 43.913 E:133 44.297
UTM	53K 371398E 7374887N

(9.8 km)

▼ **40.1 km** SP: Flynn's Grave, on right. CSA on Larapinta Dr through town.

Reverend John Flynn was founder of Royal Flying Doctor Service and established a base in Alice Springs in 1939.

SP: Flynn's Grave, on left. CSA. **6.2 km** ▲

(6.2 km)

▼ **46.3 km** Crossroads. Traffic lights and railway crossing. This is Stuart Hwy, Alice Springs. CSA for town centre. TL for Tennant Creek and Darwin. TR for Kulgera and SA border.

Zero trip meter in Alice Springs at junction of Stuart Hwy and SP: Larapinta Drive. Proceed west along Larapinta Dr SP: West MacDonnells/Desert Park. **0.0 km** ▲

GPS	S:23 42.060 E:133 52.597
UTM	53K 385472E 7378425N

REVERSE DIRECTIONS START

Gregory National Park

Victoria River near Timber Creek

TIMBER CREEK ◄► KALKARINGI 269.8 KM
1. TIMBER CREEK ◄► BULLITA HOMESTEAD 58.4/149.7 km *(easy/difficult)*
2. BULLITA HOMESTEAD ◄► KALKARINGI 211.4 km *(moderate)*

WHEN TO GO May–September **TIME** 4–6 days

Gregory National Park is named after explorer Augustus Charles Gregory, who led a British scientific expedition across northern Australia in 1855–56. The park encompasses the one-time pastoral leases of Bullita and Humbert River stations. This trek traverses old stock routes along which drovers mustered and moved large mobs of cattle on their way to saleyards in Queensland or meatworks at Wyndham in Western Australia.

Situated in the north-west of the Northern Territory, Gregory National Park lies due south of Darwin but is accessed from either Katherine (285 kilometres) or Kununurra in Western Australia (320 kilometres). The park features tropical and semi-arid plant life, spectacular range and gorge scenery, significant Aboriginal sites and evidence of early European pastoral history. Large tracts of spinifex and grassy flood plains dominate the lowlands, which are drained by several major tributaries of the Victoria River. This flat country is interspersed with rocky hills and jump-ups that offer excellent views.

The region is very remote and therefore thorough preparation and planning is essential. There are a number of creek and river crossings – two over the East Baines River are wide and require extra caution, especially at times of high water. The Humbert River crossing provides some interesting four-wheel driving as the route traverses an angled rock bar. Down on the Wickham River the crossing is often sandy. The riverbanks here provide excellent shady sites for a lunch stop or bush camp.

Fuel and supplies can be purchased at Timber Creek on the Victoria Highway at the beginning of the trek. A 3.5-kilometre Heritage Walking Trail in Timber Creek highlights the town's historic sites. Kalkaringi at the end of the trek has supplies, fuel and take-away meals.

GREGORY NATIONAL PARK

Warning sign at entrance to Gregory National Park

Services

VEHICLE ASSISTANCE
AANT   13 1111

POLICE
Kalkaringi   (08) 8975 0790
Timber Creek   (08) 8975 0733

PARKS AND RESERVES
Gregory National Park
PWCNT Gregory National Park   (08) 8975 0888

VISITOR INFORMATION
Katherine   (08) 8972 2650

Authors' note

We found Kalkaringi a friendly community. The grass-covered camping area had plenty of shade and the adjacent roadhouse did a 'mean' bucket of hot chips – a pleasant change from weeks of ham sandwiches! The locals reckon the barra fishing in the nearby Victoria River is also pretty good.

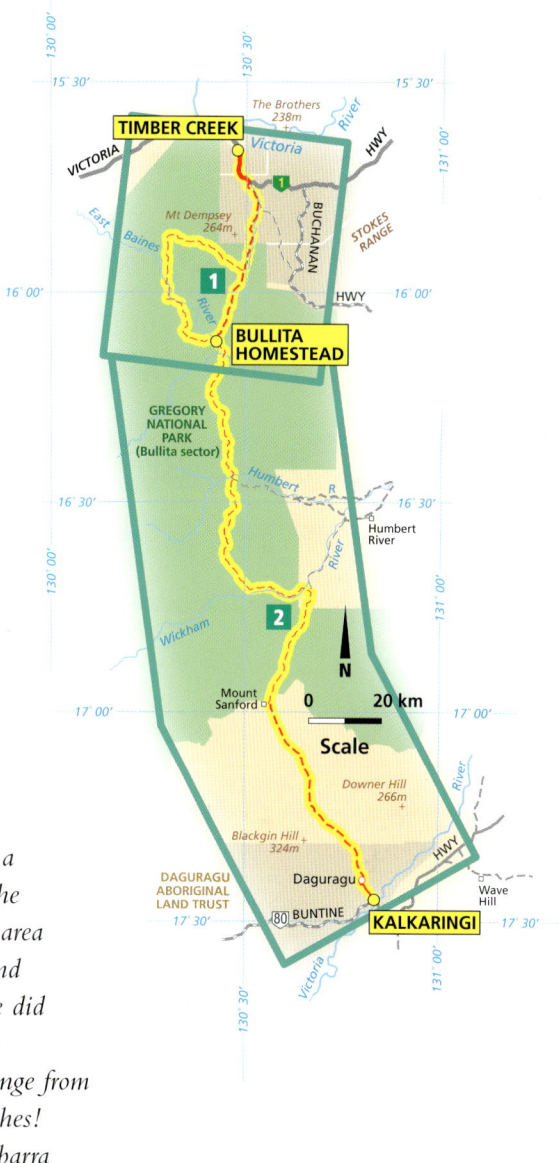

Town Facilities

	Fuel: D/P/A	Mechanical repairs	Tyre repairs	Public telephone	Public toilets	Shop/supplies	Gas refills	Ice	Visitor information	Post office	Medical centre	Police	Meals	Motel	Hotel	Cabins	Caravan park	Camping
Kalkaringi	D/P	•	•	•	•	•		•		•	•	•				•	•	•
Timber Creek	D/P/A	•	•	•	•	•	•	•		•	•	•	•	•	•	•	•	•

101

1 TIMBER CREEK ◀▶ BULLITA HOMESTEAD 58.4 KM

Start point
Timber Creek

Road atlas
357 G5

Total distance
75.4 km (includes side trip to Limestone Gorge)
149.7 km (includes side trip along Bullita Stock Route)
166.7 km (includes all side trips)

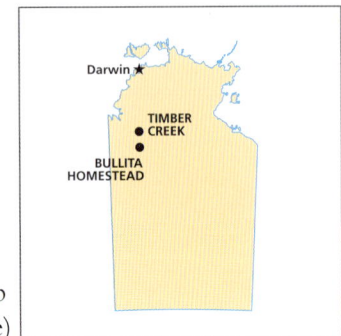

Standard
Easy
Bullita Stock Route side trip (difficult)

Time
2–3 days

Longest distance no PD (includes all options)
247.7 km (Timber Creek to Bullita Homestead and return to Timber Creek)
415.5 km (Timber Creek to Kalkaringi)

Topographic maps
Auslig 1:250 000 series: *Auvergne*; *Waterloo*

Other useful information
- PWCNT brochures: *Gregory National Park Fact Sheet*; *Gregory National Park Campgrounds and Walking Tracks*; *Gregory National Park Bird List*; *Gregory National Park Four Wheel Drive Tracks Visitor's Guide*.
- Ranger talks in Gregory National Park June–August.
- Northern Territory Discovery Trails brochure: *Timber Creek and Victoria River*.

Description

Departing from Timber Creek, the trek follows the Victoria Highway south-east for 10 kilometres before taking the gravel access road to the national park. This is Aboriginal land, which extends to the park's northern boundary. Eighteen kilometres south of the boundary a side trip to Limestone Gorge leads to a beautiful billabong and a chance of a refreshing dip. A trail from Limestone Gorge camping area offers walkers an opportunity to explore the surrounding limestone country.

The Bullita Stock Route – a difficult one-way track that explores the rugged north-west section of the park – is accessed a short distance before the homestead. Bullita Campground is 100 metres along the stock route, on the eastern bank of the East Baines River. The wide river crossing here requires careful driving and was the first obstacle drovers encountered on the long journey to the Wyndham meatworks in Western Australia. There is some interesting and at times challenging four-wheel driving as the route drops into the valley of Spring Creek, including a descent via a series of limestone steps, which makes the going fairly slow over the first 10 kilometres.

Before reaching Spring Creek Yard you pass an interesting outcrop of limestone formations. At the yard a clear waterhole provides good swimming and there is a small camping area nearby. Further on near the Spring Creek–East Baines River junction is the 'Oriental Hotel', a boab tree that offered rest and shade to weary drovers. The camping area of Drovers Rest, 11 kilometres to the west, is near the junction of the East Baines River and Barrabarrac Creek, where there is some good fishing for barramundi.

Once back at the park's main access road it is an easy return trip to Timber Creek, or drive 20 kilometres south to Bullita Homestead to start the next section of the trek. Interpretive signs and photographic displays at the homestead provide an insight into the lifestyle and hardships of the early settlers and drovers who once lived and worked in this remote country.

Advice and warnings

- Tracks generally closed November–April. The first 10 km of Bullita Stock Route is difficult and slow due to limestone steps and ridges. The East Baines River crossings have markers showing the best route so follow these markers; the second crossing has a steep entry point and the eastern side of the river is very rocky. Contact PWCNT Gregory National Park, tel. (08) 8975 0888, to check track conditions.
- Standard road tyres and all-terrain tyres are suitable. Carry two spare tyres.
- Trailers and caravans are not permitted on any four-wheel-drive tracks in the park.
- Camping is at designated sites only. Campfires only in built fireplaces.
- Carry plenty of drinking water, food and supplies.
- Rubbish bins are not provided in the park so please take your rubbish with you.
- Saltwater and freshwater crocodiles inhabit park waters so swim only in areas signposted as safe. Limestone Creek Billabong by the camping area and Spring Creek near Spring Creek Yard are considered safe swimming spots but observe any warning signs.
- This is remote country so be sure to carry some means of communication such as a satellite phone or HF radio.

TIMBER CREEK ◀▶ BULLITA HOMESTEAD

Bullita Stock Route
The first part of the track linking Bullita and Humbert River stations to the meatworks at Wyndham in Western Australia, this route was once the domain of drovers and their large mobs of cattle. Along the way stockmen regularly met and camped under the shade of boab trees (*Adansonia gibbosa*), the trunks of which were often emblazoned with the name of a favourite pub such as the 'Oriental Hotel'. Present-day travellers can follow the trail via a one-way four-wheel-drive loop, and visit old camps and cattle yards.

Limestone Gorge
The gorge is part of a corroded landscape of dramatic limestone formations created by the build-up of marine deposits more than 700 million years ago. Walking trails with interpretive signs provide access to tufa dams, rugged escarpments, stromatolites, and sweeping views over the East Baines River valley.

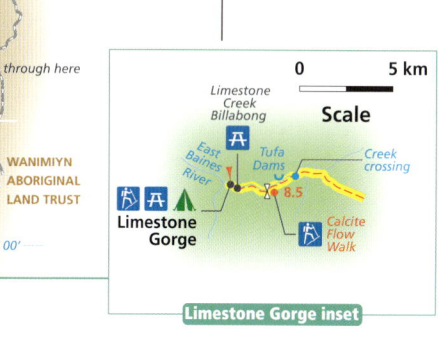

Bullita Homestead
Bullita was first taken up by Jack and Gerry Skeahan and Ambrose Durack in 1905. Located beside the East Baines River, the homestead complex includes a washhouse, meat house, numerous sheds and nearby stockyards. Informative signs give the history of the station and its surrounds.

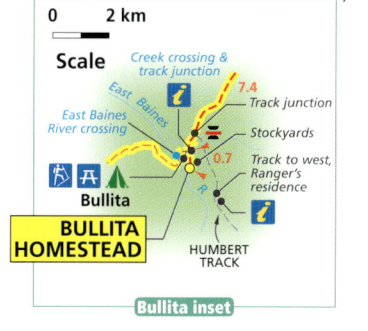

Campsite Facilities

	Toilets	Disabled access	4WD access only	Off-road trailer	Off-road caravan	Drinking water	Fee payable	Ranger patrolled	BBQ/fireplace	Campfires prohibited	Picnic tables	Shelter shed	No rubbish disposal	Public phone	Shower	Bushwalking	Swimming	Swimming not advised	Fishing	Canoeing	Dogs allowed
Baines		•						•			•				•	•					
Bullita	•		•	•	•		•	•	•		•				•			•			
Drovers Rest		•						•			•					•					
Limestone Gorge	•	•			•	•	•				•	•									
Spring Creek Yard		•						•			•				•						

103

GREGORY NATIONAL PARK

Tranquil waters of Spring Creek

Permits and bookings
- No permits or bookings required.
- A voluntary registration system is available for safety purposes, tel. 1300 650 750. This service takes note of your travel, vehicle and credit card details. When you leave the park you must deregister by midday of the following day of your planned return. If you fail to do this, action will be taken to locate you and fees may be charged.
- Bag and size limits apply to fishing. Contact Northern Territory Fisheries Department, tel. (08) 8999 2144, for details or visit their website (www.fisheries.nt.gov.au).

ROUTE DIRECTIONS

▼ **0.0 km** Zero trip meter on Victoria Hwy at Timber Creek, with information bay on left. Proceed east along highway towards Katherine.

Timber Creek. Information bay on right. **50.3 km** ▲

GPS S:15 39.751 E:130 28.810
UTM 52L 658644E 8267841N

(10.2 km)

▼ **10.2 km** Road junction. TR. SP: Gregory National Park/Bullita Access. Road SO to Katherine.

T-junction with bitumen. TL. This is Victoria Hwy. Road on right to Katherine. **40.1 km** ▲

(6.6 km)

▼ **16.8 km** Track junction. CSA. SP: Gregory National Park. Track on left.

Track junction. CSA. Track on right. **33.5 km** ▲

(0.9 km)

▼ **17.7 km** Creek crossing.

Creek crossing. **32.6 km** ▲

(13.9 km)

▼ **31.6 km** Enter SP: Gregory National Park.

Exit Gregory National Park. **18.7 km** ▲

GPS S:15 54.254 E:130 30.392
UTM 52L 661279E 8241077N

(5.3 km)

▼ **36.9 km** Track junction. CSA. SP: Bullita 20 km. Track on right SP: No Entry Authorised Vehicles Only.

Track on right is where Bullita Stock Route side trip exits. This is a one-way track only.

Track junction. CSA. SP: Timber Creek 34 km. Track on left SP: No Entry Authorised Vehicles Only. **13.4 km** ▲

GPS S:15 56.881 E:130 29.616
UTM 52L 659859E 8236242N

(4.8 km)

▼ **41.7 km** Concrete causeway.

Concrete causeway. **8.6 km** ▲

(4.2 km)

▼ **45.9 km** Concrete causeway.

Concrete causeway. **4.4 km** ▲

(2.6 km)

▼ **48.5 km** Concrete causeway.

Concrete causeway. **1.8 km** ▲

(1.8 km)

▼ **50.3 km** Track junction. Side trip to Limestone Gorge.

Zero trip meter at track junction. CSA. Track on left SP: 9 km Limestone Gorge. **0.0 km** ▲

GPS S:16 03.288 E:130 27.171
UTM 52K 655414E 8224458N

▶ **SIDE TRIP: Limestone Gorge**

▼ **0.0 km** Zero trip meter at track junction. Proceed west along track towards Limestone Gorge.

(4.6 km)

▼ **4.6 km** Creek crossing.

(0.9 km)

▼ **5.5 km** SP: Tufa Dams, on right. CSA.

Tufa dams have been created when deposits of calcium carbonate, or calcite, from the waters of Limestone Creek have built up over many years on obstructions such as rocks and tree roots.

(0.8 km)

▼ **6.3 km** Carpark on left for Calcite Flow Walk. CSA through gate.

A 600-m return walk leaves from here to views of surrounding valley and limestone structures.

(1.9 km)

▼ **8.2 km** Track junction. CSA. Track on right SP: Limestone Creek Billabong.

TIMBER CREEK ◀▶ BULLITA HOMESTEAD

	Track on right leads short distance to picnic area beside Limestone Creek Billabong, a pleasant spot for lunch and a refreshing swim. **(0.3 km)**	▼ 7.3 km	Creek crossing.
			Creek crossing. 0.1 km ▲
			(0.1 km)
▼ 8.5 km	Limestone Gorge camping area. Return to side trip start.	▼ 7.4 km	Track junction. Information board on left. Side trip along Bullita Stock Route.
	Limestone Gorge camping area has 5 individual camping bays with boabs scattered around perimeter. From camping area a walking track leads 1.8 km through limestone formations to ridge tops and good views of East Baines River valley.		Zero trip meter at track junction. CSA past information board on right. Track on left SP: Bullita Campground/Bullita Stock Route. 0.0 km ▲
			GPS S:16 06.741 E:130 25.504
			UTM 52K 652398E 8218111N
	GPS S:16 02.840 E:130 23.032	▶	**SIDE TRIP: Bullita Stock Route**
	UTM 52K 648039E 8225335N	▼ 0.0 km	Zero trip meter at track junction with information board on left. Proceed in westerly direction along track SP: Bullita Campground/Bullita Stock Route.
◀	**END SIDE TRIP**		
▼ 0.0 km	Zero trip meter at track junction. CSA. Track on right SP: 9 km Limestone Gorge.		**GPS** S:16 06.741 E:130 25.504
	Track junction. 7.4 km ▲		**UTM** 52K 652398E 8218111N
	Track on left SP: 9 km Limestone Gorge. See Limestone Gorge side trip.		**(0.1 km)**
	(4.0 km)	▼ 0.1 km	Track junction. CSA. Track on left SP: Bullita Campground.
▼ 4.0 km	Creek crossing.		Track on left leads short distance to **Bullita Campground**, a large area with 10 cleared sites set high above East Baines River. The river was named by Gregory in 1855 after one of his party, artist and explorer Thomas Baines, who is credited with its discovery.
	Creek crossing. 3.4 km ▲		
	(2.7 km)		
▼ 6.7 km	Track junction. CSA. SP: Bullita. Track on left SP: Humbert Track.		
	The Humbert Track on left leads southwards. See Gregory National Park section 2 (Bullita Homestead to Kalkaringi).		**(0.3 km)**
		▼ 0.4 km	Cross East Baines River.
	Track junction. CSA. Track on right SP: Humbert Track. 0.7 km ▲		Wide river crossing so follow markers. Caution required.
	Track on right is where section 2 exits.		**GPS** S:16 06.738 E:130 25.304
	GPS S:16 06.395 E:130 25.604		**UTM** 52K 652041E 8218119N
	UTM 52K 652581E 8218748N		**(8.8 km)**
	(0.6 km)	▼ 9.2 km	Top of Spring Creek Jump-up.

Wide crossing at the East Baines River

105

GREGORY NATIONAL PARK

Limestone outcrops along the Bullita Stock Route

Track now descends into Spring Creek Valley via a series of limestone steps and ridges. From here the going is extremely slow.

(1.3 km)

▼ 10.5 km Interesting limestone pillars in this vicinity.

(3.1 km)

▼ 13.6 km Track junction. CSA. Spring Creek Yard and track on left.

Track on left leads 0.1 km to small **Spring Creek Yard camping area**, which is ideally located next to large scenic waterhole in Spring Creek. A great spot to cool off.

GPS   S:16 05.150 E:130 20.437
UTM   52K 643384E 8221105N

(0.4 km)

▼ 14.0 km Creek crossing.

(7.5 km)

▼ 21.5 km Track junction. CSA. Track on right.
'Oriental Hotel' boab tree on track on right.

GPS   S:16 01.545 E:130 19.927
UTM   52K 642518E 8227759N

(0.1 km)

▼ 21.6 km Cross Spring Creek.
This crossing is a few hundred metres up from East Baines River junction.

(9.4 km)

▼ 31.0 km Creek crossing.

(1.1 km)

▼ 32.1 km Cross East Baines River.
Sharp entry into river. Wide river crossing so follow markers. Caution required.

GPS   S:15 58.439 E:130 17.682
UTM   52L 638550E 8233512N

(0.4 km)

▼ 32.5 km T-junction. TR. Track on left SP: Camping Area 100 m.

Track on left leads short distance to small, unprotected clearing, which is **Baines camping area**.

(2.9 km)

▼ 35.4 km Creek crossing.

(2.0 km)

▼ 37.4 km Creek crossing.

(2.4 km)

▼ 39.8 km T-junction.

GPS   S:15 54.620 E:130 17.579
UTM   52L 638410E 8240555N

▼ 0.0 km Zero trip meter at T-junction. TR. SP: Timber Creek 58 km. Track on left SP: Drovers Rest 11 km.

Track on left leads 11.1 km to **Drovers Rest camping area**, a small cleared site above Barrabarrac Creek, with a few shady trees.

(7.7 km)

▼ 7.7 km Track junction. CSA. Track on left.
Track on left leads short distance to scenic section of Barrabarrac Creek lined with pandanus palms.

GPS   S:15 51.896 E:130 19.168
UTM   52L 641277E 8245560N

(5.2 km)

▼ 12.9 km Track junction. CSA. Track on left to gate.

(17.8 km)

▼ 30.7 km T-junction with Gregory National Park main access road. TR and proceed 20.8 km to return to side trip start.
Road on left SP: Timber Creek 34 km. Road on right SP: Bullita 20 km, and also leads to start of Gregory National Park section 2 (Bullita Homestead to Kalkaringi).

GPS   S:15 56.881 E:130 29.616
UTM   52L 659859E 8236242N

◀ **END SIDE TRIP**

▼ 0.0 km Zero trip meter at track junction. CSA. Information board on left. Track on right SP: Bullita Campground/Bullita Stock Route.

Track junction. 0.7 km ▲

Track on left SP: Bullita Campground/Bullita Stock Route. This is start of Bullita Stock Route side trip.

(0.5 km)

▼ 0.5 km Stockyards on left. KR. SP: Bullita Homestead.

Track junction. KL past stockyards on right. 0.2 km ▲

(0.2 km)

▼ 0.7 km Bullita Homestead. Trek section ends.

Zero trip meter at Bullita Homestead carpark. Proceed out of homestead towards Victoria Hwy. 0.0 km ▲

GPS   S:16 07.043 E:130 25.499
UTM   52K 652385E 8217554N

REVERSE DIRECTIONS START

2 BULLITA HOMESTEAD ◄► KALKARINGI 211.4 KM

Start point
Bullita Homestead

Road atlas
357 G5

Total distance
211.4 km

Standard
Moderate

Time
2–3 days

Longest distance no PD (includes all options)
415.5 km (Timber Creek to Kalkaringi)

Topographic maps
Auslig 1:250 000 series: *Waterloo*; *Victoria River Downs*; *Wave Hill*

Other useful information
- Kalkaringi store open Monday–Friday 9am–1pm and 2–5pm and Saturday 10am–2pm, tel. (08) 8975 0788; accepts cash, EFTPOS and credit cards.
- PWCNT brochures: *Gregory National Park Fact Sheet*; *Gregory National Park Campgrounds and Walking Tracks*; *Gregory National Park Bird List*; *Gregory National Park Four Wheel Drive Tracks Visitors Guide*.

Description

The second section of this trek leaves from Bullita Homestead and follows the Humbert Track, an old packhorse trail that linked Humbert River station to Bullita. Once across the Humbert River, which can be tricky and requires careful wheel placement, you follow the Wickham Track to the Wickham River crossing – this is generally shallow with a sandy bottom and is best tackled with four-wheel-drive engaged. From here the Gibbie Creek Track leads south. The national park ends at Mount Sanford station, where navigation can be difficult at times but most of the route is signposted. From the southern boundary of Mount Sanford it is an easy drive through Aboriginal land to the town of Kalkaringi.

The country between the Humbert and Wickham rivers is characterised by large grassy flood plains and rocky hills. Flat-topped mesas – land forms common in arid and semi-arid terrain – dot the landscape. Just before the Humbert River crossing is a walking track to Police Creek Waterhole, where police from Timber Creek camped while tracking the killer of Brigalow Bill, the first white man to live on the Humbert River.

Birdlife is prolific in the park. White-breasted sea eagles are common and you may even catch a glimpse of the endangered Gouldian finch or the rarely seen purple-crowned fairy wren.

Bullita Homestead

GREGORY NATIONAL PARK

Old cattle yards are common along the route and now provide locations for bush camping. The campsite at Top Humbert Yard, just south of the Humbert River crossing, is a short walk from the scenic palm-fringed Gunbunbu Waterhole. Paperbark Yard campsite is also in a picturesque location, set beside a waterhole surrounded by palms and paperbarks. These shady trees also line the riverbanks at the Wickham River crossing campsite.

Advice and warnings

- Track closures November–April. Wickham and Gibbie Creek tracks generally comprise two wheel tracks through high grass so follow track markers. Gibbie Creek Track has numerous wash-outs and some creek crossings may be impassable after rain. There are numerous rocky creek crossings. The Humbert River crossing is over a large sloped rock shelf. Walk the crossing first to familiarise yourself with the slope and layout of the rocks. Water level of the river depends on the time of year. Contact PWCNT Gregory National Park, tel. (08) 8975 0888, to check track conditions.
- Mount Sanford station is private property so keep to main track, watch out for roaming cattle and leave all gates as found.
- Standard road tyres and all-terrain tyres are suitable. Carry two spare tyres.
- Trailers and caravans are not permitted on any of the four-wheel-drive tracks in the park.
- Camping is at designated sites only. Campfires only in built fireplaces. No camping permitted on Mount Sanford station.
- Carry plenty of drinking water, food and supplies.
- There are no rubbish bins in the national park so please take your rubbish with you.
- Saltwater and freshwater crocodiles inhabit the waters of the park so swim only in areas signposted as safe.
- This is remote country so be sure to carry some means of communication such as a satellite phone or HF radio.

Humbert River Track near the tent hills

Permits and bookings

- No permits or bookings required.
- A voluntary registration system is available for safety purposes, tel. 1300 650 750. This service takes note of your travel, vehicle and credit card details. When you leave the park you must deregister by midday of the following day of your planned return. If you fail to do this, action will be taken to locate you and fees may be charged.
- Bag and size limits apply to fishing. Contact Northern Territory Fisheries Department, tel. (08) 8999 2144, for details or visit their website (www.fisheries.nt.gov.au).

Campsite Facilities

	Toilets	Disabled access	4WD access only	Off-road trailer	Off-road caravan	Drinking water	Fee payable	Ranger patrolled	BBQ/fireplace	Campfires prohibited	Picnic tables	Shelter shed	No rubbish disposal	Public phone	Shower	Bushwalking	Swimming	Swimming not advised	Fishing	Canoeing	Dogs allowed
Bullita	•		•	•	•	•	•		•		•			•			•	•			
Fig Tree Yard			•						•				•								
Paperbark Yard			•						•				•						•		
Top Humbert Yard			•						•				•								
Wickham River			•										•						•		

BULLITA HOMESTEAD ◀▶ KALKARINGI

Top Humbert Yard
Although now in ruins, the yard complex once included stockmen's huts made from corrugated iron salvaged from World War II army water tanks. The cattle yard had a post and rail structure known as a bronco panel, to which the animals were tied while the stockmen branded, dehorned and castrated them.

Jump-ups
A jump-up or mesa is a flat-topped hill bounded by steep rock walls. Its top consists of a layer of hard capping that resists erosion. Over time this top layer begins to wear away, creating a cone-shaped 'tent hill'. The track climbs a number of jump-ups that offer spectacular views.

Jump-up on the Wickham Track

Nutwood tree

Wickham River
The bank of the Wickham River, with beautiful pandanus palms and tall paperbarks, makes a shady and cool site for an overnight camp or lunch spot. Between Dingo Yard and the river crossing there are some fine nutwood trees (*Terminalia arostrata*), a species unique to this part of Australia. The river environment is home to many birds and attracts wildlife in the evenings.

109

Humbert's Charlie Schultz

'I'll be lucky to last a bloody year', was the first comment uttered by 19-year-old Charlie Schultz when he arrived at the remote and lonely Humbert River station in 1928. Schultz did last a year; in fact he stayed on until 1971 to become one of the best-known cattlemen in the Northern Territory.

Humbert River station was a small, isolated property next to the renowned Victoria River Downs. Purchased by Charlie's father and uncle against better advice, Humbert River was remote, run down and largely in debt when Charlie arrived to take over the management. Charlie had spent most of his previous working life on cattle stations throughout Queensland and was a skilled horseman and horse breeder. Over the ensuing years his negotiation skills, work ethic, horsemanship and knowledge of stock saw the station claw its way out of debt, earning him a solid reputation among those on surrounding stations. His droving feats were legendary – it was nothing for him to move large mobs along stock routes such as the infamous Murrunji Track to Queensland, with very few if any losses of cattle en route.

Charlie married in 1941 and his wife, Hessie, moved from Queensland to Humbert River. They employed Aboriginal people to help with station work, and treated them with a respect not often present on outback properties at the time, with Charlie acknowledging that the station would not have survived and prospered without them.

Charlie Schultz died in April 1997. He gave a full account of his life at Humbert River in *Beyond the Big Run* (University of Queensland Press), written in collaboration with Darrell Lewis.

Charlie Schultz at Humbert River station in about 1928

ROUTE DIRECTIONS

▼ 0.0 km — Zero trip meter at Bullita Homestead. Proceed north towards Victoria Hwy.
Bullita Homestead. 21.9 km ▲
GPS S:16 07.043 E:130 25.499
UTM 52K 652385E 8217554N
(0.2 km)

▼ 0.2 km — Track junction. KL past stockyards on right.
Stockyards on left. KR. SP: Bullita Homestead. 21.7 km ▲
(0.5 km)

▼ 0.7 km — Track junction. CSA past information board on right. Track on left SP: Bullita Campground/Bullita Stock Route.
Information board on left and track junction. CSA. SP: Bullita Homestead. Track on right SP: Bullita Campground/Bullita Stock Route. 21.2 km ▲
(0.1 km)

▼ 0.8 km — Creek crossing.
Creek crossing. 21.1 km ▲
(0.6 km)

▼ 1.4 km — Track junction. Hard TR. SP: Humbert Track. Track SO to Victoria Hwy.
Track junction. Hard TL. SP: Bullita. 20.5 km ▲
GPS S:16 06.395 E:130 25.604
UTM 52K 652581E 8218748N
(0.4 km)

▼ 1.8 km — Concrete causeway.
Concrete causeway. 20.1 km ▲
(2.0 km)

▼ 3.8 km — Track junction. CSA. Track on right SP: Ranger Residence/Emergency Only.
Track junction. CSA. Track on left SP: Ranger Residence/Emergency Only. 18.1 km ▲
(0.3 km)

▼ 4.1 km — Information board and visitor book on left. CSA. SP: Humbert Track.
Track deteriorates from here.
SP: End of Humbert Track. Information board and visitor book on right. CSA. 17.8 km ▲
Track improves from here.
GPS S:16 07.684 E:130 26.022
UTM 52K 653309E 8216366N
(2.7 km)

▼ 6.8 km — Creek crossing.
Creek crossing. 15.1 km ▲
(0.5 km)

▼ 7.3 km — Creek crossing.
Creek crossing. 14.6 km ▲
(1.8 km)

▼ 9.1 km — Creek crossing.
Creek crossing. 12.8 km ▲
(10.7 km)

▼ 19.8 km — Creek crossing.
Large stand of boab trees in this vicinity.
Creek crossing. 2.1 km ▲
(1.2 km)

▼ 21.0 km SP: Figtree Valley Lookout, on right. CSA.

A 1.5-km, 1-hour-return walk leads to a lookout point with good views over Fig Tree Valley.

SP: Figtree Valley Lookout, on left. CSA. 0.9 km ▲

(0.9 km)

▼ 21.9 km Track junction.

Zero trip meter at track junction. CSA. Track on right SP: Fig Tree Yard 1.5 km. 0.0 km ▲

GPS S:16 14.908 E:130 24.976
UTM 52K 651353E 8203057N

▼ 0.0 km Zero trip meter at track junction. CSA. Track on left SP: Fig Tree Yard 1.5 km.

Track on left leads 1.2 km to **Fig Tree Yard camping area**, a small cleared site located beside waterhole on Fig Tree Creek.

Track junction. 27.8 km ▲

(1.0 km)

▼ 1.0 km Creek crossing.

Creek crossing. 26.8 km ▲

(1.7 km)

▼ 2.7 km Regrowth area of turpentine wattle. CSA.

Turpentine wattle was regularly burned by Aboriginal people to prevent it growing into dense thickets. Pastoralists also practised the burning method to ensure open pastures.

Regrowth area of turpentine wattle. CSA. 25.1 km ▲

(2.4 km)

▼ 5.1 km Creek crossing.

Creek crossing. 22.7 km ▲

(1.0 km)

▼ 6.1 km Track crosses over a series of limestone ridges in this vicinity.

Track crosses over a series of limestone ridges in this vicinity. 21.7 km ▲

(5.4 km)

▼ 11.5 km Fig Tree Jump-up.

This jump-up marks the point where water flows south into Humbert River and north into East Baines River. Good views from here.

Fig Tree Jump-up. 16.3 km ▲

(3.8 km)

▼ 15.3 km Creek crossing.

Creek crossing. 12.5 km ▲

(3.4 km)

▼ 18.7 km Creek crossing.

Creek crossing. 9.1 km ▲

(1.5 km)

▼ 20.2 km 2nd Drovers Camp in this vicinity.

Site where drovers camped the second night on their way from Humbert River station to Wyndham meatworks.

2nd Drovers Camp in this vicinity. 7.6 km ▲

GPS S:16 23.445 E:130 27.266
UTM 52K 655320E 8187285N

(0.2 km)

▼ 20.4 km Creek crossing.

Creek crossing. 7.4 km ▲

(0.8 km)

Signposted walking track to Police Creek Waterhole

▼ 21.2 km River crossing.

River crossing. 6.6 km ▲

(1.9 km)

▼ 23.1 km River crossing.

River crossing. 4.7 km ▲

(3.7 km)

▼ 26.8 km Walking trail to SP: Police Creek Waterhole, on left. CSA.

A 1.5-km, 1-hour-return walking trail leads to waterhole at junction of Police Creek and Humbert River.

Walking trail to SP: Police Creek Waterhole, on right. CSA. 1.0 km ▲

(0.1 km)

▼ 26.9 km Cross Humbert River.

Crossing comprises a sloped, rock ledge. Follow markers across river. It is best to walk crossing first to familiarise yourself with slope and layout of rocks.

Cross Humbert River. 0.9 km ▲

GPS S:16 26.184 E:130 28.014
UTM 52K 656615E 8182224N

(0.9 km)

GREGORY NATIONAL PARK

Remote country south of the Humbert River

▼ 27.8 km   T-junction.

         Zero trip meter at track junction. TR. Track SO SP: Top Humbert Yard 600 m.   0.0 km ▲

         GPS   S:16 26.494 E:130 27.725
         UTM   52K 656097E 8181656N

▼ 0.0 km   Zero trip meter at T-junction. TL. Track on right SP: Top Humbert Yard 600 m.

         Track on right leads 0.6 km to Top Humbert Yard camping area, a small cleared site close to old stockyards and ruins of cattlemen's huts.

         Track junction.   81.0 km ▲

         (0.3 km)

▼ 0.3 km   Track junction. TR. SP: Wickham Track/Buchanan Highway via Mount Sanford Station. Track SO SP: Humbert Track 17 km.

         Track junction. TL. SP: Humbert Track. Track on right SP: Humbert Track 17 km.   80.7 km ▲

         GPS   S:16 26.568 E:130 27.911
         UTM   52K 656427E 8181517N

         (1.1 km)

▼ 1.4 km   Creek crossing.

         Creek crossing.   79.6 km ▲

         (9.2 km)

▼ 10.6 km   Creek crossing.

         Creek crossing.   70.4 km ▲

         (5.3 km)

▼ 15.9 km   Creek crossing.

         Creek crossing.   65.1 km ▲

         (2.4 km)

▼ 18.3 km   Creek crossing.

         On left-hand side of track over creek are three cone-shaped hills, which are eroded mesas known as tent hills.

         Creek crossing.   62.7 km ▲

         (2.3 km)

▼ 20.6 km   Creek crossing. Track now climbs to top of jump-up.

         Creek crossing.   60.4 km ▲

         (4.1 km)

▼ 24.7 km   Good views from this point over surrounding plains and Upper Wickham.

         Steep descent off jump-up. Engage low range.

         Good views from this point.   56.3 km ▲

         Top of jump-up. Disengage low range.

         GPS   S:16 36.449 E:130 27.021
         UTM   52K 654712E 8163307N

         (0.3 km)

▼ 25.0 km   Base of jump-up.

         Disengage low range.

         Base of jump-up.   56.0 km ▲

         Steep climb to top of jump-up. Engage low range.

         (3.6 km)

▼ 28.6 km   Track junction. KL. Information board and track on hard right SP: Broadarrow Track.

         Track junction. KR. Track on left SP: Broadarrow Track.   52.4 km ▲

         GPS   S:16 38.287 E:130 27.036
         UTM   52K 654714E 8159917N

         (1.2 km)

BULLITA HOMESTEAD ◀▶ KALKARINGI

▼ 29.8 km   Creek crossing.
                          Creek crossing.   51.2 km ▲
(7.6 km)

▼ 37.4 km   Creek crossing.
                          Creek crossing.   43.6 km ▲
(2.9 km)

▼ 40.3 km   Creek crossing.
                          Creek crossing.   40.7 km ▲
(4.8 km)

▼ 45.1 km   Track junction. TL. Track on right leads 0.4 km to Wickham River.
            Track junction. TR. Track SO leads 0.4 km to Wickham River.   35.9 km ▲
(0.1 km)

▼ 45.2 km   Dingo Yard on left. CSA.
                          Dingo Yard on right. CSA.   35.8 km ▲

GPS   S:16 42.230 E:130 33.526
UTM   52K 666196E 8152558N

(0.2 km)

▼ 45.4 km   Creek crossing.
                          Creek crossing.   35.6 km ▲
(0.6 km)

▼ 46.0 km   Creek crossing.
                          Creek crossing.   35.0 km ▲
(2.4 km)

▼ 48.4 km   Creek crossing.
                          Creek crossing.   32.6 km ▲
(1.8 km)

▼ 50.2 km   Creek crossing.
                          Creek crossing.   30.8 km ▲
(3.1 km)

▼ 53.3 km   Creek crossing.
                          Creek crossing.   27.7 km ▲
(4.7 km)

▼ 58.0 km   Cross Wickham River.
            River crossing has sandy bottom. Water levels depend on time of year. **Wickham River bush camping** is in picturesque setting beside river among paperbark trees and pandanus palms. Prolific birdlife and good fishing.
                          Cross Wickham River.   23.0 km ▲

GPS   S:16 42.350 E:130 38.975
UTM   52K 675879E 8152259N

(2.4 km)

▼ 60.4 km   T-junction. TR. SP: Gibbie Creek Track/Mt Sanford Station – 35 km – 2 hrs. Track on left SP: Humbert River Station.
            Track junction. TL. SP: Wickham Track/Dingo Yard/Top Humbert Yard.   20.6 km ▲

GPS   S:16 42.862 E:130 40.075
UTM   52K 677826E 8151298N

(2.5 km)

▼ 62.9 km   Creek crossing.
                          Creek crossing.   18.1 km ▲
(0.8 km)

▼ 63.7 km   Creek crossing.
                          Creek crossing.   17.3 km ▲
(1.2 km)

▼ 64.9 km   Creek crossing.
                          Creek crossing.   16.1 km ▲
(0.9 km)

▼ 65.8 km   Creek crossing.
                          Creek crossing.   15.2 km ▲
(0.5 km)

▼ 66.3 km   Cross Gibbie Creek.
                          Cross Gibbie Creek.   14.7 km ▲

GPS   S:16 45.520 E:130 39.280
UTM   52K 676373E 8146408N

(0.8 km)

▼ 67.1 km   Water gauge on left. CSA.
                          Water gauge on right. CSA.   13.9 km ▲
(3.1 km)

▼ 70.2 km   Creek crossing.
                          Creek crossing.   10.8 km ▲
(2.2 km)

▼ 72.4 km   Creek crossing.
            Large waterhole on right.
                          Creek crossing.   8.6 km ▲
(1.3 km)

▼ 73.7 km   Creek crossing.
            Large waterhole on left.
                          Creek crossing.   7.3 km ▲
(3.6 km)

▼ 77.3 km   Creek crossing.
                          Creek crossing.   3.7 km ▲
(1.7 km)

▼ 79.0 km   Cross Gibbie Creek.
                          Cross Gibbie Creek.   2.0 km ▲

GPS   S:16 51.078 E:130 36.613
UTM   52K 671550E 8136196N

(1.7 km)

The Gibbie Creek Track winds through tall cane grass

■ 113

GREGORY NATIONAL PARK

Waterhole on the Wickham River

▼ 80.7 km	Creek crossing.	
	Creek crossing.	0.3 km ▲
	(0.3 km)	
▼ 81.0 km	Track junction.	
	Zero trip meter at track junction. CSA. Track on right SP: Paperbark Yard.	0.0 km ▲
	GPS S:16 51.974 E:130 36.378 **UTM** 52K 671119E 8134547N	
▼ 0.0 km	Zero trip meter at track junction. CSA. Track on left SP: Paperbark Yard.	
	Track on left leads short distance to Paperbark Yard camping area, a small cleared space beside large waterhole lined with palms and paperbark trees.	
	Track junction.	15.1 km ▲
	(1.0 km)	
▼ 1.0 km	Creek crossing.	
	Creek crossing.	14.1 km ▲
	(7.5 km)	
▼ 8.5 km	Creek crossing.	
	Creek crossing.	6.6 km ▲
	(1.4 km)	
▼ 9.9 km	Creek crossing.	
	Creek crossing.	5.2 km ▲
	(2.9 km)	
▼ 12.8 km	Gate. LAF. CSA, exiting Gregory National Park and entering SP: Mt Sanford Station.	
	Mount Sanford station is private property. Please stay on main track. Do not deviate onto any other tracks and leave all gates as found.	

	Gate. LAF. CSA entering SP: Gregory National Park. Information board on left.	2.3 km ▲
	GPS S:16 57.747 E:130 33.946 **UTM** 52K 666716E 8123934N	
	(1.5 km)	
▼ 14.3 km	Track junction. CSA on centre track. Tracks on left and right.	
	Track junction. CSA on centre track. Tracks on left and right.	0.8 km ▲
	(0.2 km)	
▼ 14.5 km	Creek crossing.	
	Creek crossing.	0.6 km ▲
	(0.4 km)	
▼ 14.9 km	Gate. LAF.	
	Gate. LAF.	0.2 km ▲
	(0.2 km)	
▼ 15.1 km	Track junction.	
	Zero trip meter at track junction. Hard TR. SP: Gregory National Park. Mount Sanford homestead on left.	0.0 km ▲
	GPS S:16 58.847 E:130 33.587 **UTM** 52K 666062E 8121911N	
▼ 0.0 km	Zero trip meter at track junction. TL. SP: Kalkaringi – 65 km – 1.5 hrs. Mount Sanford homestead opposite junction.	
	Track junction.	65.6 km ▲
	(0.3 km)	
▼ 0.3 km	Gate. LAF. Track junction through gate. KR.	
	Track junction. KL through gate. LAF.	65.3 km ▲
	(0.6 km)	

BULLITA HOMESTEAD ◀▶ KALKARINGI

▼ 0.9 km Creek crossing.

　　　　　　　　　　　　　　　　　Creek crossing. 64.7 km ▲

(0.3 km)

▼ 1.2 km Gate. LAF.

　　　　　　　　　　　　　　　　　Gate. LAF. 64.4 km ▲

(2.6 km)

▼ 3.8 km Gate. LAF.

　　　　　　　　　　　　　　　　　Gate. LAF. 61.8 km ▲

(0.5 km)

▼ 4.3 km Gate. LAF.

　　　　　　　　　　　　　　　　　Gate. LAF. 61.3 km ▲

(7.7 km)

▼ 12.0 km Gate. LAF.

　　　　　　　　　　　　　　　　　Gate. LAF. 53.6 km ▲

(3.3 km)

▼ 15.3 km Gate. LAF.

　　　　　　　　　　　　　　　　　Gate. LAF. 50.3 km ▲

(2.5 km)

▼ 17.8 km Cross Poison Creek.

　　　　　　　　　　　　　　　　Cross Poison Creek. 47.8 km ▲

```
GPS   S:17 06.510 E:130 38.650
UTM   52K 674929E 8107704N
```

(4.0 km)

▼ 21.8 km Track junction. CSA. SP: Blackgin Bore. Track on left.

　　　　　　　　　　　Track junction. CSA. Track on right. 43.8 km ▲

(2.3 km)

▼ 24.1 km Track junction. CSA. Track on left SP: No 5 Yard.

　　　　　Y-junction. KL. SP: Mt Sanford. Track on right SP: No 5 Yard. 41.5 km ▲

(2.9 km)

▼ 27.0 km Gate. LAF.

　　　　　　　　　　　　　　　　　Gate. LAF. 38.6 km ▲

(4.2 km)

▼ 31.2 km Gate. LAF.

　　　　　　　　　　　　　　　　　Gate. LAF. 34.4 km ▲

(0.1 km)

▼ 31.3 km Track junction. CSA. Track on right.

　　　　　　　　　　Y-junction. KR. SP: Mt Sanford. 34.3 km ▲

(0.2 km)

▼ 31.5 km Gate. LAF.

　　　　　　　　　　　　　　　　　Gate. LAF. 34.1 km ▲

(12.5 km)

▼ 44.0 km Creek crossing. Blackgin Waterhole on left.

　　　　　Creek crossing. Blackgin Waterhole on right. 21.6 km ▲

```
GPS   S:17 17.853 E:130 45.338
UTM   52K 686602E 8086678N
```

(1.7 km)

▼ 45.7 km Track junction. CSA to gate. Track on left SP: No 5 Yard.

　　　　　Track junction. CSA. Track on right SP: No 5 Yard. 19.9 km ▲

(0.1 km)

▼ 45.8 km Gate. LAF.

　　　　　　　　　　　　　　　　　Gate. LAF. 19.8 km ▲

(9.0 km)

▼ 54.8 km Gate. LAF.

　　　　　　　　　　　　　　　　　Gate. LAF. 10.8 km ▲

(3.1 km)

▼ 57.9 km Road junction with bitumen. KR and cross SP: Lawi Causeway. Road on left.

Road on left leads 0.6 km to Daguragu.

　　　　　Road junction. KL on dirt road. SP: Gregory National Park 65. Road on right to Daguragu. 7.7 km ▲

Track now traverses private property. Please stay on main track and leave all gates as found.

```
GPS   S:17 23.882 E:130 47.909
UTM   52K 691054E 8075515N
```

(7.4 km)

▼ 65.3 km T-junction. TR. SP: Buntine Highway/Halls Creek. Road on left SP: Katherine.

　　　　　Road junction. TL. SP: Daguragu/Gregory National Park 4 x 4 Access Only. 0.3 km ▲

(0.3 km)

▼ 65.6 km Kalkaringi store, where fuel is available, and caravan park on right.

Kalkaringi is on Buntine Hwy, which leads in north-easterly direction to Katherine.

　　　　　Zero trip meter on the Buntine Hwy at Kalkaringi. Kalkaringi store on left. Proceed in easterly direction towards Katherine. 0.0 km ▲

```
GPS   S:17 26.860 E:130 50.049
UTM   52K 694791E 8069986N
```

REVERSE DIRECTIONS START

FOLLOWING PAGES
Campsite beside the Wickham River

115

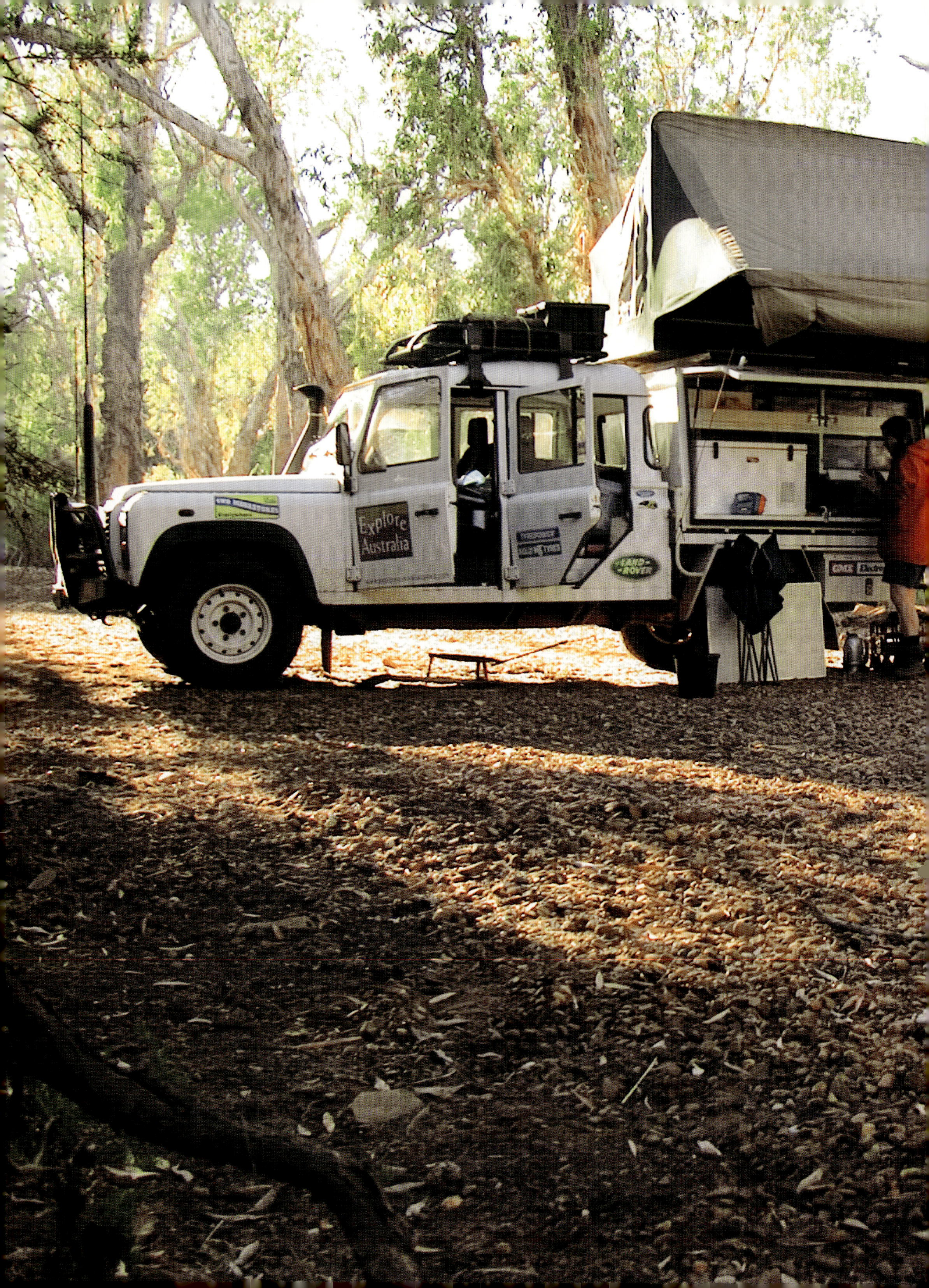
Explore Australia
LAND-ROVER

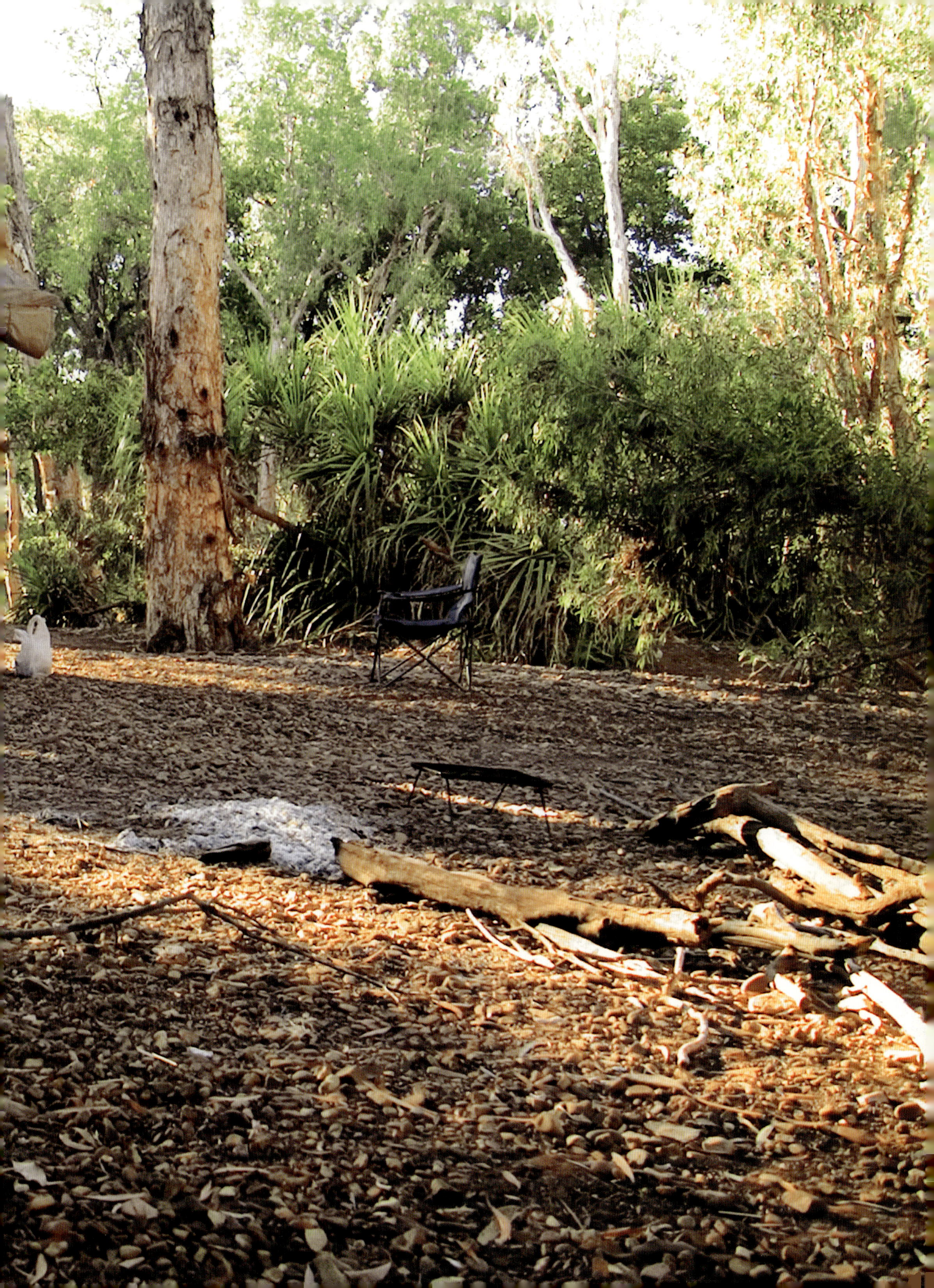

Canning Stock Route

An inscription on the remains of an old well bucket marks the turn-off to Well 34

WILUNA ◀▶ HALLS CREEK 1789.2 KM
1. WILUNA ◁▷ KUNAWARRITJI 984.6 km *(difficult)*
2. KUNAWARRITJI ◁▷ HALLS CREEK 804.6 km *(difficult)*

WHEN TO GO April–September   **TIME** 16–20 days

The Canning Stock Route exists due to the vision and efforts of one man, Alfred Canning, who surveyed the route in 1906–07 and led the well-sinking expedition during 1908–10. The appeal of the route today is its captivating mix of isolation, history, mystery and folklore. It is Australia's premier four-wheel-drive adventure.

Traversing the Little Sandy, Great Sandy and Tanami deserts, the Canning Stock Route (CSR) is a track of epic proportions, winding its way between 54 stock watering points comprising handcrafted wells, ancient springs and natural soaks that stretch north–south across more than half the continent. Waves of wind-sculptured dunes are a dominant feature of the landscape and between Wiluna and Billiluna you will cross about 700 of these sandhills, some as high as 15 metres. If you do all the suggested side trips, you will cross some 200 additional dunes. With tyre pressure appropriately reduced most high-clearance, four-wheel-drive vehicles comfortably complete the stock route with little trouble. Interspersed with the dune country are rocky plains, red sandstone hills, shimmering dry salt lakes and potentially boggy claypans.

Wiluna at the southern end of the route and Halls Creek in the north provide all services and supplies. Fuel and limited supplies are also available from the Aboriginal communities at Kunawarritji and Billiluna.

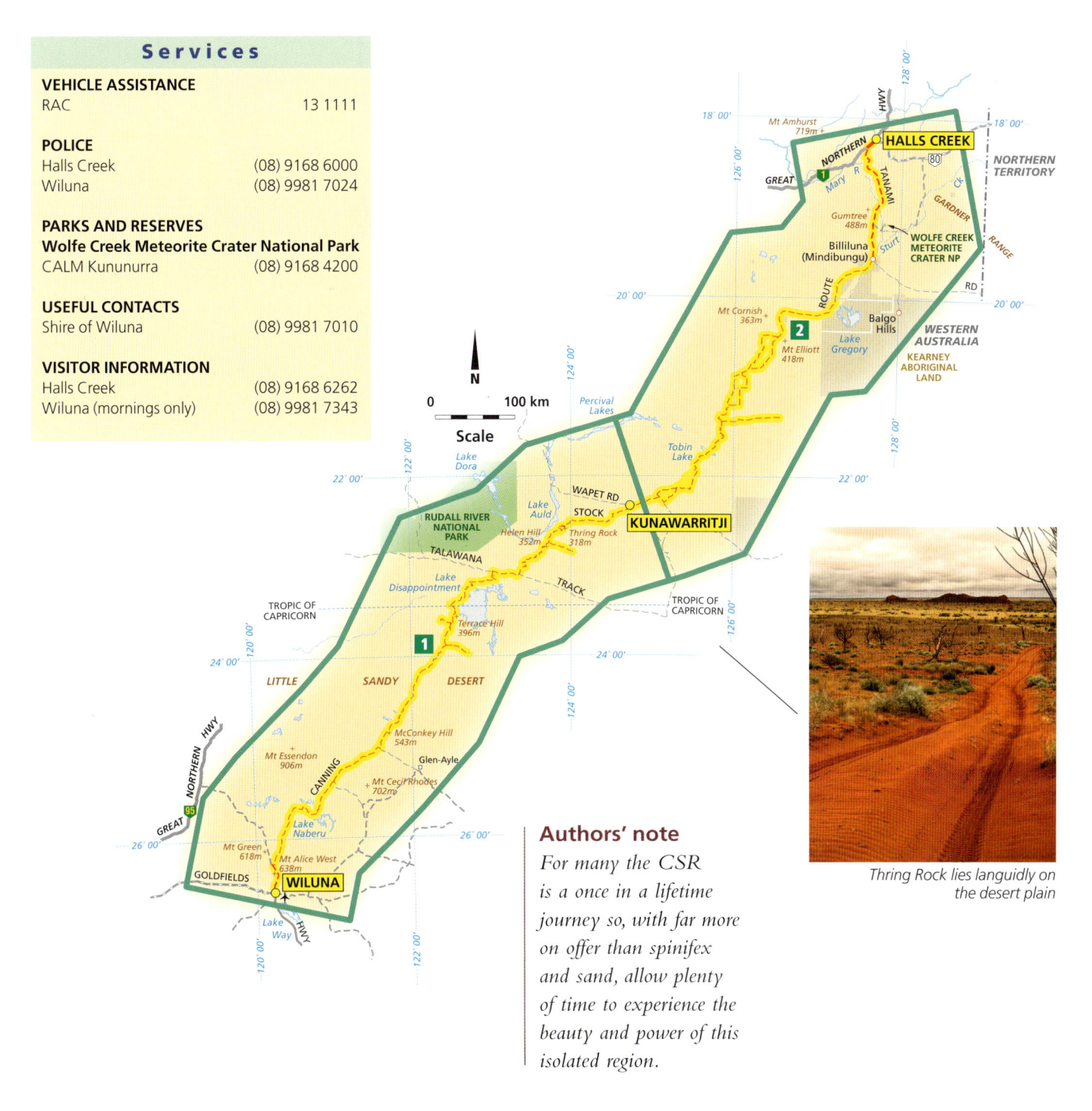

CANNING STOCK ROUTE

Services

VEHICLE ASSISTANCE
RAC   13 1111

POLICE
Halls Creek   (08) 9168 6000
Wiluna   (08) 9981 7024

PARKS AND RESERVES
Wolfe Creek Meteorite Crater National Park
CALM Kununurra   (08) 9168 4200

USEFUL CONTACTS
Shire of Wiluna   (08) 9981 7010

VISITOR INFORMATION
Halls Creek   (08) 9168 6262
Wiluna (mornings only)   (08) 9981 7343

Authors' note

For many the CSR is a once in a lifetime journey so, with far more on offer than spinifex and sand, allow plenty of time to experience the beauty and power of this isolated region.

Thring Rock lies languidly on the desert plain

Town Facilities

	Fuel: D/P/A	Mechanical repairs	Tyre repairs	Public telephone	Public toilets	Shop/supplies	Gas refills	Ice	Visitor information	Post office	Medical centre	Police	Meals	Motel	Hotel	Cabins	Caravan park	Camping
Billiluna	D/P	•	•	•	•		•			•								
Halls Creek	D/P/A	•	•	•	•	•	•	•	•	•	•	•	•	•	•	•	•	•
Kunawarritji	D/P	•	•	•	•											•		•
Wiluna	D/P	•	•	•	•	•	•	•	•	•	•	•	•		•	•	•	•

119

CANNING STOCK ROUTE

1 WILUNA ◄► KUNAWARRITJI 984.6 KM

Start point
Wiluna

Road atlas
352 A1, 358 E1, 359 F8

Total distance
1197.0 km (includes route-directed side trips)

Standard
Difficult

Time
8–10 days

Longest distance no PD (includes all options)
1344.3 km (Wiluna to Kunawarritji)
969.7 km (Wiluna to Well 23 fuel dump)

Topographic maps
Auslig 1:250 000 series: *Wiluna*; *Nabberu*; *Stanley*; *Trainor*; *Gunanya*; *Runton*; *Tabletop*; *Ural*

Other useful information
- Capricorn Roadhouse at Newman supplies fuel in 200-litre drums to dump site near Well 23; arrangement and prepayment required 6–8 weeks in advance, tel. (08) 9175 1535.
- Kunawarritji community store has petrol and diesel and a range of supplies; open Monday–Friday 8am–5pm (during peak visitor season) and Saturday 9am–12noon (closed Sunday and public holidays), tel. (08) 9176 9040; accepts cash and EFTPOS.
- Access to CSR possible at Well 5 from Granite Peak station, tel. (08) 9981 2983, and at Well 9 from Glen-Ayle station, tel. (08) 9981 2990 or (08) 9981 2989; fee applies and you must contact ahead of time (access is to or from Carnegie station on Gunbarrel Hwy).

Aboriginal rock art at Killagurra Gorge

- *Canning Stock Route: A Traveller's Guide* by Ronele and Eric Gard provides useful information and interesting history.
- Australian Geographic travel guide series: *The Canning Stock Route*.
- Wildflowers are prolific during late winter and spring so pack a wildflower identification book.

Description
In addition to the long-distance remote desert travel through a striking and ever-changing landscape, most people who traverse the Canning Stock Route do so to visit and marvel at the wells that were sunk along 1400 kilometres of the original route at intervals of about 24 kilometres. Many of these have fallen into a state of decay, their waters stagnant, with little remaining apart from rusting troughs and rotting timber, while others have been restored by various groups and provide good water for travellers.

This first section of the trek from Wiluna (see maps on pages 125 and 130–1) probably holds more scenic riches than the northern stretch beyond Kunawarritji. The route is generally straightforward until you reach Well 10, where you enter the Little Sandy Desert proper and soon encounter the first CSR sand dune. However, before this there are delightful places to visit, including the picturesque waterhole at Windich Springs and a historic fort at Well 9. Windich Springs (No. 4A Water) and Pierre Spring (Well 6) provide sheltered camping amid towering river red gums, and Well 3 also offers camping among shady trees. A climb to the top of Ingebong Hills rewards you with fantastic views and some intriguing rock strata running at unusual angles. The ubiquitous spinifex on the interdunal flats is broken in places by flowering hakea and grevillea, and elsewhere there are mulga, bloodwood and acacia species.

Once into the dunes of the Little Sandy Desert your speed of travel slows, allowing you to enjoy the scenery of low rolling sandhills. Traditionally, the dune crossings were thought to be less challenging if driving north–south, but these days few travellers differentiate and equal numbers traverse the CSR in both directions.

Travellers heading along the Canning early in the season (April–May) usually encounter prolific spinifex growth in the centre of the track. The seeds can clog your radiator and a hot exhaust can set the spinifex alight and ignite your vehicle. You need to take precautions against these dangers and make regular checks of your vehicle's undercarriage (see Advice and warnings).

In the Calvert Range and nearby Durba Hills superb natural art galleries are evidence of early Aboriginal occupation of the region. The optional side trip to the Calvert Range is highly recommended and good bush campsites are scattered around the base of the range. Within the crumbling sandstone ridges of the Durba Hills are many hidden delights. A hike to Canning's Cairn gives unsurpassed views westwards across desert dunes and mulga scrub. It is hard to resist a rest day or two at delightful Durba Springs, a well-protected campsite set in a wide gorge with large shady white gums, although it does get busy during the peak season. The rock walls of this gorge and the towering red sandstone escarpments of Killagurra Gorge are decorated with Aboriginal rock art featuring human and animal figures.

A detour to the scenic Diebil Hills and a short walk will take you to Diebil Spring, if time and fuel reserves allow, before crossing the Tropic of Capricorn and coming to the huge shimmering salt-encrusted expanse of Lake Disappointment. The western shore of the lake is fringed by forests of desert oak that provide ideal sites for bush camping. North of the lake, at Well 23 on the Talawana Track, there is a fuel dump for those who have prearranged delivery from Capricorn Roadhouse at Newman (see Other useful information).

Further north you can stretch your legs with a short climb up Thring Rock for more good views. Kunawarritji Aboriginal community just south of Well 33 is roughly the halfway point along the Canning and offers fuel and limited supplies.

Dry creek bed near Biella Spring

Advice and warnings
- This is remote country and thorough planning and preparation are required. You must be self-sufficient and carry enough fuel, water and supplies for the trip.
- Track varies from soft sand dunes to compacted earth, heavy corrugations and rocky sections. Sometimes sections of track can be closed due to floodwaters, which may be present for many years. In most places flood bypasses are in place. After rain, check all claypans prior to crossing them. At Lake Disappointment caution is required at Savory Creek crossing – it is best to walk the crossing first. Contact the Shire of Wiluna, tel. (08) 9981 7010, to check road conditions.
- Route runs through pastoral property south of Well 10 so do not deviate from track.
- Watch out for oncoming traffic over sand dunes – mount a high-flying red flag to your vehicle.
- *Spinifex warning.* Early season travellers should install radiator guards (fine mesh screens) to protect against spinifex seeds, which can quickly clog the radiator and cause your vehicle to overheat. In addition, it is sensible to check your vehicle's undercarriage at regular intervals, especially around the exhaust, for any build-up of spinifex. Hot exhaust pipes can easily ignite the resin in the spinifex causing a fire. On the few occasions that this has occurred along the CSR the vehicles have been burned out within two minutes! Petrol powered vehicles tend to be the more susceptible but modern turbo diesel vehicles often have catalytic converters, which run quite hot.
- Standard road tyres or all-terrain tyres are suitable. Tyre pressure should be lowered to allow for better ride comfort over corrugations and for ease of crossing sand dunes.
- Towing any sort of trailer or caravan along the CSR is not recommended.
- Bush camping only along the route with no facilities. All campers must be self-sufficient.
- There are no rubbish bins along the CSR so your rubbish must be carried out.
- Ensure that toilet paper is completely burned and/or buried in a hole at least 30 cm deep.
- Bucket and long rope should be carried to access water from wells. To preserve this water do not camp within 100 m of wells; always close lids on wells; do not wash or use detergents or soaps near wells; and do not remove any well equipment. Boil water or use Puritabs.
- Long distance communications equipment, such as a satellite phone or HF radio, should be carried. Use a UHF radio, generally channel 40, to make contact with other travellers on the stock route.

Permits and bookings
- No permits required to travel the CSR.
- Bookings recommended for motel accommodation at Club Hotel Wiluna, tel. (08) 9981 7012.

Alfred Canning Establishes the Canning Stock Route

The man who achieved the seemingly impossible task of establishing the world's longest stock route, a 1700-kilometre droving track through the heart of Western Australia's desert country, was surveyor Alfred Wernam Canning.

Following the West's mining boom in the 1890s, Kimberley and Northern Territory pastoralists wanted a stock route that allowed access to burgeoning southern markets. If they could reach the railhead at Meekatharra, 181 kilometres west of Wiluna, cattle could be trucked to the abattoirs near Perth.

Reports from early explorers to the region were unfavourable. In 1856 Augustus Gregory skirted the northern edges of the Great Sandy Desert but turned back in dismay when he reached a vast wasteland of dry salt lakes. Travelling by camel in 1873, Peter Warburton led an expedition from Alice Springs across the Great Sandy Desert to the north-west coast, a 6500-kilometre nightmare trek that lasted over eight months. In 1874 John Forrest led a party that made a west–east crossing from Geraldton to northern South Australia. He explored the southern reaches of today's Canning, but thought the area 'most wretched'.

In 1896 Lawrence Wells' Calvert Expedition was charged with opening a stock route in Western Australia's north. The party trekked from Geraldton to Lake Augusta (east of Wiluna), then headed north-east. At Separation Well the group split in two, agreeing to meet at Joanna Spring over 320 kilometres due north. Two men perished in the desert and Wells was fortunate to make it to the Fitzroy River. The task that had been set was considered hopeless. A young Scottish adventurer, David Carnegie, took up the challenge. In 1896–97 he made an extraordinary journey from Coolgardie to Halls Creek and back. Disappointed at what he found, Carnegie reported that a droving route was not feasible.

The construction ... was carried out by hand, taking two years to complete

Born in country Victoria in 1860, Alfred Canning had joined the New South Wales Department of Lands as a cadet surveyor. In 1884 he married Edith Maude Butcher in Sydney, staying on with the Department of Lands for ten more years before joining the Western Australian Department of Lands and Surveys as a licensed surveyor in 1893. In 1901 he was entrusted with surveying the location of a rabbit proof fence that was to run from Starvation Harbour, 90 kilometres east of Esperance on the south coast, to Cape Keraudren, east of Port Hedland. This project, covering 1890 kilometres over three years, became one of the longest continuous surveys undertaken anywhere in

Well 26 has been completely restored to its original condition

Killagurra Springs, one of several natural water sources along the Canning

the world at the time. Canning almost lost his life when his camel became exhausted 64 kilometres from Wallal telegraph station. Canning continued on foot, and after reaching the telegraph station and sending his telegram to Perth, set off again on foot back to his camp, some 129 kilometres away, in soaring temperatures.

In March 1906 the Western Australia Surveyor General requested that Canning head a party to survey a possible stock route from Wiluna to Halls Creek. The tough and tenacious Canning, by this time an excellent bushman, set off with eight men (including an Aboriginal tracker), 23 camels and two horses. The survey took 13 months to complete, at the end of which time Canning's report was favourable, advocating a series of wells be sunk at intervals along the route to water stock. Like Carnegie's expedition, the 1906 party would probably have perished without the help of local Aboriginal people, who were coerced into revealing water sources in what seemed to be a waterless barren landscape.

Canning's survey was followed up almost immediately with the construction of 51 watering points, mostly wells. The construction party, including 20 men, 62 camels, 400 goats for meat and milk, and two horses, was again headed by Canning and the work was carried out by hand, taking two years to complete.

The first mob of 150 cattle was taken down the CSR in 1911 from Halls Creek. The stock route disrupted Aboriginal lives and hostilities often erupted between the two cultures and a series of murders took place during the early years. A number of stockmen, including three members of the first droving party, met their fate along the route. Grave-site locations are detailed in the route directions.

Incredibly, at the age of 70, Alfred Canning was asked by the Public Works Department to complete a project reconditioning all CSR wells, as the contractor William Snell had failed to finish the job. On 23 March 1930 Canning and his party set off from Wiluna only to find Snell's work unsatisfactory. The new team started from scratch, reconditioning nearly all 51 watering points, and sinking three new wells, before finally returning to Perth on 20 August 1931.

Alfred Canning died on 22 May 1936 at the age of 76. As a tribute to one of Australia's greatest surveyors the Department of Mines commissioned a bronze bust of Canning, now in the offices of the Department of Lands and Surveys in Perth. Canning is buried in Perth's Karrakatta cemetery. The last mob of cattle was taken down the CSR in 1958. A four-wheel-drive party completed the first vehicle traverse in 1968.

CANNING STOCK ROUTE

ROUTE DIRECTIONS

▼ 0.0 km Zero trip meter in Wiluna at crossroads. SP: Gunbarrel Hwy, on right, and SP: Wells St, on left. Proceed in northerly direction along SP: Wotton Street.

Crossroads in Wiluna. SP: Gunbarrel Hwy, on left, and SP: Wells St, on right. 39.0 km ▲

GPS S:26 35.672 E:120 13.475
UTM 51J 223591E 7055474N

(3.8 km)

▼ 3.8 km Road junction. CSA. Track on left.
Track on left leads 3.5 km to Well 1, GPS S:26 33.476 E:120 10.873 UTM 51J 219180E 7059436N, first well sunk by Canning's party in 1908 and dug to depth of 45 feet (13.7 m) with capacity of 4125 gallons (18 752 litres) and replenishment rate of 580 gallons (2636 litres) per hour.

Road junction. CSA. Track on right to Well 1. 35.2 km ▲

GPS S:26 33.705 E:120 12.938
UTM 51J 222620E 7059088N

(6.6 km)

▼ 10.4 km Road junction. CSA. Road on left SP: North Pool.
Road on left leads 10.0 km to North Pool (Water 1A), GPS S:26 26.772 E:120 08.868 UTM 51J 215574E 7071746N, and small bush campsite.

Road junction. CSA. Road on right SP: North Pool. 28.6 km ▲

(28.6 km)

▼ 39.0 km Road junction.

Zero trip meter at T-junction. TL. 0.0 km ▲

GPS S:26 16.752 E:120 11.186
UTM 51J 219025E 7090340N

Rusting remains of stock watering troughs are a common sight at old wells

▼ 0.0 km Zero trip meter at road junction. TR. SP: Canning Stock Route Heritage Trail.
Track deteriorates from here.

T-junction. 71.1 km ▲
Maintained road from here.

(2.3 km)

▼ 2.3 km Well 2 on right. CSA.
Well 2 was dug to depth of 65 feet (19.8 m) with capacity of 4200 gallons (19 093 litres) and replenishment rate of 600 gallons (2727 litres) per hour.

Well 2 on left. CSA. 68.8 km ▲

GPS S:26 16.973 E:120 12.463
UTM 51J 221160E 7089978N

(37.3 km)

▼ 39.6 km Track junction. CSA. Track on right SP: CSR Well 2A 60 m.
Track on right leads 60 m to Well 2A (The Granites), a large rock pool and last well sunk by Canning's party on their return to Wiluna in 1910. Well 2A, GPS S:26 00.308 E:120 19.237 UTM 51J 231805E 7120997N, was blasted out of solid rock and is 16 feet long by 10 feet wide by 10 feet deep (4.8 x 3 x 3 m) with capacity of 9600 gallons (43 642 litres).

Track junction. CSA. Track on left SP: CSR Well 2A 60 m. 31.5 km ▲

(31.5 km)

▼ 71.1 km Track junction.

Zero trip meter at track junction. CSA. Track on left. 0.0 km ▲
Track on left leads 0.1 km to Well 3.

GPS S:25 46.511 E:120 24.765
UTM 51J 240528E 7146664N

▼ 0.0 km Zero trip meter at track junction. CSA. Track on right.
Track on right leads 0.1 km to **Well 3** and **bush camping area**, comprising a number of small sites among shady trees. Well 3, GPS S:25 46.541 E:120 24.819 UTM 51J 240619E 7146611N, was dug to depth of 43 feet (13.1 m) with a 39-foot 6-inch (12-m) shaft, with capacity of 8475 gallons (38 528 litres) and replenishment rate of 130 gallons (590 litres) per hour. Water available.

Track junction. 76.6 km ▲

(4.2 km)

▼ 4.2 km Creek crossing.

Creek crossing. 72.4 km ▲

(2.2 km)

▼ 6.4 km Windmill and tank on right. This is White Well. Stockyards on left. CSA.

White Well on left and stockyards on right. CSA. 70.2 km ▲

(0.2 km)

▼ 6.6 km Creek crossing.

Creek crossing. 70.0 km ▲

(5.1 km)

▼ 11.7 km Windmill, tank and stockyards on right. This is Corners Well. CSA.

WILUNA ◀▶ KUNAWARRITJI

Windich Springs
Named in 1874 by explorer John Forrest after an Aboriginal guide in his party, this scenic waterhole surrounded by river red gums attracts masses of birds, including pink and grey galahs, corellas and zebra finches. In the spring the surrounding plains are carpeted with wildflowers such as yellow oval-leaf cassia, pink mulla mulla and white flannel bush.

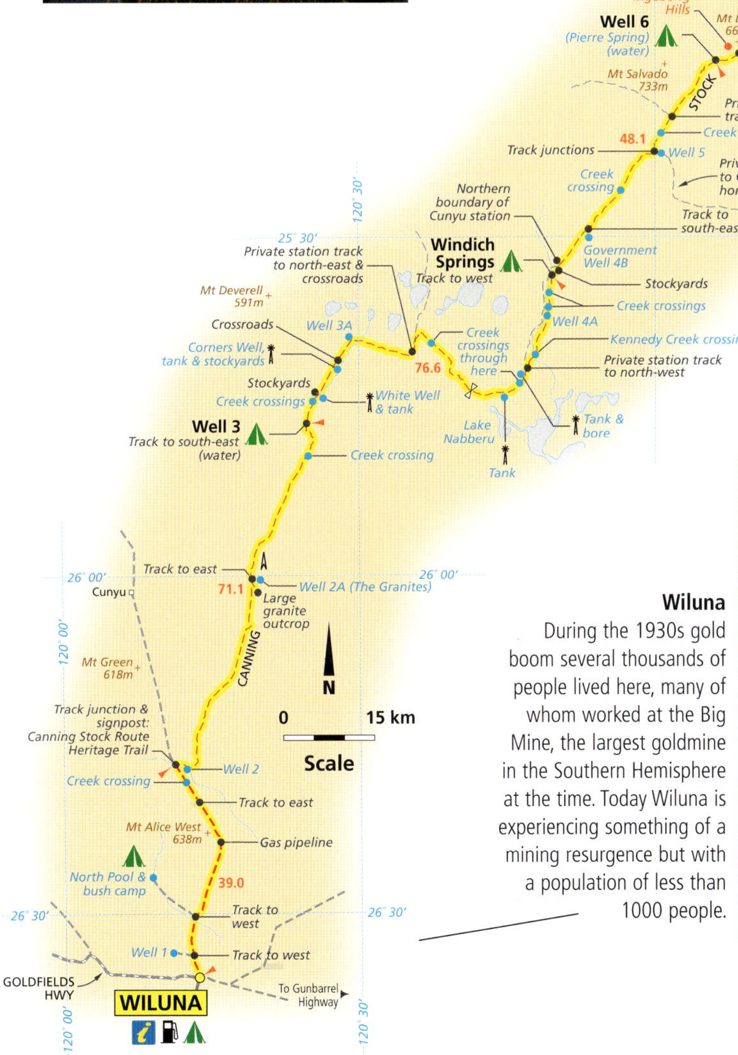

Well Water
Water is available at some wells, indicated on the maps by (water) and in the route directions by (water available). Water quality varies from year to year so boil it before drinking or cooking.

Wiluna
During the 1930s gold boom several thousands of people lived here, many of whom worked at the Big Mine, the largest goldmine in the Southern Hemisphere at the time. Today Wiluna is experiencing something of a mining resurgence but with a population of less than 1000 people.

North Pool near Wiluna

125

CANNING STOCK ROUTE

Corners Well on left. CSA. **64.9 km** ▲

(0.2 km)

▼ **11.9 km** Crossroads. CSA. SP: CSR.

Crossroads. CSA. SP: CSR. **64.7 km** ▲

(4.6 km)

▼ **16.5 km** Well 3A on left. CSA.

Well 3A, sunk by William Snell's party in 1929, was dug to depth of 40 feet (12.2 m) with capacity of 1800 gallons (8182 litres) and replenishment rate of 100 gallons (454 litres) per hour. This part of route leads through Cunyu station so stay on main track. No camping until Windich Springs.

Well 3A on right. CSA. **60.1 km** ▲

GPS S:25 39.167 E:120 29.275
UTM 51J 247811E 7160373N

(11.5 km)

▼ **28.0 km** Y-junction. KL. Track on right SP: Private Station Track.

Track junction. CSA. SP: CSR. Track on left. **48.6 km** ▲

(0.6 km)

▼ **28.6 km** Crossroads. CSA. SP: CSR.

Crossroads. CSA. SP: CSR. **48.0 km** ▲

(8.0 km)

▼ **36.6 km** Creek crossing.

Creek crossing. **40.0 km** ▲

(2.3 km)

▼ **38.9 km** Creek crossing.

Creek crossing. **37.7 km** ▲

(7.8 km)

▼ **46.7 km** Gate. SP: Please shut gate.

Gate. SP: Please shut gate. **29.9 km** ▲

GPS S:25 43.705 E:120 41.343
UTM 51J 268157E 7152361N

(5.5 km)

▼ **52.2 km** Creek crossing.

Creek crossing. **24.4 km** ▲

(0.8 km)

▼ **53.0 km** Windmill and tank on right. CSA.

Windmill and tank on left. CSA. **23.6 km** ▲

(4.9 km)

▼ **57.9 km** Windmill and tank on left. CSA.

Windmill and tank on right. CSA. **18.7 km** ▲

(1.4 km)

▼ **59.3 km** Y-junction. KR. SP: CSR. Track on left SP: Private Station Track.

Track junction. CSA. Track on right SP: Private Station Track. **17.3 km** ▲

(2.9 km)

▼ **62.2 km** Cross Kennedy Creek.

Cross Kennedy Creek. **14.4 km** ▲

GPS S:25 40.491 E:120 47.907
UTM 51J 279037E 7158484N

(7.1 km)

▼ **69.3 km** Well 4A on left. CSA.

Well 4A, sunk by William Snell's party in 1929, was dug to depth of 33 feet (10 m) with capacity of 2000 gallons (9092 litres) and replenishment rate of 5000 gallons (22 730 litres) per hour.

Well 4A on right. CSA. **7.3 km** ▲

GPS S:25 37.066 E:120 49.123
UTM 51J 280967E 7164842N

(1.5 km)

▼ **70.8 km** Creek crossing.

Creek crossing. **5.8 km** ▲

(2.7 km)

▼ **73.5 km** Creek crossing.

Creek crossing. **3.1 km** ▲

(3.1 km)

▼ **76.6 km** Track junction.

Zero trip meter at track junction. CSA. Track on right SP: Windich Springs. **0.0 km** ▲

Track on right leads short distance to Windich Springs and good bush camping.

GPS S:25 33.446 E:120 49.583
UTM 51J 281628E 7171539N

▼ **0.0 km** Zero trip meter at track junction. CSA. Track on left SP: Windich Springs.

Track on left leads short distance to Windich Springs (No. 4A Water), GPS S:25 33.432 E:120 49.541 UTM 51J 281557E 7171563N. **Windich Springs** has good **bush camping** beside scenic waterhole rimmed by river red gums.

Track junction. **48.1 km** ▲

(1.4 km)

▼ **1.4 km** Cattle yards on right. CSA.

Cattle yards on left. CSA. **46.7 km** ▲

(0.8 km)

▼ **2.2 km** Sign on left. Northern boundary of Cunyu station. CSA.

Sign on right. From here track travels through Cunyu station. Stay on main track. Camping only at Windich Springs. CSA. **45.9 km** ▲

(8.1 km)

▼ **10.3 km** Track junction. CSA. Track on right SP: CSR Govt 4B 900 m.

Track on right leads 0.8 km to Government Well 4B, GPS S:25 29.692 E:120 53.116 UTM 51J 287435E 7178566N, sunk by William Snell's party in 1929 and dug to depth of 42 feet (12.8 m) with capacity of 2500 gallons (11 365 litres).

Track junction. CSA. Track on left SP: CSR Govt 4B 900 m. **37.8 km** ▲

GPS S:25 29.444 E:120 53.190
UTM 51J 287552E 7179025N

(18.2 km)

▼ **28.5 km** Track junction. CSA. Track on right.

Track on right leads 0.7 km to Well 5, GPS S:25 22.603 E:121 00.253 UTM 51J 299199E 7191839N, deepest well along CSR and dug to depth of 104 feet 6 inches (31.8 m) with additional shaft of 2 feet 6 inches wide by 5 feet high and 28 feet long (0.8 x 1.5 x 8.5 m) with capacity of 1200 gallons (5455 litres) and replenishment rate of 60 gallons (272 litres) per hour. Track past Well 5 is private access track to Granite Peak homestead. Access fee applies to use this track (see Other useful information, page 120).

    Track junction. CSA. Track on left to Well 5. 19.6 km ▲

GPS S:25 22.599 E:120 59.845
UTM 51J 298514E 7191836N

(0.3 km)

▼ **28.8 km** Crossroads. CSA. Track on right leads 0.7 km to Well 5.

    Crossroads. CSA. 19.3 km ▲
    Track on left leads 0.7 km to Well 5.

(3.4 km)

▼ **32.2 km** Creek crossing.

    Creek crossing. 15.9 km ▲

(3.6 km)

▼ **35.8 km** Track junction. CSA. Private station track on left.

    Track junction. CSA. Private station track on right. 12.3 km ▲

(12.3 km)

▼ **48.1 km** Track junction.

    Zero trip meter at track junction. CSA. Well 6 on left. Track on right. 0.0 km ▲
    Track on right leads to camping area.

GPS S:25 14.453 E:121 05.967
UTM 51J 308569E 7207025N

▼ **0.0 km** Zero trip meter at track junction. CSA. Well 6 on right and track on left.

Track on left leads to **Well 6 camping area** beneath tall river red gums. Well 6 (Pierre Spring) was dug to depth of 11 feet (3.3 m) with capacity of 825 gallons (3750 litres) and replenishment rate of 1800 gallons (8182 litres) per hour. Well 6 was fully restored in July 1991. Water available.

    Track junction. 61.8 km ▲

(4.5 km)

▼ **4.5 km** Track junction. CSA. SP: CSR. Track on left SP: Ingebong Hills.

Track on left leads 0.3 km to carpark at base of Ingebong Hills. From carpark a short walk leads to top of hills, with some interesting rock formations and expansive views over surrounding plains. Best approach to summit is from north-east.

    Track junction. CSA. SP: CSR. Track on right SP: Ingebong Hills. 57.3 km ▲

(1.2 km)

▼ **5.7 km** Dome-shaped hill approximately 2.0 km to left of track is Mt Davis.

    Dome-shaped hill approximately 2.0 km to right of track is Mt Davis. 56.1 km ▲

(6.8 km)

▼ **12.5 km** Cross small sand dune.

    Cross small sand dune. 49.3 km ▲

(10.6 km)

Well 5 was sunk through 31 metres of solid rock

▼ **23.1 km** Track junction. CSA. Track on left.

Track on left leads 0.2 km to Well 7, situated among large, dense stand of mulga, providing good sheltered camping. Well 7, GPS S:25 09.498 E:121 17.426 UTM 51J 327693E 7216431N, was dug to depth of 70 feet (21.3 m) with capacity of 8250 gallons (37 505 litres) and replenishment rate of 160 gallons (727 litres) per hour.

    Track junction. CSA. Track on right leads to Well 7. 38.7 km ▲

GPS S:25 09.575 E:121 17.379
UTM 51J 327616E 7216288N

(5.0 km)

▼ **28.1 km** Willy Willy Bore on left. CSA.

    Willy Willy Bore on right. CSA. 33.7 km ▲

(1.6 km)

▼ **29.7 km** Track junction. CSA. Track on left.

    Y-junction. KL. SP: CSR. Track on right. 32.1 km ▲

(6.2 km)

▼ **35.9 km** Y-junction. KL. SP: CSR Well 8 200 m. Track on right.

    Track junction. CSA. Track on left. 25.9 km ▲

(0.2 km)

▼ **36.1 km** Well 8 on right. CSA. SP: CSR.

Well 8 was dug to depth of 60 feet (18.2 m) with capacity of 3450 gallons (15 684 litres) and replenishment rate of 550 gallons (2500 litres) per hour. Bush camping in vicinity.

    Well 8 on left. CSA. SP: CSR. 25.7 km ▲

GPS S: 25 06.359 E:121 23.211
UTM 51J 337344E 7222345N

(8.1 km)

▼ **44.2 km** Y-junction. KL. SP: CSR. Track on right.

    Track junction. CSA. Track on left. 17.6 km ▲

(8.8 km)

CANNING STOCK ROUTE

▼ 53.0 km   Creek crossing.

         Creek crossing.   8.8 km ▲

(5.7 km)

▼ 58.7 km   Creek crossing.

         Creek crossing.   3.1 km ▲

(0.9 km)

▼ 59.6 km   Track junction. CSA. SP: CSR. Track on left.

         Y-junction. KL. SP: CSR. Track on right.   2.2 km ▲

(2.2 km)

▼ 61.8 km   Track junction.

         Zero trip meter at track junction. TR. SP: CSR To Wiluna. On left is Well 9 and track to Forrest Fort.   0.0 km ▲

GPS   S:25 01.045 E:121 35.194
UTM   51J 357382E 7232380N

▼ 0.0 km   Zero trip meter at track junction. TL. SP: CSR To Halls Creek. Well 9 and Forrest Fort on right.

Well 9, GPS S:25 01.087 E:121 35.179 UTM 51J 357357E 7232302N, was dug to depth of 14 feet (4.2 m) with capacity of 900 gallons (4091 litres) and replenishment rate of 1360 gallons (6182 litres) per hour. Camping is possible in this vicinity, but do *not* camp near well as it is stock watering point. Please note this area is pastoral property so be sure to take your rubbish out. Forrest Fort is remains of stone 'fort' built in 1874 by explorer John Forrest and his party as protection against attacks from Aboriginal people.

         Track junction.   71.5 km ▲

(1.1 km)

▼ 1.1 km   Track junction. CSA. Track on right.

Track on right is private access track to Glen-Ayle station. This property, over 300 000 ha, was settled by the Ward family in late 1940s. Access fee applies (see Other useful information, page 120).

         Y-junction. KR. Track on left to Glen-Ayle station.   70.4 km ▲

(7.7 km)

▼ 8.8 km   Y-junction. KR. Track on left to Joes Bore.

Track now deteriorates as not maintained from here.

         Track junction. CSA. Track on right.   62.7 km ▲

         Track improves from here as generally maintained.

GPS   S:24 56.879 E:121 35.502
UTM   51J 357820E 7240075N

(2.5 km)

▼ 11.3 km   Creek crossing.

         Creek crossing.   60.2 km ▲

(10.4 km)

▼ 21.7 km   Well 10 on right. CSA.

Well 10, also known as Lucky Well, was dug to depth of 70 feet 6 inches (21.5 m), with additional right-angled shaft 12 feet long (3.6 m), and with capacity of 7275 gallons (33 072 litres) and replenishment rate of 250 gallons (1136 litres) per hour. Bush camping in this vicinity among mulga trees.

         Well 10 on left. CSA.   49.8 km ▲

GPS   S:24 51.134 E:121 39.165
UTM   51J 363879E 7250741N

(2.3 km)

▼ 24.0 km   Track junction. KR. Track on left.

Track on left leads to well-protected bush campsite among mulga trees.

         Track junction. CSA. Track on right to bush campsite.   47.5 km ▲

(1.3 km)

▼ 25.3 km   Hill on right of track with small cairn is McConkey Hill.

         Hill on left of track with small cairn is McConkey Hill.   46.2 km ▲

(3.1 km)

▼ 28.4 km   Cross first sand dune.

         Cross last sand dune.   43.1 km ▲

GPS   S:24 48.538 E:121 41.562
UTM   51J 367870E 7255572N

(8.4 km)

▼ 36.8 km   Well 11 and 'Notice to Travellers' sign on left. CSA.

Well 11 was dug to depth of 8 feet 6 inches (2.6 m) with capacity of 750 gallons (3409 litres) and replenishment rate of 4300 gallons (19 548 litres) per hour.

         Well 11 on right. CSA.   34.7 km ▲

GPS   S:24 44.946 E:121 44.038
UTM   51J 371980E 7262241N

(4.8 km)

▼ 41.6 km   Protected bush camping in this vicinity. CSA.

Bush campsites among mulga trees that offer good protection.

         Protected bush camping in this vicinity. CSA.   29.9 km ▲

(12.0 km)

▼ 53.6 km   Bush campsite on left. CSA.

         Bush campsite on right. CSA.   17.9 km ▲

(4.6 km)

▼ 58.2 km   Southern edge of Lake Aerodrome.

Track skirts around eastern edge of lake. Not realising dangers inherent in its surface, William Snell (see page 123) thought this lake might serve as an airstrip.

         Southern edge of Lake Aerodrome.   13.3 km ▲

GPS   S:24 40.263 E:121 49.658
UTM   51J 381378E 7270969N

(7.7 km)

▼ 65.9 km   Northern edge of Lake Aerodrome.

         Northern end of Lake Aerodrome.   5.6 km ▲

         Track skirts around eastern edge of lake.

(5.6 km)

▼ 71.5 km   Y-junction.

         Zero trip meter at Y-junction. KL. Track on right.   0.0 km ▲

         Track on right leads 0.5 km to Well 12.

GPS   S:24 35.617 E:121 52.678
UTM   51J 386402E 7279586N

▼ 0.0 km   Zero trip meter at Y-junction. KR. Track on left.

WILUNA ◀▶ KUNAWARRITJI

Bark of the mineritchie or red mulga (Acacia cyperophylla)

Track on left leads 0.5 km to Well 12 and bush campsite under desert oaks. Well 12, GPS S:24 35.651 E:121 52.361 UTM 51J 385867E 7279519N, was dug to depth of 25 feet (7.6 m) with capacity of 1800 gallons (8182 litres) and replenishment rate of 1250 gallons (5682 litres) per hour. Well 12 was fully restored in July 2003. Water available.

Y-junction. **71.1 km** ▲

(5.2 km)

▼ **5.2 km** Bush camping in this vicinity.
Numerous protected campsites in this vicinity among mulga trees.

Bush camping in this vicinity. **65.9 km** ▲

(20.8 km)

▼ **26.0 km** Track junction. TL. SP: Well 13 – 2 km. Track SO.
Track SO is continuation of main CSR and leads 1.3 km to join route directions at upcoming 29.7-km mark.

T-junction. TR. **45.1 km** ▲
Route rejoins main CSR at this junction.

(2.1 km)

▼ **28.1 km** Well 13 on left. CSA.
Well 13 bush camping among mulga trees in this vicinity. Area can get very boggy in wet conditions. Well 13 was dug to depth of 25 feet (7.6 m) with capacity of 1875 gallons (8523 litres) and replenishment rate of 1250 gallons (5682 litres) per hour.

Well 13 on right. CSA. SP: CSR. **43.0 km** ▲

GPS S:24 25.318 E:121 59.294
UTM 51J 397427E 7298680N

(1.6 km)

▼ **29.7 km** Track junction. CSA. SP: CSR. Track on right.
Route rejoins main CSR at this junction. Good sheltered camping amid mulga trees on right.

Track junction. TR. SP: Well 13 – 2 km. **41.4 km** ▲
Track on left.
Track on left is continuation of main CSR and leads 1.3 km to join route directions at upcoming 45.1-km mark.

(8.8 km)

▼ **38.5 km** Creek crossing.

Creek crossing. **32.6 km** ▲

(7.7 km)

▼ **46.2 km** Well 14 on right. CSA.
Well 14 was dug to depth of 50 feet 6 inches (15.4 m) with capacity of 4425 gallons (20 116 litres) and replenishment rate of 320 gallons (1454 litres) per hour.

Well 14 on left. CSA. **24.9 km** ▲

GPS S:24 17.144 E:122 03.193
UTM 51J 403913E 7313812N

(16.7 km)

▼ **62.9 km** Track junction. CSA. Track on left.
Track on left leads 0.3 km to parking area with short walk to top of rocky outcrop and lookout.

Track junction. CSA. Track on right. **8.2 km** ▲

(8.2 km)

▼ **71.1 km** Track junction.

Zero trip meter at track junction. KR. SP: **0.0 km** ▲
CSR. Track on left leads 0.2 km to Well 15.

GPS S:24 08.371 E:122 12.041
UTM 51J 418787E 7330095N

▼ **0.0 km** Zero trip meter at track junction. KL. Track SO.
Track SO leads 0.2 km to Well 15 and Joseph Edward Wilkins memorial. He was killed in 1936 by Aboriginal people 15 miles east of well. Well 15, GPS S:24 08.475 E:122 12.120 UTM 51J 418922E 7329904N, was dug to depth of 22 feet (6.7 m) with capacity of 1200 gallons (5455 litres) and replenishment rate of 1800 gallons (8182 litres) per hour. Bush camping near well. Water available.

Track junction. **46.2 km** ▲

(20.1 km)

▼ **20.1 km** Track junction. CSA. Track on left to bush campsite.

Track junction. CSA. Track on right to **26.1 km** ▲
bush campsite.

(2.6 km)

▼ **22.7 km** Short rocky section.

Short rocky section. **23.5 km** ▲

(0.2 km)

▼ **22.9 km** Bush campsite on right. CSA.

Bush campsite on left. CSA. **23.3 km** ▲

(15.3 km)

▼ **38.2 km** Track junction. CSA. Track on left SP: CSR Well 16 – 400 m.
Track on left leads 0.5 km to **Well 16** and **bush camping** on small site with some shelter. Well 16, GPS S:23 54.491 E:122 23.009 UTM 51K 437248E 7355802N, was dug to depth of 55 feet 6 inches (16.9 m) with capacity of 5475 gallons (24 889 litres) and replenishment rate of 240 gallons (1091 litres) per hour.

■ 129

CANNING STOCK ROUTE

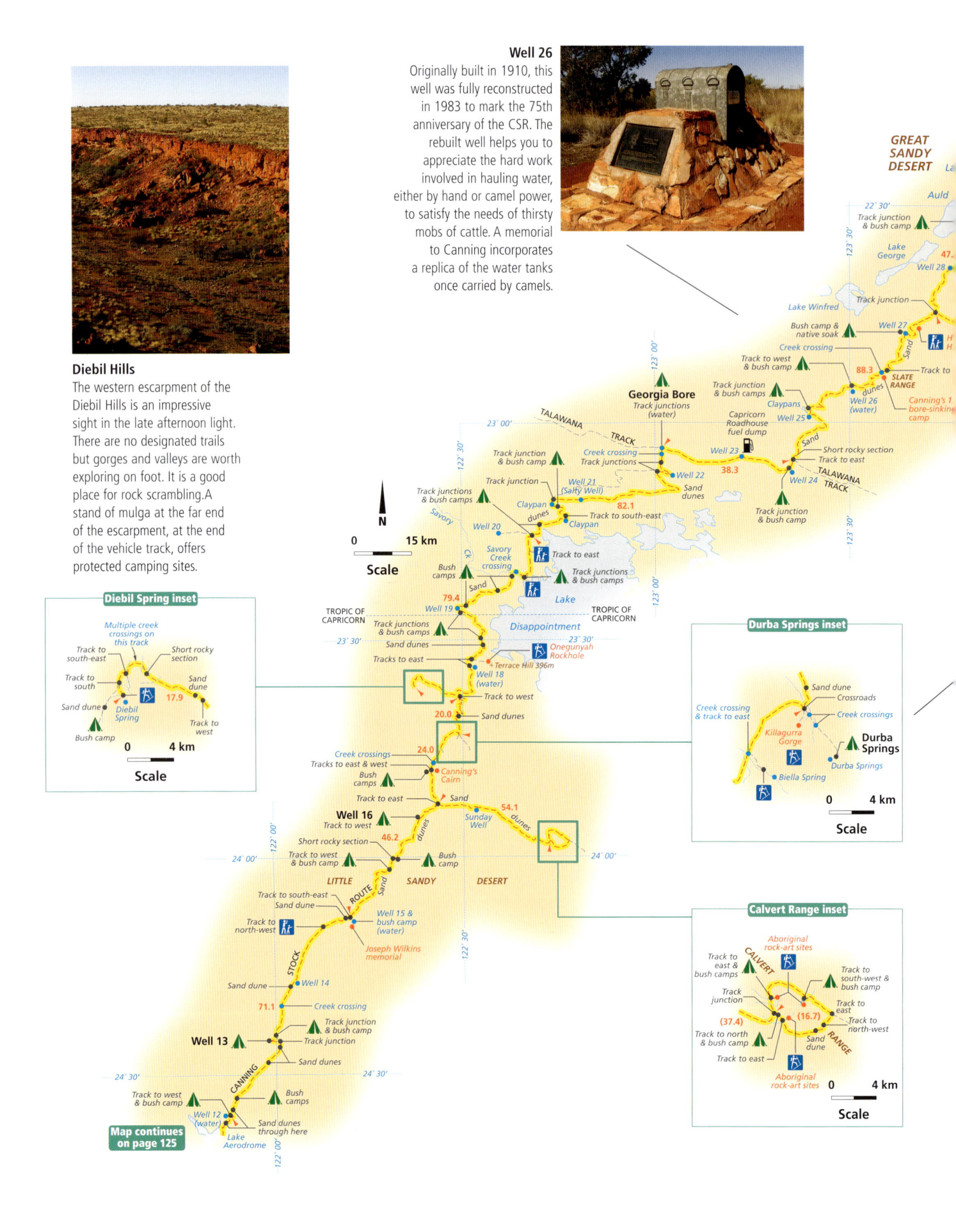

Diebil Hills

The western escarpment of the Diebil Hills is an impressive sight in the late afternoon light. There are no designated trails but gorges and valleys are worth exploring on foot. It is a good place for rock scrambling. A stand of mulga at the far end of the escarpment, at the end of the vehicle track, offers protected camping sites.

Well 26

Originally built in 1910, this well was fully reconstructed in 1983 to mark the 75th anniversary of the CSR. The rebuilt well helps you to appreciate the hard work involved in hauling water, either by hand or camel power, to satisfy the needs of thirsty mobs of cattle. A memorial to Canning incorporates a replica of the water tanks once carried by camels.

130

WILUNA ◀▶ KUNAWARRITJI

Lake Disappointment

The first European to discover the lake was Lawrence Wells, who trekked across its 50-kilometre expanse in 1896. The lake was named the following year by pastoralist and explorer Frank Hann after he failed to find good water. Hann had walked off his Lawn Hill station in the Gulf of Carpentaria, penniless from poor seasons and, with six Aboriginal companions and 67 horses, overlanded to Western Australia in search of suitable pastoral country. For today's four-wheel-drive explorers, the generally dry lake provides some magnificent views across to a horizon that on some days is indistinguishable from the shimmering heat haze and white salt.

Durba Springs

Once used by drovers to rest their cattle, the wide grass-covered valley at the entrance to Durba Springs is now a popular camping spot, protected by sandstone cliffs and shaded by white gums. Gorges dissect the surrounding Durba Hills, their rock walls adorned with Aboriginal rock art and carved initials of early stockmen.

Campsite Facilities

	Toilets	Disabled access	4WD access only	Off-road trailer	Off-road caravan	Drinking water	Fee payable	Ranger patrolled	BBQ/fireplace	Campfires prohibited	Picnic tables	Shelter shed	No rubbish disposal	Public phone	Shower	Bushwalking	Swimming	Swimming not advised	Fishing	Canoeing	Dogs allowed
Durba Springs		•	•							•											
Georgia Bore			•							•											
Well 3			•	•						•											
Well 6	•		•	•						•											
Well 13			•							•											
Well 16			•							•											
Well 30			•							•											
Well 31			•							•											
Windich Springs			•							•											

131

CANNING STOCK ROUTE

Western escarpment of the Calvert Range

	Track junction. CSA. Track on right SP: CSR Well 16 – 400 m.	8.0 km ▲
	GPS S:23 54.740 E:122 23.051 **UTM** 51K 437321E 7355343N	
	(8.0 km)	

▼ 46.2 km Track junction. Side trip to Calvert Range.

Calvert Range protects Aboriginal art sites, accessible from loop track around base of hills.

	Zero trip meter at track junction. KR. SP: CSR. Track on left to Calvert Range.	0.0 km ▲
	GPS S:23 52.698 E:122 26.007 **UTM** 51K 442321E 7359132N	

▶ **SIDE TRIP: Calvert Range**

▼ 0.0 km Zero trip meter at track junction on CSR. Turn into track leading east.

From here there are 8 sand dunes to cross before next reading.

(11.8 km)

▼ 11.8 km Sunday Well on right is 20 m from track behind some tea trees.

Two of Canning's 1906 survey party were taken to this well by an Aboriginal guide. They found good clear water after digging a 13-foot (3.9-m) shaft. As it was Sunday (6 July), it was named Sunday Well. From here there are 15 sand dunes to cross before next reading.

GPS S:23 53.116 E:122 32.104
UTM 51K 452669E 7358398N

(25.6 km)

▼ 37.4 km T-junction. TR.

Track loops around Calvert Range and returns to this junction on left.

GPS S:23 57.832 E:122 43.442
UTM 51K 471923E 7349746N

(0.3 km)

▼ 37.7 km Track junction. CSA. Track on left.

Track on left leads 0.1 km to bush campsite surrounded by high rock face.

(0.8 km)

▼ 38.5 km Track junction. CSA. Track on left.

Track on left leads 0.2 km to parking area. From here walk up creek bed for 150–200 m to find Aboriginal rock-art sites along both sides of creek, including human and animal figures and concentric circle engravings.

(3.7 km)

▼ 42.2 km Sand dune.

(1.0 km)

▼ 43.2 km Y-junction. KR.

(1.4 km)

▼ 44.6 km T-junction. TL. Track on right.

Track on right continues eastwards and to a number of other Aboriginal rock-art sites.

GPS S:23 57.869 E:122 46.446
UTM 51K 477017E 7349687N

(3.2 km)

▼ 47.8 km T-junction. TR. Track on left.

Track on left leads 0.4 km to carpark and Aboriginal rock-art sites depicting human and animal figures, and 0.6 km to bush campsite.

(4.9 km)

▼ 52.7 km Track junction. KR. Track on left and campsites on left.

Track on left leads to bush camping areas and 0.3 km to Aboriginal art gallery with human and animal figures.

GPS S:23 57.114 E:122 43.285
UTM 51K 471654E 7351071N

(1.4 km)

▼ 54.1 km Track junction. This is where loop started, at 37.4-km reading. TR to return to side trip start.

◀ **END SIDE TRIP**

WILUNA ◀▶ KUNAWARRITJI

▼ 0.0 km Zero trip meter at track junction. CSA. SP: CSR. Track on right to Calvert Range.
                    Track junction. See side trip to Calvert Range. 24.0 km ▲
(9.6 km)

▼ 9.6 km Track junction. CSA. Track on left.
Track on left leads 0.3 km to bush campsites among mulga trees.
                    Track junction. CSA. Track on right. 14.4 km ▲
(0.2 km)

▼ 9.8 km Y-junction. KL. SP: CSR. Track on right.
Track on right leads 0.6 km to carpark where walk up hill leads to Canning's Cairn. For easy access to summit follow small rock cairns uphill from large square rock in second carpark.
                    Y-junction. KR. SP: CSR. Track on left. 14.2 km ▲
GPS   S:23 48.006 E:122 25.041
UTM   51K 440646E 7367783N
(2.2 km)

▼ 12.0 km Creek crossing.
                    Creek crossing. 12.0 km ▲
(0.1 km)

▼ 12.1 km Creek crossing.
                    Creek crossing. 11.9 km ▲
(4.3 km)

▼ 16.4 km Creek crossing. Track junction over creek. CSA. Track on right.
Track on right leads 2.2 km to parking area, where half-hour walk leads up creek bed to pool of water that is Biella Spring.
                    Track junction. CSA over creek. Track on left to Biella Spring. 7.6 km ▲
GPS   S:23 45.089 E:122 26.453
UTM   51K 443022E 7373175N
(7.6 km)

▼ 24.0 km Crossroads.
                    Zero trip meter at crossroads. TR. SP: CSR. Track on left to Durba Springs. Track SO to Killagurra Gorge. 0.0 km ▲
GPS   S:23 43.036 E:122 29.379
UTM   51K 447979E 7376982N

▼ 0.0 km Zero trip meter at crossroads. TL. SP: CSR. Track SO to Durba Springs. Track on right to Killagurra Gorge.
Track SO leads 5.3 km to **Durba Springs camping area**, a large grassed spot surrounded by high walls of Durba Hills and well-shaded by tall gums and date palms. Durba Springs: GPS S:23 45.268 E:122 31.039 UTM 51K 450813E 7372873N. Track on right (at crossroads) leads 1.6 km to parking area (under large rock overhang) at Killagurra Gorge, GPS S:23 43.810 E:122 29.071 UTM 51K 447460E 7375552N. A walk leads from parking area up gorge to Aboriginal rock-art sites with paintings of human figures. Killagurra Gorge is a registered sacred site, still used for traditional ceremonies, so please respect the area.
                    Crossroads. 20.0 km ▲
(20.0 km)

▼ 20.0 km Track junction. Side trip to Diebil Spring.

                    Zero trip meter at track junction. KL. Track on right SP: Diebil Spring 18 km. 0.0 km ▲
GPS   S:23 37.849 E:122 29.656
UTM   51K 448415E 7386555N

▶ **SIDE TRIP: Diebil Spring**

▼ 0.0 km Zero trip meter at track junction on CSR. Turn onto track to west SP: Diebil Spring 18 km.
(6.3 km)

▼ 6.3 km Track junction. CSA. Track on left.
(0.9 km)

▼ 7.2 km Sand dune.
(4.0 km)

▼ 11.2 km Creek crossing.
(1.0 km)

▼ 12.2 km Short rocky descent.
(0.2 km)

▼ 12.4 km Creek crossing.
(0.5 km)

▼ 12.9 km Creek crossing.
(2.0 km)

▼ 14.9 km Creek crossing.
(0.1 km)

▼ 15.0 km Creek crossing.
(0.2 km)

Picturesque Durba Springs

CANNING STOCK ROUTE

▼ 15.2 km Track junction. TR. Track SO.
Track SO leads 0.8 km to rocky gully.
(1.4 km)

▼ 16.6 km Track junction. CSA. Track on right.
Track on right leads 4.2 km to campsite set among mulga trees. GPS S:23 37.752 E:122 21.155 UTM 51K 433962E 7386676N.
(1.0 km)

▼ 17.6 km Creek crossing.
(0.3 km)

▼ 17.9 km Carpark at end of gully. Return to side trip start.
From this carpark walk 520 m in south-easterly direction up gully to smaller gully on right where Diebil Spring is located at base of sheer rock face. Some rock hopping required to reach spring-fed pool amid large boulders: GPS S:23 36.734 E:122 22.561 UTM 51K 0436482E 7388714N.

| GPS S:23 36.452 E:122 22.529 |
| UTM 51K 436288E 7389085N |

◀ **END SIDE TRIP**

▼ 0.0 km Zero trip meter at track junction. KR. Track on left SP: Diebil Spring 18 km.
Track junction. See side trip to Diebil Spring. **79.4 km** ▲
(13.8 km)

▼ 13.8 km Track junction. CSA. Track on right SP: CSR Well 18 – 1 km.
Track on right leads 1.1 km to Well 18, GPS S:23 33.805 E:122 31.707 UTM 51K 451877E 7394029N, dug to depth of 16 feet (4.8 m) with capacity of 1275 gallons (5796 litres) and replenishment rate of 2000 gallons (9092 litres) per hour. Water available.
Track junction. CSA. Track on left SP: CSR Well 18 – 1 km. **65.6 km** ▲

| GPS S:23 33.604 E:122 31.162 |
| UTM 51K 450949E 7394397N |

(3.0 km)

▼ 16.8 km Track junction. CSA. Track on right.
Views of Terrace Hill can be seen to south-east from track. Track on right leads 5.3 km to carpark and short walk to Onegunyah Rockhole and Aboriginal rock art.
Track junction. CSA. Track on left. **62.6 km** ▲
(8.2 km)

▼ 25.0 km Track junction. CSA. Track on left.
Track on left to bush campsite.
Track junction. CSA. Track on right. **54.4 km** ▲
(11.1 km)

▼ 36.1 km Cross Tropic of Capricorn.
Small plaque on left of track marks this point.
Cross Tropic of Capricorn. **43.3 km** ▲

| GPS S:23 26.495 E:122 31.013 |
| UTM 51K 450652E 7407513N |

(2.5 km)

▼ 38.6 km Track junction. CSA. Track on right.
Track on right to bush campsite.

Track junction. CSA. Track on left. **40.8 km** ▲
(1.2 km)

▼ 39.8 km Well 19. CSA.
Well 19 was dug to depth of 13 feet 6 inches (4.1 m) with capacity of 750 gallons (3409 litres) and replenishment rate of 1350 gallons (6137 litres) per hour.
Well 19. CSA. **39.6 km** ▲

| GPS S:23 25.606 E:122 29.325 |
| UTM 51K 447772E 7409143N |

(2.9 km)

▼ 42.7 km Bush campsite on right. CSA.
Bush campsite on left. CSA. **36.7 km** ▲
(12.1 km)

▼ 54.8 km Bush campsite on right under desert oaks. CSA.
Bush campsite on left. CSA. **24.6 km** ▲
(6.1 km)

▼ 60.9 km Small bush campsite on left. CSA.
Small bush campsite on right. CSA. **18.5 km** ▲
(0.9 km)

▼ 61.8 km Track junction. CSA. Track on left.
Track on left leads approximately 6 km to alternative crossing of Savory Creek, which can be used at times of high water.
Track junction. CSA. Track on right. **17.6 km** ▲
(1.2 km)

▼ 63.0 km Track junction. TL and cross Savory Creek.
Over creek, track turns to right. Savory Creek is an unexpectedly beautiful stretch of water in the middle of the desert.
Cross Savory Creek. **16.4 km** ▲
Over creek track junction. TR.

| GPS S:23 20.632 E:122 38.450 |
| UTM 51K 463286E 7418368 |

(2.8 km)

▼ 65.8 km Track junction. KL. Track on right.
Track on right follows creek around edge of Lake Disappointment to mouth of creek and 4.9 km to small headland with views across lake's vast expanse.
Track junction. CSA. Track on left. **13.6 km** ▲
(0.6 km)

▼ 66.4 km Track junction. KR. Track on left.
Track on left leads 0.1 km to bush campsite.
Track junction. KL. Track on right. **13.0 km** ▲
(2.1 km)

▼ 68.5 km Track junction. CSA. Track on left.
Track on left leads to bush campsite among desert oaks.
Track junction. CSA. Track on right. **10.9 km** ▲
(5.6 km)

▼ 74.1 km Track junction. KL. Track on right.
Track on right leads 2.8 km to parking area with good views over Lake Disappointment.
Track junction. KR. Track on left. **5.3 km** ▲
(5.3 km)

Salt build-up around the edge of Lake Disappointment

▼ 79.4 km   Track junction.

    Zero trip meter at track junction. CSA. Track on right SP: CSR Well 20 – 10 km.   **0.0 km** ▲

    GPS   S:23 15.565 E:122 40.990
    UTM   51K 467593E 7427727N

▼ 0.0 km   Zero trip meter at track junction. CSA. Track on left SP: CSR Well 20 – 10 km.

Track on left leads 9.4 km to Well 20, GPS S:23 15.230 E:122 35.806 UTM 51K 458754E 7428323N, dug to depth of 18 feet (5.5 m) with capacity of 750 gallons (3409 litres) and replenishment rate of 1350 gallons (6137 litres) per hour.

    Track junction.   **82.1 km** ▲

(0.4 km)

▼ 0.4 km   Bush campsite on right. CSA.

    Bush campsite on left. CSA.   **81.7 km** ▲

(2.1 km)

▼ 2.5 km   SP: Lake Disappointment, on right. CSA.

    SP: Lake Disappointment, on left. CSA.   **79.6 km** ▲

    GPS   S:23 15.191 E:122 42.115
    UTM   51K 469509E 7428421N

(2.2 km)

▼ 4.7 km   Track junction. CSA. Track on left.

Track on left leads 0.1 km to 2 small bush campsites underneath stand of desert oaks.

    Track junction. CSA. Track on right.   **77.4 km** ▲

(0.4 km)

▼ 5.1 km   SP: Lake Disappointment, on right. CSA.

    SP: Lake Disappointment, on left. CSA.   **77.0 km** ▲

(7.3 km)

▼ 12.4 km   Track skirts around eastern edge of claypan.

    End of claypan.   **69.7 km** ▲

(2.3 km)

▼ 14.7 km   Track junction. CSA. Track on right.

    Track junction. CSA. Track on left.   **67.4 km** ▲

(6.1 km)

▼ 20.8 km   Track junction. CSA. Track on right.

Track on right leads 0.1 km to small bush campsite among mulga trees.

    Track junction. CSA. Track on left.   **61.3 km** ▲

(2.0 km)

▼ 22.8 km   Track crosses large claypan.

If wet, diversion track runs around eastern edge of claypan. This diversion track was used at the time of field research.

    Track crosses large claypan.   **59.3 km** ▲

    GPS   S:23 11.289 E:122 44.082
    UTM   51K 472849E 7435627N

(1.9 km)

▼ 24.7 km   Track junction. TR. Track on left.

Track on left is original vehicle track.

    Track junction. TL. Track SO.   **57.4 km** ▲

(7.6 km)

▼ 32.3 km   Well 21. CSA.

Well 21, also known as 'Salty Well', was dug to depth of 51 feet (15.5 m) with capacity of 4500 gallons (20 457 litres) and replenishment rate of 150 gallons (681 litres) per hour.

    Well 21. CSA.   **49.8 km** ▲

    GPS   S:23 10.660 E:122 48.569
    UTM   51K 480501E 7436800N

(36.9 km)

▼ 69.2 km   T-junction. TR. Track on left.

Track on left is original vehicle track.

    Track junction. TL. Track SO.   **12.9 km** ▲

(3.8 km)

▼ 73.0 km   Track junction. TL. Track SO.

Track SO leads 0.4 km to Well 22, GPS S:23 07.237 E:123 02.540 UTM 51K 504334E 7443127N, dug to depth of 53 feet 6 inches (16.3 m) with capacity of 1575 gallons (7160 litres) and replenishment rate of 1000 gallons (4546 litres) per hour.

    Track junction. TR. Track on left to Well 22.   **9.1 km** ▲

    GPS   S:23 07.229 E:123 02.360
    UTM   51K 504027E 7443142N

(4.6 km)

▼ 77.6 km   Track junction. CSA. Track on left.

    Y-junction. KL. Track on right.   **4.5 km** ▲

(2.5 km)

▼ 80.1 km   Creek crossing.

    Creek crossing.   **2.0 km** ▲

(1.5 km)

▼ 81.6 km   Track junction. CSA. Track on left.

Track on left leads 0.3 km to **Georgia Bore** and **camping area**, an open spot beneath tall gum trees. GPS S:23 03.532 E:123 01.066 UTM 51K 501820E 7449964N. Water available.

    Track junction. CSA. Track on right to Georgia Bore.   **0.5 km** ▲

(0.5 km)

▼ 82.1 km   T-junction.

    Zero trip meter at track junction. TL. Track SO is Talawana Track.   **0.0 km** ▲

CANNING STOCK ROUTE

GPS	S:23 03.504 E:123 01.320
UTM	51K 502254E 7450015N

▼ 0.0 km Zero trip meter at T-junction. TR. SP: CSR. Track on left is Talawana Track.

From here to Well 23 track is heavily corrugated. Talawana Track on left leads to Rudall River National Park, Newman and the Marble Bar Rd. Talawana Track was built in 1963 by Len Beadell and his Gunbarrel Road Construction Party.

Track junction. 38.3 km ▲

(21.7 km)

▼ 21.7 km Track junction. CSA. Well 23 and track on left.

Well 23 was dug to depth of 19 feet (5.8 m) with capacity of 1275 gallons (5796 litres) and replenishment rate of 1450 gallons (6591 litres) per hour. Track on left leads 0.9 km to Capricorn Roadhouse fuel dump (see Other useful information, page 120).

Track junction. CSA. Well 23 and track on right. 16.6 km ▲

GPS	S:23 04.759 E:123 13.230
UTM	51K 522584E 7447683N

(14.0 km)

▼ 35.7 km Track junction. CSA. Track on right.

Track on right leads 0.4 km to Well 24 and bush campsites. Well 24, GPS S:23 06.567 E:123 20.606 UTM 51K 535167E 7444323N, was dug to depth of 33 feet (10 m) with capacity of 4350 gallons (19 775 litres) and replenishment rate of 360 gallons (1636 litres) per hour.

Track junction. CSA. Track on left to Well 24. 2.6 km ▲

GPS	S:23 06.355 E:123 20.567
UTM	51K 535102E 7444714N

(2.6 km)

▼ 38.3 km Track junction.

Zero trip meter at T-junction with Talawana Track. TR. SP: CSR. 0.0 km ▲

GPS	S:23 05.178 E:123 21.208
UTM	51K 536201E 7446883N

▼ 0.0 km Zero trip meter at track junction. TL. SP: CSR. Track SO SP: Windy Corner.

Track SO is Talawana Track and leads 203 km to Windy Corner.

T-junction. This is Talawana Track. 88.3 km ▲

(1.7 km)

▼ 1.7 km Short rocky climb.

Short rocky descent. 86.6 km ▲

(18.7 km)

▼ 20.4 km Track crosses number of claypans.

Number of bush campsites are located along edges of claypans.

Claypans. Bush camping in this vicinity. 67.9 km ▲

(0.9 km)

▼ 21.3 km Well 25 on left. CSA.

Well 25 was dug to depth of 37 feet 6 inches (11.4 metres) with capacity of 3000 gallons (13 638 litres) and replenishment rate of 600 gallons (2727 litres) per hour.

Well 25 on right. 67.0 km ▲
Track now crosses number of claypans.

GPS	S:22 58.965 E:123 23.812
UTM	51K 540677E 7458335N

(0.8 km)

▼ 22.1 km Track crosses large claypan.

Track crosses large claypan. 66.2 km ▲

(1.2 km)

▼ 23.3 km Track junction. TR and cross sand dune. Track on left.

Track on left leads short distance to bush campsite among mulga trees.

Track junction. TL. Track SO to bush campsite. 65.0 km ▲

(19.3 km)

▼ 42.6 km Track junction. CSA. Well 26 on right. Track on left.

Track on left leads to Well 26 camping area, an open spot with no shade so not an overly appealing place to camp. Well 26 was dug to depth of 23 feet (7 m) with capacity of 1950 gallons (8864 litres) and replenishment rate of 2000 gallons (9092 litres) per hour. This well was completely reconstructed in 1983 (see note on Well 26, page 130). Memorial to Canning nearby. Water available.

Track junction. CSA. Well 26 on left. Track on right to camping area. 45.7 km ▲

GPS	S:22 54.967 E:123 30.334
UTM	51K 551844E 7465677N

(13.4 km)

▼ 56.0 km Creek crossing.

Small plaque on right indicates this was site of Canning's 1907 bore-sinking camp.

Creek crossing. 32.3 km ▲

(1.2 km)

▼ 57.2 km Track junction. CSA. Track on right.

Track on right leads 0.4 km to base of Slate Range.

Track junction. CSA. Track on left. 31.1 km ▲

(1.1 km)

▼ 58.3 km Slate Range on right.

Slate Range on left. 30.0 km ▲

(15.3 km)

▼ 73.6 km Well 27 on left. KR. SP: CSR.

A track to left of well leads 0.7 km to native soak and to bush camping among mulga trees. To west of soak are Aboriginal artefacts such as grinding stones and stone tools. Well 27 was dug to depth of 24 feet (7.3 m) with capacity of 1800 gallons (8182 litres) and replenishment rate of 300 gallons (1363 litres) per hour.

Well 27 on right. KL. SP: CSR. 14.7 km ▲

GPS	S:22 47.684 E:123 38.655
UTM	51K 566124E 7479059N

(8.2 km)

▼ 81.8 km Helen Hill on right of track.

Good views from summit.

Helen Hill on left of track. 6.5 km ▲

(6.5 km)

WILUNA ◀▶ KUNAWARRITJI

▼ 88.3 km   Track junction. Side trip to Separation Well.

Zero trip meter at track junction. CSA. SP: Well 27 – 10 miles. Track on left to Separation Well.   0.0 km ▲

GPS   S:22 44.793 E:123 43.212
UTM   51K 573946E 7484357N

▶   SIDE TRIP: Separation Well

▼ 0.0 km   Zero trip meter at track junction on CSR. Turn into track to east SP: Separation Well.

(8.8 km)

▼ 8.8 km   Cross sand dune.

(2.9 km)

▼ 11.7 km   Cross sand dune.

(7.5 km)

▼ 19.2 km   Cross sand dune.

(0.1 km)

▼ 19.3 km   Track junction. CSA. Track on right leads short distance to small bush campsite.

(0.1 km)

▼ 19.4 km   Cross sand dune.

(14.8 km)

▼ 34.2 km   Separation Well. Return to side trip start.

Feral camels frequent this historic watering spot. First Europeans to discover the well, in 1896, were Lawrence Wells, his cousin Charles Wells and George Jones. Termed the Calvert Expedition after its sponsor, Albert Calvert, the trip ended tragically when the party separated here and Charles Wells and Jones perished in the desert (see page 122).

GPS   S:22 51.067 E:124 00.961
UTM   51K 604241E 7472602N

◀   END SIDE TRIP

▼ 0.0 km   Zero trip meter at track junction. CSA. SP: Well 28 – 14 miles. Track on right SP: Separation Well.

Track junction. See side trip to Separation Well.   47.4 km ▲

(16.3 km)

▼ 16.3 km   Well 28 on left. CSA.

Well 28 was dug to depth of 30 feet (9.1 m) with capacity of 2750 gallons (12 501 litres) and replenishment rate of 740 gallons (3364 litres) per hour.

Well 28 on right. CSA.   31.1 km ▲

GPS   S:22 38.590 E:123 45.435
UTM   51K 577808E 7495783N

(31.1 km)

▼ 47.4 km   Track junction. Route option via Thring Rock.

If not taking Thring Rock option, main route directions continue immediately following route option notes below.

Zero trip meter at track junction. CSA.   0.0 km ▲

Track on left is where Thring Rock route option (below) rejoins.

GPS   S:22 33.647 E:123 52.916
UTM   51K 590674E 7504832N

▶   ROUTE OPTION: Thring Rock

▼ 0.0 km   Zero trip meter at track junction on CSR. TR into track to east.

Track SO leads 0.9 km to Well 29.

T-junction. End route option.   5.0 km ▲

TL to continue south on CSR. Reverse directions continue at 0.0 km mark above. Track on right is main CSR track north and leads 0.9 km to Well 29.

(0.5 km)

▼ 0.5 km   Bush camping in this vicinity among mulga trees. CSA.

Bush camping in this vicinity. CSA.   4.5 km ▲

(3.6 km)

▼ 4.1 km   Track junction. CSA. Track on right.

Track on right leads to base of Thring Rock. Excellent views from summit. Bush campsites at base of rock and to east of rock. Thring Rock (and nearby Lake Auld and King Hill) named by Lawrence Wells after 3 men who had accompanied John McDouall Stuart on his south–north crossing of the continent in 1862.

Y-junction. KR. Track on left to Thring Rock.   0.9 km ▲

GPS   S:22 34.299 E:123 55.063
UTM   51K 594346E 7503607N

(0.3 km)

▼ 4.4 km   Cross sand dune.

Cross sand dune.   0.6 km ▲

(0.6 km)

▼ 5.0 km   Crossroads. This is main CSR. CSA and cross sand dune to rejoin route directions at upcoming 5.5-km reading.

Track on left is where main CSR joins.

Zero trip meter at crossroads. CSA to start route option.   0.0 km ▲

Track on right is main CSR track.

GPS   S:22 33.861 E:123 55.206
UTM   51K 594596E 7504414N

◀   END ROUTE OPTION

▼ 0.0 km   Zero trip meter at track junction. CSA. Track on right.

Track on right to Thring Rock.

Aboriginal grinding stone near Well 27

■ 137

CANNING STOCK ROUTE

	Track junction. **5.5 km** ▲	▼ 52.7 km	Track junction. CSA. Track on right SP: To Nurgurga Soak 1.2 km.
	Reverse directions to continue southwards on CSR follow after route option notes above. **(0.9 km)**		Track on right leads 1.1 km to native well.

▼ 0.9 km — Track junction. CSA on loop around Well 29, then KL at junction on way out.

Well 29, GPS S:22 33.288 E:123 52.740 UTM 51K 590376E 7505496N, was dug to depth of 45 feet (13.7 m) with capacity of 4800 gallons (21 821 litres) and replenishment rate of 230 gallons (1045 litres) per hour.

Track junction. CSA on loop around Well 29, then KR at junction on way out. **4.6 km** ▲

(4.6 km)

▼ 5.5 km — Crossroads.

Zero trip meter at crossroads. TR. Track SO. **0.0 km** ▲

Track SO is reverse directions start of Thring Rock route option. See route option notes above for details.

GPS S:22 33.861 E:123 55.206
UTM 51K 594596E 7504414N

▼ 0.0 km — Zero trip meter at crossroads. TL and cross sand dune. Track on right.

Track on right is where Thring Rock route option rejoins CSR.

Crossroads. **110.2 km** ▲

(14.8 km)

▼ 14.8 km — Small bush campsite on left. CSA.

Small bush campsite on right. CSA. **95.4 km** ▲

(12.5 km)

▼ 27.3 km — Track junction. CSA. Track on left SP: Nangabbittajarra 6.0 km.

Track on left leads 5.6 km to Nangabbittajarra Native Well.

Track junction. CSA. Track on right SP: Nangabbittajarra 6.0 km. **82.9 km** ▲

(6.1 km)

▼ 33.4 km — Track junction. CSA. Track on left.

Track on left leads to **Well 30 bush campsite** surrounded by tall bloodwood trees.

Track junction. CSA. Track on right to bush campsite. **76.8 km** ▲

(0.2 km)

▼ 33.6 km — SP: Dunda Jinnda Well 30, on left. Track junction just past well. CSA. Track on right.

Well 30 was dug to depth of 26 feet (7.9 m) with capacity of 2475 gallons (11 251 litres) and replenishment rate of 2000 gallons (9092 litres) per hour. Track on right leads 3.7 km to carpark and 75-m walk to Mujingerra Cave, used by Aboriginal people for water supply and shelter. Descending into cave is not recommended – it is home to poisonous snakes such as the king brown.

Track junction. CSA. SP: Dunda Jinnda Well 30, on right. Track on left leads to Mujingerra Cave. **76.6 km** ▲

GPS S:22 30.250 E:124 08.379
UTM 51K 617221E 7510921N

(19.1 km)

▼ 52.7 km — Track junction. CSA. Track on right SP: To Nurgurga Soak 1.2 km.

Track on right leads 1.1 km to native well.

Track junction. CSA. Track on left. **57.5 km** ▲

(7.1 km)

▼ 59.8 km — Track junction. TR. SP: CSR Well 31 – 4 km. Track SO.

Track SO is main CSR, which rejoins route directions at upcoming 69.1-km mark.

T-junction. TL. Track on right. **50.4 km** ▲

Track on right is where main CSR rejoins route directions.

GPS S:22 30.552 E:124 22.816
UTM 51K 641968E 7510155N

(3.7 km)

▼ 63.5 km — Track junction. TL. Track SO SP: To Well 31– 200 mts.

Track SO leads 0.3 km to **Well 31** and **bush camping area** shaded by tall gums. Well 31: GPS S:22 31.539 E:124 24.425 UTM 51K 644709E 7508308N.

T-junction. TR. Track on left. SP: To Well 31 – 200 mts. **46.7 km** ▲

GPS S:22 31.518 E:124 24.289
UTM 51K 644477E 7508349N

(5.6 km)

▼ 69.1 km — Track junction. KR. Track on left.

Track on left is where main CSR rejoins route directions.

Y-junction. KL. SP: To Well 31. Track on right. **41.1 km** ▲

Track on right is main CSR, which rejoins route directions at upcoming 50.4-km mark.

GPS S:22 30.311 E:124 26.355
UTM 51K 648040E 7510543N

(23.5 km)

▼ 92.6 km — Track junction. CSA. Well 32 on right of track. Track on left.

Well 32 was dug to depth of 25 feet (7.6 m) with capacity of 1875 gallons (8523 litres) and replenishment capacity of 950 gallons (4318 litres) per hour. Track on left leads 2.3 km to Mallowa Native Well.

Track junction. CSA. Well 32 on left of track. Track on right. **17.6 km** ▲

GPS S:22 24.358 E:124 35.128
UTM 51K 663198E 7521376N

(17.6 km)

▼ 110.2 km — Crossroads. Start trek section 2 (CSA). Road on left SP: 4 km Kunawarritji. Road on right leads to Gary Junction Rd via Jenkins Track.

Kunawarritji has fuel and supplies. Gary Junction Rd leads 1043.4 km to Alice Springs in NT (see Ocean to Alice, pages 84–99.)

Zero trip meter at crossroads. CSA in southerly direction. Road on right SP: 4 km Kunawarritji. Road on left leads to Gary Junction Rd. **0.0 km** ▲

GPS S:22 21.304 E:124 44.607
UTM 51K 679529E 7526832N

REVERSE DIRECTIONS START

138

2 KUNAWARRITJI ◀▶ HALLS CREEK 804.6 KM

Start point
Kunawarritji

Road atlas
354 C5

Total distance
966.2 km (includes route-directed side trips)

Standard
Difficult

Time
8–10 days

Longest distance no PD (includes all options)
1040.5 km (Kunawarritji to Billiluna)

Topographic maps
Auslig 1:250 000 series: *Ural*; *Helena*; *Percival*; *Dummer*; *Cornish*; *Mount Bannerman*; *Billiluna*; *Gordon Downs*

Other useful information
- Kunawarritji community store has fuel and a range of supplies; open Monday–Friday 8am–5pm (during peak visitor season) and Saturday 9am–12noon (closed Sunday and public holidays), tel. (08) 9176 9040; accepts cash and EFTPOS.
- Billiluna has fuel and supplies. Petrol and diesel from Billiluna Corporation, open Monday–Friday 7am–12noon and 1–3pm and Saturday 9–11am (other times possible but call-out fee applicable), tel. (08) 9168 8988; accepts cash and EFTPOS. Good range of supplies from Kururrungku store, open Monday–Friday 8–11.30am and 2–4.30pm and Saturday 9–11am, tel. (08) 9168 8076; accepts cash and EFTPOS.
- *Canning Stock Route: A Traveller's Guide* by Ronele and Eric Gard provides useful information and history.
- Australian Geographic travel guide series: *The Canning Stock Route*.
- Wildflowers are prolific during late winter and spring so pack a wildflower identification book.

Description

The northern section of the CSR (see the maps on pages 141 and 151) traverses the dune fields of the Great Sandy Desert. Some of the largest dune crossings of the entire route are encountered as the track winds its way north, and there are some enjoyable runs through valleys between the sandhills. Vegetation is often sparse in places while elsewhere wildflowers grow prolifically after winter rains.

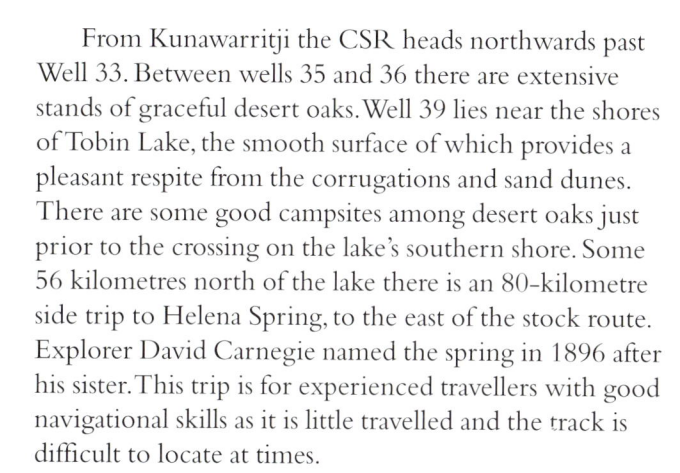

From Kunawarritji the CSR heads northwards past Well 33. Between wells 35 and 36 there are extensive stands of graceful desert oaks. Well 39 lies near the shores of Tobin Lake, the smooth surface of which provides a pleasant respite from the corrugations and sand dunes. There are some good campsites among desert oaks just prior to the crossing on the lake's southern shore. Some 56 kilometres north of the lake there is an 80-kilometre side trip to Helena Spring, to the east of the stock route. Explorer David Carnegie named the spring in 1896 after his sister. This trip is for experienced travellers with good navigational skills as it is little travelled and the track is difficult to locate at times.

There are a number of alternative track options north of the Helena Spring detour, each over 60 kilometres long so you need to decide which way you intend to travel. The first option provides access to Well 44, the second to wells 46 and 47. If you do not take the latter option, the main CSR track passes Mount Ford, a rocky bluff with excellent views over the desert – after a scramble on foot up the peak's southern side. It is also possible to access picturesque Well 46 with its good drinking water and sheltered campsites via a track that leaves the CSR to the north of Mount Ford.

Drawing water from Well 49

The approach to Well 48 skirts the west side of the imposing Breaden Hills, part of the Southesk Tablelands, where you can visit Breaden Pool and Godfreys Tank, both vital watering points during Carnegie's 1896–97 expedition. At Breaden Pool there is a hunting hide and scattered tool-making sites, evidence of previous Aboriginal occupation. Some 76 kilometres further, just south of Lake Gregory, is Well 51, the northernmost well constructed by Alfred Canning. From this point north the stock route was able to use natural watering holes and soaks.

Just north of Well 51 the CSR skirts the western edge of some small lakes, part of the Lake Gregory system, before climbing the last of the dunes on the south–north route. A short distance from Bloodwood Well there is camping at Nyarna Lake Stretch. At Billiluna, at the junction of the CSR and the Tanami Road, petrol and diesel are available. The Tanami leads to Halls Creek, but a detour to Wolfe Creek Meteorite Crater is a 'must' for those who have not visited it before (see Tanami Road, page 51). The one-time gold-rush town of Halls Creek offers all services and supplies. Located 14 kilometres east, the mudbrick ruins of the original town are worth a visit.

Advice and warnings

- This is remote country and thorough planning and preparation are required. You must be self-sufficient and carry enough fuel, water and supplies for the trip.
- Track varies from soft sand dunes to compacted earth, heavy corrugations and rocky sections. Parts of the track can be closed due to floodwaters, which may be present for many years. Generally flood bypasses are in place. After rain, check all claypans prior to crossing them. Contact either Halls Creek Visitor Information Centre, tel. (08) 9168 6262, or Halls Creek Police, tel. (08) 9168 6000, to check road conditions.
- Watch out for oncoming traffic over sand dunes – mount a high-flying red flag on your vehicle.
- *Spinifex warning*. Early season travellers should install radiator guards (fine mesh screens) to protect against spinifex seeds, which can quickly clog the radiator and cause your vehicle to overheat. In addition, it is sensible to check your vehicle's undercarriage at regular intervals, especially around the exhaust, for any build-up of spinifex. Hot exhaust pipes can easily ignite the resin in the spinifex causing a fire. On the few occasions that this has occurred along the CSR the vehicles have been burned out within two minutes! Petrol powered vehicles tend to be the more susceptible but modern turbo diesel vehicles often have catalytic converters, which run quite hot.
- Standard road tyres or all-terrain tyres are suitable. Tyre pressure should be lowered to allow better ride comfort over corrugations and for ease of crossing sand dunes.
- Towing trailers or caravans not recommended.
- Bush camping only along the route with no facilities. All campers must be self-sufficient.
- There are no rubbish bins along the track so take your rubbish with you.
- Ensure that toilet paper is completely burned and/or buried in a hole at least 30 cm deep.
- Bucket and long rope should be carried to access water from wells. To preserve this water do not camp within 100 m of wells; always close lids on wells; do not wash or use detergents or soaps near wells; and do not remove any well equipment. Boil water or use Puritabs.
- Long distance communications equipment, such as a satellite phone or HF radio, should be carried. Use a UHF radio, generally channel 40, to make contact with other travellers on the stock route.

Permits and bookings

- No permits required to travel CSR.
- Bookings required to camp at Nyarna Lake Stretch. Contact Mindibungu Aboriginal community, tel. (08) 9168 8988.

Campsite Facilities

	Toilets	Disabled access	4WD access only	Off-road trailer	Off-road caravan	Drinking water	Fee payable	Ranger patrolled	BBQ/fireplace	Campfires prohibited	Picnic tables	Shelter shed	No rubbish disposal	Public phone	Shower	Bushwalking	Swimming	Swimming not advised	Fishing	Canoeing	Dogs allowed
Nyarna Lake Stretch			•			•	•			•	•										
Well 33			•	•						•											
Well 46			•		•					•											
Well 50			•							•											
Wolfe Creek	•			•	•		•		•	•	•	•			•						

KUNAWARRITJI ◀ ▶ HALLS CREEK

Breaden Pool
The pool's namesake, Joe Breaden, a member of David Carnegie's 1896–97 expedition, found this watering spot tucked away in the Breaden Hills. Nowadays it is only a short walk from the valley carpark. Above the pool is an Aboriginal hideout, a handcrafted rock wall behind which hunters would crouch in wait to catch prey that came to the water to drink.

Well 46
One of the most picturesque wells along the CSR, Well 46 is surrounded by stands of tea tree, mulga and beautiful white eucalypts, which supply ample shade and privacy for camping. The well was restored in 1991 and good water can be fetched with a bucket and long rope.

Well 37
During the 1970s Well 37, or Libral Well, became popularly known as Haunted Well. In the vicinity are graves of drovers Christopher George Frederick Shoesmith, James Campbell Thomson and an Aboriginal man called Chinaman, who were killed here in 1911 by Aboriginal people. A fourth grave is that of John Vincent McLernon, a member of the 1922 Locke Oil Prospecting Syndicate Expedition, who was killed 56 kilometres to the south and his body brought here for burial.

141

ROUTE DIRECTIONS

▼ **0.0 km** Zero trip meter at junction crossroads with road to Kunawarritji on left and Jenkins Track on right. CSA in northerly direction along CSR.

Crossroads. Road on right SP: 4 km Kunawarritji. CSA to continue south (see trek section 1). **38.7 km** ▲

Road on left leads to Gary Junction Rd (see Ocean to Alice, pages 84–99).

GPS	S:22 21.304 E:124 44.607
UTM	51K 679529E 7526832N

(3.6 km)

▼ **3.6 km** Track junction. CSA. Well 33 on right, windmill and water tank on left.

Track on left leads to **Well 33 bush camping**, a large open area surrounded by low stunted tea trees close to windmill and water outflow. Track on right leads to airfield. Well 33 was dug to depth of 21 feet 9 inches (6.6 m) with capacity of 2400 gallons (10 910 litres) and replenishment rate of 1000 gallons (4546 litres) per hour. Water available.

Track junction. CSA. Well 33 on left, windmill and water tank on right. **35.1 km** ▲

GPS	S:22 20.513 E:124 46.512
UTM	51K 682816E 7528254N

(19.2 km)

▼ **22.8 km** Track junction. CSA. Track on left.

Track on left leads 5.1 km to Well 34, GPS S:22 15.542 E:124 54.159 UTM 51K 696060E 7537268N, dug to depth of 17 feet 6 inches (5.3 m) with capacity of 1750 gallons (7955 litres) and replenishment rate of 900 gallons (4091 litres) per hour.

Track junction. CSA. Track on right. **15.9 km** ▲

GPS	S:22 16.619 E:124 56.540
UTM	51K 700125E 7535228N

(14.3 km)

▼ **37.1 km** Rocky outcrop, approximately 2 km on right of track, is Kidson Bluff.

Kidson Bluff was named after Edward Kidson from Carnegie Institute of Washington in the United States, who carried out magnetic observations along CSR in June–October 1914.

Kidson Bluff can be seen on left of track. **1.6 km** ▲

(1.6 km)

▼ **38.7 km** T-junction. This is Callowa Track. Route option via wells 35 and 36.

If not taking option via wells 35 and 36, main route directions continue immediately following route option notes below. At time of research, wells 35 and 36 were flooded. Bypass tracks were in place and used. Stretching northwards from around Well 35 to beyond Well 36 are magnificent stands of desert oak (*Allocasuarina decaisneana*). Dubbed the Great Oak Forest, the shady trees provide pleasant, well-protected bush campsites. Canning cut wood from this forest to line Well 35 (desert oak timber is hard and termite-resistant).

Zero trip meter at track junction. TL to follow CSR southwards. **0.0 km** ▲

Tranquil scene at flooded Well 36

Track SO is where route option via wells 35 and 36 (below) rejoins. If coming from this direction TR onto CSR.

GPS	S:22 14.202 E:125 04.874
UTM	51K 714502E 7539499N

▶ **ROUTE OPTION: wells 35 and 36**

▼ **0.0 km** Zero trip meter at junction of CSR and Callowa Track. TL onto Callowa Track.

Track junction. End route option. **36.4 km** ▲

TR onto CSR to continue southwards. Reverse directions continue at 0.0 km mark above. Track SO is main CSR track north.

(3.3 km)

▼ **3.3 km** Track junction. TR. This is the flood bypass route. Track SO leads 0.7 km to Well 35.

Well 35, GPS S:22 12.735 E:125 03.062 UTM 51K 711426E 7542249N, was dug to depth of 16 feet (4.8 m) with capacity of 1350 gallons (6137 litres) and replenishment rate of 1500 gallons (6819 litres) per hour.

T-junction. TL. Track on right to Well 35. **33.1 km** ▲

GPS	S:22 13.081 E:125 03.461
UTM	51K 712102E 7541601N

(1.5 km)

▼ **4.8 km** T-junction. TR and cross small sand dune. This is where flood bypass joins dry weather access track.

Track on left leads to Well 35 and is dry weather access track.

Track junction. TL. This is the flood bypass route. Track SO leads to Well 35. **31.6 km** ▲

KUNAWARRITJI ◀▶ HALLS CREEK

	GPS S:22 12.599 E:125 03.220 **UTM** 51K 711700E 7542496N		
	(0.7 km)		
▼ 5.5 km	Cross sand dune.		
	Cross sand dune.	30.9 km ▲
	(18.1 km)		
▼ 23.6 km	Track junction. KR over sand dune.		
	Track on left leads to carpark from where short walk leads to Bungabinni Native Well.		
	Track junction. KL. Track on right.	12.8 km ▲
	(1.5 km)		
▼ 25.1 km	Track junction. KL. Track on right.		
	Track on right leads 8.8 km east to main CSR.		
	Track junction. CSA. Track on left.	11.3 km ▲
	GPS S:22 09.313 E:125 12.288 **UTM** 51K 727373E 7548342N		
	(9.3 km)		
▼ 34.4 km	Track junction. Hard TL. This is the flood bypass track.		
	Track junction. Hard TR. This is where flood bypass joins with dry weather access track.	2.0 km ▲
	GPS S:22 08.659 E:125 16.842 **UTM** 51K 735222E 7549434N		
	(1.4 km)		
▼ 35.8 km	Track junction. CSA. Track on left.		
	Track on left leads 0.2 km to Well 36, GPS S:22 08.371 E:125 17.004 UTM 51K 735508E 7549961N, dug to depth of 18 feet 6 inches (5.6 m) with replenishment rate of 900 gallons (4091 litres) per hour.		
	Y-junction. KL. Track on right.	0.6 km ▲
	GPS S:22 08.375 E:125 17.096 **UTM** 51K 735666E 7549951N		
	(0.5 km)		
▼ 36.3 km	Claypan on left. CSA.		
	Claypan on right. CSA.	0.1 km ▲
	(0.1 km)		
▼ 36.4 km	T-junction. This is CSR. TL to rejoin route directions at upcoming 36.1-km reading.		
	Zero trip meter at junction of CSR and track on right to Well 36. TR to start route option. Proceed to Well 36.	0.0 km ▲
	GPS S:22 08.387 E:125 17.471 **UTM** 51K 736311E 7549920N		
◀	**END ROUTE OPTION**		
▼ 0.0 km	Zero trip meter at T-junction. TR onto Callowa Track.		
	Track on left leads to wells 35 and 36.		
	Track junction.	36.1 km ▲
	Reverse directions to continue southwards on CSR follow after route option notes above.		
	(9.2 km)		
▼ 9.2 km	Track junction. TL. SP: CSR. Track SO leads 32.0 km to Gary Junction.		
	T-junction. This is Callowa Track. TR. Track on left to Gary Junction.	26.9 km ▲

Welding the roof rack leg

Casualty on the Canning

During field research we travelled from north to south down the Canning. What a fantastic month. En route to Billiluna we were flagged down by a carload of Aboriginal people who had a flat tyre. So we helped them out by supplying some glue – they had their own patches and scraper – and some air from the compressor. What a bunch of great people. Bridget, a very forthright female, introduced us to all her family and she and Cath enjoyed a chat about life and our trip. Because we stopped and took the time to help them out, Bridget asked her brother in-law, who is a witch doctor, to bless us. Wongambi did so, wishing us a safe journey. He also showed Cath some bush medicine and food plants.

A witch doctor's blessing and Craig's bush welding skills saved the day

Buoyed by this encounter we continued on our way. 'The Brick' performed exceptionally well, considering she weighs over 4 tonnes when fully loaded. She tackled the sand dunes with ease but we had no time for complacency. Near Well 33 we experienced the first casualty of our transcontinental journeys. One of the legs on the roof rack cracked in two. So Craig unloaded the firewood and secured the leg as best as possible. We arrived at the well to find a couple having a bush shower – naked of course. Didn't take them long to hide behind the water tank! We set up camp and Craig spent the afternoon attending to the roof rack leg, with admirable results. His bush welding skills saved the day.

CANNING STOCK ROUTE

	GPS S:22 17.977 E:125 08.243 **UTM** 51K 720193E 7532450N		
	(2.2 km)		
▼ 11.4 km	Trig marker on right.		
	Trig marker on left.	24.7 km ▲	
	(11.9 km)		
▼ 23.3 km	Trig marker on left.		
	Trig marker on right.	12.8 km ▲	
	(1.2 km)		
▼ 24.5 km	Small creek crossing.		
	Small creek crossing.	11.6 km ▲	
	(2.4 km)		
▼ 26.9 km	Small creek crossing.		
	Small creek crossing.	9.2 km ▲	
	(3.7 km)		
▼ 30.6 km	Track junction. CSA. Track on left.		
	Track on left leads 8.8 km west to 25.1-km mark on route option via wells 35 and 36.		
	Track junction. CSA. Track on right.	5.5 km ▲	
	GPS S:22 10.907 E:125 16.809 **UTM** 51K 735103E 7545285N		
	(5.5 km)		
▼ 36.1 km	Track junction.		
	Zero trip meter at track junction. CSA. Track on right leads 0.8 km to Well 36.	0.0 km ▲	
	Track on right is reverse directions start of route option via wells 35 and 36. See route option notes above for details.		
	GPS S:22 08.387 E:125 17.471 **UTM** 51K 736311E 7549920N		
▼ 0.0 km	Zero trip meter at track junction. CSA. Track on left.		
	Track on left leads 0.8 km to Well 36. This is where route option via wells 35 and 36 rejoins CSR.		
	Track junction.	22.5 km ▲	
	(1.0 km)		
▼ 1.0 km	Track junction. KR. Track on left.		
	Track junction. CSA over sand dune. Track on right.	21.5 km ▲	
	(0.1 km)		
▼ 1.1 km	Track junction. KR. Track on left is old alignment.		
	Track junction. TL. Track on right is old alignment.	21.4 km ▲	
	GPS S:22 07.973 E:125 17.729 **UTM** 51K 736766E 7550677N		
	(19.9 km)		
▼ 21.0 km	Bush campsite on right. CSA over dune.		
	Bush campsite on left. CSA.	1.5 km ▲	
	(1.2 km)		
▼ 22.2 km	Bush campsite on right. CSA.		
	Good site with plenty of shade among desert oaks.		
	Bush campsite on left. CSA.	0.3 km ▲	
	(0.3 km)		
▼ 22.5 km	Track junction.		

	Zero trip meter at track junction. CSA. Track on left.	0.0 km ▲	
	Track on left leads 0.2 km to Well 37 and grave sites of Thomson, Shoesmith, Chinaman and McLernon (see note on Well 37, page 141).		
	GPS S:22 09.181 E:125 27.505 **UTM** 51K 753543E 7548184N		
▼ 0.0 km	Zero trip meter at track junction. CSA. Track on right to Well 37.		
	Track on right leads 0.2 km to Well 37 and grave sites of Thomson, Shoesmith, Chinaman and McLernon. Well 37, GPS S:22 09.248 E:125 27.532 UTM 51K 753587E 7548060N, was dug to depth of 16 feet (4.8 m) with capacity of 1500 gallons (6819 litres) and replenishment rate of 1240 gallons (5637 litres) per hour.		
	Track junction.	88.3 km ▲	
	(0.1 km)		
▼ 0.1 km	Track junction. CSA. Track on right to Well 37.		
	Track junction. CSA. Track on left.	88.2 km ▲	
	Track on left leads 0.1 km to Well 37.		
	(18.1 km)		
▼ 18.2 km	Carpark on right. CSA.		
	From carpark a short walk leads to cave where some Aboriginal rock art, although very faint, is visible.		
	Carpark on left. CSA.	70.1 km ▲	
	(10.9 km)		
▼ 29.1 km	Carpark on right. CSA.		
	From carpark a short walk leads to Water 38 (Wardabunni Rockhole), situated in creek. After rockhole had been enlarged with blasting, and the rubble cleared, it was estimated to have capacity of 30 000 gallons (136 382 litres).		
	Carpark on left. CSA.	59.2 km ▲	
	GPS S:21 57.025 E:125 32.034 **UTM** 51K 761704 E 7570497N		
	(1.8 km)		
▼ 30.9 km	Dry creek crossing.		
	Dry creek crossing.	57.4 km ▲	
	(0.9 km)		
▼ 31.8 km	Bush campsite on right. CSA.		
	Campsite is set among tall cabbage gums.		
	Bush campsite on left. CSA.	56.5 km ▲	
	(0.2 km)		
▼ 32.0 km	Track junction. KR. Minor track on left.		
	Track on left is original track, rarely used since track to wells 37 and 38 was built in 1990.		
	Track junction. KL. SP: CSR Water 38 – 3 km. Minor track on right.	56.3 km ▲	
	GPS S:21 56.485 E:125 30.656 **UTM** 51K 759347E 7571533N		
	(23.3 km)		
▼ 55.3 km	Track junction. TL. Track SO.		
	T-junction. TR. Track on left.	33.0 km ▲	
	(0.3 km)		
▼ 55.6 km	Lookout point on left. CSA.		
	Spectacular views to north and west from here.		

KUNAWARRITJI ◀▶ HALLS CREEK

Lookout point on right. CSA. 32.7 km ▲

(0.2 km)

▼ 55.8 km Track junction. KL. Track on right.

Track junction. KR. Track on left. 32.5 km ▲

(13.0 km)

▼ 68.8 km Well 39 on right. CSA.

Well 39 was dug to depth of 15 feet 8 inches (4.8 m) with capacity of 1425 gallons (6478 litres) and replenishment rate of 1100 gallons (5000 litres) per hour.

Well 39 on left. CSA. 19.5 km ▲

| GPS | S:21 46.023 E:125 39.096 |
| UTM | 51K 774217E 7590603N |

(3.6 km)

▼ 72.4 km Track junction. CSA. Track on right.

Track on right leads to small bush campsite among desert oaks.

Track junction. CSA. Track on left to bush campsite. 15.9 km ▲

(0.4 km)

▼ 72.8 km Track junction. CSA. Track on right.

Track on right leads to large bush campsite among shady desert oaks.

Track junction. CSA. Track on left to bush campsite. 15.5 km ▲

(0.4 km)

▼ 73.2 km Southern edge of Tobin Lake. CSA and cross lake.

Large salt lake, generally dry, but sections can become extremely boggy after heavy rains. Named after Michael Tobin, who on Canning's 1906–07 expedition was fatally wounded by an Aboriginal spear – Tobin simultaneously shot and killed the spear-thrower.

Southern edge of Tobin Lake. 15.1 km ▲

| GPS | S:21 44.615 E:125 40.306 |
| UTM | 51K 776348E 7593166N |

(12.7 km)

▼ 85.9 km Northern edge of Tobin Lake. CSA.

Northern edge of Tobin Lake. CSA and cross lake. 2.4 km ▲

(2.4 km)

▼ 88.3 km T-junction.

Zero trip meter at track junction. TR. Track SO. 0.0 km ▲

Track SO leads 2.6 km to Well 40 and a further 0.6 km to grave site of Michael Tobin.

| GPS | S:21 39.944 E:125 46.011 |
| UTM | 51K 786343E 7601617N |

▼ 0.0 km Zero trip meter at T-junction. TL. Track on right.

Track on right leads 2.6 km to Well 40 and further 0.6 km to grave site of Michael Tobin. Well 40, GPS S:21 40.042 E:125 47.224 UTM 51K 788433E 7601399N, was dug to depth of 12 feet 6 inches (3.8 m) with capacity of 1275 gallons (5796 litres) and replenishment rate of 1200 gallons (5455 litres) per hour.

Track junction. 56.1 km ▲

(22.1 km)

Marble headstone near Well 40 marks burial site of Michael Tobin

▼ 22.1 km Seismic line to left and right. CSA.

Seismic line to left and right. CSA. 34.0 km ▲

(1.4 km)

▼ 23.5 km Track junction. CSA. Track on left.

Track on left leads 1.7 km to Well 41, GPS S:21 33.224 E:125 50.948 UTM 51K 795091E 7613870N, dug to depth of 19 feet 6 inches (5.9 m) with capacity of 2250 gallons (10 228 litres) and replenishment rate of 950 gallons (4318 litres) per hour.

Track junction. CSA. Track on right to Well 41. 32.6 km ▲

| GPS | S:21 33.067 E:125 51.900 |
| UTM | 51K 796740E 7614130N |

(10.7 km)

▼ 34.2 km Track junction. CSA. Track on right.

Track on right is overgrown and leads 11.5 km to Gunowarba Native Well.

Track junction. CSA. Track on left. 21.9 km ▲

(8.7 km)

▼ 42.9 km Cross large sand dune.

Cross large sand dune. 13.2 km ▲

(13.2 km)

▼ 56.1 km Track junction. Side trip to Helena Spring.

Zero trip meter at track junction. CSA. Track on left SP: 81 km Helena Spring. 0.0 km ▲

| GPS | S:21 23.548 E:125 50.215 |
| UTM | 51K 794149E 7631758N |

CANNING STOCK ROUTE

Warrabuda Native Well

▶ **SIDE TRIP: Helena Spring**

▼ **0.0 km** Zero trip meter at track junction on CSR. Turn east into track SP: 81 km Helena Spring.
(17.7 km)

▼ **17.7 km** Sand dune.
(2.6 km)

▼ **20.3 km** Sand dune.
(0.3 km)

▼ **20.6 km** Sand dune.
(0.7 km)

▼ **21.3 km** Sand dune.
(0.3 km)

▼ **21.6 km** Sand dune.
(0.1 km)

▼ **21.7 km** Track junction. CSA. Track on left SP: Warrabuda 4.7 km.
Track on left leads 4.3 km to Warrabuda Native Well.
GPS S:21 22.651 E:126 01.688
UTM 52K 191819E 7633155N
(0.7 km)

▼ **22.4 km** Sand dune.
(0.9 km)

▼ **23.3 km** Good bush camping in this vicinity between dunes.
GPS S:21 22.448 E:126 02.549
UTM 52K 193301E 7633558N
(1.0 km)

▼ **24.3 km** Sand dune.
(0.5 km)

▼ **24.8 km** Track now passes through low-lying areas for next 8.0 km.
(3.2 km)

▼ **28.0 km** Sand dune.
(4.0 km)

▼ **32.0 km** Sand dune.
(1.0 km)

▼ **33.0 km** Sand dune. Track now travels between dunes for 41.4 km.
(0.7 km)

▼ **33.7 km** Sand dune.
(2.1 km)

▼ **35.8 km** Sand dune.
(37.6)

▼ **73.4 km** Seismic line to left and right. CSA.
GPS S:21 20.363 E:126 29.799
UTM 52K 240361E 7638226N
(1.0 km)

▼ **74.4 km** Track now runs back into vegetated dune system for next few kilometres, through picturesque valley dotted with trees.
(2.9 km)

▼ **77.3 km** Track now passes through low-lying sections.
(2.4 km)

▼ **79.7 km** Cross small sand ridge.
(0.1 km)

▼ **79.8 km** Claypan. From start of claypan track follows its northern edge around to Helena Spring.
(1.0 km)

▼ **80.8 km** Helena Spring on right of track. Return to side trip start.
During his 1896–97 expedition David Carnegie named Helena Spring after his sister, who was one of his greatest supporters.
GPS S:21 20.389 E:126 33.948
UTM 52K 247537E 7638291N

◀ **END SIDE TRIP**

KUNAWARRITJI ◀▶ HALLS CREEK

▼ 0.0 km — Zero trip meter at track junction. CSA. Track on right SP: 81 km Helena Spring.

Track junction. 39.8 km ▲

Track on left SP: 81 km Helena Spring. See Helena Spring side trip.

(1.6 km)

▼ 1.6 km — Cross large sand dune.

This sand dune has a trig marker.

Cross large sand dune. 38.2 km ▲

(0.2 km)

▼ 1.8 km — Bush campsite on left. CSA.

Bush campsite on right. CSA. 38.0 km ▲

(19.9 km)

▼ 21.7 km — Well 42 on left. CSA and cross Guli Lake.

At Guli Spring (Well 42) the sandstone of the natural spring was cut into a well measuring 25 feet by 14 feet by 4 feet (7.6 x 4.2 x 1.2 m) with additional sink of 4 feet 4 inches square (1.3 m square). This is shallowest well on CSR. Guli Lake is an ephemeral salt lake.

Well 42 on right. CSA. 18.1 km ▲

GPS S:21 18.926 E:125 52.952
UTM 51K 799038E 7640206N

(5.5 km)

▼ 27.2 km — Northern edge of Guli Lake.

Northern edge of Guli Lake. CSA and cross lake. 12.6 km ▲

(12.6 km)

▼ 39.8 km — Track junction. Route option via wells 43 and 44.

If not taking option via wells 43 and 44, main route directions continue immediately following route option notes below.

Zero trip meter at track junction. KR to follow CSR southwards. 0.0 km ▲

Track on left is where route option via wells 43 and 44 (below) rejoins. If coming from this direction TL onto CSR.

GPS S:21 12.730 E:125 56.400
UTM 51K 805216E 7651536N

▶ **ROUTE OPTION: wells 43 and 44**

▼ 0.0 km — Zero trip meter at track junction. TR and head east towards Well 43.

Track junction. End route option. 69.4 km ▲

TL onto CSR to continue southwards. Reverse directions continue at 0.0 km mark above. Track to right is main CSR track north.

(3.6 km)

▼ 3.6 km — Track junction. KL. Track on right.

Track on right leads short distance to Well 43, GPS S:21 12.796 E:125 58.425 UTM 51K 808720E 7651349N, dug to depth of 19 feet 6 inches (5.9 m) with capacity of 1900 gallons (8637 litres) and replenishment rate of 1000 gallons (4546 litres) per hour. Bush camping possible in this vicinity.

Track junction. KR. Track on left to Well 43. 65.8 km ▲

GPS S:21 12.768 E:125 58.403
UTM 51K 808683E 7651401N

(19.5 km)

▼ 23.1 km — Possible bush camping on right between dunes. CSA.

Possible bush camping on left between dunes. CSA. 46.3 km ▲

(11.4 km)

▼ 34.5 km — Track junction. TR. Minor track on left.

Track on left leads 7.0 km to main CSR track but is very overgrown.

Track junction. TL. Minor track SO. 34.9 km ▲

GPS S:21 01.031 E:126 03.565
UTM 52K 194323E 7673136N

(9.7 km)

▼ 44.2 km — Well 44 on right. CSA.

Well 44 was dug to depth of 43 feet (13.1 m) with replenishment rate of 1000 gallons (4546 litres) per hour.

Well 44 on left. CSA. 25.2 km ▲

GPS S:21 00.818 E:126 09.002
UTM 52K 203742E 7673700N

(14.4 km)

▼ 58.6 km — Pijallinga Claypan. CSA.

At this claypan Canning's construction party, until this point surviving on flour and water rations, shot a large number of ducks. They made themselves ill after gorging on the subsequent duck feast.

Pijallinga Claypan. CSA. 10.8 km ▲

GPS S:20 53.868 E:126 09.122
UTM 52K 203722E 7686535N

(8.1 km)

▼ 66.7 km — Rocky outcrop on right. CSA.

This outcrop has numerous caves to explore.

Rocky outcrop on left. CSA. 2.7 km ▲

(0.1 km)

▼ 66.8 km — Sand dune.

Sand dune. 2.6 km ▲

(0.3 km)

▼ 67.1 km — Sand dune.

Sand dune. 2.3 km ▲

(0.5 km)

▼ 67.6 km — Cross Gravity Lake.

Bush camping on right prior to lake. Gravity Lakes comprise 2 salt lakes. Track crosses the larger Gravity Lake.

Eastern edge of Gravity Lake. 1.8 km ▲

GPS S:20 51.727 E:126 05.330
UTM 52K 197071E 7690370N

(1.1 km)

▼ 68.7 km — North-western edge of Gravity Lake.

Bush camping possible behind dune system on lake's northern shore.

Cross Gravity Lake. 0.7 km ▲

(0.7 km)

▼ 69.4 km — T-junction. This is main CSR. TR to rejoin route directions at upcoming 66.3-km reading.

■ 147

CANNING STOCK ROUTE

Tracks across Gravity Lake

	Zero trip meter at track junction. TL to start route option. Proceed east to Gravity Lake. Track SO is main CSR.	0.0 km ▲

GPS S:20 51.025 E:126 04.740
UTM 52K 196024E 7691647N

◀ **END ROUTE OPTION**

▼ 0.0 km Zero trip meter at track junction. KL.
Track on right leads to wells 43 and 44.

Track junction. 66.3 km ▲

Reverse directions to continue southwards on CSR follow after route option notes above.

(0.6 km)

▼ 0.6 km Possible bush campsite on left. CSA.

Possible bush campsite on right. CSA. 65.7 km ▲

(31.1 km)

▼ 31.7 km Track junction. CSA. Track on right.
Track on right leads 17.0 km to Well 44, but overgrown and not used at time of research.

Track junction. CSA. Track on left. 34.6 km ▲

GPS S:21 01 027 E:125 59.728
UTM 51K 811386E 7673037N

(34.6 km)

▼ 66.3 km Track junction.

Zero trip meter at track junction. CSA. Track on left leads 0.7 km to Gravity Lake. 0.0 km ▲

Track on left is reverse directions start of route option via wells 43 and 44. See route option notes above for details.

GPS S:20 51.025 E:126 04.740
UTM 52K 196024E 7691647N

▼ 0.0 km Zero trip meter at track junction. CSA. Track on right.
Track on right leads 0.7 km to Gravity Lake. This is where route option via wells 43 and 44 rejoins CSR.

Track junction. 14.9 km ▲

(14.9 km)

▼ 14.9 km Track junction. Well 45 on right. Route option via wells 46 and 47.

If not taking option to wells 46 and 47, main route directions continue immediately following route option notes below. Well 45 was dug to depth of 28 feet (8.5 m) with capacity of 2250 gallons (10 228 litres) and replenishment rate of 1000 gallons (4546 litres) per hour. If taking route option, note that lake bypass was used as lake (currently unnamed) was flooded at the time of research.

Zero trip meter at track junction and Well 45 on left. CSA to follow CSR southwards. 0.0 km ▲

Track on right is where route option via wells 46 and 47 (below) rejoins. If coming from this direction, Well 45 is opposite junction and you TR onto CSR.

GPS S:20 47.624 E:126 10.480
UTM 52K 205875E 7698104N

▶ **ROUTE OPTION: wells 46 and 47**

▼ 0.0 km Zero trip meter at track junction with Well 45 on right. TL and head westwards.

Track junction. End route option. 26.4 km ▲

TR onto CSR to continue southwards. Reverse directions continue at 0.0 km mark above.
Track to left is main CSR track north.

(10.0 km)

▼ 10.0 km Track junction. TR. This is lake bypass. Track SO.
Track SO is dry weather access route to lake.

Track junction. TL. This is end of lake bypass. 16.4 km ▲
Track on right leads to lake.

GPS S:20 43.840 E:126 13.733
UTM 52K 211403E 7705188N

(6.8 km)

▼ 16.8 km Track junction. KR. This is end of lake bypass. Track on left leads to lake.
Track on left is dry weather access route.

Track junction. KL. This is the lake bypass. 9.6 km ▲
Track on right leads to lake.

(9.4 km)

▼ 26.2 km Well 46 on right. CSA.

Well 46 bush camping has some delightful campsites in this vicinity among shady white gums. Water available.

Well 46 on left. CSA. 0.2 km ▲

GPS S:20 38.510 E:126 17.258
UTM 52K 217360E 7715131N

(0.2 km)

▼ 26.4 km Track junction.

Zero trip meter at track junction. TR. Track on left. 0.0 km ▲

Track on left leads 14.4 km to main CSR track.

GPS S:20 38.445 E:126 17.344
UTM 52K 217508E 7715254N

▼ 0.0 km Zero trip meter at track junction. TL. Track SO.
Track SO leads 14.4 km to main CSR track.

KUNAWARRITJI ◀▶ HALLS CREEK

	Track junction.	50.9 km ▲	
(5.2 km)			
▼ 5.2 km	Cross first sand dune of route option.		
	Cross last sand dune of route option.	45.7 km ▲	
(12.5 km)			
▼ 17.7 km	Gravity Junction.		
	This is junction of 6 seismic lines.		
	Gravity Junction.	33.2 km ▲	

GPS   S:20 31.932 E:126 19.220
UTM   52K 220570E 7727331N

(10.3 km)

▼ 28.0 km Cross sand dune.
                                         Cross sand dune. 22.9 km ▲

(0.9 km)

▼ 28.9 km T-junction. TR. Track on left.
Track on left leads 3.7 km to Well 47, GPS S:20 25.834 E:126 17.495 UTM 52K 217384E 7738538N, dug to depth of 24 feet 6 inches (7.5 m) with capacity of 1500 gallons (6819 litres) and replenishment rate of 1250 gallons (5682 litres) per hour.
               Track junction. TL. Track SO to Well 47. 22.0 km ▲

GPS   S:20 25.979 E:126 19.840
UTM   52K 220842E 7738327N

(9.0 km)

▼ 37.9 km Cross last sand dune of route option.
                       Cross first sand dune of route option. 13.0 km ▲

(13.0 km)

▼ 50.9 km T-junction. This is main CSR. TL to rejoin route directions at upcoming 64.9-km reading.
               Zero trip meter at track junction. Track on right SP: Well 47 – 26 km. TR to start route option. Proceed west towards Well 47. 0.0 km ▲

GPS   S:20 26.708 E:126 31.465
UTM   52K 241716E 7737309N

◀ **END ROUTE OPTION**

Unnamed lake between wells 45 and 46

▼ 0.0 km Zero trip meter at track junction. CSA SP: CSR. Well 45 on right and track on left.
Track on left leads to wells 46 and 47.
                    Track junction. Well 45 on left. 64.9 km ▲
                    Reverse directions to continue southwards on CSR follow after route option notes above.

(16.0 km)

▼ 16.0 km Track junction. CSA. Track on left to bush campsite.
                    Track junction. CSA. Track on right to bush campsite. 48.9 km ▲

(4.2 km)

▼ 20.2 km SP: Mount Ford, on right. CSA.
Magnificent 360-degree views of vast surrounding low-lying areas from top of Mt Ford. Best access via southern face of mountain.
                    SP: Mount Ford, on left. CSA. 44.7 km ▲

GPS   S:20 45.867 E:126 20.933
UTM   52K 223968E 7701656N

(11.4 km)

▼ 31.6 km Track junction. CSA. Track on left.
Track on left leads 14.4 km to Well 46.
                    Track junction. CSA. Track on right. 33.3 km ▲

GPS   S:20 41.402 E:126 24.415
UTM   52K 229882E 7709996N

(1.2 km)

▼ 32.8 km Track junction. CSA. Track on left.
Track on left leads short distance to carpark and short walk to trig on Crescent Ridge.
                    Track junction. CSA. Track on right. 32.1 km ▲

(26.8 km)

▼ 59.6 km Small aluminium plaque on right reads: 'Colonel Peter Egerton-Warburton with his exploration party crossed here on 2/9/1873'.
                    Small aluminium plaque on left. 5.3 km ▲

GPS   S:20 28.748 E:126 29.446
UTM   52K 238261E 7733490N

(1.4 km)

▼ 61.0 km Mt Romilly on right. CSA.
Mt Romilly was named by David Carnegie during his 1896–97 expedition after one of his brothers-in-law.
                    Mt Romilly on left. CSA. 3.9 km ▲

(3.9 km)

▼ 64.9 km Track junction.
                    Zero trip meter at track junction. CSA. Track on right SP: Well 47 26 km. 0.0 km ▲
                    Track on right leads 25.7 km to Well 47 and is reverse directions start of route option via wells 46 and 47. See route option notes above for details.

GPS   S:20 26.708 E:126 31.465
UTM   52K 241716E 7737309N

▼ 0.0 km Zero trip meter at track junction. CSA. Track on left SP: Well 47 26 km.

■ 149

CANNING STOCK ROUTE

Impressive peaks of Twin Heads

	Track on left leads 25.7 km to Well 47. This is where route option via wells 46 and 47 rejoins CSR.		
	Track junction.	**24.4 km** ▲	
	(6.4 km)		
▼ **6.4 km**	Last of larger sand dunes.		
	First of larger sand dunes.	**18.0 km** ▲	
	(14.8 km)		
▼ **21.2 km**	Creek crossing.		
	Creek crossing.	**3.2 km** ▲	
	(3.2 km)		
▼ **24.4 km**	Track junction.		
	Zero trip meter at track junction. CSA. Track on left.	**0.0 km** ▲	
	Track on left leads 4.5 km to carpark at end of Breaden Valley.		
	GPS S:20 15.691 E:126 32.363 **UTM 52K 242974E 7757667N**		
▼ **0.0 km**	Zero trip meter at track junction. CSA. Track on right.		
	Track on right leads 4.5 km to carpark at north-eastern end of Breaden Valley. Short walk from carpark leads to Breaden Pool, and longer walk (10–15 minutes one way) leads to Godfreys Tank. Bush camping possible in vicinity of carpark.		
	Track junction.	**1.6 km** ▲	
	(0.3 km)		
▼ **0.3 km**	Track junction. CSA. Track on right.		
	Track on right leads 2.8 km up valley to small bush campsite.		

	Track junction. CSA. Track on left.	**1.3 km** ▲	
	(1.3 km)		
▼ **1.6 km**	Track junction.		
	Zero trip meter at track junction. CSA. Track on right.	**0.0 km** ▲	
	Track on right leads 1.0 km to Well 48.		
	GPS S:20 14.956 E:126 31.958 **UTM 52K 242248E 7759013N**		
▼ **0.0 km**	Zero trip meter at track junction. CSA. Track on left.		
	Track on left leads 1.0 km to Well 48, GPS S:20 14.903 E:126 31.411 UTM 52K 241294E 7759096N, dug to depth of 65 feet 6 inches (19.9 m) with additional shaft of 14 by 6 by 3 feet (4.2 x 1.8 x 0.9 m), allowing total capacity of 7650 gallons (34 777 litres) and replenishment rate of 130 gallons (591 litres) per hour.		
	Track junction.	**55.9 km** ▲	
	(3.0 km)		
▼ **3.0 km**	Twin Heads on right. CSA.		
	Almost identical rocky outcrops providing good photo opportunities in the late afternoon.		
	Twin Heads on left. CSA.	**52.9 km** ▲	
	(2.0 km)		
▼ **5.0 km**	Creek crossing.		
	Creek crossing.	**50.9 km** ▲	
	(5.5 km)		
▼ **10.5 km**	Track junction. CSA. Track on left.		
	Track on left leads 0.1 km to carpark at base of Mt Ernest (Chinamans Hat).		

KUNAWARRITJI ◀▶ HALLS CREEK

Halls Creek
Historic Halls Creek in the south-east of the Kimberley was the site of Western Australia's first gold rush in 1885. The town managed to survive after the gold petered out and today is a centre for the surrounding beef cattle district and a gateway to major attractions such as the intriguing dome-shaped hills of Purnululu National Park to the north-east.

Lake Gregory
This large lake system was named after explorer Augustus Gregory who in 1855–56 led an expedition charged with finding new land for settlement. Leaving from the Victoria River in the Northern Territory, Gregory trekked south-west in early 1856, through present-day Gregory National Park and along Sturt Creek for nearly 500 kilometres, giving up when the creek disappeared into the 'unbounded waste' of a great salt lake.

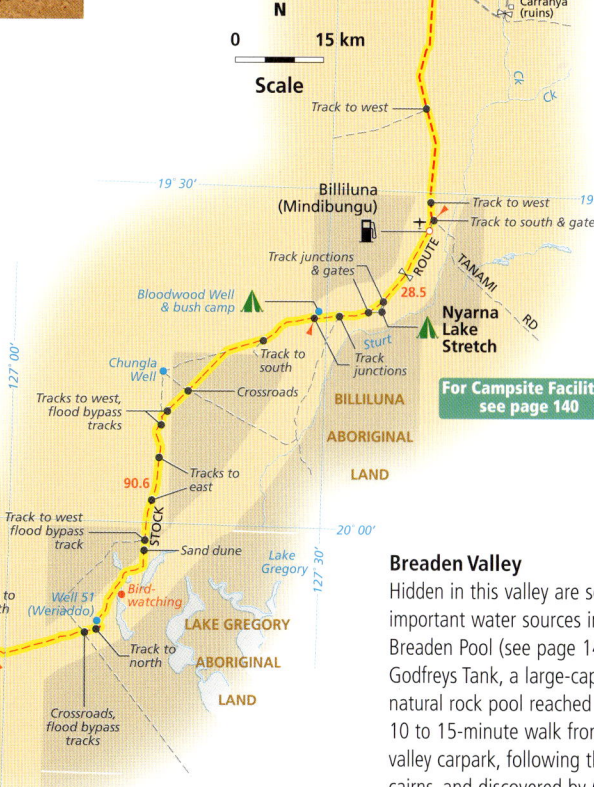

Breaden Valley
Hidden in this valley are several important water sources including Breaden Pool (see page 141) and Godfreys Tank, a large-capacity natural rock pool reached via a 10 to 15-minute walk from the valley carpark, following the rock cairns, and discovered by Godfrey Massie, a member of Carnegie's 1896–97 exploring party.

CANNING STOCK ROUTE

	Track junction. CSA. Track and Mt Ernest (Chinamans Hat) on right.	45.4 km ▲
	GPS S:20 10.064 E:126 34.051 **UTM** 52K 245762E 7768096N	
	(2.3 km)	
▼ 12.8 km	Creek crossing.	
	Creek crossing.	43.1 km ▲
	(10.8 km)	
▼ 23.6 km	Well 49 on right. Bush camping on left. CSA.	
	Well 49, restored in July 2001, was dug to depth of 50 feet (15.2 m) with capacity of 4800 gallons (21 821 litres) and replenishment rate of 500 gallons (2273 litres) per hour. Behind well is grave site of Jack Smith. Water available.	
	Well 49 on left. Bush camping on right. CSA.	32.3 km ▲
	GPS S:20 09.854 E:126 40.878 **UTM** 52K 257654E 7768653N	
	(6.1 km)	
▼ 29.7 km	Track junction. 'Notice to Travellers' on left. CSA. Track on left.	
	Track on left leads to bush campsite.	
	Track junction. 'Notice to Travellers' on right. CSA. Track on right.	26.2 km ▲
	(0.1 km)	
▼ 29.8 km	Track junction. CSA. Track on left.	
	Track on left leads short distance to bush campsite amid stand of desert oak.	
	Track junction. CSA. Track on right to bush campsite.	26.1 km ▲
	(0.5 km)	
▼ 30.3 km	Track junction. CSA. Track on left.	
	Track on left leads 0.1 km to good campsite well shaded by stand of desert oak.	
	Track junction. CSA. Track on right to bush campsite.	25.6 km ▲
	(25.6 km)	
▼ 55.9 km	Track junction.	
	Zero trip meter at track junction. CSA. Track on left to camping area.	0.0 km ▲
	GPS S:20 11.932 E:126 58.785 **UTM** 52K 288904E 7765226N	
▼ 0.0 km	Zero trip meter at track junction. CSA. Track on right.	
	Track on right leads 2.0 km to large shaded **Well 50 camping area**, then further 0.3 km to Well 50 and further 4.1 km to carpark. From carpark a walk leads up creek bed to Culvida Soak. Well 50, GPS S:20 12.553 E:126 57.861 UTM 52K 287309E 7764061N, was dug to depth of 62 feet (18.9 m) with capacity of 3300 gallons (15 000 litres) and replenishment rate of 500 gallons (2273 litres) per hour.	
	Track junction.	90.6 km ▲
	(16.3 km)	
▼ 16.3 km	Crossroads. CSA. SP: 51. Tracks on left and right are flood bypass tracks.	
	Crossroads. CSA. SP: 50.	74.3 km ▲
	(2.0 km)	
▼ 18.3 km	Track junction. CSA. Track on left.	

	Track junction. CSA. Track on right.	72.3 km ▲
	(1.9 km)	
▼ 20.2 km	SP: Weriaddo Well, on left. CSA.	
	Weriaddo Well (Well 51) was dug to depth of 22 feet (6.7 m) with capacity of 900 gallons (4091 litres) and replenishment rate of 1750 gallons (7955 litres) per hour. Well 51, northernmost well on stock route, is filled in.	
	SP: Weriaddo Well, on right. CSA.	70.4 km ▲
	GPS S:20 08.870 E:127 08.768 **UTM** 52K 306232E 7771079N	
	(6.1 km)	
▼ 26.3 km	Lake on right. CSA.	
	Lake on right is part of Lake Gregory system. Heavy rains sometimes fill lakes, enticing waterbirds such as cranes, ducks, cockatoos and brolgas. Wonderful site for birdwatching.	
	Lake on left. CSA.	64.3 km ▲
	(9.3 km)	
▼ 35.6 km	Last sand dune on CSR.	
	First sand dune on CSR.	55.0 km ▲
	GPS S:20 02.435 E:127 12.958 **UTM** 52K 313405E 7783032N	
	(1.7 km)	
▼ 37.3 km	Track junction. CSA. Track on left is flood bypass track.	
	Track junction. CSA. Track on right is flood bypass track.	53.3 km ▲
	(6.7 km)	
▼ 44.0 km	Track junction. CSA. Track on right.	
	Track junction. CSA. Track on left.	46.6 km ▲
	(15.8 km)	
▼ 59.8 km	Track junction. CSA. Track on left is flood bypass track.	
	Track junction. CSA. Track on right is flood bypass track.	30.8 km ▲
	(0.8 km)	

Flat-topped hills surround the entrance to Breaden Valley

KUNAWARRITJI ◀▶ HALLS CREEK

▼ 60.6 km Track junction. CSA. Track on left is flood bypass track.

    Track junction. CSA. Track on right is flood bypass track. 30.0 km ▲

(5.3 km)

▼ 65.9 km Crossroads. CSA. SP: CSR.
Track on left leads 7.0 km to Chungla Well.

    Crossroads. CSA. SP: CSR. 24.7 km ▲

GPS   S:19 47.726 E:127 17.185
UTM   52K 320499E 7810247N

(24.5 km)

▼ 90.4 km Y-junction. KR. Track on left.

    Track junction. CSA. Track on right. 0.2 km ▲

(0.2 km)

▼ 90.6 km Track junction.

    Zero trip meter at track junction. CSA. Track on right leads to Bloodwood Well. 0.0 km ▲

GPS   S:19 41.497 E:127 28.877
UTM   52K 340813E 7821933N

▼ 0.0 km Zero trip meter at junction. CSA. Track on left.
Track on left leads 0.2 km to Bloodwood Well and windmill. Possible bush camping.

    Track junction. 28.5 km ▲

(4.2 km)

▼ 4.2 km Track junction. CSA. Track on right.

    Track junction. CSA. Track on left. 24.3 km ▲

(5.0 km)

▼ 9.2 km Gate. LAF. Through gate Y-junction. KL. Track on right SP: Nyarna Lake Stretch.
Track on right leads 2.4 km to **Nyarna Lake Stretch camping area** with well-shaded sites near lake, on Sturt Creek. Bookings required to camp here (see Permits and bookings).

    Track junction. CSA through gate. LAF. Track on left. 19.3 km ▲

GPS   S:19 40.773 E:127 33.973
UTM   52K 349705E 7823346N

(3.0 km)

▼ 12.2 km Track junction. CSA through gate. LAF. Track on right to Nyarna Lake Stretch camping area.

    Gate. LAF. Through gate Y-junction. KR. Track on left to Nyarna Lake Stretch camping area. 16.3 km ▲

(6.0 km)

▼ 18.2 km Track junction. CSA through gate. LAF. Track on right.

    Gate. LAF. Through gate Y-junction. KR. Track on left. 10.3 km ▲

(7.8 km)

▼ 26.0 km Y-junction. KL. Track on right.

    Track junction. CSA. Track on left. 2.5 km ▲

(0.5 km)

▼ 26.5 km Crossroads. CSA. SP: Tanami Highway.
Track on right leads 0.1 km to Billiluna store.

    Crossroads. CSA. SP: Canning Stock Route. 2.0 km ▲

GPS   S:19 33.306 E:127 39.531
UTM   52K 359309E 7837199N

(0.7 km)

▼ 27.2 km Track junction. CSA. Track on right.

    Y-junction. KR. SP: Canning Stock Route. Track on left SP: Residents Only. 1.3 km ▲

(0.8 km)

▼ 28.0 km Track junction. CSA. Track on left.

    Track junction. CSA. Track on right. 0.5 km ▲

(0.5 km)

▼ 28.5 km T-junction. This is Tanami Rd.

    Zero trip meter at road junction. TR. SP: Billiluna Station. Road SO. 0.0 km ▲
Road SO to Sturt Creek and Alice Springs.

GPS   S:19 32.380 E:127 40.045
UTM   52K 360194E 7838914N

▼ 0.0 km Zero trip meter at T-junction with Tanami Rd. TL.
Road on right leads 3.5 km to Sturt Creek, and Alice Springs (see Tanami Road, pages 46–55).

    Road junction. 172.0 km ▲

(42.2 km)

▼ 42.2 km Road junction. CSA over grid. Road on right leads to Wolfe Creek Meteorite Crater.
Road on right leads 23.0 km to **Wolfe Creek Meteorite camping area** and carpark. Camping area is open space with individual camping bays. (See Tanami Road, pages 51 and 55, for more details on crater.)

    Road junction. CSA. Road on left leads to Wolfe Creek Meteorite Crater. 129.8 km ▲

GPS   S:19 10.401 E:127 38.941
UTM   52K 357947E 7879441N

(112.8 km)

▼ 155.0 km Quarantine bin on left. CSA.
Bin is for disposal of all fresh fruit, vegetables, nuts and honey brought into WA from NT.

    Quarantine bin on right. CSA. 17.0 km ▲

(0.4 km)

▼ 155.4 km T-junction with bitumen. This is Great Northern Hwy. TR. SP: Halls Creek 18. Road on left SP: 282 Fitzroy Crossing.

    Road junction. TL onto gravel road. SP: Tanami Rd/Alice Springs. 16.6 km ▲

GPS   S:18 19.475 E:127 33.281
UTM   52K 347264E 7973297N

(16.6 km)

▼ 172.0 km Halls Creek. SP: Hall Street, and Visitor Information Centre on right.

    Zero trip meter in Halls Creek on Great Northern Hwy. SP: Hall Street, and Visitor Information Centre on left. Proceed in southerly direction along highway towards Fitzroy Crossing. 0.0 km ▲

GPS   S:18 13.469 E:127 40.047
UTM   52K 359102E 7984466N

REVERSE DIRECTIONS START

FOLLOWING PAGES
Stand of grasstrees south of Well 6

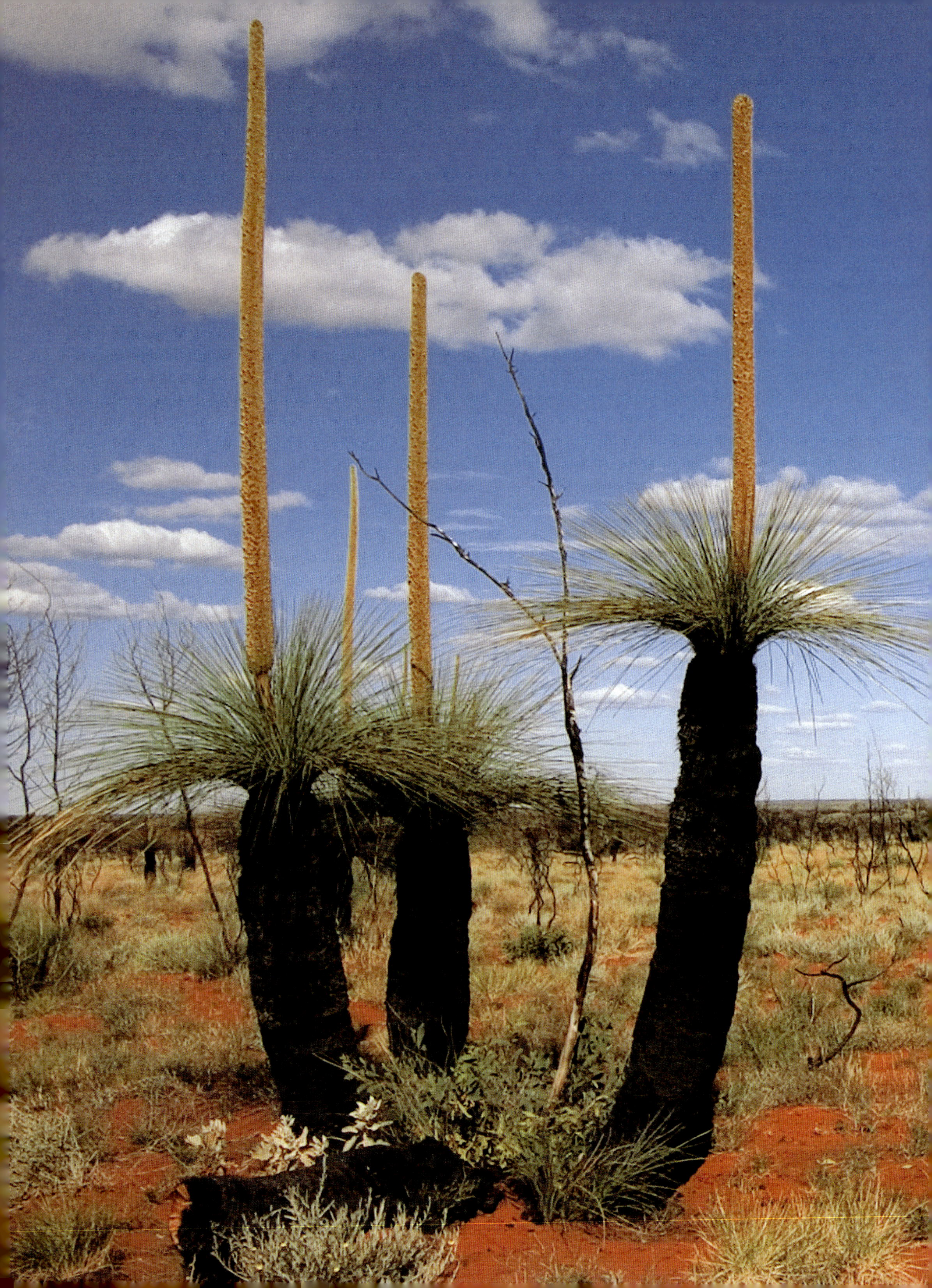

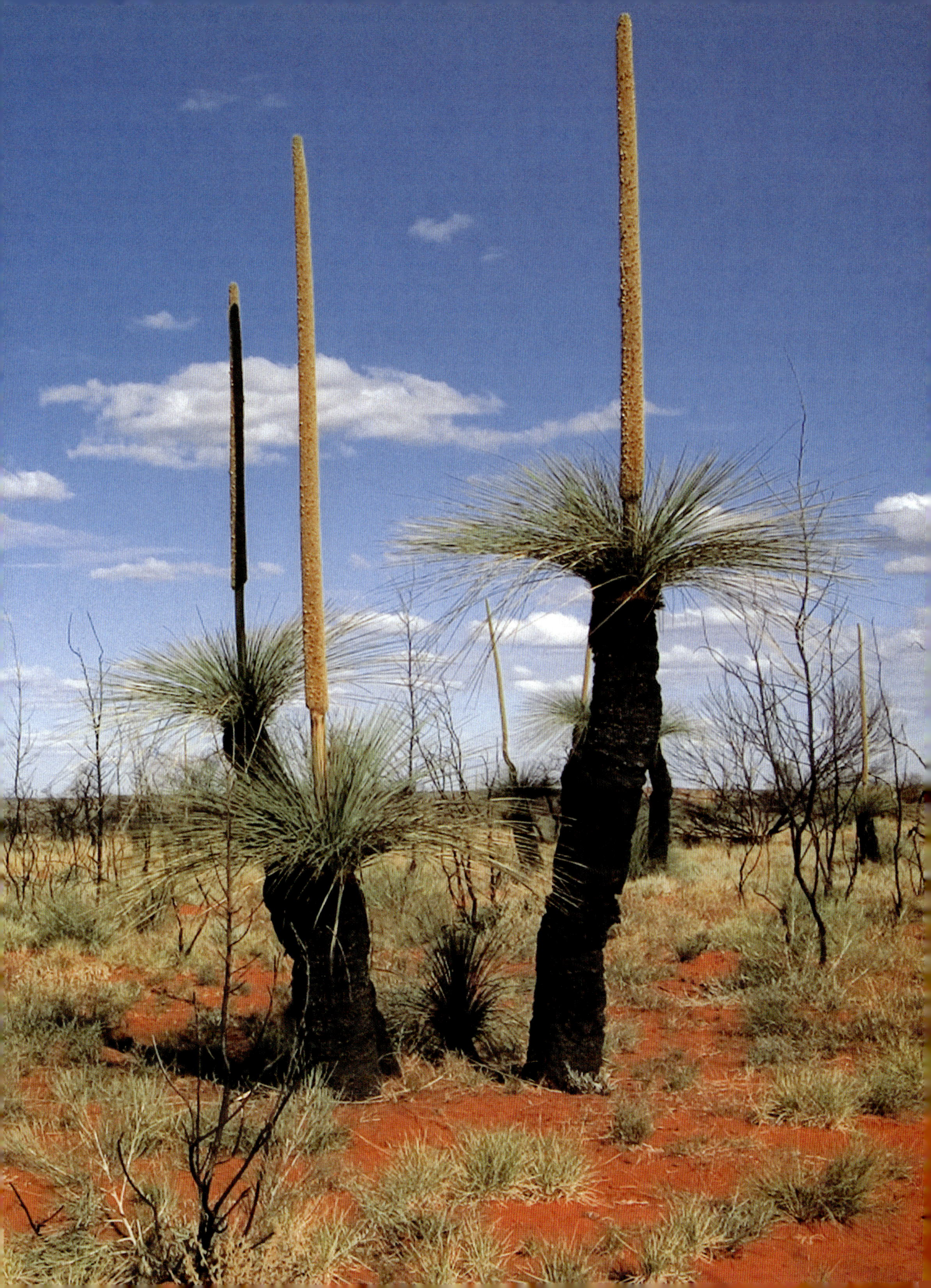

Holland Track

Wave Rock near Hyden

HYDEN ◄►COOLGARDIE 321.5 KM
ONE SECTION ONLY *(easy)*
WHEN TO GO March–November **TIME** 3–4 days

Following the route of early prospectors, the remote Holland Track offers four-wheel-drive travellers an opportunity to explore the heathlands, sand plains and woodlands that were opened up during the rush to Western Australia's goldfields in the late 1800s.

The 530-kilometre track dates from April 1893, when John Holland set out from Broomehill (about 150 kilometres north of Albany) with a small party of men to establish a shorter route for prospectors between the port of Albany and the goldfields of Coolgardie. In a little over two months a route was forged, and was to be used by around 18 000 fortune-seekers before being abandoned when the goldfields were linked to Perth by rail. In 1992, to mark the centenary of Holland's achievement, Graeme Newbey and Adrian Malloy cut a new track, which followed the original as closely as possible.

The trek described in these pages covers the north-eastern section of the Holland Track, from Hyden in the south to Coolgardie in the north. It passes numerous granite outcrops and rock holes that provided vital water supplies to prospectors and travellers. Vegetation varies from low stunted heath in the south to stands of majestic salmon gum and open woodlands of gimlet in the north. Despite the remote and at times inhospitable terrain, the journey is not particularly difficult.

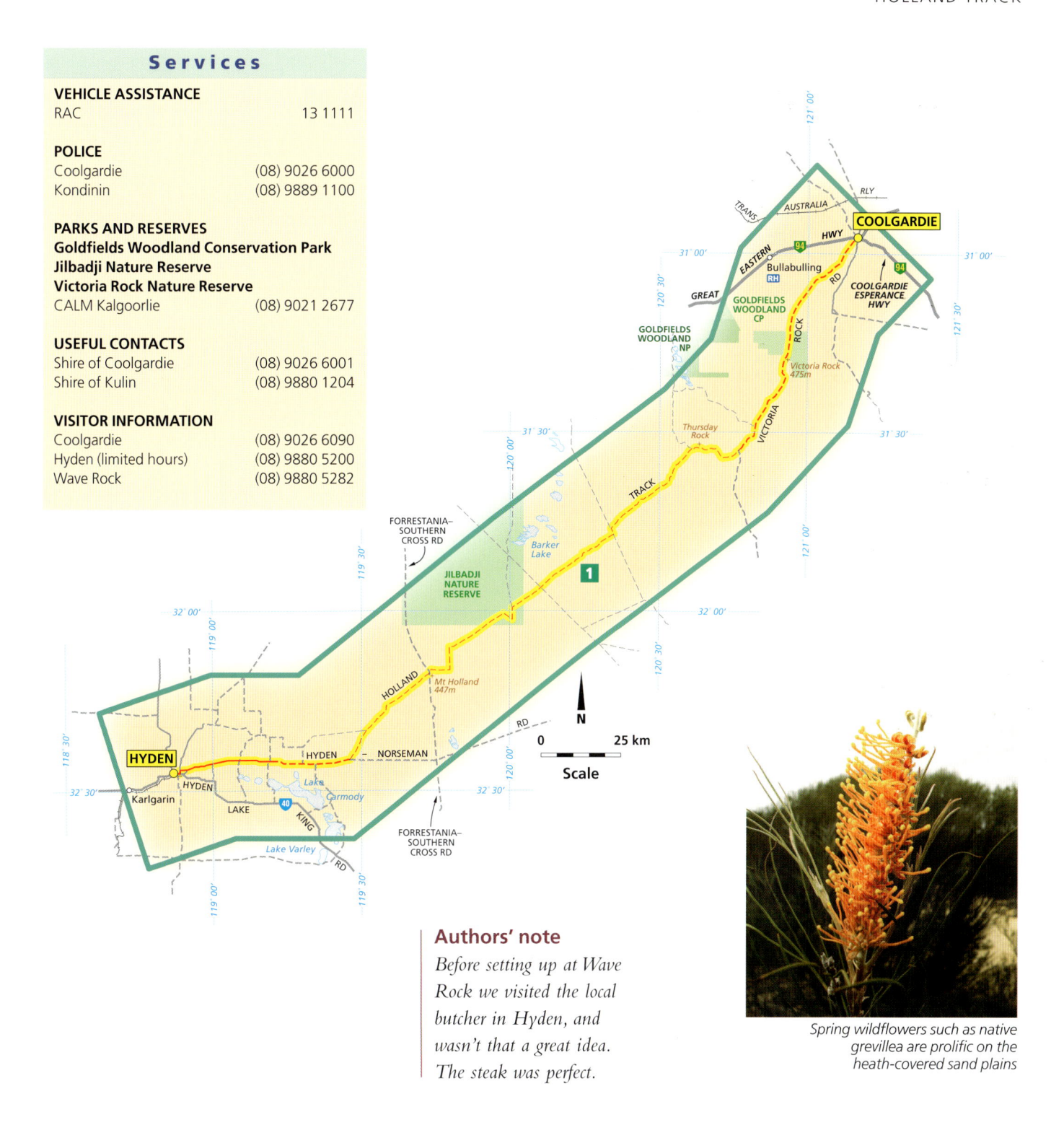

HOLLAND TRACK

Services

VEHICLE ASSISTANCE
RAC 13 1111

POLICE
Coolgardie (08) 9026 6000
Kondinin (08) 9889 1100

PARKS AND RESERVES
Goldfields Woodland Conservation Park
Jilbadji Nature Reserve
Victoria Rock Nature Reserve
CALM Kalgoorlie (08) 9021 2677

USEFUL CONTACTS
Shire of Coolgardie (08) 9026 6001
Shire of Kulin (08) 9880 1204

VISITOR INFORMATION
Coolgardie (08) 9026 6090
Hyden (limited hours) (08) 9880 5200
Wave Rock (08) 9880 5282

Authors' note

Before setting up at Wave Rock we visited the local butcher in Hyden, and wasn't that a great idea. The steak was perfect.

Spring wildflowers such as native grevillea are prolific on the heath-covered sand plains

Town Facilities

	Fuel: D/P/A	Mechanical repairs	Tyre repairs	Public telephone	Public toilets	Shop/supplies	Gas refills	Ice	Visitor information	Post office	Medical centre	Police	Meals	Motel	Hotel	Cabins	Caravan park	Camping
Coolgardie	DPA	•	•	•	•	•	•	•	•	•	•	•	•	•	•	•	•	•
Hyden	DPA	•	•	•	•	•	•	•		•	•		•	•	•	•	•	•

157

HOLLAND TRACK

HYDEN ◀▶ COOLGARDIE 321.5 KM

Start point
Hyden

Road atlas
352 B5, 358 F4

Total distance
322.7 km (includes route-directed side trip)

Standard
Easy

Time
3–4 days

Longest distance no PD (includes all options)
347.5 km (Hyden to Coolgardie)

Topographic maps
Auslig 1:250 000 series: *Hyden*; *Lake Johnston*; *Boorabbin*

Other useful information
- CALM brochure: *The Goldfields*.
- Tourist flyer: *Holland Track: Broomehill to Bayley's Rush 1893–1993*, available from Hyden Visitor Information Centre.

Description
The Hyden–Coolgardie section of the Holland Track traverses remote country. Characterised by heath-covered sand plains in the south, it gradually gives way to dense scrubland around Mount Holland and then to woodlands of gimlet and salmon gum, which continue through to Victoria Rock Nature Reserve towards the end of the trek. Throughout the route there are outcrops of granite, some towering high above the surrounding plains, with natural water catchments in the form of gnamma holes that quenched the thirst of early travellers and prospectors on their way to the goldfields. The names of natural features along the track often recall the four men who were first to cut their way through: John Holland, Rudolph and David Krakouer and John Carmody.

The entire route is generally easy, except for a few boggy sections that hold water for some time after rain, but many of these have by-pass tracks. There are some stretches of deep, soft sand and some lightly corrugated areas, mostly on the sand plains. Trackside scrub is overgrown in places so be prepared for some minor damage to your vehicle's paintwork.

Shortly after leaving Hyden you will see the signpost to Wave Rock, one of Western Australia's most photographed natural attractions – the middle of the day can often provide the best light for pictures of this ancient granite formation. Continuing eastwards on the Hyden–Norseman Road you reach the Holland Track almost 50 kilometres from Hyden. Veering north-eastwards it makes its way across the plains – if you travel in spring, these are carpeted in wildflowers. Past Wattle Rocks is a mallee fowl nest, located near the side of the track.

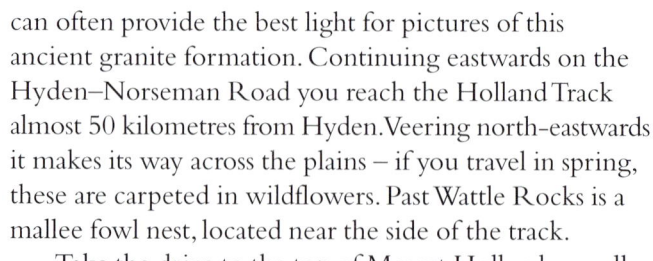

Take the drive to the top of Mount Holland or walk part of the way. The panoramic views from the summit are worth the effort. John Holland's party climbed the rocky peak in May 1893 and it was later named in his memory. He thought the surrounding country looked auriferous, but despite searching the party found no gold. Today the nearby Bounty Gold Mine is a successful operation, and numerous mine access roads criss-cross the route in this vicinity. After Victoria Rock Nature Reserve the road improves, although it remains gravel, for the short run to the historic goldmining town of Coolgardie.

Take time to explore the natural features of this landscape, particularly the granite outcrops. The largest of these, Thursday Rock and Victoria Rock, provide dramatic 360-degree views from their summits. At Thursday Rock a collection of weathered boulders, all sizes and shapes, is strewn haphazardly on the summit. The massive granite outcrop of Victoria Rock, named by Holland, was a landmark to prospectors using the track. Various lizard species inhabit these rocky areas, and you may spot a thorny devil out on the sand plains.

Except for established campgrounds and caravan parks around Hyden and Coolgardie, Victoria Rock has the only campsite with facilities. However, you should try some of the inviting bush camping spots mentioned in the route directions. The majestic salmon gum and bronze-trunked gimlet of the woodlands create delightful bush campsites.

Advice and warnings
- Sections of the route are difficult and impassable during and after rain so avoid travel at these times. The narrow and winding track makes it difficult to see oncoming traffic, and there are sections where it is not possible to pull over. Overhanging vegetation in places may cause scratches to vehicle paintwork. Contact CALM Kalgoorlie, tel. (08) 9021 2677, or Shire of Coolgardie, tel (08) 9026 6001, to check track conditions.
- Standard road tyres or all-terrain tyres are suitable.
- Towing off-road camper trailers is possible but pulling over for oncoming traffic on the narrow track is particularly difficult in some sections.

HYDEN ◀▶ COOLGARDIE

Weathered boulder on Thursday Rock

- Drinking water is not available at bush campsites so carry enough for drinking, cooking and washing needs.
- Along last section of track between Gnarlbine Rock and Coolgardie there are numerous working mine operations with open mine shafts and unstable excavations. Take care near mining sites. Nothing is to be taken or disturbed at these sites.

Permits and bookings
- No permits required.
- Camping fees apply at Wave Rock caravan park.

ROUTE DIRECTIONS

▼ 0.0 km Zero trip meter in Hyden at junction of SP: Lynch Street, and Hyden–Lake King Rd. Hyden Memorial Hall and CWA on left. CSA in easterly direction towards Wave Rock.

Hyden. SP: Lynch Street, and Memorial Hall on right. 4.1 km ▲

GPS S:32 26.950 E:118 51.917
UTM 50H 675335E 6408244N

(2.0 km)

▼ 2.0 km Road junction. TL. SP: 2 Wave Rock/181 Southern Cross.

T-junction. TR. SP: Hyden 2. 2.1 km ▲

(1.0 km)

▼ 3.0 km Road junction. TR. SP: Wave Rock Resort. Road SO SP: The Humps 18/Mulkas Cave 18.

T-junction. TL. SP: 3 Hyden. 1.1 km ▲

(0.8 km)

▼ 3.8 km SP: Breakers Picnic Area, on right. CSA.
Picnic area has tables, electric barbecue and toilets.

Picnic area on left. CSA. 0.3 km ▲

(0.3 km)

▼ 4.1 km Road junction.

Zero trip meter at road junction. Road on left to Wave Rock and caravan park. CSA. 0.0 km ▲

GPS S:32 26.470 E:118 53.889
UTM 50H 678441E 6409082N

▼ 0.0 km Zero trip meter at road junction. CSA. SP: Hippos Yawn. Road on right leads 100 m to SP: Wave Rock carpark and caravan park.

Road junction. 66.2 km ▲

(0.5 km)

▼ 0.5 km Road junction. CSA. Road on right leads 200 m to SP: Hippos Yawn.
Hippos Yawn is large rock sculptured by wind and weather into shape of yawning hippopotamus' mouth.

Track junction. CSA. Road on left SP: Hippos Yawn. 65.7 km ▲

(0.7 km)

▼ 1.2 km T-junction. TL. SP: Norseman 295. Road on right SP: Lake King/Hyden.

Road junction. TR. SP: Wave Rock 1.2. 65.0 km ▲

GPS S:32 26.458 E:118 54.654
UTM 50H 679640E 6409077N

(17.5 km)

▼ 18.7 km Crossroads. CSA. SP: Lake Varley 77.

Crossroads. CSA. SP: 23 Hyden. 47.5 km ▲

(9.1 km)

▼ 27.8 km Road junction. CSA. SP: Hyden Norseman Rd. Road on right SP: Lake O'Connor Rd.

Road junction. CSA. SP: 31 Hyden/93 Kondinin. Road on left SP: Lake O'Connor Rd. 38.4 km ▲

(21.0 km)

▼ 48.8 km Pass through State Barrier Fence.
The State Barrier Fence was built in the early 1900s to help control the rabbit population, but proved unsuccessful. When completed in 1905, the fence stretched from Cape Keraudren to Starvation Boat Harbour, a total of 1822 km.

Pass through State Barrier Fence. 17.4 km ▲

GPS S:32 25.408 E:119 24.500
UTM 50H 726457E 6410072N

(4.9 km)

▼ 53.7 km Crossroads. TL. SP: Holland Track 4WD Only.
Track is marked by old letterbox and monument.

Crossroads. TR. This is Hyden–Norseman Rd. 12.5 km ▲

GPS S:32 24.845 E:119 27.537
UTM 50H 731242E 6411004N

(7.5 km)

▼ 61.2 km Track junction. CSA. Track on left.

Y-junction. KL. SP: HT. 5.0 km ▲

(3.2 km)

▼ 64.4 km Track junction. KR. Minor track on left.

159

HOLLAND TRACK

Travelling along the Holland Track

Agnes Gnamma Hole
This rock hole containing water was named after John Holland's wife, Agnes, who died of typhoid in 1894 aged 20 years and 8 months. She travelled the track with her husband in 1893, probably the first European woman to traverse the route.

Hyden
The town of Hyden, gateway to Wave Rock, is a service centre for the surrounding farming district and provides all facilities and supplies.

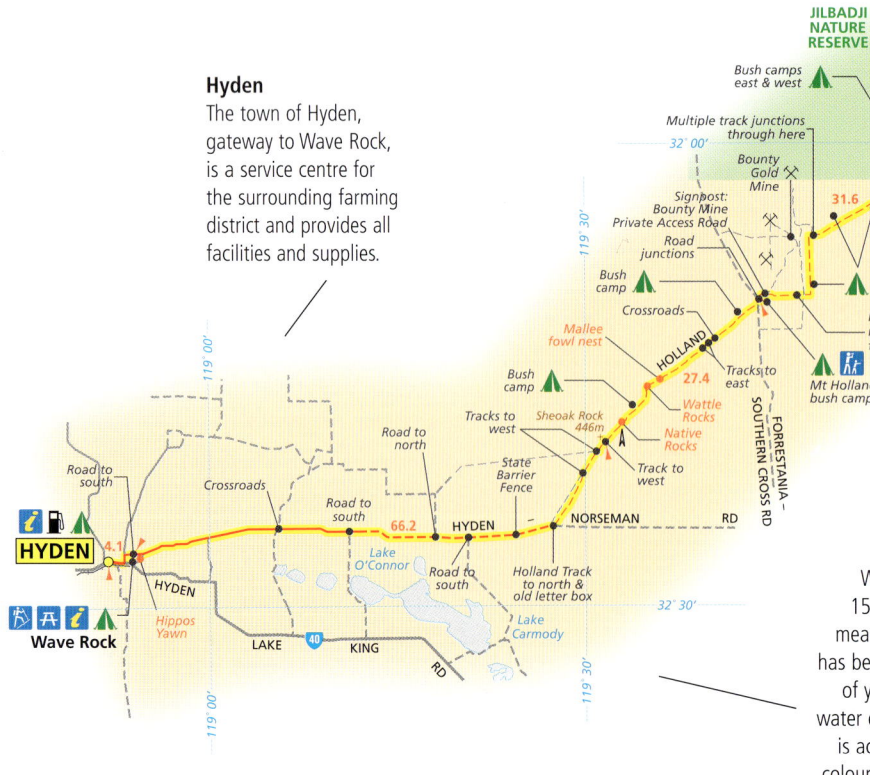

Wave Rock
Wave Rock, an awesome 15-metre-high granite cliff measuring 110 metres long, has been shaped over millions of years by weathering and water erosion. The wave effect is accentuated by streaks of colour, the result of dissolving minerals during rain.

HYDEN ◀▶ COOLGARDIE

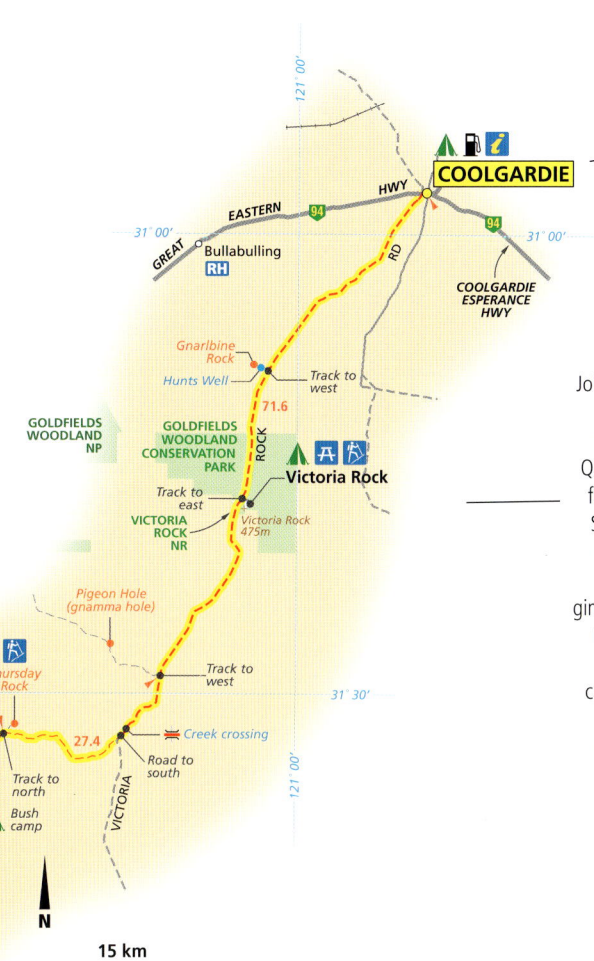

Coolgardie
Coolgardie is an interesting place to spend a few hours. Its grand buildings and mining relics testify to its former boomtown status. Once a centre of 15 000 people in the early 1900s, its population is now around 1000.

Victoria Rock
John Holland named the large granite outcrop of Victoria Rock on 13 June 1893 after Queen Victoria, and erected a flagpole on its highest point. Surrounding this spectacular rock are regrowth forests of salmon gum, redwood and gimlet, which were clear-felled in the 1920s. Fine examples of salmon gum woodlands can be seen elsewhere along the track, particularly near Centenary Rocks (pictured).

Mallee Fowl Nest
A large mallee fowl mound just north of Wattle Rocks is maintained by a male bird for ten months of the year. Built from sticks, plants, leaves and dirt, the mound is a well-designed incubator for the eggs laid by the female. The heat generated by the decomposing plants and leaves keeps the eggs warm. The male, which has a tongue that can gauge temperature, is able to keep the mound at a constant 33–34 degrees Celsius by removing or adding sand. After 49 days of incubation the chicks hatch, dig their way out of the mound and then must fend for themselves.

Campsite Facilities

	Toilets	Disabled access	4WD access only	Off-road trailer	Off-road caravan	Drinking water	Fee payable	Ranger patrolled	BBQ/fireplace	Campfires prohibited	Picnic tables	Shelter shed	No rubbish disposal	Public phone	Shower	Bushwalking	Swimming	Swimming not advised	Fishing	Canoeing	Dogs allowed
Victoria Rock	•		•	•			•		•		•	•			•						
Wave Rock	•	•		•	•	•	•		•		•		•	•	•						•

HOLLAND TRACK

		Track junction. KL. Minor track on right.	1.8 km ▲
	(1.8 km)		
▼ 66.2 km	Track junction.		
		Zero trip meter at track junction. CSA. Track on right to Sheoak Rock.	0.0 km ▲
	GPS S:32 19.392 E:119 31.677 **UTM** 50H 737970E 6420931N		
▼ 0.0 km	Zero trip meter at track junction. CSA. Track on left.		
	Track on left leads 0.5 km to Sheoak Rock and trig point.		
		Track junction.	27.4 km ▲
	(2.7 km)		
▼ 2.7 km	Communications tower on right. CSA.		
		Communications tower on left. CSA.	24.7 km ▲
	(0.4 km)		
▼ 3.1 km	Track skirts around edge of Native Rocks.		
		Track skirts around edge of Native Rocks.	24.3 km ▲
	(2.7 km)		
▼ 5.8 km	Possible bush camping on left. CSA.		
		Possible bush camping on right. CSA.	21.6 km ▲
	(3.6 km)		
▼ 9.4 km	Wattle Rocks.		
		Wattle Rocks.	18.0 km ▲
	(1.8 km)		
▼ 11.2 km	Mallee fowl nest on left. CSA.		
		Mallee fowl nest on right. CSA.	16.2 km ▲
	GPS S:32 15.337 E:119 35.970 **UTM** 50H 744889E 6428264N		
	(6.7 km)		
▼ 17.9 km	Track junction. CSA. Track on right.		
		Track junction. CSA. Track on left.	9.5 km ▲
	(1.0 km)		
▼ 18.9 km	Track junction. CSA. Minor track on right.		
		Track junction. CSA. Minor track on left.	8.5 km ▲
	(1.0 km)		
▼ 19.9 km	Crossroads. CSA.		
		Crossroads. CSA.	7.5 km ▲
	(4.3 km)		
▼ 24.2 km	Possible bush campsite on left. CSA.		
		Possible bush campsite on right. CSA.	3.2 km ▲
	(3.0 km)		
▼ 27.2 km	Y-junction. KR. SP: Holland Track.		
		Track junction. CSA. Track on right.	0.2 km ▲
	(0.1 km)		
▼ 27.3 km	T-junction. TL. SP: HT. This is Southern Cross Rd.		
		Track junction. TR. SP: HT.	0.1 km ▲
	GPS S:32 10.200 E:119 43.844 **UTM** 50H 757498E 6437452N		
	(0.1 km)		
▼ 27.4 km	Road junction. Side trip to Mount Holland.		
		Zero trip meter at road junction. CSA. Track on left to Mt Holland and bush campsites.	0.0 km ▲
	GPS S:32 10.133 E:119 43.877 **UTM** 50H 757553E 6437575N		

▶	**SIDE TRIP: Mount Holland**		
▼ 0.0 km	Zero trip meter at road junction. Turn onto track to east.		
	(0.1 km)		
▼ 0.1 km	Track junction. TR. Road SO leads to bush camping areas.		
	(0.4 km)		
▼ 0.5 km	Track junction. Track on right leads up steep incline to summit of Mt Holland.		
	It is recommended that you park here and walk to summit, which is a small area and suitable only for one vehicle at a time.		
	(0.1 km)		
▼ 0.6 km	Mt Holland summit (486 m). Return to side trip start.		
	GPS S:32 10.265 E:119 44.087 **UTM** 50H 757877E 6437322N		
◀	**END SIDE TRIP**		
▼ 0.0 km	Zero trip meter at road junction. CSA. Track on right to Mt Holland and bush campsites.		
	Road junction. See side trip to Mount Holland.		31.6 km ▲
	(0.2 km)		
▼ 0.2 km	Y-junction. KR. SP: Holland Track. Road on left SP: Southern Cross.		
	Entering SP: Bounty Mine Private Access Road. Please drive with caution. On left after junction are some waterholes found by John Holland.		
		Road junction. TL. SP: Hyden.	31.4 km ▲
	GPS S:32 10.027 E:119 43.853 **UTM** 50H 757520E 6437772N		
	(0.9 km)		
▼ 1.1 km	Y-junction. KR. SP: Holland Track. Road SO SP: Bounty Gold Mine.		
		Track junction. CSA. Minor track on left, and track on right SP: Bounty Gold Mine.	30.5 km ▲
	(2.3 km)		
▼ 3.4 km	Track junction. CSA. Track on right.		
		Track junction. CSA. Track on left.	28.2 km ▲
	(2.0 km)		
▼ 5.4 km	Track junction. CSA. Tracks on right and left.		
		Track junction. CSA. Tracks on right and left.	26.2 km ▲
	(0.6 km)		
▼ 6.0 km	Y-junction. KR. SP: Holland Track.		
		Track junction. CSA. Track on right.	25.6 km ▲
	(0.2 km)		
▼ 6.2 km	Crossroads. CSA.		
		Crossroads. CSA.	25.4 km ▲
	(0.2 km)		
▼ 6.4 km	Crossroads. CSA.		
		Crossroads. CSA.	25.2 km ▲
	(0.5 km)		
▼ 6.9 km	Track junction. TL. SP: Holland Track.		
		Track junction. TR. SP: HT.	24.7 km ▲
	GPS S:32 09.864 E:119 47.880 **UTM** 50H 763859E 6437910N		
	(1.3 km)		

John Holland's Extraordinary Trek

The discovery of gold in 1892 at Bayley's Find, later Coolgardie, was the start of Western Australia's gold-rush period. To reach the goldfields, fortune-seekers flocked to Perth from the eastern states and elsewhere, while those living in the far south of the state had to travel via Northam, only 100 kilometres from the capital. For southerners, and sea travellers from the east, a more direct route from the port of Albany would substantially shorten the journey.

On 14 April 1893 John Holland, Rudolph and David Krakouer and John Carmody left Broomehill. Their aim was to cut a cart track through remote country to the main water supply point for the goldfields at Gnarlbine Rock. For the first few days they travelled through farmland but on 18 April they ventured into unknown territory, with just a compass to guide them. Constant problems were lack of water and feed for the horses. The party discovered that many of the granite outcrops were natural catchments, yielding good volumes of water for considerable periods after rain. After cutting their way through dense scrub the group arrived at King Rock on 15 May. Finding plenty of spring grasses, they rested until 18 May before continuing through scrub with no signs of water or food for the horses.

The men soon happened upon a large hill, later named Mount Holland. Near its base they found a gnamma hole containing good water. Holland thought the surrounding terrain looked auriferous, but the party was not lucky enough to find gold. Today, Mount Holland is the centre of extensive goldmining activity. The men left Mount Holland on 24 May, and two days later heavy rain alleviated water problems for the remainder of the journey. On 27 May they came across a large area of about 100 acres with excellent horse feed, a soak and a large stand of sandalwood. They named the place Sandalwood Camp and rested here for a few days. On 14 June the party approached a large granite outcrop, which they named Victoria Rock. On its highest peak Holland erected a flagpole inscribed with his name.

Gnarlbine Rock was the destination of Holland and his companions

The party discovered that many of the granite outcrops were natural catchments, yielding good volumes of water

The party left here on 16 June (John Carmody's 21st birthday) and, much to their surprise and delight, arrived shortly after at Gnarlbine Rock. They reached Bayley's Find on 18 June, the day after Paddy Hannan reported his discovery of gold at what is now Kalgoorlie.

John Holland and his party had covered nearly 530 kilometres in two months and four days. Their cart road shortened the arduous overland journey to the goldfields by almost a fortnight, and many hopefuls disembarked at Albany and used the Holland Track in preference to the longer route via the port of Fremantle. Most prospectors travelled the track on foot, with many pushing their possessions on crudely made wheelbarrows. The track remained in use until around 1915.

HOLLAND TRACK

▼ 8.2 km　T-junction. TL. SP: Holland Track.

Possible bush campsite on right 50 m prior to junction.

　　　　　　　　Track junction. TR. SP: HT.　23.4 km ▲

(5.8 km)

▼ 14.0 km　Track junction. TR. SP: Holland Track.

　　　　　　　　Track junction. TL. SP: HT.　17.6 km ▲

GPS	S:32 06.036 E:119 47.747
UTM	50H 763834E 6444991N

(0.7 km)

▼ 14.7 km　Y-junction. KL. SP: Holland Track.

　　　　　　Track junction. CSA. Track on left.　16.9 km ▲

(0.7 km)

▼ 15.4 km　Y-junction. KL. SP: Holland Track.

　　　　　　Y-junction. KR. SP: Holland Track.　16.2 km ▲

(2.5 km)

▼ 17.9 km　Possible bush campsites on left. CSA.

　　　　　　Possible bush campsites on right. CSA.　13.7 km ▲

(4.8 km)

▼ 22.7 km　Possible bush campsites on right. CSA.

　　　　　　　Possible bush campsites on left. CSA.　8.9 km ▲

(3.5 km)

▼ 26.2 km　Crossroads. CSA. Now entering Jilbadji Nature Reserve.

The 200 000-hectare Jilbadji Nature Reserve protects range of flora and fauna not found elsewhere. Plants include native pomegranate, *Banksia audax* and species of mallee (*Eucalyptus steedmanii*). Birds and animals include mallee fowl, honeyeaters, thornbills and thorny devils.

　　　　　　　　　　　　Crossroads. CSA.　5.4 km ▲

(1.3 km)

▼ 27.5 km　Crossroads. CSA.

　　　　　　　　　　　　Crossroads. CSA.　4.1 km ▲

(1.9 km)

▼ 29.4 km　Possible bush campsites on left and right. CSA.

　　　Possible bush campsites on left and right. CSA.　2.2 km ▲

(2.2 km)

▼ 31.6 km　Track junction.

　　　　Zero trip meter at track junction. CSA.　0.0 km ▲
　　　SP: HT. Track on left to Sandalwood Rocks.

GPS	S:32 01.213 E:119 57.077
UTM	50H 778758E 6453515N

▼ 0.0 km　Zero trip meter at track junction. CSA. SP: HT. Track on right SP: Sandalwood Rocks 1 km.

Track on right leads 1.0 km to SP: Sandalwood Rocks, where bush camping is possible.

　　　　　　　　　　　　Track junction.　93.2 km ▲

(6.3 km)

▼ 6.3 km　State Barrier Fence. TL onto eastern side of fence.

Follow fence line in northerly direction, keeping fence on left.

　　　　　　　End of State Barrier Fence. TR.　86.9 km ▲

GPS	S:32 01.391 E:120 00.443
UTM	51H 217346E 6453078N

Blazed tree near Centenary Rocks

(3.7 km)

▼ 10.0 km　Track junction. TR. SP: HT.

　　　　　　　　Track junction. TL. SP: HT.　83.2 km ▲

(7.2 km)

▼ 17.2 km　Possible bush campsite on right. CSA.

　　　　　　　Possible bush campsite on left. CSA.　76.0 km ▲

(4.3 km)

▼ 21.5 km　Crossroads. CSA. SP: Holland Track. Track on left and right is Banker–Mt Day Rd.

Monument commemorating centenary of Holland Track is here with a visitor book.

　　　　　　　　　　　　Crossroads. CSA.　71.7 km ▲

GPS	S:31 55.978 E:120 06.289
UTM	51J 226284E 6463335N

(21.8 km)

▼ 43.3 km　Track junction. CSA. Minor track on right.

　　　　　　Track junction. CSA. Minor track on left.　49.9 km ▲

(0.6 km)

▼ 43.9 km　Track junction. CSA. Track on left. On right is Centenary Rocks, named to commemorate 1992 Centenary Expedition.

Track on left leads to bush campsites and old trees with blazed scars, probably made by early pioneers.

　　　　　Track junction. CSA. Track on right to　49.3 km ▲
　　　　　bush campsites.

HYDEN ◀ ▶ COOLGARDIE

GPS	S:31 49.317 E:120 17.019
UTM	51J 242889E 6476084N

(2.0 km)

▼ 45.9 km — Track junction. CSA. Track on left to possible bush campsites.

Track junction. CSA. Track on right. 47.3 km ▲

(5.5 km)

▼ 51.4 km — T-junction. TL.

Track junction. TR. 41.8 km ▲

(2.0 km)

▼ 53.4 km — Track junction. TR. SP: HT.

T-junction. TL. SP: HT. 39.8 km ▲

(10.1 km)

▼ 63.5 km — Krakouer Rock on left. CSA.

Krakouer Rock on right. CSA. 29.7 km ▲

GPS	S:31 42.513 E:120 24.819
UTM	51J 254898E 6488960N

(0.2 km)

▼ 63.7 km — Track junction. KL. Track on right joins main track after short distance.

Track junction. CSA. 29.5 km ▲

(0.2 km)

▼ 63.9 km — Track junction. CSA.

Track junction. KR. Track on left joins main track after short distance. 29.3 km ▲

(15.5 km)

▼ 79.4 km — Agnes Gnamma Hole on left. CSA.

Agnes Gnamma Hole on right. CSA. 13.8 km ▲

GPS	S:31 37.615 E:120 31.987
UTM	51J 266018E 6498274N

(5.2 km)

▼ 84.6 km — Diamond Rock on left. CSA. Short walk to rock. Possible bush campsite on right.

Diamond Rock on right. CSA. 8.6 km ▲

GPS	S:31 35.423 E:120 33.576
UTM	51J 268440E 6502382N

(6.9 km)

▼ 91.5 km — Salt lake on left. CSA.

Salt lake on right. CSA. 1.7 km ▲

(0.2 km)

▼ 91.7 km — Track junction. KR. A T-junction is 40 m further on. TR.

Bush camping in this vicinity.

Track junction. TL. SP: HT. A Y-junction is 40 m further on. KL. 1.5 km ▲

GPS	S:31 32.783 E:120 36.480
UTM	51J 272927E 6507362N

(1.5 km)

▼ 93.2 km — Track junction.

Zero trip meter at track junction. TL. SP: HT. Track on right to Thursday Rock. 0.0 km ▲

GPS	S:31 32.612 E:120 37.169
UTM	51J 274011E 6507702N

▼ 0.0 km — Zero trip meter at track junction. TR. SP: HT. Track on left to Thursday Rock.

Track on left leads 1.9 km to carpark and short walk to Thursday Rock. Holland arrived here on a Thursday in 1893, hence the name.

Track junction. 27.4 km ▲

(17.7 km)

▼ 17.7 km — T-junction. TL. This is Victoria Rock Rd.

Road junction. TR. SP: HT. 9.7 km ▲

GPS	S:31 32.787 E:120 46.356
UTM	51J 288557E 6507684N

(9.7 km)

▼ 27.4 km — Road junction.

Zero trip meter at road junction. CSA. Track on right leads 9.0 km to Pigeon Hole. 0.0 km ▲

GPS	S:31 28.844 E:120 49.473
UTM	51J 293345E 6515069N

▼ 0.0 km — Zero trip meter at road junction. CSA. Track on left leads 9.0 km to Pigeon Hole (gnamma hole).

Road junction. 71.6 km ▲

(25.4 km)

▼ 25.4 km — Road junction. CSA. Track on right SP: Victoria Rock Picnic Site.

Track on right leads short distance to picnic site and **Victoria Rock camping area**, a small place at base of east side of rock, among thickets of rock she-oak.

Road junction. CSA. Track on left SP: Victoria Rock Picnic Site. 46.2 km ▲

GPS	S:31 17.256 E:120 55.678
UTM	51J 302767E 6536671N

(16.0 km)

▼ 41.4 km — Road junction. CSA. Road on left SP: Gnarlbine Rock.

Gnarlbine Rock was discovered in 1863 by H. M. Lefroy. In 1864 C. C. Hunt camped here and improved access to the waterhole, which was used by later explorers and prospectors. The soak at Gnarlbine became the main water supply for Coolgardie goldfields.

Road junction. CSA. Road on right SP: Gnarlbine Rock. 30.2 km ▲

GPS	S:31 08.905 E:120 57.597
UTM	51J 305528E 6552158N

(29.5 km)

▼ 70.9 km — Crossroads. TR. This is Great Eastern Hwy. Road on left SP: Southern Cross 188/Perth 557.

Crossroads. TL. SP: Gnarlbine Rock 29 km/ Queen Victoria Rock 45 km. 0.7 km ▲

GPS	S:30 57.288 E:121 09.498
UTM	51J 324083E 6573953N

(0.7 km)

▼ 71.6 km — Coolgardie Post Office on left and SP: Hunt St, on right.

Zero trip meter in Coolgardie on Great Eastern Hwy with post office on right and SP: Hunt St, on left. CSA in westerly direction along Great Eastern Hwy towards Southern Cross. 0.0 km ▲

GPS	S:30 57.273 E:121 09.938
UTM	51J 324783E 6573992N

REVERSE DIRECTIONS START

■ 165

Gunbarrel Highway

Plaque at Len Beadell Tree

WARBURTON ◄► WILUNA 835.3 KM
ONE SECTION ONLY (*moderate*)
WHEN TO GO April–September **TIME** 3–4 days

The Gunbarrel Highway is the best known of all the roads built by pioneering trailblazer Len Beadell and his Gunbarrel Road Construction Party. Completed in 1958, it originally stretched from Victory Downs station, south-west of Kulgera in the Northern Territory, to Carnegie station in Western Australia, thus linking central Australia with Western Australia's road network and becoming the first road constructed at these latitudes.

Much of the original eastern part of the Gunbarrel Highway now passes through Aboriginal lands and a permit is required. The trek described here takes you along the only remaining section of the highway that is easily accessible to the general public. Many of the natural features, tracks and places were named by or after early explorers and pioneers. The route takes in diverse desert landscapes as well as large tracts of grazing country west of Carnegie station.

About halfway between Warburton and Carnegie the highway veers northwards through the largely uninhabited country of the Gibson Desert and track conditions range from well-made gravel to long stretches of teeth-shattering corrugations. Take your time here to place less strain on your vehicle and your temper! There are some good opportunities for walking, including hikes to the summit of Mount William Lambert and Mount Beadell, both of which afford great views of the desert terrain.

Warburton, at the start of the trek, has a roadhouse with a campground, supplies and fuel (diesel and avgas only). Wiluna, at journey's end, has all facilities and supplies, while Carnegie station, at the trek's mid-way point, has fuel, limited supplies and a campground.

GUNBARREL HIGHWAY

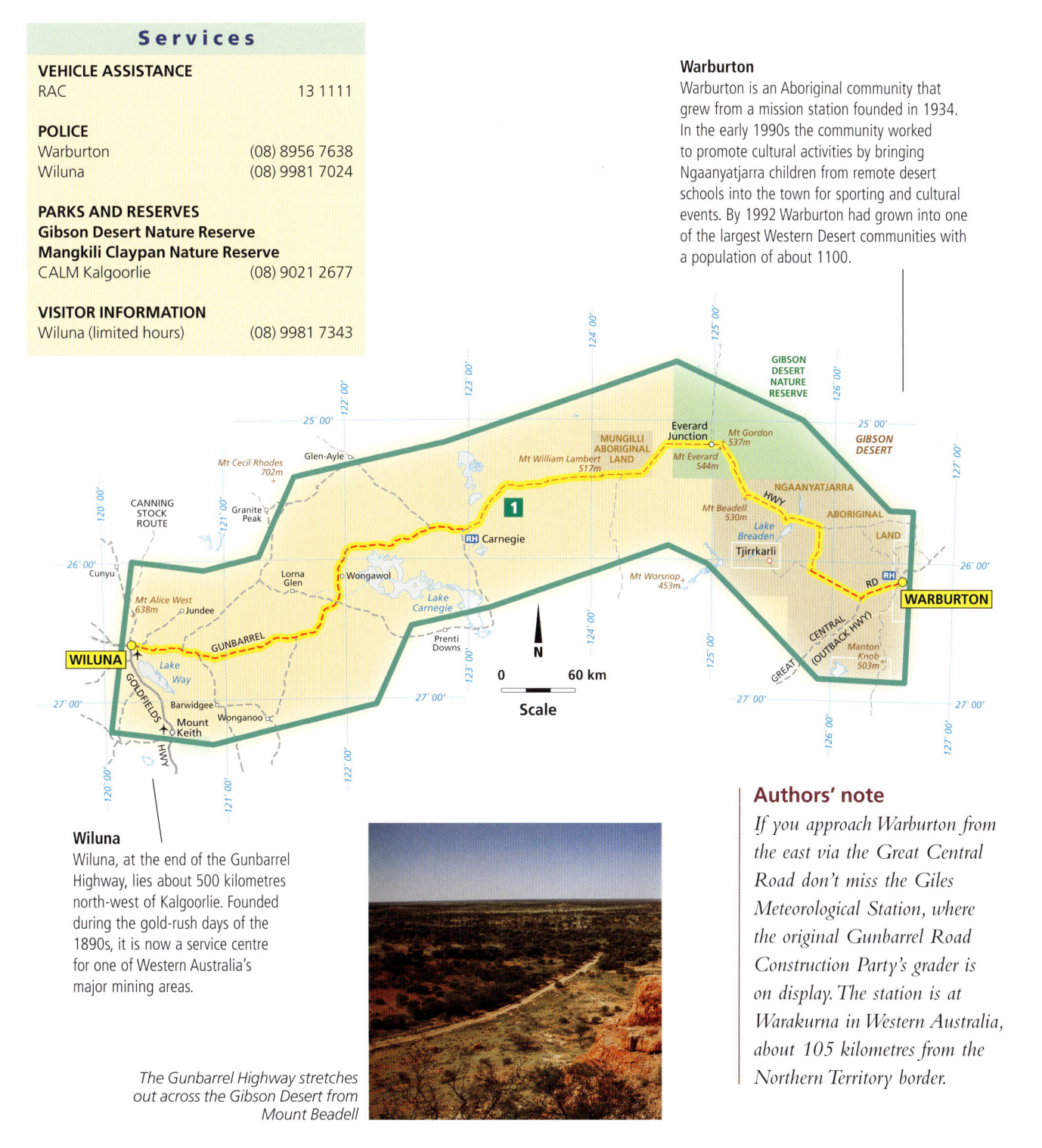

Services

VEHICLE ASSISTANCE
RAC   13 1111

POLICE
Warburton   (08) 8956 7638
Wiluna   (08) 9981 7024

PARKS AND RESERVES
Gibson Desert Nature Reserve
Mangkili Claypan Nature Reserve
CALM Kalgoorlie   (08) 9021 2677

VISITOR INFORMATION
Wiluna (limited hours) (08) 9981 7343

Warburton
Warburton is an Aboriginal community that grew from a mission station founded in 1934. In the early 1990s the community worked to promote cultural activities by bringing Ngaanyatjarra children from remote desert schools into the town for sporting and cultural events. By 1992 Warburton had grown into one of the largest Western Desert communities with a population of about 1100.

Wiluna
Wiluna, at the end of the Gunbarrel Highway, lies about 500 kilometres north-west of Kalgoorlie. Founded during the gold-rush days of the 1890s, it is now a service centre for one of Western Australia's major mining areas.

The Gunbarrel Highway stretches out across the Gibson Desert from Mount Beadell

Authors' note
If you approach Warburton from the east via the Great Central Road don't miss the Giles Meteorological Station, where the original Gunbarrel Road Construction Party's grader is on display. The station is at Warakurna in Western Australia, about 105 kilometres from the Northern Territory border.

Town Facilities

	Fuel: D/P/A	Mechanical repairs	Tyre repairs	Public telephone	Public toilets	Shop/supplies	Gas refills	Ice	Visitor information	Post office	Medical centre	Police	Meals	Motel	Hotel	Cabins	Caravan park	Camping
Warburton	D			•	•	•	•			•		•				•	•	•
Wiluna	D/P	•	•	•	•	•	•	•	•	•		•	•		•		•	•

167

GUNBARREL HIGHWAY

WARBURTON ◄►WILUNA 835.3 KM

Start point
Warburton

Road atlas
352 E1, 354 E8

Total distance
835.3 km

Standard
Moderate

Time
3–4 days

Longest distance no PD (includes all options)
495.2 km (Warburton to Carnegie station)

Topographic maps
Auslig 1:250 000 series: *Wiluna*; *Kingston*; *Stanley*; *Herbert*; *Browne*; *Yowalga*; *Talbot*

Other useful information
- Warburton Roadhouse has supplies, diesel and avgas (no petrol); open Monday–Friday 8am–5pm and Saturday–Sunday 9am–3pm, tel. (08) 8956 7656; accepts cash, EFTPOS and credit cards.
- Carnegie station offers minor mechanical repairs, tyre repairs, petrol, diesel and limited supplies, tel. (08) 9981 2991; accepts cash only.

Corrugated section of track near Len Beadell Tree

Description

For the most part this trek is relatively straightforward, with the exception of severely corrugated sections along the Heather Highway and on the Gunbarrel Highway between the Heather Highway and Carnegie station. The short stretch along the Great Central Road and the much longer Carnegie station to Wiluna section are generally well maintained. The journey can be completed comfortably in three to four days.

This trek traverses the section of the Gunbarrel that runs between the Heather Highway and the frontier town of Wiluna. Starting from the Aboriginal community of Warburton the route heads south-west along the Great Central Road before turning onto the Heather Highway at Steptoes Corner. The road remains in fair condition for about 48 kilometres then a turn to the north marks the start of the corrugations. At Mount Samuel Junction you reach the Gunbarrel Highway and turn west. The continuation of the Gunbarrel to the east includes a now abandoned section of road, which requires a permit to traverse.

Travelling in a north-westerly direction the route passes Mount Beadell with its memorial to the great outback road builder before reaching Everard Junction, where the Gary Highway, another of Beadell's roads, strikes off to the north. On 27 April 1963 a Len Beadell plaque was erected here. Beadell named the junction after the 544-metre-high Mount Everard, located just to the east, which was named by explorer David Carnegie during his 1896–97 expedition. There is a visitor book at the junction for modern-day travellers to leave their mark. The surrounding area is part of the scenic Gibson Desert Nature Reserve, with spinifex-covered plains and stands of mulga woodland.

Past Geraldton Bore is another scenic spot, the Mangkili Claypan Nature Reserve, a small sanctuary protecting tree-rimmed wetlands. Once you approach Carnegie station, the point where the Gunbarrel Highway first joined with the Western Australian road network, the track begins to improve. Carnegie is a welcome oasis after the bone-shaking corrugations and from here to Wiluna the trek passes mainly grazing country, with a number of picturesque watercourses lined by river red gums, such as Harry Johnston Water and Wongawol Creek.

Camels are often seen and it is not uncommon for these beasts to trot along the route in front of your vehicle for anything up to 20 kilometres, with no opportunity to pass them on the narrow track. There is a wide variety of bush camping opportunities available and the better sites are noted in the route directions.

The Gunbarrel Road Construction Party

The Gunbarrel Road Construction Party (GRCP) was founded in 1955 when army surveyor Len Beadell recruited six men to assist with road-building projects in the remote heart of outback Australia. Previously Beadell had been involved with establishing the atomic bomb-testing sites at both Emu and Maralinga in South Australia. The original members of the GRCP were surveyor Len Beadell, bulldozer driver Doug Stoneham, grader driver Scotty Boord, supply driver Bill Lloyd, general mechanic Rex Flatman, cherry picker Willy Appleton and cook Paul Christensen. During the life of the construction party several members left or were replaced and over time the following men belonged to the team: supply driver Frank Quinn, cooks Cyril Koch and Tom Roberts, grader driver Shorty Williams and cherry picker Eric Graefling.

The party's first-completed and best-known road is the Gunbarrel Highway, named because large sections of it were 'straight as a gunbarrel'. Construction commenced in the Northern Territory in November 1955, with the first leg of the road from Victory Downs on the original Stuart Highway west to Mulga Park homestead. In December of the same year Beadell selected the site for the Giles Meteorological Station. This remote weather station, which still records daily weather observations, was essential for the proposed weapons testing. Work continued on the Gunbarrel along with other road-building projects during 1956 and 1957. In 1958 the highway was eventually completed when it reached Carnegie station.

During the building of these roads Beadell would push ahead of the construction group on solo reconnaissance trips in his long-suffering Land Rover, surveying the best route through trackless deserts, at times for several hundred kilometres. He would then return to base camp to direct the road-making party through the surveyed region. Often stranded in remote areas due to mechanical failures, the GRCP became extremely proficient in bush mechanics and was able to have its equipment up and running as soon as possible. When all else failed a crew member would drive thousands of kilometres to pick up a spare part.

The Gunbarrel Road Construction Party's grader at Giles Meteorological Station

When all else failed a crew member would drive thousands of kilometres to pick up a spare part before the party could continue

During its working life from 1955 to 1963, the GRCP was responsible for building more than 6000 kilometres of outback roads, which opened up 2.5 million square kilometres of the Great Victoria, Great Sandy, Little Sandy and Gibson deserts for the first time.

Len Beadell (1923–95) was recognised nationally and internationally for the network of roads he created, receiving a British Empire Medal in 1958 and the Order of Australia in 1988, and having an asteroid named after him by Mount Palomar Observatory in California in 1987. Beadell led the GRCP for ten years, accompanied in the 1960s by his wife and newly born child. During his road surveys he established routes over dune fields and between salt lakes, located and frequently restored outback wells and left a legacy of aluminium-plated signposts, which later generations of desert travellers visit as a mark of homage to this extraordinary Australian.

GUNBARREL HIGHWAY

Early Explorers

A number of European explorers had passed through this remote region by the end of the 1800s. In 1874 John Forrest, later to become the country's first native-born baronet, led the first west–east expedition through the central deserts. In 1876 Ernest Giles achieved a similar feat, taking a more northerly route than Forrest, trekking through the harsh expanses of the Gibson Desert. In 1896 Lawrence Wells' Calvert Expedition reached Lake Carnegie before veering north on its ill-fated exploration. David Carnegie, son of a Scottish earl, came looking for gold and in 1896–97 went on to complete one of the most daring desert journeys – from Coolgardie to Halls Creek and back, through the Gibson and Great Sandy deserts. Along the way he named many features of the landscape, including Mount Everard and Mount Gordon.

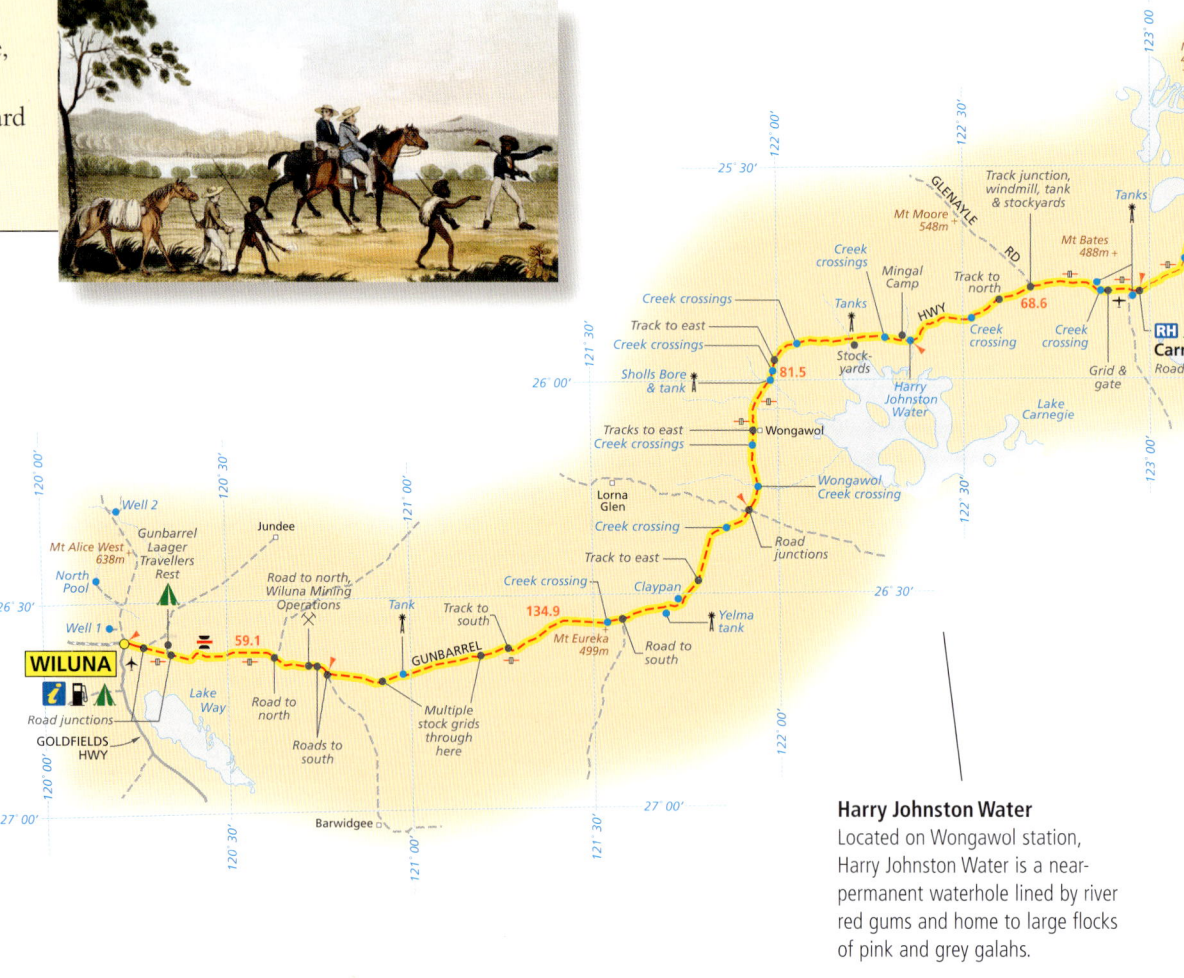

Harry Johnston Water
Located on Wongawol station, Harry Johnston Water is a near-permanent waterhole lined by river red gums and home to large flocks of pink and grey galahs.

WARBURTON ◀▶ WILUNA

Mount Beadell
Named in honour of Len Beadell, this peak offers excellent views from its summit, which is accessible by vehicle or a steep walking track that leads from a large information shelter at the mountain's base. A memorial in the form of a stainless steel theodolite, a replica of surveying equipment used by Beadell, was erected on 12 May 1996, the first anniversary of his death.

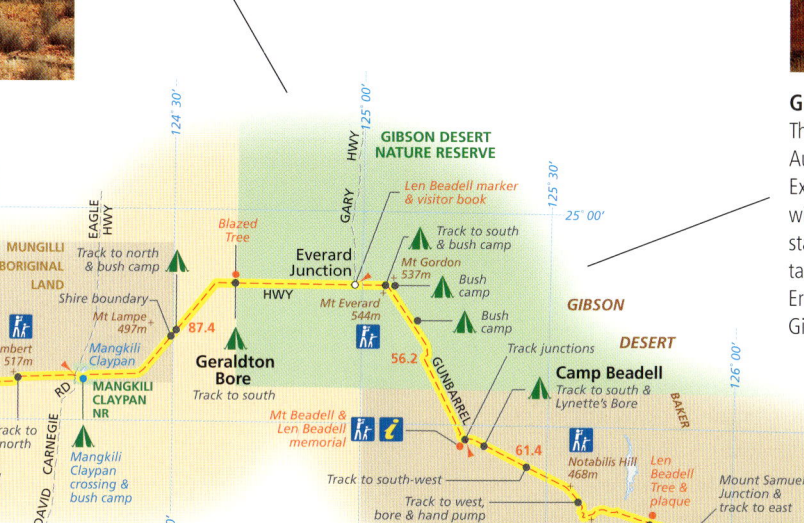

Gibson Desert Nature Reserve
The reserve protects a part of Australia's fifth largest desert. Extensive spinifex plains are interlaced with sand dunes and dotted with stands of hardy mulga. The desert takes its name from a member of Ernest Giles' 1874 expedition, Alfred Gibson, who died here.

Mangkili Claypan Nature Reserve
Located within the Gibson Desert, this small reserve was established in 1977 to protect what is a rare ephemeral wetland in the harsh arid environment. The large claypan holds water for considerable time after rain, allowing the growth of plant species not normally found in the region, such as the river red gum.

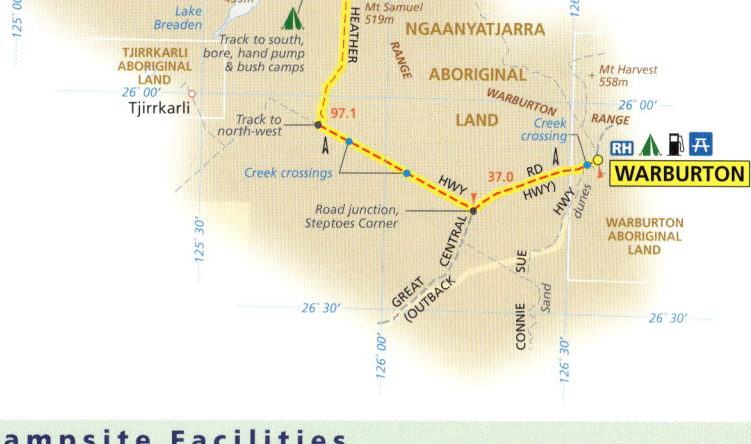

Campsite Facilities

	Toilets	Disabled access	4WD access only	Off-road trailer	Off-road caravan	Drinking water	Fee payable	Ranger patrolled	BBQ/fireplace	Campfires prohibited	Picnic tables	Shelter shed	No rubbish disposal	Public phone	Shower	Bushwalking	Swimming	Swimming not advised	Fishing	Canoeing	Dogs allowed
Camp Beadell		•	•						•												•
Carnegie	•		•	•	•	•	•		•			•	•	•							
Geraldton Bore		•	•						•												•
Warburton Roadhouse	•			•	•		•		•		•	•	•								
Wiluna Club Hotel	•								•				•	•							•

171

GUNBARREL HIGHWAY

Road sign at Wiluna

Advice and warnings
- Possible track closures at times of wet weather. In heavily corrugated sections, bypass and side tracks are usually available. There are large wash-outs, dips in the road and a number of cattle grids. Mangkili Claypan may be impassable during and after rains – check track prior to crossing as detour may be necessary in wet weather. Road not maintained from Heather Highway to Wiluna Shire boundary, and from boundary to Carnegie station it is irregularly maintained. Road is well maintained from Carnegie to Wiluna. Contact Shire of Wiluna, tel. (08) 9981 7010, and Ngaanyatjarra Council, tel. (08) 8950 1711, to check road conditions.
- Highway passes through sections of pastoral lease and Aboriginal land so do not deviate from main road.
- Watch out for large cattle trucks.
- Watch out for roaming cattle, kangaroos and camels on the road.
- Standard road tyres are suitable.
- Towing off-road trailers and off-road caravans is possible, but be well prepared for heavy corrugations and rough conditions.
- Camping is possible at bush campsites mentioned in the route notes, as well as at designated sites.
- Do not rely on water from bores. All bore water should be boiled for at least three minutes before using. Carry a long rope and a small container to access water from bores. Carry plenty of water for drinking, washing and cooking needs.

Permits and bookings
- No permits required.
- Bookings recommended for units at Carnegie station, tel. (08) 9981 2991. Camp bookings are not necessary here for individuals but are recommended for groups.

ROUTE DIRECTIONS

▼ **0.0 km** — Zero trip meter at Warburton on Great Central Rd. Warburton Roadhouse and camping area on right. Proceed in south-westerly direction towards Laverton along Great Central Rd.

Warburton Roadhouse and camping area on left. — **37.0 km** ▲

Warburton Roadhouse camping area is a pleasant, grassed spot behind the roadhouse, with some shade.

GPS	S:26 07.931 E:126 34.154
UTM	52J 256962E 7107406N

(0.8 km)

▼ **0.8 km** — Road junction. CSA. Road on left.

Road on left leads to Warburton community. No access.

Y-junction. KL. SP: Warburton Roadhouse. Road on right. — **36.2 km** ▲

(2.1 km)

▼ **2.9 km** — Creek crossing.

Creek crossing. — **34.1 km** ▲

(0.9 km)

▼ **3.8 km** — Road junction. CSA. Track on left SP: Connie Sue Highway.

Track on left is Connie Sue Hwy, see pages 176–85.

Road junction. CSA. Track on right SP: Connie Sue Highway. — **33.2 km** ▲

GPS	S:26 08.958 E:126 32.328
UTM	52J 253954E 7105452N

(33.2 km)

▼ **37.0 km** — Road junction.

Zero trip meter at T-junction. This is Great Central Rd. TL. SP: Warburton 42. Road on right to Laverton. — **0.0 km** ▲

GPS	S:26 15.757 E:126 14.448
UTM	52J 224417E 7092295N

▼ **0.0 km** — Zero trip meter at road junction. TR. SP: Tjirrkarli Community. This is Heather Hwy. Road SO.

Road SO leads 530 km to Laverton.

T-junction. — **97.1 km** ▲

(48.3 km)

▼ **48.3 km** — Road junction. TR. Road SO to Tjirrkarli community.

Road deteriorates from here.

Road junction. TL. Road on right to Tjirrkarli community. — **48.8 km** ▲

Road improves from here.

GPS	S:26 04.132 E:125 48.911
UTM	51J 781643E 7113647N

(37.9 km)

▼ **86.2 km** — T-junction. TL. SP: 720 Wiluna. This is Gunbarrel Hwy. Track on right.

Track on right is continuation of Gunbarrel Hwy. Permits and regulations apply to travel this section. Contact Ngaanyatjarra Council, tel. (08) 8950 1711, for details.

Track junction. TR. SP: Warburton 126. This is Heather Hwy. Track SO. — **10.9 km** ▲

WARBURTON ◀▶ WILUNA

	GPS S:25 45.152 E:125 52.985 **UTM** 51J 789211E 7148558N	
(10.9 km)		
▼ 97.1 km	Track junction.	
	Zero trip meter at track junction. CSA. Len Beadell Tree and plaque on left. Track on right.	0.0 km ▲
	GPS S:25 43.336 E:125 46.918 **UTM** 51J 779133E 7152130N	
▼ 0.0 km	Zero trip meter at track junction. CSA. Len Beadell Tree and plaque on right. Track on left.	
	Track on left leads 0.5 km to bore (dry in August 2003) and bush campsites. Plaque on Len Beadell Tree dated 17 September 1958.	
	Track junction.	61.4 km ▲
(25.1 km)		
▼ 25.1 km	Track junction. CSA. Track on left.	
	Track on left leads to bore and hand pump. Water available August 2003.	
	Track junction. CSA. Track on right.	36.3 km ▲
(5.1 km)		
▼ 30.2 km	Trig marker on Notabilis Hill on right. CSA.	
	Good views of Gibson Desert.	
	Trig marker on left. CSA.	31.2 km ▲
	GPS S:25 38.561 E:125 33.226 **UTM** 51J 756397E 7161412N	
(12.1 km)		
▼ 42.3 km	Track junction. CSA. Track on left SP: Tjirrkarli 61 km.	
	Track junction. CSA. Track on right.	19.1 km ▲
(12.8 km)		
▼ 55.1 km	Track junction. CSA. Track on left.	
	Track on left leads 0.2 km to **Camp Beadell camping area** and Lynette's Bore. Bush camping among stands of desert oak. Lynette's Bore was dug by CRA Exploration in April 1989; water at 43.5 m.	
	Track junction. CSA. Track on right.	6.3 km ▲
	GPS S:25 32.838 E:125 19.954 **UTM** 51J 734366E 7172390N	
(6.1 km)		
▼ 61.2 km	Track junction. CSA. Track on left.	
	Track on left leads 0.7 km to summit of Mt Beadell and to Len Beadell memorial. Excellent views from summit.	
	Track junction. CSA. Track on right.	0.2 km ▲
(0.2 km)		
▼ 61.4 km	Track junction.	
	Zero trip meter at track junction. CSA. Track on right to base of Mt Beadell and information board.	0.0 km ▲
	GPS S:25 32.066 E:125 16.554 **UTM** 51J 728695E 7173915N	
▼ 0.0 km	Zero trip meter at track junction. CSA. Track on left.	
	Track on left leads short distance to base of Mt Beadell and information board about Len Beadell. Walking track from here leads to summit.	
	Track junction.	56.2 km ▲
(15.4 km)		
▼ 15.4 km	Enter SP: Gibson Desert Nature Reserve. CSA.	
	Exit Gibson Desert Nature Reserve. CSA.	40.8 km ▲
(20.1 km)		
▼ 35.5 km	Bush campsite on right. CSA.	
	Bush campsite on left. CSA.	20.7 km ▲
(11.9 km)		
▼ 47.4 km	Bush campsite on right. CSA.	
	Bush campsite on left. CSA.	8.8 km ▲
(0.5 km)		
▼ 47.9 km	Track junction. CSA. Track on left.	
	Track on left leads short distance to base of Mt Everard. Walk to summit for excellent views. Bush camping in this vicinity.	
	Track junction. CSA. Track on right.	8.3 km ▲
(8.3 km)		
▼ 56.2 km	Track junction.	
	Zero trip meter at junction. This is Everard Junction. CSA. Len Beadell marker and visitor book on right. Track on left SP: Kidson and Windy Corner.	0.0 km ▲
	GPS S:25 10.457 E:124 58.830 **UTM** 51J 699594E 7214286N	
▼ 0.0 km	Zero trip meter at junction. This is Everard Junction. CSA. Len Beadell marker and visitor book on left. Track on right SP: Kidson and Windy Corner.	
	Len Beadell marker placed 27 April 1963. Track on right is Gary Hwy.	
	Track junction.	87.4 km ▲
(31.8 km)		
▼ 31.8 km	Exit Gibson Desert Nature Reserve. CSA.	
	Enter SP: Gibson Desert Nature Reserve.	55.6 km ▲
(0.5 km)		
▼ 32.3 km	Track junction. CSA. Track on left SP: Water.	
	Track on left is Hunt Oil Rd and leads 0.1 km to **Geraldton Bore camping area**. Bore was drilled by CRA Exploration in April 1989. It is suitable for emergency use; water is at 16 m.	
	Track junction. CSA. Track on right SP: Water.	55.1 km ▲

Mount Everard offers good views from its summit

■ 173

GUNBARREL HIGHWAY

	GPS S:25 10.438 E:124 39.866 **UTM** 51J 667735E 7214752N		▼ 26.9 km	Old football oval and posts on left of track. CSA.	
	(0.5 km)			Old football oval and posts on right of track. CSA.	20.0 km ▲
▼ 32.8 km	Blazed tree on right. CSA.			(20.0 km)	
	This tree has exact replica of plaque placed here by Len Beadell on 14 October 1958. (Like many of his plaques, the original of this one has unfortunately disappeared.)		▼ 46.9 km	Road junction.	
				Zero trip meter at road junction. CSA. Track on left.	0.0 km ▲
	Blazed tree on left. CSA.	54.6 km ▲		Track on left leads 0.3 km along rocky 4WD track to trig point on Mt Nossiter.	
	GPS S:25 10.432 E:124 39.584 **UTM** 51J 667262E 7214769N			**GPS** S:25 25.516 E:123 47.054 **UTM** 51J 578864E 7187730N	
	(21.3 km)		▼ 0.0 km	Zero trip meter at road junction. CSA. Track on right.	
▼ 54.1 km	Track junction. CSA. Track on right. Track on right leads short distance to bush campsite.			Track on right leads 0.3 km along rocky 4WD track to trig point on Mt Nossiter.	
	Track junction. CSA. Track on left.	33.3 km ▲		Road junction.	105.2 km ▲
	(2.2 km)			(29.8 km)	
▼ 56.3 km	Enter SP: Shire of Wiluna. Road conditions improve.		▼ 29.8 km	Creek crossing.	
				Creek crossing.	75.4 km ▲
	Exit Shire of Wiluna.	31.1 km ▲		**GPS** S:25 28.054 E:123 30.609 **UTM** 51J 551283E 7183179N	
	Road conditions deteriorate.			(75.3 km)	
	GPS S:25 18.024 E:124 29.710 **UTM** 51J 650519E 7200949N		▼ 105.1 km	T-junction. TL.	
	(23.9 km)			Road junction. TR. SP: Gunbarrel Hwy/ Warburton 493/Giles 724/Alice Springs 1533.	0.1 km ▲
▼ 80.2 km	Enter SP: Mungilli Claypan Nature Reserve. Correct name is Mangkili Claypan Nature Reserve.			(0.1 km)	
			▼ 105.2 km	T-junction.	
	Exit Mangkili Claypan Nature Reserve.	7.2 km ▲		Zero trip meter at road junction. TL. Road SO to Carnegie station.	0.0 km ▲
	(4.8 km)			**GPS** S:25 47.753 E:122 58.407 **UTM** 51J 497338E 7146920N	
▼ 85.0 km	Cross Mangkili Claypan. Possible bush camping around edge of claypan.		▼ 0.0 km	Zero trip meter at T-junction. TR. SP: Wiluna 353/Perth 1320. Road on left.	
	Cross Mangkili Claypan.	2.4 km ▲		Road on left leads short distance to **Carnegie camping area**, a large grassed site located behind station store and campers' kitchen.	
	GPS S:25 24.179 E:124 15.673 **UTM** 51J 626857E 7189830N			Road junction.	68.6 km ▲
	(2.4 km)			(10.8 km)	
▼ 87.4 km	Crossroads.		▼ 10.8 km	Creek crossing.	
	Zero trip meter at crossroads. CSA. Road on right SP: Empress Springs 174/David Carnegie Rd 4x4 Only. Road on left is Eagle Hwy.	0.0 km ▲		Creek crossing.	57.8 km ▲
	GPS S:25 23.708 E:124 14.413 **UTM** 51J 624753E 7190719N			(19.5 km)	
▼ 0.0 km	Zero trip meter at crossroads. CSA. Road on left SP: Empress Springs 174/David Carnegie Rd 4x4 Only. Road on right is Eagle Hwy.		▼ 30.3 km	Road junction. KL. Road on right SP: 91 Glen Ayle.	
				Road junction. CSA. Road on left SP: 91 Glen Ayle.	38.3 km ▲
	Crossroads.	46.9 km ▲		(38.3 km)	
	(0.4 km)		▼ 68.6 km	Creek crossing.	
▼ 0.4 km	Exit Mangkili Claypan Nature Reserve.			Zero trip meter at creek crossing. This is Harry Johnston Water. CSA.	0.0 km ▲
	Enter SP: Mungilli Claypan Nature Reserve.	46.5 km ▲		On left prior to crossing is Mingal Camp. This is a stock camp and public camping is prohibited.	
	Correct name is Mangkili.				
	(15.2 km)			**GPS** S:25 54.583 E:122 21.537 **UTM** 51J 435795E 7134157N	
▼ 15.6 km	Road junction. CSA. Track on right. Track on right leads 0.2 km to carpark. It is a short walk from carpark to summit of Mt William Lambert for extensive views.		▼ 0.0 km	Zero trip meter at creek crossing. This is Harry Johnston Water. CSA.	
				On right over creek crossing is Mingal Camp, a stock camp that is not available for public camping.	
	Track junction. CSA. Track on left.	31.3 km ▲			
	GPS S:25 24.071 E:124 05.200 **UTM** 51J 609301E 7190184N				
	(11.3 km)				

WARBURTON ◀▶ WILUNA

Harry Johnston Water

▼ 0.0 km — Zero trip meter at road junction. CSA. Road on left SP: Prenti Downs 106/Windidda 32.
    Road junction. **134.9 km** ▲
(32.1 km)

▼ 32.1 km — Large claypan on right often filled with water. CSA.
    Large claypan on left. CSA. **102.8 km** ▲
(5.7 km)

▼ 37.8 km — Yelma tank and windmill on left. This is site of old Yelma station. CSA.
    Yelma tank and windmill on right. This is site of old Yelma station. CSA. **97.1 km** ▲

GPS	S:26 31.920 E:121 41.493
UTM	51J 369642E 7064733N

(11.8 km)

▼ 49.6 km — Road junction. CSA. Road on left.
    Road junction. CSA. Road on right. **85.3 km** ▲
(85.3 km)

▼ 134.9 km — T-junction.
    Zero trip meter at road junction. TL. SP: 294 Carnegie Stn. Road SO SP: Barwidgee Stn. **0.0 km** ▲

GPS	S:26 40.681 E:120 46.405
UTM	51J 278430E 7047293N

▼ 0.0 km — Zero trip meter at T-junction. TR. SP: Jundee. Road on left SP: Bronzewing.
    Road junction. **59.1 km** ▲
(6.1 km)

▼ 6.1 km — Road junction. CSA. Road on right to Wiluna Mining Operations.
    Road junction. CSA. Road on left. **53.0 km** ▲
(10.3 km)

▼ 16.4 km — Road junction. CSA. Road on right SP: 10 Lake Violet Stn/228 Glenayle Stn.
    Road junction. CSA. SP: Carnegie Stn 311. Road on left. **42.7 km** ▲

GPS	S:26 38.127 E:120 37.698
UTM	51J 263897E 7051749N

(30.7 km)

▼ 47.1 km — Road junction. CSA. Road on right SP: Gunbarrel Laager Travellers Rest.
Road on right leads 2.4 km to vineyard and privately run camping area. Fees apply.
    Road junction. CSA. Road on left SP: Gunbarrel Laager Travellers Rest. **12.0 km** ▲
(6.8 km)

▼ 53.9 km — Offset crossroads. CSA. SP: Wiluna 5. Road on right to Jundee Gold Mine. Road on left to Wiluna Gold Mine.
    Offset crossroads. CSA. SP: Granite Peak. **5.2 km** ▲
(5.2 km)

▼ 59.1 km — Crossroads. Wiluna. Road on left and right SP: Wotton Street.
Wiluna Club Hotel camping area and caravan park is a large open space behind the hotel at northern end of town on Wotton St.
    Zero trip meter in Wiluna at junction of Wotton and Wells sts. Turn into road heading east SP: Gunbarrel Hwy. **0.0 km** ▲

GPS	S:26 35.659 E:120 13.490
UTM	51J 223615E 7055499N

REVERSE DIRECTIONS START

    Creek crossing. **81.5 km** ▲
(7.2 km)

▼ 7.2 km — Creek crossing.
    Creek crossing. **74.3 km** ▲
(9.6 km)

▼ 16.8 km — Creek crossing.
    Creek crossing. **64.7 km** ▲
(1.8 km)

▼ 18.6 km — Creek crossing.
    Creek crossing. **62.9 km** ▲
(26.8 km)

▼ 45.4 km — Creek crossing.
    Creek crossing. **36.1 km** ▲

GPS	S:26 00.245 E:121 58.734
UTM	51J 397811E 7123465N

(13.8 km)

▼ 59.2 km — Y-junction. KR. SP: Wiluna. Track on left.
    Road junction. CSA. Track on right. **22.3 km** ▲
(1.3 km)

▼ 60.5 km — Road junction. CSA. Road on left.
Road on left to Wongawol station.
    Road junction. CSA. Road on right. **21.0 km** ▲
(14.4 km)

▼ 74.9 km — Cross Wongawol Creek.
Possible lunch spot on right prior to crossing.
    Cross Wongawol Creek. **6.6 km** ▲

GPS	S:26 15.025 E:121 56.650
UTM	51J 394556E 7096154N

(6.6 km)

▼ 81.5 km — Road junction.
    Zero trip meter at road junction. CSA. Road on right SP: Prenti Downs 106/Windidda 32. **0.0 km** ▲

GPS	S:26 18.256 E:121 55.244
UTM	51J 392265E 7090170N

■ 175

Connie Sue Highway

Connie Sue Highway

WARBURTON ◀▶ RAWLINNA 648.8 KM
ONE SECTION ONLY *(moderate)*
WHEN TO GO May–September   **TIME** 4–5 days

The Connie Sue Highway, constructed and named in 1962 by legendary road builder Len Beadell after his daughter, runs north–south through the south-eastern deserts of Western Australia. Although not a difficult trek, the country is arid and isolated, ranging from the spinifex-clad dunes of the Great Victoria Desert to the featureless plains of the western Nullarbor.

The Connie Sue was completed with the aim of linking the small railway siding of Rawlinna to the Aboriginal mission at Warburton. The highway's namesake, Len's young daughter, was just five months old when she accompanied Len and his wife, Anne, on the road-making expedition. The completed highway, blazed through 650 kilometres of almost waterless country, was a remarkable achievement.

Today the track surface varies from soft sandy stretches to rocky limestone sections and is often heavily corrugated, particularly between Warburton and Neale Junction. There are some magnificent panoramic views, particularly over MacKenzie and Harkness gorges, and from the top of Hanns Tabletop Hill. The rolling dunes of the Great Victoria Desert, the majestic marble gums around Neale Junction and the vastness of the western Nullarbor add to the trek's scenic splendour.

The Aboriginal community of Warburton at the start of the trek has a well-stocked roadhouse, but supplies diesel and avgas fuel only. Rawlinna does not cater for travellers. The closest facilities are available 144 kilometres to the south at Cocklebiddy on the Eyre Highway via Carlisle Road or 380 kilometres to the west at Kalgoorlie along the Trans Australia Railway Access Road.

Services

VEHICLE ASSISTANCE
RAC   13 1111

POLICE
Warburton   (08) 8956 7638

PARKS AND RESERVES
Neale Junction Nature Reserve
CALM Kalgoorlie   (08) 9021 2677

VISITOR INFORMATION
Ngaanyatjarra Council (08) 8950 1711

Authors' note
Manton Knob and vantage points overlooking Harkness and MacKenzie gorges are good spots to take a break from the incessant corrugations of the northern section of this trek.

Warburton
The Aboriginal community of Warburton, located 565 kilometres north-east of Laverton on the Great Central Road, is the administrative centre for the region. The town has an interesting and informative cultural centre located in the shire council building.

Rawlinna
A one-time settlement for railway maintenance workers and their families, Rawlinna today is little more than a siding on the Trans Australia Railway and the base for a nearby large-scale lime mine. Trains still pass through Rawlinna, but only stop for oncoming railway traffic and to pick up customers, generally mine workers or local farmers who have a booked ticket.

Old Station Master's Office at Rawlinna

Native Tomato
Some species of the native tomato were important foods for Aboriginal people of the central deserts but other species, particularly in northern Australia, are poisonous. The plant pictured is *Solanum phlomoides*, which is inedible.

Town Facilities

	Fuel: D/P/A	Mechanical repairs	Tyre repairs	Public telephone	Public toilets	Shop/supplies	Gas refills	Ice	Visitor information	Post office	Medical centre	Police	Meals	Motel	Hotel	Cabins	Caravan park	Camping
Cocklebiddy	D/P/A	•	•	•			•	•				•	•	•		•	•
Rawlinna			•	•													•	
Warburton	D			•	•	•	•	•		•	•	•				•	•	•

CONNIE SUE HIGHWAY

WARBURTON ◀▶ RAWLINNA 648.8 KM

Start point
Warburton

Road atlas
352 E1, 354 E8

Total distance
648.8 km

Standard
Moderate

Time
4–5 days

Longest distance no PD (includes all options)
797.0 km (Warburton to Cocklebiddy on Eyre Highway)

Topographic maps
Auslig 1:250 000 series: *Talbot*; *Lennis*; *Vernon*; *Neale*; *Plumridge*; *Seemore*; *Naretha*

Other useful information
- Warburton Roadhouse has supplies, diesel and avgas (no petrol); open Monday–Friday 8am–5pm and Saturday–Sunday 9am–3pm, tel. (08) 8956 7656; accepts cash, EFTPOS and credit cards.
- Cocklebiddy Roadhouse open Monday–Saturday 6.30am–10pm and Sunday 6.30am–9pm, tel. (08) 9039 3462; accepts cash, EFTPOS and credit cards.
- Wildflowers are prolific during late winter and spring so carry a wildflower identification guide.
- Desert wildlife is amazingly varied and nature enthusiasts should carry bird, reptile and mammal identification guides.

Description
Departing from Warburton, the trek heads south. Spinifex and mulga dominate in a landscape of rolling dunes, rocky outcrops and scenic breakaways. The route ascends a number of rocky rises, the highest being Manton Knob, which provides good views, while a short distance further, on the west of the highway, you can gaze out over the MacKenzie and Harkness gorges. Stands of mulga and red mulga grow in the gorges and along the rims. Although the trek traverses dune fields with sections of soft sand and corrugations, most are easily negotiated with a slight reduction of tyre pressure.

On the approach to Neale Junction the harsh desert begins to give way to an almost park-like setting, with stands of marble gum. Surprisingly, the largest stands of this imposing tree are found here in the Great Victoria Desert. Neale Junction itself, which is marked with one of Len Beadell's plaques, is the intersection of the east–west Anne Beadell and the north–south Connie Sue highways and is surrounded by Neale Junction Nature Reserve.

Heading south from the junction, bluebush plains and stands of hardy mallee begin to appear at the southernmost fringes of the desert before you reach the sparsely vegetated Nullarbor Plain. Travel is slow here as you make your way over rough limestone stretches on the Nullarbor. A number of tracks leave the main highway, which can make navigation tricky as most are not signposted. Follow the route directions carefully.

Nature enthusiasts and photographers will find this region fascinating with its surprising range of fauna and landforms. There are ample opportunities to stretch your legs – a 'must' is a scramble up Hanns Tabletop Hill for superb views across the surrounding desert country.

Warburton Roadhouse camping area is the only site with facilities – all other overnight stops on this trek are at bush campsites and as such have no facilities. Numerous natural clearings beside the track provide shelter for camping, but remember to be self-sufficient and please take all your rubbish with you. Camping is possible at Rawlinna, at the end of the highway, but again there are no facilities.

Campsite Facilities

	Toilets	Disabled access	4WD access only	Off-road trailer	Off-road caravan	Drinking water	Fee payable	Ranger patrolled	BBQ/fireplace	Campfires prohibited	Picnic tables	Shelter shed	No rubbish disposal	Public phone	Shower	Bushwalking	Swimming	Swimming not advised	Fishing	Canoeing	Dogs allowed
Neale Junction			•	•							•										
Rawlinna			•	•					•			•									•
Warburton Roadhouse	•			•	•	•	•	•		•	•		•	•							

WARBURTON ◀▶ RAWLINNA

MacKenzie Gorge
Pastoralist, prospector and explorer Frank Hann crossed this region many times between 1903 and 1908, naming more than 100 features in the Great Victoria Desert. MacKenzie Gorge, named by Hann after Montgomery MacKenzie, a resident of Laverton, is part of some magnificent ironstone breakaway country with natural rock stacks and arches.

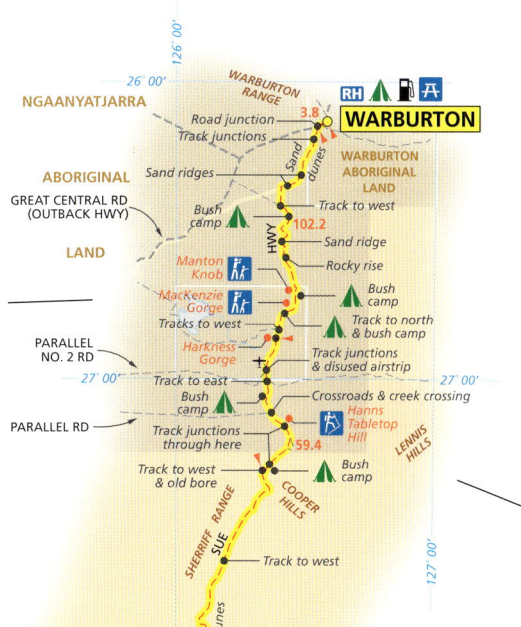

Hanns Tabletop Hill
Frank Hann climbed this flat-topped hill in 1903. Today visitors can also climb to its summit and enjoy the magnificent 360-degree views over the Great Victoria Desert. Easiest access to the summit is from the eastern side.

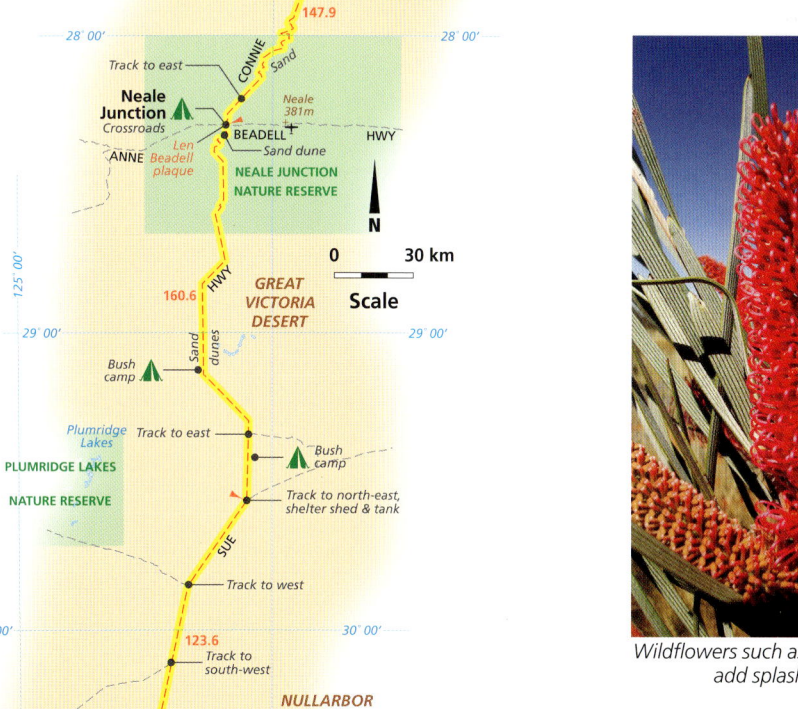

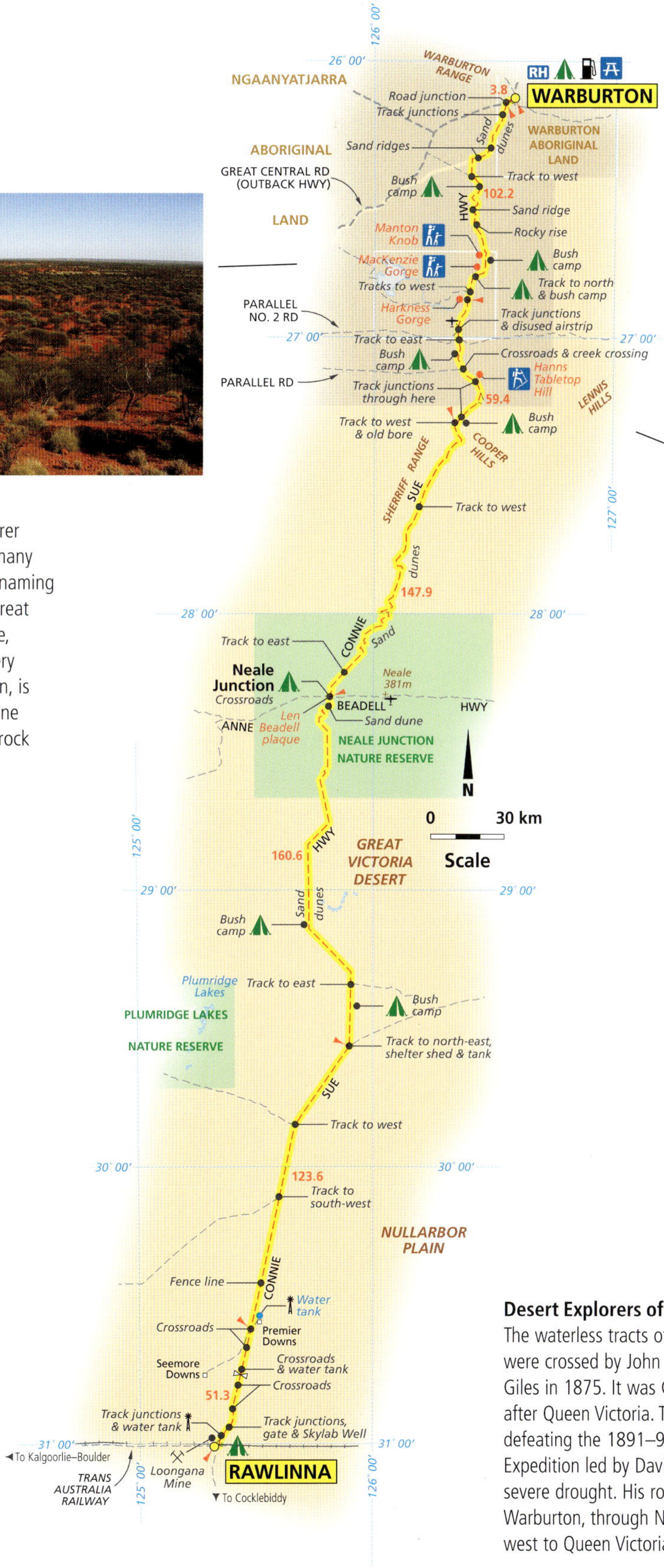

Wildflowers such as Hakea francisiana *add splashes of colour to the desert landscape*

Desert Explorers of the 1800s
The waterless tracts of the Great Victoria Desert were crossed by John Forrest in 1874 and Ernest Giles in 1875. It was Giles who named the desert after Queen Victoria. The region came close to defeating the 1891–92 Elder Scientific Exploring Expedition led by David Lindsay in a period of severe drought. His route passed to the east of Warburton, through Neale Junction then south-west to Queen Victoria Spring.

Hanns Tabletop Hill

Advice and warnings

- This is a remote area so you need to be totally self-sufficient and your vehicle well equipped. Carry plenty of water, food and fuel.
- Possible track closures during and after rain and sections of the track hold water for some time after wet weather. The northern part of the track has sandy sections, heavy corrugations, wash-outs, sand dunes, narrow stretches and rocky rises. The southern section crosses limestone and rocky areas. For road conditions in the north contact Warburton Roadhouse, tel. (08) 8956 7656, Ngaanyatjarra Council, tel. (08) 8950 1711, or CALM Kalgoorlie, tel. (08) 9021 2677; for road conditions in the south contact Cocklebiddy Roadhouse, tel. (08) 9039 3462, or Dundas Shire Council, tel. (08) 9039 1205.
- Numerous bypass tracks lead off the highway but the route directions follow the main road.
- In the south the track passes through outback stations so watch out for roaming stock, leave all gates as found and do not disturb cattle or watering points.
- The track passes through privately owned Aboriginal lands and pastoral leases so do not leave the main track without prior permission.
- Standard road tyres are suitable.
- Towing off-road trailers is possible.
- Bush camping only along the highway and 'no trace' camping applies. At the end of the trek camping is possible at Rawlinna but campfires are not permitted so use gas/fuel stoves.
- Rubbish bins are not provided along the track so please take your rubbish with you.
- All buildings in Rawlinna are private.

Permits and bookings

- Permit required to travel through Ngaanyatjarra land (Yupuparra Aboriginal Land Reserve No. 40787, which is located 84 kilometres south of Warburton and stretches for around 37 kilometres). Permit is free and available from Ngaanyatjarra Council, tel. (08) 8950 1711, or from Aboriginal Lands Trust in Perth, tel. (08) 9235 8000, or visit their website (www.dia.wa.gov.au). Allow up to four weeks for delivery of permit.
- If camping in Rawlinna, travellers must contact Loongana Mine via UHF channel 11 on arrival as a courtesy, prior to setting up.

ROUTE DIRECTIONS

▼ 0.0 km	Zero trip meter in Warburton on Great Central Rd with roadhouse on right. Head in south-westerly direction towards Laverton along Great Central Rd.	
	Warburton Roadhouse and camping area on left.	3.8 km ▲

Warburton Roadhouse camping area is a pleasant, grassed spot behind the roadhouse, with some shade.

GPS S:26 07.931 E:126 34.154
UTM 52J 256962E 7107406N

(0.8 km)

▼ 0.8 km	Road junction. CSA. Road on left.	
	Y-junction. KL. Road on right to Warburton community.	3.0 km ▲

(2.1 km)

▼ 2.9 km	Creek crossing.	
	Creek crossing.	0.9 km ▲

(0.9 km)

▼ 3.8 km	Road junction.	
	Zero trip meter at T-junction with Great Central Rd. TR.	0.0 km ▲

Road on left leads 561 km to Laverton.

GPS S:26 08.958 E:126 32.328
UTM 52J 253954E 7105452N

▼ 0.0 km	Zero trip meter at road junction. TL. SP: Connie Sue Highway.	

Road SO leads 561 km to Laverton.

	T-junction with Great Central Rd.	102.2 km ▲

(0.8 km)

▼ 0.8 km	Y-junction. KR. Track on left.	
	Track junction. CSA. Track on right.	101.4 km ▲

(2.4 km)

▼ 3.2 km	Track junction. CSA. Track on right.	
	Y-junction. KR. Track on left.	99.0 km ▲

(3.9 km)

▼ 7.1 km	Y-junction. KR. Track on left.	
	Track junction. CSA. Track on right.	95.1 km ▲

(13.3 km)

▼ 20.4 km	Cross sand ridge.	
	Cross sand ridge.	81.8 km ▲

(7.4 km)

▼ 27.8 km	Cross sand ridge.	
	Cross sand ridge.	74.4 km ▲

(10.0 km)

▼ 37.8 km Track junction. KL. SP: Neale Junction. Track on right.
Track on right leads to Great Central Rd.
                    Track junction. KR. Track on left.   64.4 km ▲
GPS   S:26 25.187 E:126 23.721
UTM   52J 240212E 7075198N
(6.0 km)

▼ 43.8 km Bush campsite on right. CSA.
                    Bush campsite on left. CSA.   58.4 km ▲
(17.7 km)

▼ 61.5 km Cross sand ridge.
                    Cross sand ridge.   40.7 km ▲
(5.0 km)

▼ 66.5 km Rocky rise.
                    Rocky rise.   35.7 km ▲
(12.6 km)

▼ 79.1 km Manton Knob. Good views from this ridge line. CSA.
                    Manton Knob. Good views from this ridge line. CSA.   23.1 km ▲
GPS   S:26 41.553 E:126 27.620
UTM   52J 247295E 7045100N
(3.4 km)

▼ 82.5 km Bush campsite on left. CSA.
                    Bush campsite on right. CSA.   19.7 km ▲
(5.2 km)

▼ 87.7 km Views over MacKenzie Gorge on right. CSA.
                    Views over MacKenzie Gorge on left. CSA.   14.5 km ▲
(4.0 km)

▼ 91.7 km Track junction. CSA. Track on right.
Track on right leads short distance to small bush campsite.
                    Track junction. CSA. Track on left.   10.5 km ▲
(5.9 km)

▼ 97.6 km Track junction. CSA. Track on right.
                    Track junction. CSA. Track on left.   4.6 km ▲
(4.6 km)

▼ 102.2 km Track junction.
                    Zero trip meter at track junction. CSA. Track on left to Harkness Gorge.   0.0 km ▲
GPS   S:26 51.997 E:126 22.972
UTM   52J 239981E 7025653N

▼ 0.0 km Zero trip meter at track junction. CSA. Track on right.
Track on right leads 0.3 km to edge of Harkness Gorge.
                    Track junction.   59.4 km ▲
(11.2 km)

▼ 11.2 km Track junction. CSA. Track on right.
Track on right leads 0.8 km to disused airstrip and old mining camp.
                    Track junction. CSA. Track on left.   48.2 km ▲
(2.2 km)

▼ 13.4 km Y-junction. KL. Track on right.
Track on right is Parallel No. 2 Rd and leads 110 km to Great Central Rd.
                    Track junction. CSA. Track on left.   46.0 km ▲

GPS   S:26 58.634 E:126 20.692
UTM   52J 236462E 7013315N
(0.5 km)

▼ 13.9 km Track junction. CSA. Track on right.
                    Y-junction. KR. Track on left is Parallel No. 2 Rd.   45.5 km ▲
(3.1 km)

▼ 17.0 km Track junction. KR. Track on left.
                    Track junction. CSA. Track on right.   42.4 km ▲
(6.4 km)

▼ 23.4 km Bush campsite on right. CSA.
                    Bush campsite on left. CSA.   36.0 km ▲
(6.3 km)

▼ 29.7 km Crossroads. CSA.
                    Crossroads. CSA.   29.7 km ▲
(0.6 km)

▼ 30.3 km Creek crossing.
                    Creek crossing.   29.1 km ▲
(6.9 km)

▼ 37.2 km Track junction. CSA. Track on left.
Track on left leads 0.8 km to carpark at base of Hanns Tabletop Hill. Best access to top of hill is from eastern side.
                    Track junction. CSA. Track on right.   22.2 km ▲
GPS   S:27 09.667 E:126 24.988
UTM   52J 243990E 6993083N
(4.1 km)

▼ 41.3 km Track junction. CSA. Track on left.
                    Track junction. CSA. Track on right.   18.1 km ▲
(1.0 km)

▼ 42.3 km Y-junction. KR. Track on left.
Track on left is a no through road.
                    Track junction. CSA. Track on right.   17.1 km ▲
(4.1 km)

▼ 46.4 km Track junction. CSA. Track on left.
Track on left is a no through road.
                    Track junction. CSA. Track on right.   13.0 km ▲
(4.6 km)

▼ 51.0 km Track junction. CSA. Track on right.
                    Track junction. CSA. Track on left.   8.4 km ▲
(4.8 km)

▼ 55.8 km Bush campsite on left. CSA.
                    Bush campsite on right. CSA.   3.6 km ▲
(0.2 km)

▼ 56.0 km Crossroads. CSA.
Old seismic line to left and right.
                    Crossroads. CSA.   3.4 km ▲
(3.4 km)

▼ 59.4 km Track junction.
                    Zero trip meter at track junction. CSA. Track on left leads to drilling exploration site.   0.0 km ▲
GPS   S:27 18.957 E:126 20.381
UTM   52J 236743E 6975764N

▼ 0.0 km Zero trip meter. Track junction. CSA. Track on right.

Sturt's desert pea (Swainsona formosa)

Track on right leads short distance to drilling exploration site. There are number of other similar sites along Connie Sue Hwy.

Track junction. **147.9 km** ▲

(41.1 km)

▼ **41.1 km** Minor track on right. CSA.

Minor track on left. CSA. **106.8 km** ▲

(16.8 km)

▼ **57.9 km** Cross sand dune.

Cross sand dune. **90.0 km** ▲

(9.5 km)

▼ **67.4 km** Cross sand dune.

Cross sand dune. **80.5 km** ▲

(30.8 km)

▼ **98.2 km** Cross sand dune.

Cross sand dune. **49.7 km** ▲

(1.1 km)

▼ **99.3 km** Enter SP: Neale Junction Nature Reserve.

Exit Neale Junction Nature Reserve. **48.6 km** ▲

GPS S:28 00.489 E:126 03.791
UTM 52J 211195E 6898417N

(48.6 km)

▼ **147.9 km** Crossroads. This is Neale Junction.

Neale Junction is intersection of Connie Sue Highway (north to south) and Anne Beadell Highway (east to west). Junction was named by Len Beadell and one of his plaques stands here. Be sure to sign visitor book.

Zero trip meter at Neale Junction crossroads. CSA. Anne Beadell Hwy to left and right. **0.0 km** ▲

GPS S:28 18.179 E:125 49.036
UTM 51J 776284E 6866012N

▼ **0.0 km** Zero trip meter at Neale Junction crossroads. CSA.

Track on left and right is Anne Beadell Hwy, see pages 186–201. Track on right leads 0.2 km to **Neale Junction camping area**, a large, well-cleared area.

Crossroads. This is Neale Junction. **160.6 km** ▲

(48.6 km)

▼ **48.6 km** Exit Neale Junction Nature Reserve.

Enter SP: Neale Junction Nature Reserve. **112.0 km** ▲

(55.6 km)

▼ **104.2 km** Bush camping in this vicinity. CSA.

Bush camping in this vicinity. CSA. **56.4 km** ▲

(31.5 km)

▼ **135.7 km** Track junction. CSA. Track on left.

Track junction. CSA. Track on right. **24.9 km** ▲

(8.7 km)

▼ **144.4 km** Bush campsite on left. CSA.

Bush campsite on right. CSA. **16.2 km** ▲

(16.2 km)

▼ **160.6 km** Track junction.

Zero trip meter at Y-junction. KL. Track on right, and shelter and rainwater tank. **0.0 km** ▲

GPS S:29 33.950 E:125 54.074
UTM 51J 781089E 6725809N

▼ **0.0 km** Zero trip meter at track junction. CSA. Track on left, and shelter and rainwater tank.

Track on left leads to Tjuntjuntjara, which is a closed community.

Y-junction. **123.6 km** ▲

(38.9 km)

WARBURTON ◀▶ RAWLINNA

▼ 38.9 km — Road junction. CSA. Track on right.
Track on right leads 85.0 km to Plumridge Lakes Nature Reserve, a popular spot for birdwatching and bush camping.
Road junction. CSA. Track on left. — 84.7 km ▲
GPS   S:29 50.977 E:125 40.311
UTM   51J 758129E 6694881N
(30.3 km)

▼ 69.2 km — Road junction. CSA onto less-used track in southerly direction. Track on right.
Track deteriorates to less-used track. Track on right leads to Kitchener siding.
Road junction. CSA. Track on left. — 54.4 km ▲
GPS   S:30 06.780 E:125 36.195
UTM   51J 750836E 6665833N
(35.3 km)

▼ 104.5 km — Pass through fence line.
Pass through fence line. — 19.1 km ▲
(18.8 km)

▼ 123.3 km — Y-junction. KL. Track on right.
Track junction. CSA. Track on left. — 0.3 km ▲
(0.3 km)

▼ 123.6 km — Crossroads.
Zero trip meter at crossroads. CSA. — 0.0 km ▲
GPS   S:30 35.327 E:125 28.784
UTM   51J 737776E 6613350N

▼ 0.0 km — Zero trip meter at crossroads. CSA.
Track on left to Premier Downs and track on right to Seemore Downs.
Crossroads. — 51.3 km ▲
(7.7 km)

▼ 7.7 km — Crossroads. CSA.
Crossroads. CSA. — 43.6 km ▲
(9.1 km)

▼ 16.8 km — Crossroads. CSA.
Crossroads. CSA. — 34.5 km ▲
(0.3 km)

▼ 17.1 km — Tank on right. CSA.
Tank on left. CSA. — 34.2 km ▲
(0.5 km)

▼ 17.6 km — Gate. LAF.
Gate. LAF. — 33.7 km ▲
(5.8 km)

▼ 23.4 km — Crossroads. CSA.
Crossroads. CSA. — 27.9 km ▲
(10.0 km)

▼ 33.4 km — Crossroads. CSA.
Crossroads. CSA. — 17.9 km ▲
(0.4 km)

▼ 33.8 km — Y-junction. KR. Track on left.
Track junction. CSA. Track on right. — 17.5 km ▲
(8.0 km)

▼ 41.8 km — Track junction. CSA through gate. LAF. Track on right. Through gate track on left. CSA.
Track on left through gate leads to Skylab Well.
Track junction. CSA through gate. LAF. Track on right to well. Through gate track on left. CSA. — 9.5 km ▲
GPS   S:30 56.608 E:125 23.017
UTM   51J 727720E 6574227N
(0.8 km)

▼ 42.6 km — Track junction. CSA. Track on left.
Y-junction. KL. Track on right. — 8.7 km ▲
(2.1 km)

▼ 44.7 km — Track junction. CSA. Track on right.
Track junction. CSA. Track on left. — 6.6 km ▲
(1.5 km)

▼ 46.2 km — Track junction. CSA. Track on right.
Track on right to windmill.
Track junction. CSA. Track on left. — 5.1 km ▲
(1.8 km)

▼ 48.0 km — Y-junction. KL. Track on right.
Track on right leads to Loongana Mine workings.
Track junction. CSA. Track on left. — 3.3 km ▲
GPS   S:30 59.210 E:125 20.783
UTM   51J 724060E 6569494N
(2.3 km)

▼ 50.3 km — Gate. LAF.
Gate. LAF. — 1.0 km ▲
(0.1 km)

▼ 50.4 km — Crossroads. CSA over railway lines.
Crossroads. CSA. — 0.9 km ▲
(0.1 km)

▼ 50.5 km — T-junction. TR.
Road junction. TL over railway lines. — 0.8 km ▲
GPS   S:31 00.531 E:125 20.426
UTM   51J 723441E 6567065N
(0.8 km)

▼ 51.3 km — Rawlinna Railway Station on right.
Rawlinna camping area is a grassed park area located at eastern edge of town. The gazetted Carlisle Rd located to west of Rawlinna leads 144 km south to Cocklebiddy on Eyre Hwy. This road leads through pastoral land so please leave all gates as found and do not disturb stock or stock watering points. Alternatively drive 375 km west along Trans Australia Railway Access Rd to Kalgoorlie. Trans Australia Railway Access Rd to east of Rawlinna is a private road and public access is not permitted.
Zero trip meter in Rawlinna with Rawlinna Railway Station on left. Proceed in easterly direction out of Rawlinna. — 0.0 km ▲
GPS   S:31 00.520 E:125 19.931
UTM   51J 722653E 6567102N

REVERSE DIRECTIONS START

FOLLOWING PAGES
Sandhill country north of Neale Junction

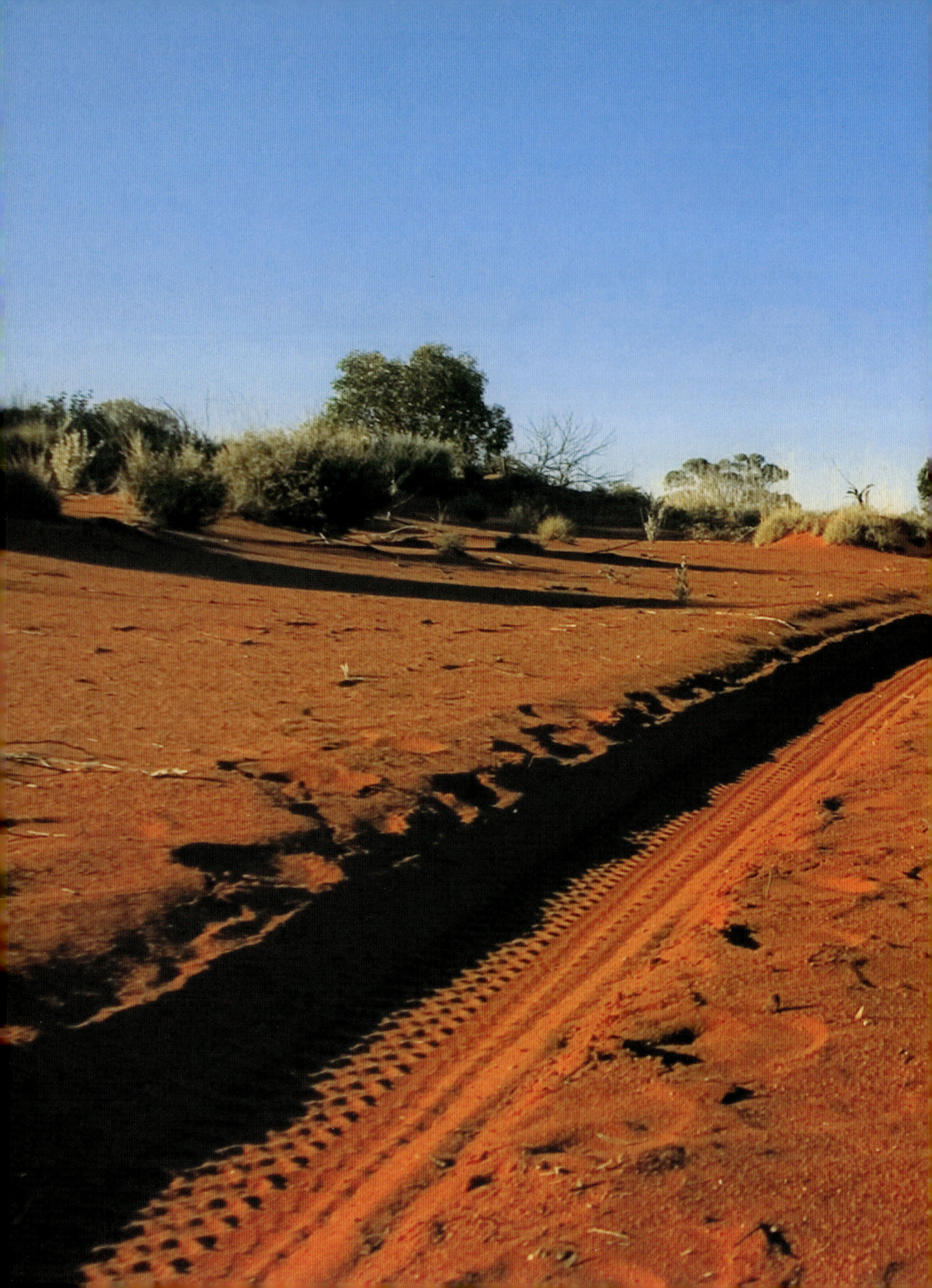

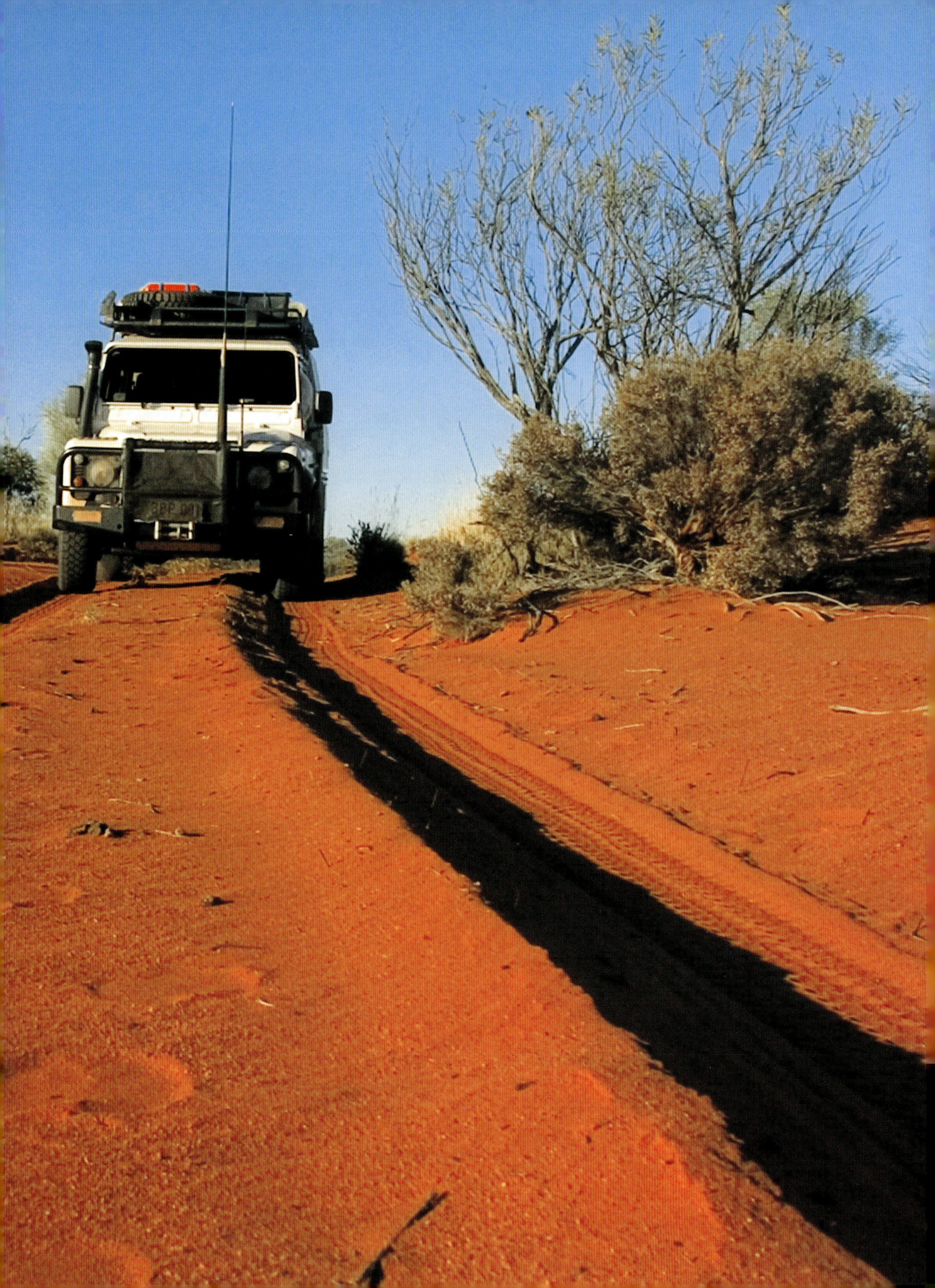

Anne Beadell Highway

Majestic marble gums are a feature of the Great Victoria Desert

COOBER PEDY ◀▶ LAVERTON 1338.4 KM
1. COOBER PEDY ◁▷ NEALE JUNCTION 958.7 km *(difficult)*
2. NEALE JUNCTION ◁▷ LAVERTON 379.7 km *(moderate)*

WHEN TO GO April–September   **TIME** 7–8 days

The Anne Beadell Highway runs from Coober Pedy in South Australia to Laverton in Western Australia and dissects the Great Victoria Desert, one of Australia's most scenic desert regions. Constructed between 1953 and 1962 by the Gunbarrel Road Construction Party led by Len Beadell, and named after his wife, the purpose of this remote road was to access the Emu Atomic Test Site.

More of a track than a highway, the Anne Beadell is generally sandy. Natural features of interest include Serpentine Lakes, a series of large salt lakes near the Western Australia–South Australia border, and the incredibly diverse desert vegetation. Old Yeo Lake homestead, a corrugated iron hut characteristic of many early pastoral homesteads, is one of the few signs of past human habitation along the track.

Emu was the location of the first atomic test explosion on mainland Australia and, although little remains, it is possible to visit concrete monuments at the sites where the bombs were detonated in 1953. As these were atomic bombs, please heed the radiation warning signs in the vicinity.

The opal-mining town of Coober Pedy at the eastern end of the trek is an interesting place to explore with its eclectic mix of cultures. It has a good selection of services for travellers and a range of accommodation including underground hotels and motels. Laverton, another mining town, at the trek's western end can also cater to your needs.

ANNE BEADELL HIGHWAY

Services

VEHICLE ASSISTANCE
RAA (SA)/RAC (WA)   13 1111

POLICE
Coober Pedy   (08) 8672 5056
Laverton   (08) 9031 1000

PARKS AND RESERVES
Neale Junction Nature Reserve
Yeo Lake Nature Reserve
CALM Kalgoorlie   (08) 9021 2677

Tallaringa Conservation Park
Unnamed Conservation Park
NPWSA Ceduna   (08) 8625 3144

VISITOR INFORMATION
Coober Pedy   (08) 8672 5298
                or 1800 637 076
Laverton   (08) 9031 1750

The thorny devil (Moloch horridus) is a slow-moving creature so watch out for it on the track

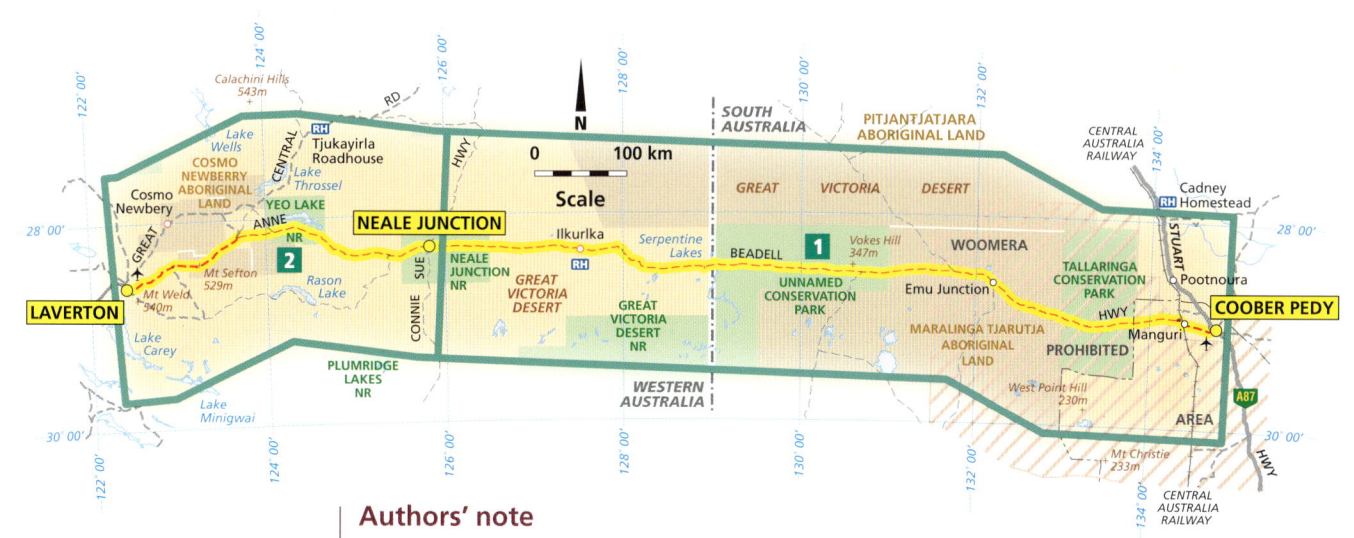

Authors' note

The stunning landscape of the Great Victoria Desert is one of our favourites. 'Desert' seems a misnomer when you see the wonderful mix of vegetation, from beautiful cream-trunked marble gums to rings of spinifex that look like designer hedges, all set against the striking red hues of surrounding dunes.

Town Facilities

	Fuel: D/P/A	Mechanical repairs	Tyre repairs	Public telephone	Public toilets	Shop/supplies	Gas refills	Ice	Visitor information	Post office	Medical centre	Police	Meals	Motel	Hotel	Cabins	Caravan park	Camping
Coober Pedy	D/P/A	•	•	•	•	•	•	•	•	•	•	•	•	•	•	•	•
Laverton	D/P	•	•	•	•	•	•	•	•	•	•	•	•	•	•	•	•

ANNE BEADELL HIGHWAY

1 COOBER PEDY ◄► NEALE JUNCTION 958.7 KM

Start point
Coober Pedy

Road atlas
353 J3

Total distance
958.7 km

Standard
Difficult

Time
4–5 days

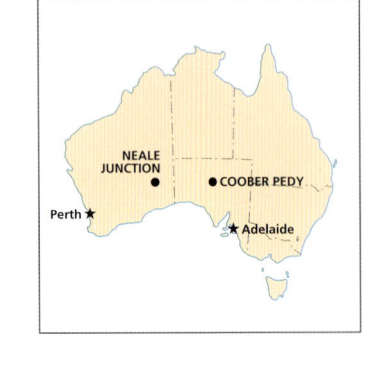

Longest distance no PD (includes all options)
810.5 km (Coober Pedy to Ilkurlka Roadhouse)

Topographic maps
Auslig 1:250 000 series: *Coober Pedy*; *Murloocoppie*; *Tallaringa*; *Giles*; *Noorina*; *Wanna*; *Vernon*; *Neale*

Other useful information
- Ilkurlka Roadhouse sells basic food supplies, local Aboriginal paintings and other items (if you require diesel or unleaded fuel, it is advisable to phone in advance to check availability); open Monday–Friday 9am–5pm and Saturday morning, tel. (08) 9037 1147; accepts cash only (EFTPOS facilities planned).
- NPWSA guide: *Unnamed Conservation Park*.
- Information booklets, brochures and maps enclosed with Desert Parks Pass (see Permits and bookings).
- Mark Shephard's *The Great Victoria Desert* is an excellent reference on the natural history, Aboriginal occupation, European exploration and nuclear-weapons testing in the region.
- This desert expanse is the habitat of a great variety of birds and wildflowers so pack identification guides for reference.

Description
The first section of the trek takes in a variety of landscapes ranging from stark moonscape-like landforms around Coober Pedy to ruby-red sand dunes in the Great Victoria Desert. The generally sandy track runs parallel to the main dune system but there are a number of small dunes to cross and some heavily corrugated stretches. Although rough in places, it is possible to tow a well-constructed off-road trailer along this route.

Leaving Coober Pedy the route strikes west, passing through Mabel Creek station on a designated Public Access Route (PAR) before entering Tallaringa Conservation Park, roughly the eastern boundary of the Great Victoria Desert. The track surface to this point is generally maintained, with signposted directions through the maze of tracks on Mabel Creek station. However, once in Tallaringa the corrugations commence and continue more or less until the South Australia–Western Australia border near Serpentine Lakes.

Emu Junction, near the sites of the first atomic bomb blasts on the Australian continent, is approximately 230 kilometres west of Coober Pedy. Little remains today and concrete plinths mark ground zero at two sites, dubbed Totem 1 and Totem 2.

West of Emu Junction the large Unnamed Conservation Park protects some of the Great Victoria Desert's diverse flora (see page 190). At the western edge of the park lies the salt-encrusted expanse of Serpentine Lakes and once across this you reach the South Australia–Western Australia border, marked by a Len Beadell plaque. From here the road gradually begins to improve as it is maintained, if somewhat irregularly. Birds of prey are often seen soaring high above the desert or occasionally perched on the branch of a tree beside the track. Other animals most commonly seen are reptiles such as lizards, and feral camels.

Between the border and eastern boundary of Neale Junction Nature Reserve the Tjuntjuntjara community have recently constructed some shelters with water tanks and toilets beside the track and you can camp within range of these facilities.

Before entering Neale Junction Nature Reserve a moderately difficult detour over a number of sand dunes takes you to the wreckage of a small plane that put down in the desert while en route from Warburton to Kalgoorlie in the early 1990s. Neale Junction, the intersection of the Connie Sue and Anne Beadell highways, is surrounded by a stand of majestic marble gums. Camping is not permitted in the immediate vicinity, but there is an informal camping area located a couple of hundred metres to the west of the junction. Travellers have the option here to continue west along the Anne Beadell Highway (see trek section 2) or travel north to Warburton or south to Rawlinna via the Connie Sue Highway (see pages 176–85).

Appealing bush campsites are dotted along the highway, including some good sheltered sites around Vokes Hill Corner in the Unnamed Conservation Park. You need to be totally self-sufficient with all your camping requirements, particularly water – there are no reliable supplies en route.

Christmas tree mulga

Advice and warnings
- There are no facilities between Coober Pedy and Ilkurlka so you need to be totally self-sufficient and your vehicle well equipped. Carry plenty of food, water and fuel.
- Tracks may be impassable after heavy rains. There are sections of soft sand, heavy corrugations, small dunes, wash-outs and overgrown vegetation. For track conditions in South Australia, contact South Australian road report hotline, tel. 1300 361 033, or NPWSA Port Augusta, tel. 1800 816 078, or NPWSA Ceduna, tel. (08) 8625 3144. For track conditions in Western Australia, contact Shire of Laverton, tel. (08) 9031 1202, or CALM Kalgoorlie, tel. (08) 9021 2677.
- Travel through Mabel Creek station is via Public Access Route (PAR). Station holders request that the following regulations are observed: no camping, no deviating from the main access track, leave all gates as found, observe all advisory signs, use grids where provided, no disturbing of stock or wildlife, no polluting or damaging of stock water supplies or other station improvements, no shooting or carrying firearms, no alcohol to be consumed or carried openly and no rubbish disposal along the route.
- Track passes through Tjuntjuntjara land so stay on main access track.
- Standard road tyres are suitable. It is recommended that you carry two spare tyres.
- Towing an off-road trailer is possible but a heavy-duty model is recommended.
- In South Australia, bush camping is permitted along the highway in natural clearings, for up to 100 metres on either side of the track, except within the signposted 50-kilometre no-camping zone (in Unnamed Conservation Park) and on Mabel Creek station.
- In Western Australia, bush camping is permitted along the length of the highway in natural clearings, for up to 50 metres on either side of the track.
- No rubbish disposal along the track so please carry your rubbish with you.
- Do not take any items from the Emu bomb sites and take heed of radiation warnings.
- Travellers driving from east to west must observe the fresh food quarantine, which prohibits taking fresh fruit, vegetables, nuts or honey into Western Australia. West–east travellers must not take fresh fruit or vegetables into South Australia.

Permits and bookings
- Desert Parks Pass required per vehicle to travel through Tallaringa Conservation Park. This pass covers a range of other outback parks in South Australia and entitles the holder to camp within these parks or at specified locations and to travel on designated park roads. The pass comes in a handy pack with information booklets, brochures and maps. Contact Desert Parks Hotline, tel. 1800 816 078, to obtain pass or for further details.
- Travel permit required to travel through Woomera Prohibited Area. Contact Defence Support Centre, PO Box 157, Woomera SA 5720, tel. (08) 8674 2311.
- Permit required to enter Maralinga Tjarutja land. Contact Maralinga Tjarutja Inc, PO Box 435, Ceduna SA 5690, tel. (08) 8625 2946.
- Camping permit required to camp in Unnamed Conservation Park. Contact NPWSA Ceduna, PO Box 569, Ceduna SA 5690, tel. (08) 8625 3144.
- Coober Pedy has a range of accommodation. Contact the visitor information centre for details.

ANNE BEADELL HIGHWAY

Serpentine Lakes
The salt lake system of Serpentine Lakes extends over an area of 100 kilometres south of the Anne Beadell Highway. Skeletal insect remains, animal footprints and sun-dried leaves make interesting patterns in the salt-encrusted surfaces. It is worth exploring the area on foot.

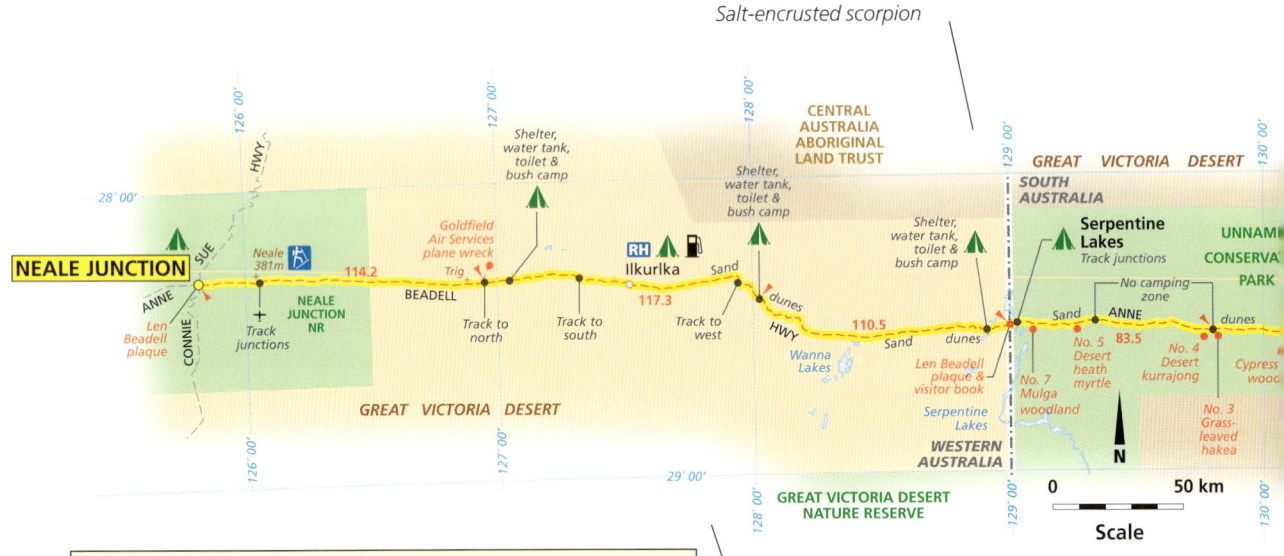

Salt-encrusted scorpion

Ilkurlka
Ilkurlka Roadhouse opened in April 2004 and now supplies basic food items. It also has fuel but you need to phone ahead to check availability. See Other useful information, page 188, for contact details.

Desert Flora

The large Unnamed Conservation Park protects some of the Great Victoria Desert's diverse flora. The vegetation found in the desert and in this park contrasts sharply with the treeless plains to the south and east. Radically different from deserts in the traditional sense, the Great Victoria features groves of marble gum (*Eucalyptus gongylocarpa*), mallee (various species but one of the most common is *Eucalyptus youngiana*), mulga woodland (various forms including a conifer-like species, Christmas tree mulga or *Acacia aneura* var. *conifera*) and cypress pine, along with small shrubs and the ever-present spinifex (*Triodia* spp.). During late winter and early spring and especially after good winter rains the desert comes alive with stunning displays of wildflowers.

Blue pincushion

190

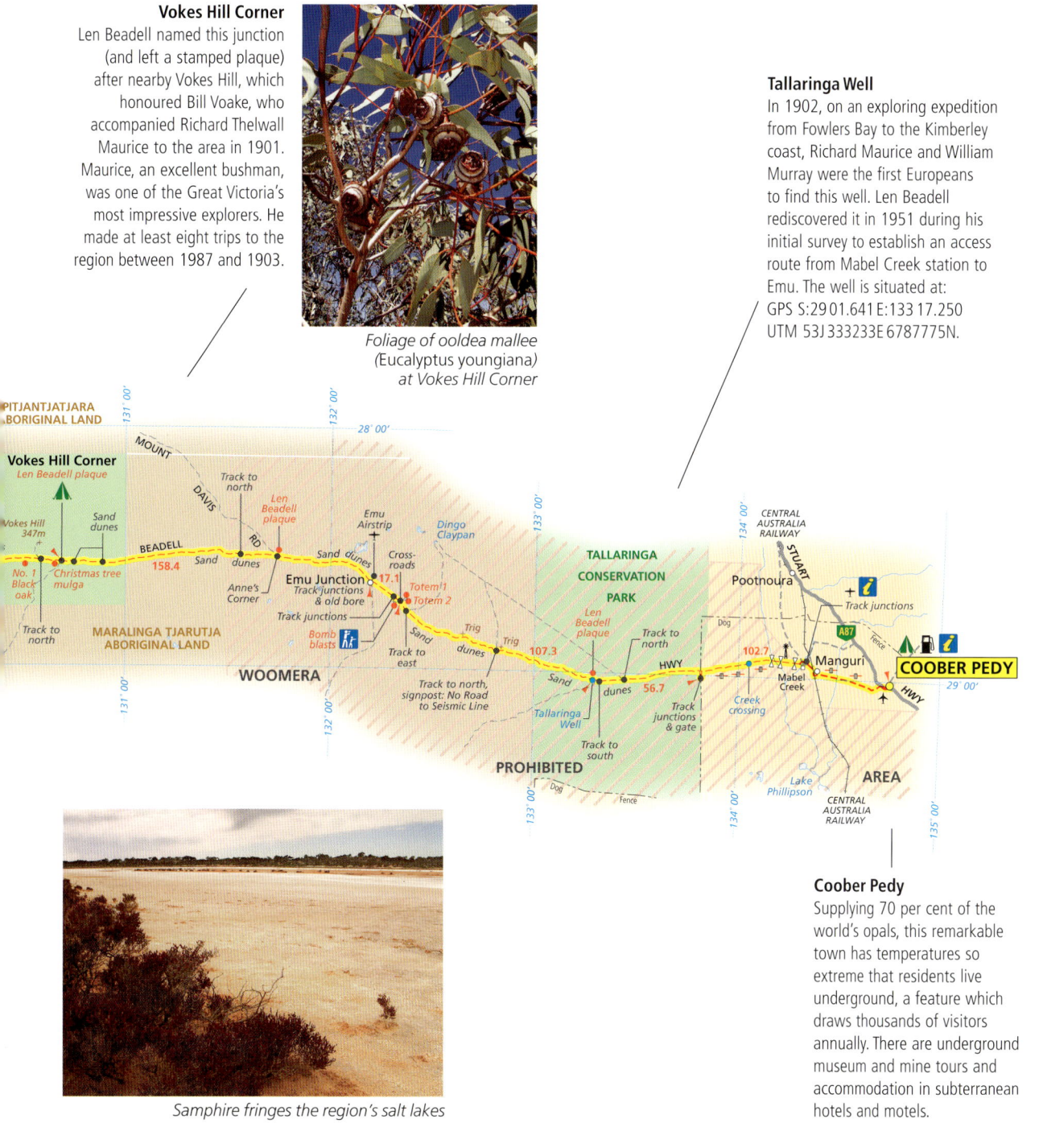

COOBER PEDY ◀▶ NEALE JUNCTION

Vokes Hill Corner
Len Beadell named this junction (and left a stamped plaque) after nearby Vokes Hill, which honoured Bill Voake, who accompanied Richard Thelwall Maurice to the area in 1901. Maurice, an excellent bushman, was one of the Great Victoria's most impressive explorers. He made at least eight trips to the region between 1987 and 1903.

Foliage of ooldea mallee (Eucalyptus youngiana) at Vokes Hill Corner

Tallaringa Well
In 1902, on an exploring expedition from Fowlers Bay to the Kimberley coast, Richard Maurice and William Murray were the first Europeans to find this well. Len Beadell rediscovered it in 1951 during his initial survey to establish an access route from Mabel Creek station to Emu. The well is situated at:
GPS S:29 01.641 E:133 17.250
UTM 53J 333233E 6787775N.

Samphire fringes the region's salt lakes

Coober Pedy
Supplying 70 per cent of the world's opals, this remarkable town has temperatures so extreme that residents live underground, a feature which draws thousands of visitors annually. There are underground museum and mine tours and accommodation in subterranean hotels and motels.

Campsite Facilities

	Toilets	Disabled access	4WD access only	Off-road trailer	Off-road caravan	Drinking water	Fee payable	Ranger patrolled	BBQ/fireplace	Campfires prohibited	Picnic tables	Shelter shed	No rubbish disposal	Public phone	Shower	Bushwalking	Swimming	Swimming not advised	Fishing	Canoeing	Dogs allowed
Neale Junction	•	•									•										
Serpentine Lakes	•	•		•							•										
Vokes Hill Corner	•	•		•							•										

191

ANNE BEADELL HIGHWAY

ROUTE DIRECTIONS

▼ 0.0 km — Zero trip meter on Stuart Hwy with Visitor Information bay on left, just south of southern entrance to Coober Pedy township. Proceed along highway in northerly direction.

Coober Pedy Visitor Information bay on right. 102.7 km ▲

GPS S:29 01.482 E:134 45.603
UTM 53J 476634E 6789254N

(0.4 km)

▼ 0.4 km — Road junction. CSA. SP: Alice Springs. Road on right SP: Hutchison Street, leads to SP: Coober Pedy/Oodnadatta.

Road junction. CSA. SP: Port Augusta. Road on left SP: Coober Pedy/Oodnadatta. 102.3 km ▲

(1.2 km)

▼ 1.6 km — Road junction. CSA. SP: Alice Springs. Road on right SP: Coober Pedy/Oodnadatta.

Road junction. CSA. SP: Port Augusta. Road on left SP: Coober Pedy/Oodnadatta. 101.1 km ▲

(1.2 km)

▼ 2.8 km — Road junction. CSA. Road on left to airport.

Road junction. CSA. Road on right to airport. 99.9 km ▲

(1.2 km)

▼ 4.0 km — Road junction. TL onto gravel road. SP: Mabel Creek HS 43.

Road now passes through mining area with numerous tracks running off main road.

T-junction with bitumen. This is Stuart Hwy. TR. 98.7 km ▲

GPS S:29 01.153 E:134 43.307
UTM 53J 472907E 6789853N

(33.5 km)

▼ 37.5 km — Y-junction. KL. Track on right.

Track junction. CSA. Track on left. 65.2 km ▲

(1.8 km)

▼ 39.3 km — Cross railway line.

Cross railway line. 63.4 km ▲

(3.9 km)

▼ 43.2 km — Track junction. CSA. Track on right.

Y-junction. KR. Track on left. 59.5 km ▲

(1.1 km)

▼ 44.3 km — Grid. Enter SP: Mabel Creek Station.

Grid. Exit Mabel Creek station. 58.4 km ▲

GPS S:28 56.877 E:134 21.346
UTM 53J 437220E 6797610N

(1.8 km)

▼ 46.1 km — Track junction. CSA. Track on left.

Track junction. CSA. Track on right. 56.6 km ▲

(1.6 km)

▼ 47.7 km — Y-junction. KR. SP: The Anne Beadell Highway/Laverton 1300 km/Tallaringa Conservation Park 54 km. Track on left SP: Mabel Creek Homestead.

Information shelter on right. It is recommended that you read all details before proceeding.

Track junction. CSA. Track on right SP: Mabel Creek Homestead. Information shelter on left. 55.0 km ▲

GPS S:28 55.812 E:134 19.622
UTM 53J 434408E 6799561N

(0.3 km)

▼ 48.0 km — Creek crossing.

Creek crossing. 54.7 km ▲

(0.6 km)

▼ 48.6 km — Y-junction. KL. SP: Vokes Hill. Track on right.

Track junction. CSA. SP: Coober Pedy. Track on left. 54.1 km ▲

(2.2 km)

▼ 50.8 km — Grid. Over grid T-junction. TR. SP: Vokes Hill. **You are now on original Anne Beadell Hwy.**

Track junction. TL over grid. SP: Coober Pedy. 51.9 km ▲

GPS S:28 56.211 E:134 18.118
UTM 53J 431969E 6798810N

(2.2 km)

▼ 53.0 km — Gate. LAF.

Gate. LAF. 49.7 km ▲

(5.9 km)

▼ 58.9 km — Gate. LAF.

Gate. LAF. 43.8 km ▲

(5.3 km)

▼ 64.2 km — Gate. LAF.

Gate. LAF. 38.5 km ▲

(0.1 km)

▼ 64.3 km — Gate. LAF. Through gate track junction. CSA. Track on right.

Track junction. CSA through gate. LAF. 38.4 km ▲

(8.9 km)

▼ 73.2 km — Creek crossing.

Creek crossing. 29.5 km ▲

(26.5 km)

▼ 99.7 km — T-junction. TL keeping Dog Fence on right. SP: Gate 3 km.

The Dog Fence is the longest fence in the world, winding 5400 km from the Great Australian Bight in South Australia, across New South Wales and into Queensland. It was erected by landholders to protect their sheep from dingoes and was built in stages, which over time were linked together.

Track junction. TR. SP: Mabel Crk Station 48 km. 3.0 km ▲

GPS S:28 58.781 E:133 49.072
UTM 53J 384833E 6793690N

(3.0 km)

▼ 102.7 km — Track junction.

Zero trip meter at track junction. TL through gate in Dog Fence and enter Mabel Creek station. Please close gate. Track SO SP: No Through Road. Through gate track junction. TL keeping Dog Fence on left. 0.0 km ▲

GPS S:29 00.391 E:133 49.156
UTM 53J 385000E 6790718N

COOBER PEDY ◀▶ NEALE JUNCTION

Spinifex rings in Tallaringa Conservation Park

▼ 0.0 km — Zero trip meter at track junction. TR through gate in Dog Fence and enter Tallaringa Conservation Park. Please close gate. Through gate track junction. TR keeping Dog Fence on right. SP: Vokes Hill 330 km. Track on left SP: No Through Road.

Track junction. 56.7 km ▲

(3.0 km)

▼ 3.0 km — Track junction. TL. Track SO SP: No Public Thoroughfare.

T-junction. TR. SP: Gate 3 km. Track on left. 53.7 km ▲

(38.2 km)

▼ 41.2 km — Track junction. CSA. Track on right.

Track junction. CSA. Track on left. 15.5 km ▲

(10.5 km)

▼ 51.7 km — Cross sand dune.

Cross sand dune. 5.0 km ▲

(3.7 km)

▼ 55.4 km — Track junction. CSA. Track on left.

Track junction. CSA. Track on right. 1.3 km ▲

(1.3 km)

▼ 56.7 km — Tallaringa Well on left and Len Beadell plaque on right.

Zero trip meter at Len Beadell plaque on left and Tallaringa Well on right. CSA. 0.0 km ▲

GPS   S:29 01.627 E:133 17.243
UTM   53J 333222E 6787800N

▼ 0.0 km — Zero trip meter at Tallaringa Well on left and Len Beadell plaque on right. CSA. SP: Emu.

Tallaringa Well is 20 m to south of Len Beadell plaque, in grove of trees. NPWSA requests no camping within 5-km radius of Tallaringa Well.

Len Beadell plaque on left and Tallaringa Well on right. 107.3 km ▲

(51.0 km)

▼ 51.0 km — Track junction. CSA. Minor track on right SP: No Road to Seismic Line.

Track junction. CSA. Minor track on left. 56.3 km ▲

(51.1 km)

▼ 102.1 km — Track junction. CSA. Track on right.

Track on right leads approximately 54.0 km to Dingo Claypan.

Track junction. CSA. Track on left. 5.2 km ▲

GPS   S:28 45.274 E:132 22.050
UTM   53J 242942E 6816364N

(5.2 km)

▼ 107.3 km — Crossroads.

Zero trip meter at crossroads. CSA. 0.0 km ▲

Track on left leads to Totem 1 and 2 where British atomic bombs were test exploded during October 1953. Track on right leads to original viewing point for bomb blasts.

GPS   S:28 43.056 E:132 20.261
UTM   53J 239938E 6820397N

▼ 0.0 km — Zero trip meter at crossroads. CSA.

Track on right leads 4.0 km to Totem 1 where British atomic bomb was test exploded on 15 October 1953, and 4.1 km to Totem 2, where second bomb was test exploded on 27 October 1953. Please take heed of radiation signs. Track on left leads 3.5 km to low rise that was original viewing point for bomb blasts.

Crossroads. 17.1 km ▲

(3.6 km)

■ 193

ANNE BEADELL HIGHWAY

▼ 3.6 km Track junction. CSA. Track on left.

　　　　　　Y-junction. KL. Track on right.　13.5 km ▲

(1.4 km)

▼ 5.0 km Track junction. CSA. Track on right.

　　　　　　Track junction. CSA. Track on left.　12.1 km ▲

(10.6 km)

▼ 15.6 km Track junction. CSA. Track on left.

　　　　　　Track junction. CSA. Track on right.　1.5 km ▲

(0.6 km)

▼ 16.2 km Old water bore on left. CSA.

　　　　　　Old water bore on right. CSA.　0.9 km ▲

(0.2 km)

▼ 16.4 km Track junction. CSA. Track on right.

Track on right leads 0.4 km to Emu Airstrip.

　　　　　　Track junction. CSA. Track on left to airstrip.　0.7 km ▲

```
GPS   S:28 38.137 E:132 12.102
UTM   53J 226436E 6829181N
```

(0.2 km)

▼ 16.6 km Track junction. TL. Track on right to airstrip.

　　　　　　Track junction. TR. Track SO.　0.5 km ▲

Track SO leads 0.5 km to Emu Airstrip.

(0.5 km)

▼ 17.1 km Crossroads. This is Emu Junction.

　　　　　　Zero trip meter at Emu Junction crossroads. TL. SP: Coober Pedy. Track SO SP: No Through Road.　0.0 km ▲

```
GPS   S:28 38.236 E:132 11.705
UTM   53J 225793E 6828983N
```

Anne Beadell Highway near Vokes Hill Corner

▼ 0.0 km Zero trip meter at Emu Junction crossroads. TR. SP: Vokes Hill. Track on left SP: No Through Road.

Track on left leads 0.4 km to site of former Emu township. Evidence of the township is visible by way of tiered flat floors where tents were erected.

　　　　　　Crossroads. This is Emu Junction.　158.4 km ▲

(50.4 km)

▼ 50.4 km Track junction. This is Anne's Corner. Len Beadell plaque on right. CSA. SP: 70 M Vokes Hill Corner. Track on right.

Old Len Beadell sign meaning 70 miles (not metres). Track on right is Mount Davis Rd.

　　　　　　Track junction. This is Anne's Corner. Len Beadell plaque on left. CSA. SP: Emu 30 M. Track on left.　108.0 km ▲

```
GPS   S:28 32.304 E:131 44.386
UTM   52J 768086E 6840090N
```

(18.5 km)

▼ 68.9 km Track junction. CSA. Track on right.

　　　　　　Track junction. CSA. Track on left.　89.5 km ▲

(57.3 km)

▼ 126.2 km Enter SP: Unnamed Conservation Park.

　　　　　　Exit Unnamed Conservation Park.　32.2 km ▲

(32.2 km)

▼ 158.4 km Track junction. This is Vokes Hill Corner.

　　　　　　Zero trip meter at Vokes Hill Corner. Len Beadell plaque on left. CSA. SP: Emu 100 Miles. Track on right SP: Cook 180 Miles.　0.0 km ▲

```
GPS   S:28 33.898 E:130 41.207
UTM   52J 664989E 6839049N
```

▼ 0.0 km Zero trip meter at Vokes Hill Corner. Len Beadell plaque on right. CSA. SP: WA Border 110 Miles. Track on left SP: Cook 180 Miles.

Vokes Hill Corner bush camping offers good camping spots in a number of natural, cleared areas near the junction, among wattle and mallee scrub.

　　　　　　Track junction. This is Vokes Hill Corner.　91.0 km ▲

(0.6 km)

▼ 0.6 km Tall thin trees on left of track are Christmas tree mulga (*Acacia aneura* var. *conifera*). CSA.

　　　　　　Tall thin trees on right of track are Christmas tree mulga. CSA.　90.4 km ▲

(9.5 km)

▼ 10.1 km Track junction. CSA. Track on right.

Track on right leads to Vokes Hill.
No public access.

　　　　　　Track junction. CSA. Track on left.　80.9 km ▲

(7.9 km)

▼ 18.0 km Track junction. CSA. Marker No. 1 and track on left.

This is good example of black oak (*Casuarina pauper*) woodland. Aboriginal people obtained life-saving water from the roots of these trees.

　　　　　　Track junction. CSA. Marker No. 1 and track on right.　73.0 km ▲

(39.9 km)

Mainland Australia's First Atomic Bomb Blasts

In June 1952 Australian Army surveyor Len Beadell was advised that he was to head a team to find a suitable site in outback Australia for a joint British–Australian operation to detonate a nuclear bomb. The brief dictated that the site be over 500 kilometres from Woomera, where long-range rocket launching had previously taken place, to prevent any radiation fallout from posing a threat to future missile testing. It was also essential that the chosen site include ground suitable to land aircraft. Some months later officials approved the site of Emu, situated 285 kilometres west of Coober Pedy in South Australia and including a claypan with a large, hard flat surface. Emu took its name from an animal footprint found in the claypan's crust.

Some 400 personnel including construction workers and scientists arrived, transforming Emu into a village complete with kitchen, mess huts, tent accommodation and water-storage tanks. Access was via aircraft only and all construction was done without earth-moving equipment. Ground access was urgently required for transportation of heavy equipment and bulk fuel supplies. During February and March of 1953 a road, which Len Beadell had previously surveyed, was pushed through Mabel Creek station near Coober Pedy, west past Tallaringa Well and onto Emu. This was the beginning of the Anne Beadell Highway, completed in June 1961 to link Coober Pedy on the Stuart Highway with Western Australia's eastern goldfields.

Once all necessary construction for bomb detonation was complete, it became a matter of waiting for ideal weather and wind conditions. On 15 October 1953 the first of two atomic bombs was detonated. This bomb, perched atop a 30-metre-tall steel tower, had an explosive yield of 10 kilotons (1 kiloton is equal to 1000 tonnes of dynamite). A second atomic bomb, with a yield of 8 kilotons, was detonated on October 27. Today these blast sites, known as Totem 1 and Totem 2, are marked by concrete plinths.

After the blasts it was decided that Emu was too remote and that a new site with easier access was required. By the end of 1953 the town of Emu had been dismantled. Len Beadell was again charged with the task of locating a site deemed suitable for atomic testing.

Totem 2 atomic test site

He suggested an area 35 kilometres north–north-west of Watson on the Trans Australia Railway line, which was to become known as Maralinga. Seven nuclear weapons were detonated here between September 1956 and October 1957.

Repercussions of this controversial period in Australian history, including innumerable surveys and reports, radioactive testing, decontamination attempts and compensation claims, have dragged out over decades, culminating in a Royal Commission in 1984. It found the United Kingdom solely responsible for decontaminating the test zone. One subsequent report cited $650 million as the figure required for a complete radiological clean-up. In 1993 the UK agreed to contribute around $45 million. At the current rate of progress, it will be at least 240 000 years before the area is fit for human habitation.

> *Repercussions of this controversial period in Australian history ... have dragged out over decades*

▼ 57.9 km   Marker No. 2 on left. CSA.

This is a good example of cypress pine woodland.

                                             Marker No. 2 on right. CSA.   33.1 km ▲

(31.1 km)

▼ 89.0 km   Marker No. 3 on left. CSA.

Examples of grass-leaved hakea (*Hakea francisiana*).

                                             Marker No. 3 on right. CSA.   2.0 km ▲

(2.0 km)

▼ 91.0 km   SP: No Camping for next 50 km, on right.

                           Zero trip meter at end of camping exclusion zone. CSA.   0.0 km ▲

GPS	S:28 29.736 E:129 20.100
UTM	52J 532786E 6847850N

▼ 0.0 km   Zero trip meter at SP: No Camping for next 50 km. CSA.

This is eastern boundary of camping exclusion zone.

                                   End of camping exclusion zone.   83.5 km ▲

(3.8 km)

▼ 3.8 km   Marker No. 4 on left. CSA.

Examples of desert kurrajong (*Brachychiton gregorii*).

                                         Marker No. 4 on right. CSA.   79.7 km ▲

(45.1 km)

▼ 48.9 km   End of camping exclusion zone. CSA.

This is western boundary of camping exclusion zone.

Desert campsite in Unnamed Conservation Park

                         SP: No Camping for next 50 km, on right. CSA.   34.6 km ▲

(7.3 km)

▼ 56.2 km   Marker No. 5 on left. CSA.

Examples of desert heath myrtle (*Thryptomene maisonneuvii*).

                                    Marker No. 5 on right. CSA.   27.3 km ▲

(17.8 km)

▼ 74.0 km   Marker No. 7 on left. CSA.

Examples of mulga (*Acacia aneura*) woodland.

                                    Marker No. 7 on right. CSA.   9.5 km ▲

(6.8 km)

▼ 80.8 km   Serpentine Lakes camping area. CSA.

Serpentine Lakes camping area is situated on both sides of track among tall mallee scrub.

                           Serpentine Lakes camping area. CSA.   2.7 km ▲

GPS	S:28 30.043 E:129 01.584
UTM	52J 502584E 6847328N

(0.2 km)

▼ 81.0 km   SP: Serpentine Lakes. CSA. This is eastern bank of lake.

                                 Eastern bank of Serpentine Lakes.   2.5 km ▲

(0.1 km)

▼ 81.1 km   Track junction. CSA. Track on right.

Track on right leads along eastern edge of northern section of Serpentine Lakes.

                                    Track junction. CSA. Track on left.   2.4 km ▲

(0.1 km)

▼ 81.2 km   Track junction. CSA. Track on right.

                                    Track junction. CSA. Track on left.   2.3 km ▲

Track on left leads along eastern edge of northern section of Serpentine Lakes.

(1.6 km)

▼ 82.8 km   Track junction on western edge of Serpentine Lakes. CSA. Track on right.

Track on right leads around western shore of northern section of Serpentine Lakes.

             Track junction on western edge of Serpentine Lakes. CSA. Track on left.   0.7 km ▲

(0.7 km)

▼ 83.5 km   SA–WA border.

           Zero trip meter at WA–SA border. Len Beadell plaque and visitor book on right. CSA into SP: Unnamed Conservation Park.   0.0 km ▲

GPS	S:28 30.515 E:129 00.057
UTM	52J 500093E 6846457N

▼ 0.0 km   Zero trip meter at SA–WA border. Len Beadell plaque and visitor book on left. CSA into SP: Shire of Laverton.

                                                     WA–SA border.   110.5 km ▲

(9.8 km)

▼ 9.8 km   Track junction. CSA. Track on left.

                                 Track junction. CSA. Track on right.   100.7 km ▲

(0.1 km)

▼ 9.9 km   Shelter, rainwater tank and toilet on left. CSA.

Bush camping in this vicinity.

COOBER PEDY ◄► NEALE JUNCTION

Nests made by spinifex ants

	Shelter, rainwater tank and toilet on right. CSA.	100.6 km ▲
(100.6 km)		
▼ 110.5 km	Shelter, rainwater tank and toilet on right.	
	Zero trip meter at shelter, rainwater tank and toilet on left. CSA.	0.0 km ▲
	GPS S:28 24.491 E:128 01.562 **UTM** 52J 404598E 6857194N	
▼ 0.0 km	Zero trip meter at shelter, rainwater tank and toilet on right. CSA. Bush camping in this vicinity.	
	Shelter, rainwater tank and toilet on left.	117.3 km ▲
(12.2 km)		
▼ 12.2 km	Track junction. CSA. Track on left.	
	Track junction. CSA. Track on right.	105.1 km ▲
(46.3 km)		
▼ 58.5 km	Crossroads. CSA. Track on left leads short distance to Ilkurlka Roadhouse. See Other useful information, page 188, for contact details.	
	Crossroads. CSA.	58.8 km ▲
	GPS S:28 21.027 E:127 31.082 **UTM** 52J 354754E 6863083N	
(0.1 km)		
▼ 58.6 km	Camping area on right. CSA. Facilities here include a toilet.	
	Camping area on left. CSA.	58.7 km ▲
(20.5 km)		

▼ 79.1 km	Track junction. CSA. Track on left.	
	Track junction. CSA. Track on right.	38.2 km ▲
(28.3 km)		
▼ 107.4 km	Shelter, rainwater tank and toilet on right. CSA. Bush camping in this vicinity.	
	Shelter, rainwater tank and toilet on left. CSA.	9.9 km ▲
(9.9 km)		
▼ 117.3 km	Track junction.	
	Zero trip meter at track junction. CSA. Track on left.	0.0 km ▲
	GPS S:28 19.744 E:126 57.031 **UTM** 52J 299081E 6864639N	
▼ 0.0 km	Zero trip meter at track junction. CSA. Track on right. Track on right leads 8.7 km to wreckage of Goldfield Air Services plane that crash-landed in January 1993 en route from Warburton to Kalgoorlie.	
	Track junction.	114.2 km ▲
(45.1 km)		
▼ 45.1 km	Enter SP: Neale Junction Nature Reserve.	
	Exit Neale Junction Nature Reserve.	69.1 km ▲
	GPS S:28 19.025 E:126 30.140 **UTM** 52J 255103E 6865139N	
(44.7 km)		
▼ 89.8 km	Cross airstrip. CSA. Walking track leads from northern end of airstrip to some interesting rock arrangements.	
	Cross airstrip. CSA.	24.4 km ▲
	GPS S:28 18.345 E:126 03.523 **UTM** 52J 211556E 6865415N	
(1.5 km)		
▼ 91.3 km	Track junction. CSA. Track on right. Track on right leads 0.4 km to rocky outcrop.	
	Track junction. CSA. Track on left.	22.9 km ▲
(22.9 km)		
▼ 114.2 km	Crossroads. This is Neale Junction (start of trek section 2). Track on left and right is Connie Sue Hwy, see pages 176–85. For **Neale Junction camping area**, CSA 0.2 km to track junction, where track on left leads short distance to large open site situated well off the road.	
	Zero trip meter at crossroads at Neale Junction. Len Beadell plaque on right. CSA. SP: 220 M [miles] SA Border/600 M [miles] Coober Pedy.	0.0 km ▲
	GPS S:28 18.179 E:125 49.036 **UTM** 51J 776284E 6866012N	

REVERSE DIRECTIONS START

■ 197

ANNE BEADELL HIGHWAY

2 NEALE JUNCTION ◀▶ LAVERTON 379.7 KM

Start point
Neale Junction

Road atlas
352 D2

Total distance
379.7 km

Standard
Moderate

Time
2–3 days

Longest distance no PD (includes all options)
575.7 km (Ilkurlka Roadhouse to Laverton)

Topographic maps
Auslig 1:250 000 series: *Neale*; *Rason*; *Laverton*

Other useful information
- Ilkurlka Roadhouse (east of Neale Junction in trek section 1) sells basic food supplies, local Aboriginal paintings and other items (if you require diesel or unleaded fuel, it is advisable to phone in advance to check availability); open Monday–Friday 9am–5pm and Saturday morning, tel. (08) 9037 1147; accepts cash only (EFTPOS facilities planned).
- Laverton Shire brochure: *Windarra Heritage Trail*.
- Mark Shephard's *The Great Victoria Desert* is an excellent reference on the natural history, Aboriginal occupation and European exploration of the region.
- This desert region is the habitat of a great variety of birds and wildflowers, so pack identification guides for reference.

Description
This short section covers just 380 kilometres from Neale Junction to Laverton and the track surface is generally good. Once out of the junction reserve, jump-ups and breakaways start to dominate the landscape. Previous attempts to utilise this western edge of the Great Victoria Desert for grazing proved unsuccessful and the now abandoned Yeo Lake homestead stands as a reminder of the futile endeavours of early pastoralists. The old homestead, a charming two-roomed corrugated-iron hut surrounded by mulga, is now maintained by CALM and is enclosed by Yeo Lake Nature Reserve. You can spend the night in the old shack or set up camp in a sheltered spot nearby. The lake from which the homestead and reserve take their names is to the north, with access via a four-wheel-drive track.

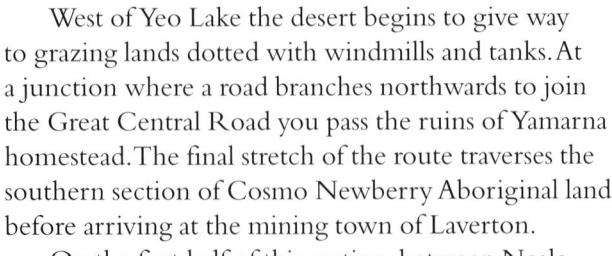

West of Yeo Lake the desert begins to give way to grazing lands dotted with windmills and tanks. At a junction where a road branches northwards to join the Great Central Road you pass the ruins of Yamarna homestead. The final stretch of the route traverses the southern section of Cosmo Newberry Aboriginal land before arriving at the mining town of Laverton.

On the first half of this section, between Neale Junction and Yeo Lake, there are a number of pleasant, shady bush campsites, but there are few campsites between Yeo Lake and Laverton. Once at Laverton, if time permits, Mount Windarra mine site, which once held the attention of the world, is only 28 kilometres to the north-west. This is where Poseidon NL found significant nickel deposits in September 1969, starting the famous Poseidon boom that took shares from 80 cents to $280 during the following five months. The Windarra Heritage Trail leads you on a walking tour at the mine site.

Advice and warnings
- There are no facilities between Neale Junction and Laverton so you need to be totally self-sufficient and your vehicle well equipped. Carry plenty of food, water and fuel.

Colourful breakaway country near Laverton

NEALE JUNCTION ◄► LAVERTON

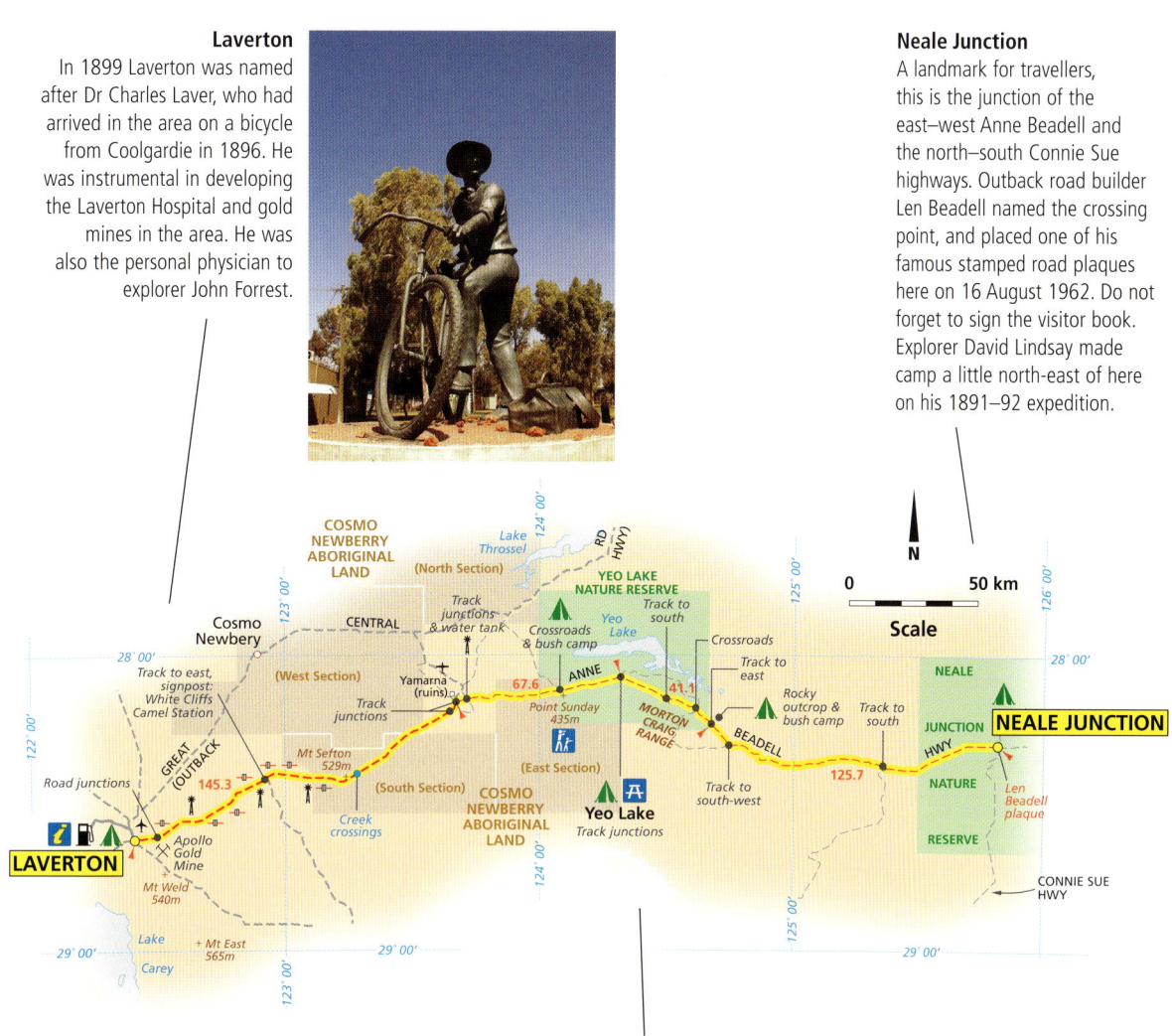

Laverton
In 1899 Laverton was named after Dr Charles Laver, who had arrived in the area on a bicycle from Coolgardie in 1896. He was instrumental in developing the Laverton Hospital and gold mines in the area. He was also the personal physician to explorer John Forrest.

Neale Junction
A landmark for travellers, this is the junction of the east–west Anne Beadell and the north–south Connie Sue highways. Outback road builder Len Beadell named the crossing point, and placed one of his famous stamped road plaques here on 16 August 1962. Do not forget to sign the visitor book. Explorer David Lindsay made camp a little north-east of here on his 1891–92 expedition.

Yeo Lake Homestead
Once the focal point of a large pastoral property, the homestead is a quaint corrugated-iron building comprising two rooms, one with a fireplace, and a verandah at the rear. Beside the homestead is an old well, from which water can be drawn by bucket – recommended for washing purposes only. Against the shed is a shower inside an old water tank, where a waterbag can be hung from an overhead rod.

Campsite Facilities

	Toilets	Disabled access	4WD access only	Off-road trailer	Off-road caravan	Drinking water	Fee payable	Ranger patrolled	BBQ/fireplace	Campfires prohibited	Picnic tables	Shelter shed	No rubbish disposal	Public phone	Shower	Bushwalking	Swimming	Swimming not advised	Fishing	Canoeing	Dogs allowed
Neale Junction			•	•						•											
Yeo Lake	•		•	•		•			•		•	•									

199

ANNE BEADELL HIGHWAY

Paddymelons flourish after rain (they are poisonous despite their enticing appearance)

- Tracks may be impassable after heavy rain. There are sections of soft sand, deep corrugations, small dunes and wash-outs. Contact Shire of Laverton, tel. (08) 9031 1202, or CALM Kalgoorlie, tel. (08) 9021 2677, to check track conditions.
- Track passes through Cosmo Newberry Aboriginal land so stay on the main access track.
- Standard road tyres are suitable. Carry two spare tyres.
- Towing an off-road trailer is possible but a heavy-duty model is recommended.
- Bush camping is permitted along the length of the highway in natural clearings, for up to 50 metres from either side of the track.
- No rubbish disposal along the track so please carry your rubbish with you.
- When visiting Yeo Lake homestead, leave buildings and surrounds in a clean, tidy condition. Ensure all fires are totally extinguished.

Permits and bookings

- Permit required to travel through Cosmo Newberry Aboriginal land (East), Reserve No. 20396, and Cosmo Newberry Aboriginal land (South), Reserve No. 25050. Permit available from Aboriginal Lands Trust in Perth, tel. (08) 9235 8000 or visit their website (www.dia.wa.gov.au). Permit is free but allow up to four weeks for delivery.
- Bookings not required for Yeo Lake homestead.

ROUTE DIRECTIONS

▼ 0.0 km — Zero trip meter at Neale Junction. Len Beadell plaque on left. CSA in westerly direction towards SP: Laverton 240 Miles.
Track on left and right is Connie Sue Hwy.
Crossroads. This is Neale Junction. 125.7 km ▲
GPS S:28 18.179 E:125 49.036
UTM 51J 776284E 6866012N
(0.2 km)

▼ 0.2 km — Track junction. CSA. Track on left.
Track on left leads short distance to **Neale Junction camping area**, a large open site situated well off the road.
Track junction. CSA. Track on right leads short distance to Neale Junction camping area. 125.5 km ▲
(33.4 km)

▼ 33.6 km — Exit Neale Junction Nature Reserve.
Enter SP: Neale Junction Nature Reserve. 92.1 km ▲
GPS S:28 23.114 E:125 30.101
UTM 51J 745134E 6857577N
(15.0 km)

▼ 48.6 km — Track junction. CSA. Track on left.
Track junction. CSA. Track on right. 77.1 km ▲
(66.4 km)

▼ 115.0 km — Track junction. CSA. Minor track on left.
Track junction. CSA. Minor track on right. 10.7 km ▲
(10.7 km)

▼ 125.7 km — Track junction.
Zero trip meter at track junction. CSA. Track on left to rocky outcrop. 0.0 km ▲
GPS S:28 14.117 E:124 40.433
UTM 51J 664235E 6875599N

▼ 0.0 km — Zero trip meter at track junction. CSA. Track on right.
Track on right leads 0.2 km to base of rocky outcrop and possible bush camping.
Track junction. 41.1 km ▲
(0.9 km)

▼ 0.9 km — Enter SP: Yeo Lake Nature Reserve.
Exit Yeo Lake Nature Reserve. 40.2 km ▲
(8.1 km)

▼ 9.0 km — Track junction. CSA. Minor track on left and right.
Track junction. CSA. Minor track on left and right. 32.1 km ▲
(12.0 km)

▼ 21.0 km — Track junction. CSA. Track on left.
Track on left leads 2.0 km to base of impressive mesa. Good views of breakaway country from here.
Track junction. CSA. Track on right. 20.1 km ▲
GPS S:28 09.001 E:124 30.060
UTM 51J 647387E 6885268N
(20.1 km)

▼ 41.1 km — Track junction.
Zero trip meter at track junction. CSA. Track on left to SP: Yeo Lake Homestead. 0.0 km ▲

NEALE JUNCTION ◀▶ LAVERTON

▼ 0.0 km
GPS   S:28 04.603 E:124 19.098
UTM   51J 629533E 6893598N

Zero trip meter at track junction. CSA. Track on right to SP: Yeo Lake Homestead.

Yeo Lake homestead has some good sheltered **campsites** in its vicinity.

Track junction. 67.6 km ▲

(1.0 km)

▼ 1.0 km Track junction. CSA. Track on left.

Track junction. CSA. Track on right. 66.6 km ▲

(23.7 km)

▼ 24.7 km Crossroads. CSA.

Road on right is Point Sunday Rd and leads 36 km to Great Central Rd. Road on left leads 0.2 km to base of Point Sunday, possible bush camping and views from Point Sunday.

Crossroads. CSA. 42.9 km ▲

GPS   S:28 07.371 E:124 04.944
UTM   51J 606307E 6888715N

(0.4 km)

▼ 25.1 km Exit Yeo Lake Nature Reserve.

Enter SP: Yeo Lake Nature Reserve. 42.5 km ▲

(37.2 km)

▼ 62.3 km Track junction. CSA. Track on left.

Track junction. CSA. Track on right. 5.3 km ▲

(1.2 km)

▼ 63.5 km Windmill and tank on right. CSA.

Windmill and tank on left. CSA. 4.1 km ▲

(2.8 km)

▼ 66.3 km Track junction. KR. Minor track on left.

Track junction. CSA. Minor track on right. 1.3 km ▲

(1.3 km)

▼ 67.6 km Track junction.

Zero trip meter at track junction. Yamarna station ruins. TR. SP: Neale Junction. 0.0 km ▲

GPS   S:28 09.542 E:123 40.206
UTM   51J 565790E 6884999N

▼ 0.0 km Zero trip meter at track junction. Yamarna station ruins. TL.

Track junction. 145.3 km ▲

(4.9 km)

▼ 4.9 km Road junction. CSA. Track on left.

Road junction. CSA. Track on right. 140.4 km ▲

(81.6 km)

▼ 86.5 km Road junction. CSA. Road on left SP: White Cliffs Camel Station/Private Road.

Y-junction. KL. Road on right SP: White Cliffs Camel Station/Private Road. 58.8 km ▲

GPS   S:28 25.245 E:122 55.179
UTM   51J 492131E 6856185N

(50.4 km)

▼ 136.9 km Road junction. CSA. Road on left SP: Apollo Gold Mine.

Road junction. CSA. Road on right. 8.4 km ▲

(6.8 km)

▼ 143.7 km T-junction with bitumen. This is SP: Crawford Soak Rd. TL.

Road junction. TR onto gravel road. 1.6 km ▲

GPS   S:28 37.275 E:122 25.116
UTM   51J 443166E 6833837N

(1.3 km)

▼ 145.0 km T-junction. TR then immediately TL into SP: Augusta Street.

Road junction. TR then immediately TL. This is Great Central Rd. 0.3 km ▲

(0.3 km)

▼ 145.3 km Laverton. Post office and Visitor Information Centre on left.

Zero trip meter on Augusta St in Laverton with post office and Visitor Information Centre on right and Desert Inn Hotel on left. Proceed along Augusta St in easterly direction. 0.0 km ▲

GPS   S:28 37.548 E:122 24.245
UTM   51J 441749E 6833326N

REVERSE DIRECTIONS START

Impressive mesa near Yeo Lake homestead

■ 201

Googs Track

Eastern section of Googs Lake

CEDUNA ◄► GLENDAMBO 370.7 KM
ONE SECTION ONLY *(difficult)*
WHEN TO GO April–October **TIME** 2–3 days

Googs Track in South Australia is a testament to the Denton family, who established this route through remote and isolated desert country during the 1970s. They started track clearing in 1973, worked on weekends and holidays, and finally completed the mammoth task three years later, linking up with an old track near Mount Finke that had been cut by hand during the 1950s.

The trek strikes north from Ceduna to Malbooma, a route characterised by rolling sandhills with some dunes reaching 25 metres high. Most vehicles will conquer the dunes comfortably with lowered tyre pressure.

Apart from the numerous dune crossings, Googs Lake is a major highlight of the trip. The main lake in a large salt lake system, it stretches for a vast 15 kilometres. The impressive bulk of Mount Finke lies approximately 40 kilometres south of Malbooma and was named in 1858 by John McDouall Stuart who, on climbing the summit to survey the surrounding countryside, wrote in his diary that 'nothing meets the eye save black scrub as dismal as midnight … a fearful country'.

The one-time bustling towns of Tarcoola and Kingoonya on the Trans Australia Railway line are now virtually ghost towns and as such are interesting places to spend some time. The picturesque bayside town of Ceduna offers a full range of services and supplies while Glendambo, on the Stuart Highway, has all types of fuel and limited supplies.

GOOGS TRACK

Services

VEHICLE ASSISTANCE
RAA   13 1111

POLICE
Ceduna   (08) 8626 2020

PARKS AND RESERVES
Yellabinna Regional Reserve
Yumbarra Conservation Park
NPWSA Ceduna   (08) 8625 3144

VISITOR INFORMATION
Ceduna   1800 639 413
Glendambo   (08) 8672 1030

Authors' note
Googs Track has been described as a mini version of the Canning Stock Route or Simpson Desert crossing. If you want an introduction to desert travel then this short but challenging jaunt is ideal.

The Dentons of Lone Oak
John (Goog) Denton and his wife, Jenny, lived at Lone Oak, a station on the southern edge of Yumbarra Conservation Park. The story goes that one of the reasons for their three-year toil on the track's construction was to provide a shortcut to the annual picnic race meeting at Tarcoola. Lone Oak is no longer owned by the Denton family.

Town Facilities

	Fuel: D/P/A	Mechanical repairs	Tyre repairs	Public telephone	Public toilets	Shop/supplies	Gas refills	Ice	Visitor information	Post office	Medical centre	Police	Meals	Motel	Hotel	Cabins	Caravan park	Camping
Ceduna	D/P/A	•	•	•	•	•	•	•	•	•	•	•	•	•	•	•	•	•
Glendambo	D/P/A	•	•	•		•	•	•				•	•	•			•	•
Kingoonya			•	•									•		•			
Tarcoola				•														

203

CEDUNA ◀▶ GLENDAMBO 370.7 KM

Start point
Ceduna

Road atlas
353 I5

Total distance
370.7 km

Standard
Difficult

Time
2–3 days

Longest distance no PD (includes all options)
419.1 km (Ceduna to Glendambo)

Topographic maps
Auslig 1:250 000 series: *Streaky Bay*; *Childara*; *Tarcoola*; *Kingoonya*

Other useful information
- Glendambo Roadhouse has fuel; open seven days 6.45am–10.30pm, tel. (08) 8672 1092; accepts cash, EFTPOS and credit cards.
- Woodys service station at Glendambo has fuel and limited grocery supplies; open seven days 7am–10pm, tel. (08) 8672 1035; accepts cash, EFTPOS and credit cards.
- Kingoonya hotel has accommodation and meals, tel. (08) 8672 1073.
- NPWSA information sheets: *Yumbarra Conservation Park: 4 Wheel Drive Vehicles Only*; *Yumbarra Conservation Park and Yellabinna Regional Reserve: Googs Track*.
- Wildflowers grow along the edge of the track through the dunes so pack a wildflower identification guide.

Description

Leaving the fishing and oyster-farming town of Ceduna, Kalanbie Road takes you through grain-growing country typical of the western Eyre Peninsula, with wheat being the staple crop. The ubiquitous spinifex of the inland deserts and mallee scrub soon replace the farmlands as you enter Yumbarra Conservation Park. From this point rolling sand dunes predominate and the route twists and turns through forests of mallee as it negotiates the sandhills. Overall track conditions are good, but there are corrugated sections and 'scalloping' on some of the dune approaches.

A stop at Googs Lake provides a welcome diversion from the roller-coaster ride over the dunes. It is well worth exploring the area on foot. Just past here the track enters Yellabinna Regional Reserve, picking up the sand dunes again for the run towards Mount Finke. In the vicinity of the mountain, the mallee begins to give way to stands of mulga. During late winter and early spring the reserve becomes awash with wildflowers, transforming the otherwise muted tones into a vibrant sea of colour. Yumbarra protects rare species of grevillea and hakea and provides an ideal habitat for the Major Mitchell cockatoo. This beautiful pale pink bird is also found in Yellabinna, along with other desert dwellers such as thorny devils, mallee fowl and sandhill dunnarts.

At 361 metres, Mount Finke is a notable landmark in this otherwise flat country. Those who choose to tackle the strenuous climb to the peak are rewarded by an outstanding 360-degree desert panorama. Be sure to sign the visitor book at the summit.

Once out of Yellabinna Regional Reserve you enter Malbooma station, where the pastoral landscape returns. It is not long before you pick up the well-maintained Trans Australia Railway Access Road to Tarcoola. This town and Kingoonya, further to the east, were once important railway centres but now have only a handful of residents. Kingoonya was on the original Stuart Highway but when this was realigned to the east in the early 1980s the town rapidly declined. Neither place offers fuel or supplies for travellers.

Reducing tyre pressure before tackling the dunes

Crossing a salt lake near Mount Finke

Much of this trek is confined to vehicle-based exploration, but the surrounds of Googs Lake present a notable exception. The lake's south-west shores offer plenty of pleasant campsites amid stands of black oak, while camping is also possible in the vicinity of Mount Finke. There are no facilities at either of these locations so you need to be totally self-sufficient.

Advice and warnings
- Recommended direction of travel is south to north to reduce the chance of head-on collisions on the dune crests. If travelling from north to south, you must stop at the Quarantine Inspection Station on arrival in Ceduna. If you have fresh fruit or vegetables, it is an idea to keep receipts of purchase as proof that these items did not come from Western Australia.
- Dry weather access only. Possible track closures after heavy rain and during periods of fire danger. Track is sandy, corrugated and crosses innumerable dunes. Contact NPWSA Ceduna, tel. (08) 8625 3144, to check track conditions. For up-to-date information on road conditions between Tarcoola and Glendambo, contact Glendambo Visitor Centre, tel. (08) 8671 1030.
- Route passes through the Dog Fence at the northern and southern ends of Googs Track. Please ensure the gates are closed securely.
- Signposted maximum speed limit in Yellabinna Regional Reserve is 40 kilometres per hour. Watch for oncoming traffic over sand dunes – mount a high-flying red flag to your vehicle and tune CB/UHF radio to channel 18.
- Sections of the track pass through private property so please respect landholders and leave all gates as found.
- Do not drive on Googs Lake.
- Standard road tyres are suitable. Reduce tyre pressure at beginning of the track as noted in route directions.
- Towing off-roads trailers is possible but not recommended.
- Self-sufficient, 'no trace' camping applies at the two designated campsites and other numerous bush campsites along the track.
- Drinking water is not available so carry enough for your drinking, cooking and washing needs.
- Rubbish bins are not provided on this trip so carry your rubbish with you.
- Fire restrictions apply November–April. Contact NPWSA Ceduna, tel. (08) 8625 3144, for further details.

Permits and bookings
- No permit required to travel these roads.
- Permit required to camp in Yumbarra Conservation Park and Yellabinna Regional Reserve, obtainable from NPWSA, 11 McKenzie St, Ceduna SA 5690, tel. (08) 8625 3144.

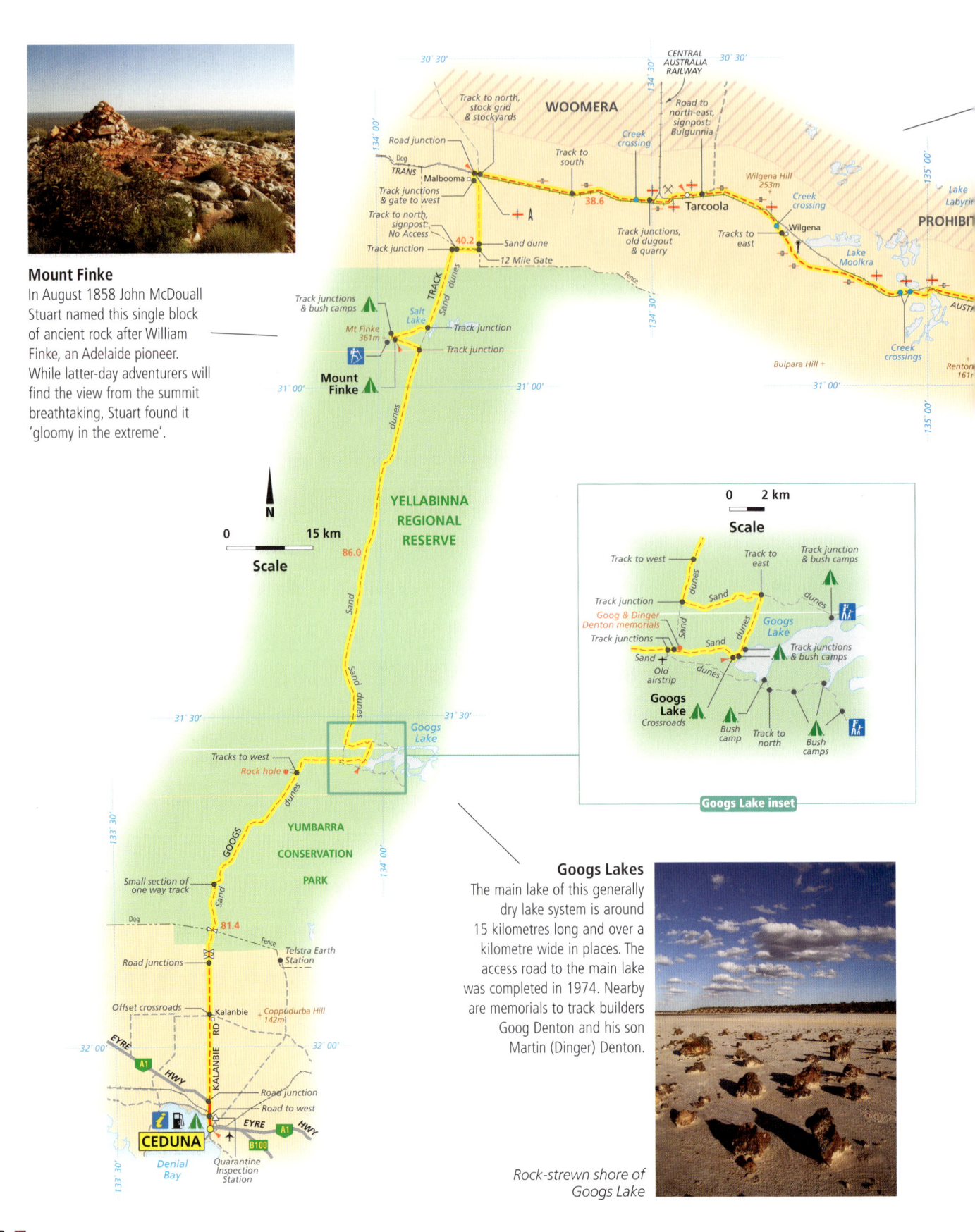

GOOGS TRACK

Mount Finke
In August 1858 John McDouall Stuart named this single block of ancient rock after William Finke, an Adelaide pioneer. While latter-day adventurers will find the view from the summit breathtaking, Stuart found it 'gloomy in the extreme'.

Googs Lakes
The main lake of this generally dry lake system is around 15 kilometres long and over a kilometre wide in places. The access road to the main lake was completed in 1974. Nearby are memorials to track builders Goog Denton and his son Martin (Dinger) Denton.

Rock-strewn shore of Googs Lake

CEDUNA ◀▶ GLENDAMBO

Tarcoola

Tarcoola was named after the horse that won the Melbourne Cup in 1893, the same year gold was discovered in the area. Once a thriving railway settlement, Tarcoola is now a virtual ghost town. Numerous buildings remain, including a hotel, school, hospital and a scattering of residential houses, but only a couple of people live here. There are no facilities for visitors.

Old hotel in Tarcoola

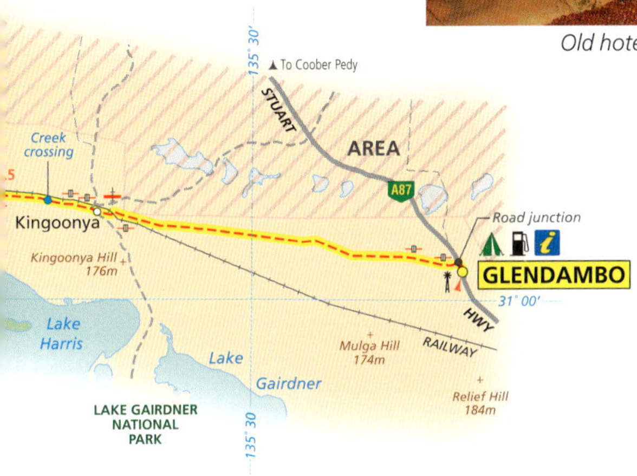

World's Longest Fence

The Dog Fence that cuts across both ends of Googs Track is the longest fence in the world, winding 5400 kilometres across South Australia, New South Wales and Queensland. The 2225-kilometre section in South Australia starts from the cliffs of the Great Australian Bight, runs eastwards to the north of Ceduna then heads north-west to do a loop around Coober Pedy, before winding its way back east through the salt lakes to New South Wales, at a point east of Lake Frome.

The unbroken barrier was built by landholders to protect their sheep from predatory dingoes

Two metres high, the unbroken barrier was built by landholders to protect their sheep from predatory dingoes. Constructed in stages between 1850 and 1940, individual sections were linked over time. In 1946 the South Australian government passed the *Dog Fence Act*, providing for a continuous dog-proof fence across the state. Today, landholders receive a government subsidy for maintenance of the fence.

Spring wildflowers add colour to the track

Campsite Facilities

	Toilets	Disabled access	4WD access only	Off-road trailer	Off-road caravan	Drinking water	Fee payable	Ranger patrolled	BBQ/fireplace	Campfires prohibited	Picnic tables	Shelter shed	No rubbish disposal	Public phone	Shower	Bushwalking	Swimming	Swimming not advised	Fishing	Canoeing	Dogs allowed
Googs Lake	•			•					•												
Mount Finke	•			•					•												

207

GOOGS TRACK

ROUTE DIRECTIONS

▼ 0.0 km — Zero trip meter in Ceduna at roundabout. Junction of SP: McKenzie Street, to left and right, and SP: Poynton Street. Proceed in westerly direction through shopping centre along Poynton St towards SP: Perth 1964.

Ceduna. Roundabout. SP: McKenzie Street, to left and right. Road on left SP: Adelaide 781. — 81.4 km ▲

```
GPS   S:32 07.559 E:133 40.420
UTM   53H 374887E 6444830N
```

(1.9 km)

▼ 1.9 km — Quarantine (fruit fly) Inspection Station on right. CSA.

Quarantine (fruit fly) Inspection Station. Stop for inspection. CSA. — 79.5 km ▲

Mandatory disposal of fresh fruit and vegetables at this station if carried in from WA.

(0.3 km)

▼ 2.2 km — Road junction. CSA. SP: Penong. Road on left SP: 10 Denial Bay.

Road junction. CSA. SP: Ceduna. Road on right SP: 10 Denial Bay. — 79.2 km ▲

(0.7 km)

▼ 2.9 km — Cross railway line.

Cross railway line. — 78.5 km ▲

(1.9 km)

▼ 4.8 km — Road junction. TR onto gravel road. SP: Kalanbie 15.

T-junction with bitumen. This is Eyre Hwy. TL. — 76.6 km ▲

```
GPS   S:32 04.992 E:133 40.226
UTM   53H 374524E 6449569N
```

(15.0 km)

▼ 19.8 km — Offset crossroads. CSA. Road on left SP: 14 O'Loughlin Tank. Road on right SP: Goode Hall 19.

Offset crossroads. CSA. — 61.6 km ▲

(8.6 km)

▼ 28.4 km — Road junction. CSA. Track on right to homestead.

Road junction. CSA. Track on left. — 53.0 km ▲

(0.2 km)

▼ 28.6 km — Road junction. CSA through gate. LAF. SP: Googs Track. Road on left.

Road junction. CSA through gate. LAF. Road on right. — 52.8 km ▲

```
GPS   S:31 52.227 E:133 40.519
UTM   53J 374696E 6473159N
```

(1.7 km)

▼ 30.3 km — Gate. LAF. CSA entering SP: Conservation Park.

Gate. LAF. Entering private property. Stay on main track. — 51.1 km ▲

(3.8 km)

▼ 34.1 km — Gate in Dog Fence. Please close. CSA. SP: Googs Track/4WD Track Only. Entering SP: Yumbarra Conservation Park.

Reduce tyre pressure here.

Gate in Dog Fence. Please close. CSA. — 47.3 km ▲

Increase tyre pressure here.

```
GPS   S:31 49.359 E:133 40.939
UTM   53J 375294E 6478466N
```

(8.2 km)

▼ 42.3 km — Y-junction. KL. SP: Keep to left.

Track junction. CSA. Track on right. — 39.1 km ▲

(0.6 km)

▼ 42.9 km — Track junction. CSA. Track on right.

Y-junction. KL. SP: Keep to left. — 38.5 km ▲

(25.0 km)

▼ 67.9 km — Track junction. CSA. Track on left.

Track on left leads 1.9 km to rock hole.

Track junction. CSA. Track on right. — 13.5 km ▲

(0.5 km)

▼ 68.4 km — Track junction. CSA. Track on left.

Track junction. CSA. Track on right. — 13.0 km ▲

Track on left leads 2.5 km to rock hole.

(9.0 km)

▼ 77.4 km — Track junction. CSA. Track on right.

Track on right leads 14.5 km along south-west edge of Googs Lake. Track leads to numerous bush campsites and lookout points.

Track junction. CSA. Track on left. — 4.0 km ▲

(0.2 km)

▼ 77.6 km — Y-junction. KR. SP: Memorials/Googs Lake. Track on left SP: Mount Finke 79 km.

Track on left leads 2.9 km to join route directions at upcoming 9.2-km mark.

Track junction. CSA. Track on right. — 3.8 km ▲

```
GPS   S:31 33.996 E:133 55.584
UTM   53J 398116E 6507102N
```

(0.2 km)

Cresting a sand dune on Googs Track

Flowering pigface in the desert sand

▼ 77.8 km　Track junction and memorials on left. CSA. SP: Googs Lake 4 km. Track on left SP: Mount Finke 78 km.

Memorials to builders of Googs Track, John 'Goog' Denton and his son Martin 'Dinger' Denton, on the left.

　　　　　Track junction. CSA. Memorials and track on right SP: Mount Finke 78 km.　3.6 km ▲

(3.6 km)

▼ 81.4 km　Crossroads.

　　　　　Zero trip meter at crossroads. TR. Track on left SP: Googs Lake.　0.0 km ▲

GPS	S:31 34.195 E:133 57.806
UTM	53J 401634E 6506768N

▼ 0.0 km　Zero trip meter at crossroads. TL. Track SO SP: Googs Lake.

Track SO leads 0.1 km to edge of **Googs Lake** with scattered bush **campsites** beneath shady black oaks. Excellent bush camping in vicinity.

　　　　　Crossroads.　86.0 km ▲

(0.4 km)

▼ 0.4 km　Track junction. CSA. Track on right.

Track on right leads 0.1 km to bush campsites.

　　　　　Track junction. CSA. Track on left.　85.6 km ▲

(0.3 km)

▼ 0.7 km　Track junction. CSA. Track on right.

Track on right leads 0.2 km to lake's edge and bush campsites.

　　　　　Track junction. CSA. Track on left.　85.3 km ▲

(3.3 km)

▼ 4.0 km　T-junction. TL. Track on right.

Track on right leads 4.9 km to Y-junction. Track on left leads 0.5 km to track on right, which leads short distance to high point over Googs Lake, with good views to north and south of lake. Track on right at Y-junction leads 0.3 km to bush campsite on lake's edge.

　　　　　Track junction. TR. SP: Googs Lake 4 km.　82.0 km ▲

GPS	S:31 32.343 E:133 58.864
UTM	53J 403276E 6510205N

(5.2 km)

▼ 9.2 km　T-junction. TR. SP: Mount Finke 74 km. Track on left SP: Memorials 4 km/Googs Lake 8 km.

　　　　　Track junction. TL. Track SO.　76.8 km ▲

Track SO leads 2.9 km to join route directions at upcoming 3.8-km mark.

GPS	S:31 32.542 E:133 55.976
UTM	53J 398710E 6509794N

(2.6 km)

▼ 11.8 km　Track junction. CSA. Track on left.

　　　　　Track junction. CSA. Track on right.　74.2 km ▲

(68.1 km)

▼ 79.9 km　Track junction. TL. SP: Mount Finke 7 km. Track SO.

Track SO leads 4.1 km to join route directions at upcoming 7.5-km mark.

　　　　　T-junction. TR.　6.1 km ▲

GPS	S:30 56.615 E:134 04.619
UTM	53J 411830E 6576285N

(5.8 km)

GOOGS TRACK

Stone tank beside the Tarcoola–Kingoonya Road

▼ 85.7 km	Bush camping in this vicinity. CSA. **Mount Finke** bush **campsites** are in clearings amid shady trees.	
	Bush camping in this vicinity. CSA.	0.3 km ▲
	(0.3 km)	
▼ 86.0 km	Track junction.	
	Zero trip meter at track junction. TL. Track on right SP: Mount Finke.	0.0 km ▲
	GPS S:30 55.380 E:134 01.572 UTM 53J 406958E 6578525N	
▼ 0.0 km	Zero trip meter. Track junction. TR. Track on left SP: Mount Finke.	
	Track on left leads 1.6 km to carpark at base of Mt Finke. From carpark a walking trail leads to summit of Mt Finke. Allow 1–1.5 hours return for this steep climb.	
	Track junction.	40.2 km ▲
	(0.3 km)	
▼ 0.3 km	Bush camping in this vicinity. CSA.	
	Bush camping in this vicinity. CSA.	39.9 km ▲
	(0.1 km)	
▼ 0.4 km	Track junction. TR. Track SO.	
	Track SO leads to bush campsites on north-east side of Mt Finke.	
	Track junction. TL.	39.8 km ▲
	(6.0 km)	
▼ 6.4 km	Cross salt lake.	
	Western edge of salt lake.	33.8 km ▲
	(1.1 km)	
▼ 7.5 km	T-junction. TL. Track on right.	
	Track junction. TR. SP: Mount Finke 7 km/Salt Lakes. Track SO.	32.7 km ▲

	Track SO leads 4.1 km to join route directions at upcoming 6.1-km mark.	
	GPS S:30 54.588 E:134 05.567 UTM 53J 413308E 6580042N	
	(12.4 km)	
▼ 19.9 km	Exit Yellabinna Regional Reserve. Increase tyre pressure here.	
	Enter SP: Yellabinna Regional Reserve. Reduce tyre pressure here.	20.3 km ▲
	(1.8 km)	
▼ 21.7 km	Track junction. KR. Track SO.	
	Track junction. CSA. Track on right.	18.5 km ▲
	(0.8 km)	
▼ 22.5 km	Track junction. CSA keeping Dog Fence on left side. SP: Tarcoola. Track on left SP: No Access.	
	Track junction. CSA. SP: Ceduna via Googs Track. Track on right SP: No Access.	17.7 km ▲
	(4.0 km)	
▼ 26.5 km	Track junction. TL through SP: 12 Mile Gate. Please close. Dog Fence now on right side. SP: Tarcoola. Track on right SP: No Access.	
	12 Mile Gate. Please close. Through gate TR keeping Dog Fence on right. SP: Ceduna via Googs Track. Track SO SP: No Access.	13.7 km ▲
	GPS S:30 47.512 E:134 11.270 UTM 53J 422297E 6593181N	
	(12.2 km)	
▼ 38.7 km	Track junction. KR keeping Malbooma outstation on left. Tracks on left.	
	Track junction. KL. SP: Googs Track. Malbooma outstation and tracks on right.	1.5 km ▲
	(1.3 km)	

CEDUNA ◀▶ GLENDAMBO

▼ 40.0 km	Cross railway line.		
		Cross railway line.	0.2 km ▲
(0.2 km)			
▼ 40.2 km	T-junction.		
	Zero trip meter at road junction. TL. SP: Googs Track.		0.0 km ▲
	GPS S:30 40.419 E:134 10.888 **UTM** 53J 421592E 6606279N		
▼ 0.0 km	Zero trip meter at T-junction. TR.		
		Road junction.	38.6 km ▲
(31.2 km)			
▼ 31.2 km	Road junction. CSA. Track on left.		
	Track on left leads 0.1 km to old wood-lined dugout. Dugouts were used by rail-construction companies for storing explosives, which were for blasting in quarries such as the one on the south side of the track. These quarries provided ballast for the railway line. Please ensure door of dugout is kept closed to help maintain wood lining and to keep out animals.		
		Road junction. CSA. Track on right.	7.4 km ▲
	GPS S:30 42.982 E:134 29.774 **UTM** 53J 451765E 6601723N		
(0.9 km)			
▼ 32.1 km	Cross railway line.		
		Cross railway line.	6.5 km ▲
(3.2 km)			
▼ 35.3 km	Cross railway line.		
		Cross railway line.	3.3 km ▲
(3.3 km)			
▼ 38.6 km	Tarcoola. Crossroads.		
	Zero trip meter in Tarcoola at crossroads. CSA. SP: 94 Mulgathing HS.		0.0 km ▲
	GPS S:30 42.536 E:134 34.064 **UTM** 53J 458608E 6602575N		
▼ 0.0 km	Zero trip meter in Tarcoola at crossroads. CSA.		
		Tarcoola. Crossroads.	124.5 km ▲
(2.4 km)			
▼ 2.4 km	Road junction. CSA. SP: Kingoonya 82. Road on left SP: 81 Bulgunnia.		
	Road junction. CSA. SP: 2 Tarcoola. Road on right SP: 81 Bulgunnia.		122.1 km ▲
(11.0 km)			
▼ 13.4 km	Cross railway line.		
		Cross railway line.	111.1 km ▲
(6.4 km)			
▼ 19.8 km	Road junction. CSA. Road on left SP: 1 Wilgena HS.		
		Road junction. CSA. Road on right.	104.7 km ▲
(18.7 km)			
▼ 38.5 km	Cross railway line.		
		Cross railway line.	86.0 km ▲
(6.5 km)			
▼ 45.0 km	Cross railway line.		
		Cross railway line.	79.5 km ▲
(5.7 km)			
▼ 50.7 km	Cross railway line.		

		Cross railway line.	73.8 km ▲
(10.1 km)			
▼ 60.8 km	Cross railway line.		
		Cross railway line.	63.7 km ▲
(19.5 km)			
▼ 80.3 km	Road junction. CSA. Road on left SP: 280 Coober Pedy.		
	Road junction. CSA. SP: Tarcoola 82. Road on right SP: 280 Coober Pedy.		44.2 km ▲
(0.8 km)			
▼ 81.1 km	Kingoonya. CSA. Road on right.		
		Kingoonya. CSA. Road on left.	43.4 km ▲
	GPS S:30 54.768 E:135 19.005 **UTM** 53J 530266E 6580019N		
(0.3 km)			
▼ 81.4 km	Road junction. CSA. SP: Glendambo 44. Road on right SP: Wirrulla 250/Kokatha 48.		
	Road junction. CSA. SP: 80 Tarcoola/232 Coober Pedy. Road on left.		43.1 km ▲
(1.6 km)			
▼ 83.0 km	Cross railway line.		
		Cross railway line.	41.5 km ▲
(40.5 km)			
▼ 123.5 km	T-intersection with bitumen. This is Stuart Hwy. TR. SP: Pt Augusta. Road on left SP: Coober Pedy.		
	Road on left leads 252 km to Coober Pedy.		
	Road junction. TL onto gravel road. SP: Kingoonya/Tarcoola.		1.0 km ▲
	GPS S:30 57.719 E:135 44.675 **UTM** 53J 571112E 6574374N		
(0.5 km)			
▼ 124.0 km	Road junction. TL. SP: Glendambo.		
		T-junction with Stuart Hwy. TR.	0.5 km ▲
(0.5 km)			
▼ 124.5 km	Glendambo. Information bay and rest area on right. Glendambo Hotel on left.		
	Zero trip meter at Glendambo. Information bay and rest area on left, Glendambo Hotel on right. Proceed in northerly direction towards Coober Pedy.		0.0 km ▲
	GPS S:30 58.168 E:135 44.969 **UTM** 53J 571574E 6573541N		
		REVERSE DIRECTIONS START	

■ 211

Victoria's High Country

Summer snowfall on Nunniong Road near Bentley Plain

CORRYONG ◄► MANSFIELD 529.3 KM
1. CORRYONG ◄►OMEO 241.6 km *(difficult)*
2. OMEO ◄►FARM JUNCTION 89.4 km *(moderate)*
3. FARM JUNCTION ◄►MANSFIELD 198.3 km *(difficult)*

WHEN TO GO December–May **TIME** 5–8 days

The High Country of Victoria is characterised by steep, winding tracks, stunning mountain views, numerous river crossings and a plethora of great campsites. Steeped in history and folklore, the mountain terrain offers everything to those seeking an insight into our pioneering past as well as providing a great four-wheel-drive experience that is at times challenging.

This alpine environment holds attractions almost too numerous to mention, from the picturesque Howqua Hills, remote Howitt Plains, fabled Zeka Spur Track and magnificent Wonnangatta Valley to the Crooked River goldfields and one-time gold-rush towns of Talbotville and Grant, which in the boom times of the late 1800s boasted banks, hotels, newspapers and populations numbering in the thousands. The route climbs spectacular Mount Pinnibar for 360-degree panoramas, winds its way across alpine meadows on Davies Plain, passes the headwaters of the mighty Murray River and, south-east of Omeo, visits Moscow Villa on Bentley Plain. If you have limited time available you can start or finish at either Omeo or Farm Junction near Dargo.

There is a huge choice of camping places along the route, from town caravan parks with amenities to secluded bush campsites beside crystal-clear mountain streams. Corryong at the start and Mansfield at journey's end have all facilities and supplies. Omeo has slightly fewer services while Dargo has limited shop supplies, fuel, mechanical repairs and a hotel.

VICTORIA'S HIGH COUNTRY

Services

VEHICLE ASSISTANCE	
NRMA (NSW)/RACV (Vic)	13 1111

POLICE
Corryong	(02) 6076 1666
Mansfield	(03) 5775 2555
Omeo	(03) 5159 1222

PARKS AND RESERVES
Alpine National Park
Parks Vic Dargo	(03) 5140 1243
Parks Vic Mansfield	(03) 5733 1200
Parks Vic Omeo	(03) 5159 1660
Parks Vic Swifts Creek	(03) 5159 5100

Kosciuszko National Park
NPWS Khancoban	(02) 6076 9373

Grant Historic Area
Parks Vic Dargo	(03) 5140 1243

PARKS AND RESERVES (continued)
Oriental Claims Historic Area
Victoria Falls Historic Area
Parks Vic Omeo	(03) 5159 1660

Howqua Hills Historic Area
Parks Vic Mansfield	(03) 5733 1200

Dogs Grave Reserve
Nunniong State Forest
DSE Swifts Creek	(03) 5159 5100

VISITOR INFORMATION
Corryong	(02) 6076 2277
Dargo	(03) 5140 1219
Mansfield	(03) 5775 1464
www.mansfield-mtbuller.com.au	
Omeo	(03) 5159 1552
www.omeo.net/region	

Authors' note
The route we follow in this trek takes you on a 'grand tour' of Victoria's magical High Country. It also offers some of the very best four-wheel driving in the Australian alpine region.

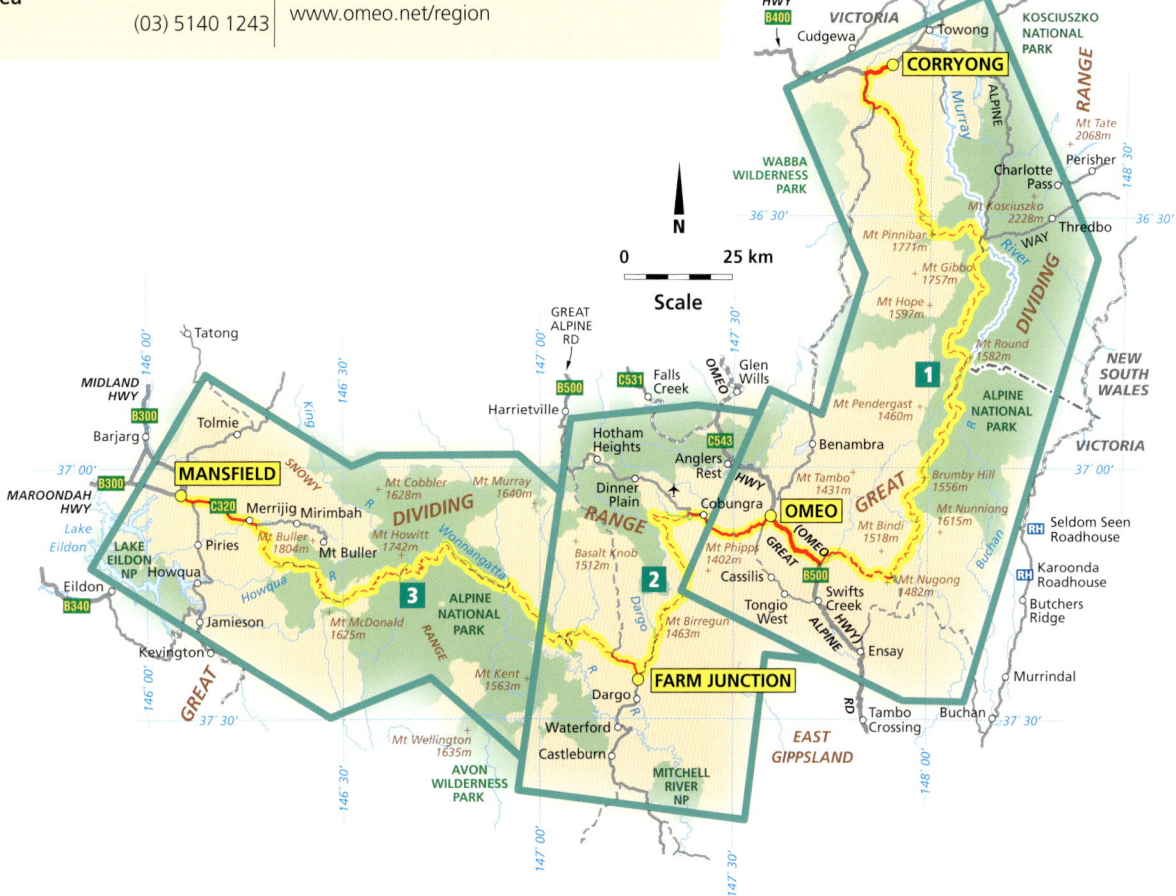

Town Facilities

	Fuel: D/P/A	Mechanical repairs	Tyre repairs	Public telephone	Public toilets	Shop/supplies	Gas refills	Ice	Visitor information	Post office	Medical centre	Police	Meals	Motel	Hotel	Cabins	Caravan park	Camping
Corryong	D/P	•	•	•	•	•	•	•	•	•	•	•	•	•	•	•	•	•
Dargo	D/P	•		•	•	•	•		•	•			•		•	•		•
Mansfield	D/P/A	•	•	•	•	•	•	•	•	•	•	•	•	•	•	•	•	•
Omeo	D/P/A	•	•	•	•	•	•	•	•	•	•	•	•	•	•	•	•	•

213

VICTORIA'S HIGH COUNTRY

1 CORRYONG ◀▶ OMEO 241.6 KM

Start point
Corryong

Road atlas
349 H6

Total distance
241.6 km

Standard
Difficult

Time
2–3 days

Longest distance no PD (includes all options)
262.3 km (Corryong to Omeo)

Topographic maps
Auslig 1:250 000 series: *Tallangatta*; *Bairnsdale*

Other useful information
- Parks Victoria brochure: *Alpine National Park*.
- Parks Victoria park notes: *Alpine National Park: Source of the rivers around Mitta Mitta, Omeo, Tallangatta and Corryong*; *Alpine National Park: Wilderness and the Snowy around Benambra, Buchan and Bonang*; *Alpine National Park: The High Country around Bright, Mt Beauty, Omeo and Dargo*.
- Envirobook: *Wild Guide: Plants and Animals of the Australian Alps* by Barbara Cameron-Smith.
- Booklet: *The Man from Snowy River*, available from Corryong Visitor Centre, tells the story of Jack Riley.
- Pack sturdy shoes, binoculars, sunscreen and hats.
- Keen anglers should pack fishing rods as many of the rivers and streams are stocked with trout.

Description

From the Upper Murray town of Corryong the trek heads southwards, taking in stunning views back over the Main Range and Mount Kosciuszko from the summit of Mount Pinnibar before dropping down to the Murray River via the lush pastures of Tom Groggin station. Areas of this northern part of the state's alpine region were burned by bushfires in early 2003. As you travel through you will be amazed at nature's ability to regenerate.

From Tom Groggin it is possible to ford the river into New South Wales and join the Alpine Way, but our route enters Alpine National Park, climbing steeply at times along Davies Plain Track through forests of towering ash to the alpine meadows of Davies Plain, with its historic hut and delightful camping areas nestled among snow gums. Wild horses, or brumbies, are often sighted in the vicinity of Davies Plain and the area is still grazed in summer by cattle from Tom Groggin station.

The track traverses the smaller Charlies Creek Plain, and other small snow plains fringed by snow gums and

Lush green meadow of Charlies Creek Plain

black sallies, before the descent to the Murray River at McCarthys, also known as The Poplars. The snow plains and meadows are ablaze with wildflowers over the summer months, a total transformation from the snow blanket they wear in winter. The route now follows Limestone Creek Track to the Benambra–Black Mountain Road, running parallel to Limestone Creek for much of the way.

A short distance along Benambra–Black Mountain Road the track turns south into Native Cat Track, before picking up the well-maintained Nunniong Road. It is worth taking the short detour to Moscow Villa hut and Bentley Plain. The historic steam-powered Washington winch makes an interesting stop before you join the Swifts Creek–Omeo Road for the run to Omeo.

There are plenty of camping opportunities along this section of the trek with the best being those at Davies and Bentley plains. You will have no difficulty finding secluded bush campsites along other stretches of the route. Road conditions on this section vary from well-maintained gravel through to steep, narrow and winding bush tracks such as those encountered in the vicinity of Mount Pinnibar, and the Tom Groggin and Davies Plain tracks.

Advice and warnings
- This route is through alpine country so be prepared for dramatic changes to weather conditions, even in summer when snow can fall. Carry wet weather gear and warm clothing.
- Sections of the route can be difficult and impassable during and after rain so travel at these times is best avoided.
- Seasonal road closures apply to the Mt Pinnibar, Tom Groggin, Davies Plain, Charlies Creek and Limestone Creek tracks. Closure dates vary from year to year but general rule of thumb is mid-June – early November. Contact Parks Victoria Omeo, tel. (03) 5159 1660, to check road conditions and closures.
- Murray River crossing at Tom Groggin can be difficult and high after heavy rain and snowfalls so contact Parks Victoria Omeo, tel. (03) 5159 1660, or NPWS (NSW) Khancoban, tel. (02) 6076 9373, to check conditions.
- Sections of the route pass through private property. Stay on and do not deviate from the track, obey all signage and leave all gates as found. Tom Groggin is a privately owned working cattle station. Access through the property is via the designated track. No access to private areas.
- Standard road or all-terrain tyres are suitable.
- Towing off-road trailers or caravans along the route is not recommended.
- Camping is at designated camping areas as well as at a number of bush campsites noted in route directions.
- Carry plenty of drinking water, food and supplies.

Inside Moscow Villa hut

- Rubbish bins are not provided in the national parks so please take your rubbish with you.
- Carry your own firewood and do not cut down any alpine vegetation. Pack a gas/fuel stove.
- Waters in these alpine regions can be very cold and can have numerous underwater obstructions. Always check conditions prior to swimming. Diving into these waters is not advised and can be extremely dangerous.
- March flies are prevalent during the summer months so carry good insect repellent.

Permits and bookings
- No permits required.
- No bookings required for camping areas.
- A park use and camping fee applies to camp at Tom Groggin camping area in Kosciuszko National Park in NSW. Contact NPWS Khancoban, tel. (02) 6076 9373, for further details.
- Bookings recommended for accommodation in Omeo during peak holiday periods such as Christmas, New Year and Easter.
- Recreational fishing licence is required in Victoria and NSW. Contact Fisheries and Aquaculture, Victorian Department of Natural Resources and Environment, tel. 13 6186, or visit their website (www.nre.vic.gov.au), or NSW Fisheries, tel. (02) 9527 8411, or visit their website (www.fisheries.nsw.gov.au), to check details.

VICTORIA'S HIGH COUNTRY

ROUTE DIRECTIONS

▼ **0.0 km** Zero trip meter in Corryong on Murray Valley Hwy with post office on right. PSA in south-westerly direction towards Tallangatta.

Corryong. Post office on left. **81.5 km** ▲

GPS S:36 11.761 E:147 54.258
UTM 55H 581301E 5993933N

(1.2 km)

▼ **1.2 km** Road junction. CSA. Road on left SP: Pioneer Ave/Jack Riley's Grave.

Road on left leads 0.7 km to grave of Jack Riley, the man on whom A. B. 'Banjo' Paterson based his poem 'The Man from Snowy River'.

Road junction. CSA. Road on right SP: Jack Riley's Grave. **80.3 km** ▲

(6.3 km)

▼ **7.5 km** Bridge over Nariel Creek. Over bridge road junction. TL. SP: Omeo/C545. Road SO SP: Wodonga.

T-junction. TR. SP: Corryong. Road on left SP: Wodonga. **74.0 km** ▲

GPS S:36 12.967 E:147 49.818
UTM 55H 574629E 5991761N

(3.0 km)

▼ **10.5 km** Road junction. CSA. Road on left SP: Nariel Creek Recreation Reserve.

Road on left leads short distance to **Nariel Creek** Recreation Reserve **camping area**, a large, grassy space beside creek.

Road junction. CSA. Road on right SP: Nariel Creek Recreation Reserve. **71.0 km** ▲

GPS S:36 14.529 E:147 49.884
UTM 55H 574703E 5988873N

(4.3 km)

▼ **14.8 km** SP: Nankervis's Bridge, over Nariel Creek.

Nankervis's Bridge. **66.7 km** ▲

(2.0 km)

▼ **16.8 km** Road junction. TL. SP: Thougla. This is Nariel Gap Rd.

T-junction with bitumen. TR. SP: Corryong 17. **64.7 km** ▲

GPS S:36 17.110 E:147 51.142
UTM 55H 576545E 5984083N

(2.1 km)

▼ **18.9 km** Road junction. This is Nariel Gap. CSA. Track on right SP: Nariel Gap Tk, and track on left.

Road junction. CSA. Track on left and right. **62.6 km** ▲

(4.1 km)

▼ **23.0 km** Road junction with bitumen. KR. SP: Thougla. Road on left SP: 18 Corryong.

Road junction. TL onto gravel road. SP: Nariel. Road on right SP: 18 Corryong. **58.5 km** ▲

GPS S:36 18.250 E:147 54.006
UTM 55H 580812E 5981938N

(1.8 km)

▼ **24.8 km** Bridge.

Bridge. **56.7 km** ▲

(2.1 km)

▼ **26.9 km** Track junction. CSA over bridge. Track on left SP: Grays Tk.

Bridge. Over bridge track junction. CSA. Track on right SP: Grays Tk. **54.6 km** ▲

(0.1 km)

▼ **27.0 km** Track junction. CSA. Track on left to possible bush campsite.

Track junction. CSA. Track on right to possible bush campsite. **54.5 km** ▲

(1.8 km)

Campsite Facilities

	Toilets	Disabled access	4WD access only	Off-road trailer	Off-road caravan	Drinking water	Fee payable	Ranger patrolled	BBQ/fireplace	Campfires prohibited	Picnic tables	Shelter shed	No rubbish disposal	Public phone	Shower	Bushwalking	Swimming	Swimming not advised	Fishing	Canoeing	Dogs allowed
Bentley Plain	•								•	•	•				•						
Buckwong Creek		•							•		•					•					
Charlies Creek Plain	•	•							•	•			•						•		
Davies Plain	•	•							•				•								
Dogmans Hut	•	•							•				•								
Limestone Creek	•	•							•				•		•		•				
McCarthys	•	•							•		•						•				
Moscow Villa	•								•				•								
Nariel Creek	•			•	•			•										•	•		•
Native Dog Flat	•						•			•			•								
Tom Groggin	•	•		•	•		•	•	•		•		•				•		•		

216

CORRYONG ◀▶ OMEO

Davies Plain Hut
Its pioneering past and remote setting make this one of the High Country's most popular destinations. Originally built in 1939 by the Gibson family, the hut has been rebuilt and restored numerous times using traditional construction methods to maintain its authenticity.

Spar tree on Nunniong Road

The Washington Winch
The steam-powered winch on Nunniong Road was used to snig logs out of the nearby gully with the assistance of spar trees, which supported the overhead rigging. Interpretive boards detail the process used to remove timber from the deep gullies of the forest. (See also page 223.)

Moscow Villa
The delightful and welcoming log-style Moscow Villa was built by local bushman Bill Ah Chow in the early 1940s. Ah Chow allegedly named the villa at the time of Hitler's advance towards Moscow during World War II. In 1957 during the Cold War, Ah Chow was paid a visit by government officials unhappy with the name of his hut. Not to be defeated, Ah Chow devised the acronym 'My Own Summer Cottage Officially Welcomes Visitors Inside Light Lunch Available'. All are still welcome to spend some time in Bill's hut.

VICTORIA'S HIGH COUNTRY

▼ **28.8 km** Track junction. CSA. Track on right SP: Stockwell Tk, and track on left.

        Track junction. CSA. Track on left and right.   **52.7 km** ▲

(1.6 km)

▼ **30.4 km** Bridge. Possible bush campsite on right before and over bridge.

        Bridge.   **51.1 km** ▲

GPS S:36 21.089 E:147 55.377
UTM 55H 582814E 5976670N

(2.6 km)

▼ **33.0 km** Track junction. CSA. Track on right SP: Gentle Annie Tk.

        Track junction. CSA. Track on left.   **48.5 km** ▲

(11.7 km)

▼ **44.7 km** Track junction. CSA. Track on right SP: Gentle Annie Tk.

        Track junction. CSA. Track on left.   **36.8 km** ▲

(1.9 km)

▼ **46.6 km** Track junction. This is SP: Gibsons Gap. KR on Walkers Logging Rd. Tracks on left SP: Mt Baldy Tk/Mt Elliot Ridge Tk/Dam Tk.

        Track junction. KL. Tracks on right.   **34.9 km** ▲

GPS S:36 25.704 E:147 57.826
UTM 55H 586391E 5968103N

(1.4 km)

▼ **48.0 km** Track junction. CSA. Track on left SP: Dam Tk, and track on right.

        Track junction. CSA. Track on left and right.   **33.5 km** ▲

(2.4 km)

▼ **50.4 km** Track junction. CSA. SP: Marginal Rd. Track on left SP: Tempest Logging Rd.

        Track junction. CSA. Track on right.   **31.1 km** ▲

(0.2 km)

▼ **50.6 km** Track junction. CSA. SP: Marginal Rd. Track on left SP: Boebuck Tk.

        Track junction. CSA. Track on right.   **30.9 km** ▲

(2.2 km)

▼ **52.8 km** Track junction. KL. SP: Dead Finish Tk. Track on right SP: Marginal Rd.

        Track junction. CSA SP: Marginal Rd. Track on left.   **28.7 km** ▲

GPS S:36 28.599 E:147 58.222
UTM 55H 586929E 5962744N

(3.6 km)

▼ **56.4 km** Track junction. CSA. SP: Dead Finish Tk. Track on left.

        Track junction. CSA. SP: Dead Finish Tk. Track on right.   **25.1 km** ▲

(1.6 km)

▼ **58.0 km** Crossroads. TL. SP: Pinnibar Jeep Tk.

        Crossroads. TR. SP: Dead Finish Tk.   **23.5 km** ▲

GPS S:36 30.145 E:147 58.261
UTM 55H 586958E 5959884N

(0.9 km)

▼ **58.9 km** Track junction. KR. SP: Pinnibar Tk. Track on left SP: Link Tk.

        Track junction. CSA. SP: Pinnibar Tk. Track on right.   **22.6 km** ▲

(5.2 km)

▼ **64.1 km** Mt Pinnibar. CSA. Trig marker and SP: Shady Ck Upper Tk, on right.

        Mt Pinnibar. CSA. Trig marker and SP: Shady Ck Upper Tk, on left.   **17.4 km** ▲

GPS S:36 32.135 E:148 00.218
UTM 55H 589841E 5956176N

(1.5 km)

▼ **65.6 km** Track junction. TL. SP: Tom Groggin Tk. Track SO SP: Pinnibar Gibbo Tk.

        Track junction. TR uphill.   **15.9 km** ▲

GPS S:36 32.248 E:148 01.102
UTM 55H 591158E 5955954N

(10.2 km)

▼ **75.8 km** Exit Alpine National Park and enter SP: Tom Groggin Station.

Now travelling through private property. Keep to signposted tracks.

        Exit Tom Groggin station and enter SP: Alpine National Park.   **5.7 km** ▲

GPS S:36 31.248 E:148 06.339
UTM 55H 598992E 5957716N

(0.5 km)

▼ **76.3 km** Gate. LAF. Through gate track junction. TR. SP: To Tom Groggin Tck/To Davies Plain Tck/To Alpine Way. Track on right SP: No public access.

        Track junction. TL through gate. LAF. SP: To Mt Pinnibar Tck.   **5.2 km** ▲

(0.4 km)

▼ **76.7 km** Grid. Over grid track junction. TR. SP: To Tom Groggin Tck/To Davies Plain Tck/To Alpine Way. Track SO SP: No Public Access.

        Track junction. TL over grid. SP: To Mt Pinnibar Tck.   **4.8 km** ▲

(1.1 km)

▼ **77.8 km** Gate. LAF. Proceed to junction. At junction TL. SP: Tom Groggin Tck/To Alpine Way/To Davies Plain Track. Now entering Alpine National Park.

        Track junction. TR and proceed through gate. LAF. SP: To Mt Pinnibar Tck. Now entering SP: Tom Groggin Station private property.   **3.7 km** ▲

GPS S:36 31.101 E:148 06.525
UTM 55H 599251E 5956136N

(0.4 km)

▼ **78.2 km** Track junction. TR. SP: Tom Groggin Tck. Track SO SP: No Public Access.

        Track junction. TL. SP: Tom Groggin Tck/ To Mt Pinnibar Tck.   **3.3 km** ▲

(1.7 km)

▼ **79.9 km** Track junction. CSA. SP: To Davies Plain Tck. Track on left SP: Camping Area.

Track on left leads 0.4 km to **Dogmans Hut camping area**, a small site in vicinity of hut.

        Track junction. CSA. SP: To Mt Pinnibar Tck. Track on right. SP: To Camping Area.   **1.6 km** ▲

(1.1 km)

▼ **81.0 km** Creek crossing.

        Creek crossing.   **0.5 km** ▲

(0.5 km)

▼ **81.5 km** Track junction.

CORRYONG ◀ ▶ OMEO

Near the summit of Mount Pinnibar

		Zero trip meter at track junction. TL. SP: Tom Groggin Tck/To Mt Pinnibar Tck. Track on right to Murray River and NSW.	0.0 km ▲		**GPS** S:36 34.286 E:148 07.777 **UTM** 55H 601072E 5952075N	
	GPS S:36 33.129 E:148 07.464 **UTM** 55H 600630E 5954219N				(0.8 km)	
▼ 0.0 km	Zero trip meter at track junction. CSA. SP: Davies Plain Tck. Track on left to Murray River and NSW.			▼ 3.7 km	Seasonal closure gates.	
					Seasonal closure gates.	12.7 km ▲
				(12.1 km)		
				▼ 15.8 km	Enter snow plain.	
	Track on left crosses Murray River and leads 1.1 km to Tom Groggin camping area (in Kosciuszko National Park), a very large area of grassland suitable for groups, and also leads 2.1 km to Alpine Way.				Exit snow plain and enter forest.	0.6 km ▲
				(0.3 km)		
				▼ 16.1 km	Cross Davies Plain Creek.	
					Cross Davies Plain Creek.	0.3 km ▲
		Track junction.	16.4 km ▲	(0.3 km)		
	(0.7 km)			▼ 16.4 km	Track junction.	
▼ 0.7 km	Seasonal closure gates.				Zero trip meter at track junction. KL. Track on right SP: Davies Plain Camping Area.	0.0 km ▲
		Seasonal closure gates.	15.7 km ▲		**GPS** S:36 39.030 E:148 07.541 **UTM** 55H 600617E 5943308N	
	(0.4 km)					
▼ 1.1 km	Track junction. CSA. Track on left.			▼ 0.0 km	Zero trip meter at track junction. KR keeping cattle yards on left. Track on left SP: Davies Plain Camping Area.	
		Track junction. CSA. Track on right.	15.3 km ▲			
	(0.6 km)					
▼ 1.7 km	Track junction. CSA. Track on left.				**Track on left leads short distance to Davies Plain camping area**, a large grassy area encircled by snow gums, in the vicinity of Davies Plain Hut.	
		Track junction. CSA. Track on right.	14.7 km ▲			
	(1.2 km)					
▼ 2.9 km	Cross Buckwong Creek. Over creek camping on left and right.				Track junction.	39.4 km ▲
				(7.0 km)		
	Buckwong Creek camping area is a small spot beside creek, suitable for 1 or 2 sites.			▼ 7.0 km	Cross snow plain.	
					Cross snow plain.	32.4 km ▲
		Camping on left and right. CSA over Buckwong Creek.	13.5 km ▲	(1.1 km)		

219

VICTORIA'S HIGH COUNTRY

▼ 8.1 km   Track junction. CSA. Track on left is Kings Plain Track.

     Track junction. CSA. SP: Davies Plain Tk. Track on right.   31.3 km ▲

(4.6 km)

▼ 12.7 km   Seasonal closure gate.

     Seasonal closure gate.   26.7 km ▲

(0.1 km)

▼ 12.8 km   Cross SP: Charlie's Creek.

     Cross SP: Charlie's Creek.   26.6 km ▲

```
GPS   S:36 43.946 E:148 03.874
UTM   55H 595053E 5934281N
```

(0.2 km)

▼ 13.0 km   Charlies Creek Plain camping area. CSA.

Charlies Creek Plain camping area is an area of grassland amid snow gums, suitable for groups.

     Charlies Creek Plain camping area. CSA.   26.4 km ▲

(0.1 km)

▼ 13.1 km   Track junction. CSA. Track on left.

Track on left leads 0.3 km to site of Charlies Hut, which was destroyed by bushfires in 2003.

     Track junction. CSA. Track on right.   26.3 km ▲

(2.4 km)

▼ 15.5 km   Crossroads. TL. SP: McCarthy Tk. Track on right SP: Buckwong Tk. Track SO SP: Misery Trail.

     Crossroads. TR. SP: Davies Plain Tk.   23.9 km ▲

```
GPS   S:36 44.694 E:148 02.650
UTM   55H 593217E 5932918N
```

(5.6 km)

▼ 21.1 km   Track junction. CSA. SP: McCarthys Tk. Track on right SP: Mac's Creek Tk.

     Track junction. CSA. Track on left.   18.3 km ▲

(3.3 km)

▼ 24.4 km   Track junction. TR. SP: Limestone Creek Tk. Track SO is McCarthys Tk.

Track SO leads 1.2 km to **McCarthys camping area**, which has scattered campsites beside Murray River.

     Track junction. TL. SP: McCarthys Tk. Track on right leads 1.2 km to camping area.   15.0 km ▲

```
GPS   S:36 46.761 E:148 05.843
UTM   55H 597924E 5929043N
```

(0.7 km)

▼ 25.1 km   Creek crossing.

     Creek crossing.   14.3 km ▲

(5.0 km)

▼ 30.1 km   Creek crossing.

     Creek crossing.   9.3 km ▲

(2.8 km)

▼ 32.9 km   Creek crossing.

     Creek crossing.   6.5 km ▲

(0.7 km)

▼ 33.6 km   Creek crossing.

     Creek crossing.   5.8 km ▲

(1.4 km)

Crossing Davies Plain Creek

▼ 35.0 km   Track junction. TL. Track on right to bush campsites.

     Track junction. TR.   4.4 km ▲

(0.8 km)

▼ 35.8 km   Seasonal closure gate.

     Seasonal closure gate.   3.6 km ▲

(1.2 km)

▼ 37.0 km   Track junction. CSA. Track on right SP: Limestone Creek Camping Area.

Track on right leads short distance to **Limestone Creek camping area**, a large area of open grassland close to Limestone Creek.

     Track junction. CSA. Track on left SP: Limestone Creek Camping Area.   2.4 km ▲

```
GPS   S:36 51.315 E:148 03.309
UTM   55H 594062E 5920665N
```

(2.4 km)

▼ 39.4 km   Track junction. This is the Limestone–Black Mountain Rd.

     Zero trip meter at road junction. TR. SP: Limestone Ck Tck/Dry Weather 4WD.   0.0 km ▲

```
GPS   S:36 52.362 E:148 03.116
UTM   55H 593754E 5918733N
```

▼ 0.0 km   Zero trip meter at track junction. TL onto Limestone–Black Mountain Rd. Road on right leads 41 km to Benambra.

     Road junction.   60.6 km ▲

(3.6 km)

CORRYONG ◀▶ OMEO

▼ 3.6 km Road junction. TR. SP: Native Cat Tck/Dry Weather Only. Road SO.

Road SO leads 3.0 km to Native Dog Flat camping area, which has a number of sites amid snow gums.

Track junction. TL. This is the Limestone–Black Mountain Rd.   57.0 km ▲

Road on right leads 3.0 km to Native Dog Flat camping area.

GPS S:36 52.671 E:148 04.622
UTM 55H 595985E 5918137N

(7.5 km)

▼ 11.1 km Native Cat Flat. CSA.

Native Cat Flat. CSA.   49.5 km ▲

(6.4 km)

▼ 17.5 km Track junction. CSA. Track on left.

Track junction. CSA. Track on right.   43.1 km ▲

(3.5 km)

▼ 21.0 km Track junction. TL through seasonal closure gates. This is Nunniong Rd.

Track junction. TR. SP: Native Cat Tk.   39.6 km ▲

GPS S:36 59.053 E:147 59.889
UTM 55H 588831E 5906413N

(4.4 km)

▼ 25.4 km Brumby Hill trig point on left. CSA.

Trig point on right. CSA.   35.2 km ▲

(2.8 km)

▼ 28.2 km Track junction. CSA. SP: Nunniong Road. Track on right SP: Brumby Rocks Tk.

Brumby Rocks on left. Views from this point.

Track junction. CSA. Track on left.   32.4 km ▲

(4.4 km)

▼ 32.6 km Track junction. KL. SP: Nunniong Rd. Track on right SP: Garrons Point Tk.

Track junction. KR. SP: Nunniong Rd. Track on left.   28.0 km ▲

(3.9 km)

▼ 36.5 km Track junction. KR. SP: Nunniong Rd. Track SO SP: Jam Tin Flat Tk.

Track junction. KL. SP: Nunniong Rd. Track on right.   24.1 km ▲

GPS S:37 05.820 E:147 57.548
UTM 55H 585246E 5895301N

(5.0 km)

▼ 41.5 km Bridge over SP: Blue Shirt Creek.

Bridge.   19.1 km ▲

(0.2 km)

▼ 41.7 km Track junction. KR. Track on left.

Track junction. CSA. Track on right.   18.9 km ▲

(0.4 km)

▼ 42.1 km Track junction. CSA. Track on left.

Track junction. CSA. Track on right.   18.5 km ▲

(1.8 km)

▼ 43.9 km Track junction. CSA. SP: Nunniong Rd. Track on left SP: Old Wheatfields Tk.

Track junction. CSA. SP: Nunniong Rd. Track on right.   16.7 km ▲

(1.2 km)

▼ 45.1 km Track junction. CSA. Track on left.

Track junction. KL uphill SP: Nunniong Rd. Track on right SP: Wheatfields Tk.   15.5 km ▲

(1.2 km)

▼ 46.3 km Track junction. CSA. SP: Nunniong Rd. Track on left SP: Nunnet Rd.

Track junction. CSA. SP: Nunniong Rd. Track on right.   14.3 km ▲

(0.9 km)

▼ 47.2 km Nunniong Plains on right. CSA.

Nunniong Plains on left. CSA.   13.4 km ▲

(0.3 km)

▼ 47.5 km Crossroads. CSA. Track on right SP: Nunniong Plains Tk.

Crossroads. CSA. SP: Nunniong Road. Track on left SP: Nunniong Plains Tk.   13.1 km ▲

(3.0 km)

▼ 50.5 km Track junction. CSA. SP: Nunniong Rd. Track on right SP: Lake Hill Tk.

Track junction. CSA. Track on left.   10.1 km ▲

(1.9 km)

▼ 52.4 km Track junction. CSA. SP: Nunniong Rd. Track on left SP: Ski Road.

Track junction. CSA. Track on right.   8.2 km ▲

(1.3 km)

▼ 53.7 km Bridge over SP: Back River.

Bridge.   6.9 km ▲

(0.6 km)

▼ 54.3 km Track junction. CSA. SP: Nunniong Rd. Track on right SP: Granite Flat Road.

Track junction. CSA. Track on left.   6.3 km ▲

(2.7 km)

▼ 57.0 km Track junction. CSA. SP: Nunniong Rd. Track on left SP: Dobbys Tk.

Track junction. CSA. SP: Nunniong Rd. Track on right SP: Dobbys Tk. KL at next track junction.   3.6 km ▲

(0.7 km)

▼ 57.7 km Track junction. CSA. SP: Nunniong Rd. Track on right SP: Sawpit Road.

Track junction. CSA. Track on left.   2.9 km ▲

(2.9 km)

▼ 60.6 km T-junction.

Zero trip meter at road junction. TL. SP: Nunniong Road. Road SO SP: Bentley Plain Road.   0.0 km ▲

GPS S:37 13.234 E:147 54.407
UTM 55H 580449E 5880274N

▼ 0.0 km Zero trip meter at T-junction. TR. Road on left SP: Bentley Plain Road.

Road on left leads 3.3 km to Moscow Villa hut and **camping area**, a small location in vicinity of delightful hut built by Bill Ah Chow, and 3.5 km to scenic **Bentley Plain camping area**, a large space with centrally positioned shelter shed and hut.

Road junction.   43.7 km ▲

(0.5 km)

▼ 0.5 km Crossroads. CSA. SP: Nunniong Rd. Track on left SP: South Escarpment Tk/Nugong Tower. Track on right SP: Escarpment Tk.

■ 221

VICTORIA'S HIGH COUNTRY

Moscow Villa hut on Bentley Plain

		Crossroads. CSA.	**43.2 km** ▲	▼ **20.2 km**	Bridge over Tambo River.	
	(1.9 km)				Bridge over Tambo River.	**23.5 km** ▲
▼ **2.4 km**	SP: The Washington, on right. CSA.				**(0.4 km)**	
		SP: The Washington, on left. CSA.	**41.3 km** ▲	▼ **20.6 km**	Road junction. TL. This is Bindi Rd.	
	GPS S:37 12.760 E:147 53.025				Road junction. KR. SP: Nunniong Road/ Forest Drive.	**23.1 km** ▲
	UTM 55H 578414E 5881170N					
	(5.0 km)				**GPS** S:37 10.136 E:147 45.572	
▼ **7.4 km**	Road junction. CSA. SP: Nunniong Rd. Track on left SP: Great White Hope Road/ No Through Road.				**UTM** 55H 567431E 5886117N	
					(4.9 km)	
				▼ **25.5 km**	Road junction. This is Omeo Hwy. TR. Road on left leads 8.6 km to Swifts Creek.	
		Road junction. CSA. Track on right.	**36.3 km** ▲			
	(2.1 km)				Road junction. TL. SP: Tambo Valley Golf Club 8.	**18.2 km** ▲
▼ **9.5 km**	Road junction. CSA over grid. SP: Nunniong Rd. Track on left SP: Low Saddle Tk.				**GPS** S:37 11.488 E:147 43.460	
					UTM 55H 564287E 5883642N	
		Road junction. CSA. Track on right.	**34.2 km** ▲		**(17.6 km)**	
	(6.6 km)			▼ **43.1 km**	T-junction. TL. SP: Day Ave/Omeo Town Centre.	
▼ **16.1 km**	Road junction. CSA. Track on right.				Road junction. TR. SP: B500/Bairnsdale/Orbost.	**0.6 km** ▲
		Road junction. KR. Track on left.	**27.6 km** ▲			
	(2.5 km)				**(0.6 km)**	
▼ **18.6 km**	Road junction. CSA onto bitumen. Road on right SP: Golf Course.			▼ **43.7 km**	Road junction in Omeo. Golden Age Motel and SP: Tongio Rd, on left (start of trek section 2).	
		Road junction. CSA onto gravel. SP: Nunniong Rd. Road on left SP: Golf Course.	**25.1 km** ▲		Zero trip meter in Omeo on main road, Day Ave, at junction with SP: Tongio Rd, on right. Golden Age Motel on right. PSA through town in easterly direction towards Bairnsdale.	**0.0 km** ▲
	(1.0 km)					
▼ **19.6 km**	Road junction. KL on bitumen.				**GPS** S:37 06.480 E:147 35.453	
		Road junction. KR on bitumen.	**24.1 km** ▲		**UTM** 55H 552505E 5893782N	
	(0.6 km)					
					REVERSE DIRECTIONS START	

The Washington Steam Winch

Located alongside Nunniong Road, the impressive Washington steam winch was one of two of its type to be brought to Australia from the United States in the early 1920s for use at the Karri Timber Mills in Western Australia. After serving their time in the west both winches were relocated to Victoria and used in the Powelltown and Noojee areas before the Washington was purchased in 1959 by the Ezard's Sawmill in Swifts Creek.

After arriving in Swifts Creek a considerable amount of time was spent preparing the winch for its new mountain location. On completion of the work, the winch was moved to the bush and carefully positioned on the top side of Nunniong Road, beside a permanent spring-fed stream. The water from the stream was used to feed the boiler. Once the winch was in place an area on the opposite side of the road was clear-felled, leaving only a couple of large spar trees. The spar trees, opposite the winch, supported the overhead, or 'skyline', rigging. This apparatus was used to pull logs out of the gully and up to the road for loading onto logging trucks.

To prepare a spar tree a rigger had to climb the selected tree and cut off every branch, leaving the tree as a straight pole. The rigger wore a special belt that held pieces of rope plus a one-person crosscut saw. A spare belt was also carried just in case! In addition to the belt, the rigger had special leggings fitted with a sharp steel spike attached to a steel bar on each inside leg. To climb the tree the belt was placed around the tree trunk and the rigger lifted the belt as high as possible and slowly 'walked' up the tree, pushing the leg spikes into the trunk to secure himself. Once all the branches were cut, usually to a height of about 45 metres, the rigger would descend the tree in the same fashion. It was then necessary to climb back up the spar tree and attach the pulleys and ropes.

The historic Washington winch is in the process of being restored

During its brief period of use the Washington hauled just over 9000 cubic metres of timber from the forest

The Washington was only used for a short time due to the ever-increasing deepening of the ruts created by snigging, or dragging, the logs. Another problem was that the logs being dragged often jammed on rocks in the gully below. During its brief period of use, however, the Washington winch hauled just over 9000 cubic metres of timber from the forest. It has been placed on the heritage list and is now in the process of being restored. Recent renovations include the erection of new spar trees and associated rigging.

VICTORIA'S HIGH COUNTRY

2 OMEO ◀▶ FARM JUNCTION 89.4 KM

Start point
Omeo

Road atlas
349 H7

Total distance
95.2 km (includes route-directed side trip)

Standard
Moderate

Time
1–2 days

Longest distance no PD (includes all options)
103.6 km (Omeo to Dargo)

Topographic map
Auslig 1:250 000 series: *Bairnsdale*

Old mine workings at the Oriental Claims Historic Area

Other useful information
- Dargo store open seven days 8.30am–6pm, tel. (03) 5140 1219; accepts cash, EFTPOS and credit cards.
- D. Guy Autos at Waterford, 10 kilometres south of Dargo on Lindenow Rd, offers mechanical and tyre repairs and 4WD vehicle recovery service, tel. (03) 5140 1265.
- Parks Victoria brochure: *Alpine National Park*.
- Parks Victoria park notes: *Alpine National Park: Source of the rivers around Mitta Mitta, Omeo, Tallangatta and Corryong*; *Alpine National Park: Our mountain heritage around Heyfield, Licola and Dargo in the Wonnangatta–Moroka Area*; *Alpine National Park: The High Country around Bright, Mt Beauty, Omeo and Dargo*.
- Parks Victoria Heritage Notes: *Oriental Claims Historic Area: Edge of the High Country*.
- Envirobook: *Wild Guide: Plants and Animals of the Australian Alps* by Barbara Cameron-Smith.
- Good bushwalking opportunities so pack sturdy shoes, binoculars, sunscreen and hats.

Description

This trek section runs from Omeo, a picturesque service town located beside Livingstone Creek, to just short of Dargo, a delightful village nestled in a valley beside the Dargo River. Just west of Omeo is the Oriental Claims Historic Area, where large-scale hydraulic sluicing for gold was carried out during the latter part of the 1800s. Omeo was once a mining town at the centre of this goldfield. From here the route follows the Great Alpine Road westwards to Cobungra, where you can visit Victoria Falls Historic Area, the site of the state's first hydro-electric-power scheme. The falls are located a few kilometres on from the picnic and camping area.

A little further west you leave the Great Alpine Road and turn onto the Victoria River Track, which passes through part of Cobungra station. There are a number of gates in this section – please leave these as found. Victoria River Track, and Dinner Plain Track, which it soon joins, are relatively easy going in the dry season but are difficult in the wet as they have a clay base. There is a pleasant bush campsite just before the junction of these two tracks.

Dinner Plain Track joins with the all-weather gravel Birregun Road, passing a monument and small camping area at Dogs Grave and skirting the summit of Mount Birregun, where a short detour provides good views towards Mount Hotham and the surrounding area. Past here turn into the steep and narrow Stock Route Spur Track that leads down to the Dargo River at Collins Flat.

224

OMEO ◀▶ FARM JUNCTION

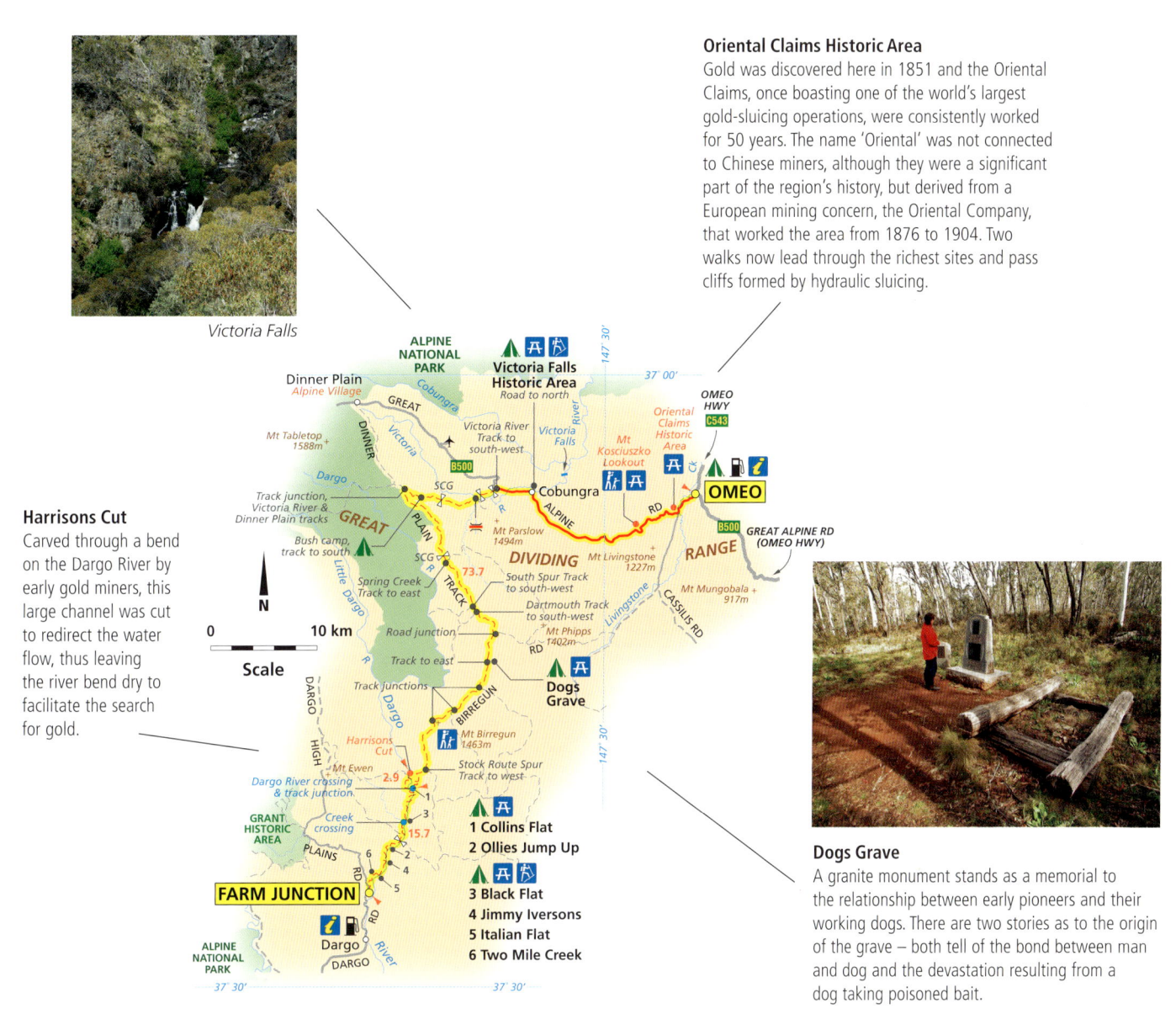

Victoria Falls

Oriental Claims Historic Area
Gold was discovered here in 1851 and the Oriental Claims, once boasting one of the world's largest gold-sluicing operations, were consistently worked for 50 years. The name 'Oriental' was not connected to Chinese miners, although they were a significant part of the region's history, but derived from a European mining concern, the Oriental Company, that worked the area from 1876 to 1904. Two walks now lead through the richest sites and pass cliffs formed by hydraulic sluicing.

Harrisons Cut
Carved through a bend on the Dargo River by early gold miners, this large channel was cut to redirect the water flow, thus leaving the river bend dry to facilitate the search for gold.

Dogs Grave
A granite monument stands as a memorial to the relationship between early pioneers and their working dogs. There are two stories as to the origin of the grave – both tell of the bond between man and dog and the devastation resulting from a dog taking poisoned bait.

Campsite Facilities

	Toilets	Disabled access	4WD access only	Off-road trailer	Off-road caravan	Drinking water	Fee payable	Ranger patrolled	BBQ/fireplace	Campfires prohibited	Picnic tables	Shelter shed	No rubbish disposal	Public phone	Shower	Bushwalking	Swimming	Swimming not advised	Fishing	Canoeing	Dogs allowed
Black Flat	•					•	•		•		•		•							•	
Collins Flat		•					•		•		•								•	•	
Dogs Grave	•		•				•		•		•									•	
Italian Flat	•		•	•		•	•		•		•		•	•					•	•	
Jimmy Iversons	•					•			•		•										
Ollies Jump Up	•		•	•		•	•		•		•				•				•	•	
Two Mile Creek	•		•	•		•	•		•		•				•				•	•	
Victoria Falls	•			•		•	•		•		•		•							•	

225

Omeo on the Great Alpine Road

Outlaws at Omeo

Included in the hordes of prospectors who flocked to Omeo in the 1850s was an assortment of villains. One of the area's more sinister characters was Tom Toke, who allegedly murdered young gold prospector Ballarat Harry at nearby Haunted Stream in 1857, after Harry confided in Toke that he was in possession of a sum of money. Toke was never convicted of the crime but rumour has it that Ballarat Harry was an alias used by the well-heeled Roger Tichborne. Heir to a baronetcy in England, Tichborne went missing until 1865 when a Wagga Wagga butcher laid claim to the title. Accepted by the mother but disputed by the family, the butcher was imprisoned for perjury in 1872.

The crossing of the river can be deep after rain so be prepared to check the crossing on foot first. Once across the river there is camping at Collins Flat. The route-directed side trip to Harrisons Cut, a water diversion constructed by early gold miners and carved through a bend in the Dargo River, leaves from here.

Continuing on towards Farm Junction finds you on Upper Dargo Road, which begins to improve as the track strikes south, closely following the course of the river. There are a number of very good camping areas along this stretch, with Italian Flat and Ollies Jump Up being two of the more popular. The route directions for this section conclude at Farm Junction, a road junction on the Dargo High Plains Road, but it is only a little over 5 kilometres to the township of Dargo if you wish to break your journey here.

Advice and warnings

- This route is through alpine country so be prepared for dramatic changes to weather conditions, even in summer when snow can fall. Carry wet weather gear and warm clothing.
- Sections of the route can be difficult and impassable during and after rain so travel at these times is best avoided.
- Seasonal road closures apply to the Victoria River and Dinner Plain tracks. Closure dates vary from year to year but the general rule of thumb is mid-June – early November. Contact Parks Victoria Omeo, tel. (03) 5159 1660, to check road conditions and closures. The Dargo River crossing at the bottom of Stock Route Spur Track can be impassable after heavy rain or during the spring snow melt so contact Parks Victoria and Department of Sustainability & Environment Dargo, tel. (03) 5140 1243, for details.
- Sections of the route pass through private property. Stay on and do not deviate from the track, obey all signage and leave all gates as found.
- Standard road or all-terrain tyres are suitable.
- Towing off-road trailers or caravans along the route is not recommended.
- Camping is at designated camping areas as well as at a number of bush campsites noted in route directions.
- Carry plenty of drinking water, food and supplies.
- Rubbish bins are not provided on this trek section so please take your rubbish with you.
- Carry your own firewood and do not cut down any alpine vegetation. Pack a gas/fuel stove.
- Waters in these alpine regions can be very cold and can have numerous underwater obstructions. Always check conditions prior to swimming. Diving into these waters is not advised and can be extremely dangerous.
- March flies are prevalent during the summer months so carry good insect repellent.

Permits and bookings

- No permits required.
- No bookings required for camping areas.
- Bookings recommended for accommodation in Omeo and Dargo during peak holiday periods such as Christmas, New Year and Easter.
- Recreational fishing licence is required in Victoria. For further details contact Fisheries and Aquaculture, Victorian Department of Natural Resources and Environment, tel. 13 6186, or visit their website (www.nre.vic.gov.au).

ROUTE DIRECTIONS

▼ **0.0 km** — Zero trip meter in Omeo at junction of Day Ave (Great Alpine Rd) and SP: Tongio Rd, on left. Golden Age Motel on left. PSA in westerly direction towards Mt Hotham.

Omeo. SP: Tongio Rd and Golden Age Motel on right (start of trek section 1). **73.7 km** ▲

GPS S:S37 06.480 E:147 35.453
UTM 55H 552505E 5893782N

(1.9 km)

OMEO ◄► FARM JUNCTION

▼ **1.9 km** Road junction. CSA. Road on right SP: Oriental Claims Historic Area.

Road on right leads short distance to carpark and walking track to historic Oriental Claims, the site of a large gold-sluicing operation.

Road junction. CSA. Road on left SP: Oriental Claims Historic Area. **71.8 km** ▲

(0.2 km)

▼ **2.1 km** Road junction. CSA. SP: Mt Hotham. Road on left SP: Cassilis Rd.

Road junction. CSA. SP: Omeo. Road on right. **71.6 km** ▲

(5.4 km)

▼ **7.5 km** Road junction. CSA. Road on right SP: Mt Kosciuszko Lookout.

Road on right leads short distance to Mt Kosciuszko Lookout and picnic area. Views to NSW, Main Range and Mt Kosciuszko.

Road junction. CSA. Road on left SP: Mt Kosciuszko Lookout. **66.2 km** ▲

(12.5 km)

▼ **20.0 km** Road junction. CSA. Road on right SP: Victoria Falls Rd/Victoria Falls Historic Area.

Road on right leads 0.6 km to **Victoria Falls Historic Area campground** and picnic area, a scenic grassy site among snow gums.

Road junction. CSA. Road on left SP: Victoria Falls Historic Area. **53.7 km** ▲

GPS S:37 05.863 E:147 25.479
UTM 55H 537735E 5894203N

(3.6 km)

▼ **23.6 km** Road junction. TL onto gravel road. SP: Victoria River Tk/McMillan Walking Track/To Woods Point 200 km. This is a seasonal closure track.

T-junction with bitumen. This is Great Alpine Road. TR. **50.1 km** ▲

GPS S:37 05.572 E:147 23.152
UTM 55H 534291E 5894756N

(0.2 km)

▼ **23.8 km** Gate. LAF.

Gate. LAF. **49.9 km** ▲

(1.8 km)

▼ **25.6 km** Gate. LAF. Through gate track junction. KL. Track on right.

Track junction. CSA through gate. LAF. Track on left. **48.1 km** ▲

(0.1 km)

▼ **25.7 km** Y-junction. KR. SP: Victoria River Tk.

Track junction. CSA. Track on right. **48.0 km** ▲

(0.1 km)

▼ **25.8 km** Bridge. CSA through gate. LAF.

Gate. LAF. CSA over bridge. **47.9 km** ▲

(3.7 km)

▼ **29.5 km** Seasonal closure gate.

Seasonal closure gate. **44.2 km** ▲

(2.1 km)

▼ **31.6 km** Track junction. KR. Track on left leads 0.1 km to bush campsite.

Track junction. Track on right to bush campsite. **42.1 km** ▲

(2.3 km)

▼ **33.9 km** Track junction. TL. SP: Dinner Plain Tk.

Track junction. TR. SP: Victoria River Tk. **39.8 km** ▲

GPS S:37 05.595 E:147 17.393
UTM 55H 525761E 5894744N

(9.0 km)

▼ **42.9 km** Seasonal closure gate.

Seasonal closure gate. **30.8 km** ▲

(0.1 km)

Climbing a rise on Dinner Plain Track

▼ 43.0 km   Track junction. CSA. Track on left SP: Spring Creek Tk.
           Track junction. CSA. Track on right.   30.7 km ▲
(5.8 km)

▼ 48.8 km   Track junction. CSA. Track on right SP: South Spur Tk.
           Track junction. CSA. Track on left.   24.9 km ▲
(0.6 km)

▼ 49.4 km   Track junction. CSA. Track on right SP: Dartmouth Tk.
           Track junction. CSA. Track on left.   24.3 km ▲
(3.4 km)

▼ 52.8 km   T-junction. TR. SP: Birregun Road.
           Track junction. TL. SP: Dinner Plain Tk.   20.9 km ▲
GPS S:37 12.699 E:147 23.129
UTM 55H 534204E 5881579N
(2.7 km)

▼ 55.5 km   Track junction. TL. SP: Dogs Grave.
           T-junction. TR. This is Birregun Rd.   18.2 km ▲
(0.3 km)

▼ 55.8 km   Track junction. KR. Track on left.
Track on left leads short distance to monument and **Dogs Grave** picnic and **camping area**, a small sheltered space amid trees with short walk to creek.
           Track junction. KL. Track on right to monument and picnic and camping area.   17.9 km ▲
GPS S:37 14.030 E:147 22.824
UTM 55H 533743E 5879119N
(0.4 km)

▼ 56.2 km   T-junction. This is Birregun Rd. TL.
           Track junction. TR. SP: Dogs Grave.   17.5 km ▲
(2.5 km)

▼ 58.7 km   Track junction. CSA. Track on left is Messmate Spur Track.
           Track junction. CSA. Track on right.   15.0 km ▲
(3.4 km)

▼ 62.1 km   Track junction. CSA. Track on left SP: Dane Tk.
           Track junction. CSA. Track on right.   11.6 km ▲
(2.4 km)

▼ 64.5 km   Track junction. CSA. Track on left.
Track on left leads 0.4 km to Mt Birregun summit with goods views to east.
           Track junction. CSA. Track on right to Mt Birregun summit.   9.2 km ▲
(5.5 km)

▼ 70.0 km   Track junction. TR. SP: Stock Route Spur Tk.
Track descends steeply from here for 3.4 km.
           T-junction. This is Birregun Rd. TL.   3.7 km ▲
GPS S:37 19.354 E:147 18.770
UTM 55H 527717E 5869297N
(2.1 km)

▼ 72.1 km   Y-junction. KL. Track on right SP: Private Property.
           Track junction. CSA uphill. Track on left.   1.6 km ▲
(1.3 km)

▼ 73.4 km   Dargo River crossing.
Bush camping in vicinity over river.
           Dargo River crossing.   0.3 km ▲
GPS S:37 20.281 E:147 17.970
UTM 55H 526530E 5867587N
(0.3 km)

▼ 73.7 km   Track junction. Side trip to Harrisons Cut.
           Zero trip meter at track junction. KR. SP: Stock Route SP [Spur]. Track SO SP: Matherson SP [Spur].   0.0 km ▲
GPS S:37 20.369 E:147 17.835
UTM 55H 526330E 5867425N

▶   **SIDE TRIP: Harrisons Cut**

▼ 0.0 km   Track junction. Turn into track SP: Matherson SP [Spur].
(0.5 km)

▼ 0.5 km   Y-junction. KL. SP: Matherson SP [Spur]/Harrisons. Track on right leads to private property.
(1.4 km)

▼ 1.9 km   Track junction. CSA. Track on right.
(0.3 km)

▼ 2.2 km   Track junction. CSA. Track on right.
(0.6 km)

▼ 2.8 km   Track junction. CSA. SP: Harrisons Cut. Track on left SP: Matherson Tk.
(0.1 km)

Harrisons Cut on the Dargo River

OMEO ◀▶ FARM JUNCTION

▼ 2.9 km Small parking area. Harrisons Cut on opposite side of river. Return to side trip start.
GPS   S:37 19.538 E:147 17.799
UTM   55H 526282E 5868962N

◀ **END SIDE TRIP**

▼ 0.0 km Zero trip meter at track junction. CSA. SP: Dargo. Proceed past SP: Collins Flat Camping Area, on left. Track on right SP: Matherson SP.
Collins Flat camping area is a large and open grassy site close to river.

Track junction. 15.7 km ▲
Track SO is side trip to Harrisons Cut.
(0.3 km)

▼ 0.3 km Gate. LAF.
Gate. LAF. 15.4 km ▲
(4.5 km)

▼ 4.8 km Track junction. CSA. Track on left SP: Black Flat Camping Area.
Black Flat camping area is a well-shaded site on a bend in river.

Track junction. CSA. Track on right to camping area. 10.9 km ▲
(0.4 km)

▼ 5.2 km Creek crossing.
Creek crossing. 10.5 km ▲
(1.6 km)

▼ 6.8 km Track junction. CSA. SP: Farm Tk, on right.
Track junction. CSA. Track on left. 8.9 km ▲
(0.8 km)

▼ 7.6 km Gate. LAF.
Gate. LAF. 8.1 km ▲
(0.1 km)

▼ 7.7 km Track junction. CSA. Track on left SP: Swifts Creek/Omeo.
Y-junction. KL. SP: Upper Dargo. 8.0 km ▲
(1.2 km)

▼ 8.9 km Track junction. CSA. Track on left SP: Ollie's Jump Up Camping Area.
Track on left leads short distance to Ollies Jump Up camping area, an open space with numerous sites beside river.

Track junction. CSA. Track on right to camping area. 6.8 km ▲
(2.6 km)

▼ 11.5 km Track junction. CSA. Track on left SP: Jimmy Iverson's Camping Area. Track on right SP: Mt Ewen Tk.
Track on left leads short distance to Jimmy Iversons camping area, an open grassy area close to river.

Track junction. CSA. Track on right to camping area and track on left. 4.2 km ▲
(1.3 km)

▼ 12.8 km Track junction. CSA. Track on left SP: Italian Flat Camping Area.
Track on left leads short distance to Italian Flat camping area, a very large area of grassland with sites spread along river.

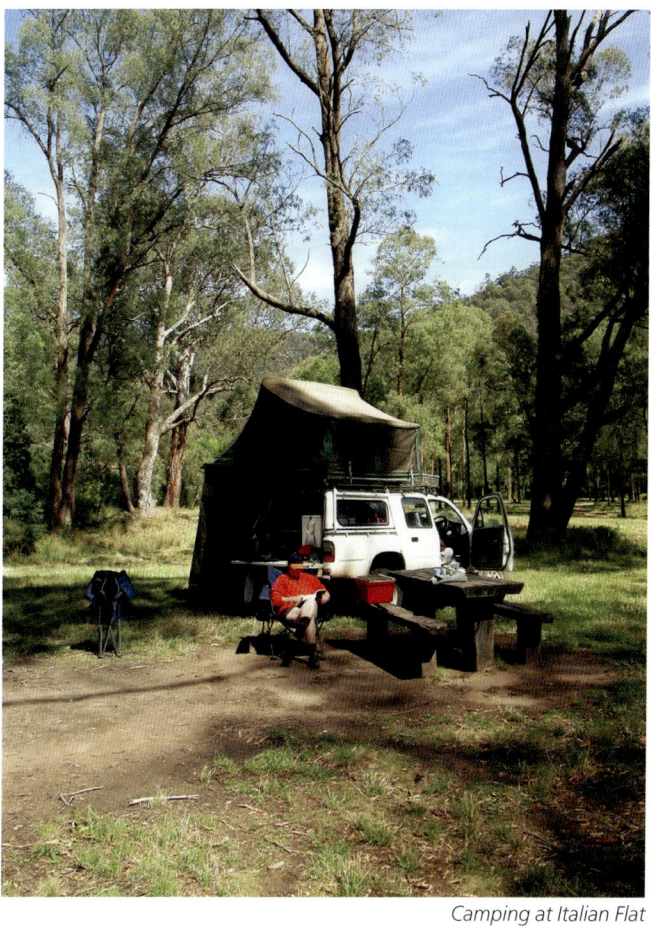

Camping at Italian Flat

Track junction. CSA. Track on right to camping area. 2.9 km ▲
(0.8 km)

▼ 13.6 km Causeway. Over causeway track junction. CSA. Track on right.
Track on right leads short distance to **Two Mile Creek camping area**, a small grassy spot.

Track junction. CSA over causeway. Track on left to camping area. 2.1 km ▲
(2.1 km)

▼ 15.7 km T-junction with bitumen. This is Dargo High Plains Rd and Farm Junction. (Road on right is start of trek section 3.)
Road on left leads 5.7 km to Dargo.

Zero trip meter at Farm Junction at junction of Dargo High Plains Rd and Upper Dargo Rd. Turn into Upper Dargo Rd. 0.0 km ▲
GPS   S:37 25.366 E:147 15.240
UTM   55H 522474E 5858197N

REVERSE DIRECTIONS START

VICTORIA'S HIGH COUNTRY

3 FARM JUNCTION ◀▶ MANSFIELD 198.3 KM

Start point
Farm Junction

Road atlas
349 G7

Total distance
198.3 km

Standard
Difficult

Time
2–3 days

Longest distance no PD (includes all options)
227.1 km (Dargo to Mansfield)

Topographic maps
Auslig 1:250 000 series: *Bairnsdale*; *Warburton*

Other useful information
- Dargo store open seven days 8.30am–6pm, tel. (03) 5140 1219; accepts cash, EFTPOS and credit cards.
- D. Guy Autos at Waterford, 10 kilometres south of Dargo on Lindenow Rd, offers mechanical and tyre repairs and 4WD vehicle recovery service, tel. (03) 5140 1265.
- Parks Victoria brochure: *Alpine National Park*.
- Parks Victoria park notes: *Alpine National Park: Valleys and bluffs around Mansfield and Whitfield*; *Alpine National Park: Our mountain heritage around Heyfield, Licola and Dargo in the Wonnangatta–Moroka area*; *Grant Historic Area: Around Dargo and the Crooked River Goldfields*; *Alpine National Park: The High Country around Bright, Mt Beauty, Omeo and Dargo*; *Howqua Hills Visitor Guide*.
- Envirobook: *Wild Guide: Plants and Animals of the Australian Alps* by Barbara Cameron-Smith.
- Warrior Press: *The Wonnangatta Mystery – An Inquiry into the Unsolved Murders* by Keith Leydon and Michael Ray.
- Research Publications: *Secrets of Ghost Towns of the High Country* by Luke Steenhuis.
- Good bushwalking opportunities so pack sturdy shoes, binoculars, sunscreen and hats.

Description
The final trek section takes in some of the best-known four-wheel-drive touring destinations in Victoria's alpine region. Leaving Farm Junction the route leads north-west to Grant, former 'capital' of the Crooked River goldfields, then hugs the mountainside as it drops into the Crooked River valley to Talbotville via McMillan Road. Like Grant, Talbotville was the site of goldmining activity during the 1860s, but little remains today. One legacy is the cleared former township site, which provides a large grassy camping area beside the river. A drive along the Crooked River Track upstream from Talbotville provides access to a number of former mining areas as well as an energetic but worthwhile walk to the ruins of New Good Hope Mine.

From Talbotville the trek meanders downstream, crossing Crooked River on two occasions before turning into Racecourse Track, which again follows the river, this time on the opposite bank. The route climbs Cynthia Range Track to Wombat Range Track, where it runs along the ridge line before a steep descent into Wonnangatta Valley. Most of the tracks in this area have narrow, steep sections that require sustained use of low-range four-wheel drive. Once down in the valley there are a number of river crossings to negotiate before you come out into the valley proper at the site of old Wonnangatta homestead near Conglomerate Creek. Vegetation in this part of the High Country comprises mixed eucalypt forest on the lower slopes and forests of ash in the higher areas.

A mecca to four-wheel-drive travellers, the open and picturesque Wonnangatta Valley offers plenty of camping locations and is a great spot to spend a day or two relaxing beside the river. Another intriguing aspect of the place is its infamy as the scene of two mysterious and still unsolved murders in 1917–18 (see pages 236–7).

The fabled Zeka Spur Track is used to exit the Wonnangatta Valley on the long uphill haul to Howitt Plains. Zeka Spur Track requires the use of low-range in sections, with a number of small rocky ledges to negotiate, but with care most drivers should have little trouble. Once on Howitt Plains it is only a short distance to Howitt Hut, where there is bush camping. Travellers with a little extra time may like to walk to Gantner Hut and Macalister Springs near Mount Howitt.

From Howitt Plains the route strikes west on Brocks Road and heads towards Mansfield. The first part of this stretch is rough in sections but improves as you approach Sheepyard Flat in Howqua Hills Historic Area, another former goldmining spot. En route you can visit Upper Jamieson Hut as well as choose from a host of delightful camping places spread along the banks of the Howqua River. From Sheepyard Flat it is only a short detour to Frys Hut on Frys Flat or you can follow the marked walking trail. This area is popular with fisherfolk chasing those elusive trout. Mansfield, at the end of the trek, has a full range of facilities and supplies.

FARM JUNCTION ◀▶ MANSFIELD

Crossing the Wombat Range

- Camping is at designated camping areas as well as at a number of bush campsites noted in route directions.
- Carry plenty of drinking water, food and supplies.
- Rubbish bins are not provided along this trek so please take your rubbish with you.
- Carry your own firewood and do not cut down any alpine vegetation. Pack a gas/fuel stove.
- Waters in these alpine regions can be very cold and can have numerous underwater obstructions. Always check conditions prior to swimming. Diving into these waters is not advised and can be extremely dangerous.
- March flies are prevalent during the summer months so carry good insect repellent.

Permits and bookings

- No permits required.
- No bookings required for camping areas.
- Bookings recommended for accommodation in Dargo during peak holiday periods such as Christmas, New Year and Easter.
- Recreational fishing licence is required in Victoria. For further details contact Fisheries and Aquaculture, Victorian Department of Natural Resources and Environment, tel. 13 6186, or visit their website (www.nre.vic.gov.au).

Advice and warnings

- This route is through alpine country so be prepared for dramatic changes to weather conditions, even in summer when snow can fall. Carry wet weather gear and warm clothing.
- Sections of the route can be difficult and impassable during and after rain so travel at these times is best avoided.
- Seasonal road closures apply to the Wombat Range/Spur and Zeka Spur tracks as well as sections of Howitt and Brocks roads. Closure dates vary from year to year but general rule of thumb is mid-June – early November. Contact Parks Victoria and Department of Sustainability & Environment (DSE) Dargo, tel. (03) 5140 1243, or Parks Victoria and DSE Mansfield, tel. (03) 5733 1200, to check road conditions and closures.
- Seasonal closures apply to Noonans Flat and Frys Flat camping areas. Contact Parks Victoria Mansfield, tel. (03) 5733 1200, to check details.
- Numerous river crossings can become impassable after heavy rain. Check conditions before crossing.
- Sections of the route pass through private property. Stay on and do not deviate from the track, obey all signage and leave all gates as found.
- Standard road or all-terrain tyres are suitable.
- Towing off-road trailers or caravans along the route is not recommended.

ROUTE DIRECTIONS

▼ 0.0 km — Zero trip meter at Farm Junction at junction of Upper Dargo Rd and Dargo High Plains Rd. Proceed along Dargo High Plains Rd in northerly direction towards Mt Hotham.

Zero trip meter at road junction. Road on left is Upper Dargo Rd (start trek section 2). — 16.6 km ▲

Road SO leads 5.7 km to Dargo.

GPS S:37 25.366 E:147 15.240
UTM 55H 522474E 5858197N

(10.0 km)

▼ 10.0 km — Road junction. CSA. Road on left SP: Hibernia Road/Jungle Creek Falls.

Road junction. CSA. Road on right. — 6.6 km ▲

(1.1 km)

▼ 11.1 km — Road junction. TL. SP: McMillan Rd/Grant/Historic Gold Mining Town Site.

T-junction with bitumen. This is Dargo High Plains Rd. TR. SP: Dargo 17. — 5.5 km ▲

GPS S:37 22.423 E:147 11.172
UTM 55H 516486E 5863652N

(3.1 km)

▼ 14.2 km — Track junction. CSA. Track on right SP: Jolly Sailor.

Track junction. CSA. Track on left. — 2.4 km ▲

(0.7 km)

▼ 14.9 km — SP: Grant Cemetery on right. CSA.

Cemetery on left. CSA. — 1.7 km ▲

(1.4 km)

231

VICTORIA'S HIGH COUNTRY

Old mining equipment at New Good Hope Mine near Talbotville

1 Eight Mile
2 Seven Mile
3 Tunnel Bend Flat
4 Noonans Flat
5 Pickerings Flat
6 Davons
7 Sheepyard Flat
8 Frys Flat
9 Blackbird Flat

Frys Hut
Frys Hut was built in the 1940s from split timber by legendary bushman Fred Fry. He was renowned for his skills as a bush carpenter and axeman. Fred also cut and split timber for other huts he built in the region including the Upper Jamieson, Ritchies, Gardiners and Schusters huts.

Frys Hut on Frys Flat beside the Howqua River

FARM JUNCTION ◀▶ MANSFIELD

Wonnangatta Valley
The magnificent and remote Wonnangatta Valley is well hidden among mountain ranges. The fame of the valley is two-fold: its spectacular scenery and the mysterious murders in 1917–18 (see pages 236–7).

Grant Historic Area
During its heydays in the late 1800s, Grant had a population of 2000, 15 hotels, four banks, newspaper office, courthouse, police station and numerous stores. However, the boom was short-lived and the majority of businesses had closed by 1867, with the last residents leaving in 1916. Walks include a heritage trail, a stroll to the Jolly Sailor Mine and a visit to the cemetery and the water-filled tunnel of the Jeweller Shop Mine.

Campsite Facilities

	Toilets	Disabled access	4WD access only	Off-road trailer	Off-road caravan	Drinking water	Fee payable	Ranger patrolled	BBQ/fireplace	Campfires prohibited	Picnic tables	Shelter shed	No rubbish disposal	Public phone	Shower	Bushwalking	Swimming	Swimming not advised	Fishing	Canoeing	Dogs allowed
Blackbird Flat	•		•								•					•		•	•		
Davons	•		•			•					•				•	•		•	•		
Eight Mile	•		•			•	•								•	•			•		
Frys Flat	•		•				•								•	•			•		
Grant	•		•			•	•	•							•				•		
Noonans Flat	•		•				•								•	•			•		
Pickerings Flat	•		•				•								•	•			•		
Seven Mile	•		•			•	•								•	•			•		
Sheepyard Flat	•		•			•	•	•							•				•	•	
Talbotville	•		•			•	•								•				•	•	
Tunnel Bend Flat	•		•				•								•	•			•	•	
Upper Jamieson Hut		•							•	•						•					
Wonnangatta	•		•			•					•	•				•			•		

233

VICTORIA'S HIGH COUNTRY

▼ 16.3 km   Y-junction. KR. SP: Grant Township Site.

                     Track junction. CSA. Track on right.   0.3 km ▲

(0.3 km)

▼ 16.6 km   Track junction. This is site of Grant township.

            Zero trip meter at track junction at Grant   0.0 km ▲
township site. KR. Track on left to camping area.

GPS   S:37 20.639 E:147 09.224
UTM   55H 513617E 5866956N

▼ 0.0 km   Zero trip meter at track junction at Grant township site. KL. Track on right leads 0.2 km to camping and picnic area, information board and walks.

Grant camping area has a number of sites located among shady trees.

         Track junction. This is site of Grant township.   10.4 km ▲

(0.4 km)

▼ 0.4 km   Track junction. CSA. Track on right.

Track on right leads 0.2 km to picnic area and Jeweller Shop Mine, where a short walk leads to mine tunnel in side of hill.

                              Track junction. CSA.   10.0 km ▲
Track on left to picnic area.

(0.2 km)

▼ 0.6 km   Track junction. TR. SP: McMillan Rd/Talbotville.

                 Y-junction. KL. SP: Grant Township Site.   9.8 km ▲

GPS   S:37 20.559 E:147 08.861
UTM   55H 513081E 5867105N

(1.3 km)

▼ 1.9 km   Lookout point on right. CSA.

                         Lookout point on left. CSA.   8.5 km ▲

(0.3 km)

▼ 2.2 km   Track junction. KR. SP: Talbotville. Track on left SP: Collingwood Spur Tk.

                   Track junction. CSA. Track on right.   8.2 km ▲

(2.8 km)

▼ 5.0 km   Track junction. KL. SP: McMillans Rd. Track on right SP: Bulltown Spur.

                         Track junction. KR. Track on left.   5.4 km ▲

(5.2 km)

▼ 10.2 km   SP: Talbotville Cemetery on left. CSA.

                             Cemetery on right. CSA.   0.2 km ▲

(0.2 km)

▼ 10.4 km   Track junction. This is Talbotville.

             Zero trip meter at track junction at Talbotville.   0.0 km ▲
TR. SP: McMillan Rd/Dargo 33/Grant.

GPS   S:37 20.032 E:147 04.045
UTM   55H 505972E 5868088N

▼ 0.0 km   Zero trip meter at track junction at Talbotville. TL.

Talbotville camping area in this vicinity is a very large grassy area located along the banks of Crooked River. Track on right leads to Bulltown and South Basalt Knob and 3.3 km, including 12 crossings of Crooked River, to New Good Hope Mine.

                          Track junction at Talbotville.   41.7 km ▲

(0.2 km)

▼ 0.2 km   Cross Crooked River. Over river track junction. CSA. SP: Crooked River Rd. Track on right SP: Brewery Ck Tk.

Numerous bush campsites beside river for 1 km along Crooked River Rd.

           Track junction. KR and cross river. Track on left   41.5 km ▲
SP: Brewery Creek Tk.

(1.8 km)

▼ 2.0 km   Cross river.

                                  Cross river.   39.7 km ▲

(1.2 km)

▼ 3.2 km   Track junction. TR. SP: Racecourse Tk.

                         Track junction. TL. SP: 38.5 km ▲
Crooked River Tk/Talbotville.

GPS   S:37 21.303 E:147 04.664
UTM   55H 506884E 5865737N

(0.3 km)

▼ 3.5 km   Cross Wongungarra River.

                     Cross Wongungarra River.   38.2 km ▲

(2.7 km)

▼ 6.2 km   Gate. LAF.

                                  Gate. LAF.   35.5 km ▲

(1.3 km)

▼ 7.5 km   Track junction. This area is known as Pioneer Racecourse. TL. SP: Station Tk.

Campsite on right. Station Track climbs steeply to next reading.

                 Track junction. TR. SP: Racecourse Tk.   34.2 km ▲

GPS   S:37 20.074 E:147 03.098
UTM   55H 504574E 5868011N

(2.9 km)

▼ 10.4 km   T-junction. TR. SP: Cynthia Range Tk.

                 Track junction. TL. SP: Station Tk.   31.3 km ▲

Station Track drops steeply to next reading.

GPS   S:37 20.879 E:147 02.018
UTM   55H 502979E 5866523N

(3.1 km)

▼ 13.5 km   Track junction on Mt Cynthia. TR. SP: Wombat Range Tk. Track SO SP: Eaglevale Tk.

              T-junction. TL. SP: Cynthia Range Tk.   28.2 km ▲

Crossing the Crooked River

GPS	S:37 20.169 E:147 00.365
UTM	55H 500539E 5867836N

(7.4 km)

▼ 20.9 km Track junction. CSA. Track on left.

Track on left leads 1.1 km to Mt Von Guerard with views over valley.

Track junction. CSA. Track on right.   20.8 km ▲

(4.9 km)

▼ 25.8 km Track junction. CSA. SP: Wombat Spur Tk. Track on left SP: Herne Spur Tk.

Wombat Spur Track drops steeply from here.

Track junction. CSA. SP: Wombat Spur Tk.   15.9 km ▲
Track on right SP: Herne Spur Tk.

(4.2 km)

▼ 30.0 km Track junction. Hard TL through seasonal closure gate. Track SO SP: Mt Hart Tk.

Track junction. Hard TR. SP: Wombat Range Tk.   11.7 km ▲
Track on left SP: Mt Hart Tk.

Wombat Range Track climbs steeply from here.

GPS	S:37 13.771 E:146 55.424
UTM	55H 493235E 5879663N

(0.2 km)

▼ 30.2 km Track junction. CSA. SP: Humffray Riv Tk. Track on right.

Track junction. KR. SP: To Wombat Range.   11.5 km ▲

(0.2 km)

▼ 30.4 km Cross Humffray River.

Cross Humffray River.   11.3 km ▲

GPS	S:37 13.945 E:146 55.301
UTM	55H 493053E 5879341N

(0.1 km)

▼ 30.5 km Small bush campsite on right. CSA.

Small bush campsite on left. CSA.   11.2 km ▲

(0.5 km)

▼ 31.0 km Cross Humffray River.

Cross Humffray River.   10.7 km ▲

(1.2 km)

▼ 32.2 km Cross Humffray River.

Cross Humffray River.   9.5 km ▲

(0.4 km)

▼ 32.6 km Track junction. CSA over Wonnangatta River. SP: Wonnangatta Tk. Track on left SP: Herne Spur.

Cross Wonnangatta River. Over river track   9.1 km ▲
junction. KL. SP: Humffray River Tk.

GPS	S:37 14.390 E:146 54.392
UTM	55H 491710E 5878518N

(0.4 km)

▼ 33.0 km Bush campsite on right. CSA.

Bush campsite on left. CSA.   8.7 km ▲

(5.7 km)

▼ 38.7 km Track junction. CSA. Track on right.

Track junction. CSA. Track on left.   3.0 km ▲

(1.4 km)

▼ 40.1 km Track junction. CSA. Track on right to bush campsites.

Track junction. CSA. Track on left.   1.6 km ▲

(0.9 km)

Alpine woodlands surround the Wonnangatta Valley

▼ 41.0 km Track junction. CSA and cross creek. Over creek track junction. KL.

Tracks on right before and over creek lead to bush campsites.

Creek crossing. Over creek track junction.   0.7 km ▲
KR. SP: Dargo.

GPS	S:37 12.625 E:146 50.286
UTM	55H 485635E 5881773N

(0.6 km)

▼ 41.6 km Track junction. CSA and cross Conglomerate Creek. Track on left.

Track on left to bush camping area.

Track junction. CSA. Track on right to   0.1 km ▲
bush camping area.

(0.1 km)

▼ 41.7 km Track junction over Conglomerate Creek. This is Wonnangatta Valley.

Zero trip meter at track junction before   0.0 km ▲
Conglomerate Creek. CSA and cross creek.
Track on right to hut and old homestead site.

GPS	S:37 12.444 E:146 49.950
UTM	55H 485137E 5882107N

▼ 0.0 km Zero trip meter at track junction over Conglomerate Creek. CSA through valley.

Track on left to hut and old homestead site. Numerous tracks on right lead to **Wonnangatta** station **camping area**, with campsites beside river.

Track junction before Conglomerate Creek.   94.5 km ▲

(0.4 km)

235

The Wonnangatta Murder Mystery

Jim Barclay, a well-liked horse trainer and cattle trader, and his employee John Bamford, a farm hand with a bad temper, were murdered in this remote and tranquil valley nearly 87 years ago. Jim Barclay was born in 1869 in Hastings, Victoria, and spent much of his life roaming from job to job in both Victoria and Queensland before finally settling in the Mansfield district in 1909. He undertook various labouring jobs and gained a reputation for his expertise as a horse and cattle handler. He married in 1910 but his wife died at the age of 20 in September 1911, only seven months after giving birth to a son, the couple's only child.

In April 1915 Jim Barclay took on the role of manager at Wonnangatta station, which had been acquired by a Mansfield syndicate headed by Arthur Phillips. In those days access to the remote and rugged Wonnangatta Valley was a good three-day trip by foot or horse. However, life was not entirely solitary for Barclay as his nearest neighbour and good friend, Harry Smith from Eaglevale, visited regularly.

In mid-December 1917 Barclay hired John Bamford, a 61-year-old Yorkshireman who had migrated to Australia at the age of 18 but about whom not much was known. On Thursday 20 December, a week after Bamford started work, both men rode to Talbotville to vote in the national referendum on conscription. When in town Barclay was overheard saying that his crop still needed another 14 days before harvesting. Harry Smith was also in town and apparently questioned his friend Barclay about Bamford. In a reference to Bamford's alleged bad temper he asked, 'What sort of bugger have you hired?' to which Barclay replied, 'He was all I could get'.

Barclay visited his friend Albert Stout, the local postmaster and store owner. He received some Christmas mail from his son who was staying with his sister Molly. Barclay answered the mail then he and Bamford spent the evening with Stout and his wife. Leaving the next morning, on 21 December, the two Wonnangatta men were never seen alive again.

Nearly a month later, on the evening of 23 January 1918, Smith, who had not seen his friend Barclay since December, made the 25-kilometre ride on horseback from Eaglevale to Wonnangatta station, arriving around 6pm. He had some mail for Barclay that he had collected in Talbotville. However, when he arrived he found no one about. A message written on the kitchen door, which he believed had been left by Bamford, read 'home tonight'. Smith cooked himself a meal and stayed the night, expecting his friend's return. When neither Barclay nor Bamford appeared, Smith left the mail on the table and returned home.

Three weeks later Smith returned to Wonnangatta, on 14 February, to find the mail he had delivered earlier still on the table unopened. This time Barclay's favourite dog, Baron, was running loose and obviously very hungry and Smith realised something was wrong. Smith stayed overnight and, after doing a quick search around the homestead and yards, left the next morning taking Baron with him. Smith arranged for a telegram to be sent to Arthur Phillips.

Phillips and Jack Jebb arrived at Wonnangatta station on 22 February and found that the homestead had not been occupied for some time. The next day they rode to Eaglevale and spent the night with Harry Smith. On Sunday 24 the three men returned to Wonnangatta, arriving late in the afternoon, and searched the area around the homestead. The next day they searched along

> *Who committed these crimes and why is as much a mystery today as it was after the gruesome discoveries in February and November 1918*

John Bamford's body was found near Howitt Hut

Remote and tranquil Wonnangatta Valley, the scene of two unsolved murders

the banks of Conglomerate Creek, or Home Creek as it was known then. Here they found a red blanket covering a human skull. Further inspection found that the skull was attached to a body in a shallow grave. After digging sand away from the remains they were able to identify Jim Barclay from the pants and boots on the body. Phillips and Jebb left for Mansfield to advise the police. Harry Smith returned to Eaglevale.

The police investigation team, headed by Detective Alex McKerral, arrived at Wonnangatta on 2 March and was met by Harry Smith and Constable Hayes. Arrangements were made for Barclay's body to be taken to Mansfield for an autopsy. McKerral conducted a search and in Barclay's room found that a gun had recently been fired, a struggle had occurred and that scratches across the floor were consistent with the dragging of boots. In Bamford's room he found a pile of clothes on the floor as though hurriedly taken off, and a blue blanket missing. The autopsy on Jim Barclay found that he had 15 bullet pellets in his body and that the shot or shots had come from behind. Barclay was buried at Hastings cemetery on 9 March 1918. He was 48 years old.

The inquest into Barclay's death commenced on 25 April 1918. Deputy Coroner Harrie Amor's official finding was that: 'James Barclay died at Wonnangatta Station between the twenty first day of December 1917 and the fourth day of January 1918, from a gunshot wound in the back' and that he 'was murdered by some person or persons unknown'.

The missing Bamford was touted as the main suspect in Barclay's murder. A reward was posted and a notice sent to police stations throughout Australia. In the spring of 1918 Harry Smith advised police that he thought Bamford could be found in the Mount Howitt area.

In November of 1918 a group including Harry Smith, Constable Daniel Hayes, Wonnangatta's new manager Bill Hearn and his helper Jim Fry rode to Howitt Hut where they spent the night. The next day they started their search at a nearby area known as Terrible Hollow. After finding nothing they decided to return to the hut but en route Hearn spotted the remains of a fire. A pair of boots was found protruding from beneath a log. John Bamford's body was discovered, buried beneath logs, sticks and stones.

A subsequent autopsy found evidence of a bullet wound on the left side of the temple, a small bullet lodged in the skull and that the shot causing instant death was not self-inflicted but was fired from a distance. The inquest into Bamford's death was held in December and coroner Mr Grey found that: 'The deceased John Bamford met his death between December 1917 and January 1918 and was wilfully murdered by some person or persons unknown'. John Bamford was buried in Dargo cemetery.

Who committed these crimes and why is as much a mystery today as it was after the gruesome discoveries in February and November 1918. Rumours and theories about the case are still a topic of conversation in the area.

VICTORIA'S HIGH COUNTRY

▼ 0.4 km   Track junction. CSA. Track on left to cemetery.
           Track junction. CSA. Track on right to cemetery.   94.1 km ▲
(2.9 km)

▼ 3.3 km   Track junction. CSA. Track on left SP: Dry River Track.
           Track junction. CSA. Track on right.   91.2 km ▲
(0.4 km)

▼ 3.7 km   Cross SP: Dry River.
           Cross SP: Dry River.   90.8 km ▲

GPS   S:37 11.327 E:146 48.163
UTM   55H 482490E 5884167N

(3.5 km)

▼ 7.2 km   Track junction. CSA. SP: Howitt Plain. This is Zeka Spur Track. Track on right SP: Rileys Creek Tk/Myrtleford.
           Track junction. CSA. SP: Wonnangatta Stn.   87.3 km ▲
           Track on left SP: Myrtleford.

GPS   S:37 10.171 E:146 46.544
UTM   55H 480090E 5886299N

(22.2 km)

▼ 29.4 km   Seasonal closure gate.
           Seasonal closure gate.   65.1 km ▲
(0.2 km)

▼ 29.6 km   T-junction with SP: Howitt Road. TR. SP: Mansfield/4WD Only. Road on left SP: Licola.
Road on left leads 2.2 km to Howitt Hut and bush camping in vicinity of hut.
           Road junction. TL. SP: Zeka Spur Tk.   64.9 km ▲

GPS   S:37 12.741 E:146 41.624
UTM   55H 472825E 5881527N

(0.3 km)

▼ 29.9 km   Road junction. CSA. Track on left SP: Butcher Country Trk.
           Road junction. CSA. Track on right.   64.6 km ▲
(1.1 km)

▼ 31.0 km   Road junction. CSA. Carpark on right SP: Howitt.
From carpark a 5-km walk leads to Macalister Springs, passing Gantner Hut on the way, and a 7-km walk leads to Mt Howitt.
           Road junction. CSA. Carpark and walks on left.   63.5 km ▲
(6.6 km)

▼ 37.6 km   Road junction. CSA. Track on right.
           Road junction. CSA uphill. Track on left.   56.9 km ▲
(0.8 km)

▼ 38.4 km   Seasonal closure gate. CSA over bridge over Macalister River.
           Bridge. CSA through seasonal closure gate.   56.1 km ▲

GPS   S:37 12.782 E:146 38.868
UTM   55H 468750E 5881437N

(0.7 km)

▼ 39.1 km   Creek crossing. Over creek track junction. KR. SP: To Brocks Road.
           Creek crossing.   55.4 km ▲
(0.6 km)

▼ 39.7 km   Bridge.
           Bridge.   54.8 km ▲
(6.6 km)

▼ 46.3 km   Track junction. This is King Billy Saddle. CSA. SP: Brocks Rd. Track on right SP: Lovicks.
           Track junction. CSA. Track on left SP: Lovicks.   48.2 km ▲

GPS   S:37 12.928 E:146 36.355
UTM   55H 465035E 5881152N

(10.7 km)

▼ 57.0 km   Seasonal closure gate.
           Seasonal closure gate.   37.5 km ▲
(1.3 km)

▼ 58.3 km   Track junction. CSA. Track on right SP: Cairn Ck Tk.
           Y-junction. KR. SP: Brocks Rd.   36.2 km ▲
(6.0 km)

▼ 64.3 km   Bridge.
           Bridge.   30.2 km ▲
(0.2 km)

▼ 64.5 km   Track junction. CSA. Track on left.
           Y-junction. KL.   30.0 km ▲
(0.8 km)

▼ 65.3 km   Bridge.
           Bridge.   29.2 km ▲
(1.8 km)

▼ 67.1 km   Track junction. CSA. Track on right.
           Track junction. CSA. Track on left.   27.4 km ▲
(0.7 km)

▼ 67.8 km   Track junction. CSA. Track on left SP: Low Saddle Rd.
           Y-junction. KL. SP: Brocks Rd.   26.7 km ▲

GPS   S:37 15.565 E:146 28.016
UTM   55H 452731E 5876216N

(1.2 km)

▼ 69.0 km   Track junction. CSA. Track on left.
Track on left leads 0.8 km to Upper Jamieson Hut. Deep crossing of Jamieson River to reach hut and **Upper Jamieson Hut camping area**, which is well shaded and close to the river and hut. This is our favourite hut in this area and we always try to spend a night here when visiting the region.
           Track junction. KL. Track on right.   25.5 km ▲
(6.7 km)

▼ 75.7 km   Road junction at SP: Eight Mile Gap. TL. SP: Brocks Road/Sheepyard Ft. Track on right is Bluff Link Rd.
           Road junction at SP: Eight Mile Gap. TR. SP: 18.8 km ▲
           Brocks Road.

GPS   S:37 13.929 E:146 26.622
UTM   55H 450653E 5879229N

(7.9 km)

▼ 83.6 km   Road junction. CSA. Track on right SP: Eight Mile.
Track on right leads 0.5 km to **Eight Mile camping area**, a large grassed area with some shady sites located over small creek crossing.
           Road junction. CSA. Track on left   10.9 km ▲
           SP: Eight Mile.
(1.3 km)

▼ 84.9 km   Road junction. CSA. Track on right SP: Seven Mile.

FARM JUNCTION ◀▶ MANSFIELD

Upper Jamieson Hut

	Track on right leads 0.5 km to **Seven Mile camping area**, with 2 camping sections – a walk-in section and a section with sites stretched along the riverbank.	
	Road junction. CSA. Track on left SP: Seven Mile.	9.6 km ▲
	(1.8 km)	
▼ 86.7 km	Road junction. CSA. Track on right SP: Six Mile.	
	Road junction. CSA. Track on left SP: Six Mile.	7.8 km ▲
	(4.0 km)	
▼ 90.7 km	Road junction. CSA. Track on right.	
	Road junction. KR uphill. Track on left.	3.8 km ▲
	(1.1 km)	
▼ 91.8 km	Carpark and SP: Tunnel Bend, on right. CSA. From carpark a short 50-m walk leads to tunnel through hill.	
	Carpark and SP: Tunnel Bend, on left. CSA.	2.7 km ▲
	GPS S:37 11.285 E:146 22.358 **UTM** 55H 444317E 5884078N	
	(0.6 km)	
▼ 92.4 km	Road junction. CSA. Track on right SP: Tunnel Bend Flat camping area.	
	Track on right leads short distance to **Tunnel Bend Flat camping area**, a very large open place beside the river with shady trees.	
	Road junction. CSA. Track on left to camping area.	2.1 km ▲
	(0.4 km)	
▼ 92.8 km	Road junction. CSA. Track on right SP: Noonan's Flat.	
	Track on right leads 0.1 km to **Noonans Flat camping area**, located above the river and suitable for 10 sites. Camping area subject to seasonal closure.	
	Road junction. CSA. Track on left to camping area.	1.7 km ▲
	(0.7 km)	
▼ 93.5 km	Road junction. CSA. Track on right SP: Pickerings Flat.	
	Track on right leads short distance to **Pickerings Flat camping area**, a very large location with numerous sites stretched along the river.	
	Road junction. CSA. Track on left to camping area.	1.0 km ▲
	(0.4 km)	
▼ 93.9 km	Road junction. CSA. Track on right SP: Davons.	
	Track on right leads to **Davons camping area**, a well-shaded place with numerous sites along the river.	
	Road junction. CSA. Track on left to camping area.	0.6 km ▲
	(0.6 km)	
▼ 94.5 km	Crossroads.	
	Zero trip meter at crossroads over bridge over Howqua River. CSA. Track on left and right SP: Sheepyard Flat.	0.0 km ▲
	GPS S:37 11.621 E:146 20.796 **UTM** 55H 442010E 5883442N	
▼ 0.0 km	Zero trip meter at crossroads. CSA across bridge over Howqua River. Track on left and right SP: Sheepyard Flat camping area.	
	Track on left and right leads to very large and scenic **Sheepyard Flat camping area** beside the river among shady trees. Track on left also leads 2.4 km to Frys Hut and **Frys Flat camping area**, a very large space along the river in vicinity of hut.	
	Crossroads.	35.1 km ▲
	(0.2 km)	
▼ 0.2 km	Road junction. CSA. Track on left SP: Blackbird Flat and track on right SP: Doughtys Rd.	
	Track on left leads 0.2 km to **Blackbird Flat camping area** where scattered bush campsites are located among trees by the river.	
	Road junction. CSA across bridge over Howqua River. Track on left SP: Doughtys Rd, and track on right SP: Blackbird Flat.	34.9 km ▲
	(16.2 km)	
▼ 16.4 km	T-junction with bitumen. This is Mansfield–Mount Buller Rd. TL. SP: 2 Merrijig/21 Mansfield. Road on right SP: Mt Buller 27.	
	Road junction. TR onto gravel road. SP: Howqua Track/Sheepyard Flat.	18.7 km ▲
	GPS S:37 06.718 E:146 16.751 **UTM** 55H 435958E 5892464N	
	(2.0 km)	
▼ 18.4 km	Road junction. CSA. Road on left to Merrijig and Club Hunt Hotel.	
	Road junction. CSA. Road on right to Merrijig and Club Hunt Hotel.	16.7 km ▲
	(16.7 km)	
▼ 35.1 km	Mansfield Chalet Roadhouse on right. CSA into Mansfield.	
	Zero trip meter on Mansfield–Mount Buller Rd with Mansfield Chalet Roadhouse on left. Proceed in easterly direction towards Mt Buller.	0.0 km ▲
	GPS S:37 03.612 E:146 05.867 **UTM** 55H 419787E 5898069N	
	REVERSE DIRECTIONS START	

Corner Country

Track to Haddon Corner

TIBOOBURRA ◀▶ WINDORAH 914.9 KM
1. TIBOOBURRA ◁▷ INNAMINCKA 458.2 km *(easy)*
2. INNAMINCKA ◁▷ WINDORAH 456.7 km *(easy)*

WHEN TO GO April–October **TIME** 4–6 days

Corner Country runs along both sides of the border of north-east South Australia, from south of Cameron Corner where three states meet, to north of Haddon Corner. It encompasses the north-west corner of New South Wales, the edge of Queensland's Channel Country and the fringe of Sturt Stony Desert. This is a driving adventure that visits three states – all in one day.

Often overlooked as a four-wheel-drive touring destination, Corner Country hosts some of Australia's finest outback scenery along with an interesting mix of Aboriginal and European history and culture. Spend time exploring Sturt National Park, named after explorer Charles Sturt who led an expedition to the region in 1844–45. Soak up the tranquillity along the legendary Cooper Creek, a focal point in the tragic Burke and Wills saga of 1860–61. Visit the two corner posts and consider the work of surveyor John Cameron and his party, who surveyed the New South Wales–Queensland border between 1879 and 1881.

Driving this trek is generally easy but conditions vary from black soil plains to desert dunes and unforgiving gibber plains. Roads close after rain, sometimes for periods of up to a week or more. In the south most pastoral land is taken up with sheep, while huge cattle stations dominate to the north. The region also contains untold natural wealth in the way of oil and gas fields surrounding Moomba in South Australia. Historic towns include the former gold-rush centres of Tibooburra and Milparinka as well as lonely Innamincka on the banks of the Cooper. Tibooburra, Innamincka and Windorah have all supplies and services.

CORNER COUNTRY

Authors' note
In Windorah we stayed at the council-run caravan park and it turned out to be really good value for money. It was great to have a hot shower after a couple of days on the road.

Shearer at Mount Browne, south-west of Milparinka

Services

VEHICLE ASSISTANCE
NRMA (NSW)/RAA (SA)/RACQ (Qld)   13 1111

POLICE
Tibooburra   (08) 8091 3303
Windorah   (07) 4656 3133

PARKS AND RESERVES
Dig Tree Reserve
Dig Tree Ranger   (07) 4655 4323

Innamincka Regional Reserve
NPWSA Innamincka   (08) 8675 9909

Sturt National Park
NPWS Tibooburra   (08) 8091 3308

VISITOR INFORMATION
Tibooburra NPWS   (08) 8091 3308
Windorah   (07) 4656 3063
www.barcooshire.com

Town Facilities

	Fuel: D/P/A	Mechanical repairs	Tyre repairs	Public telephone	Public toilets	Shop/supplies	Gas refills	Ice	Visitor information	Post office	Medical centre	Police	Meals	Motel	Hotel	Cabins	Caravan park	Camping
Cameron Corner	D/P			•	•		•	•					•		•	•		•
Innamincka	D/P	•	•	•	•	•	•	•	•	•			•		•	•	•	•
Milparinka	D/P			•	•		•						•		•		•	•
Tibooburra	D/P	•	•	•	•	•	•	•	•	•		•	•	•	•	•	•	•
Windorah	D/P	•	•	•	•	•	•	•	•	•	•	•	•	•	•	•	•	•

241

CORNER COUNTRY

1 TIBOOBURRA ◄► INNAMINCKA 458.2 KM

Start point
Tibooburra

Road atlas
348 E1, 350 E8

Total distance
503.0 km (includes route-directed side trips)

Standard
Easy

Time
2–3 days

Longest distance no PD (includes all options)
257.0 km (Milparinka to Cameron Corner)

Topographic maps
Auslig 1:250 000 series: *Milparinka*; *Callabonna*; *Tickalara*; *Strzelecki*; *Innamincka*

Other useful information
- Albert Hotel at Milparinka has limited supplies and can arrange minor mechanical and tyre repairs; open seven days 10am–late, tel. (08) 8091 3863; accepts cash, EFTPOS and credit cards.
- Cameron Corner Store has limited supplies and can arrange minor mechanical and tyre repairs; open seven days 7am–late, tel. (08) 8091 3872; accepts cash, EFTPOS and credit cards.
- Innamincka Trading Post store open seven days 8am–6pm, tel. (08) 8675 9900; accepts cash, EFTPOS and credit cards.
- NPWSA park guide: *Innamincka Regional Reserve*.
- NSW NPWS brochure: *Sturt National Park*.
- NSW NPWS information sheet: *Historic Milparinka*.
- Tourist brochures: *Corner Country: Far Western New South Wales Tour Guide*; *Innamincka on the Banks of the Cooper – Burke & Wills Country*; *Milparinka Heritage Trail* (latter available from Milparinka courthouse).
- Information booklets, brochures and maps enclosed with Desert Parks Pass (see Permits and bookings).
- Sturt National Park and Cooper Creek provide an ideal habitat for large numbers of birds so pack an identification guide and binoculars.
- There are good opportunities to explore some areas on foot so pack your camera, hat, sunscreen and sturdy walking shoes.

Description
The trek start point is the one-time goldmining town of Tibooburra in the north-west corner of New South Wales. Originally called The Granites, Tibooburra is generally regarded as the hottest town in New South Wales with summer temperatures often exceeding 40 degrees Celsius. Stop in at the Family Hotel – adorning its walls are murals by famous artists Clifton Pugh and Russell Drysdale. Also worth a visit is the interesting natural history display at the NPWS office.

The route heads south from Tibooburra on the partly sealed Silver City Highway to the small township of Milparinka. In the 1880s this was the main centre for the surrounding Albert and Mount Browne goldfields. Today the Albert Hotel, the last remaining pub in town, is a friendly spot to meet the locals, while plenty of sheltered campsites are available nearby at Evelyn Creek, named by explorer Charles Sturt after his sister.

Campsite Facilities

	Toilets	Disabled access	4WD access only	Off-road trailer	Off-road caravan	Drinking water	Fee payable	Ranger patrolled	BBQ/fireplace	Campfires prohibited	Picnic tables	Shelter shed	No rubbish disposal	Public phone	Shower	Bushwalking	Swimming	Swimming not advised	Fishing	Canoeing	Dogs allowed
Cameron Corner	•			•	•		•	•				•		•							•
Dead Horse Gully	•	•		•	•		•	•	•		•	•		•							
Evelyn Creek				•	•							•									•
Fort Grey	•			•	•		•		•	•	•			•							
Innamincka Common*	•			•	•		•	•				•			•			•	•	•	•

*See Strzelecki Track, pages 12–13, for more campsites in Innamincka Regional Reserve.

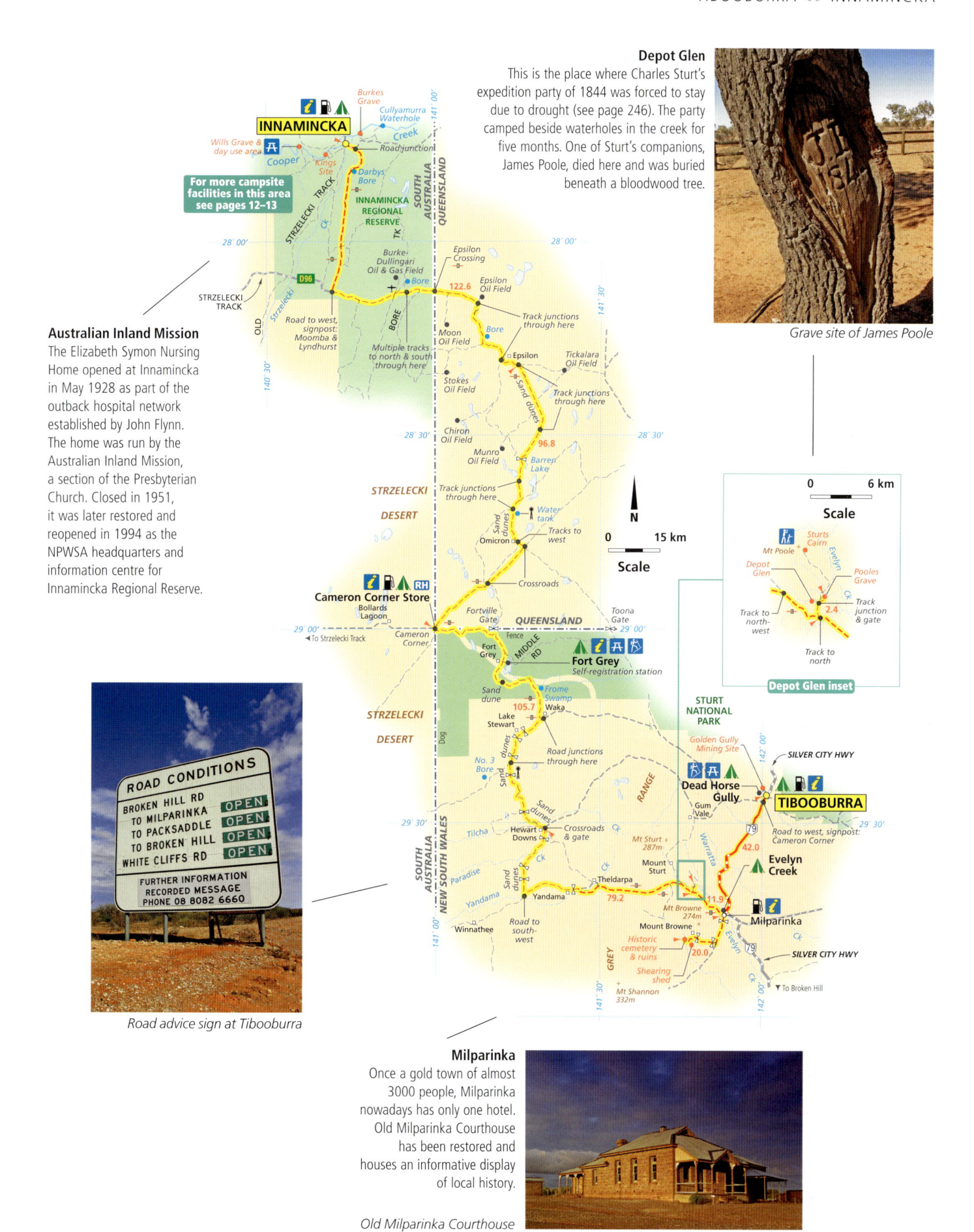

TIBOOBURRA ◀▶ INNAMINCKA

Depot Glen
This is the place where Charles Sturt's expedition party of 1844 was forced to stay due to drought (see page 246). The party camped beside waterholes in the creek for five months. One of Sturt's companions, James Poole, died here and was buried beneath a bloodwood tree.

Grave site of James Poole

Australian Inland Mission
The Elizabeth Symon Nursing Home opened at Innamincka in May 1928 as part of the outback hospital network established by John Flynn. The home was run by the Australian Inland Mission, a section of the Presbyterian Church. Closed in 1951, it was later restored and reopened in 1994 as the NPWSA headquarters and information centre for Innamincka Regional Reserve.

Road advice sign at Tibooburra

Milparinka
Once a gold town of almost 3000 people, Milparinka nowadays has only one hotel. Old Milparinka Courthouse has been restored and houses an informative display of local history.

Old Milparinka Courthouse

243

Latter-day fortune-seekers can still find gold in the Milparinka area and the pick-and-shovel-wielding miners of times past have been replaced by high-tech hopefuls, scanning the surrounding terrain and old mullock heaps with metal detectors. Enquire at the pub for directions to the best prospecting sites. From town there is an optional side trip to the now deserted Mount Browne goldfields and station ruins.

A little over 12 kilometres from Milparinka is Depot Glen, the site of Sturt's encampment during his 1844–45 expedition (see page 246). Here you can visit the grave of James Poole, Sturt's second-in-command, and take a short walk from the parking area at the base of Mount Poole to a cairn constructed by Sturt's party on the summit, from where there are stunning views over the surrounding country.

Striking west along the Hawker Gate Road, you pass a number of sheep properties before turning north onto the Hawker Gate–Cameron Corner Road. The track deteriorates from this point, crossing black soil plains that are impassable in the wet as well as a number of low-lying claypans that hold water for a considerable time after rain. Near Hewart Downs homestead the landscape changes and sand dunes start to dominate, with mulga and the occasional coolibah scattered on the low-lying flats. Apart from sheep, kangaroos are the most commonly sighted animals in these parts. Wedge-tailed eagles, pink and grey galahs and corellas are the main bird species.

Driving across the normally dry Evelyn Creek

Around 10 kilometres past Lake Stewart homestead the route joins with the Tibooburra–Cameron Corner Road. This well-maintained gravel and earth track shortly enters Sturt National Park, where it is worth spending some time. There are good visitor facilities here at Fort Grey, including camping. From the fort a 30-kilometre roller-coaster ride across the dunes takes you to Cameron Corner, the point where the three states of New South Wales, Queensland and South Australia meet. The local Corner Store (in Queensland) has fuel, limited supplies, meals, a bar and camping nearby.

The trek pushes northwards on the Queensland side of the border, before swinging west past some large cattle stations to cross into South Australia. There are a number of sand dunes and you will see several gas wells before picking up the well-maintained Strzelecki Track for the run into Innamincka. The banks of Cooper Creek, with campsites amid shady river red gums, make this area a great base for exploring the attractions of Innamincka Regional Reserve, including the numerous historic sites associated with Burke and Wills.

Advice and warnings

- This is a remote area so you need to be totally self-sufficient and your vehicle well equipped. Carry plenty of fuel, water and food. Be sure to carry some means of communication such as a satellite phone, UHF and/or HF radio.
- Possible road closures during and after heavy rains and many rivers and creeks are impassable after heavy localised rain. Severe fines apply to unauthorised use of closed roads. Ring recorded message services of the Unincorporated Districts Road Conditions Hotline, tel. (08) 8082 6660, the South Australian road report hotline, tel. 1300 361 033, or RACQ road reporting service, tel. 1300 130 595, to check road closures and conditions.
- Track passes through unfenced pastoral and leased property so keep to and do not deviate from track and do not camp without permission from landowners. Leave all gates as found or as signposted.
- Watch for roaming stock and kangaroos. If possible avoid driving between dusk and dawn.
- Standard road tyres or all-terrain tyres are suitable. Carry two spare tyres.
- Towing off-road trailers or off-road caravans is possible.
- Camping is at designated sites only. Campfires are prohibited in Sturt National Park so carry a gas/fuel stove. Free gas barbecues are located at Dead Horse Gully and Fort Grey camping areas.
- When camping along Cooper Creek, do not camp directly beneath branches of river red gums as they are prone to falling without warning.

- Bush flies are prolific so carry insect repellent. Head nets are useful to keep flies and mosquitoes at bay.

Permits and bookings
- Park use fee and camping fee apply in Sturt National Park and are payable at self-registration stations in camping areas.
- Desert Parks Pass required per vehicle to travel through Innamincka Regional Reserve. This pass covers a range of other outback parks in South Australia and entitles holder to camp within these parks or at specified locations and to travel on designated park roads. Contact Desert Parks Hotline, tel. 1800 816 078, to obtain a pass or for further details, or the NPWSA Innamincka, tel. (08) 8675 9909. Alternatively, a visitor day pass can be purchased. Innamincka Town Common has an honesty box system.
- To camp and fossick at the Mount Browne goldfields, permission is required from the landholder, tel. (08) 8091 3588. Fossicking licence not required.
- Advance bookings recommended for rooms at Albert Hotel, Milparinka, tel. (08) 8091 3863; Cameron Corner Store, tel. (08) 8091 3872; and Innamincka Hotel Motel, tel. (08) 8675 9901.
- Advance bookings recommended for station stays at Theldarpa, tel. (08) 8091 2552, and Epsilon, tel. (07) 4655 4324.
- Recreational fishing licence is not required for fishing in the Cooper Creek in South Australia but bag and size limits apply. For further details contact South Australia Fisheries, tel. (08) 8347 6107, or visit their website (www.pir.sa.gov.au/fishing).

ROUTE DIRECTIONS

▼ **0.0 km** Zero trip meter in Tibooburra along Silver City Hwy with NPWS office on left. Proceed in southerly direction along highway towards Broken Hill.

Tibooburra. NPWS office on right. **42.0 km** ▲

Dead Horse Gully camping area, 1.0 km north of Tibooburra on Hawker Gate Rd, is an open space with good facilities.

GPS S:29 25.800 E:142 00.664
UTM 54J 598070E 6743947N

(1.9 km)

▼ **1.9 km** Road junction. CSA. SP: Broken Hill 336. Road on right SP: Cameron Corner 138.

Road junction. CSA. Road on left SP: Cameron Corner 138. **40.1 km** ▲

(38.4 km)

▼ **40.3 km** Road junction. TR. SP: Historic Milparinka 2/ Depot Glen 15. Road SO SP: Broken Hill 294.

T-junction with SP: Silver City Highway. TL. SP: 40 Tibooburra. Road on right SP: Broken Hill 294. **1.7 km** ▲

The hardships of being stranded at the Milparinka pub

Marooned at Milparinka

We left Tibooburra heading in a southerly direction to Milparinka, where it started to rain. So we decided to sit and wait it out. However, we ended up sitting for five days and four nights before we could finally continue. During that time we stayed at the Albert Hotel at Milparinka and were well and truly looked after by John and Barb, 'temporary publicans' while the owners were interstate, and we enjoyed their company and that of local identity Joe, and Dog the dog.

We had a number of convivial nights at this friendly place, spending time and chatting with one of the shearing teams in the area as well as the locals and stranded fellow travellers. I know you're all thinking we have such bad luck – fancy being rained in at a pub!

Milparinka, the first town on the Albert goldfields, is quite a fascinating place, once boasting a courthouse, police station and cells, a post office, public school, two hotels, a bank and general store. Nowadays only one hotel, the Albert, survives but the remains of other buildings are worth visiting. The Milparinka Heritage and Tourism Association is in the process of reconstructing the police station. Grab a copy of the *Milparinka Heritage Trail* brochure and take a walk around the town's historic sites or take the side trip out to nearby Mount Browne goldfields.

> *I know you're all thinking we have such bad luck – fancy being rained in at a pub!*

Sturt's Unrelenting Search for an Inland Sea

The search for an inland sea preoccupied Australian explorers for the first half of the 19th century. Initially they followed the courses of the inland rivers, expecting them to flow into a vast ocean somewhere in the interior of the continent. In 1829 English explorer Charles Sturt sailed down the Murrumbidgee River to its junction with the Murray River, then travelled down the Murray to Lake Alexandrina, where the Murray flows into the sea. The belief that the network of inland rivers in New South Wales flowed into an inland sea now seemed fanciful, but Sturt and others still held to their convictions.

In an attempt to prove his theory, Sturt led an expedition from Adelaide in 1844–45, trekking north-east as far as Menindee to try and avoid the salt lakes that had defeated Edward Eyre in 1840. Travelling during severe drought and in the height of summer, Sturt was forced to camp near permanent water at Depot Glen for five months. During this time he instructed the expedition's second-in-command, James Poole, to have the men build a stone cairn on a nearby hill, now known as Mount Poole. Rain came in July and Sturt and a small party of men set off, pushing north-east, while the remainder of the party retreated to the south. Suffering from scurvy, James Poole died within a day of leaving camp with the retreating party. He was brought back to Depot Glen and buried. Sturt later wrote in his journal:

> … to give the men occupation, and to keep them in health I employed them in erecting a pyramid of stone on the summit of Red Hill … I had little thought when I engaged in that work, that I was erecting Mr Poole's monument, but so it was, that rude structure looks over his lonely grave, and will stand for ages as a record of all we suffered in the dreary region to which we were so long confined.

'I had little thought when I engaged in [building a stone cairn], that I was erecting Mr Poole's monument'

Sturt's hopes of finding an easier route inland were dramatically dashed. He was confronted by more salt lakes and then had to endure the harsh gibber expanse of what is now Sturt Stony Desert. By the time the party reached the eastern edge of the Simpson Desert, west of present-day Birdsville, they had little water remaining and were forced to retreat to Fort Grey (now part of Sturt National Park) and then back to their former encampment at Depot Glen. Sick and dispirited, Sturt gave up his quest and returned to Adelaide. Failing eyesight and ill-health caused his early retirement from further exploration.

Sturt's party found food and water at Depot Glen

	GPS S:29 43.859 E:141 53.608 **UTM** 54J 586407E 6710689N	
	(0.5 km)	
▼ 40.8 km	Milparinka Community Art Piece on left. CSA.	
	Milparinka Community Art Piece on right. CSA.	1.2 km ▲
	(0.5 km)	
▼ 41.3 km	Road junction. CSA over SP: Evelyn Creek. Tracks on right.	
	Tracks on right lead to **Evelyn Creek camping area**, with numerous bush campsites along creek among red gums.	
	Road junction over Evelyn Creek. CSA. Tracks on left.	0.7 km ▲
	(0.3 km)	
▼ 41.6 km	Road junction. TL. SP: Historic Milparinka. Road SO SP: 96 Hawker Gate/13 Depot Glen.	
	T-junction. TR. SP: Tibooburra 42/ Broken Hill 296.	0.4 km ▲
	(0.4 km)	
▼ 42.0 km	Milparinka. Albert Hotel on left. Side trip to Mount Browne goldfields.	
	Zero trip meter in Milparinka. Albert Hotel on right. Proceed in northerly direction towards Tibooburra.	0.0 km ▲
	GPS S:29 44.294 E:141 53.031 **UTM** 54J 585470E 6709893N	
▶	**SIDE TRIP: Mount Browne goldfields**	
▼ 0.0 km	Zero trip meter in Milparinka with Albert Hotel on left. Proceed past hotel and at crossroads TR. Road on left SP: Thompson St.	
	(1.8 km)	
▼ 1.8 km	Gate. LAF.	
	(7.1 km)	
▼ 8.9 km	Road junction. TR. SP: Mt Browne Woolshed & Goldfields.	
	GPS S:29 48.839 E:141 51 539 **UTM** 54J 583003E 6701517N	
	(1.2 km)	
▼ 10.1 km	Gate. LAF. Through gate track junction. CSA. Track on right.	
	(5.3 km)	
▼ 15.4 km	Gate. LAF.	
	(1.0 km)	
▼ 16.4 km	Gate. LAF.	
	(0.2 km)	
▼ 16.6 km	Shearing shed and quarters on left. Old Mt Browne homestead on right. CSA.	
	(2.9 km)	
▼ 19.5 km	Building ruins on left and right. CSA.	
	(0.5 km)	
▼ 20.0 km	Historic cemetery on right. Return to side trip start.	
	There are 11 grave sites here but only a few are marked, with dates as early as 1881.	
	GPS S:29 48.037 E:141 45.728 **UTM** 54J 573654E 6703064N	
◀	**END SIDE TRIP**	

Sturt's Cairn on the summit of Mount Poole

▼ 0.0 km	Zero trip meter in Milparinka with Albert Hotel on right. Proceed in northerly direction towards Tibooburra.	
	Milparinka. Albert Hotel on left.	11.9 km ▲
	(0.4 km)	
▼ 0.4 km	T-junction. TL. SP: 96 Hawker Gate/13 Depot Glen. Road on right SP: Tibooburra 42/Broken Hill 296.	
	Road junction. TR. SP: Historic Milparinka.	11.5 km ▲
	(11.5 km)	
▼ 11.9 km	Road junction. Side trip to Depot Glen.	
	Zero trip meter at road junction. CSA. Road on left SP: Depot Glen 2/Pooles Grave 3/ Sturts Cairn 8.	0.0 km ▲
	GPS S:29 40.810 E:141 47.455 **UTM** 54J 576527E 6716392N	
▶	**SIDE TRIP: Depot Glen**	
▼ 0.0 km	Zero trip meter at road junction. Turn north into road SP: Depot Glen 2/Pooles Grave 3/ Sturts Cairn 8.	
	(1.5 km)	
▼ 1.5 km	Y-junction. KR through old gate. SP: Pooles Grave 1/Sturts Cairn 7. Track on left.	
	Track on left leads 0.4 km to Depot Glen waterhole.	
	(0.1 km)	
▼ 1.6 km	Y-junction. KR. SP: 1 Pooles Grave. Road on left SP: 7 Sturts Cairn.	
	Road on left leads 6.5 km to base of Mt Poole, where a 15-minute one-way walk leads to summit and to Sturt's Cairn. Magnificent 360-degree views from summit.	
	(0.8 km)	
▼ 2.4 km	Carpark at Poole's Grave and Depot Glen. Return to side trip start.	
	James Poole was buried under a bloodwood tree. Blaze in tree can still be easily read.	
	GPS S:29 39.744 E:141 47.630 **UTM** 54J 576822E 6718359N	
◀	**END SIDE TRIP**	

CORNER COUNTRY

▼ 0.0 km — Zero trip meter at road junction. CSA. Road on right SP: Depot Glen 2/Pooles Grave 3/Sturts Cairn 8.

Road junction. Side trip to Depot Glen. **79.2 km** ▲

(4.7 km)

▼ 4.7 km — Y-junction. KL. Track on right SP: Mt Sturt.

Road junction. CSA. Track on left SP: Mt Sturt. **74.5 km** ▲

(26.0 km)

▼ 30.7 km — Road junction. KL. Track on right SP: Theldarpa.

Track on right leads to Theldarpa station, a working sheep station that offers farmstay accommodation from campsites to B&B in shearers quarters, tel. (08) 8091 2552.

Road junction. CSA. Track on left SP: Theldarpa. **48.5 km** ▲

```
GPS   S:29 39.853 E:141 29.791
UTM   54J 548049E 6718318N
```

(1.2 km)

▼ 31.9 km — Road junction. CSA. Track on right SP: Theldarpa.

Road junction. CSA. Track on left SP: Theldarpa. **47.3 km** ▲

(5.4 km)

▼ 37.3 km — Creek crossing.

Creek crossing. **41.9 km** ▲

(2.3 km)

▼ 39.6 km — Gate. LAF. Through gate road junction. CSA. Road on left SP: Yandama.

Road on left leads to Yandama homestead. Yandama shearing shed on right.

Road junction. CSA through gate. LAF. Road on right SP: Yandama. **39.6 km** ▲

```
GPS   S:29 40.383 E:141 25.172
UTM   54J 540595E 6717369N
```

(16.2 km)

▼ 55.8 km — Road junction. TR. SP: Camerons Corner 127. Road SO SP: Broken Hill 310.

T-junction. TL. SP: 68 Milparinka. Road on right SP: Broken Hill 310. **23.4 km** ▲

```
GPS   S:29 41.434 E:141 16.167
UTM   54J 526068E 6715471N
```

(5.3 km)

Tin dog on Hawker Gate Road

▼ 61.1 km — Gate. LAF.

Gate. LAF. **18.1 km** ▲

(4.4 km)

▼ 65.5 km — Gate. LAF.

Gate. LAF. **13.7 km** ▲

(9.3 km)

▼ 74.8 km — Y-junction. KL. Track on right.

Road junction. KR. Track on left. **4.4 km** ▲

(0.7 km)

▼ 75.5 km — Gate. LAF.

Gate. LAF. **3.7 km** ▲

(2.9 km)

▼ 78.4 km — Road junction. CSA. SP: Camerons Corner. Track on right.

Y-junction. KR. Track on left. **0.8 km** ▲

```
GPS   S:29 31.214 E:141 20.001
UTM   54J 532304E 6734328N
```

(0.6 km)

▼ 79.0 km — Road junction. CSA through fence line. Track on left.

Y-junction. KL. Track on right. **0.2 km** ▲

(0.2 km)

▼ 79.2 km — Crossroads.

Zero trip meter at crossroads. TR. SP: Broken Hill 332. Road on left SP: Tibooburra 72. **0.0 km** ▲

```
GPS   S:29 30.825 E:141 19.899
UTM   54J 532142E 6735047N
```

▼ 0.0 km — Zero trip meter at crossroads. TL. SP: 105 Cameron Corner. Road SO SP: Tibooburra 72.

Hewart Downs homestead on left at crossroads.

Crossroads. **105.7 km** ▲

(0.5 km)

▼ 0.5 km — Gate. LAF.

Gate. LAF. **105.2 km** ▲

(0.9 km)

▼ 1.4 km — Road junction. CSA. Track on left.

Road junction. CSA. Track on right. **104.3 km** ▲

(7.1 km)

▼ 8.5 km — Gate. LAF. Now entering SP: Lake Stewart Station.

Gate. LAF. Now entering SP: Hewart Downs Station. **97.2 km** ▲

```
GPS   S:29 28.355 E:141 16.145
UTM   54J 526089E 6739624N
```

(14.3 km)

▼ 22.8 km — Gate. LAF.

Gate. LAF. **82.9 km** ▲

(0.9 km)

▼ 23.7 km — Road junction. CSA. Track on right.

Y-junction. KR. Track on left. **82.0 km** ▲

(2.7 km)

▼ 26.4 km — Road junction. CSA. Track on left SP: No 3 Bore.

Y-junction. KL. Track on right SP: No 3 Bore. **79.3 km** ▲

```
GPS   S:29 20.792 E:141 13.759
UTM   54J 522261E 6753599N
```

(2.2 km)

▼ 28.6 km	Gate. LAF.		
	Gate. LAF.	77.1 km	▲
(5.9 km)			
▼ 34.5 km	Gate. LAF.		
	Gate. LAF.	71.2 km	▲
(0.6 km)			
▼ 35.1 km	Y-junction. CSA. SP: Cameron Corner. Track on left.		
	Track on left leads to Lake Stewart homestead.		
	Y-junction. CSA. SP: Broken Hill. Track on right.	70.6 km	▲

```
GPS   S:29 16.544 E:141 15.274
UTM   54J 524729E 6761438N
```

(1.9 km)

▼ 37.0 km — Gate. LAF. Through gate track junction. KR. Track SO is station track.

Gate. LAF. Entering SP: Lake Stewart. — 68.7 km ▲

(4.0 km)

▼ 41.0 km — Road junction. CSA. Track on right.

Y-junction. KR. Track on left. — 64.7 km ▲

(3.6 km)

▼ 44.6 km — Road junction. TL. SP: 60 Cameron Corner. Road SO SP: 79 Tibooburra.

Road junction. TR. SP: Lake Stewart 10. Road SO SP: 79 Tibooburra. — 61.1 km ▲

```
GPS   S:29 13.922 E:141 19.635
UTM   54J 531803E 6766262N
```

(6.8 km)

▼ 51.4 km — Grid. Enter SP: Sturt National Park.

Grid. Exit Sturt National Park. — 54.3 km ▲

(23.1 km)

▼ 74.5 km — Offset crossroads. CSA. Track on right SP: Fort Grey Campground.

Track on left leads to park ranger base. Track on right leads 0.8 km to **Fort Grey campground**, a spacious area with scattered coolibahs offering limited shade.

Offset crossroads. CSA. Track on left SP: Fort Grey Campground. — 31.2 km ▲

```
GPS   S:29 05.283 E:141 12.306
UTM   54J 519960E 6782242N
```

(2.7 km)

▼ 77.2 km — Road junction. CSA. SP: Cameron Corner 32 km. Track on right SP: Middle Road.

Road junction. CSA. SP: Fort Grey 2 km. Track on left SP: Middle Road. — 28.5 km ▲

(6.5 km)

▼ 83.7 km — Y-junction. KL. SP: Cameron Corner 22 km. Road on right SP: Fortville 1 km/Fortville Gate.

Road junction. CSA. SP: Tibooburra 117 km. Road on left SP: Fortville 1 km/Fortville Gate. — 22.0 km ▲

(21.4 km)

▼ 105.1 km — Gate in Dog Fence. Please close gate. CSA entering South Australia.

The Dog Fence is a 5400-kilometre barrier stretching from the Great Australian Bight, through the north-west corner of NSW and into Qld. It was constructed to protect sheep from dingoes (see page 207).

Cameron Corner post and plaque

Cameron Corner

The point where the borders of New South Wales, Queensland and South Australia meet, Cameron Corner was named after surveyor John Cameron, who was employed by the NSW Lands Department to lead the first survey party along the New South Wales–Queensland border between 1879 and 1881. Starting the survey from the New South Wales town of Barringun on 2 September 1879, Cameron and his party set out west towards the South Australian border. Taking 12 months to complete the arduous task and hampered by searing heat, drought and flood, the party arrived at the intersection of the three states in September 1880. On arrival at the junction Cameron erected a wooden post engraved 'Lat 29', along with the inscription 'Cameron'. This original wooden post is on display at the Tibooburra NPWS office. The party returned to Barringun and then started their survey to the east towards the MacIntyre River, finally completing the New South Wales–Queensland border survey in October 1881. Of all the state border intersecting points on the Australian mainland, the most easily accessible is Cameron Corner, making it a popular destination for four-wheel drivers who use this route to travel to places further west.

> *Of all the state border intersecting points on the Australian mainland, the most easily accessible is Cameron Corner*

CORNER COUNTRY

	Gate in Dog Fence. Please close gate. CSA entering New South Wales.	0.6 km ▲	
	GPS S:29 00.041 E:140 59.959 UTM 54J 499933E 6791939N		
	(0.3 km)		
▼ 105.4 km	Road junction. TR. Road SO SP: Strzelecki Track.		
	T-junction. TL.	0.3 km ▲	
	(0.2 km)		
▼ 105.6 km	Carpark on right. CSA over grid entering Queensland.		
	From carpark it is a short walk to the corner post of the three states.		
	Grid. Enter South Australia. Over grid carpark on left. CSA.	0.1 km ▲	
	(0.1 km)		
▼ 105.7 km	Crossroads.		
	Zero trip meter at crossroads at Cameron Corner. Road on right to Corner Store. Road on left to camping area. CSA over grid into South Australia.	0.0 km ▲	
	GPS S:28 59.881 E:140 59.958 UTM 54J 499932E 6792234N		
▼ 0.0 km	Zero trip meter at crossroads at Cameron Corner. CSA. SP: Omicron. Road on left to Corner Store. Road on right to camping area.		
	Cameron Corner Store camping area offers scattered bush camping amid red sand dunes close to store and amenities.		
	Crossroads.	96.8 km ▲	
	(0.9 km)		
▼ 0.9 km	Road junction. CSA. Track on right SP: Sports Ground.		
	Road junction. CSA. Track on left SP: Sports Ground.	95.9 km ▲	
	(36.0 km)		
▼ 36.9 km	Crossroads. CSA. SP: Naryilco. Road on right SP: Toona Gate.		
	Crossroads. CSA. SP: Cameron Corner. Road on left SP: Toona Gate.	59.9 km ▲	
	(0.3 km)		

The gate in the Dog Fence near Cameron Corner

▼ 37.2 km	Road junction. TL. SP: Omicron/Epsilon.		
	T-junction. TR.	59.6 km ▲	
	GPS S:28 47.222 E:141 16.302 UTM 54J 526518E 6815579N		
	(1.0 km)		
▼ 38.2 km	Track junction. CSA. Track on left.		
	Y-junction. KL. Track on right.	58.6 km ▲	
	(2.5 km)		
▼ 40.7 km	Track junction. CSA. Track on left.		
	Track on left to Omicron homestead.		
	Track junction. CSA. Track on right.	56.1 km ▲	
	GPS S:28 46.135 E:141 14.625 UTM 54J 523794E 6817592N		
	(0.8 km)		
▼ 41.5 km	Track junction. CSA. SP: Epsilon. Track on left.		
	Track junction. CSA. Track on right.	55.3 km ▲	
	(22.8 km)		
▼ 64.3 km	Barren Lake on right.		
	Barren Lake on left.	32.5 km ▲	
	(1.4 km)		
▼ 65.7 km	Gate. LAF.		
	Gate. LAF.	31.1 km ▲	
	(10.4 km)		
▼ 76.1 km	Track junction. CSA. Track on right.		
	Track junction. CSA. Track on left.	20.7 km ▲	
	(8.2 km)		
▼ 84.3 km	Track junction. CSA. Track on left SP: Munro 1.		
	Track junction. CSA. Track on right.	12.5 km ▲	
	(0.8 km)		
▼ 85.1 km	Track junction. CSA. SP: Mooliampah. Track on right SP: Tickalara Field.		
	Track junction. CSA. SP: Munro. Track on left.	11.7 km ▲	
	GPS S:28 24.764 E:141 18.199 UTM 54J 529709E 6857038N		
	(7.0 km)		
▼ 92.1 km	Track junction. CSA. Track on left.		
	Track junction. CSA. Track on right.	4.7 km ▲	
	(1.6 km)		
▼ 93.7 km	Track junction. CSA. Track on right.		
	Track junction. CSA. Track on left.	3.1 km ▲	
	(3.1 km)		
▼ 96.8 km	Track junction.		
	Zero trip meter at Y-junction. KR. SP: Omicron. Road on left SP: Tickalara 2.	0.0 km ▲	
	GPS S:28 19.151 E:141 15.073 UTM 54J 524627E 6867414N		
▼ 0.0 km	Zero trip meter at track junction. CSA. SP: Epsilon. Road on right SP: Tickalara 2.		
	Y-junction.	122.6 km ▲	
	(6.1 km)		
▼ 6.1 km	Road junction. KR. Track on left SP: Chiron.		
	Road junction. KL. SP: Jackson/Tickalara. Track on right SP: Chiron.	116.5 km ▲	
	(0.7 km)		
▼ 6.8 km	Road junction. CSA. SP: Innamincka/Moomba. Road on right SP: Epsilon 1 km.		

TIBOOBURRA ◀▶ INNAMINCKA

Burke-Dullingari gas fields near Innamincka

Road on right leads to Epsilon station, a working cattle property that offers air-conditioned accommodation, tel. (07) 4655 4324.

Road junction. CSA. SP: Santos/Omicron. Road on left SP: Epsilon 1 km. **115.8 km** ▲

GPS S:28 17.973 E:141 12.127
UTM 54J 519817E 6869598N

(8.5 km)

▼ **15.3 km** Y-junction. KR. Track on left SP: Stokes.

Y-junction. KL. Track on right SP: Stokes. **107.3 km** ▲

(13.0 km)

▼ **28.3 km** T-junction. TL. SP: Moomba/Dullingari. Road on right SP: Epsilon 3.

Road junction. TR. SP: Epsilon Homestead/ Tickalara. Road SO SP: Epsilon 3. **94.3 km** ▲

GPS S:28 09.673 E:141 07.832
UTM 54J 512815E 6884932N

(14.3 km)

▼ **42.6 km** Grid. This is Epsilon Crossing. CSA, entering South Australia and SP: Innamincka Regional Reserve.

Grid. This is Epsilon Crossing. CSA, entering Queensland. **80.0 km** ▲

GPS S:28 07.682 E:140 59.683
UTM 54J 499481E 6888615N

(8.0 km)

▼ **50.6 km** Road junction. CSA. SP: Innamincka/Bore Track. Track on left SP: Bore Track.

Road junction. CSA. SP: Epsilon. Track on right SP: Bore Track. **72.0 km** ▲

(0.5 km)

▼ **51.1 km** Road junction. CSA. SP: Moomba/Dullingari. Road on right SP: Bore Track/Innamincka.

Road junction. CSA. SP: Bore Track/Epsilon/ Tibooburra. Road on left SP: Bore Track/Innamincka. **71.5 km** ▲

(3.0 km)

▼ **54.1 km** T-junction. TL. SP: Dullingari/Moomba.

Road junction. TR. SP: Epsilon. **68.5 km** ▲

GPS S:28 07.999 E:140 52.889
UTM 54J 488361E 6888024N

(1.1 km)

▼ **55.2 km** Road junction. TR. SP: Moomba. Road SO SP: Toolachee/Brumby.

T-junction. TL. SP: Jackson/Epsilon. Road on right SP: Toolachee/Brumby. **67.4 km** ▲

(19.3 km)

▼ **74.5 km** Road junction. TR. SP: Innamincka. Road SO SP: Lyndhurst/Moomba.

T-junction. TL. Road on right SP: Lyndhurst/Moomba. **48.1 km** ▲

GPS S:28 07.755 E:140 41.682
UTM 54J 470018E 6888442N

(44.8 km)

▼ **119.3 km** Road junction. CSA. SP: Innamincka 4. Road on right SP: Thargomindah 372/Nappa Merrie 49.

Road junction. CSA. SP: 465 Lyndhurst. Road on left SP: Thargomindah 372/ Nappa Merrie 49. **3.3 km** ▲

(3.3 km)

▼ **122.6 km** Innamincka. Hotel and Trading Post store on right.

For Innamincka Town Common, PSA past hotel on right to T-junction. TL and continue 0.6 km to junction. Access track on right leads to **Innamincka Town Common camping area**, a large space with shady river red gums stretching along Cooper Creek. For more campsites in this area, see Strzelecki Track, pages 12–13.

Zero trip meter in Innamincka on Strzelecki Track with hotel and Trading Post on left. Proceed along Strzelecki Track in south-easterly direction towards Moomba. **0.0 km** ▲

GPS S:27 44.872 E:140 44.266
UTM 54J 474157E 6930700N

REVERSE DIRECTIONS START

The Burke and Wills Saga

In a blaze of enthusiasm the Victorian Exploring Expedition left Melbourne's Royal Park on Monday 20 August 1860 in a bid to be the first to cross the Australian continent from south to north. The expedition party was headed by an inexperienced leader, Robert O'Hara Burke.

After arriving in Menindee on the Darling River in early October Burke split the party into two, with one group remaining in Menindee to await fresh supplies before moving on to Cooper Creek. Burke, against the advice of other expedition members, set off with seven men to Cooper Creek. They arrived there on 20 November. Although the creek was not flowing there were large pools of water and plenty of shade and the men would have been reasonably comfortable until the end of summer before proceeding further north.

However, Burke's irrepressible ambition and impulsiveness, along with urging from the Expedition Committee, prompted him to make a decision that was to cost him and others their lives. Leaving four men behind at the base camp, Burke set off in the heat of summer on 16 December with his second-in-command William John Wills, Charles Gray and John King. They took Burke's faithful horse Billy and six camels loaded with supplies for three months.

William Brahe was left in charge of Depot LXV (65) on Cooper Creek with instructions to build a timber stockade, Fort Wills, while waiting for the main party to arrive with supplies from Menindee. Burke advised Brahe that if he did not return within three months then Brahe was to return to Melbourne.

Burke and his companions reached the brackish Little Bynoe River, about 50 kilometres south of the Gulf, on 9 February 1961. There had been heavy rain and the camels became bogged. Burke and Wills decided to make a final dash to the sea, leaving Gray and King to await their return. The two leaders proceeded north and on 11 February crossed extensive marshes and arrived at a tidal saltwater channel. They had reached the coast. Their journey from Cooper Creek had taken nearly two months and had consumed over two-thirds of their supplies.

On the return journey torrential wet-season rains hampered their progress. Burke was forced to reduce the party's daily rations. Weak and delirious, Charles Gray died on 17 April 1861. After four months and five days the remaining three men arrived back at Fort Wills at 7.30pm on 21 April to find the depot deserted. A freshly blazed tree advised them to DIG 3FT NW APR 21, 1861.

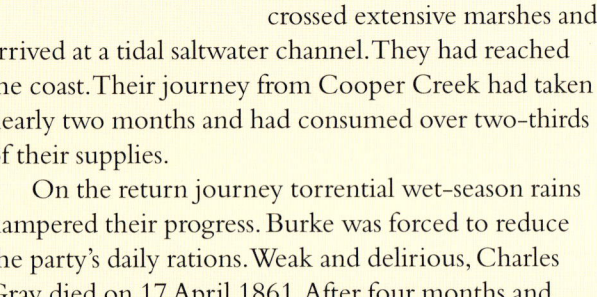

Burke's irrepressible ambition and impulsiveness ... prompted him to make a decision that was to cost him and others their lives

The exploring expedition leaves Melbourne in high spirits

The men found a cache of flour, oatmeal, sugar, rice, dried meat and other items. While they enjoyed a meal of oatmeal porridge and sugar they read the note from Brahe advising that the supply party, which was showing signs of scurvy, had left the fort earlier the same day. He had waited four months, not three as advised, and had received no messages from the outside world or the promised supplies from Menindee.

Burke's first thought was to chase Brahe, but the party and camels were totally exhausted. The men decided to follow Cooper Creek west then head south to the newly established police outpost at Mount Hopeless, 240 kilometres away. They rested for two days, feasting on the supplies left behind, and buried a message under the Dig Tree, with details of their journey north to the coast and their intention to head for Mount Hopeless. They carefully raked the ground but failed to leave a new blaze on the tree advising any rescuers to dig for their message. They left Fort Wills on 23 April, moving slowly west along the creek, and befriended a group of Aboriginal people who gave them fish and bread, called nardoo, in exchange for items of clothing. However, on 10 May, when the men realised that to survive they needed to live with the Aboriginal people, they could not find them. The three men were alone.

In the meantime William Brahe, on returning to Menindee, worried that Burke could have returned. On 3 May Brahe and local stockman William Wright made a 129-kilometre dash back to Fort Wills. On their arrival on 8 May it appeared that nothing had changed since Brahe had left in April. Satisfied that the party had not returned, Brahe and Wright travelled back to Menindee. Burke, Wills and King were only some 48 kilometres down the creek.

Wills decided to return to the depot to leave his journals and a letter detailing their location. Arriving

Burke, Wills and King return to Cooper Creek

on 30 May he found no trace of anyone. He deposited his journals, once again leaving no new markings on the tree, and arrived back at Burke and King's camp on 6 June. The two men had received supplies from their Aboriginal friends. By 22 June, living mainly on nardoo, which offered little nourishment, Wills was unable to stand. Burke and King left him in the hope of getting help from the Aboriginal people. However, on the evening of 29 June Burke lay down, wrote a note to the exploration committee, then asked King to place his pistol in his hand, telling him to continue on his own. Burke died early the next morning.

King wandered for days, existing on nardoo, before finally managing to shoot four birds, three of which he took back to Wills, but Wills was dead. King followed the creek upstream, finding an Aboriginal group with whom he lived for two months before being rescued on 15 September by a party led by Alfred Howitt. King, the sole survivor of the ill-fated Victorian Exploring Expedition, was taken back to Melbourne to tell the world his tragic tale. A public funeral was held in Melbourne for Burke and Wills in January 1863.

CORNER COUNTRY

2 INNAMINCKA ◄► WINDORAH 456.7 KM

Start point
Innamincka

Road atlas
350 D7

Total distance
484.7 km (includes route-directed side trip)

Standard
Easy

Time
2–3 days

Longest distance no PD (includes all options)
546.5 km (Innamincka to Windorah)

Topographic maps
Auslig 1:250 000 series: *Innamincka*; *Durham Downs*; *Barrolka*; *Cordillo*; *Canterbury*; *Windorah*

Other useful information
- Innamincka Trading Post store open seven days 8am–6pm, tel. (08) 8675 9900; accepts cash, EFTPOS and credit cards.
- NPWSA park guide: *Innamincka Regional Reserve*.
- Bulloo Shire Council brochure: *The Adventure Way to the famous Burke & Wills 'Dig Tree', Cooper Creek*.
- Tourist brochures: *Innamincka on the Banks of the Cooper – Burke & Wills Country*; *South West Queensland: The Essence of the Outback*; *Windorah: Heart of the Channel Country*.
- Sara Murgatroyd's *The Dig Tree* is a great read.
- Information booklets, brochures and maps enclosed with Desert Parks Pass (see Permits and bookings).

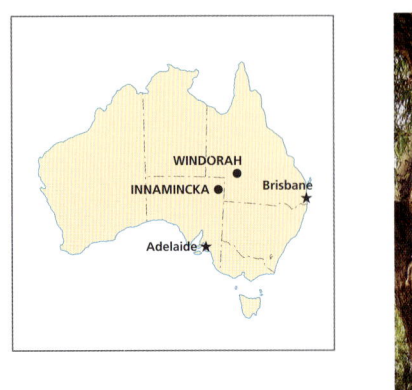

Camping at Cullyamurra Waterhole

- Cooper Creek is visited by large numbers of birds so pack an identification guide and binoculars.
- There are good opportunities to explore some areas on foot so pack your camera, hat, sunscreen and sturdy walking shoes.

Description
Established as a customs post in the 1800s, Innamincka had become a ghost town by the 1950s but gained a new lease of life from the exploration of petroleum oil and gas deposits in the Cooper Creek Basin in the 1960s.

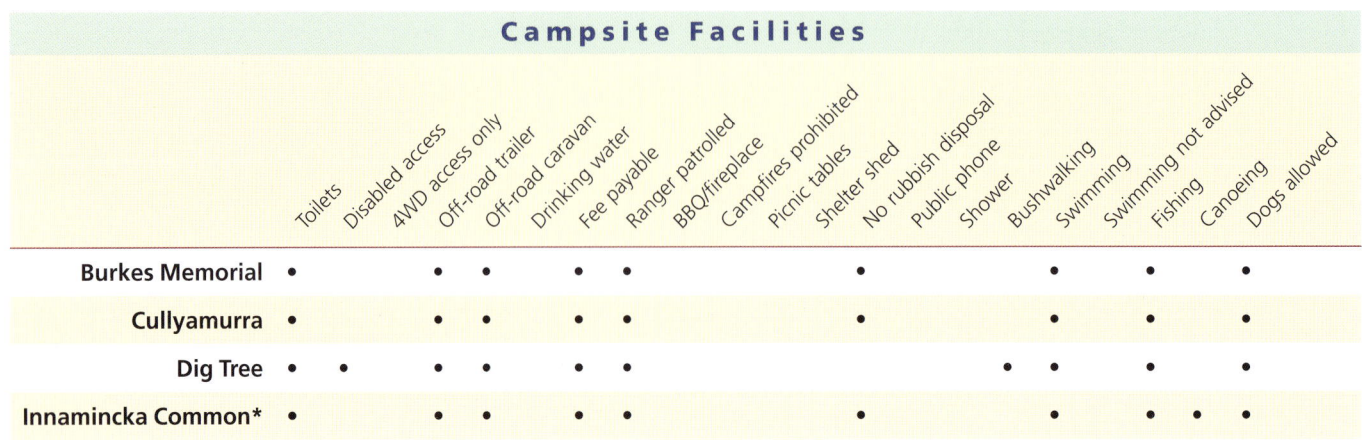

Campsite Facilities

	Toilets	Disabled access	4WD access only	Off-road trailer	Off-road caravan	Drinking water	Fee payable	Ranger patrolled	BBQ/fireplace	Campfires prohibited	Picnic tables	Shelter shed	No rubbish disposal	Public phone	Shower	Bushwalking	Swimming	Swimming not advised	Fishing	Canoeing	Dogs allowed
Burkes Memorial	•			•	•		•	•					•				•		•		•
Cullyamurra	•			•	•		•	•					•				•		•		•
Dig Tree	•	•		•	•		•							•	•		•				•
Innamincka Common*	•			•	•		•						•				•			•	•

*See Strzelecki Track, pages 12–13, for more campsites in Innamincka Regional Reserve.

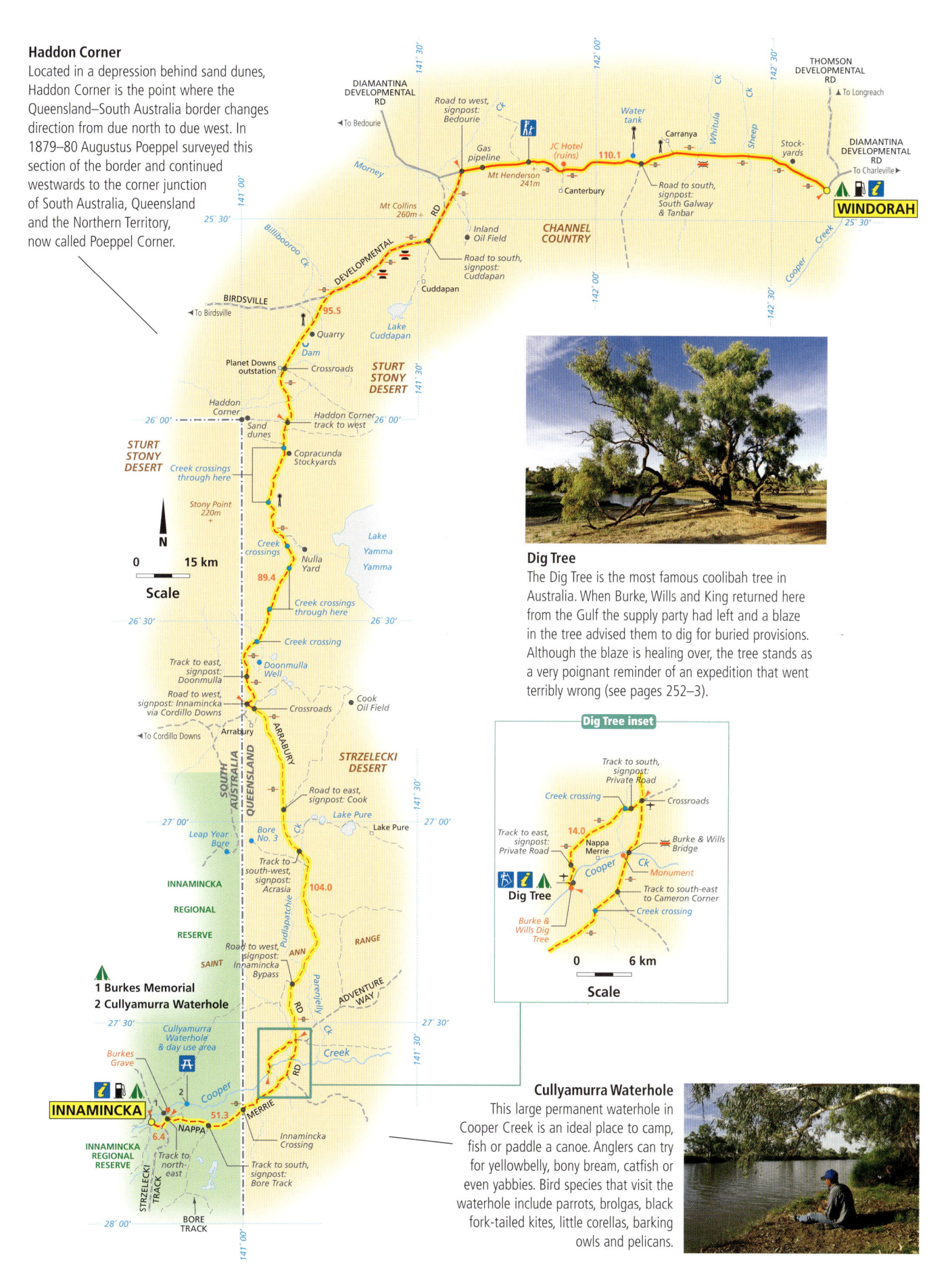

INNAMINCKA ◀▶ WINDORAH

Haddon Corner
Located in a depression behind sand dunes, Haddon Corner is the point where the Queensland–South Australia border changes direction from due north to due west. In 1879–80 Augustus Poeppel surveyed this section of the border and continued westwards to the corner junction of South Australia, Queensland and the Northern Territory, now called Poeppel Corner.

Dig Tree
The Dig Tree is the most famous coolibah tree in Australia. When Burke, Wills and King returned here from the Gulf the supply party had left and a blaze in the tree advised them to dig for buried provisions. Although the blaze is healing over, the tree stands as a very poignant reminder of an expedition that went terribly wrong (see pages 252–3).

Cullyamurra Waterhole
This large permanent waterhole in Cooper Creek is an ideal place to camp, fish or paddle a canoe. Anglers can try for yellowbelly, bony bream, catfish or even yabbies. Bird species that visit the waterhole include parrots, brolgas, black fork-tailed kites, little corellas, barking owls and pelicans.

255

Innamincka is now a popular destination for campers, and anglers who come to fish the waterholes of Cooper Creek, as well as a centre for workers from nearby cattle stations and the oil and gas fields.

You leave Innamincka via the Strzelecki Track before turning east onto the Nappa Merrie Road, which provides access to the lonely site of explorer Robert O'Hara Burke's last hours beneath a coolibah tree. The large and scenic Cullyamurra Waterhole, with innumerable campsites, is nearby. From here you cross Cooper Creek via the Burke and Wills Bridge and a signposted turn takes you 14 kilometres through Nappa Merrie station to the Dig Tree, a sprawling coolibah on the northern bank of Cooper Creek and the site of one of Australia's most famous exploration blunders (see pages 252–3). Campsites are located upstream from the Dig Tree.

Back on the main track, which at this point is known as Adventure Way, you veer north on Arrabury Road (Adventure Way continues east towards Thargomindah). After traversing vast gibber plains, the route passes through the picturesque Saint Ann Range before entering sand dune country, where the track runs parallel to the dunes. After the turn-off to Arrabury homestead the road surface begins to improve as the route leads over more gibber plains, occasionally intersected by mainly dry creek beds. If you want to visit Haddon Corner, the signposted track heads west for 13 kilometres across black soil plains, crossing two moderately sized sand dunes before arriving at the corner post. Surveyed by Augustus Poeppel in 1879, Haddon Corner is the extreme north-east point of South Australia.

From the Haddon Corner turn-off the trek continues north to join the Birdsville Developmental Road. To the west lies Birdsville via Beetota, but you turn east to pick up the bitumen on the Diamantina Developmental Road, which gives you an easy run to the Channel Country town of Windorah.

Advice and warnings

- This is a remote area so you need to be totally self-sufficient and your vehicle well equipped. Carry plenty of fuel, water and food. Be sure to carry some means of communication such as a satellite phone, UHF and/or HF radio.
- Possible road closures during and after heavy rains and many rivers and creeks are impassable after heavy localised rain. Severe fines apply to unauthorised use of closed roads. Ring recorded message services of the South Australian road report hotline, tel. 1300 361 033, and RACQ road reporting service, tel. 1300 130 595, to check road closures and conditions.
- Track passes through unfenced pastoral and leased property so keep to and do not deviate from track and do not camp without permission from landowners. Leave all gates as found or as signposted.
- Watch for roaming stock and kangaroos. If possible avoid driving between dusk and dawn.
- Standard road tyres or all-terrain tyres are suitable. Carry two spare tyres.
- Towing off-road trailers or off-road caravans is possible. Off-road caravans not recommended on the track out to Haddon Corner.
- Camping is at designated sites only.
- Bush flies are prolific so carry insect repellent. Head nets are useful to keep flies and mosquitoes at bay.

Permits and bookings

- Desert Parks Pass required per vehicle to travel through Innamincka Regional Reserve. This pass covers a range of other outback parks in South Australia and entitles holder to camp within these parks or at specified locations and to travel on designated park roads. Contact Desert Parks Hotline, tel. 1800 816 078, to obtain a pass or for further details, or the NPWSA Innamincka, tel. (08) 8675 9909. Alternatively, a visitor day pass can be purchased. Innamincka Town Common has an honesty box system.
- Entrance fee applies to visit Dig Tree Reserve, payable at honesty box on site or to patrolling ranger.
- Advance bookings recommended for rooms at Innamincka Hotel Motel, tel. (08) 8675 9901; Cooper Cabins at Windorah, tel. (07) 4656 3101; and Western Star Hotel Motel at Windorah, tel. (07) 4656 3166.
- Recreational fishing licence not required for fishing in Cooper Creek (South Australia). Bag and size limits apply. Contact South Australia Fisheries, tel. (08) 8347 6107, or visit their website (www.pir.sa.gov.au/fishing).

Taking a break along Arrabury Road

INNAMINCKA ◀▶ WINDORAH

Queerbidie Waterhole at Innamincka

ROUTE DIRECTIONS

▼ 0.0 km Zero trip meter at Innamincka on the Strzelecki Track with Trading Post and hotel on left. Proceed in easterly direction along Strzelecki Track towards SP: Dig Tree 69 km/Cullyamurra Waterhole 14 km/Burkes Grave 11 km.

Innamincka. Trading Post and hotel on right.   6.4 km ▲

For Innamincka Town Common, PSA past hotel on right to T-junction. TL and continue 0.6 km to junction. Access track on right leads to **Innamincka Town Common camping area**, a large space with shady river red gums along Cooper Creek. For more campsites in this area, see pages 12–13.

GPS S:27 44.872 E:140 44.266
UTM 54J 474157E 6930700N

(3.4 km)

▼ 3.4 km Road junction. TL. SP: Dig Tree 66 km/Cullyamurra Waterhole 11 km/Burkes Grave 8 km. Road SO SP: 465 Lyndhurst.

T-junction. TR. SP: Innamincka 4. Road on left SP: 465 Lyndhurst.   3.0 km ▲

(3.0 km)

▼ 6.4 km Road junction.

Zero trip meter at road junction. CSA. SP: Innamincka 6 km. Road on right SP: Cullyamurra Waterhole 8 km/Burkes Grave 5 km.   0.0 km ▲

GPS S:27 44.376 E:140 46.960
UTM 54J 478580E 6931624N

▼ 0.0 km Zero trip meter at road junction. CSA. SP: Nappamerry. Road on left SP: Cullyamurra Waterhole 8 km/Burkes Grave 5 km.

Road on left leads 4.4 km to carpark and walk to Burkes Memorial, and 4.4 km to **Burkes Memorial camping area**, a large area with scattered bush campsites along banks of Cooper Creek, and 8.1 km to **Cullyamurra Waterhole camping area**, a spacious location with campsites along bank of scenic waterhole.

Road junction.   51.3 km ▲

(12.3 km)

▼ 12.3 km Road junction. CSA. SP: Nappamerry. Road on right SP: Bore Track.

Road junction. CSA. SP: 19 Innamincka. Road on left SP: Bore Track.   39.0 km ▲

(11.1 km)

▼ 23.4 km Grid. This is Innamincka Crossing. Enter Queensland.

Grid. This is Innamincka Crossing. Enter South Australia.   27.9 km ▲

GPS S:27 43.165 E:140 59.738
UTM 54J 499570E 6933879N

(4.2 km)

▼ 27.6 km Creek crossing.

Creek crossing.   23.7 km ▲

(13.4 km)

▼ 41.0 km T-junction. TL. SP: Dig Tree via Burke & Wills Bridge 25 km. Road on right SP: Cameron Corner via Orientos 256 km.

Road junction. TR. SP: Innamincka 56 km. Road SO SP: Cameron Corner via Orientos 256 km.   10.3 km ▲

GPS S:27 37.772 E:141 07.669
UTM 54J 512610E 6943829N

(4.3 km)

■ 257

CORNER COUNTRY

▼ 45.3 km	Cross Burke & Wills Bridge.		
	Cross Burke & Wills Bridge.	6.0 km ▲	
(6.0 km)			
▼ 51.3 km	Crossroads. Side trip to Dig Tree.		
	Zero trip meter at crossroads. CSA. SP: Innamincka 67 km. Road on left SP: Thargomindah. Road on right SP: Dig Tree 14 km.	0.0 km ▲	

GPS   S:27 32.536 E:141 09.203
UTM   54J 515144E 6953492N

▶ **SIDE TRIP: Dig Tree**

▼ 0.0 km	Zero trip meter at crossroads. Turn south-west into track SP: Dig Tree 14 km.	
(1.5 km)		
▼ 1.5 km	Road junction. CSA. SP: Dig Tree. Road on left SP: Nappa Merrie/Private Road.	
(0.6 km)		
▼ 2.1 km	Creek crossing.	
(9.3 km)		
▼ 11.4 km	Track junction. CSA over creek. SP: Dig Tree. Track on left SP: Private Road.	
(2.3 km)		
▼ 13.7 km	Gate. Enter Dig Tree Reserve.	
	Information shelter and honesty box for fees on right.	
(0.3 km)		
▼ 14.0 km	Track junction. Carpark and picnic area on right. Short walk to Dig Tree on right. Return to side trip start.	
	Track on left leads 0.1 km to **Dig Tree** Reserve **camping area**, which has scattered bush campsites along banks of Cooper Creek.	

GPS   S:27 37.404 E:141 04.535
UTM   54J 507457E 6944512N

◀ **END SIDE TRIP**

▼ 0.0 km	Zero trip meter at crossroads. CSA. SP: Arrabury 97 km. Road on right SP: Thargomindah. Road on left SP: Dig Tree 14 km.		
	Crossroads. Side trip to Dig Tree.	104.0 km ▲	
(14.8 km)			
▼ 14.8 km	Road junction. CSA. SP: Arrabury. Road on left SP: Innamincka By-pass/Bookabourdie.		
	Road junction. CSA. SP: Innamincka/Nappa Merrie. Road on right SP: Innamincka By-pass.	89.2 km ▲	
(41.7 km)			
▼ 56.5 km	Road junction. CSA. Track on left SP: Acrasia.		
	Road junction. CSA. Track on right SP: Acrasia.	47.5 km ▲	

GPS   S:27 04.827 E:141 10.211
UTM   54J 516873E 7004643N

(14.1 km)

▼ 70.6 km	Road junction. CSA. SP: Arrabury. Road on right SP: Cook.		
	Road junction. CSA. SP: Innamincka. Road on left SP: Cook.	33.4 km ▲	
(30.9 km)			
▼ 101.5 km	Crossroads. CSA. SP: Cordillo 56 km. Road on left SP: Private Property/No Through Road.		
	Crossroads. CSA. Road on right SP: Private Property/No Through Road.	2.5 km ▲	
(2.5 km)			
▼ 104.0 km	T-junction.		
	Zero trip meter at road junction. TL. SP: 155 Innamincka via Nappa Merrie/Arrabury. Road SO SP: Innamincka via Cordillo Downs.	0.0 km ▲	

Track to Haddon Corner

258

INNAMINCKA ◀▶ WINDORAH

| GPS | S:26 42.457 E:141 00.873 |
| UTM | 54J 501447E 7045948N |

▼ 0.0 km Zero trip meter at T-junction. TR. SP: Windorah/Birdsville. Road on left SP: Innamincka via Cordillo Downs.

　　　　　　　　　　　　　Road junction.　89.4 km ▲

(20.9 km)

▼ 20.9 km Creek crossing.

　　　　　　　　　　　　　Creek crossing.　68.5 km ▲

(10.2 km)

▼ 31.1 km Creek crossing.

　　　　　　　　　　　　　Creek crossing.　58.3 km ▲

(41.8 km)

▼ 72.9 km Creek crossing.

　　　　　　　　　　　　　Creek crossing.　16.5 km ▲

(16.5 km)

▼ 89.4 km Road junction.

　　Zero trip meter at road junction. CSA. Track on right SP: 15 Haddon Corner.　0.0 km ▲

| GPS | S:26 00.443 E:141 07.815 |
| UTM | 54J 513034E 7123492N |

▼ 0.0 km Zero trip meter at road junction. CSA. Track on left SP: 15 Haddon Corner.

Track on left leads 13.5 km to corner post at Haddon Corner. In last 2.0 km before corner, you cross two large sand dunes.

　　　　　　　　　　　　　Road junction.　95.5 km ▲

(16.9 km)

▼ 16.9 km Crossroads. CSA. Track on left.

Track on left leads to Planet Downs outstation.

　　Crossroads. CSA. Track on right to outstation.　78.6 km ▲

(23.7 km)

▼ 40.6 km T-junction. This is Birdsville Developmental Rd. TR. SP: Windorah 164. Road on left SP: 222 Birdsville.

　　Road junction. TL. SP: 290 Innamincka/Arrabury. Road SO SP: 222 Birdsville.　54.9 km ▲

| GPS | S:25 41.547 E:141 14.624 |
| UTM | 54J 524455E 7158352N |

(33.3 km)

▼ 73.9 km Road junction. CSA. SP: Windorah. Road on right SP: Cuddapan.

　　Road junction. CSA. SP: Arrabury/Beetoota/Birdsville. Road on left SP: Cuddapan.　21.6 km ▲

(21.6 km)

▼ 95.5 km T-junction.

　　Zero trip meter at road junction. TL. SP: Birdsville. This is Birdsville Developmental Rd. Road SO SP: 279 Bedourie.　0.0 km ▲

| GPS | S:25 22.908 E:141 37.113 |
| UTM | 54J 562224E 7192631N |

▼ 0.0 km Zero trip meter at T-junction. This is Diamantina Developmental Rd. TR. SP: Windorah 117. Road on left SP: 279 Bedourie.

　　　　　　　　　　　　　Road junction.　110.1 km ▲

(19.2 km)

Haddon Corner surrounded by water

▼ 19.2 km Views to south towards Mt Henderson.

　　Views to south towards Mt Henderson.　90.9 km ▲

(10.4 km)

▼ 29.6 km Road junction. CSA. Track on left SP: JC Hotel Ruins.

Track on left leads 0.4 km to ruins of JC Hotel, once part of township of Canterbury.

　　Road junction. CSA. Track on right SP: JC Hotel Ruins.　80.5 km ▲

| GPS | S:25 22.820 E:141 54.049 |
| UTM | 54J 590622E 7192632N |

(23.9 km)

▼ 53.5 km Road junction. CSA. SP: Windorah. Road on right SP: South Galway/Tanbar.

　　Road junction. CSA. SP: Bedourie. Road on left SP: South Galway/Tanbar.　56.6 km ▲

(56.6 km)

▼ 110.1 km Windorah. Western Star Hotel on left.

　　Zero trip meter along Diamantina Developmental Rd in Windorah. Western Star Hotel on right. Proceed in north-westerly direction along Diamantina Developmental Rd towards Bedourie.　0.0 km ▲

| GPS | S:25 25.320 E:142 39.299 |
| UTM | 54J 666444E 7187291N |

REVERSE DIRECTIONS START

FOLLOWING PAGES
Track to the Dig Tree

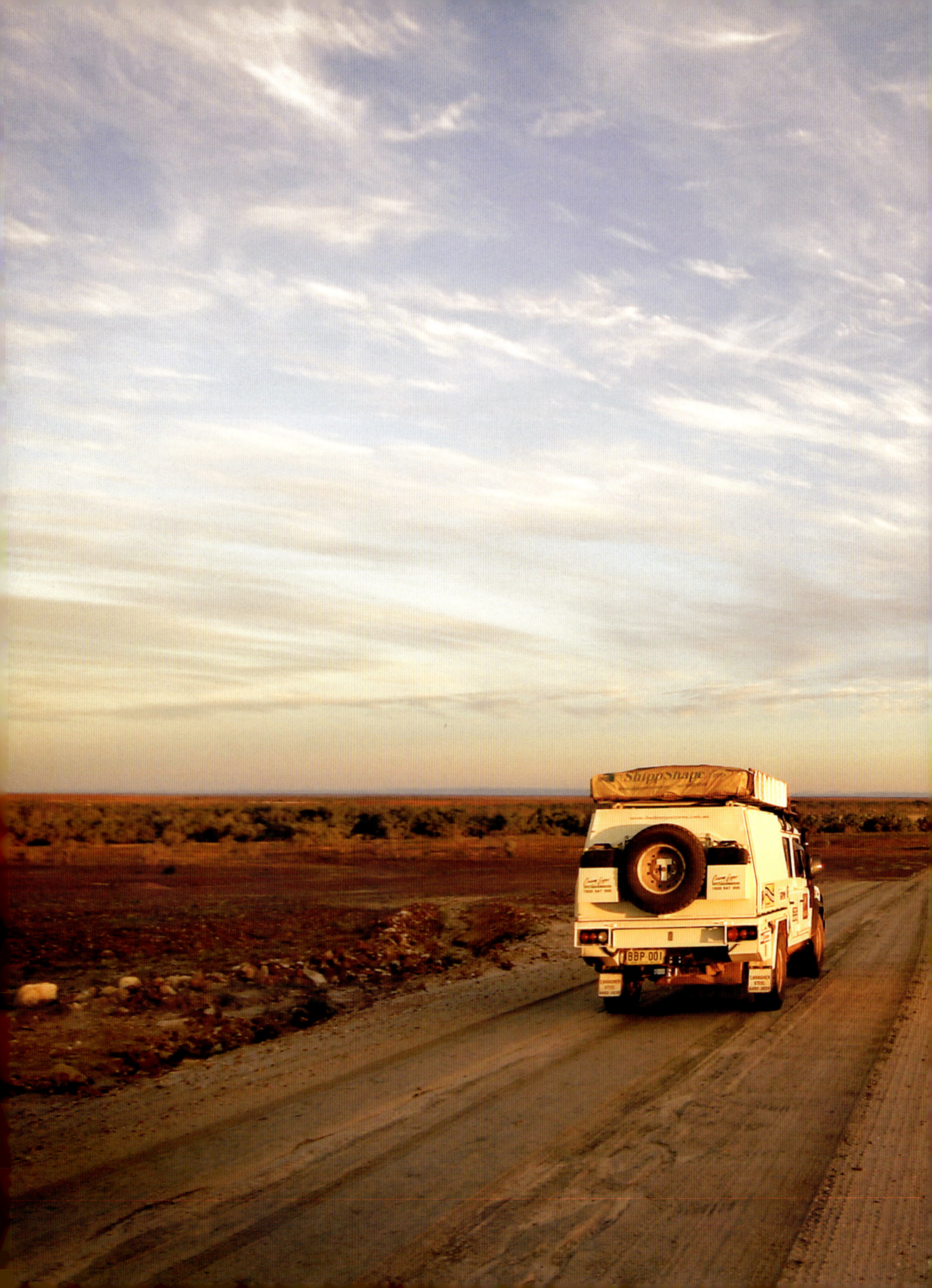

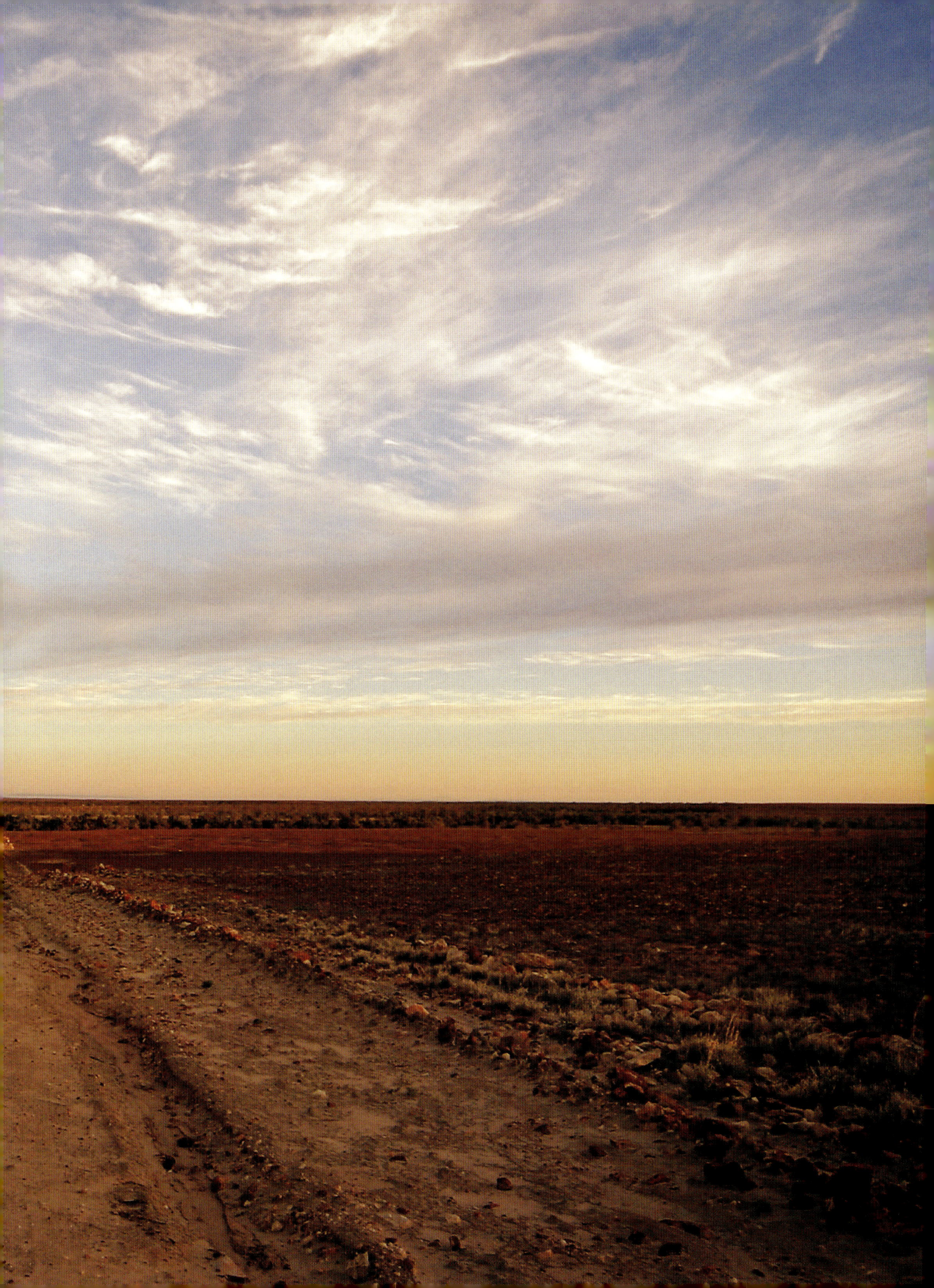

Cape York Peninsula

Isabella Falls on Battle Camp Road

COOKTOWN ◀▶ BAMAGA 844.0 KM

1. COOKTOWN ◁▷ MUSGRAVE ROADHOUSE 279.1 km *(easy)*
2. MUSGRAVE ROADHOUSE ◁▷ BRAMWELL JUNCTION 341.7 km *(easy)*
3. BRAMWELL JUNCTION ◁▷ BAMAGA 202.5/223.2 km *(difficult/easy–moderate)*

WHEN TO GO Mid-May–September **TIME** 5–8 days

The delights of Cape York Peninsula include rugged landscapes, verdant forests, pristine rivers and scenic waterfalls. Taking in the vast Lakefield and Jardine River national parks, exploring this area rates as one of Australia's top three four-wheel-drive adventures, on a par with tours of the Kimberley and the Canning Stock Route.

Not a journey to be undertaken lightly, road access along the peninsula is only possible during the northern dry season, which can start in April and extend to early November. During the Wet the rivers and creeks become impassable. North of Bramwell Junction, in trek section three, you can choose from two alternative routes. The Telegraph Track is the more difficult option to the top and is best tackled in a well-set-up vehicle with a range of recovery gear while both the Southern and Northern by-pass roads are much less demanding but often plagued by severely corrugated sections. Despite numerous river and creek crossings, off-road trailers are commonplace and towing well-constructed off-road caravans to the top via the Southern and Northern by-pass roads is possible.

Campsites vary from those with facilities, at towns and roadhouses, to secluded bush settings beside rivers and creeks. The main centres of Cooktown, Coen, Weipa, Bamaga and Seisia offer a range of supplies and services and several roadhouses and stations sell fuel and basic provisions. Aboriginal communities are scattered throughout the peninsula, with a number providing services and facilities to travellers.

CAPE YORK PENINSULA

Services

VEHICLE ASSISTANCE
RACQ   13 1111

POLICE
Bamaga   (07) 4069 3156
Coen   (07) 4060 1150
Cooktown   (07) 4069 5320
Weipa   (07) 4069 9119

PARKS AND RESERVES
Lakefield National Park
QPWS Cooktown   (07) 4069 5777
QPWS Lakefield   (07) 4060 3271
QPWS New Laura   (07) 4060 3260

Mungkan Kandju National Park
QPWS Cooktown   (07) 4069 5777

Iron Range National Park
QPWS Iron Range   (07) 4060 7170

Heathlands Resource Reserve
Jardine River National Park
QPWS Cooktown   (07) 4069 5777
QPWS Heathlands Ranger Base   (07) 4060 3241

USEFUL CONTACTS
Bamaga Island Council   (07) 4069 3121
Injinoo Community Council   (07) 4069 3252
www.injinoo.com
New Mapoon Aboriginal
  Council   (07) 4069 3277
Seisia Island Council   (07) 4069 3133
Umagico Aboriginal Council   (07) 4069 3266

VISITOR INFORMATION
Bamaga   (07) 4069 3777
Coen   (07) 4060 1135
Cooktown   (07) 4069 6004
Weipa   (07) 4069 7871

Authors' note

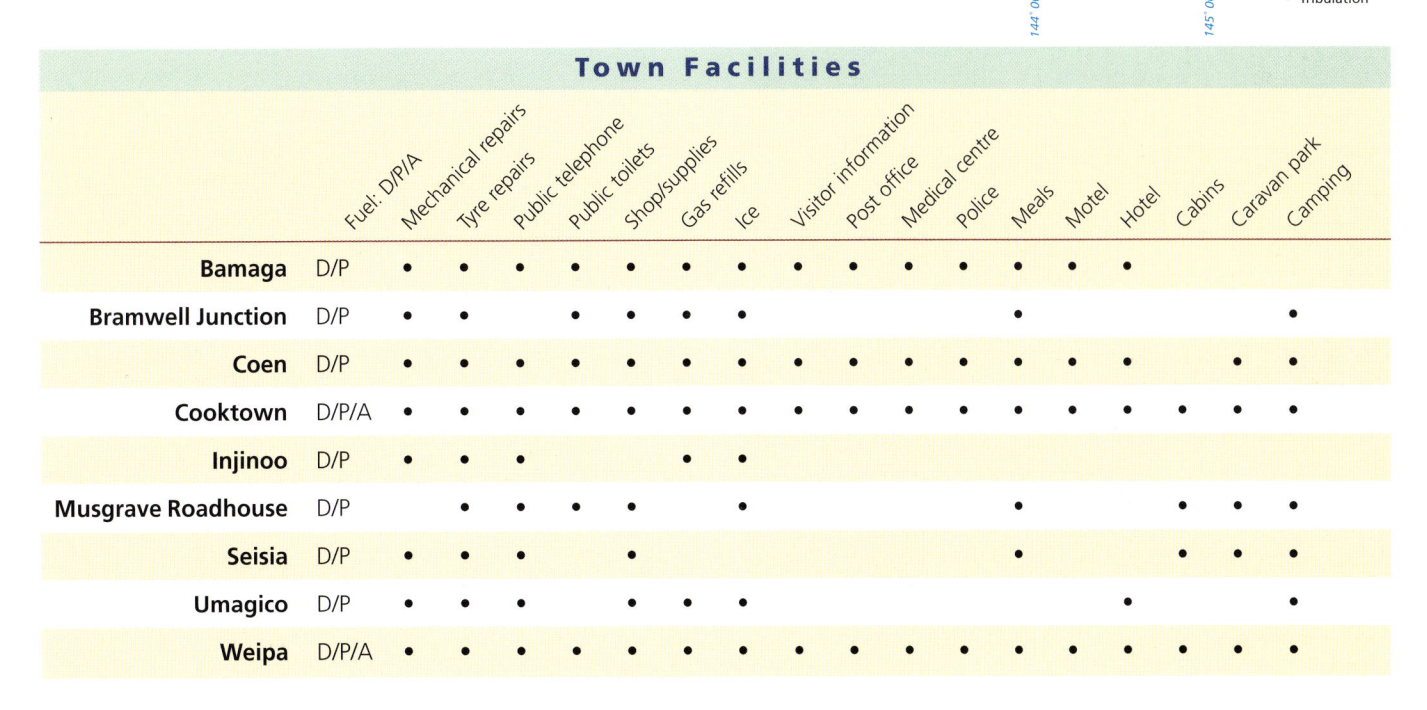

Don't miss the delightful cascades at Isabella, Fruit Bat, Eliot and Twin falls. There is camping near Eliot Falls — a great spot to base yourself for a day or two — and it's only a short walk from here to Twin Falls.

Town Facilities

	Fuel: D/P/A	Mechanical repairs	Tyre repairs	Public telephone	Public toilets	Shop/supplies	Gas refills	Ice	Visitor information	Post office	Medical centre	Police	Meals	Motel	Hotel	Cabins	Caravan park	Camping
Bamaga	D/P	•	•	•	•	•	•	•	•	•	•	•	•	•				
Bramwell Junction	D/P	•	•		•	•	•						•					•
Coen	D/P	•	•	•	•	•	•	•	•	•	•	•	•		•	•	•	•
Cooktown	D/P/A	•	•	•	•	•	•	•	•	•	•	•	•	•	•	•	•	•
Injinoo	D/P	•	•	•		•	•											
Musgrave Roadhouse	D/P	•			•	•	•						•					•
Seisia	D/P	•	•	•	•	•						•			•		•	•
Umagico	D/P	•	•		•	•									•			•
Weipa	D/P/A	•	•	•	•	•	•	•	•	•	•	•	•	•	•	•	•	•

263

1 COOKTOWN ◀▶ MUSGRAVE ROADHOUSE 279.1 KM

Start point
Cooktown

Road atlas
360 F5

Total distance
287.6 km (via Seven Mile Waterhole)

Standard
Easy

Time
2–3 days

Longest distance no PD (includes all options)
500.3 km (Endeavour Falls Tourist Park to Musgrave Roadhouse)

Topographic maps
Auslig 1:250 000 series: *Cooktown*; *Cape Melville*; *Ebagoola*

Other useful information
- Endeavour Falls Tourist Park has petrol, diesel, groceries, ice, gas bottle refills, take-away meals and cabins, caravan and camping sites. Shop open seven days 7am–8pm, tel. (07) 4069 5431; accepts cash, EFTPOS and credit cards.
- Musgrave Roadhouse offers fuel, minor mechanical and tyre repairs and accommodation, including units with two single beds, caravan and camping sites. Shop has limited supplies, serves take-away and eat-in meals and is licensed. Open seven days 7.30am–10pm, tel. (07) 4060 3229; accepts cash, EFTPOS and credit cards.
- Bizant Ranger Station and surrounding section of Lakefield National Park has been returned to local Aboriginal people so despite road signs this is now an Aboriginal outstation and no longer operates as a ranger station.
- Tourist brochures: *Cooktown Visitor Guide*; *Cooktown Town Stroll and Walking Tracks*, which includes town map.
- QPWS guide: *Lakefield National Park*.
- Lakefield National Park wetlands attract large numbers of waterbirds so pack a bird identification book and binoculars.

Description

Departing historic Cooktown, the route follows Battle Camp Road westwards to the vast Lakefield National Park and rambling Old Laura homestead, crossing a number of creeks and rivers – take care while negotiating the wide Normanby and Laura rivers (both can be impassable until early in the dry season). From Battle Camp Road there are some good views northwards to the coast and to Battle Camp Range in the west.

From Old Laura the Lakefield Road, which can be extremely corrugated in places, takes you past a number of secluded riverside fishing and camping areas on the way to New Laura Ranger Station. Most of the rivers and creeks in the park are fringed by shady paperbarks. The southern section of the park tends to be a little less crowded than the north. Kalpowar Crossing, a wide causeway over the Normanby River with a delightful camping area on the western shore, is near Lakefield Ranger Station. It is advisable to book ahead if you want to stay here. Keen anglers can throw in a line on the Normanby close to the crossing, but remember to be crocodile-wise – there have been numerous sightings of crocs in this area. Kalpowar Crossing also provides access north to Bathurst Head and Cape Melville National Park.

Shortly after Kalpowar Crossing there is an alternative route option via Seven Mile Waterhole, where there are ten camping areas. The main route passes lagoons covered with waterlilies, home to waterbirds such as herons and magpie geese, before crossing the North Kennedy River at the bumpy but easy Hann Crossing. There are plenty of shady campsites stretching downstream from the crossing

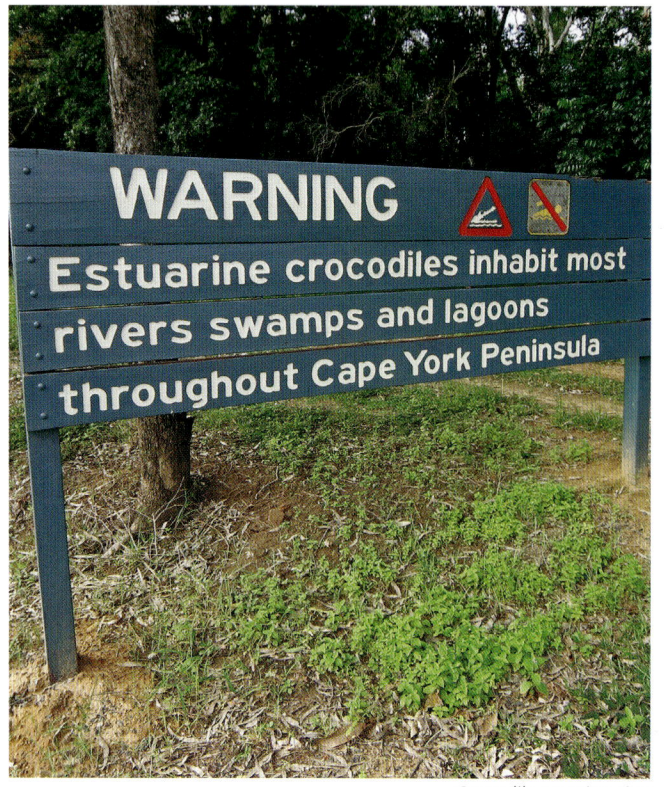

Crocodile warning sign

Normanby River crossing on Battle Camp Road

and the barramundi fishing here is reputedly good. Above the crossing the river is fresh water while downstream below the small falls the river is tidal and the habitat of crocodiles. Fishing enthusiasts with plenty of time can take advantage of a number of remote riverside campsites north-east of Bizant outstation.

After Hann Crossing, which was named for explorer William Hann, the route sweeps in an arc north, traversing the vast treeless Nifold Plain before arriving at the paperbark-lined Saltwater Creek. There is camping here in the vicinity of the crossing. Once out of the national park it is an easy run to Musgrave Roadhouse located on Peninsula Developmental Road.

Advice and warnings

- Battle Camp Road and roads within the national park have corrugated stretches and sandy sections. River and creek crossings usually have low water levels or are dry. The track from Lakefield National Park to Musgrave Roadhouse has a gravel surface that is generally maintained. Sections of the park can be closed for management purposes so observe all signs. Contact QPWS Cooktown, tel. (07) 4069 5777, New Laura Ranger Station, tel. (07) 4060 3260, or Lakefield Ranger Station, tel. (07) 4060 3271, to check track conditions.
- Due to poor visibility caused by dust it is recommended you drive with your headlights on. Exercise caution when overtaking and approaching other vehicles as it may be necessary to stop and wait for dust to settle. Always move over or stop for oncoming road trains.
- Watch out for roaming stock as the track passes through sections of unfenced pastoral land.
- Standard road tyres or all-terrain tyres are suitable. It is advisable to carry two spare tyres. Roads can be heavily corrugated so lower tyre pressure for personal comfort and to avoid damaging the track.
- Towing off-road trailers and off-road caravans is possible but ensure they are well prepared for corrugations.
- Camping is at designated sites only. Light campfires in built fireplaces or existing fire sites.
- Drinking water is not available at any campsites except Musgrave so carry enough for your own needs.
- Rubbish bins are not provided in the national parks so please take your rubbish with you.
- Carry cash as phone lines and/or power systems for credit card and EFTPOS facilities can at times be down.
- Saltwater and freshwater crocodiles inhabit the waters of the national park. There is no swimming in the park.
- Mosquitoes and sandflies are prevalent so carry plenty of good insect repellent.

CAPE YORK PENINSULA

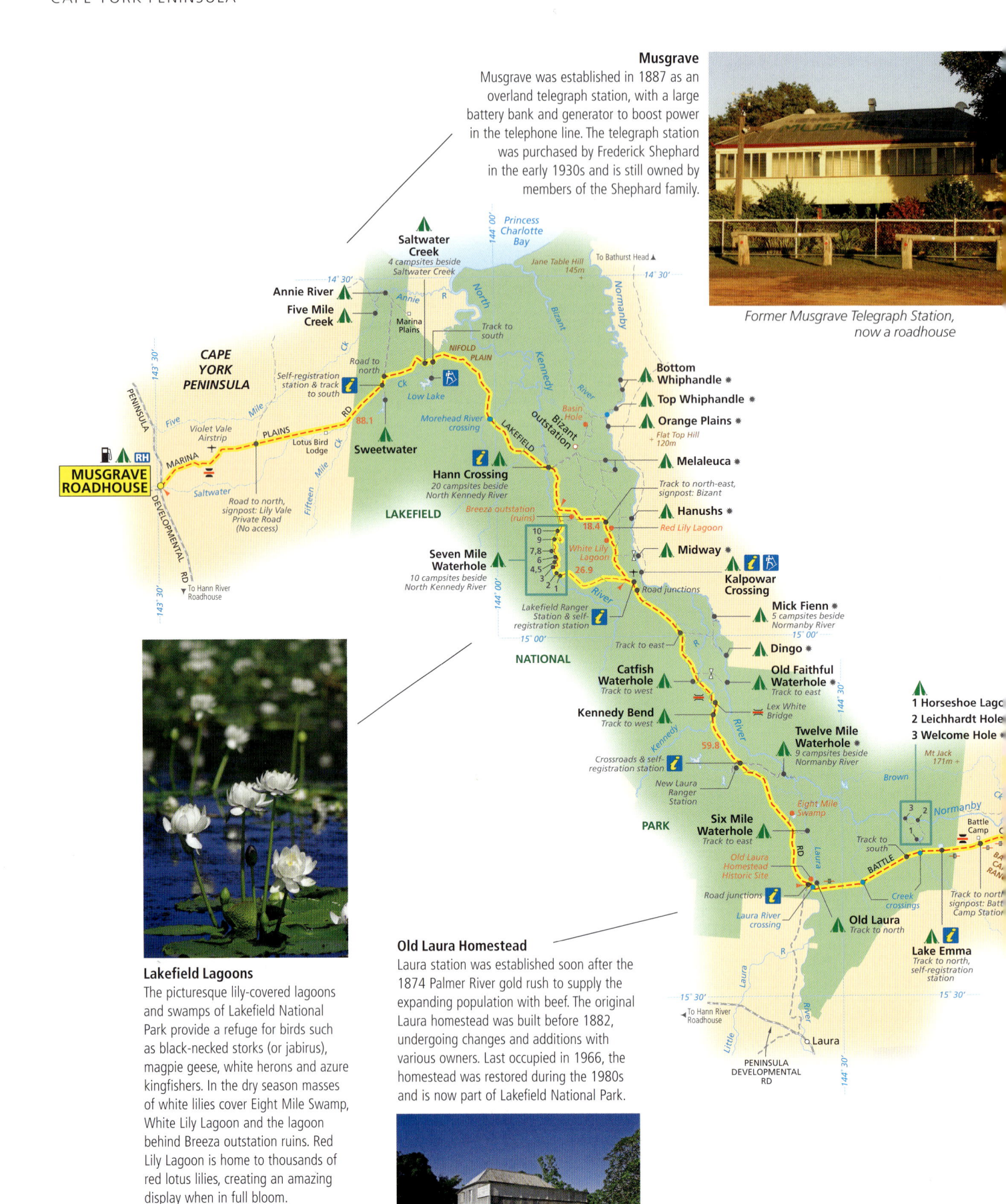

Musgrave
Musgrave was established in 1887 as an overland telegraph station, with a large battery bank and generator to boost power in the telephone line. The telegraph station was purchased by Frederick Shephard in the early 1930s and is still owned by members of the Shephard family.

Former Musgrave Telegraph Station, now a roadhouse

Lakefield Lagoons
The picturesque lily-covered lagoons and swamps of Lakefield National Park provide a refuge for birds such as black-necked storks (or jabirus), magpie geese, white herons and azure kingfishers. In the dry season masses of white lilies cover Eight Mile Swamp, White Lily Lagoon and the lagoon behind Breeza outstation ruins. Red Lily Lagoon is home to thousands of red lotus lilies, creating an amazing display when in full bloom.

Old Laura Homestead
Laura station was established soon after the 1874 Palmer River gold rush to supply the expanding population with beef. The original Laura homestead was built before 1882, undergoing changes and additions with various owners. Last occupied in 1966, the homestead was restored during the 1980s and is now part of Lakefield National Park.

Campsite Facilities

	Toilets	Disabled access	4WD access only	Off-road trailer	Off-road caravan	Drinking water	Fee payable	Ranger patrolled	BBQ/fireplace	Campfires prohibited	Picnic tables	Shelter shed	No rubbish disposal	Public phone	Shower	Bushwalking	Swimming	Swimming not advised	Fishing	Canoeing	Dogs allowed
Annie River		•	•			•	•										•	•			
Catfish Waterhole		•	•			•												•	•		
Five Mile Creek		•				•	•											•	•		
Hann Crossing	•	•	•			•	•											•	•		
Kalpowar Crossing	•	•	•			•	•	•						•	•			•	•		
Kennedy Bend		•	•			•												•	•		
Lake Emma		•	•			•	•											•	•		
Musgrave Roadhouse	•	•		•	•	•	•	•	•				•	•	•						•
Normanby River*																					
Old Laura		•	•	•		•	•											•	•		
Saltwater Creek		•	•			•	•											•	•		
Seven Mile Waterhole		•	•			•	•											•	•		
Six Mile Waterhole		•				•	•											•	•		
Sweetwater		•	•			•	•											•	•		

*Normanby River listing here relates to all campsites with an asterisk on map opposite.

Cook's Town

In 1770, Captain James Cook's *Endeavour* struck the Great Barrier Reef, requiring a massive effort by the ship's crew to refloat the vessel. Seeking shelter and safety at the mouth of a river, which Cook subsequently named after his ship, the *Endeavour* was beached, repairs carried out and botanical specimens collected. After 47 days Cook set sail in the newly repaired vessel, heading north through the treacherous reef and naming the peninsula Cape York. A little over 100 years later, in 1873, Cook's Town was established when gold was found on the Palmer River. Today the town boasts many memorials to its famous visitor: a plaque on the waterfront commemorates the landing site; a museum houses Cook treasures, diaries, charts and discarded cannons; and at the annual Cooktown Discovery Festival, held on the banks of the Endeavour River, Cook's landing is celebrated with a re-enactment.

Captain Cook statue in Cooktown

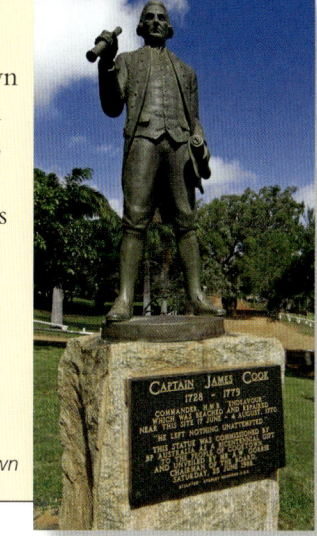

Cooktown

Cooktown is the gateway to Cape York and a frontier settlement enmeshed in gold rush and pioneer history. The wild mining town of the 1870s supported 37 pubs, but now relies on fishing, tourism and three hotels.

Permits and bookings

- No permits required to travel this route.
- Camping permits are required and fees are payable within the national park. Permits obtainable and fees payable at self-registration stations throughout the park. The following self-registration stations are those recommended for the campgrounds that follow in brackets. Where a reservation board exists, be sure to fill in the details required. *Lake Emma* (Lake Emma, Horseshoe Lagoon, Leichhardt Hole, Welcome Hole, Old Laura, Six Mile Waterhole); *New Laura Ranger Station* and reservation board (Twelve Mile Waterhole, Kennedy Bend, Old Faithful Waterhole, Catfish Waterhole, Dingo, Mick Fienn); *Lakefield Ranger Station* and reservation board (Kalpowar Crossing, Midway, Hanushs, Melaleuca, Seven Mile Waterhole, Hann Crossing, Orange Plains, Top Whiphandle, Bottom Whiphandle); *Sweetwater Lake* (Saltwater Creek, Annie River, Five Mile Creek, Sweetwater).
- Advance bookings are possible for camping areas within Lakefield National Park. Contact Lakefield Ranger Station, tel. (07) 4060 3271, with campground name and dates.
- Maximum stay of three weeks at camping areas within Lakefield National Park.
- Bookings recommended for cabins at Endeavour Falls Tourist Park, tel. (07) 4069 5431.
- Bookings recommended for units at Musgrave Roadhouse, tel. (07) 4060 3229.
- Recreational fishing is permitted within the national park. Fishing licence not required but bag and size limits apply. Contact Queensland Fisheries, tel. (07) 3225 1843, or visit their website (www.dpi.qld.gov.au/fishweb), to check restrictions and regulations.

ROUTE DIRECTIONS

▼ 0.0 km — Zero trip meter in Cooktown along Charlotte St with SP: Green St, on left, and post office and Cook Shire Council office on right. Proceed in southerly direction along Charlotte St.

Cooktown. Post office on left and SP: Green St, on right. **112.2 km ▲**

GPS S:15 27.957 E:145 14.994
UTM 55L 312240E 8289372N

(1.8 km)

▼ 1.8 km — Road junction. CSA. Road on right SP: Cemetery.

Road on right leads short distance to Cooktown's historic cemetery with poignant memorials to pioneer children, Chinese from the Palmer goldfields and shipwreck victims.

Road junction. CSA. Road on left SP: Cemetery. **110.4 km ▲**

(9.3 km)

▼ 11.1 km — Bridge over SP: Endeavour River.

Bridge over SP: Endeavour River. **101.1 km ▲**

(19.6 km)

▼ 30.7 km — Bridge over SP: Isabella Creek.

Bridge over SP: Isabella Creek. **81.5 km ▲**

(1.9 km)

▼ 32.6 km — SP: Endeavour Falls Tourist Park, on right. CSA.

Endeavour Falls are located a short walk from behind tourist park office. Call into office as a courtesy prior to walking to falls.

SP: Endeavour Falls Tourist Park, on left. CSA. **79.6 km ▲**

(4.4 km)

▼ 37.0 km — Road junction. TL. SP: Laura 100/Lakefield National Park 55. Road SO SP: 10 Hope Vale.

T-junction. TR. SP: Cooktown 35. Road on left SP: 10 Hope Vale. **75.2 km ▲**

GPS S:15 19.976 E:145 02.090
UTM 55L 289024E 8303893N

(5.5 km)

▼ 42.5 km — Isabella Creek crossing.

Isabella Falls are to left of crossing.

Isabella Creek crossing. **69.7 km ▲**

(2.7 km)

▼ 45.2 km — Road junction. CSA. SP: Battle Camp. Track on right SP: McIvor Valley.

Road junction. CSA. SP: Cooktown. Track on left SP: McIvor Valley. **67.0 km ▲**

(19.1 km)

Termite mound on the Lakefield Road

COOKTOWN ◄► MUSGRAVE ROADHOUSE

Early morning mist on Horseshoe Lagoon

▼ **64.3 km** Road junction. CSA. Track on right SP: Henwood Road.

    Road junction. CSA. Track on left SP: Henwood Road.   47.9 km ▲

(0.8 km)

▼ **65.1 km** Cross SP: Normanby River.

    Cross SP: Normanby River.   47.1 km ▲

GPS S:15 17.405 E:144 50.670
UTM 55L 268536E 8308441N

(17.5 km)

▼ **82.6 km** Road junction. CSA. Track on right SP: Battle Camp Station.

    Road junction. CSA. Track on left SP: Battle Camp Station.   29.6 km ▲

(5.6 km)

▼ **88.2 km** Enter SP: Lakefield National Park.

    Exit national park.   24.0 km ▲

(0.6 km)

▼ **88.8 km** Road junction. CSA. Track on right SP: Lake Emma Camping Area 600 m.

Track on right leads 0.4 km to **Lake Emma camping area**, a small bush campsite among paperbarks beside lake.

    Road junction. CSA. Track on left SP: Lake Emma Camping Area 600 m.   23.4 km ▲

GPS S:15 18.021 E:144 38.857
UTM 55L 247396E 8307085N

(3.0 km)

▼ **91.8 km** Road junction. CSA. Track on right.

Track on right leads 2.2 km to **Horseshoe Lagoon camping area** with bush campsites scattered around edge of scenic lagoon, a further 4.5 km to **Leichhardt Hole camping area**, a small sandy site located above river, and 6.5 km to **Welcome Hole camping area**, a small site at end of track by waterhole in river.

    Road junction. CSA. Track on left.   20.4 km ▲

(0.5 km)

▼ **92.3 km** Creek crossing.

    Creek crossing.   19.9 km ▲

(2.5 km)

▼ **94.8 km** Track junction. CSA. Track on left.

    Track junction. CSA. Track on right.   17.4 km ▲

(8.0 km)

▼ **102.8 km** Creek crossing.

    Creek crossing.   9.4 km ▲

(8.3 km)

▼ **111.1 km** Cross SP: Laura River.

    Cross SP: Laura River.   1.1 km ▲

GPS S:15 20.900 E:144 27.409
UTM 55L 226959E 8301542N

(0.2 km)

▼ **111.3 km** Road junction. CSA. Track on right.

Track on right leads 0.1 km to **Old Laura camping area**, with bush camping among shady trees.

    Road junction. CSA. Track on left.   0.9 km ▲

(0.4 km)

CAPE YORK PENINSULA

Gnarled tree roots exposed by erosion

▼ **111.7 km** Road junction. CSA. Track on right SP: Old Laura Homestead Historic Site Parking Area.

Track on right leads 0.3 km to Old Laura Homestead Historic Site and short walk to homestead and other buildings.

Y-junction. KR. SP: Cooktown 110. Track on left SP: Old Laura Homestead Historic Site Parking Area.   0.5 km ▲

(0.5 km)

▼ **112.2 km** T-junction.

Zero trip meter at Y-junction. KL. SP: Old Laura 1 km/Cooktown 110 km. This is Battle Camp Rd. Road on right SP: Laura 25 km.   0.0 km ▲

```
GPS    S:15 20.880 E:144 26.929
UTM    55L 226099E 8301568N
```

▼ **0.0 km** Zero trip meter at T-junction. TR. SP: New Laura Ranger Station 25 km/Musgrave via Lakefield 172 km. Road on left SP: Laura 25 km.

Y-junction.   59.8 km ▲

(9.0 km)

▼ **9.0 km** Road junction. CSA. Track on right SP: Six Mile Waterhole 3 km.

Road on right leads 2.9 km to **Six Mile Waterhole camping area**, a small sandy spot suitable for 1 or 2 campsites above the bank of the waterhole.

Road junction. CSA. Track on left SP: Six Mile Waterhole 3 km.   50.8 km ▲

(1.8 km)

▼ **10.8 km** Road junction. CSA. Track on right SP: Eight Mile Swamp 1 km.

Track on right leads 1.7 km to Eight Mile Swamp, a large, scenic swamp with masses of beautiful white waterlilies and birdlife.

Road junction. CSA. Track on left SP: Eight Mile Swamp 1 km.   49.0 km ▲

(13.0 km)

▼ **23.8 km** Crossroads. CSA. Track on right SP: Twelve Mile Waterhole 15 km. Track on left SP: New Laura Ranger Station. Self-registration station on left.

Track on right leads 8.5 km to start of **Twelve Mile Waterhole camping area**, with 9 large individual campsites shaded by paperbark trees stretching out along the banks of the Normanby River.

Crossroads. CSA. Track on right SP: New Laura Ranger Station. Track on left SP: Twelve Mile Waterhole 15 km.   36.0 km ▲

```
GPS    S:15 10.635 E:144 21.090
UTM    55L 215414E 8320346N
```

(8.9 km)

▼ **32.7 km** Road junction. CSA. Track on left SP: Kennedy Bend Camping Area.

Track on left leads short distance to **Kennedy Bend camping area**, with 4 bush campsites on the riverbank.

Road junction. CSA. Track on right SP: Kennedy Bend Camping Area.   27.1 km ▲

(1.8 km)

▼ **34.5 km** Bridge.

Bridge.   25.3 km ▲

(0.3 km)

▼ **34.8 km** Cross SP: Lex White Bridge, over SP: Sandy Creek.

Cross SP: Lex White Bridge, over SP: Sandy Creek.   25.0 km ▲

(1.7 km)

▼ **36.5 km** Bridge over SP: Kennedy River.

Bridge over SP: Kennedy River.   23.3 km ▲

```
GPS    S:15 04.829 E:144 18.622
UTM    55L 210860E 8331006N
```

(2.6 km)

▼ **39.1 km** Road junction. CSA. Track on left SP: Catfish Waterhole 1 km.

Track on left leads 1.2 km to **Catfish Waterhole camping area**, a large shady site beside Catfish Creek.

Road junction. CSA. Track on right SP: Catfish Waterhole 1 km.   20.7 km ▲

(1.4 km)

▼ **40.5 km** Road junction. CSA. Track on right SP: Old Faithful Waterhole 6 km.

Track on right leads 5.7 km to **Old Faithful Waterhole camping area**, with 3 large individual well-shaded sites along a large waterhole in the Normanby River.

Road junction. CSA. Track on left SP: Old Faithful Waterhole 6 km.   19.3 km ▲

(7.1 km)

COOKTOWN ◄► MUSGRAVE ROADHOUSE

▼ 47.6 km   Road junction. CSA. Track on right SP: Mick Fienn Camp Area 9 km.

Track on right leads 5.4 km to T-junction, from where track on left leads 3.6 km to Mick Fienn campsites 1 and 2 and 2.7 km to Mick Fienn campsites 3, 4 and 5. **Mick Fienn campsites** are well-shaded sites along Normanby River. At T-junction, track on right leads 4.4 km to **Dingo camping area**, a small site located among trees beside a waterhole.

Road junction. CSA. Track on left SP: Mick Fienn Camp Area 9 km.   12.2 km ▲

(9.5 km)

▼ 57.1 km   Y-junction. KL. SP: Lakefield Ranger Base 1 km/Musgrave 113 km. Track on right SP: Kalpowar Crossing Camping Area.

Track on right leads 3.2 km to **Kalpowar Crossing camping area** with 12 large, grass-covered and well-shaded sites, mainly suitable for tent-based camping.

Track junction. CSA. Track on left.   2.7 km ▲

GPS   S:14 56.304 E:144 12.283
UTM   55L 199296E 8346595N

(0.2 km)

▼ 57.3 km   Road junction. CSA. Track on right.

Y-junction. KR. Track on left SP: Kalpowar Crossing Camping Area 3 km.   2.5 km ▲

(1.3 km)

▼ 58.6 km   SP: Ranger Station, on right. This is Lakefield Ranger Station and self-registration station. CSA. SP: Bizant Ranger Station 28 km/Hann Crossing 25 km/Musgrave 112 km.

Bizant Ranger Station is now an Aboriginal outstation. See Other useful information.

SP: Ranger Station, and self-registration station on left. CSA. SP: Laura 85 km/New Laura Ranger Station 35 km.   1.2 km ▲

GPS   S:14 55.569 E:144 11.955
UTM   55L 198691E 8347944N

(1.2 km)

▼ 59.8 km   Road junction.

Zero trip meter at road junction. CSA. Track on right SP: North Kennedy Seven Mile 12 km.   0.0 km ▲

Track on right is where alternative route option via Seven Mile Waterhole joins.

GPS   S:14 55.312 E:144 11.365
UTM   55L 197626E 8348405N

▼ 0.0 km   Zero trip meter at road junction. CSA. Track on left SP: North Kennedy Seven Mile 12 km.

Track on left is alternative route option via Seven Mile Waterhole (see route option notes following the 18.4-km reading on page 272).

Road junction.   18.4 km ▲

(4.5 km)

▼ 4.5 km   Road junction. CSA. Track on right SP: Midway Camping Area.

Track on right leads 3.7 km to **Midway camping area** with 1 shaded sandy site.

Road junction. CSA. Track on left SP: Midway Camping Area.   13.9 km ▲

(1.1 km)

▼ 5.6 km   Road junction. CSA. Track on right SP: Hanushs Camping Area 8 km/Melaleuca Camping Area 16 km.

Track on right leads 7.5 km to **Hanushs camping area** with 3 well-shaded sites set high above the river, and a further 11.4 km to **Melaleuca camping area** with 4 sites set well apart along the river.

Road junction. CSA. Track on left SP: Hanushs Camping Area 8 km/Melaleuca Camping Area 16 km.   12.8 km ▲

(1.8 km)

Fishing on the Normanby River

271

CAPE YORK PENINSULA

Magpie geese at Red Lily Lagoon

▼ 7.4 km   SP: White Lily Lagoon on left. CSA.

White Lily Lagoon is a large lagoon with masses of lilies.

         SP: White Lily Lagoon on right. CSA.   11.0 km ▲

(1.0 km)

▼ 8.4 km   Road junction. CSA. Track on right SP: Red Lily Lagoon.

Track on right leads 1.0 km to carpark and walk to viewing platform over Red Lily Lagoon. When red lotus lilies are in bloom this lagoon is a magical sight.

         Road junction. CSA. Track on left SP: Red Lily Lagoon.   10.0 km ▲

GPS	S:14 51.324 E:144 09.814
UTM	55L 194749E 8355729N

(1.6 km)

▼ 10.0 km   Y-junction. KL. SP: Hann Crossing 15 km/ Musgrave 100 km. Road on right SP: Bizant Ranger Base 14 km.

         Road junction. CSA. Road on left SP: Bizant Ranger Base 14 km.   8.4 km ▲

(4.4 km)

▼ 14.4 km   Road junction. CSA. SP: Hann Crossing Camping Area. Track on left.

         Road junction. CSA. SP: Lakefield Ranger Base 14 km. Track on right.   4.0 km ▲

(1.7 km)

▼ 16.1 km   Road junction. CSA. Track on left SP: Breeza.

Track on left leads short distance to Breeza outstation ruins located on a large lagoon.

         Road junction. CSA. Track on right SP: Breeza.   2.3 km ▲

(2.3 km)

▼ 18.4 km   Road junction.

Track on left is where route option via Seven Mile Waterhole joins. Main route directions continue after end of route option notes.

         Zero trip meter at road junction. CSA. Track on right.   0.0 km ▲

Track on right is alternative route option via Seven Mile Waterhole (see below).

GPS	S:14 49.407 E:144 05.494
UTM	55L 186949E 8359167N

▶   **ROUTE OPTION: Seven Mile Waterhole**

▼ 0.0 km   Zero trip meter at road junction (see 59.8-km reading on page 271). Proceed west along track SP: North Kennedy Seven Mile 12 km.

         T-junction. TR and join main route notes at the 0.0-km reverse direction reading on page 271.   26.9 km ▲

(12.1 km)

▼ 12.1 km   Campsite 1 on left. CSA.

This is the first of 10 numbered sites comprising **Seven Mile Waterhole camping area**.

         Campsite 1 on right. CSA.   14.8 km ▲

(0.3 km)

▼ 12.4 km   Campsite 2 on left. CSA.

         Campsite 2 on right. CSA.   14.5 km ▲

(1.5 km)

▼ 13.9 km   Track junction. CSA. Track on left.

Track on left leads 0.5 km to Campsite 3.

         Track junction. CSA. Track on right.   13.0 km ▲

(1.1 km)

COOKTOWN ◄► MUSGRAVE ROADHOUSE

▼ 15.0 km	Campsite 4 on left. CSA.		
	Campsite 4 on right. CSA.	11.9 km ▲	
(0.2 km)			
▼ 15.2 km	Track junction. CSA. Track on left. Track on left leads 0.5 km to Campsite 5.		
	Track junction. CSA. Track on right.	11.7 km ▲	
(0.8 km)			
▼ 16.0 km	Campsite 6 on left. CSA.		
	Campsite 6 on right. CSA.	10.9 km ▲	
(0.9 km)			
▼ 16.9 km	Track junction. CSA. Track on left. Track on left leads 0.1 km to Campsite 7.		
	Track junction. CSA. Track on right.	10.0 km ▲	
(0.4 km)			
▼ 17.3 km	Track junction. CSA. Track on left. Track on left leads 0.3 km to Campsite 8.		
	Track junction. CSA. Track on right.	9.6 km ▲	
(1.7 km)			
▼ 19.0 km	Campsite 9 on left. CSA.		
	Campsite 9 on right. CSA.	7.9 km ▲	
(3.2 km)			
▼ 22.2 km	Campsite 10 on left. CSA.		
	Campsite 10 on right. CSA.	4.7 km ▲	
(2.2 km)			
▼ 24.4 km	T-junction. TL.		
	Track junction. TR.	2.5 km ▲	
	GPS S:14 50.268 E:144 05.584 **UTM** 55L 187131E 8357580N		
(1.9 km)			
▼ 26.3 km	T-junction. TR.		
	Track junction. TL.	0.6 km ▲	
	GPS S:14 49.429 E:144 05.180 **UTM** 55L 186386E 8359119N		
(0.6 km)			
▼ 26.9 km	T-junction. TL northwards to join main route notes below.		
	Zero trip meter at road junction. TR.	0.0 km ▲	
◄	**END ROUTE OPTION**		
▼ 0.0 km	Zero trip meter at road junction. CSA. Track on left is where alternative route option via Seven Mile Waterhole joins.		
	Road junction.	88.7 km ▲	
	Track on right is alternative route option via Seven Mile Waterhole (see above). Main route directions continue preceding route option notes above.		
(6.9 km)			
▼ 6.9 km	T-junction. TL. SP: Musgrave 85 km. Road on right. Road on right leads 17.4 km to **Orange Plains camping area**, a further 1.8 km to **Top Whiphandle camping area**, and a further 5.3 km to **Bottom Whiphandle camping area**, all of which have bush campsites scattered along the river. After turning left at T-junction, track on right leads to **Hann Crossing campsites 1–4**, which are bush campsites scattered along the North Kennedy River.		
	Road junction. TR. SP: Lakefield Ranger Base 25 km/Laura via Lakefield 110 km/Cooktown via Battle Camp 205 km.	81.8 km ▲	
	GPS S:14 45.947 E:144 04.916 **UTM** 55L 185828E 8365539N		
(0.2 km)			
▼ 7.1 km	Road junction. CSA across Hann Crossing over North Kennedy River. Track on left SP: Campsites 5–7. Track on left leads short distance to **Hann Crossing campsites 5–7**, all situated along banks of the North Kennedy River.		
	Road junction over Hann Crossing. Track on right to campsites.	81.6 km ▲	
(0.4 km)			
▼ 7.5 km	Road junction. CSA. SP: Musgrave 85 km. Track on right SP: Hann Crossing Camping Area Campsites 8–20. Track on right runs parallel to North Kennedy River to **Hann Crossing campsites 8–20**, all of which are located above banks of the river, some with excellent shade and good access to the river for fishing.		
	Road junction. CSA. SP: North Kennedy River/Hann Crossing Camping Area. Track on left SP: Hann Crossing Campsites 8–20.	81.2 km ▲	
(5.0 km)			
▼ 12.5 km	Creek crossing.		
	Creek crossing.	76.2 km ▲	
(7.8 km)			
▼ 20.3 km	Cross SP: Morehead River.		
	Cross SP: Morehead River.	68.4 km ▲	
	GPS S:14 41.810 E:143 59.498 **UTM** 54L 822200E 8373070N		
(5.7 km)			
▼ 26.0 km	Cross SP: Nifold Plain. Nifold Plain is large treeless grass plain dotted with termite mounds. On right, views across to Jane Table Hill to the north-east.		
	Southern edge of Nifold Plain.	62.7 km ▲	
(8.9 km)			
▼ 34.9 km	Western edge of Nifold Plain.		
	Cross SP: Nifold Plain.	53.8 km ▲	
(1.9 km)			
▼ 36.8 km	Road junction. CSA. Track on left SP: Low Lake 3 km. Track on left leads 2.5 km to small parking area and short walk to spectacular blue waters of Low Lake.		
	Road junction. CSA. Track on right SP: Low Lake 3 km.	51.9 km ▲	
(1.2 km)			
▼ 38.0 km	Road junction. CSA. Track on left SP: Saltwater Creek Campsites 1–2 150 M. Track on left leads 0.2 km to **Saltwater Creek campsite 1** and a further 0.3 km to **campsite 2**, both well-shaded spots located above creek bank.		
	Road junction. CSA. Track on right SP: Saltwater Creek Campsites 1–2 150 M.	50.7 km ▲	
(0.2 km)			

CAPE YORK PENINSULA

Hann Crossing on the North Kennedy River

▼ **38.2 km** Causeway over Saltwater Creek.

Causeway over Saltwater Creek. 50.5 km ▲

GPS S:14 37.095 E:143 53.905
UTM 54L 812264E 8381902N

(0.1 km)

▼ **38.3 km** Road junction. CSA. Track on right SP: Campsite 3–4 1 km.

Track on right leads 1.2 km to **Saltwater Creek campsite 3** and a further 0.3 km to **campsite 4**, both located beside Saltwater Creek with good shade.

Road junction. CSA. Track on left SP: Campsite 3–4 1 km. 50.4 km ▲

(8.0 km)

▼ **46.3 km** T-junction. TL. SP: Musgrave. This is Marina Plains Road. Road on right.

Road on right leads 11.8 km to road junction. TL here and a further 1.9 km is **Annie River camping area** on right, an open campsite beside the river. Continue past Annie River camping area for 2.6 km to a track junction. At track junction KL and follow along river for 2.7 km to small bush campsite among paperbark trees beside large waterhole in the river. This is **Five Mile Creek camping area**. Access to Five Mile Creek camping area is not suitable for off-road trailers.

Road junction. TR. SP: Bizant Ranger Station 48 km/Lakefield Ranger Station 67 km/Hann Crossing Camping Area 42 km. 42.4 km ▲

Bizant Ranger Station is now an Aboriginal outstation. See Other useful information.

GPS S:14 38.117 E:143 50.252
UTM 54L 805677E 8380099N

(1.4 km)

▼ **47.7 km** Road junction. CSA. Track on left SP: Sweetwater Camping Area 2.5 km. QPWS information and self-registration station on right.

Track on left leads 2.0 km to **Sweetwater camping area** with 2 campsites located beside a large lake surrounded by paperbark trees.

Road junction. CSA. Track on right SP: Sweetwater Camping Area 2.5 km. QPWS information and self-registration station on left. 41.0 km ▲

(5.4 km)

▼ **53.1 km** Exit Lakefield National Park.

Enter SP: Lakefield National Park. 35.6 km ▲

(17.7 km)

▼ **70.8 km** Road junction. CSA. Road on right SP: Lily Vale Private Rd/No Access.

Road junction. CSA. Road on left SP: Lily Vale Private Rd/No Access. 17.9 km ▲

(17.9 km)

▼ **88.7 km** Crossroads. Musgrave Roadhouse opposite.

Road on right, SP: Coen, is start of trek section 2. Road on left SP: Laura/Lakeland.

Zero trip meter at crossroads at Musgrave Roadhouse. Proceed east along SP: Marina Plains Road. Road to north SP: Coen. Road to south SP: Laura/Lakefield. 0.0 km ▲

GPS S:14 46.903 E:143 30.287
UTM 54L 769629E 8364312N

REVERSE DIRECTIONS START

274

2 MUSGRAVE RH ◄► BRAMWELL JUNCTION 341.7 KM

Start point
Musgrave Roadhouse

Road atlas
360 D5

Total distance
595.1 km (includes route-directed side trip)

Standard
Easy

Time
1–2 days

Longest distance no PD (includes all options)
478.0 km (Archer River Roadhouse to Bramwell Junction)

Topographic maps
Auslig 1:250 000 series: *Ebagoola*; *Coen*; *Cape Weymouth*

Other useful information
- Musgrave Roadhouse offers fuel, minor mechanical and tyre repairs and accommodation, including units with two single beds, caravan and camping sites. Shop has limited supplies, serves take-away and eat-in meals and is licensed. Open seven days 7.30am–10pm, tel. (07) 4060 3229; accepts cash, EFTPOS and credit cards.
- Archer River Roadhouse offers petrol, diesel, ice, limited grocery supplies, take-away and eat-in meals and is licensed. Accommodation includes four units and caravan and camping sites. Open seven days 7am–10pm during peak visitor season, tel. (07) 4060 3266; accepts cash, EFTPOS and credit cards.
- Moreton Telegraph Station offers mechanical and tyre repairs, welding, some trailer spares and a portable welding and vehicle recovery service. Shop has basic supplies, ice, meals, public telephone and public toilets. Accommodation options include safari tents and camping and unpowered caravan sites. Open seven days 7am–10pm, tel. (07) 4060 3360; accepts cash only.
- Bramwell station offers minor mechanical repairs, tyre repairs and welding. Shop has basic supplies, take-away and eat-in meals and is licensed. Accommodation options include donga and motel-style units and camping and unpowered caravan sites. Also on offer is a range of self-guided drives, limited hunting and several remote bush campsites, tel. (07) 4060 3300; accepts cash and credit cards.
- Bramwell Junction Roadhouse offers fuel, mechanical and tyre repairs and welding. Shop has basic supplies and take-away meals. Open seven days 7am–8.30pm, tel. (07) 4060 3230; accepts cash, EFTPOS and credit cards.
- Lockhart River retail store offers petrol, diesel, groceries and ice. Open Monday–Thursday 8.30am–12.30pm and 1.30–4pm, Friday 8.30am–12.30pm and 1.30–3pm and Saturday 8.30am–10.30pm, tel. (07) 4060 7192; accepts cash, EFTPOS and credit cards.
- QPWS guide: *Iron Range National Park*.
- *A Short History of Coen. Cape York* by Betty Clark, available from Coen stores.
- Iron Range National Park has a variety of birds and butterflies so pack identification guides.

Description
The route between the roadhouses at Musgrave and Bramwell Junction is relatively straightforward on gravel roads of generally good to fair quality. Covering a little over 340 kilometres, this leg, along the Peninsula Developmental Road and part of the Telegraph Road, can be comfortably tackled in a day. However, you will need more time to enjoy the side trip (four-wheel drive only) out to Iron Range National Park and Chili Beach, which are the highlights of this section.

The sands of Chili Beach are fringed with coconut palms

Peninsula Developmental Road north of Musgrave Roadhouse

From Musgrave Roadhouse, which is the only remaining intact example of a Cape York telegraph station, the route heads north, following the path of the old telegraph line that once ran between Cooktown and the Cape. Just over 100 kilometres north of Musgrave is the friendly town of Coen, with a good bush camping area just to the north of town beside the Coen River. Coen was named after Jan Pieterzoon Coen, a one-time governor of the Dutch East Indies.

In the extensive Mungkan Kandju National Park there is remote bush camping, or you can camp further north at the Archer River Roadhouse or on the Archer River near the crossing. Vegetation on this part of the Cape includes open woodlands and grasslands, which support stock from the large cattle stations. Paperbark-fringed rivers and creeks support prolific birdlife, while many species of raptor are commonly seen soaring high above the open forests.

If you take the side trip to Iron Range National Park, Portland Roads Road is generally easy as far as the Wenlock River crossing, but then begins to deteriorate and offers a slow and bumpy ride for much of its remaining length. There is some good bush camping beside the Wenlock, which is also a good spot to catch a glimpse of a cuscus, one of Cape York's nocturnal marsupials. The ruins of Batavia Goldfields, including mining relics, are on the eastern bank of the river and are worth a visit – gold was mined here from the 1930s until World War II. Further on is a wide but generally easy crossing of the Pascoe River. At the western boundary of Iron Range National Park a lookout platform provides views across to Mount Tozer, which features in an interesting Aboriginal Dreamtime story relating to the creation of the cassowary and emu.

Just after Mount Tozer the track passes through a stand of dense lowland rainforest, where the red volcanic soil of the track is often slippery and at times makes for some interesting driving. Near the picturesque and popular camping destination of Chili Beach is the tiny settlement of Portland Roads, home to approximately 40 people. In the 1930s it was a busy landing place for supplies destined for the goldfields at Iron Range then was used as a staging post for US troops during World War II. At the time the road from the jetty to the Iron Range airstrip was sealed. The bitumen road is long gone but a few small sections remain, along with a number of old bridges. Fuel and supplies in this area are available from the Aboriginal community at Lockhart River.

Fifteen kilometres north of the side trip turn-off, the Peninsula Developmental Road veers off to the bauxite-mining town of Weipa, around 140 kilometres away on the west coast of the Cape. This trek continues north via the Telegraph Road. The track surface is generally fair but the road is much narrower and it is best to slow down.

You cross the Wenlock River via a new high-level bridge before arriving at Old Moreton Telegraph Station. Camping is possible here or there is the option of accommodation in fully set-up safari-style tents. From the telegraph station it is 40 kilometres to Bramwell Junction Roadhouse.

Advice and warnings
- Peninsula Developmental Road has a maintained gravel surface, with corrugations, dust holes and sandy sections, but is generally suitable for conventional vehicles. There are a number of dips, causeways and creek crossings, some with sharp entries. Contact RACQ road reporting service, tel. 1300 130 595, and/or roadhouses en route, for current road conditions.
- Track to Iron Range National Park is maintained, but can be corrugated with wash-outs, dust holes and sandy sections. River and creek crossings generally have low water levels or are dry. East of Tozers Gap the track is red-clay based and becomes extremely slippery and eroded with rain. Contact QPWS Iron Range Ranger Base, tel. (07) 4060 7170, to check park road conditions.
- Due to poor visibility caused by dust it is recommended you drive with your headlights on. Exercise caution when overtaking and approaching other vehicles as it may be necessary to stop and wait for dust to settle. Always move over or stop for oncoming road trains.
- Trek passes through sections of pastoral lease and Aboriginal land so do not deviate from main roads.
- Standard road tyres or all-terrain tyres are suitable. It is advisable to carry two spare tyres. Roads can be heavily corrugated so lower tyre pressure for personal comfort and to avoid damaging the track.
- Towing off-road trailers and off-road caravans is suitable along this trek section but towing off-road caravans to Iron Range National Park is not recommended.
- Camping is at designated sites and at bush campsites noted in the route directions. Campfires are permitted within Iron Range National Park in existing fire sites or built fireplaces. Do not camp under coconut palms.
- There are a number of signposted rubbish pits along the route so please use these. They are at Coen; just north of the bridge over the Archer River; just south and north of Wenlock River; and 1.6 kilometres north of the Chili Beach turn-off en route to Portland Roads.
- Carry cash as phone lines and/or power systems for credit card and EFTPOS facilities are sometimes down.
- Saltwater and freshwater crocodiles inhabit the rivers and coastal waters so swimming is not recommended.
- South-bound travellers must stop at the Coen Information and Inspection Centre, where all fruit, vegetables, plants and artefacts will be inspected for any exotic pests and diseases. For further information contact the centre, tel. (07) 4060 1135.
- Alcohol restrictions apply at the Lockhart River community. Heavy fines apply. Restrictions do not apply to the access road to Iron Range National Park. Ring the Alcohol Management Program information line, tel. 1300 789 000, or visit the websites (www.mcmc.qld.gov.au *or* www.liquor.qld.gov.au/Indigenous/), for current restrictions.
- Mosquitoes and sandflies are prevalent so carry plenty of good insect repellent.

Permits and bookings
- No permits required to travel this route.
- Camping permits are required and fees are payable within the national park. Do this at self-registration station located at Iron Range Ranger Base.
- Bookings recommended for units at Musgrave Roadhouse, tel. (07) 4060 3229; for motel units at Exchange Hotel in Coen, tel. (07) 4060 1133; for units at Archer River Roadhouse, tel. (07) 4060 3266; for safari tents at Old Moreton Telegraph Station, tel. (07) 4060 3360; for dongas and units at Bramwell station, tel. (07) 4060 3300; and for Portland House at Portland Roads, tel. (07) 4060 7193 or (07) 4060 7322.
- Recreational fishing is permitted and a fishing licence is not required but bag and size limits apply. Contact Queensland Fisheries, tel. (07) 3225 1843, or visit their website (www.dpi.qld.gov.au/fishweb), for details.

Driving through the rainforest in Iron Range National Park

CAPE YORK PENINSULA

Green tree ants' nest

ROUTE DIRECTIONS

▼ **0.0 km** — Zero trip meter on Peninsula Developmental Rd with Musgrave Roadhouse on left and SP: Marina Plains Rd, on right. Proceed in northerly direction along Peninsula Developmental Rd towards SP: Coen.

Crossroads at Musgrave. **109.1 km** ▲

Roadhouse on right. Road on left, SP: Marina Plains Rd, is start of Section 1. Road SO SP: Laura 137.

GPS S:14 46.903 E:143 30.287
UTM 54L 769629E 8364312N

(8.8 km)

▼ **8.8 km** — Causeway over SP: Five Mile Creek.

Causeway over SP: Five Mile Creek. **100.3 km** ▲

(40.9 km)

▼ **49.7 km** — Concrete causeway.

Concrete causeway. **59.4 km** ▲

(31.1 km)

▼ **80.8 km** — Road junction. CSA. SP: Coen 27. Road on right SP: Port Stewart 60.

Road on right leads 60 km to Port Stewart, a popular fishing spot with a camping reserve.

Road junction. CSA. SP: 219 Laura. Road on left SP: Port Stewart 60. **28.3 km** ▲

(28.3 km)

▼ **109.1 km** — Road junction in Coen.

Zero trip meter at T-junction in Coen. TL. SP: Laura. Road on right SP: Business Centre. **0.0 km** ▲

GPS S:13 56.718 E:143 11.927
UTM 54L 737556E 8457224N

▼ **0.0 km** — Zero trip meter at road junction in Coen. TR. SP: Weipa/Bamaga 400. Road SO SP: Business Centre.

Road SO leads short distance to business centre of Coen, location of stores, fuel, hotel and caravan park.

T-junction in Coen. **102.8 km** ▲

(1.5 km)

▼ **1.5 km** — Bridge over SP: Coen River.

Bridge over SP: Coen River. **101.3 km** ▲

(1.5 km)

▼ **3.0 km** — Road junction. CSA. Road on right SP: The Bend Camping Area.

Road on right leads 0.1 km to **The Bend camping area**, a picturesque place beside the river.

Road junction. CSA. Road on left SP: The Bend Camping Area. **99.8 km** ▲

GPS S:13 55.454 E:143 11.620
UTM 54L 737025E 8459561N

(19.1 km)

▼ **22.1 km** — Coen Information and Inspection Centre on right.

Parking area on left. North-bound travellers can park here and visit centre to collect free Cape York information pack.

Coen Information and Inspection Centre. **80.7 km** ▲

South-bound traffic must stop for inspection. See Advice and warnings.

(2.8 km)

▼ **24.9 km** — Road junction. CSA. Road on left SP: Rokeby Ranger Station 6 km.

Road junction. CSA. Road on right SP: Rokeby Ranger Station 6 km. **77.9 km** ▲

(16.1 km)

▼ **41.0 km** — Concrete causeway.

Concrete causeway. **61.8 km** ▲

(25.2 km)

▼ **66.2 km** — Road junction. CSA. Road on left.

Road on left leads a short distance to **Archer River Roadhouse** and **campground**, a grass-covered and shady area beside the roadhouse.

Road junction. CSA. Road on right to roadhouse. **36.6 km** ▲

GPS S:13 26.318 E:142 56.544
UTM 54L 710297E 8513528N

(0.5 km)

▼ **66.7 km** — SP: Bill Hansen Bridge, over Archer River.

Bush camping possible in this vicinity.

SP: Bill Hansen Bridge, over Archer River. **36.1 km** ▲

GPS S:13 26.120 E:142 56.682
UTM 54L 710549E 8513891N

(2.5 km)

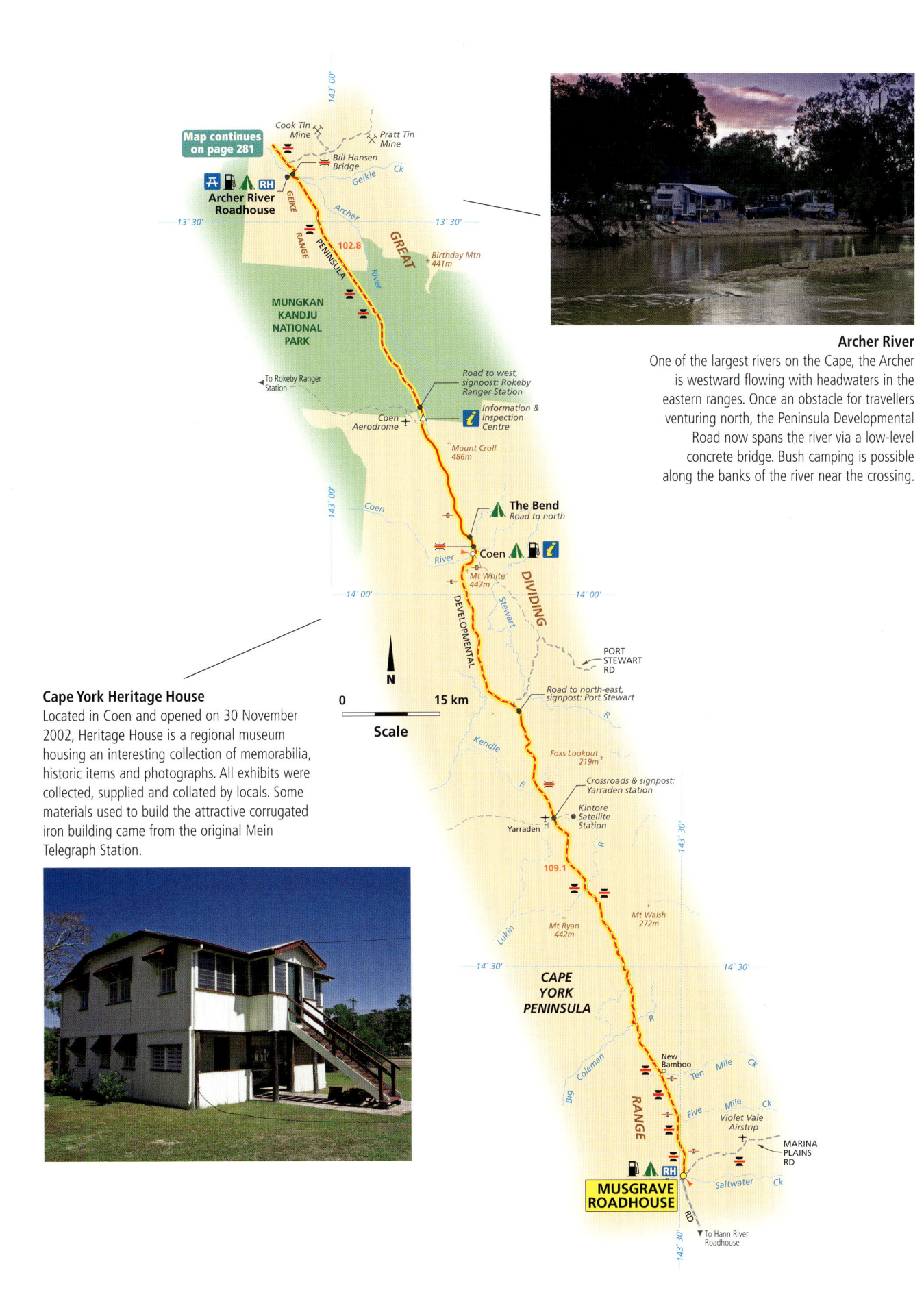

MUSGRAVE ROADHOUSE ◄►► BRAMWELL JUNCTION

Archer River
One of the largest rivers on the Cape, the Archer is westward flowing with headwaters in the eastern ranges. Once an obstacle for travellers venturing north, the Peninsula Developmental Road now spans the river via a low-level concrete bridge. Bush camping is possible along the banks of the river near the crossing.

Cape York Heritage House
Located in Coen and opened on 30 November 2002, Heritage House is a regional museum housing an interesting collection of memorabilia, historic items and photographs. All exhibits were collected, supplied and collated by locals. Some materials used to build the attractive corrugated iron building came from the original Mein Telegraph Station.

279

CAPE YORK PENINSULA

The rainbow lorikeet is a common sight on the Cape

Weipa
This remote town boasts the world's largest bauxite mine (pictured is the bauxite loading facility). Despite its isolation, Weipa offers a full range of services for travellers.

Campsite Facilities

	Toilets	Disabled access	4WD access only	Off-road trailer	Off-road caravan	Drinking water	Fee payable	Ranger patrolled	BBQ/fireplace	Campfires prohibited	Picnic tables	Shelter shed	No rubbish disposal	Public phone	Shower	Bushwalking	Swimming	Swimming not advised	Fishing	Canoeing	Dogs allowed
Archer River	•		•	•	•		•	•			•	•		•	•				•		•
The Bend	•		•	•															•		•
Bramwell Junction	•		•	•	•	•	•			•			•								•
Bramwell Station	•		•	•	•	•	•	•		•			•	•		•					•
Chili Beach	•		•	•			•	•				•						•	•		
Cooks Hut	•		•	•			•				•										
Gordon Creek			•				•	•				•		•							
Musgrave Roadhouse	•	•		•	•	•	•	•				•	•							•	
Old Moreton	•		•	•	•	•	•					•						•	•	•	
Rainforest			•			•	•					•		•							

280

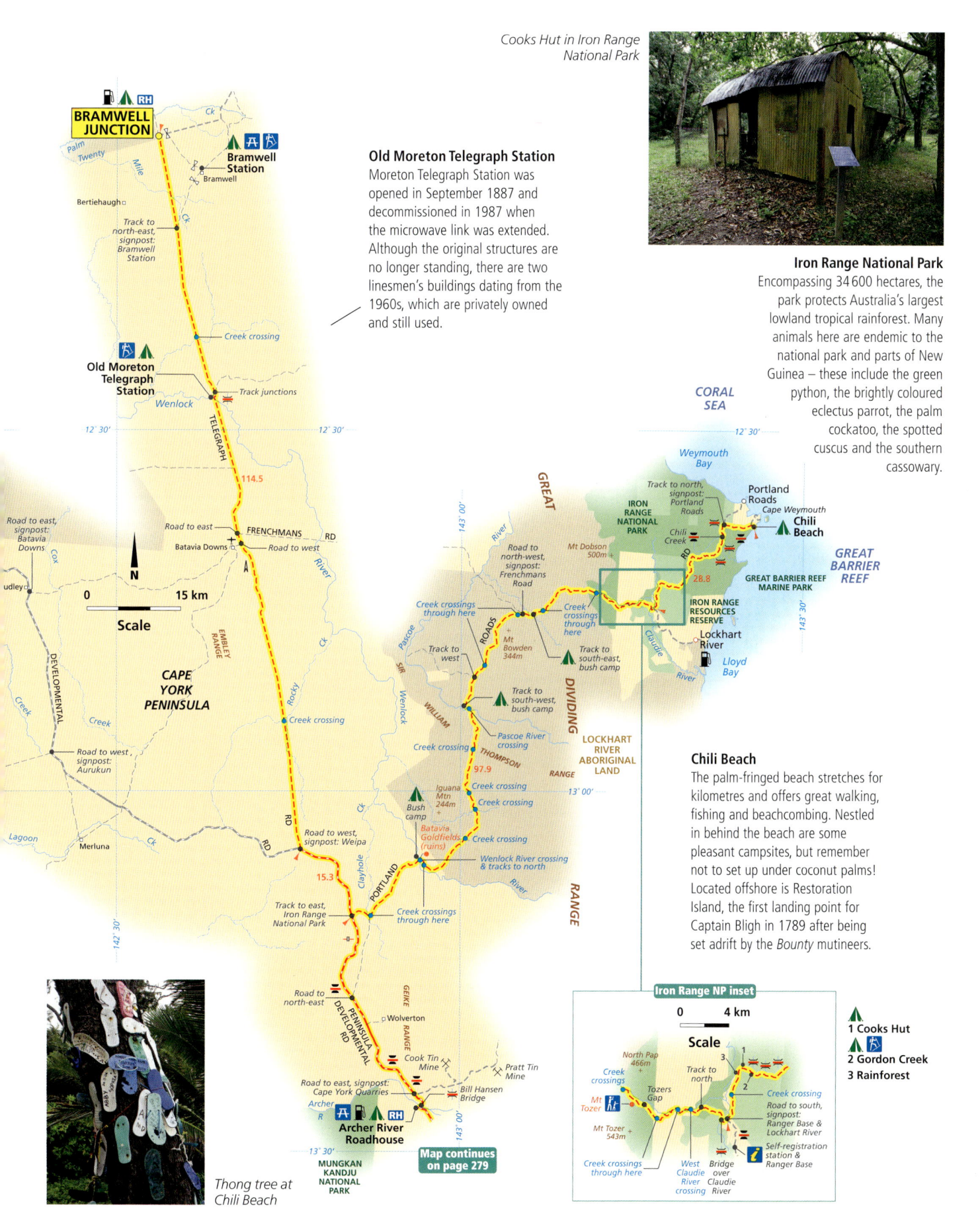

MUSGRAVE ROADHOUSE ◀▶ BRAMWELL JUNCTION

Cooks Hut in Iron Range National Park

Old Moreton Telegraph Station
Moreton Telegraph Station was opened in September 1887 and decommissioned in 1987 when the microwave link was extended. Although the original structures are no longer standing, there are two linesmen's buildings dating from the 1960s, which are privately owned and still used.

Iron Range National Park
Encompassing 34 600 hectares, the park protects Australia's largest lowland tropical rainforest. Many animals here are endemic to the national park and parts of New Guinea – these include the green python, the brightly coloured eclectus parrot, the palm cockatoo, the spotted cuscus and the southern cassowary.

Chili Beach
The palm-fringed beach stretches for kilometres and offers great walking, fishing and beachcombing. Nestled in behind the beach are some pleasant campsites, but remember not to set up under coconut palms! Located offshore is Restoration Island, the first landing point for Captain Bligh in 1789 after being set adrift by the *Bounty* mutineers.

Thong tree at Chili Beach

Iron Range NP inset

1 Cooks Hut
2 Gordon Creek
3 Rainforest

CAPE YORK PENINSULA

Crossing the Pascoe River on Portland Roads Road

▼ **69.2 km** Road junction. CSA. Road on right SP: Cape York Quarries.

    Road junction. CSA. Road on left SP: Cape York Quarries.   **33.6 km** ▲

(19.2 km)

▼ **88.4 km** Road junction. CSA. Road on right.

    Road junction. CSA. Road on left.   **14.4 km** ▲

(14.4 km)

▼ **102.8 km** Road junction. Side trip to Iron Range National Park.

    Zero trip meter at road junction. Proceed in southerly direction towards SP: 101 Coen. Road on left SP: Portland Roads Rd/Lockhart River 118/Iron Range National Park.   **0.0 km** ▲

GPS S:13 10.416 E:142 50.596
UTM 54L 699778E 8542934N

▶ **SIDE TRIP: Iron Range National Park**

▼ **0.0 km** Zero trip meter on Peninsula Developmental Rd at junction with SP: Portland Roads Road. Proceed eastwards along Portland Roads Rd towards SP: Lockhart River 118/Iron Range National Park.

GPS S:13 10.416 E:142 50.596
UTM 54L 699778E 8542934N

(3.8 km)

▼ **3.8 km** Creek crossing.
(6.4 km)

▼ **10.2 km** Creek crossing.
(5.7 km)

▼ **15.9 km** Creek crossing.
(0.4 km)

▼ **16.3 km** Track junction. CSA. Track on left.

Track on left leads 0.4 km to small bush campsite above Wenlock River.
(0.1 km)

▼ **16.4 km** Wenlock River crossing.

GPS S:13 05.735 E:142 56.519
UTM 54L 710547E 8551485N

(0.1 km)

▼ **16.5 km** Track junction. CSA. Tracks on left.

Track on left closest to river leads 0.2 km to grave site on left. At grave site KR and follow track for a further 0.9 km to ruins of Batavia Goldfields, including steam engines, old boilers and other rust-coated items.
(0.4 km)

▼ **16.9 km** Creek crossing.
(13.5 km)

▼ **30.4 km** Creek crossing.
(1.8 km)

▼ **32.2 km** Creek crossing.
(12.9 km)

▼ **45.1 km** Creek crossing.
(5.3 km)

▼ **50.4 km** Track junction. CSA. Track on left.

Track on left leads 0.1 km to bush campsite.
(0.2 km)

▼ **50.6 km** Pascoe River crossing.

GPS S:12 53.000 E:143 00.651
UTM 54L 718201E 8574912N

(0.4 km)

▼ **51.0 km** Track junction. CSA. Track on left.

MUSGRAVE ROADHOUSE ◀▶ BRAMWELL JUNCTION

	Track on left leads 0.5 km to small bush campsite. **(5.2 km)**
▼ 56.2 km	Track junction. CSA. Track on left. **(4.6 km)**
▼ 60.8 km	Creek crossing. **(1.9 km)**
▼ 62.7 km	Creek crossing. **(7.6 km)**
▼ 70.3 km	Creek crossing. **(0.1 km)**
▼ 70.4 km	Track junction. CSA. Track on left SP: Frenchmans Road. Track on left leads 10.6 km to a crossing of the Pascoe River. This crossing recommended only for experienced drivers with well set-up vehicles (preferably two) with high clearance and recovery equipment. This crossing is not recommended for trailers. Once over Pascoe River the route traverses Frenchmans Rd for 42 km to join main route north, Telegraph Rd, at the 50.7-km reading (see page 285). Permission to deviate from Frenchmans Rd is required from the Batavia Downs homestead, tel. (07) 4060 3272. **GPS S:12 45.296 E:143 05.246** **UTM 54L 726630E 8589053N** **(1.7 km)**
▼ 72.1 km	Creek crossing. **(0.4 km)**
▼ 72.5 km	Track junction. CSA over creek. Track on right. Track on right leads 0.1 km to small bush campsite. **(1.8 km)**
▼ 74.3 km	Creek crossing. **(4.8 km)**
▼ 79.1 km	Creek crossing. **(1.8 km)**
▼ 80.9 km	Creek crossing. Remains of old bridge, built during World War II, can be seen on left while crossing creek. **(2.3 km)**
▼ 83.2 km	Creek crossing. **(1.5 km)**
▼ 84.7 km	Boundary of SP: Iron Range National Park. **(1.4 km)**
▼ 86.1 km	Creek crossing. **(0.8 km)**
▼ 86.9 km	Creek crossing. **(0.6 km)**
▼ 87.5 km	Mt Tozer Lookout on right. From carpark a 70-m walk leads to lookout and viewing platform. **GPS S:12 43.961 E:143 12.767** **UTM 54L 740266E 8591403N** **(0.3 km)**

Cath and Craig with the RockVegas crew at the entrance to the Lions Den Hotel

Conviviality on the Cape

We travelled from Cairns to Cooktown via the beautiful Daintree and while we didn't get to see a cassowary we did meet the RockVegas crew from Rockhampton and enjoyed their company at a couple of camps.

From Cooktown it was another three weeks travelling to the very tip of the continent. What a marvellous experience, in part due to the wonderful bunch of people we met along the way. As we were all heading to the one 'pointy' part of the peninsula we ran into each other several times. Needless to say there were quite a few nights spent yarning and drinking with new friends.

Needless to say there were a few nights spent yarning and drinking with new friends

Considering we live in such a big country it's amazing the people you meet. Cath ran into a couple of families who came from Sydney – they lived just around the corner from where she grew up so there was much to catch up on. Well, we may not have seen a cassowary in the Daintree but we did see a cuscus (not to be confused with cous cous) while in Iron Range National Park. Only problem was it was way too quick for us to get the camera out to photograph.

CAPE YORK PENINSULA

▼ 87.8 km Creek crossing.
(0.2 km)

▼ 88.0 km Creek crossing.
(0.4 km)

▼ 88.4 km SP: Tozers Gap.
(2.9 km)

▼ 91.3 km Creek crossing.
(1.1 km)

▼ 92.4 km Creek crossing.
(1.4 km)

▼ 93.8 km Cross SP: West Claudie River.
(1.2 km)

▼ 95.0 km Track junction. CSA. Track on left to small clearing.
(2.3 km)

▼ 97.3 km Bridge over SP: Claudie River.
GPS   S:12 44.779 E:143 16.606
UTM   54L 747203E 8589834N
(0.6 km)

▼ 97.9 km T-junction.
GPS   S:12 44.728 E:143 16.870
UTM   54L 747682E 8589924N

▼ 0.0 km Zero trip meter at T-junction. TL. SP: Portland Roads 29 km. Track on right SP: Ranger Base 3 km/Lockhart River 11 km.
Track on right leads 2.6 km to Iron Range National Park Ranger Base and self-registration station, where campers must register and pay fees prior to camping in the park, and a further 8 km to Lockhart River community.
(2.1 km)

▼ 2.1 km Creek crossing.
(1.9 km)

▼ 4.0 km Track junction. CSA. Track on left SP: Rainforest Campgrounds 300 m.
Track on left leads 0.3 km to **Rainforest campground**, a small spot in clearing amid rainforest, suitable for 2 campsites.
(0.5 km)

▼ 4.5 km Track junction. CSA. Track on left SP: Cooks Hut Camping Area.
Track on left leads short distance to **Cooks Hut camping area**, a grassy area shaded by mango trees near Cooks Hut, which was built by gold miner Reg Cook after World War II from materials scavenged from local mine sites.
(0.7 km)

▼ 5.2 km Track junction. CSA. Track on right SP: Gordon Creek Camping Area.
Track on right leads short distance to **Gordon Creek camping area**, a small clearing set above the road, suitable for 2 campsites.
(0.1 km)

▼ 5.3 km Bridge over SP: Gordon Creek.
GPS   S:12 42.781 E:143 17.940
UTM   54L 749651E 8593498N
(0.2 km)

▼ 5.5 km SP: Gordon Creek Camping Area, on right. CSA.
Camping is in small clearing above the road.
(0.7 km)

▼ 6.2 km Bridge.
(1.6 km)

▼ 7.8 km Bridge.
(11.0 km)

▼ 18.8 km Bridge.
(1.6 km)

▼ 20.4 km Bridge.
(1.0 km)

▼ 21.4 km Rock causeway over SP: Chili Creek.
GPS   S:12 38.777 E:143 22.856
UTM   54L 758620E 8600803N
(2.2 km)

▼ 23.6 km Track junction. TR. SP: Chili Beach camping area 6.2 km. Track SO SP: Portland Roads.
Track SO leads 5.6 km to scenic and delightful port of Portland Roads.
GPS   S:12 37.756 E:143 22.998
UTM   54L 758895E 8602684N
(2.9 km)

▼ 26.5 km Causeway.
(1.8 km)

▼ 28.3 km T-junction. TR. SP: Chili Beach.
(0.5 km)

▼ 28.8 km Y-junction. Chili Beach. Tracks on right and left lead to campsites. Return to side trip start.
Chili Beach camping area is located in scenic position with numerous sites behind beach, well sheltered by shrubs with towering coconut palms. Note that water from well at camping area is not suitable for drinking.
GPS   S:12 37.879 E:143 25.608
UTM   54L 763620E 8602414N

◀ **END SIDE TRIP**

▼ 0.0 km Zero trip meter at road junction. Proceed in northerly direction towards SP: Weipa 159. Road on right SP: Portland Roads Rd/Lockhart River 118/Iron Range National Park.
Road junction. Road on left is side trip to Iron Range National Park.   15.3 km ▲
(15.3 km)

▼ 15.3 km Road junction.
Zero trip meter at T-junction. TL. SP: Peninsula Developmental Road/116 Coen. Road on right SP: Weipa 145.   0.0 km ▲
Road on right leads 145 km to Weipa, which has all services and facilities.
GPS   S:13 04.839 E:142 46.114
UTM   54L 691751E 8553276N

▼ 0.0 km Zero trip meter at road junction. TR. SP: Cape York (Pajinka). Road SO SP: Weipa 145.
Road SO leads 145 km to Weipa, which has all services and facilities.

MUSGRAVE ROADHOUSE ◄► BRAMWELL JUNCTION

Beachfront at Portland Roads

(20.0 km)

▼ **20.0 km** Creek crossing.

(29.0 km)

▼ **49.0 km** Road junction. CSA. Road on left.

Road on left leads past Batavia Downs homestead and meets with Peninsula Developmental Rd after 40 km, approximately 70 km east of Weipa.

(1.7 km)

▼ **50.7 km** Road junction. CSA. Track on right.

Track on right is Frenchmans Rd, a short cut to and from Iron Range National Park. Permission is required from Batavia Downs homestead, tel. (07) 4060 3272, to deviate from this road. See warning about Pascoe River crossing in route directions for Iron Range National Park (at the 70.4-km reading, page 283).

GPS	S:12 38.596 E:142 40.531
UTM	54L 681975E 8601731N

(21.9 km)

▼ **72.6 km** Bridge over SP: Wenlock River.

GPS	S:12 27.355 E:142 38.449
UTM	54L 678334E 8622480N

(0.2 km)

▼ **72.8 km** Y-junction. KR. Track on left SP: Old Moreton Telegraph Station.

Track on left leads 0.4 km to **Old Moreton Telegraph Station** and **campground**, an open grassy area near old buildings used by telegraph linesmen.

T-junction. **114.5 km** ▲

Creek crossing. **94.5 km** ▲

Road junction. CSA. Road on right. **65.5 km** ▲

Road junction. CSA. Track on left. **63.8 km** ▲

Bridge over SP: Wenlock River. **41.9 km** ▲

Road junction. KL. Track on right to Old Moreton Telegraph Station. **41.7 km** ▲

(10.0 km)

▼ **82.8 km** Creek crossing.

(17.2 km)

▼ **100.0 km** Road junction. CSA. Road on right SP: Bramwell Station.

Road on right leads 10.1 km to **Bramwell Station** and **campground**, a large and shaded grassy area close to the homestead, which offers self-guided drives, some hunting and remote bush camping.

Creek crossing. **31.7 km** ▲

Road junction. CSA. Road on left SP: Bramwell Station. **14.5 km** ▲

(14.5 km)

▼ **114.5 km** Y-junction. Bramwell Junction Roadhouse and campground. Trek section 2 ends.

Bramwell Junction campground is a large, open, grassy area behind the roadhouse, with some shady trees.

Zero trip meter at track junction at Bramwell Junction. Proceed in southerly direction.

Track on left, SP: Bypass Track to Bamaga, is where route option via bypass road joins (see trek section 3).

GPS	S:12 05.641 E:142 33.529
UTM	54L 669652E 8662567N

REVERSE DIRECTIONS START

■ 285

3 BRAMWELL JUNCTION ◀▶ BAMAGA 202.5/223.2 KM

Start point
Bramwell Junction

Road atlas
360 D2

Total distance
280.1 km (via Telegraph Track, including route-directed side trip)
358.6 km (via Southern and Northern bypass roads, including route-directed side trips)

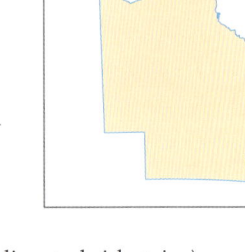

Standard
Via Telegraph Track: difficult
Via Southern and Northern bypass roads: easy–moderate

Time
2–3 days

Longest distance no PD (includes all options)
204.9 km (Bramwell Junction to Jardine River Ferry, via Telegraph Track)
293.4 km (Bramwell Junction to Jardine River Ferry, via Southern and Northern bypass roads)

Topographic maps
Auslig 1:250 000 series: *Cape Weymouth*; *Orford Bay*; *Jardine River*; *Thursday Island*; *Cape York*

Other useful information
- Bramwell Junction Roadhouse offers fuel, mechanical and tyre repairs and welding. Shop has basic supplies and meals. Open seven days 7am–8.30pm, tel. (07) 4060 3230; accepts cash, EFTPOS and credit cards.
- Jardine River ferry operates seven days 8am–5pm but closed for lunch 12noon–1pm, tel. (07) 4069 1369 (ferry supervisor). Ferry fee incorporates return trip, camping fees for bush campsites on Injinoo land (details in *Injinoo Handbook*, which is also included). Store has fuel, cold drinks and ice creams.
- A current *Northern Peninsula Area Business, Community and Tourist Directory* is a handy reference.
- QPWS guide: *Jardine River National Park*.
- Information brochures: *Lockerbie Homestead. Cape York*; *Somerset. Cape York*.
- Bird life is abundant so pack a bird identification guide and binoculars.

Description
This trek section from Bramwell Junction is where the real Cape York adventure begins, especially for those choosing to head due north along the challenging Telegraph Track. The less demanding Southern Bypass Road veers off to the east. Separate route directions are given for both routes, which join 23 kilometres south of the Jardine River ferry crossing. You may choose to tackle one track heading north then return by the alternative route.

The Telegraph Track heads north on the western side of the roadhouse and negotiates 14 river crossings before reaching the Jardine River ferry. There is good bush camping along the length of the route, particularly at Dulhunty River, Cockatoo Creek – also one of the deeper river crossings – Eliot Falls, Nolan Brook and at the old Jardine River ford. A short distance before Eliot Falls is a turn-off to delightful Fruit Bat Falls. The emerald green waters of the wide, single falls cascade into deep pools that are ideal for swimming. Those with a keen eye will spot numerous pitcher plants along the edge of the boardwalk to the falls. If you plan on camping at nearby Eliot Falls, it

Negotiating the difficult Telegraph Track

is best to grab a site by lunchtime during the peak visitor season, especially during school holiday periods as it is a prime spot for families.

The notorious Gunshot Creek crossing claims a number of vehicles each season despite being only a shadow of its former self, and it is recommended you take the easy detour via the Gunshot Bypass Track. Many river and creek crossings, along with their entry and exit points, vary in difficulty from season to season and are often a little chopped out and more demanding late in the season. The difficult and potentially disastrous vehicle-destroying Jardine River crossing at the old ford is best avoided and you are strongly advised to cross the river via the ferry crossing. The route directions detail all the river and creek crossings along this track.

For those opting for the easier trek north via the bypass roads (also known as the Bamaga Road), the Southern Bypass heads eastwards from Bramwell Junction Roadhouse. Originally the only vehicular access to the tip of Cape York was via the Telegraph Track with it numerous creek crossings but, when the Cape's communication systems were modernised, Telecom (now Telstra) constructed the bypass roads to provide better access for work crews.

About 67 kilometres north of Bramwell Junction there is a side trip to Captain Billy Landing, an enjoyable detour. From the beach-facing camping ground you can see the remains of the old landing, once used for unloading supplies for Heathlands station, now a ranger base and part of Heathlands Resource Reserve. The track to Captain Billy Landing, which is within Jardine River National Park, is generally in good condition and offers welcome relief from the bone-jarring corrugations of the bypass road.

The Southern Bypass eventually joins the Telegraph Track, continuing north as one road for almost 10 kilometres before the Northern Bypass strikes away to the west. Even if you only travel to and from Cape York via the bypass roads it is highly recommended you take the side trip to Eliot Falls – the crystal-clear waters of picturesque Fruit Bat and Twin falls are the most inviting for a refreshing dip. Swimming is not advisable below Eliot Falls due to the possible presence of estuarine crocodiles and strong, turbulent currents. The Northern Bypass is generally a straightforward run to the Jardine River ferry, but at times can be extremely corrugated with occasional wash-outs that require driver care.

Once at Bamaga many visitors choose to stay at one of the established commercial campgrounds in the area such as Seisia, Loyalty Beach or Punsand Bay, but there are also a number of delightful bush campsites scattered across the top of the peninsula, including those at Somerset,

Camping at Bramwell Junction

Mutee Head and near the mouth of the Jardine River. The Islander communities of Bamaga and Seisia and the Aboriginal communities of Injinoo, Umagico and New Mapoon offer a range of services and supplies for travellers including fuel, mechanical repairs and groceries.

From Bamaga the 35 kilometres to the tip of Cape York are detailed as a side trip in the route directions. You pass through remnants of the dense Lockerbie Scrub rainforest before arriving at the parking area where a 15-minute walk leads to the northernmost point of the Australian mainland. The track out to scenic and historic Somerset is also described.

Advice and warnings

- The Telegraph Track is a narrow winding track with sandy sections and corrugations. It is suggested you drive at a speed between 20 and 30 kilometres per hour and with your headlights on. There are numerous creek crossings that can have high water levels early in the season. It is best to check all creek-crossing depths and inspect entry and exit points prior to driving across. The Southern and Northern bypass roads are wide tracks with sandy sections, heavy corrugations and wash-outs. Watch out for oncoming and overtaking traffic and drive with your headlights on. The track north from the Jardine River ferry improves and is generally maintained. Contact the RACQ road reporting service, tel. 1300 130 595, and/or Bramwell Junction Roadhouse, tel. (07) 4060 3230, to check current track conditions.
- Exercise caution when overtaking and approaching other vehicles as it may be necessary to stop and wait for dust to settle.
- Standard road tyres or all-terrain tyres are suitable. It is advisable to carry two spare tyres. Roads can be heavily corrugated so lower tyre pressure for personal comfort and to avoid damaging the track.

- Keep your UHF radio in scan mode to listen for oncoming traffic and hazard warnings.
- Towing off-road trailers is suitable along the Telegraph Track as far north as Eliot Falls. Beyond this point it is not recommended due to difficult entry and exit points at creek crossings. Towing off-road trailers or off-road caravans is possible along the entire route to the Cape via the bypass roads.
- Camping is at designated sites and at bush campsites noted in the route directions.
- Please use the signposted rubbish pits along the route, located north of Cockatoo Creek and on the access road to Fruit Bat Falls.
- Carry cash as phone lines and/or power systems for credit card and EFTPOS facilities can be down.
- Saltwater and freshwater crocodiles inhabit the rivers and coastal waters so swimming is not recommended. Swimming is possible at Fruit Bat Falls and at the pools of Twin Falls, but is not recommended at Eliot Falls.
- Alcohol restrictions apply at all communities and lands of the Northern Peninsula Area, including Bamaga, Seisia, Injinoo, Umagico and New Mapoon. Heavy fines apply. Contact the Alcohol Management Program information line, tel. 1300 789 000, or visit the websites (www.mcmc.qld.gov.au or www.liquor.qld.gov.au/Indigenous/), for current restrictions.
- Mosquitoes and sandflies are prevalent so carry plenty of good insect repellent.
- Wear sunscreen and hats.
- Keen anglers should pack their fishing gear.

Permits and bookings
- No permits required to travel this route.
- Camping permits required and fees payable for Jardine River National Park. Self-registration stations at Heathlands Ranger Base, Eliot Falls camping area and Captain Billy Landing camping area.
- Bookings recommended for campsites and villa or lodge accommodation at Seisia Holiday Park, especially for June–August, tel. (07) 4069 3243 or 1800 653 243.
- Bookings recommended for lodge accommodation and campsites at Loyalty Beach Campground and Fishing Lodge, especially for June–August, tel. (07) 4069 3372.
- Bookings recommended for on-site tents, dongas and campsites at Punsand Bay Safari and Fishing Lodge, especially for June–August, tel. (07) 4069 1722.
- Bookings recommended for Resort Bamaga, tel. (07) 4069 3050.
- Advance bookings are necessary for ferry trips to Thursday Island. Book direct with the ferry company, Peddells Thursday Island Tours, tel. (07) 4069 1551, or through their Cape York agents: Cape York Ice n Tackle, tel. (07) 4069 3695; Loyalty Beach Camping and Fishing Lodge, tel. (07) 4069 3372; Punsand Bay Safari and Fishing Lodge, tel. (07) 4069 1722; and Seisia Holiday Park, tel. (07) 4069 3243.
- Recreational fishing is permitted and a fishing licence is not required but bag and size limits apply. Contact Queensland Fisheries, tel. (07) 3225 1843, or visit their website (www.dpi.qld.gov.au/fishweb), for current restrictions and regulations.

Campsite Facilities

	Toilets	Disabled access	4WD access only	Off-road trailer	Off-road caravan	Drinking water	Fee payable	Ranger patrolled	BBQ/fireplace	Campfires prohibited	Picnic tables	Shelter shed	No rubbish disposal	Public phone	Shower	Bush walking	Swimming	Swimming not advised	Fishing	Canoeing	Dogs allowed
Bramwell Junction	•		•	•	•	•	•	•			•			•					•		
Bramwell Station	•		•	•	•	•	•	•		•	•			•	•				•		•
Captain Billy Landing	•	•	•	•	•					•	•	•						•	•		
Eliot Falls	•		•	•			•	•			•		•	•	•						
Jardine River Ferry	•		•	•	•		•	•			•			•					•	•	•
Loyalty Beach	•			•	•	•	•	•			•			•	•				•	•	•
Mutee Head			•	•				•											•	•	
Punsand Bay	•		•	•	•	•	•	•						•	•	•	•				•
Seisia	•			•	•	•	•	•						•	•				•	•	
Umagico	•			•	•	•	•	•						•	•			•	•		•

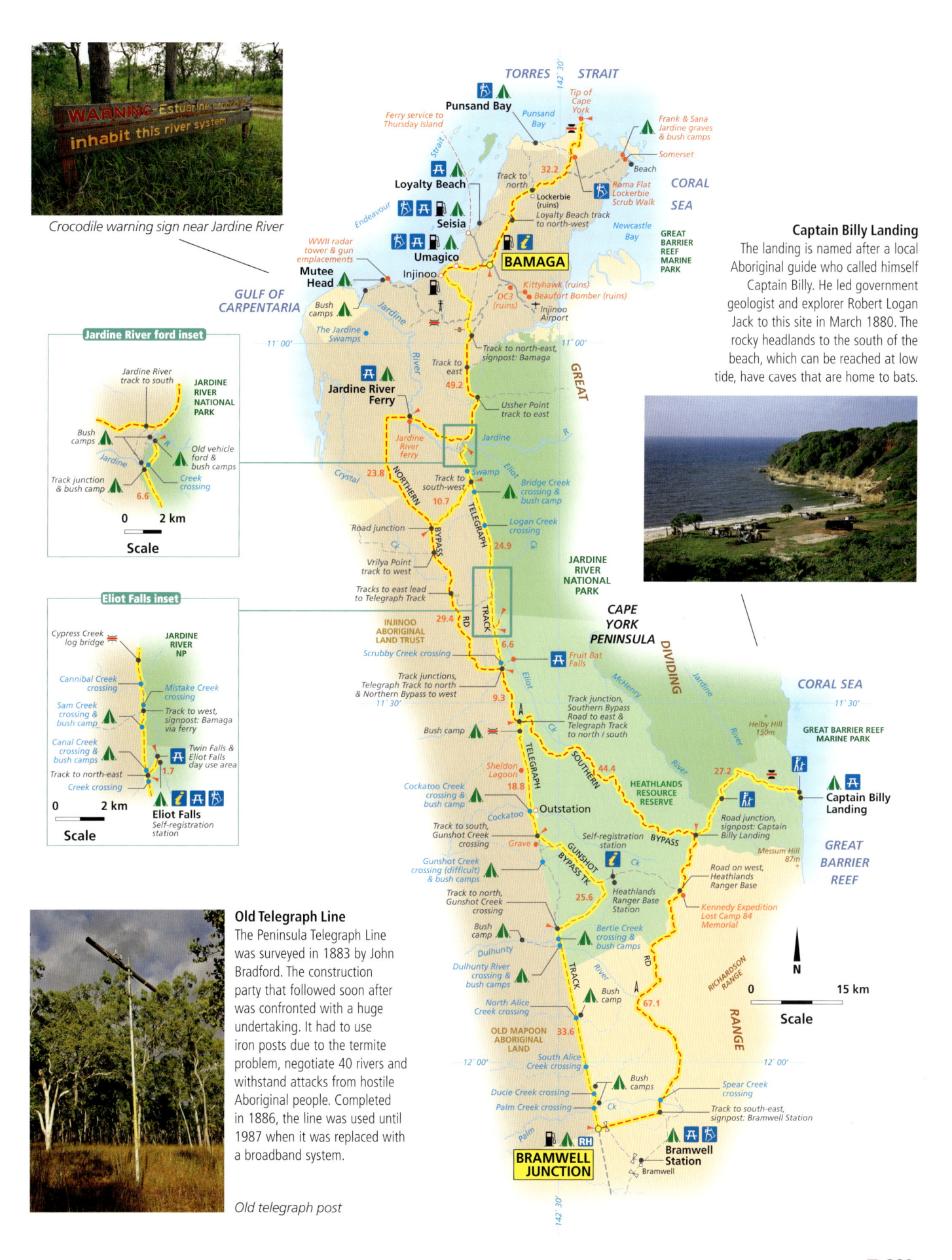

BRAMWELL JUNCTION ◀▶ BAMAGA

Crocodile warning sign near Jardine River

Captain Billy Landing

The landing is named after a local Aboriginal guide who called himself Captain Billy. He led government geologist and explorer Robert Logan Jack to this site in March 1880. The rocky headlands to the south of the beach, which can be reached at low tide, have caves that are home to bats.

Old Telegraph Line

The Peninsula Telegraph Line was surveyed in 1883 by John Bradford. The construction party that followed soon after was confronted with a huge undertaking. It had to use iron posts due to the termite problem, negotiate 40 rivers and withstand attacks from hostile Aboriginal people. Completed in 1886, the line was used until 1987 when it was replaced with a broadband system.

Old telegraph post

289

CAPE YORK PENINSULA

ROUTE DIRECTIONS

▶ **ROUTE OPTION: Telegraph Track**

▼ **0.0 km** Zero trip meter at Y-junction at Bramwell Junction. KL. SP: Telegraph Track to Bamaga. Road on right SP: Bypass track to Bamaga.

Road on right is route option via Southern Bypass Rd, see page 294.

Track junction. Bramwell Junction Roadhouse and campground. 33.6 km ▲

Bramwell Junction campground is a large, open, grassy area behind the roadhouse, with some shady trees. Road on left is where route option via Southern Bypass Rd joins. Road SO is start of trek section 2.

GPS S:12 05.641 E:142 33.529
UTM 54L 669652E 8662567N

(3.4 km)

▼ **3.4 km** Cross Palm Creek.

Southern side of creek has some eroded sections and a few drops while northern side can be steep and slippery. Small bush campsite on right over creek.

Cross Palm Creek. 30.2 km ▲

GPS S:12 03.878 E:142 33.119
UTM 54L 668926E 8665821N

(2.6 km)

▼ **6.0 km** Cross Ducie Creek.

Wide crossing, with both southern and northern sides eroded. Small bush campsite on right over creek.

Cross Ducie Creek. 27.6 km ▲

GPS S:12 02.670 E:142 33.126
UTM 54L 668951E 8668048N

(4.7 km)

▼ **10.7 km** Cross South Alice Creek.

Small crossing, which generally stops flowing in dry season.

Cross South Alice Creek. 22.9 km ▲

GPS S:12 00.417 E:142 32.416
UTM 54L 667686E 8672209N

(7.8 km)

▼ **18.5 km** Cross North Alice Creek.

Southern side of creek is washed out. There are two entry/exit points on southern side of creek – eastern one is eroded. Small bush campsite over creek.

Cross North Alice Creek. 15.1 km ▲

GPS S:11 56.342 E:142 31.546
UTM 54L 666149E 8679730N

(8.4 km)

▼ **26.9 km** Enter SP: Heathlands Reserve.

Exit Heathlands Reserve. 6.7 km ▲

(2.8 km)

▼ **29.7 km** Track junction. CSA. Track on left.

Track on left leads 7.3 km to large clearing beside the Dulhunty River, suitable for bush camping.

Track junction. CSA. Track on right. 3.9 km ▲

(0.6 km)

▼ **30.3 km** Track junction. CSA. Tracks on left and bush campsite on right.

Tracks on left lead to numerous bush campsites beside and in vicinity of Dulhunty River, a very popular camping spot.

Track junction. CSA. Tracks on right and bush campsite on left. 3.3 km ▲

(0.1 km)

▼ **30.4 km** Dulhunty River crossing.

Solid rock slab crossing with a sandy northern bank. There are three exit points on the northern side. The one on the far right is easiest while the other two are badly eroded. Bush campsites located on the northern banks.

Dulhunty River crossing. 3.2 km ▲

GPS S:11 50.280 E:142 30.106
UTM 54L 663595E 8690920N

(1.4 km)

▼ **31.8 km** Cross Bertie Creek.

Track makes a dogleg and crosses creek 30 m upstream (east). Solid rock slab crossing. Bush camping on left prior to creek and on right over creek.

Cross Bertie Creek. 1.8 km ▲

GPS S:11 49.738 E:142 29.982
UTM 54L 663375E 8691920N

(1.8 km)

▼ **33.6 km** Track junction.

Zero trip meter at T-junction. TL. This is Telegraph Track. Track on right leads to Gunshot Creek. 0.0 km ▲

GPS S:11 48.876 E:142 29.890
UTM 54L 663217E 8693510N

▼ **0.0 km** Zero trip meter at track junction. TR. SP: Heathlands Ranger Base 15 km. This is Gunshot Bypass Track. Track SO.

Track SO leads 12.3 km to Gunshot Creek crossing, a difficult crossing that varies from year to year. Our advice is to use the bypass route as every season some vehicles come to grief at the crossing. If you want to view the crossing, the quickest and easiest route is from the northern side.

T-junction. 25.6 km ▲

(11.9 km)

▼ **11.9 km** Track junction. TL. Track on right.

Track on right leads 1.9 km to Heathlands Ranger Base information board and camping self-registration station.

Track junction. TR. Track SO to Ranger Base. 13.7 km ▲

GPS S:11 44.980 E:142 33.835
UTM 54L 670422E 8700654N

(10.7 km)

▼ **22.6 km** Track junction. KR.

Track SO leads 2.0 km to Telegraph Track.

Track junction. CSA. Track on right. 3.0 km ▲

(3.0 km)

▼ **25.6 km** Track junction.

Zero trip meter at track junction. KL. This is Gunshot Bypass Track. Track SO. 0.0 km ▲

BRAMWELL JUNCTION ◄ ► BAMAGA

Crossing the Dulhunty River

Track SO leads 5.2 km to Gunshot Creek crossing, a difficult crossing that varies from year to year. Our advice is to use the bypass route as several vehicles come to grief at the crossing every season. (If you want to view the crossing, this route from the north offers the easiest access.)

GPS S:11 41.135 E:142 28.138
UTM 54L 660110E 8707798N

▼ 0.0 km Zero trip meter at track junction. CSA. This is the Telegraph Track. Track on left.

Track on left leads 1.7 km to grave site, on west side of track, of ex-PMG linesman W. J. Brown, and a further 3.5 km to Gunshot Creek crossing and camping area with bush campsites scattered among shady trees, high above creek.

Track junction.   18.8 km ▲

(3.8 km)

▼ 3.8 km Creek crossing.

Creek crossing.   15.0 km ▲

(0.5 km)

▼ 4.3 km Cross Cockatoo Creek.

Southern bank is steep and at times eroded. A wide crossing of 30–40 m across a rock bar with a number of potholes. Walk across first to pick best route. Bush camping on southern side of creek, with good site on right prior to crossing. Note signposted rubbish pit 500 m on northern side of creek.

Cross Cockatoo Creek.   14.5 km ▲

GPS S:11 39.046 E:142 27.468
UTM 54L 658912E 8711655N

(0.3 km)

▼ 4.6 km Small Aboriginal outstation on right.

This outstation is occupied all year. From time to time 'Old Kevin's Stall' operates, with fruit for sale.

Small Aboriginal outstation on left.   14.2 km ▲

(6.2 km)

▼ 10.8 km SP: Sheldon Lagoon, on left. CSA.

SP: Sheldon Lagoon, on right. CSA.   8.0 km ▲

(6.3 km)

▼ 17.1 km Bridge over Sailor Creek.

Bridge over Sailor Creek.   1.7 km ▲

GPS S:11 32.433 E:142 26.592
UTM 54L 657382E 8723854N

(0.1 km)

▼ 17.2 km Track junction. CSA. Track on left.

Track on left leads to small bush campsite.

Track junction. CSA. Track on right.   1.6 km ▲

(1.6 km)

▼ 18.8 km T-junction.

Zero trip meter at Y-junction. KR. This is Telegraph Track. Road on left.   0.0 km ▲

Road on left is route option via Southern Bypass Rd.

GPS S:11 31.570 E:142 26.535
UTM 54L 657286E 8725445N

291

CAPE YORK PENINSULA

The cascading waters of Twin Falls drop into pools that are ideal for swimming

▼ 0.0 km — Zero trip meter at T-junction. TL. This is Southern Bypass Rd.

Route option via Southern Bypass Rd joins Telegraph Track at this T-junction.

Y-junction. 9.3 km ▲

(9.3 km)

▼ 9.3 km — Road junction.

Zero trip meter at road junction. CSA. Road on right SP: Bypass track via ferry. 0.0 km ▲

GPS	S:11 27.265 E:142 25.073
UTM	54L 654668E 8733395N

▼ 0.0 km — Zero trip meter at road junction. KR. SP: Telegraph Track/Eliot Falls 8 km. Road on left SP: Bypass track via ferry.

Road on left is route option via Northern Bypass Rd.

Road junction. 6.6 km ▲

(0.1 km)

▼ 0.1 km — Track junction. CSA. Track on right SP: Fruit Bat Falls 2.6 km.

Track on right leads 2.7 km to delightful and scenic Fruit Bat Falls, an ideal swimming spot to cool off. Picnic area with toilets and tables located at carpark. Note signposted rubbish pit along this track.

Track junction. CSA. Track on left SP: Fruit Bat Falls 2.6 km. 6.5 km ▲

(0.9 km)

▼ 1.0 km — Cross Scrubby Creek.

Cross Scrubby Creek. 5.6 km ▲

(5.0 km)

▼ 6.0 km — Creek crossing, which is generally dry.

Creek crossing, which is generally dry. 0.6 km ▲

(0.6 km)

▼ 6.6 km — Y-junction.

Zero trip meter at T-junction. TR. Track on left SP: Eliot Falls 1.5 km. 0.0 km ▲

GPS	S:11 23.772 E:142 24.380
UTM	54L 653439E 8739840N

▼ 0.0 km — Zero trip meter at Y-junction. KL. Track on right SP: Eliot Falls 1.5 km.

Track on right leads 1.4 km to **Eliot Falls camping area**, a large area with individual campsites set among shady trees and only a short walk to falls. A further 0.4 km leads to Eliot Falls Day Use Area, with short walk to scenic Eliot and Twin falls. Swimming is recommended only in pools of Twin Falls.

T-junction. 24.9 km ▲

(0.3 km)

▼ 0.3 km — Cross Canal Creek.

Southern and northern sides of creek can be rough so choose the best entry/exit point.

Cross Canal Creek. 24.6 km ▲

GPS	S:11 23.639 E:142 24.339
UTM	54L 653365E 8740085N

(1.9 km)

▼ 2.2 km — Enter SP: Jardine River National Park.

Enter SP: Heathlands Reserve. 22.7 km ▲

(1.9 km)

▼ 4.1 km — Cross Sam Creek.

BRAMWELL JUNCTION ◀ ▶ BAMAGA

Southern side of creek is bumpy and northern side is through a canal. Bush camping on left over creek.

	Cross Sam Creek.	20.8 km ▲

GPS S:11 21.808 E:142 24.108
UTM 54L 652962E 8743463N

(1.5 km)

▼ 5.6 km Track junction. CSA. SP: Jardine River 25 km. Track on left SP: Bamaga via ferry 89 km.

Track on left leads to route option via Northern Bypass Rd, either 8.7 km to join at the 17.5-km reading north of Eliot Falls turn-off, or 9.3 km to join at the 17.8-km reading north of Eliot Falls turn-off (see page 296).

	Track junction. CSA. Track on right SP: Bamaga via ferry 89 km.	19.3 km ▲

GPS S:11 21.126 E:142 24.175
UTM 54L 653089E 8744719N

(0.3 km)

▼ 5.9 km Cross Mistake Creek.

Crossing has generally easy entry and exit, and sandy bottom with a few rocks.

	Cross Mistake Creek.	19.0 km ▲

GPS S:11 20.974 E:142 24.139
UTM 54L 653025E 8745000N

(2.0 km)

▼ 7.9 km Cross Cannibal Creek.

Northern bank very eroded so can be difficult at times. Caution required.

	Cross Cannibal Creek.	17.0 km ▲

GPS S:11 20.000 E:142 24.129
UTM 54L 653016E 8746795N

(2.0 km)

▼ 9.9 km Log bridge over Cypress Creek.

Guidance required to cross over this log bridge to ensure wheels are placed correctly.

	Log bridge over Cypress Creek.	15.0 km ▲

GPS S:11 19.024 E:142 23.947
UTM 54L 652693E 8748596N

(7.7 km)

▼ 17.6 km Cross Logan Creek.

	Cross Logan Creek.	7.3 km ▲

GPS S:11 15.217 E:142 23.523
UTM 54L 651955E 8755617N

(5.5 km)

▼ 23.1 km Cross Bridge Creek, also known as Nolan Brook. Over creek track junction. TR and cross minor creek.

Bridge Creek crossing has generally easy entry and exit, but creek can be deep so walk across first to check depth. Bush campsites on left over creek.

	Cross Bridge Creek, also known as Nolan Brook.	1.8 km ▲

GPS S:11 12.445 E:142 22.612
UTM 54L 650322E 8760735N

(1.8 km)

▼ 24.9 km Track junction. Side trip to Jardine River ford.

	Zero trip meter at T-junction. TR. This is the Telegraph Track.	0.0 km ▲

GPS S:11 11.594 E:142 22.318
UTM 54L 649794E 8762306N

▶ **SIDE TRIP: Jardine River ford**

▼ 0.0 km Zero trip meter at track junction. Track to west SP: Bamaga via Ferry. Proceed in northerly direction along Telegraph Track.

(2.1 km)

▼ 2.1 km Track crosses over swampy section.

(2.7 km)

▼ 4.8 km Y-junction. SP: Jardine River National Park. KR.

Track on left leads 0.3 km to Jardine River, where telegraph line crossed river to northern side. Good bush camping in this vicinity, suitable for 3 or 4 vehicles.

GPS S:11 09.245 E:142 21.365
UTM 54L 648079E 8766644N

(0.1 km)

▼ 4.9 km Creek crossing.

(1.7 km)

▼ 6.6 km Old vehicle ford across Jardine River. Return to side trip start.

Good bush camping in vicinity of old ford and along sandy banks of the river.

GPS S:11 08.441 E:142 21.683
UTM 54L 648665E 8768124N

◀ **END SIDE TRIP**

Crossing Cypress Creek

293

CAPE YORK PENINSULA

Signpost at Bramwell Junction

▼ 0.0 km — Zero trip meter at track junction. TL. SP: Bamaga via Ferry. Track SO.

    T-junction. Side trip to Jardine River ford.   10.7 km ▲

(10.7 km)

▼ 10.7 km — T-junction. Zero trip meter. TR. This is Northern Bypass Rd. End of route option.

Road on left is where route option via Northern Bypass Rd joins. Route continues on page 296.

    Zero trip meter at road junction. TL.   0.0 km ▲

    Road SO is route option south via Northern Bypass Rd.

GPS S:11 15.456 E:142 18.872
UTM 54L 643490E 8755216N

▶ **ROUTE OPTION: Southern and Northern bypass roads**

▼ 0.0 km — Zero trip meter at Y-junction at Bramwell Junction. KR. SP: Bypass track to Bamaga. Track on left SP: Telegraph Track to Bamaga.

Track on left is route option via Telegraph Track.

    Track junction at Bramwell Junction.   67.1 km ▲

Road on right is where route option via Telegraph Track joins. Road SO is start of trek section 2.

GPS S:12 05.641 E:142 33.529
UTM 54L 669652E 8662567N

(1.3 km)

▼ 1.3 km — Road junction. CSA. Track on right SP: Bramwell Station.

Track on right leads 8.3 km to **Bramwell Station** and **campground**, a large and shaded grassy area close to homestead, which offers self-guided drives, some hunting and remote bush camping.

    Road junction. CSA. Track on left SP: Bramwell Station.   65.8 km ▲

(9.1 km)

▼ 10.4 km — Road junction. CSA. Track on right SP: Bramwell Station Shortcut/Patrons only.

    Road junction. CSA. Track on left SP: Bramwell Station Shortcut/Patrons only.   56.7 km ▲

Track on left is short-cut access route to Bramwell station for those spending a night at station campground.

(1.9 km)

▼ 12.3 km — Cross Spear Creek.

    Cross Spear Creek.   54.8 km ▲

GPS S:12 03.201 E:142 39.041
UTM 54L 679679E 8667006N

(43.8 km)

▼ 56.1 km — Road junction. CSA. Track on right.

Track on right leads 0.1 km to foundation memorial, a tribute to Kennedy Expedition Lost Camp LXXXIV (Camp 84), where 3 members of Edmund Kennedy's 1848 exploring party lost their lives. Kennedy's party of 13 departed from just north of Townsville and headed for Cape York. Defeated by the harsh jungle terrain, 8 men were left at Weymouth Bay and another 3 at Shelburne Bay. Close to the tip Kennedy was killed by a Yadhaigana man. Kennedy's Aboriginal companion Jackey Jackey made it to the waiting ship at the Cape, but of the men left behind on the journey only 2 were found.

    Road junction. CSA. Track on left.   11.0 km ▲

(0.2 km)

▼ 56.3 km — Y-junction. KR. Track on left SP: Old Telegraph Track 28 km/Heathlands Ranger Base 13 km.

Track on left leads 13.0 km to Heathlands Ranger Base, information board and camping self-registration station.

    Road junction. CSA. Road on right SP: Heathlands Ranger Base 13 km.   10.8 km ▲

GPS S:11 45.692 E:142 40.713
UTM 54L 682909E 8699269N

(10.8 km)

▼ 67.1 km — Road junction. Side trip to Captain Billy Landing.

    Zero trip meter at road junction. KR. Track on left SP: Captain Billy Landing 30 km.   0.0 km ▲

GPS S:11 41.061 E:142 42.124
UTM 54L 685523E 8707792N

▶ **SIDE TRIP: Captain Billy Landing**

▼ 0.0 km — Zero trip meter on Southern Bypass Rd at junction with road to east SP: Captain Billy Landing 30 km. Proceed eastwards along this road.

(8.1 km)

▼ 8.1 km — Lookout point on right.

(12.5 km)

▼ 20.6 km — Concrete causeway.

GPS S:11 36.963 E:142 48.530
UTM 54L 697212E 8715275N

(3.0 km)

294

▼ 23.6 km Creek crossing.
(2.8 km)

▼ 26.4 km Lookout point on left.
Excellent views across beach and ocean and above camping area.
(0.8 km)

▼ 27.2 km Captain Billy Landing Camping Area. Return to side trip start.
Although susceptible to onshore winds, **Captain Billy Landing camping area** is a lovely, large circular area right on the beach.

GPS   S:11 37.921 E:142 51.366
UTM   54L 702356E 8713476N

◀ END SIDE TRIP

▼ 0.0 km Zero trip meter at road junction. KL. SP: Bamaga/Cape York. Track on right SP: Captain Billy Landing 30 km.
Road junction. Track on left is side trip to Captain Billy Landing.   44.4 km ▲
(44.4 km)

▼ 44.4 km Road junction.
Zero trip meter at Y-junction. KL. This is Southern Bypass Rd. Track on right.   0.0 km ▲
Track on right is route option via Telegraph Track.

GPS   S:11 31.570 E:142 26.535
UTM   54L 657286E 8725445N

▼ 0.0 km Zero trip meter at road junction. CSA. Track on left.
Track on left is where route option via Telegraph Track joins.
Y-junction.   9.3 km ▲
(9.3 km)

▼ 9.3 km Road junction. Side trip to Eliot Falls.
Zero trip meter at road junction. KR. Track on left SP: Telegraph Track/Eliot Falls 8 km.   0.0 km ▲
Track on left is where route option via Telegraph Track joins. It also leads 8.3 km to Eliot Falls.

GPS   S:11 27.265 E:142 25.073
UTM   54L 654668E 8733395N

▶ SIDE TRIP: Eliot Falls

▼ 0.0 km Zero trip meter at road junction. Proceed northwards along track SP: Telegraph Track/Eliot Falls 8 km.
(0.1 km)

▼ 0.1 km Track junction. CSA. Track on right SP: Fruit Bat Falls 2.6 km.
Track on right leads 2.7 km to delightful and scenic Fruit Bat Falls, an ideal swimming spot to cool off. Picnic area with toilets and tables located at carpark. Note signposted rubbish pit along this track.
(0.9 km)

▼ 1.0 km Cross Scrubby Creek.
(5.0 km)

The Jardines of Somerset

Somerset, first settled to aid shipwrecked sailors on the remote north coast, was Cape York Peninsula's official Government Residency from 1864 to 1877. Captain John Jardine, a police magistrate, was the first Government Resident. His two oldest sons, Frank and Alexander, soon joined him, undertaking a ten-month trek from Carpentaria Downs station near Rockhampton with 41 horses and 250 head of cattle, arriving at Somerset in March 1865. In 1867, in recognition of this remarkable feat, Frank was granted a parcel of grazing land west of Somerset, which he named Lockerbie.

Captain John Jardine remained Government Resident until 1866 and in 1868 Frank was offered the position, which he held until 1873. With his Samoan wife, Sana, Frank then moved from Somerset to pursue pearling interests. However, in 1877 the government administration was transferred to Thursday Island, and Frank and Sana returned to Somerset, taking up a 99-year lease. Frank continued to run cattle but pearling was his main interest. Frank died in 1919 and Sana in 1923. Their final resting place is on the scenic foreshore below the old residency site. Members of the Jardine family lived at Somerset until the outbreak of World War II, when they were evacuated. They never returned and the homestead burned down in the 1960s. Today, the family name lives on in one of the Cape's major waterways, the Jardine River.

> *Frank and Alexander [made] a ten-month trek from Carpentaria Downs station near Rockhampton with 41 horses and 250 head of cattle*

Grave of Frank Jardine

CAPE YORK PENINSULA

▼ **6.0 km** — Creek crossing, which is generally dry.
(0.6 km)

▼ **6.6 km** — Y-junction. KR. SP: Eliot Falls 1.5 km.
Track on left is continuation of alternative route option via Telegraph Track.

```
GPS   S:11 23.772 E:142 24.380
UTM   54L 653439E 8739840N
```
(1.3 km)

▼ **7.9 km** — Track junction. CSA. SP: Eliot Falls Day Use Area. Track on right SP: Eliot Falls Camping Area.
Track on right leads 0.1 km to **Eliot Falls camping area**, a large area with individual campsites among shady trees.
(0.4 km)

▼ **8.3 km** — Eliot Falls Day Use Area. Return to side trip start.
Picnic tables. From carpark a short walk leads to Twin Falls – where swimming is possible in the pools – and to Eliot Falls.

```
GPS   S:11 23.027 E:142 24.782
UTM   54L 654177E 8741210N
```

◄ **END SIDE TRIP**

▼ **0.0 km** — Zero trip meter at road junction. KL. SP: Bypass track via ferry. This is Northern Bypass Rd. Track on right (north) SP: Telegraph Track/Eliot Falls 8 km.
Road junction. Track on left is Eliot Falls side trip.   **29.4 km** ▲
(17.5 km)

Swimmers at Fruit Bat Falls

▼ **17.5 km** — Road junction. CSA. Track on right.
Track on right leads 8.7 km to route option via Telegraph Track, just north of Sam Creek at the 5.6-km reading (see page 293).
Road junction. CSA. Track on left.   **11.9 km** ▲

```
GPS   S:11 21.040 E:142 20.708
UTM   54L 646784E 8744908N
```
(0.3 km)

▼ **17.8 km** — Road junction. CSA. Track on right.
Track on right leads 9.3 km to route option via Telegraph Track, just north of Sam Creek at the 5.6-km reading (see page 293).
Road junction. CSA. Track on left.   **11.6 km** ▲
(7.8 km)

▼ **25.6 km** — Road junction. CSA. Track on left.
Track on left leads approximately 30 km to Vrilya Point and beach camping sites.
Road junction. CSA. Track on right.   **3.8 km** ▲

```
GPS   S:11 17.484 E:142 19.104
UTM   54L 643896E 8751476N
```
(3.8 km)

▼ **29.4 km** — Road junction. Route options converge.
Zero trip meter at road junction. CSA. Track on left.   **0.0 km** ▲
Track on left is route option via Telegraph Track.

```
GPS   S:11 15.456 E:142 18.872
UTM   54L 643490E 8755216N
```

► **ROUTE OPTIONS CONVERGE**

▼ **0.0 km** — Zero trip meter at road junction. Proceed in northerly direction.
Track to east is where route option via Telegraph Track joins.
Road junction. Route options separate.   **23.8 km** ▲
(23.8 km)

▼ **23.8 km** — Jardine River ferry, service station and camping area.
Jardine River Ferry camping area is a large area above bank of river with plenty of shade.
Zero trip meter on southern bank of Jardine River as exiting ferry. PSA past service station and camping area on left.   **0.0 km** ▲

```
GPS   S:11 06.234 E:142 16.987
UTM   54L 640134E 8772230N
```

▼ **0.0 km** — Zero trip meter on northern bank of Jardine River as exiting ferry. PSA.
Jardine River ferry.   **49.2 km** ▲
(9.3 km)

▼ **9.3 km** — Road junction. CSA. Track on right.
Road junction. CSA. Track on left.   **39.9 km** ▲
(0.6 km)

▼ **9.9 km** — Road junction. CSA. Track on right.
Track on right leads 0.4 km to track junction. TR and follow track for 0.7 km to another junction. PSA at this junction for 1.0 km to Jardine River and some excellent bush campsites near old hut, once used by linesmen. TL at this junction and travel 0.4 km to campsites on right and a further 0.2 km to old vehicle ford over Jardine River.

BRAMWELL JUNCTION ◀▶ BAMAGA

Tropical sunset on Jardine River

	Road junction. CSA. SP: Bypass Track. Track on left.	39.3 km ▲

GPS   S:11 08.037 E:142 21.736
UTM 54L 648765E 8768868N

(7.3 km)

▼ 17.2 km Road junction. CSA. Track on right.

Track on right leads approximately 70 km to Ussher Point camping area located on beach.

	Road junction. CSA. Track on left.	32.0 km ▲

(5.6 km)

▼ 22.8 km Road junction. CSA. Track on right.

	Road junction. CSA. Track on left.	26.4 km ▲

(5.2 km)

▼ 28.0 km Road junction. KL. SP: Injinoo. Track on right SP: Bamaga.

	Road junction. CSA. Track on left.	21.2 km ▲

GPS   S:10 59.402 E:142 22.360
UTM 54L 649974E 8784780N

(2.8 km)

▼ 30.8 km Crossroads. CSA.

Track on left leads 18.8 km to **Mutee Head camping area**, a scenic well-shaded beach location, and a further 0.4 km to track junction just before grid. TR and drive 0.4 km to World War II radar tower and gun emplacements. Proceed over grid for 4.8 km to bush campsites beside Jardine River, just upstream from where the river meets the ocean.

	Crossroads. CSA.	18.4 km ▲

GPS   S:10 58.004 E:142 22.082
UTM 54L 649479E 8787359N

(9.6 km)

▼ 40.4 km T-junction with bitumen in Injinoo. TR. SP: Bamaga.

	Road junction. TL. SP: Jardine Ferry/Cairns.	8.8 km ▲

(3.2 km)

▼ 43.6 km Road junction. CSA. SP: 4 Bamaga. Road on left SP: Umagico.

Road on left leads short distance to Umagico supermarket and further 1.5 km to **Umagico campground**, a large informal camping area located on the beach.

	Road junction. CSA. SP: Injinoo 3. Road on right SP: Umagico.	5.6 km ▲

(4.0 km)

▼ 47.6 km T-junction. TL.

	Road junction. TR. SP: Injinoo Aboriginal Community 8 km/Umagico Aboriginal Community 4 km.	1.6 km ▲

(0.1 km)

▼ 47.7 km Road junction. TR. SP: Historical Centre & Tourist Information Centre. Road SO SP: Seisia 6 km.

Road SO leads to Bamaga shopping centre; **Seisia Caravan Park**, a large formal caravan park overlooking Endeavour Strait; Seisia wharf and shopping centre; and **Loyalty Beach campground**, an informal camping area located on Endeavour Strait.

■ 297

Frangipani Beach near the tip of the Cape

At the Tip of the Top

The ultimate goal for all Cape York adventurers is to reach the northernmost point of Australia, the tip of the top. The views are outstanding and deserve to be taken in over some time, so don't rush when you get there. When we finally reached this awesome spot we were extremely lucky that there was no one else to be seen as we got there late afternoon. What a delight. We were able to relax and take in the spectacular views without another soul … oh, except for the guy who came running up the beach from his yacht and wanted us to take a photo of him at the tip, which we quickly did and then he was gone again.

	T-junction. TL. Road on right SP: Seisia 6 km.	1.5 km ▲
	(1.4 km)	
▼ 49.1 km	Road junction. CSA. Road on left SP: Cape York/Punsand Bay.	
	Road junction. CSA. Road on right SP: Cape York/Punsand Bay.	0.1 km ▲
	(0.1 km)	
▼ 49.2 km	Bamaga Visitor Centre on left. Side trip to Cape York.	
	Zero trip meter on Liu St in Bamaga with Bamaga Visitor Centre on right. Proceed in westerly direction towards Bamaga shopping centre.	0.0 km ▲

GPS	S:10 53.542 E:142 24.003
UTM	54L 653016E 8795568N

▶ **SIDE TRIP: Cape York**

▼ 0.0 km	Zero trip meter in Bamaga on Liu St with Bamaga Visitor Centre on right. Proceed in westerly direction towards Bamaga shopping centre.
	(0.1 km)
▼ 0.1 km	Road junction. TR. SP: Punsand Bay/Cape York.
	(3.3 km)
▼ 3.4 km	Road junction. CSA. Road on left.
	Road on left leads 3.8 km to Bamaga.
	(4.8 km)
▼ 8.2 km	Road junction. CSA. Track on left SP: Loyalty Beach Campground.
	Track on left leads 7.0 km to Loyalty Beach camping area.
	(7.3 km)

BRAMWELL JUNCTION ◀▶ BAMAGA

▼ 15.5 km Road junction. CSA. SP: Pajinka. Track on left SP: Punsand Bay.

Souvenir shop is on left at this junction. On right are remains of fourth Lockerbie homestead, built in 1940s by Cyril T. Holland. Track on left leads 11.4 km to **Punsand Bay** Safari and Fishing Lodge with scenic beachside **camping area**.

(6.9 km)

▼ 22.4 km Y-junction. KL. Track on right leads to Somerset.

Track on right leads 10.8 km to a track junction. At junction, track on left leads 0.4 km to beautiful protected beach with bush campsites tucked behind it, where graves of Frank Jardine and his wife, Sana, are located. At low tide it is possible to walk around rocky headland at northern end of the beach to sandstone overhang adorned with Aboriginal rock paintings. At junction, track SO leads 0.2 km to site of Somerset Government Residency, built in 1863. All that remains is a flagpole and 3 ancient cannons.

| GPS | S:10 45.813 E:142 30.547 |
| UTM | 54L 665010E 8809759N |

(2.1 km)

▼ 24.5 km Creek crossing.

(0.6 km)

▼ 25.1 km SP: Roma Flat Lockerbie Scrub Walk, on right. Parking area on left.

Roma Flat Lockerbie Scrub Walk is a self-guided 1–2-hour walk through rainforest.

(0.1 km)

▼ 25.2 km Track junction. CSA. Track on left.

Track on left leads 7.0 km to Punsand Bay.

(3.3 km)

▼ 28.5 km Track junction. CSA. Track on right.

(3.7 km)

▼ 32.2 km Parking area. Walk to the tip of the Cape from here. Return to side trip start.

From parking area a boardwalk to west winds through rainforest. Once out of rainforest you can either follow beach, depending on tides, or walk up and over the rocky headland to the tip.

| GPS | S:10 41.772 E:142 31.928 |
| UTM | 54L 667564E 8817196N |

◀ **END SIDE TRIP**

Gun emplacement at Green Hill Fort

Thursday Island Sojourn

A day trip to Thursday Island by ferry is a great way to finish the trek north but be sure to book your passage when you arrive in Seisia. We hadn't booked and had to wait around for a few days before we could get seats. Once on the island, which is about an hour's trip from Seisia, we took a bus tour, which we had organised from the mainland. It was a great way to see all the historic sites. From Green Hill Fort, the views over the town and across the beautiful blue waters to the surrounding islands are just wonderful. There are a couple of places that serve lunch but most visitors stop off at one of the island's three pubs. But remember to keep an eye on your watch. We heard that three of our fellow Cape York travellers lingered a little too long over their meal and missed the return ferry in the afternoon. That evening in the front bar of one of the pubs they managed to arrange a ride back to the mainland the following morning with a local – in a 14-foot tinnie. Three hours and three hundred dollars later they stepped ashore after a rather rough and damp crossing of Endeavour Strait!

FOLLOWING PAGES
Picturesque Eliot Falls

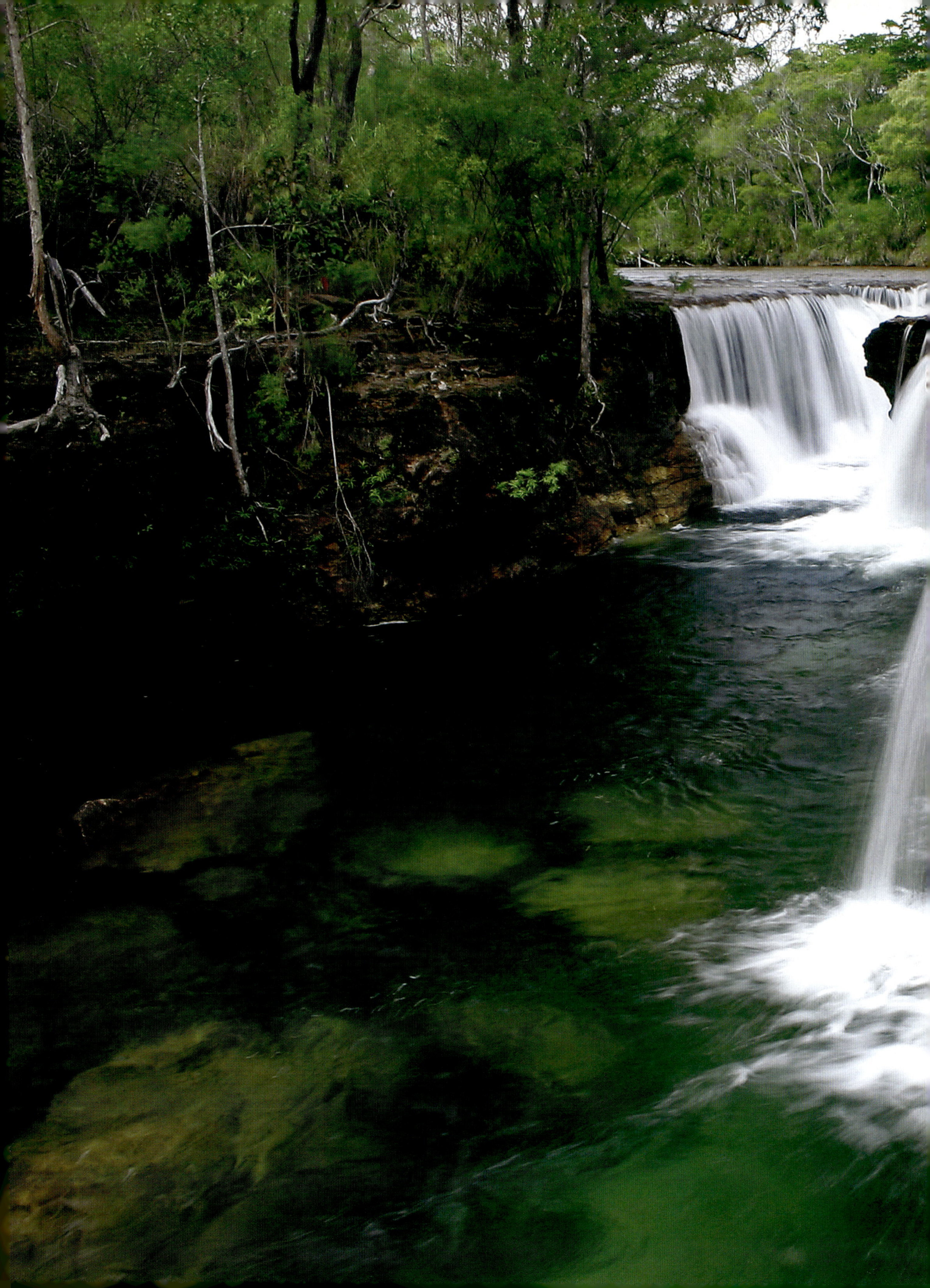

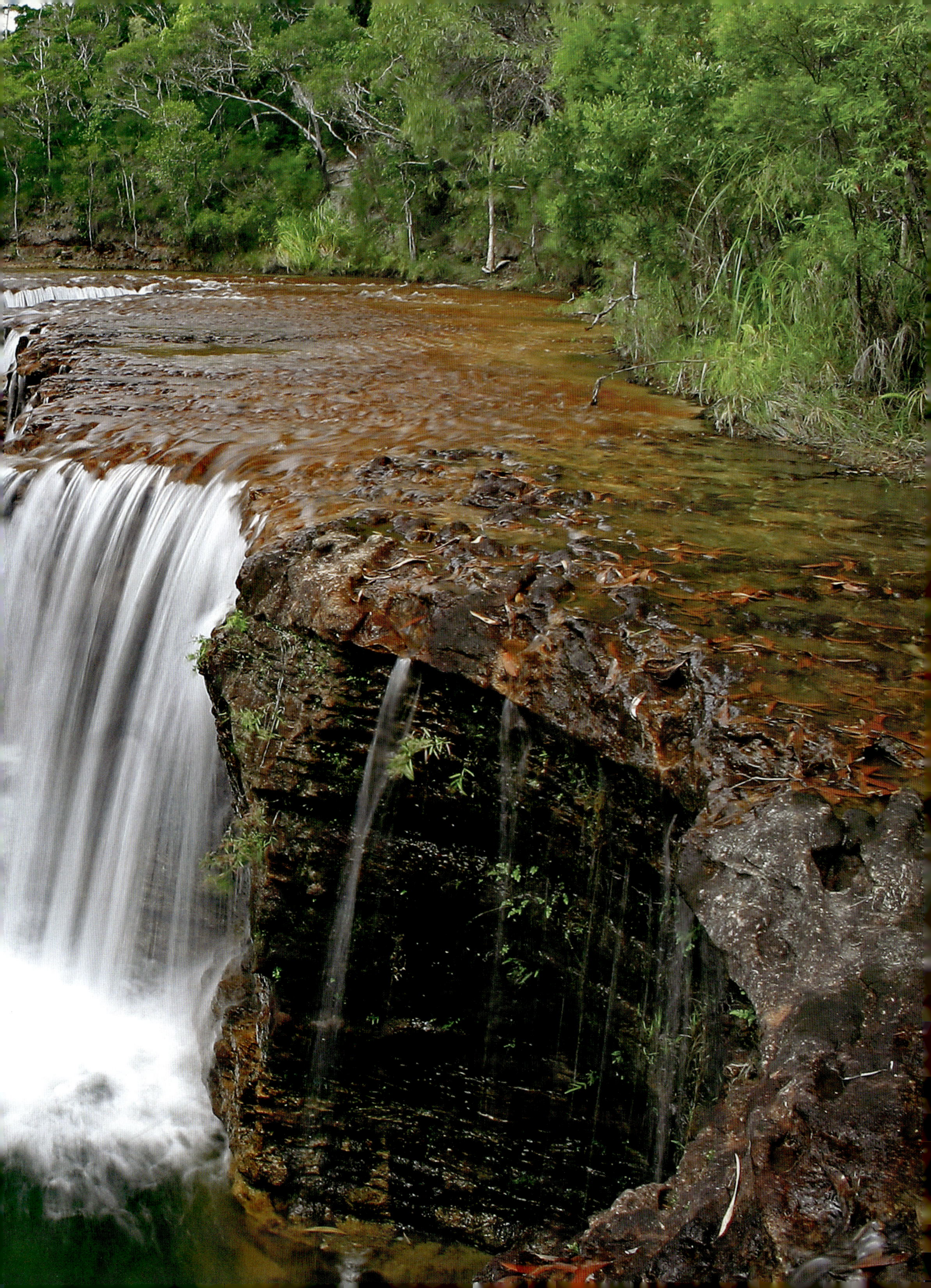

Across the Gulf

Crossing the vast Gulf plains

NORMANTON ◀▶ MATARANKA 1282.3 KM

1. NORMANTON ◁▷ BORROLOOLA 727.7 km *(easy)*
2. BORROLOOLA ◁▷ MATARANKA 554.6 km *(easy)*

WHEN TO GO May–October **TIME** 4–6 days

Starting from Queensland's Normanton in the south-east of the Gulf of Carpentaria, and ending at Mataranka in the Northern Territory, this trek covers some of the Gulf's most spectacular scenery, including vast shimmering plains, collections of towering rock formations known as 'Lost Cities', watercourses teeming with fish and rugged ranges hiding secrets from the Aboriginal Dreamtime.

The Gulf track has rough, often corrugated sections along with numerous river crossings. It leads you in the footsteps of some of our more intrepid and ill-fated explorers, such as the eccentric German Ludwig Leichhardt and the inexperienced Irish-born Robert O'Hara Burke. Legendary drover Nat Buchanan moved 1200 head through the uncharted terrain in 1878 and followed with a drive of 20 000 a few years later, one of the biggest cattle drives ever undertaken in Australia. When gold was discovered in the Northern Territory and Kimberley, the Gulf track became the favoured route from the dwindling fields of Cape York and it is lined with lonely graves of miners who succumbed to the unforgiving heat and hardships of the road.

Frontier towns such as Normanton, Burketown and Borroloola, originally the only settlements in this remote and often lawless stretch of country, today provide supplies for travellers, many of whom come to fish the rivers for mighty barramundi, wily salmon and elusive mud crabs. Fuel and limited supplies are also available at several roadhouses. There are campgrounds with facilities at roadhouses and some stations, while those who prefer bush camping will find plenty of shady sites along the route.

ACROSS THE GULF

Kris, a 26-foot crocodile replica in Normanton, is a fearsome warning of the dangers lurking in Gulf waters

Services

VEHICLE ASSISTANCE
AANT (NT)/RACQ (Qld) — 13 1111

POLICE
Borroloola	(08) 8975 8770
Burketown	(07) 4745 5120
Doomadgee	(07) 4745 8222
Mataranka	(08) 8975 4511
Ngukurr	(08) 8975 4644
Normanton	(07) 4745 1133

PARKS AND RESERVES
Bitter Springs
Elsey National Park
PWCNT Mataranka — (08) 8975 4560

Limmen National Park
PWCNT Nathan River — (08) 8975 9940

USEFUL CONTACTS
Matataranka Community Government Council — (08) 8975 4576

VISITOR INFORMATION
Burketown — (07) 4745 5111
Normanton — (07) 4745 1065

Authors' note

When you get to Burketown don't forget to drop into the visitor centre and have a chat with Frank. Along with his great local knowledge he's on for a yarn and a laugh — we were there for over an hour!

Town Facilities

Town	Fuel: D/P/A	Mechanical repairs	Tyre repairs	Public telephone	Public toilets	Shop/supplies	Gas refills	Ice	Visitor information	Post office	Medical centre	Police	Meals	Motel	Hotel	Cabins	Caravan park	Camping
Borroloola	D/P	•	•	•	•	•	•	•	•	•	•	•	•	•	•	•	•	•
Burketown	D/P	•	•	•	•	•	•	•	•	•	•	•	•	•	•	•	•	•
Mataranka	D/P/A	•	•	•	•	•	•	•	•	•	•	•	•	•	•	•	•	•
Normanton	D/P	•	•	•	•	•	•	•	•	•	•	•	•	•	•	•	•	•
Roper Bar	D/P		•	•	•	•				•	•					•	•

303

ACROSS THE GULF

1 NORMANTON ◄► BORROLOOLA 727.7 KM

Start point
Normanton

Road atlas
360 C7

Total distance
727.7 km

Standard
Easy

Time
2–3 days

Longest distance no PD (includes all options)
277.3 km (Wollogorang Roadhouse to Borroloola)

Topographic maps
Auslig 1:250 000 series: *Normanton*; *Donors Hill*; *Burketown*; *Lawn Hill*; *West Moreland*; *Calvert Hills*; *Robinson River Special*; *Bauhinia Downs*

Other useful information
- Tirranna Roadhouse has petrol, diesel, public telephone, groceries, ice, take-away and eat-in meals, motel-type accommodation and campground. Shop open seven days 8am–8pm, tel. (07) 4748 5657; accepts cash, EFTPOS and credit cards.
- Escott Barramundi Lodge offers minor mechanical repairs, tyre repairs and basic welding for patrons, along with licensed restaurant, swimming pool and fishing tours. Office hours 8am–6pm, tel. (07) 4748 5577; accepts cash, EFTPOS and credit cards.
- Doomadgee store has petrol, diesel and a good range of groceries. Open Monday–Friday 9am–4.30pm and Saturday 9am–12noon, tel. (07) 4745 8183; accepts cash, EFTPOS and credit cards.
- Hells Gate Roadhouse offers petrol, diesel, tyre repairs, limited supplies, ice, take-away and eat-in meals (also free coffee if you make it yourself), licensed restaurant, motel-type accommodation and campground. Open seven days 7am–10pm, tel. (07) 4745 8258; accepts cash, EFTPOS and credit cards.
- Wollogorang Roadhouse has petrol, diesel, mechanical and tyre repairs, limited supplies, ice, take-away and eat-in meals, licensed restaurant, motel-type accommodation and campground (also offers four-wheel-drive access to Tully and Massacre inlets on Wollogorang station, where there is remote bush camping and fishing – daily fee and rubbish bond payable at roadhouse). Open seven days 7am–9pm, tel. (08) 8975 9944; accepts cash, EFTPOS and credit cards.
- Visitor brochure: *Inland Queensland Tourist Guide*.
- Government brochure: *Take the Road Less Travelled: Savannah Way*.
- Carpentaria Shire Council brochure: *Normanton and Karumba: Queensland's Gulf Country*.
- Burke Shire booklet: *Burke Shire – Beyond the Bitumen* gives details of regional history.
- J.W. Knowles' *Lonely Rails in the Gulf Country* is a history of the Normanton to Croydon railway and the *Gulflander* tourist train.
- Discovery Trail brochure: *Northern Territory Discovery Trails: Borroloola & the Gulf Country*.
- National Trust (NT) brochures: *Borroloola Heritage Trail*; *Old Police Station Borroloola*. Both available from Old Police Station Museum.
- Birdlife is prolific on rivers and lagoons so pack a bird identification guide and binoculars.

Description
The flat and featureless Gulf Savannah country stretches west from Cairns to the Northern Territory border. There are a multitude of rivers and, fed by Gulf waters, the magnificent tidal estuaries thread through mangrove wetlands and salt flats into immense grass-covered plains. During the wet season the area can be transformed into an inland sea. The landscape is ancient and pristine and has only a small and scattered population in outback towns, remote cattle stations and Aboriginal settlements. The roads are generally maintained and include sections of bitumen, good-quality gravel and rough, corrugated dirt with long stretches of bulldust.

Normanton, where this trek starts, is home to the historic *Gulflander* train and the iconic National Hotel, better known as the Purple Pub. Once on the track, you pass monuments to Burke and Wills and explorer Fredrick Walker, and a river and falls named after Leichhardt, although the falls usually stop flowing early in the dry season.

Take fishing gear because many overnight stops – some at bush campsites beside rivers, others on cattle stations – are excellent fishing spots. Remember to be crocodile-wise when fishing and camping. Burketown lies by the Albert River, dividing the wetlands from the grass plains to the south. The only settlement of any size between Normanton and Borroloola, it offers good fishing and camping by the river. Another good spot, further on, is Wollogorang station, just across the border in the Northern Territory, which offers camping and fishing near Tully and Massacre inlets (see Other useful information for contact details).

Road train crossing the Leichhardt River

After leaving Burketown you pass the turn-off to Escott Barramundi Lodge before crossing the Gregory and Nicholson rivers via concrete causeways. The lush vegetation and prolific birdlife on the Gregory River creates a pleasant setting but the presence of saltwater crocodiles makes swimming impossible.

The track from Hells Gate winds its way across the border into Territory Gulf country and follows the Gulf of Carpentaria coastline past vast cattle stations. West of Wollogorang Roadhouse the route passes through more undulating country, a pleasant change from the flat, scrubby terrain. You cross a number of larger rivers before arriving at Borroloola. It pays to take care on this section, especially early in the dry when the waters can be quite deep. Once again, this is crocodile country so there is no swimming.

Advice and warnings

- The road is a mixture of bitumen, maintained gravel with bulldust holes, corrugations and sand. Contact RACQ road reporting service, tel. 1300 130 595, and Northern Territory road information service, tel. 1800 246 199, or visit their website (www.nt.gov.au/dtw/roadconditions), to check road conditions.
- Rivers can hold water for some time into the dry season so slow down on approaching the numerous creek and river crossings. Some have steep, sharp entries.
- Exercise caution when overtaking and approaching other vehicles and drive with your headlights on.
- Watch out for roaming stock as track passes through sections of unfenced pastoral land.
- Standard road tyres or all-terrain tyres are suitable. It is advisable to carry two spare tyres.
- Towing off-road trailers and off-road caravans is possible along the length of the route.
- Camping is at designated areas and at a number of bush campsites noted in the route directions.
- Drinking water is not available at bush campsites so carry enough for your own drinking, cooking and washing needs.
- Rubbish bins are not provided en route so please take your rubbish with you.
- Saltwater and freshwater crocodiles inhabit rivers and coastal waters. Swimming is not recommended.
- Alcohol restrictions apply at Doomadgee community. Heavy fines apply. Contact Alcohol Management Program information line, tel. 1300 789 000, or visit the websites (www.mcmc.qld.gov.au *or* www.liquor.qld.gov.au/Indigenous/), for details on current restrictions.
- Carry cash as phone lines and/or power systems for credit card and EFTPOS facilities are sometimes down.
- Mosquitoes and sandflies are prevalent so carry plenty of good insect repellent.

Permits and bookings

- No permits required to travel this route.
- No permit required to drive direct to Doomadgee store but permits required to visit other areas belonging to the community.
- No access allowed to Floraville homestead when visiting the Frederick Walker Memorial so observe the route-direction signs.
- Visitors to the vast salt flats at Burketown must complete a Trip Intention Form prior to travelling. Forms are available at the entrance to the flats.
- Bookings recommended for camping, donga and motel accommodation during May–August at Escott Barramundi Lodge, tel. (07) 4748 5577.
- Bookings recommended for motel accommodation at Tirranna Roadhouse, tel. (07) 4748 5657; Hells Gate Roadhouse, tel. (07) 4745 8258; and Wollogorang Roadhouse, tel. (08) 8975 9944.
- Bookings recommended for the *Gulflander* during peak visitor season. Contact Normanton Railway Station, tel. (07) 4745 1391, for details.
- Remote fishing and camping is possible on the Greenbank property, located to the east of Borroloola. Call into Snake Lagoon homestead first for details and payment of fees or tel. (08) 8975 9825.
- Recreational fishing is permitted and no fishing licence is required in either Queensland or the Northern Territory but bag and size limits apply. To check restrictions and regulations, contact Queensland Fisheries, tel. (07) 3225 1843, or visit their website (www.dpi.qld.gov.au/fishweb); and Northern Territory Fisheries Department, tel. (08) 8999 2372, or visit their website (www.fisheries.nt.gov.au).

ACROSS THE GULF

Hells Gate
Hells Gate is the name of a gap between two rocky outcrops, which the road passes through. During the days of early settlement the police, then based at Corinda on the Nicholson River, would escort west-bound travellers and settlers to this point, after which they were on their own until they reached police protection at Katherine in the Northern Territory.

Burketown
Burketown was officially established in July 1865 when the *Jacmel Packet* arrived at the Albert River and off-loaded supplies for nearby cattle stations. The story goes that before the police arrived in 1866, everyone carried a pistol and successful shopkeepers were those who excelled at riding, shooting and throwing a punch. Nowadays the town still services surrounding cattle stations, as well as seasonal tourists and anglers. On the riverbank are the rusting remains (pictured) of the town's once prosperous boiling-down works.

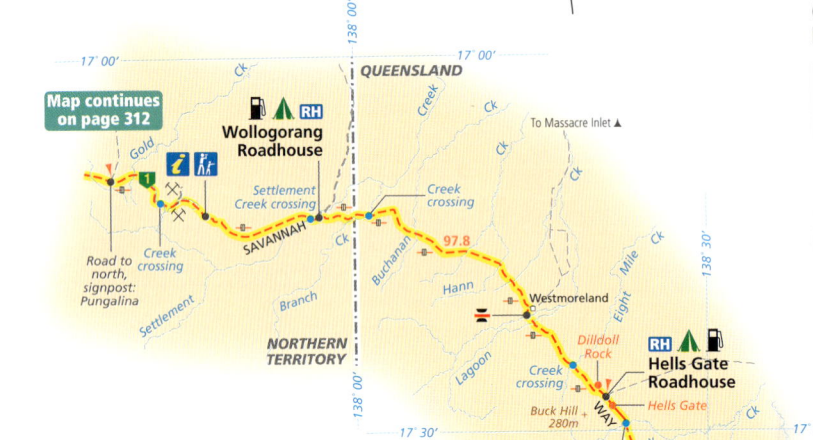

Causeway crossing at the Gregory River

Campsite Facilities

	Toilets	Disabled access	4WD access only	Off-road trailer	Off-road caravan	Drinking water	Fee payable	Ranger patrolled	BBQ/fireplace	Campfires prohibited	Picnic tables	Shelter shed	No rubbish disposal	Public phone	Shower	Bushwalking	Swimming	Swimming not advised	Fishing	Canoeing	Dogs allowed
Escott Lodge	•		•	•	•	•			•				•	•	•	•	•				
Hells Gate	•		•	•	•	•			•			•		•							•
Snake Lagoon	•		•	•		•								•			•			•	
Wollogorang	•		•	•	•	•							•	•							

NORMANTON ◀▶ BORROLOOLA

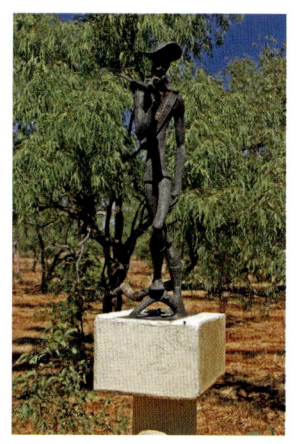

Frederick Walker Memorial
Frederick Walker was employed by the Queensland government in 1861 to lead a search party for Burke and Wills. His was the only one of the three parties in the Gulf region to find traces of the missing explorers. Walker died from gulf fever at Floraville crossing in 1866, while surveying a route for a telegraph line. A statue of Walker (pictured) stands at Floraville station.

Normanton's Purple Pub

The Albert River at Burketown

Burke and Wills Camp
On 9 February 1861 Burke, Wills, Gray and King set up Camp 119 on the southern banks of the Little Bynoe River, the northernmost camp of their expedition. The next day, leaving Gray and King, Burke and Wills set off for the coast, returning two days later after reportedly sighting the sea. On 13 February all four men left the camp to return to Cooper Creek (see pages 252–3). A monument marks the location of Camp 119.

307

ACROSS THE GULF

ROUTE DIRECTIONS

▼ 0.0 km — Zero trip meter on Landsborough St (main street) in Normanton with post office on right. Proceed in south-westerly direction along Landsborough St passing Purple Pub on left.

Normanton. Post office on left. 71.2 km ▲

GPS   S:17 40.185 E:141 04.778
UTM   54K 508446E 8046350N

(0.8 km)

▼ 0.8 km — Road junction. CSA over railway tracks SP: Cloncurry/Cairns. Road on right, SP: Matilda Street, leads 0.2 km to *Gulflander* railway station.

Railway crossing. Road junction over crossing. CSA. Road on left SP: Matilda Street. 70.4 km ▲

(4.9 km)

▼ 5.7 km — Road junction. TR onto gravel. SP: Burketown.
Road SO leads to Matilda Hwy.

T-junction with bitumen. TL. SP: Normanton. 65.5 km ▲

GPS   S:17 42.530 E:141 02.882
UTM   54K 505093E 8042027N

(31.5 km)

▼ 37.2 km — Road junction. CSA. Track on left SP: 2 Burke & Wills Monument.
Track on left leads 1.6 km to Burke & Wills Monument, marking Camp 119. Track to right of monument leads short distance to bush campsites along banks of the Little Bynoe River.

Road junction. CSA. Track on right SP: Burke & Wills Monument 2. 34.0 km ▲

GPS   S:17 51.957 E:140 49.719
UTM   54K 481847E 8024637N

(0.3 km)

▼ 37.5 km — Causeway over SP: Little Bynoe River.

Causeway over SP: Little Bynoe River. 33.7 km ▲

(0.2 km)

▼ 37.7 km — Road junction. CSA. Track on left.
Track on left leads to bush campsites by river.

Road junction. CSA. Track on right. 33.5 km ▲

(2.4 km)

▼ 40.1 km — Causeway over SP: Bynoe River.

Causeway over SP: Bynoe River. 31.1 km ▲

GPS   S:17 51.721 E:140 48.131
UTM   54K 479042E 8025069N

(2.9 km)

▼ 43.0 km — Causeway over SP: Flinders River.

Causeway over SP: Flinders River. 28.2 km ▲

(9.9 km)

▼ 52.9 km — Causeway over SP: Armstrong Ck.

Causeway over SP: Armstrong Ck. 18.3 km ▲

(18.1 km)

▼ 71.0 km — Y-junction. KL. Track on right.
Track on right leads to homestead.

Road junction. CSA. Track on left. 0.2 km ▲

(0.2 km)

▼ 71.2 km — Crossroads.

Zero trip meter at crossroads. CSA. Track on right SP: 29 km McAllister. 0.0 km ▲

GPS   S:18 00.769 E:140 33.829
UTM   54K 453827E 8008342N

▼ 0.0 km — Zero trip meter at crossroads. CSA. Track on left SP: 29 km McAllister.

Crossroads. 85.0 km ▲

(0.4 km)

▼ 0.4 km — Concrete causeway.

Concrete causeway. 84.6 km ▲

(26.7 km)

▼ 27.1 km — Y-junction. KR. Track on left.
Track on left leads to homestead.

Road junction. CSA. Track on right. 57.9 km ▲

(6.0 km)

▼ 33.1 km — Creek crossing, usually dry.

Creek crossing. 51.9 km ▲

(42.2 km)

▼ 75.3 km — Road junction. CSA. Track on right SP: Wernadinga 8.

Y-junction. KR. Track on left SP: Wernadinga 8. 9.7 km ▲

GPS   S:18 10.413 E:139 54.992
UTM   54K 385409E 7990275N

(6.1 km)

▼ 81.4 km — Road junction. CSA. Track on right.

Road junction. CSA. Track on left. 3.6 km ▲

(0.3 km)

▼ 81.7 km — Causeway over Alexandra River.

Causeway over Alexandra River. 3.3 km ▲

GPS   S:18 13.508 E:139 53.889
UTM   54K 383498E 7984556N

(0.7 km)

The Gulflander *crossing the Norman River*

NORMANTON ◀▶ BORROLOOLA

▼ 82.4 km   T-junction. TR. SP: Savannah Way/Burketown.

         Road junction. TL. SP: 15 Wernadinga/   2.6 km ▲
         160 Normanton.

GPS   S:18 13.776 E:139 53.598
UTM   54K 382989E 7984059N

(2.0 km)

▼ 84.4 km   Causeway over SP: Leichhardt River.

Bush camping to right of causeway among trees. Leichhardt Falls, to right of causeway, generally not flowing in the Dry.

         Causeway over SP: Leichhardt River.   0.6 km ▲

GPS   S:18 13.318 E:139 52.676
UTM   54K 381358E 7984893N

(0.6 km)

▼ 85.0 km   Road junction.

         Zero trip meter at road junction. CSA.   0.0 km ▲
         Track on right SP: Historic Site/
         Frederick Walker Monument.

GPS   S:18 13.129 E:139 52.406
UTM   54K 380880E 7985239N

▼ 0.0 km   Zero trip meter at road junction. CSA. Track on left SP: Historic Site/Frederick Walker Monument. Information board at junction.

Track on left leads 1.2 km to Frederick Walker memorial.

         Road junction.   71.4 km ▲

(62.6 km)

▼ 62.6 km   Causeway over SP: Harris Lake, and SP: Pear Tree Creek.

         Causeway over SP: Harris Lake, and SP: 8.8 km ▲
         Pear Tree Creek.

(5.5 km)

▼ 68.1 km   Bridge over SP: Albert River.

         Bridge over SP: Albert River.   3.3 km ▲

GPS   S:17 45.980 E:139 33.674
UTM   54K 347476E 8035082N

(3.3 km)

▼ 71.4 km   Road junction in Burketown.

         Zero trip meter in Burketown at T-junction   0.0 km ▲
         with Burketown Pub on left. TR. SP:
         Beames St, and proceed in
         south-easterly direction.

GPS   S:17 44.463 E:139 32.873
UTM   54K 346039E 8037869N

▼ 0.0 km   Zero trip meter at junction of SP: Musgrave St, and SP: Beames St, in Burketown. Burketown Pub at junction. Proceed west along SP: Musgrave Street, towards SP: Gregory.

         T-junction in Burketown.   94.7 km ▲

(5.5 km)

▼ 5.5 km   Road junction. CSA. Road on right SP: Escott Barramundi Lodge 12 km.

Road on right leads 11.8 km to Escott Barramundi Lodge and campground, a large grassy area shaded by tall trees close to homestead.

         Road junction. CSA. Road on left SP: Escott   89.2 km ▲
         Barramundi Lodge 12 km.

(20.6 km)

Gulflander driver and tour guide Ken Millard

Historic *Gulflander*

At Normanton, again in the name of research, we took an overnight trip on the *Gulflander* to Croydon. Once a week passengers and mail are transported on a leisurely five-hour journey, with mail drops along the way and a stop at Blackbull Siding for a delightful morning tea of freshly baked scones. What a wonderful trip. The train driver, Ken Millard, would have to be one of the best tour guides ever. His passion for the train and the route was evident from his inspiring commentary.

The train driver, Ken Millard, would have to be one of the best tour guides ever

To step aboard the historic 1950s locomotive is to step back in time. The 152 kilometres of track, between the port at Normanton and the gold-rush town of Croydon, were laid in 1888–91. According to Ken, many of the original 260 000 revolutionary steel sleepers are still in position. Once in Croydon, we explored on our own, discovering the exciting boom and bust story of the mining and fossicking days. We stayed at the Club Hotel where the upstairs rooms are great, although we didn't venture into the 'haunted' room. The hotel served up an excellent feed next morning then we hopped back on the train for our return trip.

You can do this memorable journey in a day but you have to return by bus in the afternoon. In April–September the train also runs a range of short trips from Normanton including a popular billy tea and damper excursion and a Thursday evening sunset sizzle barbecue outing.

ACROSS THE GULF

Extensive saltpan near Burketown

▼ **26.1 km** T-junction. TR. SP: Doomadgee 76/Hells Gate 156/Northern Territory Border 206. Road on left SP: Gregory Downs 94/Savannah Way Alt. Route.

Road on left leads 193 km to Lawn Hill National Park via Gregory Downs.

Road junction. TL. SP: 26 Burketown. Road on right SP: Gregory Downs 94.   68.6 km ▲

GPS   S:17 52.093 E:139 20.802
UTM   54K 324828E 8023619N

(8.0 km)

▼ **34.1 km** Tirranna Roadhouse on right. CSA.

Camping available behind roadhouse. Call in at office first.

Tirranna Roadhouse on left. CSA.   60.6 km ▲

(1.2 km)

▼ **35.3 km** Causeway over Gregory River.

Track on left prior to crossing leads to bush campsite. Over river numerous tracks on left lead to several bush campsites beside the river.

Causeway over Gregory River.   59.4 km ▲

GPS   S:17 53.501 E:139 17.209
UTM   54K 318505E 8020964N

(4.5 km)

▼ **39.8 km** Bridge.

Bridge.   54.9 km ▲

(49.8 km)

▼ **89.6 km** Road junction. CSA. Road on left SP: Savannah Way Alt. Route.

Road junction. CSA. Road on right SP: Savannah Way Alt. Route.   5.1 km ▲

(4.0 km)

▼ **93.6 km** Causeway over Nicholson River.

Causeway over Nicholson River.   1.1 km ▲

GPS   S:17 57.828 E:138 50.811
UTM   54K 271972E 8012498N

(1.1 km)

▼ **94.7 km** Road junction.

Zero trip meter at road junction. CSA. Road on right SP: Doomadgee.   0.0 km ▲

GPS   S:17 57.411 E:138 51.111
UTM   54K 272493E 8013273N

▼ **0.0 km** Zero trip meter at road junction. CSA. Road on left SP: Doomadgee.

Road on left leads 3.3 km to Doomadgee store. No permit required to drive direct to store but permits required to visit other community areas.

Road junction.   84.3 km ▲

(32.9 km)

▼ **32.9 km** Road junction. CSA. SP: Hells Gate/NT Border. Road on left SP: Kingfisher Camp 42 km.

Road on left leads approximately 42 km to Kingfisher Camp, where there is camping and fishing on Nicholson River, tel. (07) 4745 8212.

Road junction. CSA. Road on right SP: Kingfisher Camp 42 km.   51.4 km ▲

GPS   S:17 49.725 E:138 35.241
UTM   54K 244283E 8027112N

(33.3 km)

▼ **66.2 km** Creek crossing.

Creek crossing.   18.1 km ▲

(6.7 km)

▼ **72.9 km** Creek crossing.

310

NORMANTON ◀▶ BORROLOOLA

		Creek crossing.	11.4 km ▲	▼ 68.2 km	Creek crossing.	
	(9.8 km)				Creek crossing.	29.6 km ▲
▼ 82.7 km	Road passes through two rocky outcrops. This is Hells Gate. CSA.			(10.5 km)		
				▼ 78.7 km	Lookout and information boards on right.	
	Road passes through two rocky outcrops. This is Hells Gate. CSA.		1.6 km ▲		Lookout and information boards on left.	19.1 km ▲

GPS S:17 27.999 E:138 21.867
UTM 54K 220086E 8066887N

GPS S:17 12.507 E:137 47.104
UTM 53K 796219E 8095254N

(1.6 km)

(8.5 km)

▼ 84.3 km Hells Gate Roadhouse on right.

▼ 87.2 km Creek crossing.

Zero trip meter with Hells Gate Roadhouse on left. Proceed in south-easterly direction towards SP: 182 Burketown/80 Doomadgee.   0.0 km ▲

Creek crossing.   10.6 km ▲

(10.6 km)

GPS S:17 27.324 E:138 21.370
UTM 54K 219188E 8068121N

▼ 97.8 km Road junction.

Zero trip meter at road junction. CSA. Track on left SP: Pungalina 64.   0.0 km ▲

▼ 0.0 km Zero trip meter with Hells Gate Roadhouse on right. Proceed in north-westerly direction towards SP: NT Border 50.

GPS S:17 09.642 E:137 38.988
UTM 53K 781895E 8100743N

Hells Gate Roadhouse campground is a large, shaded area of grassland located close to the roadhouse.

▼ 0.0 km Zero trip meter at road junction. CSA. Track on right SP: Pungalina 64.

Hells Gate Roadhouse on left.   97.8 km ▲

Road junction.   122.9 km ▲

(1.8 km)

(12.0 km)

▼ 1.8 km Dilldoll Rock on right.

▼ 12.0 km Cross SP: Karns Creek.

From the Northern Territory side, rock is said to resemble the profile of an Aboriginal woman.

Cross SP: Karns Creek.   110.9 km ▲

(7.1 km)

Dilldoll Rock on left.   96.0 km ▲

▼ 19.1 km Road junction. CSA. SP: Borroloola/Cape Crawford. Road on left SP: Calvert Hills/Calvert Road.

(5.4 km)

▼ 7.2 km Creek crossing.

Road junction. CSA. SP: Wollogorang/Qld Border. Road on right SP: Calvert Hills/Calvert Road.   103.8 km ▲

Creek crossing.   90.6 km ▲

(8.9 km)

▼ 16.1 km Creek crossing.

GPS S:17 05.441 E:137 29.478
UTM 53K 765124E 8108718N

Creek crossing.   81.7 km ▲

(22.6 km)

(1.6 km)

▼ 41.7 km Road junction. CSA. Track on left.

▼ 17.7 km Concrete causeway.

Track on left leads 0.4 km to bush campsite beside the Calvert River. Small area suitable for 2 tents. Track not suitable for trailers or vans.

Concrete causeway.   80.1 km ▲

(33.1 km)

Road junction. CSA. Track on right.   81.2 km ▲

▼ 50.8 km Creek crossing.

(0.3 km)

Creek crossing.   47.0 km ▲

▼ 42.0 km Cross SP: Calvert River.

(2.9 km)

Cross SP: Calvert River.   80.9 km ▲

▼ 53.7 km Grid. Enter Northern Territory.

GPS S:16 56.074 E:137 21.601
UTM 53K 751354E 8126175N

Grid. Enter Queensland.   44.1 km ▲

GPS S:17 12.801 E:137 59.702
UTM 53K 818559E 8094377N

(0.2 km)

▼ 42.2 km Road junction. CSA. Track on right.

(5.1 km)

Track on right leads 0.1 km to bush campsite and information boards.

▼ 58.8 km Road junction. CSA. Road on right SP: Wollogorang Roadhouse.

Road junction. CSA. Track on left.   80.7 km ▲

Road on right leads 0.4 km to **Wollogorang Roadhouse** and **campground**, a large and open area of grassland with little shade, in vicinity of roadhouse.

(17.7 km)

▼ 59.9 km Road junction. CSA. Track on left.

Track on left leads 0.3 km to possible bush campsite.

Road junction. CSA. Road on left SP: Wollogorang Roadhouse.   39.0 km ▲

Road junction. CSA. Track on right.   63.0 km ▲

(1.5 km)

(0.3 km)

▼ 60.3 km Cross SP: Settlement Creek.

▼ 60.2 km Cross SP: Surprise Creek.

Cross SP: Settlement Creek.   37.5 km ▲

Cross SP: Surprise Creek.   62.7 km ▲

GPS S:17 12.877 E:137 56.191
UTM 53K 812328E 8094333N

GPS S:16 51.342 E:137 13.081
UTM 53K 736322E 8135081N

(7.9 km)

(0.4 km)

■ 311

ACROSS THE GULF

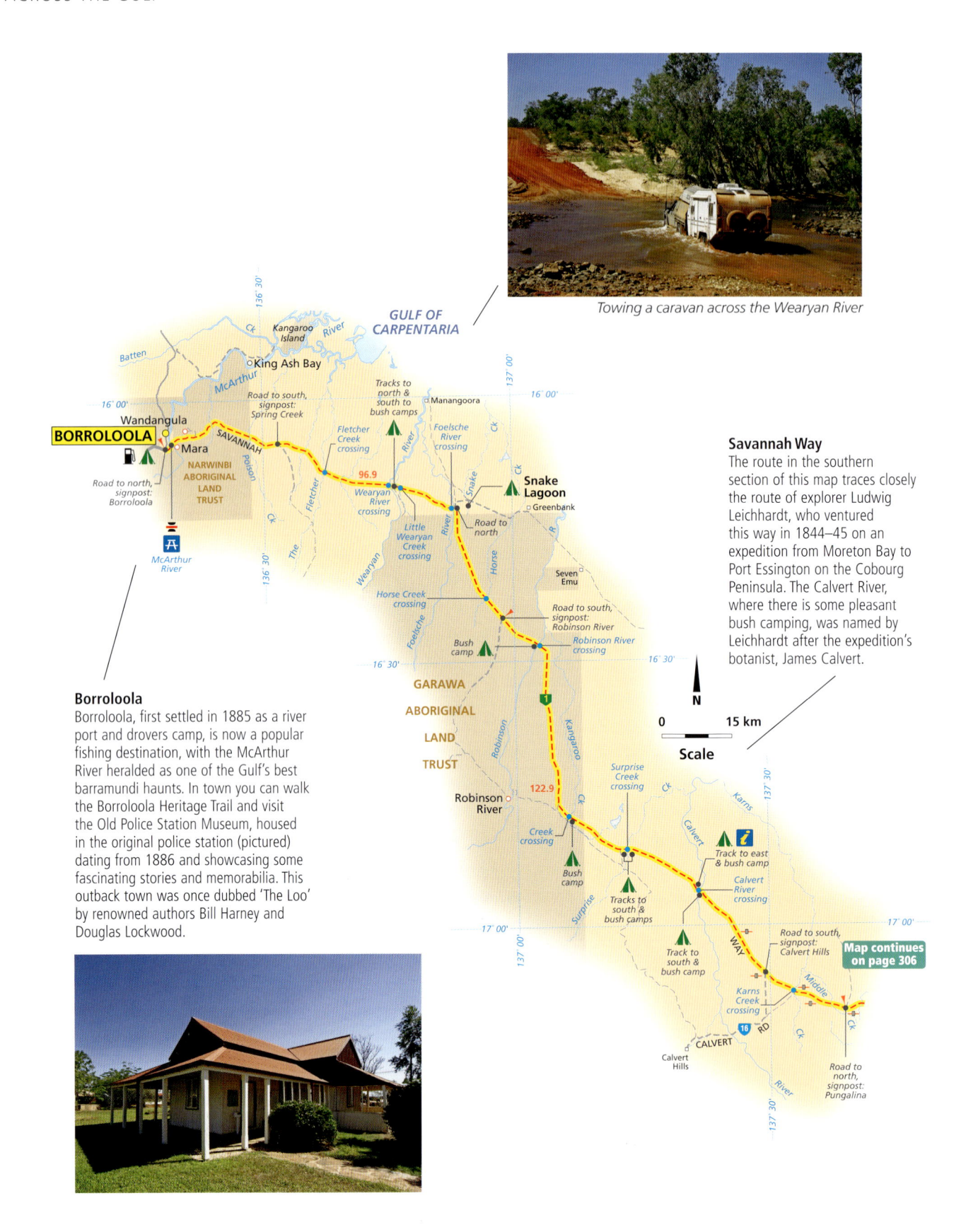

Towing a caravan across the Wearyan River

Savannah Way
The route in the southern section of this map traces closely the route of explorer Ludwig Leichhardt, who ventured this way in 1844–45 on an expedition from Moreton Bay to Port Essington on the Cobourg Peninsula. The Calvert River, where there is some pleasant bush camping, was named by Leichhardt after the expedition's botanist, James Calvert.

Borroloola
Borroloola, first settled in 1885 as a river port and drovers camp, is now a popular fishing destination, with the McArthur River heralded as one of the Gulf's best barramundi haunts. In town you can walk the Borroloola Heritage Trail and visit the Old Police Station Museum, housed in the original police station (pictured) dating from 1886 and showcasing some fascinating stories and memorabilia. This outback town was once dubbed 'The Loo' by renowned authors Bill Harney and Douglas Lockwood.

312

NORMANTON ◀▶ BORROLOOLA

▼ 60.6 km Road junction. CSA. Track on left.
Track on left leads to possible bush campsites.
Road junction. CSA. Track on right. 62.3 km ▲
(14.4 km)

▼ 75.0 km Creek crossing.
Pleasant shady bush camping on left prior to creek.
Creek crossing. 47.9 km ▲
(37.9 km)

▼ 112.9 km Cross SP: Robinson River.
Limited bush camping on rocky bank on left over river, best suited for trailers or vans.
Cross SP: Robinson River. 10.0 km ▲

GPS S:16 28.272 E:137 02.976
UTM 53K 718808E 8177832N

(10.0 km)

▼ 122.9 km Road junction.
Zero trip meter at road junction. CSA. SP: 165 Wollogorang. Road on right SP: 45 Robinson River. 0.0 km ▲

GPS S:16 25.115 E:136 58.606
UTM 53K 711087E 8183733N

▼ 0.0 km Zero trip meter at road junction. CSA. SP: 95 Borroloola. Road on left SP: 45 Robinson River.
Road junction. 96.9 km ▲
(5.5 km)

▼ 5.5 km Cross SP: Horse Creek.
Cross SP: Horse Creek. 91.4 km ▲
(20.6 km)

▼ 26.1 km Road junction. CSA. SP: Borroloola 69. Road on right SP: 25 Manangoora/Greenbank/Camp Area 5 km.
Road on right leads 1.3 km to road junction. TR here and after 2.7 km TR again at SP: Camp Area. A further 0.8 km leads to **Snake Lagoon** homestead and **camping area**, an open, grass-covered spot beside the lagoon. Call in here if continuing on to Greenbank for remote fishing and camping (see Permits and bookings for contact details).
Road junction. CSA. SP: 191 Wollogorang. Road on left SP: 25 Manangoora/Greenbank/ Camp Area 5 km. 70.8 km ▲
(0.2 km)

▼ 26.3 km Cross SP: Foelshe River.
Cross SP: Foelshe River. 70.6 km ▲

GPS S:16 12.649 E: 136 53.013
UTM 53K 701342E 8206821N

(13.1 km)

▼ 39.4 km Cross SP: Little Wearyan.
Cross SP: Little Wearyan. 57.5 km ▲
(1.4 km)

▼ 40.8 km Road junction. CSA. Track on left and right.
Track on left leads 0.6 km to a rough bush campsite and track on right leads 0.9 km to several bush campsites.
Road junction. CSA. Track on left and right. 56.1 km ▲
(0.3 km)

▼ 41.1 km Cross SP: Wearyan River.
Cross SP: Wearyan River. 55.8 km ▲

GPS S:16 10.029 E:136 45.498
UTM 53K 687991E 8211772N

(15.1 km)

▼ 56.2 km Cross SP: Fletcher Creek.
Cross SP: Fletcher Creek. 40.7 km ▲
(12.8 km)

▼ 69.0 km Road junction. CSA. SP: 28 Borroloola. Road on left SP: 61 Spring Creek.
Road junction. CSA. SP: 234 Wollogorang. Road on right SP: 61 Spring Creek. 27.9 km ▲
(26.1 km)

▼ 95.1 km Causeway over SP: McArthur River.
Picnic area on left over river.
Causeway over SP: McArthur River. 1.8 km ▲

GPS S:16 04.800 E:136 19.042
UTM 53K 640902E 8221767N

(1.8 km)

▼ 96.9 km Road junction. Road SO SP: Cape Crawford (start of trek section 2).
Road on right, SP: Borroloola, leads 3.5 km to town centre.
Zero trip meter at road junction on SP: Carpentaria Highway, and road on left SP: Borroloola. Proceed in easterly direction towards SP: Wollogorang. 0.0 km ▲

GPS S:16 05.285 E:136 18.307
UTM 53K 639585E 8220881N

REVERSE DIRECTIONS START

Crossing the Wearyan River

ACROSS THE GULF

2 BORROLOOLA ◀▶ MATARANKA 554.6 KM

Start point
Borroloola

Road atlas
357 K5

Total distance
565.4 km (includes route-directed side trip)

Standard
Easy

Time
2–3 days

Longest distance no PD (includes all options)
442.2 km (Borroloola to Roper Bar)

Topographic maps
Auslig 1:250 000 series: *Bauhinia Downs*; *Mount Young*; *Roper River*; *Urapunga*; *Katherine*

Other useful information
- Old Police Station Museum at Borroloola open Monday–Friday 8am–5pm (outside these times key available from several businesses listed on museum door); entry is by gold coin donation.
- Roper Bar store open Monday–Saturday 9am–6pm and Sunday 1–6pm, tel. (08) 8975 4636; accepts cash, EFTPOS and credit cards.
- Elsey National Park has canoe hire. On-site managers present at Jalmurark campground April–October, tel. (08) 8975 4789. Park also hosts ranger campfire talks once a week at Jalmurark campground during peak visitor season. Contact NTPWC Mataranka, tel. (08) 8975 4560, for current day and time.
- Government brochure: *Take the Road Less Travelled: Savannah Way*.
- NTPWC fact sheets: *Proposed Limmen National Park*; *Elsey National Park*.
- Discovery Trail brochure: *Northern Territory Discovery Trails: Mataranka*
- Birdlife is prolific around rivers and lagoons so pack an identification guide and binoculars.

Description

Borroloola, the starting point of this trek section, is perched on a rise above the McArthur River. Departing town you follow the often rough and corrugated Nathan River Road (also called Savannah Way), soon reaching the newly gazetted Limmen National Park, which stretches from just north of Cape Crawford almost to Roper Bar.

The sparse, undulating country on this part of the trek is broken by patches of scrub and rocky escarpments. Protected within the national park and among its highlights are extraordinary collections of towering sandstone stacks, millions of years old. We visited one called the Southern Lost City. There is a pleasant camping area and delightful swimming hole at Butterfly Springs, good bush camping at Lomarieum Lagoon near St Vidgeon station ruins and good fishing in many of the park's tidal rivers. Keen anglers may like to visit the Limmen Bight River Fishing Camp (see Permits and bookings) located on the park's eastern boundary.

At the Hodgson River crossing, near the northern exit to the park, a rough bush track leads a little over 3 kilometres southwards to an old ford, Rocky Bar Crossing. A little downstream from here is an interesting collection of petroglyphs, or Aboriginal rock engravings.

Back on Nathan River Road it is only a short distance to the turn-off to Roper Bar, which has a caravan park, campground and general store with fuel and supplies. The river here is a popular fishing spot and the ruins of the former Roper Bar police outpost are nearby. The rock bar divides the tidal from the freshwater Roper and both river and bar were named after John Roper, a member of Ludwig Leichhardt's 1845 expedition. From Roper Bar the road to Mataranka is single-lane bitumen most of the way and passes through country of little scenic interest. A number of information signs at the rest stops along this stretch relate to the area's most famous figure, author Jeannie Gunn, and her well-known novel *We of the Never Never*. Once at Mataranka you can explore nearby Elsey National Park and take a relaxing dip in the thermal springs.

The emu apple (Owenia vernicosa) produces hard inedible nuts

BORROLOOLA ◀▶ MATARANKA

Advice and warnings

- The road is a mixture of bitumen, maintained gravel with bulldust holes, corrugations and sand. Contact the Northern Territory road information service, tel. 1800 246 199, or visit their website (www.nt.gov.au/dtw/roadconditions), to check road conditions.
- Rivers can hold water for some time into the dry season so slow down on approaching the numerous creek and river crossings. Some have steep, sharp entries.
- Exercise caution when overtaking and approaching other vehicles and drive with your headlights on.
- Watch out for roaming stock as track passes through sections of unfenced pastoral land.
- Standard road tyres or all-terrain tyres are suitable. It is advisable to carry two spare tyres.
- Towing off-road trailers and off-road caravans is possible but towing trailers or caravans to the Southern Lost City in Limmen National Park is not recommended.
- Camping is only permitted at designated areas and bush campsites noted in the route directions.
- Drinking water is not available at bush campsites so carry enough for your own drinking, cooking and washing needs.
- Rubbish bins are not provided en route so please take your rubbish with you.
- Saltwater and freshwater crocodiles inhabit rivers and coastal waters. Swimming is not recommended.
- Swimming is possible in Elsey National Park at the thermal springs and in the Roper River near the campground.
- A 15-horsepower limit applies to outboards on the Roper River in Elsey National Park.
- Carry cash as phone lines and/or power systems for credit card and EFTPOS facilities can be down.
- Mosquitoes and sandflies are prevalent so carry plenty of good insect repellent.

Permits and bookings

- No permits required to travel this route.
- Advance bookings recommended for cabins at Limmen Bight River Fishing Camp, tel. (08) 8975 9844.
- Bookings recommended for motel and cabin accommodation during May–August at Mataranka Homestead Resort, tel. (08) 8975 4544.
- Lorella Springs offers camping and fishing. Bookings recommended, tel. (08) 8932 4943, or visit their website (www.lorellasprings.com) for information.
- Recreational fishing is permitted in Northern Territory waters. Fishing licence is not required but bag and size limits apply. Contact Northern Territory Fisheries Department, tel. (08) 8999 2372, or visit their website (www.fisheries.nt.gov.au), to check current restrictions and regulations.

Petroglyphs at Rocky Bar Crossing

ROUTE DIRECTIONS

▼ **0.0 km** — Zero trip meter at road junction on SP: Carpentaria Highway, and road on right SP: Borroloola. Proceed in westerly direction towards SP: Cape Crawford.

Road junction. Road SO SP: Wollogorang (start of trek section 1). **88.4 km** ▲

Road on left, SP: Borroloola, leads 3.5 km to town centre.

GPS S:16 05.285 E:136 18.307
UTM 53K 639585E 8220881N

(8.3 km)

▼ **8.3 km** — T-junction. TL. SP: Cape Crawford/Carpentaria Highway. Road on right SP: Bing Bong.

Road junction. TR. SP: Borroloola. Road SO SP: Bing Bong. **80.1 km** ▲

(18.2 km)

▼ **26.5 km** — Road junction. TR onto gravel road. SP: Roper Bar. Road SO SP: Cape Crawford.

T-junction with bitumen. TL. SP: Borroloola. Road on right SP: Cape Crawford. **61.9 km** ▲

GPS S:16 08.595 E:136 05.220
UTM 53K 616223E 8214912N

(12.2 km)

▼ **38.7 km** — Creek crossing.

Creek crossing. **49.7 km** ▲

(1.1 km)

315

ACROSS THE GULF

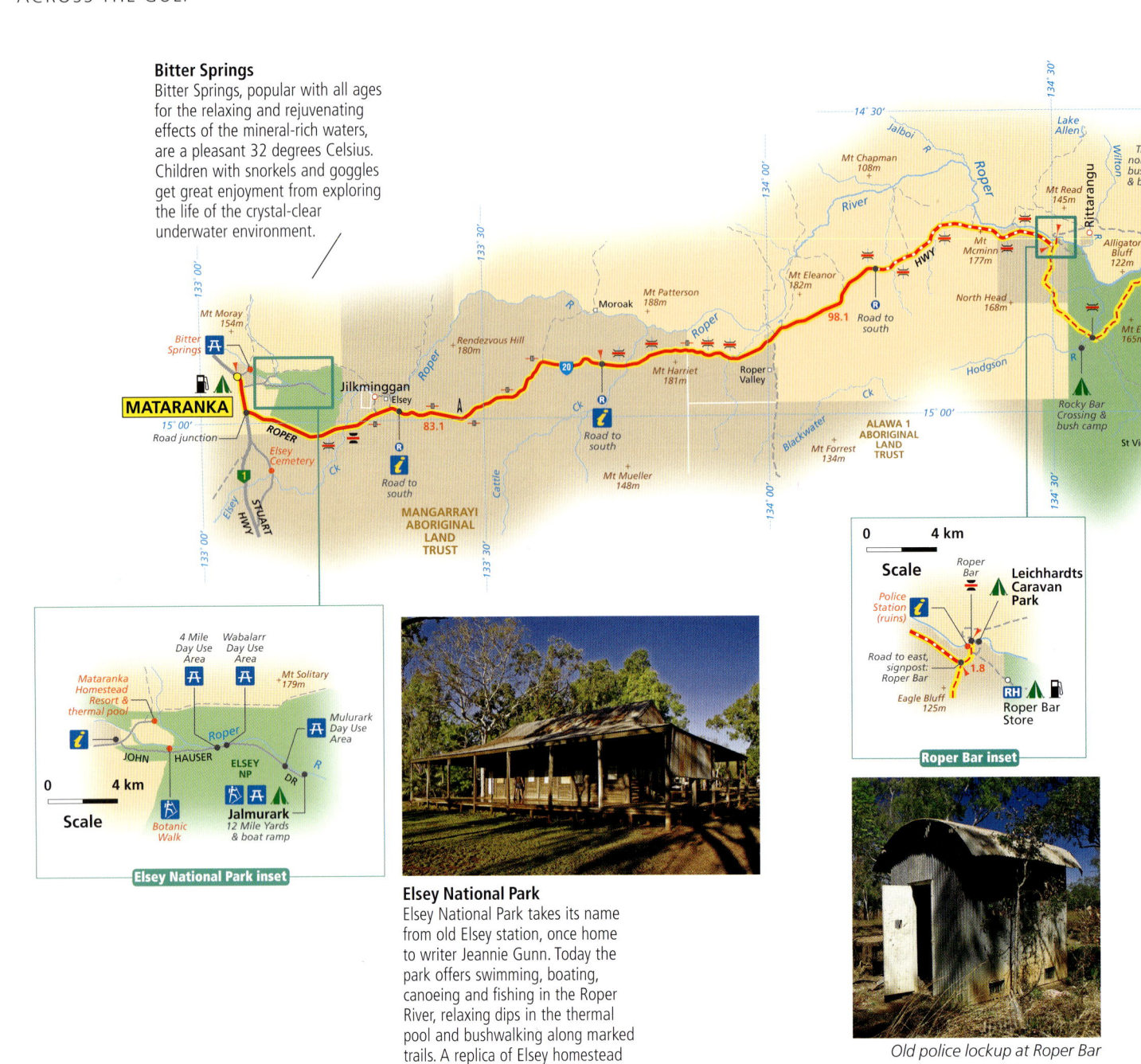

Bitter Springs
Bitter Springs, popular with all ages for the relaxing and rejuvenating effects of the mineral-rich waters, are a pleasant 32 degrees Celsius. Children with snorkels and goggles get great enjoyment from exploring the life of the crystal-clear underwater environment.

Elsey National Park
Elsey National Park takes its name from old Elsey station, once home to writer Jeannie Gunn. Today the park offers swimming, boating, canoeing and fishing in the Roper River, relaxing dips in the thermal pool and bushwalking along marked trails. A replica of Elsey homestead (pictured) is located near the pool.

Old police lockup at Roper Bar

Campsite Facilities

	Toilets	Disabled access	4WD access only	Off-road trailer	Off-road caravan	Drinking water	Fee payable	Ranger patrolled	BBQ/fireplace	Campfires prohibited	Picnic tables	Shelter shed	No rubbish disposal	Public phone	Shower	Bushwalking	Swimming	Swimming not advised	Fishing	Canoeing	Dogs allowed
Butterfly Springs	•		•	•			•	•		•	•					•					
Jalmurark	•	•		•	•	•	•		•					•	•		•		•	•	
Leichhardts	•			•	•	•	•	•						•			•		•	•	•
Limmen Bight River	•		•	•	•		•	•			•		•	•			•			•	•
Towns River	•	•	•	•			•			•							•	•			

BORROLOOLA ◀▶ MATARANKA

Lomarieum Lagoon
Lomarieum Lagoon, a beautiful elongated stretch of water, provides an ideal habitat for fish and waterbirds. Waterlilies adorn the lagoon's surface and its edges are rimmed by paperbarks. During the wet season the lagoon floods out to the Roper River, allowing crocodiles to inhabit its waters.

Southern Lost City
Once a sandstone escarpment that eroded over thousands of years, the towering narrow stacks that remain give the appearance of a lost city. A walking trail leads through these spectacular formations.

Waterlilies at Butterfly Springs

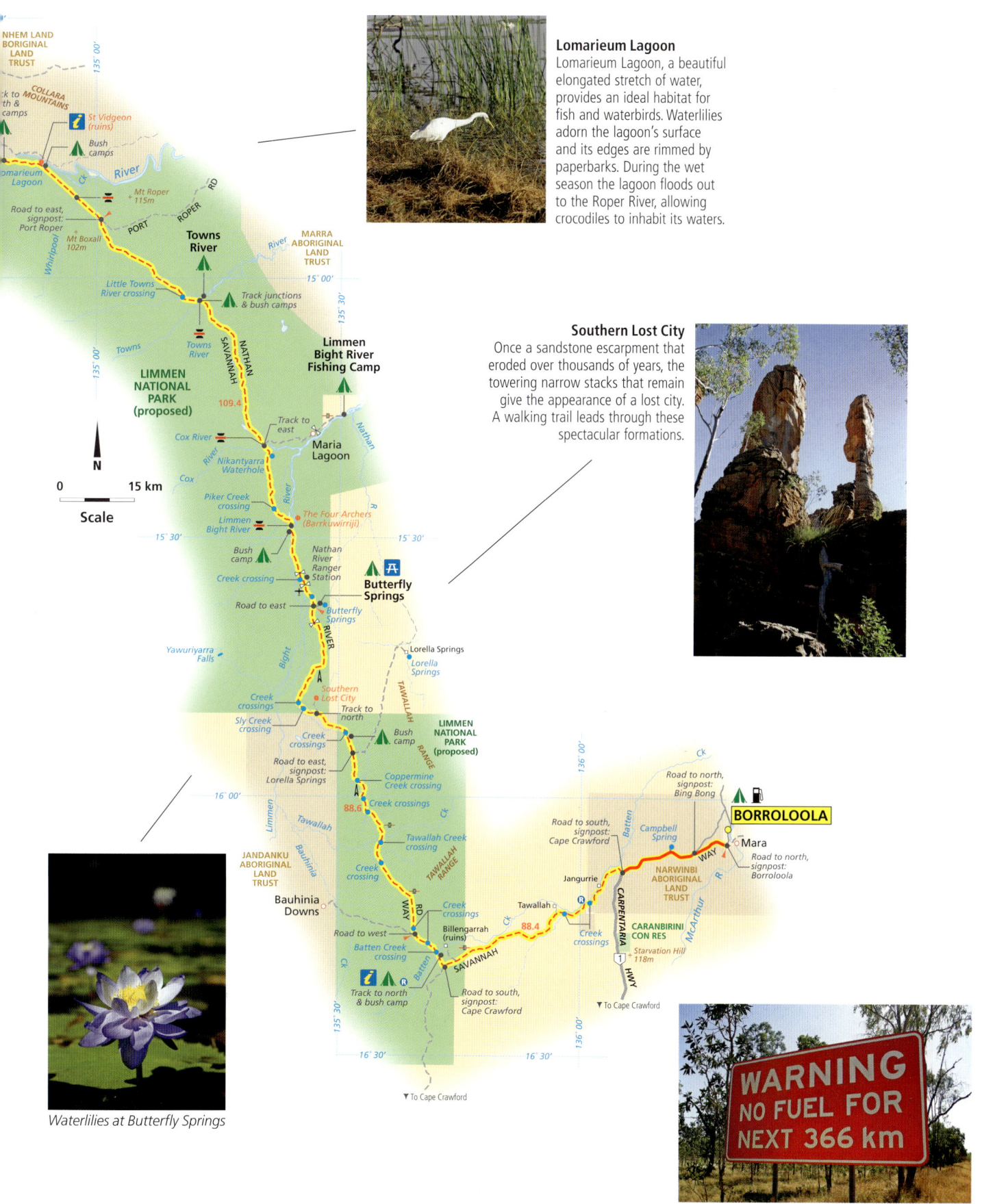

Warning sign on Nathan River Road

317

ACROSS THE GULF

Southern Lost City rock formations

▼ **39.8 km** Road junction. CSA. Track on right.
Track on right leads 0.1 km to shaded spot beside waterhole, ideal for a lunch stop.
Road junction. CSA. Track on left. **48.6 km** ▲
(5.9 km)

▼ **45.7 km** Creek crossing.
Creek crossing. **42.7 km** ▲
(27.3 km)

▼ **73.0 km** Grid. Enter SP: Limmen National Park.
Grid. Exit Limmen National Park. **15.4 km** ▲
(5.1 km)

▼ **78.1 km** Road junction. TR. SP: Nathan River Road/Roper Bar 315. Road SO SP: Cape Crawford.
T-junction. TL. SP: Borroloola. Road on right SP: Cape Crawford. **10.3 km** ▲
GPS S:16 19.743 E:135 43.367
UTM 53K 577206E 8194529N
(3.4 km)

▼ **81.5 km** Road junction. CSA. Track on right.
Track on right leads 0.2 km to rest area/bush camping spot, a sheltered place beside creek with information boards.
Road junction. CSA. Track on left. **6.9 km** ▲
(0.1 km)

▼ **81.6 km** Cross SP: Batten Creek.
Cross SP: Batten Creek. **6.8 km** ▲
(1.5 km)

▼ **83.1 km** Creek crossing.
Creek crossing. **5.3 km** ▲
(1.7 km)

▼ **84.8 km** Creek crossing.
Creek crossing. **3.6 km** ▲
(3.6 km)

▼ **88.4 km** Road junction.
Zero trip meter at road junction. CSA. Road on right SP: 24 Bauhinia Downs Stn. **0.0 km** ▲
GPS S:16 15.933 E:135 39.577
UTM 53K 570481E 8201577N

▼ **0.0 km** Zero trip meter at road junction. CSA. Road on left SP: 24 Bauhinia Downs Stn.
Road junction. **88.6 km** ▲
(0.4 km)

▼ **0.4 km** Creek crossing.
Creek crossing. **88.2 km** ▲
(18.1 km)

▼ **18.5 km** Creek crossing.
Creek crossing. **70.1 km** ▲
(4.9 km)

▼ **23.4 km** Cross SP: Tawallah Creek.
Cross SP: Tawallah Creek. **65.2 km** ▲
GPS S:16 05.335 E:135 35.281
UTM 53K 562886E 8221140N
(11.5 km)

▼ **34.9 km** Creek crossing.
Creek crossing. **53.7 km** ▲
(2.6 km)

▼ **37.5 km** Creek crossing.
Creek crossing. **51.1 km** ▲
(2.3 km)

BORROLOOLA ◀▶ MATARANKA

▼ 39.8 km Cross SP: Coppermine Creek.
Cross SP: Coppermine Creek. 48.8 km ▲
(6.3 km)

▼ 46.1 km Road junction. CSA. Road on right SP: Lorella Springs Stn 35.
Road junction. CSA. Road on left SP: Lorella Springs Stn 35. 42.5 km ▲
(4.1 km)

▼ 50.2 km Creek crossing.
Possible bush camping on right prior to creek. Best suited for vans and trailers because of rocky banks.
Creek crossing. 38.4 km ▲

GPS S:15 52.879 E:135 30.987
UTM 53L 555289E 8244124N

(1.8 km)

▼ 52.0 km Creek crossing.
Creek crossing. 36.6 km ▲
(7.1 km)

▼ 59.1 km Road junction. CSA. Track on right SP: Southern Lost City.
Track on right leads 4.2 km to interesting rock formations. Track is not suitable for trailers or caravans. At time of research, PWCNT were upgrading the track to the Southern Lost City and were building a designated walking trail and camping area.
Road junction. CSA. Track on left SP: Southern Lost City. 29.5 km ▲

GPS S:15 50.409 E:135 27.296
UTM 53L 548713E 8248693N

(3.2 km)

▼ 62.3 km Cross SP: Sly Creek.
Cross SP: Sly Creek. 26.3 km ▲
(1.9 km)

▼ 64.2 km Creek crossing.
Creek crossing. 24.4 km ▲
(3.0 km)

▼ 67.2 km Creek crossing.
Creek crossing. 21.4 km ▲
(17.7 km)

▼ 84.9 km Gate. LAF.
Gate. LAF. 3.7 km ▲
(3.7 km)

▼ 88.6 km Road junction.
Zero trip meter at road junction. CSA. Track on left SP: Butterfly Springs. 0.0 km ▲

GPS S:15 37.961 E:135 26.856
UTM 53L 547976E 8271644N

▼ 0.0 km Zero trip meter at road junction. CSA. Track on right SP: Butterfly Springs.
Track on right leads 1.8 km to **Butterfly Springs camping area**, with 6 individual sites surrounded by grevilleas and paperbarks, and a short walk to delightful waterfall and waterhole suitable for swimming.
Road junction. 109.4 km ▲
(6.1 km)

▼ 6.1 km Gate. LAF. T-junction through gate. TL. SP: 192 Roper Bar. Road on right SP: No Through Road.
Road on right leads short distance to Nathan River ranger station.
Road junction. CSA through gate. LAF. SP: Borroloola/Cape Crawford. Road on left SP: No Through Road. 103.3 km ▲
(1.2 km)

▼ 7.3 km Creek crossing.
Creek crossing. 102.1 km ▲
(0.3 km)

▼ 7.6 km Gate. LAF.
Gate. LAF. 101.8 km ▲
(11.3 km)

▼ 18.9 km Causeway over SP: Limmen Bight River.
Possible bush camping on left prior to crossing, on sandy banks.
Causeway over SP: Limmen Bight River. 90.5 km ▲

GPS S:15 28.842 E:135 24.053
UTM 53L 543000E 8288465N

(6.3 km)

▼ 25.2 km Cross SP: Piker Creek.
Cross SP: Piker Creek. 84.2 km ▲
(12.5 km)

▼ 37.7 km Nikantyarra Waterhole on right.
Waterhole offers ideal photo opportunity with lilies and prolific birdlife.
Nikantyarra Waterhole on left. 71.7 km ▲

GPS S:15 20.467 E:135 21.317
UTM 53L 538135E 8303913N

(2.6 km)

▼ 40.3 km Causeway over SP: Cox River.
Causeway over SP: Cox River. 69.1 km ▲
(0.2 km)

▼ 40.5 km Road junction. CSA. Road on right SP: Maria Lagoon 12.
Road on right leads 20.5 km to **Limmen Bight River Fishing Camp**, with large campground high above the river. Popular with fisherfolk (see Permits and bookings for details).
Road junction. CSA. Road on left SP: Maria Lagoon 12. 68.9 km ▲

GPS S:15 19.275 E:135 20.672
UTM 53L 536984E 8306112N

(37.8 km)

▼ 78.3 km Road junction. CSA. Track on right SP: Towns River.
Track on right leads 1.3 km to **Towns River camping area**, with scattered bush campsites close to the river.
Road junction. CSA. Track on left SP: Towns River. 31.1 km ▲

GPS S:15 02.551 E:135 12.788
UTM 53L 522909E 8336960N

(0.1 km)

▼ 78.4 km Road junction. CSA. Track on left.
Track on left leads 0.3 km to small bush campsite.

319

ACROSS THE GULF

		Road junction. CSA. Track on right.	31.0 km ▲		Road junction. CSA. Track on left to river.	52.1 km ▲

(0.1 km)

▼ 78.5 km Causeway over SP: Towns River.
　　　　　　　　Causeway over SP: Towns River.　30.9 km ▲

GPS S:15 02.591 E:135 12.679
UTM 53L 522714E 8336887N

(0.1 km)

▼ 78.6 km Road junction. CSA. Track on left and right.

Track on left and right leads short distance to possible bush campsites.

　　　　　Road junction. CSA. Track on left and right.　30.8 km ▲

(3.9 km)

▼ 82.5 km Creek crossing.
　　　　　　　　　　　　　Creek crossing.　26.9 km ▲

(0.1 km)

▼ 82.6 km Cross SP: Little Towns River.
　　　　　　　　Cross SP: Little Towns River.　26.8 km ▲

(26.8 km)

▼ 109.4 km T-junction.
　　　　Zero trip meter at road junction. TR. SP: Borroloola 300. Road SO SP: Port Roper 42.　0.0 km ▲

GPS S:14 53.248 E:135 00.574
UTM 53L 501029E 8354121N

▼ 0.0 km Zero trip meter at T-junction. TL. SP: 90 Roper Bar/Savannah Way. Road on right SP: Port Roper 42.

Port Roper is a popular and remote fishing area with no services or facilities.

　　　　　　　　　　　　Road junction.　87.0 km ▲

(7.3 km)

▼ 7.3 km Causeway over SP: Whirlpool Creek.
　　　　Causeway over SP: Whirlpool Creek.　79.7 km ▲

(10.5 km)

▼ 17.8 km Road junction. CSA. St Vidgeon homestead ruins and track on right.

Information boards on right at ruins. Track on right leads 0.3 km to bush campsites at edge of Lomarieum Lagoon, a beautiful large waterhole rimmed with paperbarks.

　　　Road junction. CSA. St Vidgeon homestead ruins and track on left.　69.2 km ▲

GPS S:14 47.013 E:134 53.216
UTM 53L 487832E 8365611N

(8.6 km)

▼ 26.4 km Road junction. CSA. Track on right.

Track on right leads to Roper River. Numerous tracks on right lead to bush campsites at water's edge.

　　　　　Road junction. CSA. Track on left.　60.6 km ▲

(2.1 km)

▼ 28.5 km Causeway over SP: Mountain Creek.
　　　　Causeway over SP: Mountain Creek.　58.5 km ▲

(2.9 km)

▼ 31.4 km Road junction. CSA. Track on right to river.
　　　Road junction. CSA. Track on left to river.　55.6 km ▲

(3.5 km)

▼ 34.9 km Road junction. CSA. Track on right to river.

(8.3 km)

▼ 43.2 km Road junction. CSA. Track on right.

Track on right leads short distance to boat ramp and bush campsites. Very popular site for caravan travellers and anglers during dry season. Campers advised to be self-sufficient and have their own chemical toilets.

　　　　　　Road junction. CSA. Track on left.　43.8 km ▲

GPS S:14 44.824 E:134 41.543
UTM 53L 466890E 8369627N

(21.8 km)

▼ 65.0 km Road junction. CSA. Track on left.

Track on left leads 3.7 km to old ford known as Rocky Bar Crossing and nearby bush camping area suitable for 2–3 vehicles. Track not suitable for caravans. Aboriginal petroglyphs (engravings) visible on the southern bank of the river downstream, or east, of crossing.

　　　　　　Road junction. CSA. Track on right.　22.0 km ▲

GPS S:14 52.719 E:134 34.119
UTM 53L 453600E 8355051N

(0.4 km)

▼ 65.4 km Bridge over SP: Hodgson River.
　　　　　Bridge over SP: Hodgson River.　21.6 km ▲

(0.6 km)

▼ 66.0 km Exit Limmen National Park.
　　　　　Enter SP: Limmen National Park.　21.0 km ▲

(21.0 km)

▼ 87.0 km T-junction. Side trip to Roper River.
　　Zero trip meter at road junction. TR. SP: Savannah Way. Road SO SP: Roper Bar.　0.0 km ▲

GPS S:14 43.502 E:134 30.102
UTM 53L 446361E 8372027N

▶ **SIDE TRIP: Roper River**

▼ 0.0 km Zero trip meter at road junction. Proceed in northerly direction towards SP: Roper Bar.

(1.0 km)

▼ 1.0 km Road junction. CSA. Road on right SP: Roper Bar.

Road on right leads 0.3 km to turn-off to **Leichhardts Caravan Park**, a large and informal grassy park with shaded sites above the Roper River, and leads a further 2.6 km to the Roper Bar store.

(0.5 km)

▼ 1.5 km Police station ruins on left. Information boards.

(0.3 km)

▼ 1.8 km Causeway over Roper River. Known as Roper Bar. Return to side trip start.

GPS S:14 42.789 E:134 30.469
UTM 53L 447016E 8373343N

◀ **END SIDE TRIP**

▼ 0.0 km Zero trip meter at T-junction. TL. SP: Savannah Way/Roper Highway/Stuart Hwy. Road on right SP: Roper Bar.

BORROLOOLA ◀▶ MATARANKA

Reflections highlight the beauty of Bitter Springs

	Road on right leads to the Roper River and Roper Bar Store.	
	Road junction. Side trip to Roper Bar.	98.1 km ▲

(38.7 km)

▼ 38.7 km Rest area on left. CSA.

Tables, shelter, fireplace, bins and emergency water.

	Rest area on right. CSA.	59.4 km ▲

(59.4 km)

▼ 98.1 km Rest area on left.

	Zero trip meter with rest area on right. CSA.	0.0 km ▲

GPS S:14 54.777 E:133 42.667
UTM 53L 361369E 8350901N

▼ 0.0 km Zero trip meter with rest area on left. CSA.

Tables, shelter, fireplace, bins, emergency water and information boards.

	Rest area on right.	83.1 km ▲

(44.8 km)

▼ 44.8 km Rest area on left. CSA.

Tables, shelter, fireplace, bins, emergency water and information boards.

	Rest area on right. CSA.	38.3 km ▲

(11.4 km)

▼ 56.2 km Causeway over SP: Elsey Creek.

	Causeway over SP: Elsey Creek.	26.9 km ▲

(19.9 km)

▼ 76.1 km T-junction with SP: Stuart Highway. TR. SP: Katherine. Road on left SP: Tennant Creek.

	Road junction. TL. SP: Roper Highway/Roper Bar. Road SO SP: Tennant Creek.	7.0 km ▲

GPS S:14 58.911 E:133 04.775
UTM 53L 293490E 8342787N

(4.9 km)

▼ 81.0 km Road junction. CSA. SP: Katherine. Road on right SP: Elsey National Park/Mataranka Thermal Pool.

Road on right leads 4.3 km to road junction. TR into John Hauser Dr, which leads 12.7 km to Elsey National Park's **Jalmurark campground**, a pleasant and shady grass-covered area only a short walk from swimming pontoons on the Roper River. At road junction, road SO leads 2.7 km to Mataranka Homestead Resort and thermal pool, with free access for day visitors.

	Road junction. CSA. SP: Tennant Creek. Road on left SP: Elsey National Park/Mataranka Thermal Pool.	2.1 km ▲

GPS S:14 56.324 E:133 04.350
UTM 53L 292686E 8347551N

(2.1 km)

▼ 83.1 km Crossroads in Mataranka. Police station on left. Road on right SP: Elsey National Park/Bitter Springs.

Road on right leads 3.0 km to crystal-clear waters of Bitter Springs thermal pool.

	Zero trip meter on Stuart Hwy at crossroads at northern end of Mataranka township. Road on left SP: Elsey National Park/Bitter Springs. Police station on right. Proceed in southerly direction along Stuart Hwy through town.	0.0 km ▲

GPS S:14 55.309 E:133 03.927
UTM 53L 291912E 8349417N

REVERSE DIRECTIONS START

FOLLOWING PAGES
Crossing the rock-strewn bed of the Wearyan River

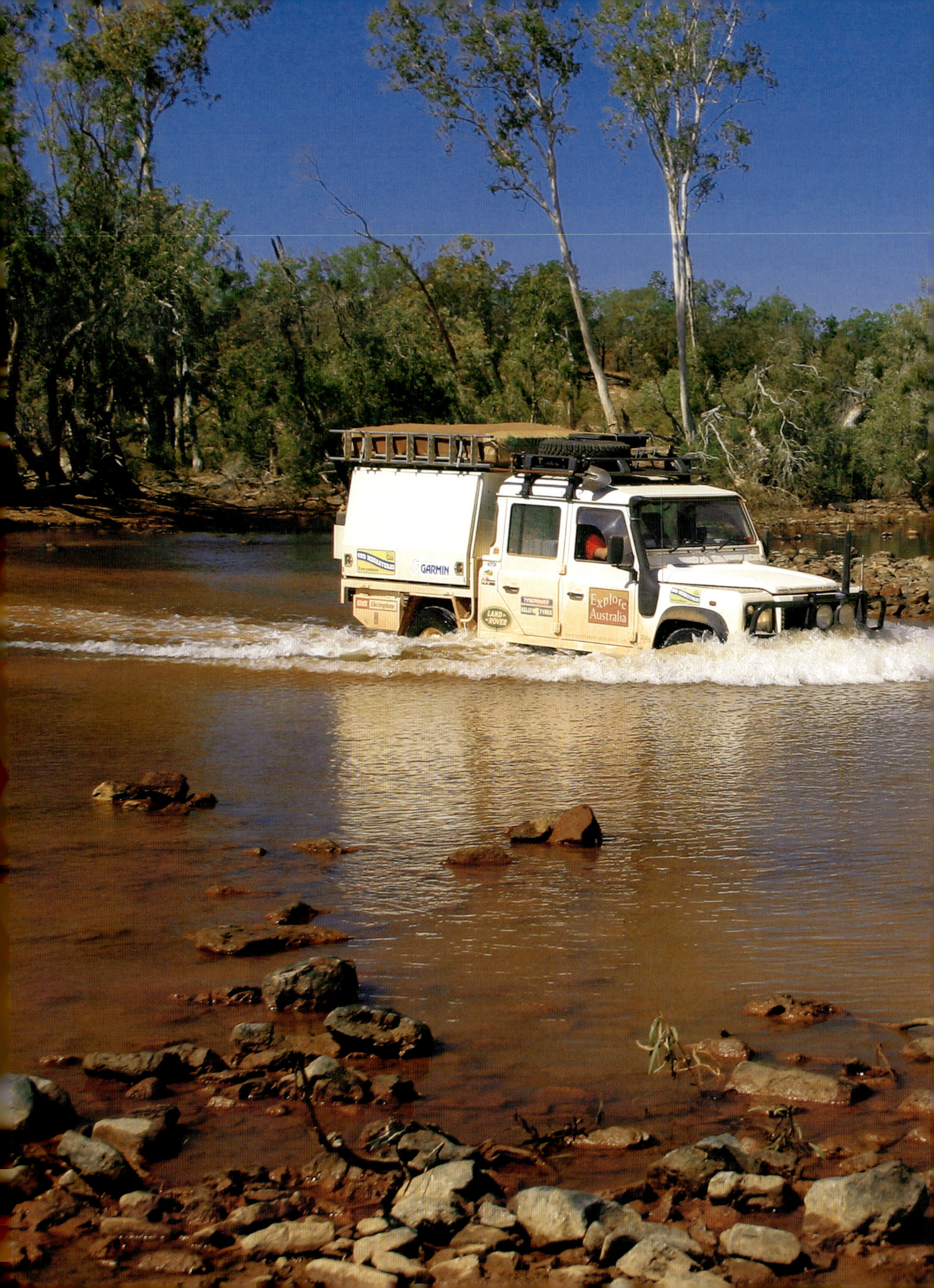
GARMIN
Explore
Australia

Making the Most of Your Trip

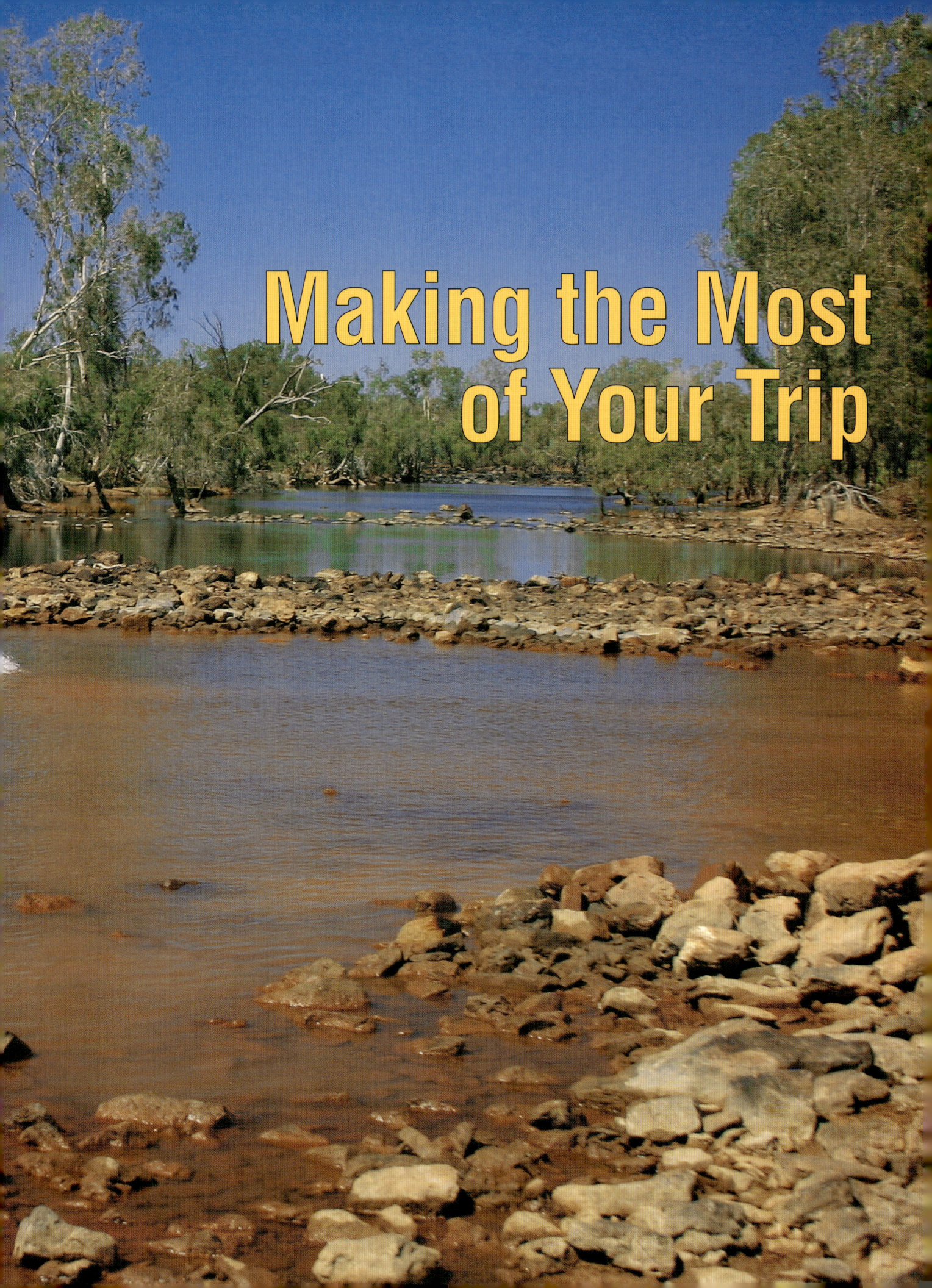

Preparing for Your Trip

Planning and preparation are essential ingredients for a safe and enjoyable four-wheel-drive adventure, whether it be a week-long jaunt into the magical High Country of Victoria, a two-month trip taking in the Tanami Road, Canning Stock Route and Gunbarrel Highway or the experience of a lifetime tackling most or all of the great treks in this book. In the following pages we outline a number of issues that you need to consider before you leave, discuss camping gear and the like, give you some things to think about when setting up your vehicle and offer ideas and hints for when you are on the road. For checklists to download and further discussion on setting up your vehicle, including equipment reviews and a host of additional resources, visit the website (www.exploreaustraliaby4wd.com).

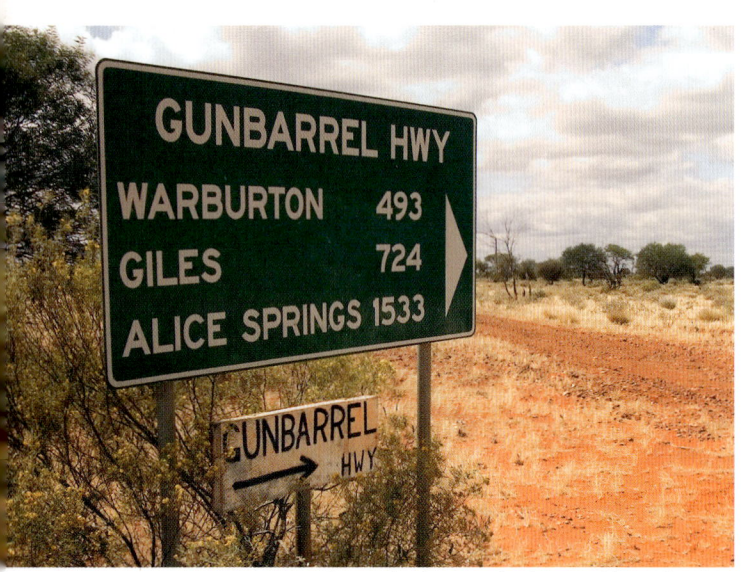

Assess the time required to travel long distances

Time and distance

Be realistic about how much time you have available and how far you should aim to travel. An estimate of the time you should allow is provided at the start of each trek. Be sure to take into consideration the degree of difficulty and the distance to be covered and check that each section of a trek is possible within a realistic time frame. Once you are on the road you will discover some places of interest that you would like to visit and others that may disappoint you. Build flexibility into your plans and be prepared to stay a while in some places.

Money

It goes without saying that travel always costs more than you expect. Make a daily or weekly budget so that you can calculate average costs for fuel, food, repairs, camping fees, admission charges, eating out, treats and so on.

Checklist

If you will be away for some time, or are going to remote areas, take:
- cash to use in case of emergencies – you may not be able to use automatic teller machines, EFTPOS facilities or cheques in some rural areas; some outback areas experience down time with electronic banking systems, necessitating payment in cash
- two credit cards, at least, for the automatic teller machine in case one card does not work
- one credit card that is widely accepted (VISA, MasterCard or Bankcard)
- personal identification that includes your photograph, such as a driver's licence or passport.

Vehicle insurance and roadside assistance

Check that your vehicle insurance covers the activities you have planned and the areas in which you intend to travel. Some policies may not cover travel on ungazetted roads. Remember to carry copies of all policies with you.

PREPARING FOR YOUR TRIP

Some insurance policies do not cover travel on ungazetted roads

Check your roadside breakdown policy and the level of assistance for which you are covered. Some policies may not cover specific locations, types of terrain or types of vehicle. If you have basic roadside assistance cover it may be worthwhile upgrading to one of the 'plus' options before travelling. Many new vehicles have a 24-hour roadside-service warranty, but it is important to check that help will be available while travelling in remote areas.

Health and first aid

Check what your health insurance cover provides in an emergency and take your medical insurance card (and any necessary details) with you. At the least you should join an ambulance service. If you take prescribed medications ensure these are safely packed, and if you plan on travelling for extended periods visit your doctor to obtain prescriptions that will last your entire trip. If you wear prescription glasses, it is a good idea to pack a second pair (or more) in case of loss or breakage. It is imperative that you have a basic knowledge of first aid and know how to perform CPR (if necessary, take a course with St John Ambulance Australia or a similar organisation).

Choosing your route

Consider the following factors when deciding your route:
- how much time do you have available? (remember to allow time to get to your destination and home again)
- type and quality of road surfaces (travel is slower on gravel roads than on bitumen)
- time of year that you plan to travel (summer in northern Australia means monsoonal rain, and some roads are impassable)
- whether you are travelling unaccompanied or with a companion vehicle

- fuel availability and distances between fuelling points (after establishing fuel consumption under both *easy* and *difficult* driving conditions, work on the basis of covering only 80 per cent of that distance in the outback, to give yourself a margin of safety)
- access to restricted areas (allow plenty of time to obtain permits if required – many can take up to six weeks to issue and deliver)
- whether pets are permitted
- access to the attractions you want to visit
- access to services you or your passengers may need
- type of vehicle(s) you are using
- your four-wheel driving skills and on-road experience.

Travel is slower on gravel roads than on bitumen

Navigation and travel aids

Navigation skills are a must. You should have basic navigation and direction-finding skills before setting out on a trip into remote or unfamiliar territory. There are a number of useful reference books on this subject and these are generally available from specialist map outlets and stores specialising in outdoor equipment and travel.

Always have at least one good compass in your vehicle and be able to read a compass in conjunction with a map. You should also be able to find north without the aid of a compass, day or night.

Maps

The maps in this book are produced from GPS data collected in the field and cover the trip discribed in the route directions. However, if you require more detailed maps, the relevant 1:250 000 topographic maps available are listed at the start of each trek. Plastic or canvas wallets are a good way to store your maps while travelling. Heavy-duty cardboard mailing tubes, available at post offices, are ideal for storing rolled maps.

MAKING THE MOST OF YOUR TRIP

Digital mapping and GPS
Computer-based or digital maps are now widely available and are growing in popularity, especially with outback travellers. *GPS Vehicle Navigation in Australia* by Robert Pepper (Boiling Billy Publications) provides details on choosing, setting up and using GPS and digital-map-based systems. If you do have these facilities, you should also carry conventional paper maps to use in case of a systems breakdown.

Global positioning system, or GPS, is a popular navigational aid for recreational travellers to determine their current position on a map to within a couple of metres. GPS is a satellite-based navigation system developed and maintained by the United States Department of Defense. A GPS receiver determines the user's current position by collecting distance/time measurements from satellites via an antenna. A GPS unit (receiver and antenna) can also be used to store your current position, navigate to your destination and display and track the course travelled. It can be run either from a vehicle's electrical system or from rechargeable or disposable batteries.

Brochures
Relevant visitor brochures and national park notes and fact sheets are listed for each trek. These provide additional information on certain aspects of the region and are generally available at visitor information centres and park offices in the area.

Permits
Entry permits are required for many national parks and some Aboriginal and Department of Defence lands. Because the granting of a permit is not automatic, you may have to wait several weeks before you receive permission to travel (relevant contact details are provided for each trek in Permits and bookings).

Bush mechanics
When travelling in remote areas you need a range of skills to cope with unexpected problems. You should be able to:
- strip a tyre from a wheel and mend a puncture
- repair a broken brake line and bleed brakes
- mend a hole in a ruptured fuel tank or radiator
- replace a blocked fuel filter
- bleed air from a diesel-engine fuel line
- extricate a bogged vehicle.

A GPS receiver (left) and an in-vehicle digital mapping display (right) are popular navigational aids

If you do not already have these skills, it is a good idea to join a reputable four-wheel-drive club that has a strong education program or take a four-wheel-drive driver-training course (check the yellow pages telephone directory for listings).

Camping
All the treks in this guide are based around camping out, and there is detailed information on campsites and camping facilities available for each trek. For further details on over 2500 campsites throughout Australia check out *Camping in Australia* by Cathy Savage and Craig Lewis (Explore Australia Publishing).

There are bound to be times when you feel like some extra facilities or a taste of luxury and choose to stay in a commercial caravan park, motel or hotel. Be sure to include these additional accommodation costs in your budget. Some of the options are given in these pages but

Breaking a tyre bead using a bead-breaking tool

PREPARING FOR YOUR TRIP

for a more comprehensive listing look at the directories produced by state motoring organisations – they generally rate accommodation and give details on facilities and costs.

Tents
There are many different types of tents, from basic two-person tents to family-sized domed tents, made from a variety of materials ranging from lightweight nylon to heavy-duty canvas. When choosing your tent look for: one that is easy to erect; quality material and sewing; flyscreens and ventilation; and sewn-in floors.

Large family tent

Bedding and swags
Your choice of bedding will depend on whether you camp in a tent, swag or trailer. No matter what you choose, good bedding is important, especially in alpine and desert regions where overnight temperatures can fall below zero. Quality sleeping bags have various temperature ratings, fillings and thicknesses. Camping mattresses come in a range of styles: space-saving self-inflating mattresses; blow-up mattresses, which often require a pump; and foam mattresses, which take up valuable space. Do not forget to pack pillows.

The humble swag has come a long way in recent years. Easy to set-up, it is now regarded by many as an essential item for outback travel. When choosing a swag look for a comfortable mattress and good-quality canvas. A swag with mesh screening to keep insects at bay is ideal for tropical climates.

Rooftop tents
Rooftop tents are another good option for campers. They are quick to set-up and pack-up but are restrictive if you wish to have a base camp (they have to move with your vehicle!). We have used an Australian-made ShippShape Roof Top Tent for five years and find it very comfortable and extremely practical.

Camper trailers
A number of treks in this book are suitable for well-built off-road trailers. For families, in particular, they provide additional storage and greater facilities and a more comfortable base camp than a tent.

Off-road caravans
The trend towards travelling Australia's outback towing an off-road caravan is on the increase. If you choose to travel this way then look for a purpose-built off-road model that has been manufactured to withstand the harsh conditions often encountered while touring off the beaten track. A number of treks in this guide are suitable for well-set-up off-road vans.

Additional camp furniture
The following items will make your camping experience more comfortable:
- folding camp chairs (there are some very comfortable varieties on the market)
- a small, lightweight folding table.

Dealing with insects
Insects such as flies, mosquitos, sandflies and ants can be an irritating problem when camping, especially in the tropics. While a fly veil will help keep bush flies away from your face in the outback, biting insects such as mosquitoes can be more of an annoyance. Regions such as Cape York, the Top End and parts of the Kimberley are especially prone to these creatures and you should wear long-sleeved, light-coloured, loose-fitting clothing and cover any exposed areas with a DEET-based insect repellent. We also carry a lightweight mosquito net for particularly bad areas. Screened mesh tents are another alternative.

A rooftop tent, mosquito-proof net and comfortable folding camp chairs make camping more enjoyable

MAKING THE MOST OF YOUR TRIP

Travelling with pets

Almost all national parks and many caravan parks do not allow pets (cats, dogs or birds) so the decision to take your pet will limit your choice of route and overnight stops and, in most cases, will severely restrict the number of treks available to you in this book. Many pastoral areas in the outback are regularly baited for wild dogs so extra precautions need to be taken if travelling with pets through these regions.

Refrigeration

Portable cooling units range from cheap ice-block chilled, insulated containers to expensive multi-voltage compressor-driven refrigerator-freezer combinations and 'three-way' type units that operate on 12 volts, 240 volts and bottled LP gas. Over the last 12 years we have used an Australian-made 39-litre Autofridge and a 90-litre Evakool 12-volt fridge and both have given us almost trouble-free operation. If you use a unit powered from your vehicle's electrical system we consider it essential to fit a dual-battery system – many are fitted with an automatic isolator switch to protect the starting battery from being discharged by the refrigerator. The supply battery for the refrigerator should be a deep-cycle battery, which can tolerate sustained deep discharges over a period of time. Check with a reputable 4WD accessory store or an auto-electrician about what is available.

Travelling with a pet limits your choice of route

off bottled LP gas, are also popular. Care is required when using this type of lighting as both the lantern glass and light mantles are quite fragile and prone to breaking if not handled with care. Always carry spare mantles and a spare lantern glass.

Pack at least two torches. We have found the rechargeable type (that can be recharged from your vehicle's cigarette lighter) to be good value, especially for longer trips. A hands-free head torch is also useful and is great when cooking over a fire at night.

Power sources

If you plan on staying in one place for lengthy periods, your vehicle's 12-volt electrical system – even if you have a dual-battery system fitted – can be supplemented with solar-electric-charging panels and/or a small petrol-powered generator set that has 12-volt DC output as well as 240 volts. However, you should note that some national parks do not allow generators or restrict their use to generator-only campsites. If using a generator please be mindful of other campers and observe any 'quiet times'.

Inverters – units that modify your vehicle's 12-volt power to 240 volts – are a good idea if you need to run low-draw 240-volt equipment, such as battery chargers, for video cameras and laptop computers.

Our 90-litre Evakool 12-volt fridge

Lighting

Practical 12-volt portable fluorescent lights provide good light for camps and can be placed for convenience. They draw very small amounts of power, have long-lasting light tubes and are cool to touch, which makes them safe, especially around young children. Gas lanterns, which run

Clothing

Clothing very much depends on where and when you will be travelling. Careful planning will ensure that neither too much nor too little is packed. A raincoat and sun hat should always be included, no matter where you are going.

When travelling to the northern and coastal regions during summer, cool, lightweight, loose-fitting cotton clothing will be required but warm clothes are necessary

PREPARING FOR YOUR TRIP

for cooler evenings and the occasional rainy day. Travel in the southern states requires a mixture of warm and cool-weather clothing. Close-knit woollens are ideal for cooler regions along with thermal underwear. When travelling in the deserts, warm-weather clothing is required during the day but dramatic drops in temperature at night require warm, woollen or fleece clothing or even oilskin jackets, along with a beanie and gloves.

Footwear is also important. Avoid wearing sweat-producing footwear made from synthetic materials. Wear comfortable, protective shoes and socks made of natural fibres such as cotton and wool. If you are planning on bushwalking, pack sturdy hiking boots.

Cooking equipment

Important aspects to remember when selecting your cooking equipment are the quantity and weight of each item. Everything you choose needs to be unquestionably useful and necessary. Our motto when packing an item – and this applies to everything – is that if it does not have at least three uses then it stays at home.

It is not always possible or practical to cook over an open fire so it is essential that you carry some form of portable fuel stove such as those that burn LP gas or petrol. Your gas/fuel stove should be large enough to position your kettle and pots comfortably and it should also have an effective wind guard. Always turn off gas at the bottle when the cooker is not in use. In addition to the traditional cast-iron camp oven, which is ideal for the slow-cooking of breads, roasts, curries and stews, other indispensable items include a small barbeque/grill plate, a heavy-based frying pan and a couple of saucepans and billies, heavy leather gloves and a long-handled shovel.

A camp oven and billy in use at a national park fireplace

A good-quality raincoat is essential

A good-quality metal vacuum flask is useful for hot or cold liquids that can provide a quick morning-tea break while on the road.

Utensils such as knives, forks, spoons (table, wooden and slotted), can-openers, corkscrews and so on can be carried in a plastic box with a push-on lid or, even better, a tool roll made from heavy material such as canvas with compartments that keep sharp objects separate.

The burning of wood in outback environments removes a vital habitat for small animals and insects. If you do choose to have a fire, keep it small and use as little timber as possible. Experienced camp cooks know that the best results come from small fires that consist mostly of coals. Apart from cooking, campfires provide general warmth and a pleasant focal point for a night yarning with fellow travellers. Roaring bonfires are no longer considered acceptable.

For additional information and advice, including downloadable checklists of cooking equipment, visit the website (www.exploreaustraliaby4wd.com).

The travelling larder

There is a huge range of meal options available while travelling, with many of your favourite dishes from home easily prepared while in the bush. Develop menus in advance to enable you to buy ingredients beforehand.

Foods

Your larder should contain a mix of both dried and canned foods, sauces, grains and cereals. Carry as much fresh fruit and vegetables as possible. Good choices include those that do not need refrigeration, such as potatoes, onions, sweet potatoes, pumpkin, apples, oranges and green bananas.

MAKING THE MOST OF YOUR TRIP

Cooking on a gas stove

You need to be aware of compulsory confiscation of fruit and vegetables at fruit, vine and vegetable quarantine control points. You can supplement fresh foods with a selection of dried vegetables such as peas, corn, mushrooms and carrots, and also a selection of dried fruits, nuts and seeds. Canned vegetables are a convenient alternative, but remember that cans, jars and bottles are bulky and heavy (and glass can break if not packed properly) and also adds to the rubbish-disposal problem. Carry fresh meat, chicken and fish where practicable but include smoked and salted meats, canned ham, tuna, nut meat (soy protein), camp pie and corned beef.

Storage

The most convenient way to carry your cooking equipment and non-perishable foodstuffs is in one or more lightweight plastic tubs with tight-fitting lids. It is a good idea for liquids such as cooking oils, dressings, honey, jams and sauces in glass and thin plastic containers to be decanted into tough, resilient screw-top containers (glass and brittle plastics may break or disintegrate with vibration), which can be stored in waterproof tubs, so that if anything breaks the liquid does not run through your vehicle.

We have found the best method of storing fresh meat while travelling is to have a butcher or supermarket place it in cryovac, preferably in meal-sized portions. The cryovac process, or vacuum packing, extends the 'keeping' qualities of meat when refrigerated; many cuts of beef will keep for 4 to 6 weeks while lamb, pork and chicken keep for 2 to 4 weeks.

Additional information

For a complete rundown on cooking in the bush, including equipment, techniques and a collection of over 150 mouth-watering recipes, check out our book *Australian Bush Cooking* by Cathy Savage and Craig Lewis (Boiling Billy Publications).

Photography

Many people like to record their adventures on camera, video or both. While traditional film cameras are still popular, the number of people using digital cameras is increasing. If you choose the latter there is some extra equipment required such as spare batteries, battery charger and additional storage cards or a laptop computer/portable hard-drive to store your images. While it is convenient to carry additional film, which can be easily purchased throughout the outback (but remember it can be damaged by excessive temperatures), digital images will need to be transferred from the camera's storage card once it is full.

All the photographs in this book were shot with digital camera equipment and the images transferred to a laptop computer. We used an inverter to charge the camera batteries as well as to power the laptop.

Using a tripod will improve the quality of your photographs

Equipping Your Vehicle

Your four-wheel drive needs to be in tip-top mechanical condition before you embark on any of the treks in this book. While many travellers carry out their own servicing and maintenance, a visit to a reputable four-wheel drive service centre for a thorough pre-trip overhaul and inspection is a good idea, particularly if you are not mechanically minded. That faint noise you hear from under the vehicle on your way to work – if it is not attended to before your trip – could turn into an expensive repair halfway along the Canning Stock Route! Make sure you know how to operate all your equipment, including the basic vehicle-recovery items and radio and satellite telephone communication systems. It is worth spending time on improving your skills.

Setting up your vehicle

There are numerous accessories and items that can be added to a four-wheel drive to make your trip potentially safer, more practical and more comfortable. Listed below are some items that we consider essential for four-wheel-drive touring, along with a list of non-essential items that can be added according to personal preference. When setting up a vehicle for outback travel make sure you use the best-quality equipment that your budget will allow. The remote areas of Australia are not places to find out that your gear is sub-standard. Reputable retailers such as the 4WD Megastores group offer a comprehensive range of equipment and accessories as well as expert advice on the most appropriate gear for your vehicle. For equipment reviews and a full rundown on the equipment we used to set up our Landrover Defender, 'The Brick', visit our website (www.exploreaustraliaby4wd.com).

A well-stocked first-aid kit

Essential items

- **Fire extinguishers** These are an absolute necessity and must be located in readily accessible places. Check that you have the appropriate type to be stored in a vehicle and to use for automotive fires.
- **First-aid kit** A well-stocked first-aid kit, and first-aid book, should be within easy reach. At least one person should be familiar with the use of the creams, lotions and tablets. Do a quick check before each trip and throw away out-of-date items and replenish stocks. A good-quality, high-rating sunscreen must be included.
- **Cargo barriers** These are essential for containing luggage and equipment in the rear of a station wagon to prevent objects becoming dislodged and causing possible injury.
- **Tie-down points** These are needed to secure items so they do not move around in rough road conditions.
- **Dual-battery system** It is vital to install a dual battery set-up if you run 12-volt appliances such as lights or a refrigerator. The extra appliances are powered from the auxiliary battery (which should be a deep-cycle type)

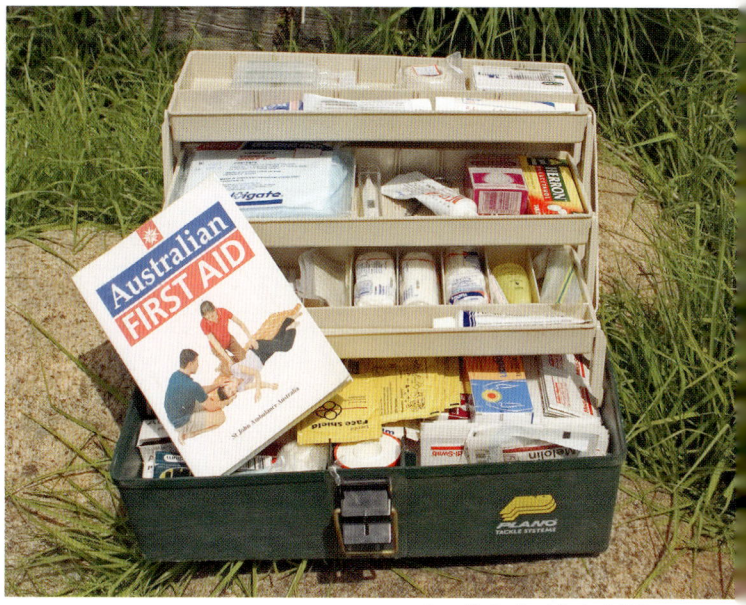

to remove the possibility of the engine-cranking battery being discharged. Dual-battery systems are wired so that both batteries are charged while the engine is running, and when the engine is at rest the batteries are not connected.
- **Vehicle recovery points** You should have these fitted to both the front and rear of your vehicle. Recovery hooks are the most common type and should be installed with high-tensile bolts and must be mounted to the chassis.

Bull bars can protect your vehicle from damage in a collision with an animal

Non-essential items
- **Bull bar** This is often the first accessory that many people fit to their vehicle. Although not essential, it may protect the vehicle from damage in a light collision with an animal or vegetation, but it can also cause chassis bending and other problems if not correctly fitted. Most good-quality aftermarket bull bars may incorporate a winch mount, jacking points, turning indicators and mounts for additional driving lights and radio aerials. Alloy bull bars are light but need specialist welding if damaged, whereas steel units weigh a little more but can be repaired readily. Do not tow or winch by connecting to a bull bar – chassis points only should be used.
- **Roof-rack** A roof-rack provides additional carrying space for lightweight items such as tents, bedding or folding chairs and table. However, any weight above roof level can seriously affect vehicle stability, especially when traversing rough, uneven terrain. A good roof-rack should have full-length runners on the legs to spread any load the full length of the gutter. Racks are available in alloy or steel.
- **Tow bar or hitch** This equipment is essential if towing off-road trailers or vans. A correctly rated and fitted tow bar is designed to handle the increased stresses that often occur during outback travel. When making your selection, ensure that the tow bar or hitch is suited to the type of weight-distribution system you are likely to use.
- **Long-range fuel tank(s)** Long-distance outback travel in remote areas often means carrying additional fuel reserves. While jerry cans are a cheap option, they often create a storage problem. If undertaking numerous long-distance trips you should consider fitting a long-range tank(s).
- **Snorkel** This is a good investment, especially for diesel-powered vehicles travelling in dusty conditions where clean air is paramount. It also helps avoid water ingestion into the motor during deep river crossings.
- **Aftermarket suspension** Many stock standard vehicle suspension set-ups are fine for bitumen road travel and the occasional weekend away carrying light loads but they are really tested when heavily loaded and constantly pounded by rough outback roads. Heavy-duty aftermarket 4WD suspension systems, such as the TJM Series 2000 kits, make for more comfortable and safer travelling in harsh conditions.
- **Driving lights** These are a good addition if you plan on driving at night (which we advise against due to the increased danger from wandering animals).

A snorkel is a worthwhile investment

Water storage

Water is essential. It is a good idea to store water in several robust containers so if one bursts you will not lose your entire supply. As water is heavy, try to place the containers forward of the back axle and, if possible, do not have the weight on one side. Take care to protect containers from chafing when travelling on rough roads. An alternative option is to fit a stainless steel tank with an external tap. Carrying water in plastic pipes or on a roof rack is not a good idea as this will contribute to vehicle instability.

Tools and spare parts

The following are basic lists of tools and spare parts that we consider essential for outback touring and should always be carried in your vehicle. If you are travelling with other vehicles, you may be able to share some of these items. A full checklist is available for download from our website (www.exploreaustraliaby4wd.com).

It is important to be aware that modern electronic engine-management systems do limit your ability to conduct roadside repairs. Most importantly, know your vehicle. Read and carry a workshop manual for your vehicle. A basic course in vehicle maintenance and emergency repairs is a good idea, and is essential for travel in remote areas.

Tools
- Adjustable spanner
- Air compressor or pump
- Battery jumper leads
- Chisel
- Hammer
- Feeler gauges
- Files, including a points file
- Hacksaw and spare blades
- Jack
- Jacking plate (2.5-centimetre-thick piece of wood, 30 centimetres square)
- Pliers
- Plug spanner
- Screwdrivers: blade and Phillips head
- Spanners: ring and open end, to suit your vehicle
- Tyre levers
- Tyre/tube repair kit
- WD40 or similar
- Wheel brace
- Wire cutters
- Tyre pressure gauge

Spare parts
- Belts: fan, air conditioner, power-steering
- Electric wire
- Filters: fuel, air and oil
- Engine oil
- Fuel pump
- Fuses
- Globes
- Hoses: heater, radiator
- Plug leads
- Points
- Spark plugs
- Tyre tube
- Water pump
- Wheel-bearing kit

Tyres

Tyre choice is generally a personal preference and this often depends on your vehicle type and the road surfaces most commonly encountered. When travelling into remote areas, you need to choose tyres carefully so that you do not spend too much time on tyre repairs.

All-terrain tyres are a good choice

For the majority of treks in this guide, standard road tyres or all-terrain tyres are suitable. However, standard road tyres are more susceptible to damage when travelling on harsh outback terrain comprising sharp stones and rocky gibber plains. For this reason many people choose to use all-terrain tyres, which generally have a high resistance to punctures and sidewall damage. When travelling on the longer, remote trips, always carry two spare tyres.

We travelled all the treks in this guide using Kelly MSR all-terrain tyres, which coped extremely well with a huge variety of surfaces from harsh gibber through to soft sand and mud.

Recovery equipment

A basic recovery kit (see below) should be carried at all times. Many of the treks in this guide traverse remote country and a well-equipped recovery kit could save your life. Additional recovery equipment, also listed, can make the job of recovery safer and almost a fuss-free experience. Remember to check all your recovery equipment for wear and tear before heading off on any trip.

Basic recovery kit
- Axe
- Bow shackles (two)
- Gloves (riggers gloves are good)
- Long-handled shovel
- Snatch strap
- Jack and jacking plate

MAKING THE MOST OF YOUR TRIP

Some essential recovery equipment

Additional equipment
- Airbag jack
- Extra shackles
- Snatch block
- Tree-protector strap
- Winch extension straps
- Winch: hand or power

Snatch strap
The snatch strap is made of polypropylene or nylon webbing, which is woven with an eye at each end. The elastic property of the webbing stretches under tension, allowing vehicles to be pulled from bogs. Snatch straps are available in a couple of lengths. If necessary, two shorter snatch straps can be joined to make a longer length. When joining two snatch straps, always loop them through each other and place a small tree branch in the knot to ensure the knot is not tightened too much. Never use metal shackles to join snatch straps.

Jack and jacking plate
A two-stage hydraulic bottle jack with a rated capacity beyond the weight of the loaded vehicle will provide good height. High-lift jacks are sometimes useful, but they are heavy, awkward to carry, tricky to use and prone to slipping. They cannot be used on vehicles that do not have rigid, flat bumpers or other suitable jacking points. A jacking plate consisting of a piece of hardwood, approximately 2.5 centimetres thick and 30 centimetres square, should be carried to place the jack on when in soft ground. Never get under a vehicle that is supported only by a jack.

Winches
Winches can be either hand or power-operated. One end of the winch cable is attached to a suitable anchor point such as a solid tree and the cable is wound in to move the vehicle. If a tree is used as an anchor, ensure that the trunk is not rotten. Attach the cable to living trees only, after first wrapping a special webbed 'tree protector' around the lower part of the truck. Winches are hazardous and must be well maintained and must be fitted to a vehicle only in an approved position and secured with rated (high-tensile) bolts. Always carry several spare shear pins.

Snatch block
This is a pulley block through which the winch cable is run to increase the efficiency of the winch. Multiple snatch blocks increase the pulling strength of the winch.

Wooden jacking plate

Using a power-operated winch

Extension straps, drag chains and D shackles
Special purpose winch extension straps are available to increase the length of winch cables. A length of tensile drag chain and a couple of approved and rated D shackles are also a good inclusion in your recovery kit.

Communication equipment
Many travellers like to stay in touch with others on the road and know how to get help if stranded. Radio equipment and telephones are the usual communication modes, and they vary considerably in price, effectiveness and availability. Organisations such as the Australia-wide HF Radio Network VKS-737 provide a range of services, including general communications, road condition reports, emergency service and weather reports, while a number of private operators such as Radtel HF Radio Network operate a HF radio telephone network, which provides direct-dial telephone services as well as emergency and message services. See page 343 for contact details of these organisations.

In almost every state, the Royal Flying Doctor Service (RFDS) has a network of HF stations that deals primarily with medical emergencies. Most HF radio sets have a RFDS emergency call alarm system fitted.

Emergency Positioning Indicating Radio Beacon (EPIRB)
When activated, these small emergency units send out an internationally recognised distress signal. Frequencies are continuously monitored. Once a signal has been received it is reported through a central command centre to local emergency services, which then activate the rescue. EPIRBs are worth considering if driving in remote areas, especially if you are not travelling with a companion vehicle.

CB radios
There are two options: amplitude modulation (AM) and ultra-high frequency (UHF), with UHF being the most commonly used by four-wheel drivers.

AM units
These units are adequate for vehicle-to-vehicle communications and are used extensively for highway communication. AM Single Side Band units boost effective output power and increase transmission distances. However, do not rely on any CB radio for distant communications.

UHF radios
UHF units have a clearer signal than AM and SSB CBs, and are not prone to the same noise levels as AM units. UHF units have a greater range and cost more to buy, and are favoured by farmers and graziers. They use a short antenna.

Antennas
Antennas determine the performance of all CB radios. Flexible antennas have the advantage of bending back when hit by overhead branches. It is best to have the antenna professionally fitted in a reasonably protected spot on the vehicle and get the installer to adjust the standing wave ratio (SWR) for optimum antenna performance.

Mobile telephones
Although a large percentage of Australia's population has access to mobile telephones, sparsely populated outback areas are not well serviced but coverage is increasing. Mobile phones, in particular the GSM digital network, generally do not operate away from population centres or away from main road routes. You will receive better coverage from the CDMA network as the number of outback towns being connected increases. In-vehicle kits provide a greater range. Contact phone service suppliers for coverage maps before you depart.

EPIRB unit

Satellite telephones
Satellite telephones will operate from almost any location in Australia. They are still relatively expensive to purchase in comparison to digital and CDMA handsets (although less expensive than HF radio units) and running costs are reasonable with call costs around $1.00 per minute (depending on plan type). Sat phones are used for reliable communication by businesses such as mining companies, and are gaining popularity with remote-area travellers because they are easy to use and carry. You might like to consider hiring a sat phone for the duration of your outback trip instead of purchasing one. Check the yellow pages telephone directory for hire outlets.

High Frequency (HF) radios
Some travellers, especially the dedicated long-term type, may prefer HF radio communication as opposed to other forms, such as sat phones, as ongoing costs are usually less. HF radios are designed for long-distance communication with reliable transmission of up to 4000 kilometres. Obtain advice from a reputable radio communications retailer.

On the Road

Four-wheel-drive touring can present various driving challenges, but many of these need not be a problem if handled with care. A mix of bad roads, sand, mud, rocks and water can present problems that novice drivers are not likely to have encountered before. Being bogged in sand or mud is usually a short-term delay whereas being stranded mid-stream with a drowned engine has the potential to destroy your vehicle. If you are inexperienced in outback travel, do as much research beforehand as you can and do not be hesitant about seeking advice. Take one or more of the courses offered by four-wheel-drive training operators or four-wheel-drive clubs. And, finally, remember to look after the environment: leave only footprints and take only photographs.

Driving techniques

Assuming that you have some warning of possible problems on the track ahead, stop the car, get out and examine a hazard before driving headlong into or over it. Consider an alternative route. When traversing steep slopes or rocky terrain, drive carefully in the correct gear, picking your way to clearer ground. The only safe way to descend a steep slope is in a straight line; if this is not possible, try an alternative route. There are times when crossing a creek bed that is dry but rocky may necessitate someone walking ahead to guide the driver. In boggy or sandy terrain, pick ground that looks most likely to provide reasonable traction.

Oncoming traffic

Slow down when oncoming vehicles approach on gravel and dirt roads. This will help avoid windscreen damage and will allow the dust to settle – otherwise your vision of the road can be obscured and you will be driving 'blind'. When road trains approach, if practical pull off to the side of the road and stop. When overtaking on gravel and dirt surfaces make sure you have clear sight for a good distance ahead (this is not always easy due to dust).

Creek crossings

Before you tackle a creek crossing it is necessary to know the depth of the water and, to a certain extent, the consistency of the creek bed. In most cases this is simply a matter of walking the crossing first, feeling around for grip for the tyres and assessing the shallowest route. However,

Creek crossings should be approached with caution

creeks in northern Australia may be inhabited by crocodiles. In these cases it is certainly not recommended that you check the depth by wading across! Where possible, choose an alternative route – and do not enter the water either in, or out of, your vehicle.

If the water level is above tyre height and there is no alternative route, wrap the front of the vehicle with a groundsheet before entering the river or creek. This will prevent the water flowing back around the radiator and drowning the engine. You may need to disconnect the fan to reduce the risk of radiator damage and to reduce spray on the engine.

Before entering the water, decide on a plan of action. Be certain that the passengers – especially children – know what to do if something goes wrong. They need to know how to get out of the car and what to do thereafter.

Once your plan of action is in place, proceed in the following way:
- engage hubs and select four-wheel-drive low-range second gear
- enter the water slowly and proceed at a constant speed, never slipping the clutch or attempting to change gear
- keep a steady pace
- check the exit beforehand – if it is steep or soft, or both, you may need to keep up the momentum once clear of the water until you reach higher and flatter ground.

If the vehicle stalls in the water and you cannot immediately restart, you will have to winch it out. Once the vehicle is on dry land check to see that no water has entered the air intake, filling one or more cylinders. If this has happened, you will have a major mechanical repair job on your hands.

Mud
Momentum is a key factor when tackling muddy conditions. If possible, avoid deep bog holes as it is impossible to tell what is lurking under the mire (like large rocks or logs). Low-range second or third gear is generally best, keeping a steady speed to avoid sinking in.

Bulldust
Bulldust occurs in some outback areas when the surface of the track breaks up into a fine, talcum-powder-like dust.

Drive steadily through bulldust

Sand driving requires reduced tyre pressures

Bulldust can also hide a badly damaged road surface lying below the deceptively smooth dust. Drive at a steady pace through bulldust patches as this helps to avoid raising large plumes of dust and choking your air filter. Check your air filter daily, and clean if necessary, when travelling in dusty conditions.

Corrugations
This phenomenon is probably one of the most despised travelling surfaces plaguing outback roads. Often it is a matter of trial and error to find the right speed to get your vehicle 'floating' over the corrugations, but this depends on many factors such as suspension set-up, tyre pressure and vehicle loads. Lowering tyre pressures, even by a small amount, helps enormously. We found with our Landrover Defender that a speed of around 60–65 kph was best.

Sand driving
The key to sand driving is flotation, which is gained by a combination of travelling slowly without stopping and using low tyre pressures. Soft, dry sand often means that the vehicle needs to maintain a constant level of power to keep travelling without digging in or stalling. Stick to existing wheel tracks where possible as the sand will be compacted already, and less damage to the environment will result. Remember that vegetated sand dunes are extremely fragile so avoid them.

When travelling in sandy country or on a beach, a tyre gauge is essential to measure tyre pressures accurately. Lower the pressure by about 10psi (from standard road pressures), even on hard-packed sand. On soft sand you may need to lower tyre pressures by as much as 15psi. In really soft sand you may have to reduce pressures slightly again. A good-quality 12-volt compressor should be carried to re-inflate tyres.

When travelling in sand dune country, attach a high mounted red warning flag (available from four-wheel-drive accessory retailers) to your vehicle to advise oncoming traffic of your presence.

You may need to experiment a little with what gears to use, depending on your vehicle and its loaded weight. Initially try four-wheel-drive high-range second gear, and see how you go. Low range usually will not be necessary, but use it if your vehicle's revs drop so that you can change down to a lower gear quickly in order to keep up momentum.

Watch tides when beach driving. You could possibly drown the engine in salt water if you are bogged and caught by an incoming tide. It is recommended that you drive on beaches only during the two-hour period before and after low tide.

A few extra checks
- Soft-sand driving can cause overheating with high temperatures building up in engine oils and coolant – try to avoid driving for long periods in soft sand by stopping to give your engine a chance to cool.
- Sand in the air filter and air intake is not good so check frequently when sand driving.
- Before beach driving, have the vehicle underbody professionally rust-proofed (do not spray with sump oil as this can contaminate beach environments).
- Hose the underbody with fresh water after all beach driving to minimise the risk of salt corrosion.

Recovering a bogged vehicle
The fastest and often easiest way to recover a bogged vehicle is to use a snatch strap. If this is not successful or practical, or you are travelling unaccompanied, then you may need to resort to a winch. Familiarise yourself with the operation before an emergency arises. If you are not familiar with vehicle recovery techniques, we recommend that you undertake a vehicle recovery course with either a recognised four-wheel-drive training operator or with a four-wheel-drive club.

Tips for handling winches
- Always pull as straight as possible in line with the vehicle (this is not always practical).
- When operating a winch and handling the cable, wear strong protective gloves – lacerations from steel splinters are very painful.
- Always keep several wraps of cable around the winch drum and do not allow the cable to cross over itself, as this will create a weak point and possibly make the cable unsafe under load.
- Keep all onlookers away from an operating winch line. When winching, a lot of force is applied to the winch cable, and if it breaks it could whip through the air and sever limbs or, at worst, cause a fatal injury. Always place some type of dampener such as a towel or blanket over the winch cable to help avoid this situation.
- Increase the vehicle engine idle speed if using an electric winch as this puts less stress on the battery.

Roadside maintenance and repairs
Here are some simple guidelines to follow on the road.
- Read your vehicle manual thoroughly before leaving.
- Keep an eye on the warning gauges and do daily checks of fuel, oil and water, and check the tension and condition of the fan belt.
- Have a look around and under your vehicle each morning before driving off to check for leaks, low tyre

Recovering a bogged vehicle using a snatch strap

A burned out vehicle, a casualty of a spinifex fire

pressures, fuel-line leaks, the movement of parts that should not move, cracks, loose components, chafing brake, fuel or radiator hoses and anything else that seems abnormal.
- When travelling over corrugated or rough terrain, check the tightness of wheel nuts (or wheel studs) on a daily basis (if nuts become loose, the wheel begins to wear the studs and can snap them off).
- Have the gate opener check the ground where the vehicle has been standing for any signs of oil or water leakage – early detection can help avoid a serious mechanical failure.
- Watch out for a fire starting where you cannot see it; in grassed areas and especially in spinifex, avoid the risk of vehicle fire by checking the exhaust system frequently as grass or seeds caught on or around the exhaust can ignite.
- Set aside adequate time at regular intervals and at an appropriate location for an overall service of the vehicle.
- Many breakdowns can be remedied by knowing how to carry out a roadside repair and success will depend on having the knowledge, the right tools and the right spares to create something temporary until you reach mechanical assistance.
- If your vehicle breaks down and you are unable to get it going again, do not leave it – this is an essential and fundamental rule in the outback. Unless you know for certain that help is close by and within easy walking distance, do not be tempted to leave the vehicle as it will be the first thing to be seen by searchers. People away from their vehicles are much harder to spot in the landscape from a plane or vehicle. Your vehicle will also offer shelter from the hot sun, either inside or underneath it.

- There are other good reasons for staying with your vehicle. For example, problems that arise in the heat of day sometimes correct themselves in the cool of the night. In particular, overheating can cause engine fuel systems to fail and the problem can correct itself after the engine has cooled.

Emergency welding

It is possible to make effective emergency welds using two batteries, a couple of jumper leads, some welding rods and a welding handpiece. A welding glass, the type used in welding helmets, makes working easier and can be taped in a piece of cardboard to act as a shield (there are also a number of 12-volt welding kits on the market). We used this method to weld a roof-rack leg that snapped about halfway along the Canning Stock Route. The weld was still holding strong when we finally had the leg reinforced with a gusset at Ceduna in South Australia after completing the Canning, Gunbarrel and Connie Sue highways and the Eyre Highway across the Nullarbor – a total of almost 3500 kilometres.

Bush welding is a useful skill in emergencies

Towing off-road trailers and off-road caravans

An off-road camper trailer or off-road caravan can provide excellent accommodation and extra facilities that are not available to those camping in tents. In cases where a number of passengers are travelling, the trailer will take some (perhaps most) of the gear and equipment that must otherwise be carried in the vehicle. However, there are certain tracks over which it is very difficult or impossible to pull trailers or caravans. On long treks this difficulty might be partly overcome by parking the trailer for a few days while you make short tours. However, if you

MAKING THE MOST OF YOUR TRIP

Towing an off-road caravan

do this, you will need to carry a tent to use while the trailer is parked. You may also need to pay site rental for the trailer while you are away. Before setting off, check state regulations regarding towing as they may vary from state to state.

Travelling safely

By observing the following precautions when travelling in Australia's outback regions, you will help contribute to your own safety and wellbeing.

Take precautions
- Whenever possible travel with a companion vehicle, especially in remote areas.
- Ensure that more than one person has first-aid knowledge and certification.
- Ensure that several people know where the first-aid kit is stored, and can operate the emergency HF radio or satellite telephone – stick the instructions and your call sign on the dashboard.
- Let people know where you are going and when you expect to arrive.
- Make sure that someone else can drive in case you are unable to do so.

Follow these safe driving techniques
- Be attentive.
- Do not travel when weary or after consuming alcohol. Observe the maxim *Stop. Revive. Survive*.
- Travel well within the limit of your ability and that of your vehicle – remember that outback travel involves long distances behind the wheel.
- Always be mindful of wandering stock on unfenced roads and tracks.

- Avoid driving at dawn and dusk as many wildlife species favour these times for moving around to search for food.

Adhere to the following etiquette
- Leave gates as you find them.
- Do not interfere with windmills, water bores or tanks.
- Never camp near stock watering points as animals will avoid coming in to drink.
- Slow down when passing another vehicle on a gravel road.
- Move to the left to allow road trains to pass.
- Check with land managers on current regulations regarding chainsaws as they are banned in most national parks and reserves.
- When crossing private property, pastoral leases or Aboriginal land, obtain permission if you wish to leave the road corridor.

Always leave gates as found

Travel with a companion vehicle in remote areas

Looking after the environment

Stay on tracks, only drive on roads open to the public and never 'bush bash'. Please respect private property and the landowner's instructions. In some locations there are special reasons for not allowing people to leave defined tracks, such as trying to limit the spread of plant diseases or noxious weeds that can be transported by tyres.

Guidelines

- Wash down the tyres and undercarriage of your vehicle or brush off excess soil before and after going into areas affected by dieback.
- Obey track closures – if a road or track is closed it should not be used.
- Drive softly and avoid tracks when they are wet and muddy – by minimising track damage you can also help reduce erosion and costly road repairs.
- Use an alternative route and bypass wet areas or wait until they dry out (this is one good reason why maps are essential items to take on your travels).
- Avoid wheel spin as wheel ruts become channels that cause erosion.
- Creek crossings should be negotiated using existing entry and exit points if there are no culverts or bridges – always check the water depth first and check for hidden obstacles such as large rocks and logs.
- If you need to operate a winch use a tree-trunk protector or ground anchors.
- Never use soaps or detergents in creeks, rivers, streams, dams or water troughs as detergents and other agents destroy water quality – wash using a bucket, at least 100 metres away from waterways.
- Campfires should be small so you do not burn large amounts of firewood and use old fireplaces instead of erecting new ones. Clear combustible material for 4 metres away from your fire site and make sure campfires are completely extinguished with water before you go.

Take heed of warning signs

Extinguish campfires with water

- Follow current fire regulations in the area.
- Never cut down vegetation, living or dead, for firewood.
- Use toilets where provided; elsewhere bury wastes at least 100 metres away from campsites and waterways, in a hole at least 15 centimetres deep. Burn toilet paper.
- Protect native flora and fauna.

Wildlife

Watch out for wildlife while travelling. To reduce the risk of damage to your vehicle and adding to the numbers of dead animals on roads, drive more slowly, watch out for animals at the side of the road and keep night, dusk and dawn driving to a minimum. In the unfortunate event that you do hit an animal, make sure it is dead instead of leaving it to die in pain. Never approach or feed wildlife. When swimming or fishing, watch out for sharks and, in northern waters, marine stingers and crocodiles.

Crocodiles

Both freshwater and estuarine (saltwater) crocodiles are found in Australia. Freshwater crocodiles, generally smaller than the estuarine species, are found in freshwater streams, billabongs and waterholes and are usually shy and placid when left alone. Saltwater crocodiles are normally found in coastal waters and tidal creeks and rivers, but they can stray into fresh water. These animals are extremely dangerous and caution is required when camping or undertaking recreational activities such as boating, canoeing or fishing in areas that are known crocodile habitats. Be crocodile-wise and follow these guidelines:

- obey all warning signs and do not leave fish scraps and bait at boat ramps or near campsites
- stand well back from the water's edge when fishing
- camp at least 50 metres away and at least 2 metres above the water's edge
- always supervise children when near the water
- do not dangle arms or legs over the side of a boat.

MAKING THE MOST OF YOUR TRIP

Take your rubbish with you

Quarantine disposal bin

Rubbish disposal

The rule of thumb to remember is: what you take in with you, make sure you take out again. The rubbish bin in the vehicle must be airtight to prevent unwelcome smells. We use a plastic tub with a tight-fitting lid stored on the roof-rack for this purpose. Dispose of all your rubbish in a legitimate dump, generally found on the outskirts of most towns, or in the bins provided. Many outback and remote national parks have no bins at bush campsites. Burying rubbish is not acceptable as wild animals can dig it up.

Quarantine

In some regions there are restrictions on the carrying of fresh fruit and vegetables across state borders. Such items may be confiscated at quarantine checkpoints. There are quarantine stations at the following locations:

- the Eyre Highway at the South Australia–Western Australia border at Eucla (westbound travellers are obliged to stop)
- the Eyre Highway at Ceduna in South Australia (eastbound travellers are obliged to stop)
- the Victoria Highway at the Northern Territory–Western Australia border east of Kununurra (westbound travellers are obliged to stop).

Other quarantine inspection points, particularly Fruit Fly Exclusion Zones, are located in other areas of Australia. It is wise to check regulations before buying fruit and vegetables to take on your journey through these areas. In other places there are signposted quarantine disposal bins beside the road. See opposite page for contact numbers of state organisations if you require further information.

PAGES 344–5
The track to Haddon Corner in Corner Country

Useful Contacts

State automobile associations
NSW NRMA, tel. 13 2132, website www.nrma.com.au
NT AANT, tel. (08) 8981 3837, website www.aant.com.au
QLD RACQ, tel. 131 905, website www.racq.com.au
SA RAA, tel. (08) 8202 4600, website www.raa.net
VIC RACV, tel. 131 955, website www.racv.com.au
WA RAC, tel. 13 1111, website www.rac.com.au

Road conditions
NSW NRMA road report, tel. 13 1122, website www.nrma.com.au
NT NT road information service, tel. 1800 246 199, website www.roadreport.nt.gov.au
QLD RACQ road reporting service, tel. 1300 130 595, website www.racq.com.au
SA SA road report hotline, tel. 1300 361 033, website www.transport.sa.gov.au
VIC VicRoads, tel. (03) 9854 2666, website www.vicroads.vic.gov.au
WA WA road condition report service, tel. 1800 013 314, website www.mrwa.wa.gov.au

State tourism associations
NSW Tourism New South Wales, tel. 13 2077, website www.visitnsw.com.au
NT Northern Territory Tourist Commission, tel. (08) 8999 3900, website www.ntholidays.com
QLD Queensland Tourism Travel Centre, tel. 13 8833, website www.queenslandholidays.com.au
SA South Australian Tourism Visitor & Travel Centre, tel. 1300 655 276, website www.southaustralia.com
VIC Tourism Victoria, tel. 13 2842, website www.visitvictoria.com
WA Western Australian Tourism Commission, tel. 1300 361 351, website www.westernaustralia.com

National parks state offices
NSW National Parks and Wildlife Service (NPWS), tel. 1300 361 967, website www.nationalparks.nsw.gov.au
NT Parks and Wildlife Commission Northern Territory (PWCNT), tel. (08) 8999 5511, website www.nt.gov.au/ipe/pwcnt
QLD Queensland Parks and Wildlife Service (QPWS), tel. 13 1304, website www.epa.qld.gov.au
SA National Parks and Wildlife South Australia (NPWSA), Department of Environment and Heritage Information, tel. (08) 8204 1910, website www.environment.sa.gov.au
VIC Parks Victoria, tel. 13 1963, website www.parkweb.vic.gov.au
WA Department of Conservation and Land Management (CALM), tel. (08) 9334 0333, website www.naturebase.net

Aboriginal land councils
NT Central Land Council, Alice Springs, tel. (08) 8951 6320, website www.clc.org.au
NT Ngaanyatjarra Aboriginal Council, Alice Springs, tel. (08) 8950 5443
NT Northern Land Council, Darwin, tel. (08) 8920 5100, website www.nlc.org.au
SA Maralinga Tjarutja Inc, Ceduna, tel. (08) 8625 2946
WA Department of Indigenous Affairs, Perth, tel. (08) 9235 8000, website www.dia.wa.gov.au

Fisheries offices
NSW Tel. (02) 9527 8411, website www.fisheries.nsw.gov.au
NT Tel. (08) 8999 2144, website www.fisheries.nt.gov.au
QLD Tel. 13 2523 or (07) 3404 6999, website www.dpi.qld.gov.au/fishweb
SA Tel. (08) 8347 6100, website www.pir.sa.gov.au
VIC Tel. 136 186, website www.nre.vic.gov.au
WA Tel. (08) 9482 7333, website www.fish.wa.gov.au

Quarantine
NSW Department of Primary Industries, tel. (02) 9764 3311 or 1800 084 881
NT Department of Primary Industries, tel. (08) 8999 2110
QLD Department of Primary Industries and Fisheries, tel. (07) 3404 6999
SA Department of Primary Industries and Resources, tel. 1300 666 010
VIC Department of Sustainability & Environment, tel. 13 6186
WA State Quarantine Office, tel. (08) 9334 1800

Radio networks
VKS-737 Radio Network, tel. (08) 8287 6222, website www.vks737.on.net

Radtel HF Radio Network, tel. (02) 4943 1745, website www.radtelnetwork.com.au

Australian Communications Authority, tel. 1300 850 115, website www.aca.gov.au

RFDS of Australia Central Operations, tel. (08) 8238 3333, website www.flyingdoctor.net

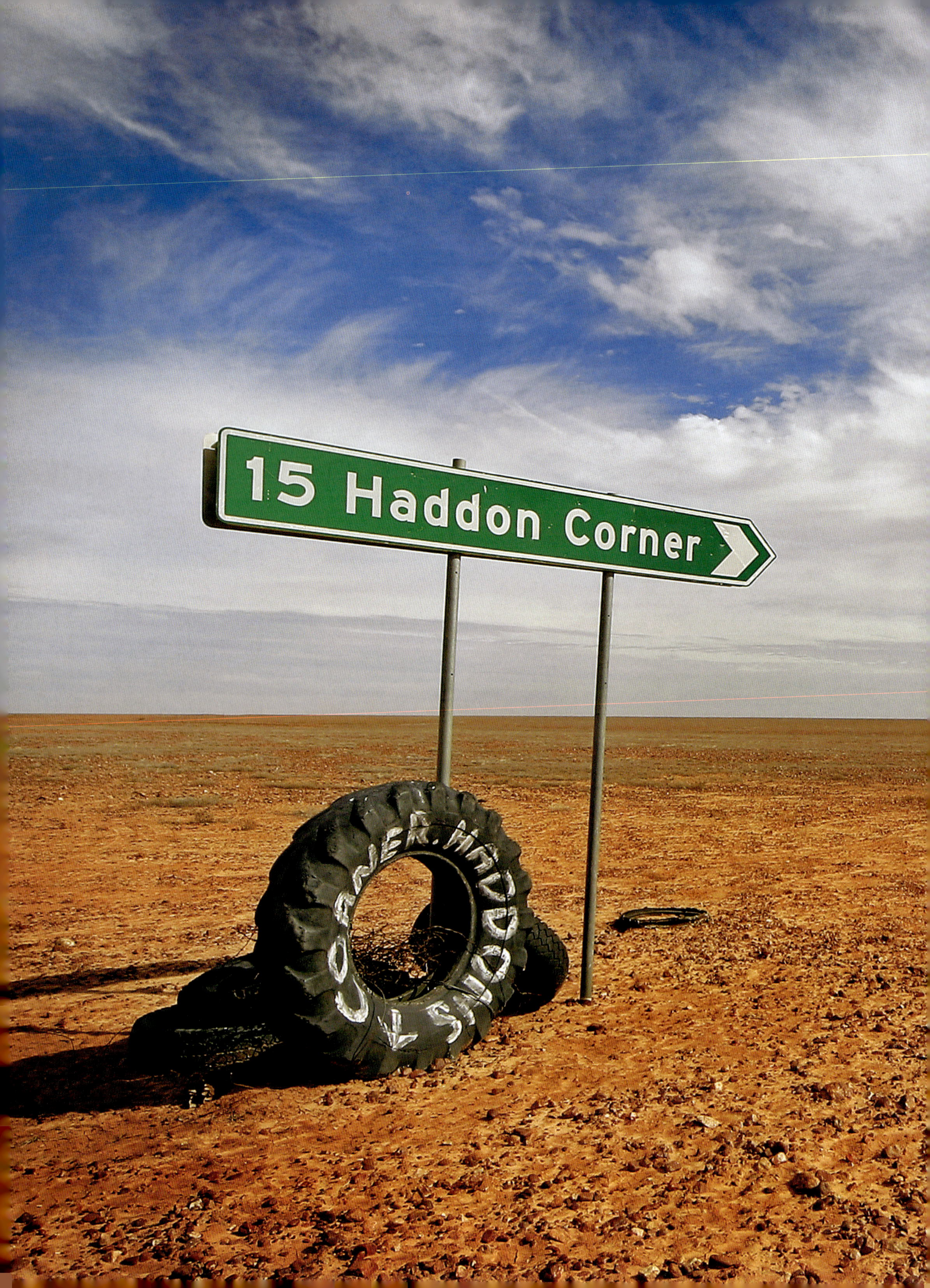
15 Haddon Corner

Road Atlas

LOCATION MAP

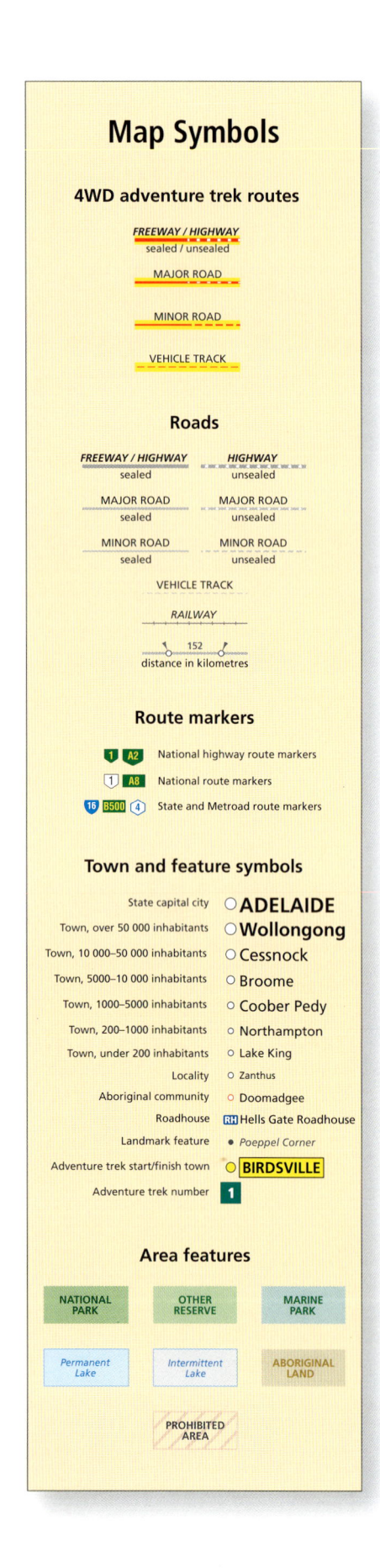

Map Symbols

4WD adventure trek routes

FREEWAY / HIGHWAY
sealed / unsealed

MAJOR ROAD

MINOR ROAD

VEHICLE TRACK

Roads

FREEWAY / HIGHWAY
sealed

HIGHWAY
unsealed

MAJOR ROAD
sealed

MAJOR ROAD
unsealed

MINOR ROAD
sealed

MINOR ROAD
unsealed

VEHICLE TRACK

RAILWAY

152
distance in kilometres

Route markers

1 A2   National highway route markers
1 A8   National route markers
16 B500 4 State and Metroad route markers

Town and feature symbols

State capital city — **ADELAIDE**
Town, over 50 000 inhabitants — **Wollongong**
Town, 10 000–50 000 inhabitants — Cessnock
Town, 5000–10 000 inhabitants — Broome
Town, 1000–5000 inhabitants — Coober Pedy
Town, 200–1000 inhabitants — Northampton
Town, under 200 inhabitants — Lake King
Locality — Zanthus
Aboriginal community — Doomadgee
Roadhouse — RH Hells Gate Roadhouse
Landmark feature — • Poeppel Corner
Adventure trek start/finish town — **BIRDSVILLE**
Adventure trek number — 1

Area features

NATIONAL PARK
OTHER RESERVE
MARINE PARK

Permanent Lake
Intermittent Lake
ABORIGINAL LAND

PROHIBITED AREA

LOCATION MAP

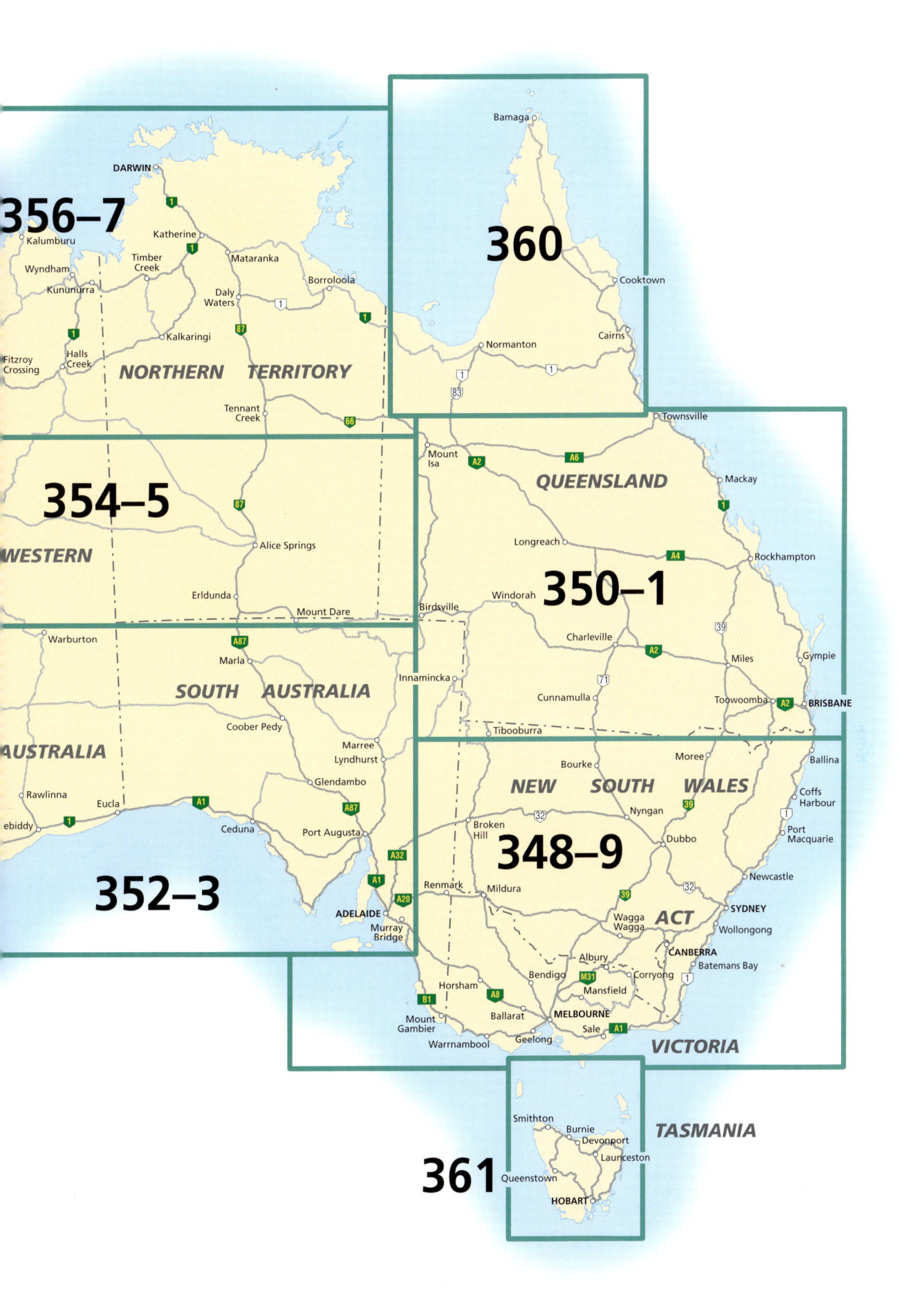

356–7
360
354–5
350–1
352–3
348–9
361

347

SOUTH EASTERN AUSTRALIA

INTER-CITY ROUTES	DISTANCE
Adelaide–Darwin via Stuart Hwy A1 A87 87 1	3026 km
Adelaide–Perth via Eyre & Great Eastern hwys A1 1 94	2700 km
Adelaide–Sydney via Sturt & Hume hwys A20 20 31	1417 km
Adelaide–Melbourne via Dukes & Western hwys M1 A8 M8	733 km
Adelaide–Melbourne via Princes Hwy M1 B1 A1 M1	906 km

348

SOUTH EASTERN AUSTRALIA

4WD Adventure Treks

1	Birdsville Track	Page 2
2	Strzelecki Track	Page 10
3	Oodnadatta Track	Page 20
14	Googs Track	Page 202
15	Victoria's High Country	Page 212
16	Corner Country	Page 240

INTER-CITY ROUTES

Route		Distance
Sydney–Melbourne via Hume Hwy/Fwy	31 M31	881 km
Sydney–Melbourne via Princes Hwy/Fwy	1 A1 M1	1037 km
Sydney–Brisbane via New England Hwy	1 15 A2	1001 km
Sydney–Brisbane via Pacific Hwy	1 1 M1	966 km
Melbourne–Adelaide via Western & Dukes hwys	M8 A8 M1	733 km
Melbourne–Adelaide via Princes Hwy	M1 A1 B1 M1	906 km
Melbourne–Brisbane via Newell Hwy	M31 A39 39 A2	1676 km

349

CENTRAL EASTERN AUSTRALIA

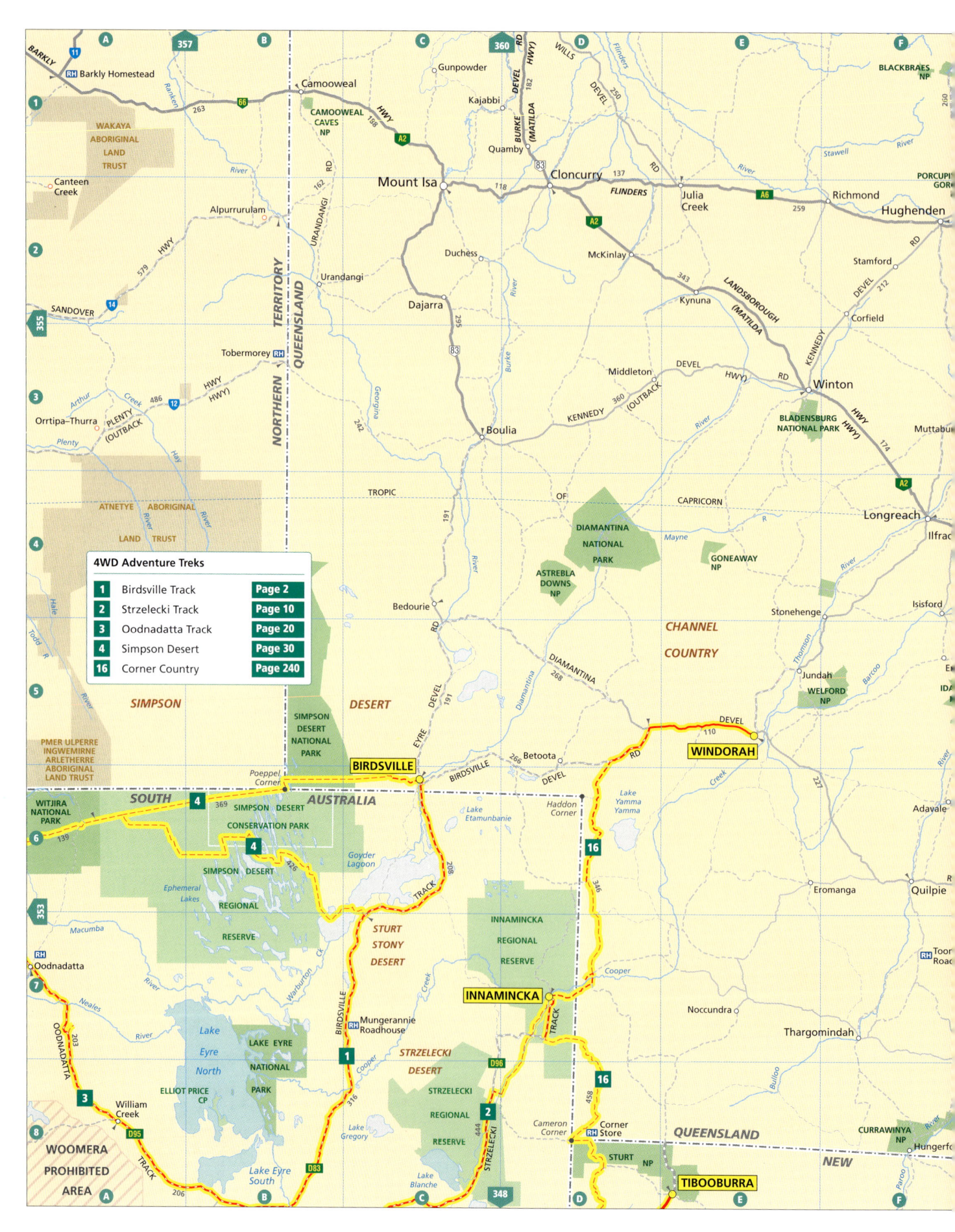

4WD Adventure Treks

1	Birdsville Track	Page 2
2	Strzelecki Track	Page 10
3	Oodnadatta Track	Page 20
4	Simpson Desert	Page 30
16	Corner Country	Page 240

CENTRAL EASTERN AUSTRALIA

INTER-CITY ROUTES	DISTANCE
Brisbane–Sydney via New England Hwy A2 15 1	1001 km
Brisbane–Sydney via Pacific Hwy M1 1 1	966 km
Brisbane–Melbourne via Newell Hwy A2 39 A39 M31	1676 km
Brisbane–Darwin via Warrego Hwy 1 87 66 A2	3406 km
Brisbane–Cairns via Bruce Hwy 1	1703 km

351

NULLARBOR PLAIN

4WD Adventure Treks	
1 Birdsville Track	Page 2
2 Strzelecki Track	Page 10
3 Oodnadatta Track	Page 20
4 Simpson Desert	Page 30
9 Canning Stock Route	Page 118
10 Holland Track	Page 156
11 Gunbarrel Highway	Page 166
12 Connie Sue Highway	Page 176
13 Anne Beadell Highway	Page 186
14 Googs Track	Page 202

NULLARBOR PLAIN

INTER-CITY ROUTES	DISTANCE
Adelaide–Darwin via Stuart Hwy A1 A87 87 1	3026 km
Adelaide–Perth via Eyre & Great Eastern hwys A1 1 94	2700 km
Adelaide–Sydney via Sturt & Hume hwys A20 20 31	1417 km
Adelaide–Melbourne via Dukes & Western hwys M1 A8 M8	733 km
Adelaide–Melbourne via Princes Hwy M1 B1 A1 M1	906 km

CENTRAL AUSTRALIA

CENTRAL AUSTRALIA

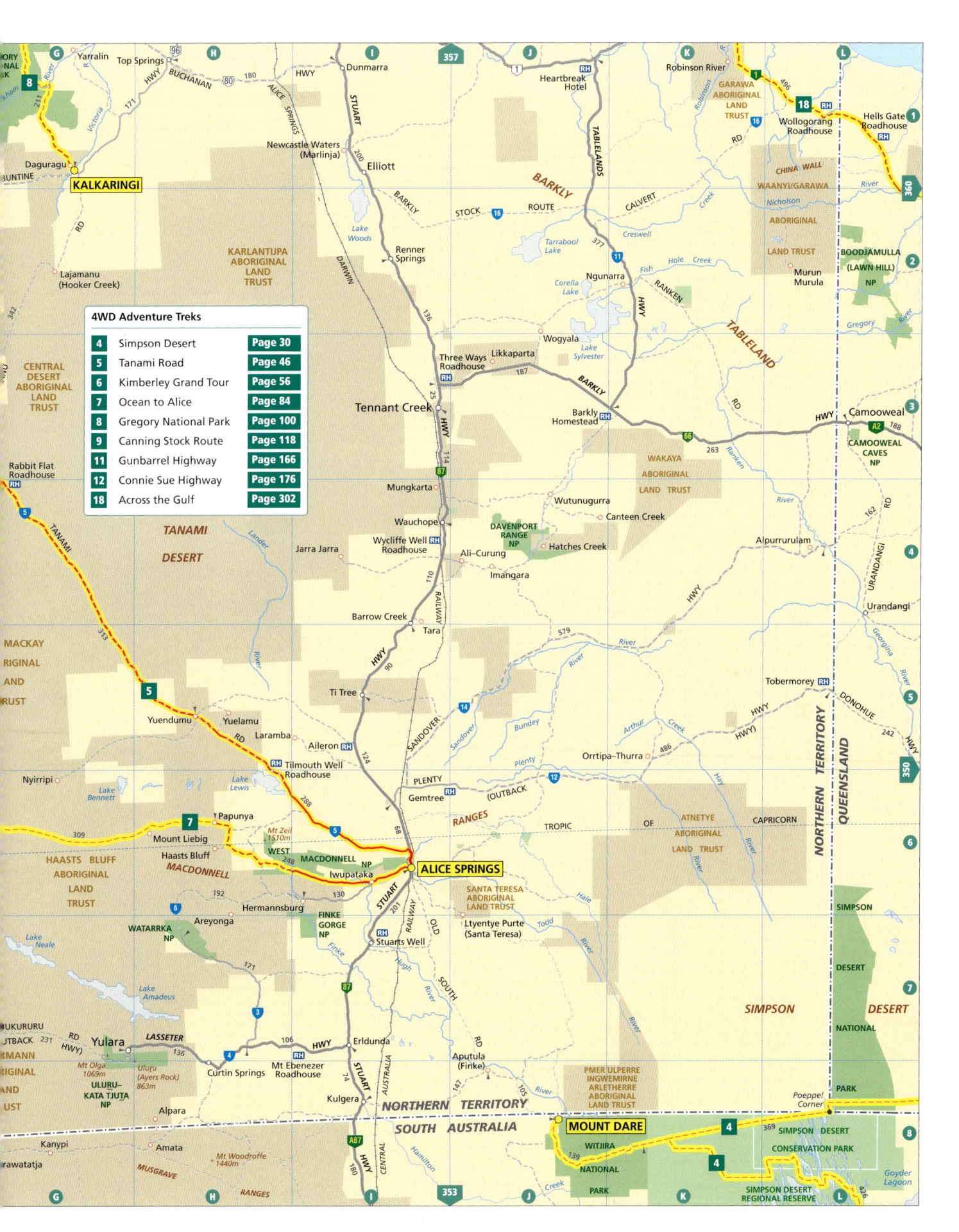

4WD Adventure Treks

4	Simpson Desert	Page 30
5	Tanami Road	Page 46
6	Kimberley Grand Tour	Page 56
7	Ocean to Alice	Page 84
8	Gregory National Park	Page 100
9	Canning Stock Route	Page 118
11	Gunbarrel Highway	Page 166
12	Connie Sue Highway	Page 176
18	Across the Gulf	Page 302

355

THE TOP END

INTER-CITY ROUTES	DISTANCE
Darwin–Adelaide via Stuart Hwy 1 87 A87 A1	3026 km
Darwin–Perth via Great Northern Hwy 1 95	4032 km
Darwin–Brisbane via Warrego Hwy 1 87 66 A2	3406 km

4WD Adventure Treks

5	Tanami Road	Page 46
6	Kimberley Grand Tour	Page 56
8	Gregory National Park	Page 100
9	Canning Stock Route	Page 118
18	Across the Gulf	Page 302

WARNINGS: In outback Australia, long distances separate some towns. Travellers should familiarise themselves with prevailing conditions before departure and take care to ensure their vehicle is roadworthy. Adequate supplies of petrol, water and food should be carried at all times.

In northern Australia, rainfall during the wet season (October to March) can make some roads impassable. Full information on road conditions should be obtained from local authorities before departure.

If visitors intend diverting off public roads within Aboriginal Land areas, a permit is required from the relevant Aboriginal authority.

Beware of crocodiles in rivers, estuaries and coastal areas.

THE TOP END

SOUTH-WESTERN WESTERN AUSTRALIA

4WD Adventure Treks

9	Canning Stock Route	Page 118
10	Holland Track	Page 156
11	Gunbarrel Highway	Page 166

INTER-CITY ROUTES — **DISTANCE**

Perth–Adelaide via Great Eastern & Eyre hwys — 2700 km
Perth–Darwin via Great Northern Hwy — 4032 km

NORTH-WESTERN WESTERN AUSTRALIA

NORTHERN QUEENSLAND

TASMANIA

INTER-CITY ROUTES		DISTANCE
Hobart–Launceston via Midland Hwy	1	200 km
Hobart–Devonport via Midland & Bass hwys	1 B52	286 km

361

Index

A

ABC Bay SA 27
Abergowrie Qld 360 F8
Aboriginal art 51, 60
Acacia NT 357 G2
Adavale Qld 350 F6
Adelaide SA 348 B5, 353 L7
Adelaide River NT 357 G3
Adria Downs Qld 40
Agnes Gnamma Hole WA 160, 165
Aileron NT 355 I5
Ains, Peter 39
Airlie Beach Qld 351 I2
Albany WA 358 E8
Albert goldfields NSW 242, 245
Albert River Qld 304, 309
Albury NSW 349 G6
Alexandra River Qld 308
Algebuckina bush camping SA 24, 25, 28
Alice Springs NT 355 I6, 22, 24, 29, 30, 36, 46, 47, 48, 49, 51, 52, 54, 84, 85, 90, 91, 96, 98, 99, 174, 192
Ali–Curung NT 355 J4
Allandale SA 29
Alpara NT 355 H8
Alpha Qld 351 H4
Alpine National Park Vic. 349 G7, 349 H7, 213, 214, 218
Alpine Way Vic. 214, 218, 219
Alpurrurulam NT 350 B2, 355 L4
Amanbidji NT 354 F1, 356 F5
Amata SA 355 H8
Andado SA 36
Andamooka SA 348 B1, 353 K4
Angurugu NT 357 K3
Anna Creek SA 27
Anne Beadell Highway SA & WA 352 C2, 178, 182, 188–201
Annes Corner SA 194
Annie River camping area Qld 266, 267, 274
Annies Creek WA 80
Aparawatatja SA 355 G8
Apollo Bay Vic. 348 E8
Apollo Gold Mine WA 201

Approdinna Attora Knolls SA 37, 38, 42
Aputula (Finke) NT 355 J8, 24, 26, 36
Aramac Qld 351 G3
Ararat Vic. 348 E7
Archer River Qld 276, 278, 279
Archer River Roadhouse Qld 360 D4, 275, 276, 278
Archer River Roadhouse campground Qld 278, 279, 280, 281
Areyonga NT 355 H6
Arkaroola SA 348 C1, 16
Armadale WA 358 C6
Armidale NSW 349 J2
Armstrong Creek Qld 308
Arno Bay SA 348 A4, 353 K6
Arrabury Qld 19, 258, 259
Art Baker Lookout SA 16
Astrebla Downs National Park Qld 350 D4
Atherton Qld 360 F7
Augathella Qld 351 H6
Augusta WA 358 C8
Aurukun Qld 360 C3
Auski Roadhouse WA 359 D5
Australian Inland Mission SA 243
Avoca Tas. 361 E5
Ayr Qld 351 H1
Ayton Qld 360 F6

B

Babinda Qld 360 F7
Back River Vic. 221
Badgingarra WA 358 C5
Baines, Thomas 105
Baines camping area NT 103, 106
Bairnsdale Vic. 349 G7, 222
Balaklava SA 348 B4, 353 L7
Balgo Hills WA 354 E3, 356 E8, 47, 48, 49, 54
Balladonia WA 352 C6
Ballarat Vic. 348 E7
Ballina NSW 349 L1, 351 L8
Balranald NSW 348 E5
Bamaga Qld 360 D1, 262, 263, 278, 285, 286, 287, 288, 290, 293, 294, 295, 297

Bamboo Creek WA 359 E3, 64
Baniyala NT 357 K3
Barcaldine Qld 351 G4
Barkly homestead NT 355 J3, 357 J8
Barnett River Gorge WA 73, 75, 76
Barrabarrac Creek NT 102, 106
Barren Lake Qld 250
Barringun NSW 351 G8
Barrow Creek NT 355 I4
Barwidgee WA 175
Batavia Downs Qld 283, 285
Batavia Goldfields Qld 276, 282
Batchelor NT 357 G3
Batemans Bay NSW 349 I6
Bathurst NSW 349 I4
Bathurst Head Qld 264
Batten Creek NT 318
Battle Camp Qld 265, 268, 269, 273
Battle Camp Range Qld 264
Bauhinia Downs NT 318
Baw Baw National Park Vic. 349 G7
Bayley's Find WA 163
Beadell, Len 92, 94, 95, 136, 166, 168, 169, 171, 173, 174, 176, 182, 186, 191, 195, 199
Beagle Bay WA 354 B1, 356 B6
Beaudesert Qld 351 K8
Beauty Point Tas. 361 D4
Bedourie Qld 350 C4, 43, 259
Beenleigh Qld 351 L7
Bega NSW 349 I7
Bell Creek camping area WA 78, 79, 80
Bell Gorge WA 73, 79, 80
Beltana SA 348 B2, 353 L4
Beltana Roadhouse SA 348 B2, 353 L4
Ben Lomond National Park Tas. 361 E5
Benalla Vic. 349 G6
Benambra Vic. 220
Benambra–Black Mountain Road Vic. 215
Bendigo Vic. 348 F6
Bentley Plain Vic. 212, 215
Bentley Plain camping area Vic. 216, 217, 221
Beresford Bore Historic Rail Siding SA 22, 26

INDEX

Bermagui NSW 349 I6
Berri SA 348 D4
Bertie Creek Qld 290
Beswick NT 357 I4
Betoota Qld 350 D5, 9, 42, 259
Beverley Springs WA 74, 76, 78
Beverley Springs camping area WA 75, 76, 78
Bicheno Tas. 361 F6
Bidyadanga WA 354 A3, 356 A8, 359 F2
Biella Spring WA 133
Big Desert Vic. 348 D5
Big Red (Nappanerica Dune) SA 30, 32, 33, 35, 40
Billabong Roadhouse WA 358 A2
Billiluna (Mindibungu) WA 354 E3, 356 E8, 47, 48, 54, 55, 118, 119, 139, 140, 153
Billiluna store WA 48, 55, 139, 153
Billy Goat Springs WA 76
Biloela Qld 351 J5
Bindoola Creek WA 64
Bindoon WA 358 C5
Bing Bong NT 315
Binnu WA 358 B3
Birdsville Qld 350 C6, 2, 3, 4, 6, 7, 9, 30, 31, 32, 33, 36, 37, 39, 40, 41, 42, 259
Birdsville Developmental Road Qld 350 C6, 259
Birdsville Inside Track SA 6, 9, 41, 43
Birdsville Track Qld & SA 350 B7, 353 L3, 2–9, 22, 33, 41, 42, 43
Birdwood Downs WA 74, 78, 83
Birdwood Downs camping area WA 78, 83
Birregun Road Vic. 224, 228
Bitter Springs NT 303, 316, 321
Bizant outstation Qld 264, 265, 271, 272, 274
Black Flat camping area Vic. 225, 229
Blackall Qld 351 G4
Blackbird Flat Vic. 239
Blackbird Flat camping area Vic. 232, 233, 239
Blackbull Qld 360 C7, 309
Blackgin Bore NT 115
Blackgin Waterhole NT 115
Blackwater Qld 351 I4
Bladensburg National Park Qld 350 E3
Blanche Cup (mound springs) SA 22, 25, 26
Blanchewater SA 10, 12, 13, 15, 16
Blina Oil Field WA 83
Bloods Creek SA 36, 39

Bloodwood Well WA 140, 153
Blue Mountains National Park NSW 349 I4
Blue Shirt Creek Vic. 221
Blue Ute Bore 1 SA 9
Blue Water Springs Roadhouse Qld 351 G1, 360 F8
Bobs Bore SA 16
Bodey's Bore SA 8
Boebuck Track Vic. 218
Bollon Qld 351 H7
Bombala NSW 349 H7
Boodjamulla (Lawn Hill) National Park Qld 355 L2, 357 L7, 360 A8
Bookabourdie SA 258
Booligal NSW 348 F4
Boorabbin National Park WA 358 E5
Border Store NT 357 H2
Border Village SA 352 F5
Bordertown SA 348 D6
Bore Track SA 19, 251, 257
Borroloola NT 357 K5, 302, 303, 304, 305, 311, 312, 313, 314, 318, 319, 320
Bothwell Tas. 361 D6
Bottom Whiphandle camping area Qld 266, 273
Boulia Qld 350 C3
Boundary Creek WA 81
Bounty Gold Mine WA 158, 162
Bourke NSW 349 G1
Bowen Qld 351 I1
Bowling Green Bay National Park Qld 351 H1
Box Creek SA 27
Brampton Island Qld 351 J2
Bramwell Junction Qld 360 D2, 262, 263, 286, 290
Bramwell Junction campground Qld 280, 281, 285, 288, 289, 290
Bramwell Junction Roadhouse Qld 275, 277, 285, 286, 287, 290
Bramwell station Qld 275, 285, 294
Bramwell Station campground Qld 280, 281, 285, 288, 289, 294
Breaden Hills WA 140, 141
Breaden Pool WA 140, 141, 150
Breaden Valley WA 150, 151
Breakfast Time (William) Creek SA 27
Breeza outstation Qld 266, 272
Bremer Bay WA 352 A8, 358 F7
Brewarrina NSW 349 H1
Brewery Creek Track Vic. 234
Bridge Creek (Nolan Brook) Qld 293
Bridgetown WA 358 D7

Bridgewater SA 348 C5, 353 L7
Bridport Tas. 361 E4
Bright Vic. 349 G6
Brisbane Qld 351 K7
Broad Arrow WA 352 B4, 358 F4
Broadarrow Track NT 112
Brocks Road Vic. 230, 231, 238
Broken Hill NSW 348 D2, 245, 247, 248, 249
Bronte Park Tas. 361 D6
Bronzewing WA 175
Brookton WA 358 D6
Broome WA 354 A2, 356 A7, 359 F1, 56, 58, 73, 83, 85, 88
Broomehill WA 358 D7, 156, 163
Browns Bore SA 42
Brumby SA 251
Brumby Hill Vic. 221
Brumby Rocks Track Vic. 221
Bryce Creek WA 76
Bubbler, The (mound springs) SA 22, 25, 26
Bucasia Qld 351 I2
Buckwong Creek Vic. 219
Buckwong Creek camping area Vic. 216, 217, 219
Buckwong Track Vic. 220
Bulahdelah NSW 349 K3
Bulgunnia SA 211
Bulla NT 357 G5
Bullakitchie NT 50
Bullita homestead NT 357 G5, 100, 102, 103, 105, 106, 107, 108, 110
Bullita Campground NT 103, 105, 106, 108, 109, 110
Bullita Stock Route NT 102, 103, 104, 105, 110
Bulltown Vic. 234
Bulltown Spur Vic. 234
Bulman NT 357 I3
Bunbury WA 358 C7
Bundaberg Qld 351 K5
Bundjalung National Park NSW 349 L1
Bungabinni Native Well WA 143
Bungadillina Creek SA 27
Buntine Highway NT 115
Burke, Robert O'Hara 10, 13, 19, 240, 244, 252–3, 255, 256, 302, 304, 307
Burkes Grave SA 13, 19, 257
Burkes Memorial camping area SA 12, 13, 19, 254, 255, 257
Burke & Wills monument and camp Qld 307, 308

INDEX

Burke & Wills Roadhouse Qld 360 B8
Burketown Qld 360 A7, 302, 303, 304, 306, 308, 309, 311
Burnett Heads Qld 351 K5
Burnie Tas. 361 C4
Burra SA 348 C4, 353 L6
Burrel Bore WA 86, 87
Burrel Bore bush camping area WA 86, 87, 88
Burt, E.A. 7
Busselton WA 358 C7
Butcher Country Track Vic. 238
Butterfly Springs camping area NT 314, 316, 317, 319
Byfield National Park Qld 351 J4
Bynoe River Qld 308
Byron Bay NSW 349 L1, 351 L8

C

Caboolture Qld 351 K7
Cadna-owie Lookout SA 28
Cadney homestead SA 353 I2
Cadoux WA 358 D5
Caiguna WA 352 D5
Cairn Creek Track Vic. 238
Cairns Qld 360 F6, 297, 308
Calcite Flow Walk NT 104
Calen Qld 351 I2
Callanna siding SA 23
Callawa station WA 88
Callowa Track WA 142, 143
Caloundra Qld 351 L7
Calvert Hills NT 311
Calvert Range WA 121, 132, 133
Calvert River NT 311, 312
Camden NSW 349 J5
Cameron, John 240, 249
Cameron Corner Qld 350 D8, 16, 17, 19, 240, 241, 242, 244, 245, 248, 249, 250, 257
Cameron Corner Store camping area Qld 242, 243, 250
Camooweal Qld 350 B1, 355 L3, 357 L8
Camooweal Caves National Park Qld 350 B1, 355 L3, 357 L8
Camp Beadell camping area WA 171, 173
Camp 119 Qld 307, 308
Campbell Town Tas. 361 E6
Canal Creek Qld 292
Canberra ACT 349 I5
Cann River Vic. 349 H7
Cannibal Creek Qld 293

Canning, Alfred 118, 122–3, 130, 132, 136, 140, 142, 145, 147
Canning Stock Route WA 354 A8, 359 F7, 55, 94, 118–53
Canning Stock Route Heritage Trail WA 124
Canning's Cairn WA 121, 133
Canteen Creek NT 350 A2, 355 J4
Canterbury Qld 259
Canunda National Park SA 348 C7
Cape Arid National Park WA 352 C6
Cape Crawford NT 357 J6, 311, 313, 314, 315, 318, 319
Cape Jervis SA 348 B5, 353 L8
Cape Le Grand National Park WA 352 B7
Cape Melville National Park Qld 360 E4, 264
Cape Tribulation Qld 360 F6
Cape York Heritage House Qld 279
Cape York Peninsula Qld 360 D4, 262–99
Cape York Quarries Qld 282
Capella Qld 351 I4
Capricorn Roadhouse WA 120, 121, 136
Captain Billy Landing Qld 287, 288, 289, 294
Captain Billy Landing camping area Qld 288, 289, 295
Cardwell Qld 360 F7
Carlisle Road WA 176
Carnamah WA 358 C4, 359 B5
Carnarvon WA 358 A1, 359 A7
Carnarvon National Park Qld 351 H5
Carnegie, David 122, 139, 140, 141, 146, 149, 151, 168, 170
Carnegie camping area WA 170, 171, 174
Carnegie homestead WA 352 B1, 354 B8, 120, 166, 168, 169, 171, 172, 174, 175
Carpentaria Highway NT 313, 315
Carson River WA 67, 72
Casino NSW 349 K1, 351 K8
Casterton Vic. 348 D7
Castlemaine Vic. 348 F7
Cataby Roadhouse WA 358 C5
Catfish Creek Qld 270
Catfish Waterhole Qld 270
Catfish Waterhole camping area Qld 266, 267, 270
Ceduna SA 353 I5, 187, 202, 203, 204, 205, 208, 210
Centenary Rocks WA 161, 164
Cessnock NSW 349 J4

Chamberlain Gorge WA 60
Chamberlain River WA 62
Channel Country Qld 350 E5, 5, 240
Chapman Hill NT 48, 50, 53
Charleville Qld 351 G6
Charlies Creek Vic. 220
Charlies Creek Plain Vic. 214
Charlies Creek Plain camping area Vic. 216, 217, 220
Charlies Creek Track Vic. 215
Charlies Hut Vic. 220
Charlton Vic. 348 E6
Charters Towers Qld 351 H1
Cheepie Qld 351 G6
Chesterton Range National Park Qld 351 H6
Childers Qld 351 K5
Chili Beach Qld 275, 276, 277, 281, 284
Chili Beach camping area Qld 280, 281, 284
Chili Creek Qld 284
Chilla Well NT 52
Chillagoe Qld 360 E7
Chinamans Hat (Mount Ernest) WA 150, 152
Chiron oilfield Qld 250
Chungla Well WA 153
Claudie River Qld 284
Clayton River SA 7
Clayton Wetlands Campsite SA 4, 5, 7
Clermont Qld 351 H3
Cleve SA 348 A4, 353 K6
Clifton Hills SA 6, 9, 33, 43
Cloncurry Qld 350 D2, 308
Cobar NSW 349 G2
Cobbler Desert SA 14
Cobungra Vic. 224
Cockatoo Creek Qld 288, 291
Cockburn SA 348 D3
Cockburn Range WA 58, 60, 64
Cocklebiddy WA 352 E5, 176, 177, 178, 183
Cocklebiddy Roadhouse WA 178, 180
Coen Qld 360 D4, 262, 263, 274, 276, 277, 278, 279, 282, 284
Coen River Qld 276, 278
Coffin Bay SA 348 A5, 353 J7
Coffin Bay National Park SA 353 J7
Coffs Harbour NSW 349 K2
Colac Vic. 348 E8
Collarenebri NSW 349 I1, 351 I8
Collie WA 358 C7
Collingwood Spur Track Vic. 234
Collins Flat Vic. 224
Collins Flat camping area Vic. 225, 229

INDEX

Collinsville Qld 351 I2
Colson, Ted 36, 39
Colson Track NT 37
Comet Qld 351 I4
Condingup WA 352 C7
Condobolin NSW 349 G4
Conglomerate Creek Vic. 230, 235
Connie Sue Highway WA 352 D4, 172, 176–83, 188, 197, 199
Coober Pedy SA 353 J3, 27, 29, 186, 187, 188, 189, 191, 192, 194, 195, 211
Cook SA 353 G4, 194, 258
Cook, James 267
Cooks Hut Qld 284
Cooks Hut camping area Qld 280, 281, 284
Cooktown Qld 360 F5, 262, 263, 264, 267, 268, 270, 273, 276, 283
Coolgardie WA 352 B5, 358 F4, 156, 157, 158, 159, 161, 163, 165, 170
Cooma NSW 349 H6
Coombah Roadhouse NSW 348 D3
Coonabarabran NSW 349 I2
Coonamble NSW 349 H2
Coongie Lakes SA 14, 19
Coongie station SA 14
Coongra Creek SA 29
Cooper Creek SA 4, 5, 6, 7, 10, 11, 13, 14, 15, 18, 19, 240, 242, 244, 245, 251, 252–3, 254, 257, 258
Cooper Creek Basin SA 16
Cooper Creek camping area SA 4, 5, 8
Coorong National Park SA 348 C6, 353 L8
Cootamundra NSW 349 H5
Coppabella Qld 351 I3
Coppermine Creek NT 319
Coral Bay WA 359 A6
Cordillo Downs SA 258, 259
Corfield Qld 350 F2
Corinna Tas. 361 B5
Corner Country NSW, Qld & SA 240–59
Corner Store Qld 350 D8
Corners Well WA 124, 126
Corrigin WA 358 D6
Corryong Vic. 349 H6, 212, 213, 214, 216
Cosmo Newberry WA 352 B2, 198, 200
Coward Springs SA 20, 21, 22, 24, 26
Coward Springs camping area SA 24, 25, 26
Cowarie SA 8, 39
Cowra NSW 349 H4
Cox River NT 319
Craigieburn Vic. 348 F7

Cranbourne Vic. 348 F7
Cranbrook WA 358 D7
Crawford Soak Road WA 201
Crescent Ridge WA 149
Croajingolong National Park Vic. 349 H7
Crooked River Vic. 234
Crooked River goldfields Vic. 212, 230
Crooked River Track Vic. 230
Crookwell NSW 349 I5
Croydon Qld 360 C7, 309
Cuddapan Qld 259
Cudmore National Park Qld 351 G4
Cue WA 358 D2
Culgoa Floodplain National Park Qld 351 H8
Culgoa National Park NSW 351 G8
Cullyamurra Waterhole SA 14, 19, 254, 255, 257
Cullyamurra Waterhole camping area SA 12, 13, 19, 254, 255, 257
Culvida Soak WA 152
Cundeelee WA 352 C4
Cunnamulla Qld 351 G7
Cunyu station WA 126
Curdimurka Railway Siding SA 25, 26
Currawinya National Park Qld 350 F8
Currie Tas. 361 A2
Curtin Springs NT 355 H8
Cynthia Range Track Vic. 230, 234
Cypress Creek Qld 293

D

Daguragu NT 355 G1, 357 G6, 115
Daintree Qld 360 F6
Daintree National Park Qld 360 F6
Dajarra Qld 350 C2
Dalby Qld 351 J7
Dalhousie Springs SA 23, 33, 34, 36, 37, 39
Dalhousie Springs camping area SA 34, 37
Dalwallinu WA 358 C4
Daly River NT 357 G3
Daly Waters NT 357 I5
Dam Track Vic. 218, 228
Damparanie Creek SA 43
Dampier WA 359 C4
Dargo Vic. 349 G7, 212, 224, 229, 230, 231, 235
Dargo High Plains Road Vic. 226, 229, 231
Dargo River Vic. 224, 225, 226, 228
Dartmouth Track Vic. 228

Darwin NT 357 G2
Davenport Range National Park NT 355 J4
Davies Plain Vic. 212
Davies Plain camping area Vic. 216, 217, 219
Davies Plain Creek Vic. 219
Davies Plain Hut Vic. 217, 219
Davies Plain Track Vic. 214, 215, 218, 219, 220
Davons camping area Vic. 232, 233, 239
Dawn Creek WA 65
Dead Bullock Soak NT 50
Dead Finish Track Vic. 218
Dead Horse Gully camping area NSW 242, 243, 244, 245
Deakin WA 352 F4
Dean Bore Creek SA 16
Deloraine Tas. 361 D5
Denham WA 358 A1, 359 A8
Denial Bay SA 208
Deniliquin NSW 348 F5
Denmark WA 358 D8
Denton, John (Goog) 202, 203, 206, 209
D'Entrecasteaux National Park WA 358 C8
Depot Glen NSW 243, 244, 245, 246, 247, 248
Derby WA 354 B2, 356 B7, 56, 57, 58, 65, 70, 73, 74, 82, 83
Derwent Bridge Tas. 361 C6
Derwent River SA 8
Deua National Park NSW 349 I6
Devonian Reef National Parks WA 354 C2, 356 C7, 57
Devonport Tas. 361 D4
Diamantina Developmental Road Qld 259
Diamantina National Park Qld 350 D4
Diamantina River Qld & SA 3, 4, 6, 9, 42
Diamond Rock WA 165
Diebil Hills WA 121, 130
Diebil Spring WA 121, 133, 134
Dig Tree Qld 10, 13, 14, 19, 252–3, 255, 257, 258
Dig Tree camping area Qld 12, 13, 19, 254, 255, 258
Diggers Rest camping area WA 59, 61, 63
Dilldoll Rock Qld 311
Dimboola Vic. 348 D6
Dimond Gorge WA 75, 77
Dingo camping area Qld 266, 271
Dingo Claypan SA 193

365

INDEX

Dingo Yard NT 109, 113
Dinner Plain Track Vic. 224, 226, 227, 228
Dipperu National Park Qld 351 I3
Djukbinj National Park NT 357 G2
Dobbys Track Vic. 221
Docker River NT 95
Dog Chain Creek WA 81
Dog Fence Qld & SA 4, 7, 15, 192, 193, 205, 207, 208, 210, 249, 250
Dogmans Hut camping area Vic. 216, 217, 218
Dogs Grave Vic. 225, 228
Dogs Grave camping area Vic. 224, 225, 228
Dogs Grave Reserve Vic. 213
Dongara WA 358 B4
Donkey Creek WA 81
Donnybrook WA 358 C7
Doomadgee Qld 360 A7, 303, 304, 305, 310, 311
Doongan WA 70
Dorrigo NSW 349 K2
Doughtys Road Vic. 239
Douglas Daly Tourist Park NT 357 G3
Dover Tas. 361 D8
Dreary Creek SA 16
Drovers Rest NT 102, 103
Drovers Rest camping area NT 103, 106
Dry River Vic. 238
Drysdale River WA 56, 58, 66, 67, 69, 70, 73
Drysdale River National Park WA 356 D4
Drysdale River station camping area WA 68, 69, 70
Dubbo NSW 349 H3
Duchess Qld 350 C2
Ducie Creek Qld 290
Duff Creek SA 27
Dulhunty River Qld 290
Dulkaninna SA 7
Dullingari SA 251
Dululu Qld 351 J4
Dumbleyung WA 358 D7
Dunda Jinnda (Well 30) WA 131, 138
Dunedoo NSW 349 I3
Dunk Island Qld 360 F7
Dunmarra NT 355 I1, 357 I6
Dunsborough WA 358 C7
Durack River WA 58, 64
Durba Hills WA 121, 131
Durba Springs WA 131, 133

Durba Springs camping area WA 130, 131, 133
Dysart Qld 351 I3

E

Eagle Highway WA 174
Eaglevale Track Vic. 234
East Baines River NT 100, 102, 103, 105, 106, 111
Echuca Vic. 348 F6
Eden NSW 349 I7
Edithburgh SA 348 B5, 353 K7
Edwards Creek SA 27
Egg Lagoon Tas. 361 A1
Eidsvold Qld 351 J5
Eight Mile camping area Vic. 232, 233, 238
Eight Mile Gap Vic. 238
Eight Mile Swamp Qld 266, 270
Eighty Mile Beach WA 359 E2, 84, 85, 86, 87, 88
Eighty Mile Beach Caravan Park and camping area WA 86, 88
Eildon Vic. 349 G7
Einasleigh Qld 360 E8
El Questro WA 58, 59, 60, 61, 62, 66
El Questro camping area WA 61, 62
Eliot Falls Qld 263, 286–7, 288, 292, 293, 295, 296
Eliot Falls camping area Qld 288, 289, 292, 296
Ellenbrae station camping areas WA 58, 59, 60, 61, 65
Ellery Creek Big Hole NT 97
Ellery Creek Big Hole camping area NT 92, 93, 98
Elliott NT 355 I1, 357 I6
Elliston SA 353 J6
Elsey Creek NT 321
Elsey National Park NT 357 I4, 303, 314, 315, 316, 321
Emerald Qld 351 I4
Emerald Springs Wayside Inn NT 357 G3
Emma Gorge WA 58, 62
Emma Gorge Resort WA 62
Emmdale Roadhouse NSW 348 F2
Emmet Qld 350 F5
Empress Springs WA 174
Emu SA 189, 193, 194, 195
Emu Air Strip SA 194
Emu Junction SA 169, 186, 188, 194
Endeavour Falls Qld 268
Endeavour Falls Tourist Park Qld 264

Endeavour River Qld 268
Endeavour Strait Qld 297
Eneabba WA 358 B4
Enngonia NSW 349 G1, 351 G8
Epsilon Qld 245, 250, 251
Epsilon Crossing Qld 251
Erabena Oil Well SA 37
Erabena Track SA 41, 42
Eringa SA 30
Erldunda NT 355 I7
Eromanga Qld 350 E6
Escarpment Track Vic. 221
Escott Barramundi Lodge Qld 304, 305, 307, 309
Escott Barramundi Lodge campground 306, 307, 309
Esperance WA 352 B7
Etadunna SA 7
Eucla WA 352 F5
Eulo Qld 350 F7
Eungella National Park Qld 351 I2
Evandale Tas. 361 E5
Evelyn Creek camping area NSW 242, 243, 247
Everard Junction WA 168, 173
Exmouth WA 359 A5
Expedition National Park Qld 351 I5
Eyre, Edward 16, 246
Eyre Creek SA 32, 33, 40
Eyre Highway SA & WA 176, 178, 183, 208
Eyre Peninsula SA 348 A4, 204

F

Farm Junction Vic. 349 G7, 212, 224, 226, 229, 230, 231
Farm Track Vic. 229
Farrands, Bruce 53
Federal SA 36
Fern Creek WA 81
Fifteen Mile Track SA 18
Fig Tree Creek NT 111
Fig Tree Valley NT 111
Fig Tree Yard camping area NT 108, 109, 111
Finke (Aputula) NT 355 J8, 24, 26, 36
Finke Gorge National Park NT 355 I7
Finke River NT 98
Fitzgerald River National Park WA 358 F7
Fitzroy Crossing WA 354 D2, 356 D7, 55, 56, 57, 73, 82, 83, 153
Fitzroy River WA 73, 77, 81
Five Mile Creek Qld 278

INDEX

Five Mile Creek camping area Qld 266, 267, 274
Flaggy Creek SA 43
Fletcher Creek NT 313
Flinders Chase National Park SA 348 A5, 353 J8
Flinders Ranges SA 10, 12, 16
Flinders Ranges National Park SA 348 B2, 353 L4
Flinders River Qld 308
Floodout Creek NT 52
Floraville Qld 305, 307
Flynn, John 93, 99, 243
Flynn's Grave NT 99
Foelsche River NT 313
Forbes NSW 349 H4
Forrest, John 122, 125, 128, 170, 179, 199
Forrest Fort WA 128
Forsayth Qld 360 D8
Forster–Tuncurry NSW 349 K3
Fort Grey NSW 244, 246
Fort Grey campground NSW 242, 243, 244, 249
Fortescue Roadhouse WA 359 B4
Fortville Gate Qld 249
Fowlers Bay SA 353 H5
Fox Trap Roadhouse Qld 351 G6
Francois Peron National Park WA 358 A1, 359 A8
Frank Hann National Park WA 352 A6, 358 F6
Franklin–Gordon Wild Rivers National Park Tas. 361 C6
Fraser Island Qld 351 L6
Frederick Walker Monument Qld 305, 307, 309
Freeth Junction SA 37
Fregon SA 353 H1
Fremantle WA 358 C6
French Line SA 32, 33, 37–41, 42
Frenchmans Road Qld 283
Freycinet Tas. 361 F6
Fruit Bat Falls Qld 263, 286, 287, 292, 295
Frys Flat Vic. 230
Frys Flat camping area Vic. 231, 232, 233, 239
Frys Hut Vic. 230, 232, 239

G

Gagebrook Tas. 361 D7
Galvans Gorge WA 76
Galwinku NT 357 J2
Gammon Ranges SA 16

Gantner Hut Vic. 230, 238
Gapuwiyak NT 357 J2
Gardiners Hut Vic. 232
Garig Gunak Barlu National Park NT 357 H1
Garrons Point Track Vic. 221
Garrthalala NT 357 K2
Gary Highway WA 168, 173
Gary Junction WA 354 D6, 90, 92, 94, 138, 143
Gascoyne Junction WA 358 B1, 359 B7
Gawler SA 348 C4, 353 L7
Gayndah Qld 351 K6
Geelong Vic. 348 F7
Geikie Gorge WA 73
Gemtree NT 355 J6
Gentle Annie Track Vic. 218
George Camp NT 357 H4
George Town Tas. 361 D4
Georges Corner SA 41
Georgetown Qld 360 D7
Georgia Bore camping area WA 130, 131, 135
Georgina Gidgee Interdunes Qld 40
Geraldton WA 358 B4
Geraldton Bore WA 168, 171
Geraldton Bore camping area WA 171, 173
Gibb River WA 70
Gibb River Crossing WA 67
Gibb River Road WA 354 C2, 356 C7, 56, 58, 59, 60, 62, 63, 64, 65, 66, 72, 73, 74, 76, 82, 83
Gibb River station WA 74
Gibbie Creek NT 113
Gibbie Creek Track NT 107, 108, 113
Gibson, Alfred 92, 171
Gibson Desert WA 354 D7, 84, 92, 166, 169, 170, 171, 173
Gibson Desert Nature Reserve WA 354 D7, 167, 168, 171, 173
Gibsons Gap Vic. 218
Gidgealpa SA 11
Giles WA 174
Giles, Ernest 28, 92, 170, 171, 179
Giles Meteorological Station WA 167, 169
Gilgandra NSW 349 H3
Gin Gin Qld 351 K5
Gingin WA 358 C5
Girringun (Lumholtz) National Park Qld 360 F7
Gladstone Qld 351 K4
Gladstone Tas. 361 F4
Glen-Ayle station WA 120, 128, 174, 175

Glen Helen Gorge NT 90, 96, 97
Glen Helen Resort and camping area NT 85, 91, 92, 93, 98
Glen Innes NSW 349 J1
Glen Joyce Rig Site SA 41
Glenbrook NSW 349 I4
Glendambo SA 348 A2, 353 J4, 202, 203, 204, 205, 211
Glendambo Roadhouse SA 204
Glenden Qld 351 I2
Glenroy homestead WA 77
Gloucester NSW 349 J3
Gnarlbine Rock WA 159, 163, 165
Gninglig WA 62
Godfreys Tank WA 140, 150, 151
Gold Coast Qld 351 L8
Goldfields Woodland Conservation Park WA 157, 161
Goldfields Woodland National Park WA 358 F5, 157, 161
Goobang National Park NSW 349 H3
Goode Hall SA 208
Goodedulla National Park Qld 351 J4
Googs Lake SA 202, 204, 205, 206, 207, 208, 209
Googs Lake campsites SA 206, 207, 209
Googs Track SA 202–11
Goolgowi NSW 349 G4
Goomalling WA 358 D5
Goondiwindi Qld 351 J8
Goongarrie National Park WA 352 B4
Gordon Tas. 361 D8
Gordon Creek Qld 284
Gordon Creek camping area Qld 280, 281, 284
Gordonvale Qld 360 F7
Gosford NSW 349 J4
Goulburn NSW 349 I5
Goulburn River National Park NSW 349 I3
Goyder Lagoon SA 6, 33
Grafton NSW 349 K1
Grampians National Park Vic. 348 D7
Granite Flat Road Vic. 221
Granite Peak (Well 5) WA 120, 126–7
Granite Peak homestead WA 127
Granites Gold Mine NT 46, 53
Grant Vic. 212, 230, 231, 234
Grant camping area Vic. 233, 234
Grant Historic Area Vic. 213, 233
Grass Patch WA 352 B6
Grassy Tas. 361 A2
Grave Creek WA 80
Gravity Junction WA 149
Gravity Lake WA 147, 148

INDEX

Gray, Charles 13, 252–3, 307
Grays Track Vic. 216
Great Alpine Road Vic. 224, 226, 227
Great Barrier Reef Marine Park Qld 360 E2
Great Basalt Wall National Park Qld 351 G1
Great Central Road WA 167, 168, 172, 177, 180, 181, 198, 201
Great Keppel Island Qld 351 K4
Great Northern Highway WA 83, 153
Great Oak Forest WA 142
Great Sandy Desert WA 359 F2, 84, 86, 118, 122, 139, 169, 170
Great Sandy National Park Qld 351 L5, 351 L6
Great Victoria Desert SA & WA 352 D3, 169, 176, 178, 179, 186, 187, 188, 190, 198
Great White Hope Road Vic. 222
Green Island Qld 360 F6
Greenbank NT 305, 313
Greenough WA 358 B4
Greenvale Qld 360 E8
Gregory Qld 360 A8, 309
Gregory, Augustus 86, 100, 105, 122, 151
Gregory Downs Qld 310
Gregory National Park NT 355 G1, 357 G5, 100–15, 151
Gregory River Qld 305, 310
Griffith NSW 349 G4
Groundrush Mine NT 50, 54
Gul Gul NT 357 H1
Gulf Country Qld & NT 302–21
Gulf Savannah Qld 360 B8, 304
Gulflander 304, 305, 308, 309
Guli Lake WA 147
Guli Spring (Well 42) WA 147
Gunbarrel Highway WA 352 A1, 354 C8, 358 F1, 359 F8, 124, 166–75
Gunbarrel Laager Travellers Rest WA 175
Gunbarrel Road Construction Party 94, 136, 166, 167, 169
Gundabooka National Park NSW 349 G2
Gunn, Jeannie 314, 316
Gunnedah NSW 349 I2
Gunowarba Native Well WA 145
Gunpowder Qld 350 C1, 360 A8
Gunshot Bypass Track Qld 290
Gunshot Creek Qld 287, 290, 291
Gunyangara NT 357 K2
Gwenneth Lakes WA 89

Gympie Qld 351 K6
Gypcrete Interdunes Qld 40

H

Haasts Bluff NT 355 H6, 90, 91, 96, 98
Haddon Corner SA 350 D6, 240, 255, 259
Hadspen Tas. 361 D5
Halfway Mill Roadhouse WA 358 C4
Halligan Bay SA 22, 27
Halls Creek WA 354 E2, 356 E7, 46, 47, 48, 49, 55, 115, 118, 119, 128, 139, 140, 151, 153, 170
Hamersley Range WA 359 C5
Hamilton Vic. 348 D7
Hamilton Island Qld 351 I2
Hann, Frank 131, 179
Hann Crossing Qld 264, 265, 271, 272
Hann Crossing campsites Qld 266, 267, 272, 273, 274
Hann River Roadhouse Qld 360 E5
Hanns Creek SA 29
Hanns Tabletop Hill WA 176, 178, 179, 181
Hanushs camping area Qld 266, 271
Harkness Gorge WA 176, 177, 178, 181
Harris Lake Qld 309
Harrisons Cut Vic. 225, 226, 228, 229
Harrisons Track Vic. 228
Harry Johnston Water WA 168, 170, 174
Harvey WA 358 C7
Hatches Creek NT 355 J4
Haunted Stream Vic. 226
Haunted Well (Well 37, Libral Well) WA 141, 144
Hawker SA 348 B2, 353 L5, 15
Hawker Gate NSW 244, 247
Hay NSW 348 F5
Hayes Creek Wayside Inn NT 357 G3
Hayman Island Qld 351 I1
Heartbreak Hotel NT 355 J1, 357 J6
Heathcote NSW 349 J5
Heather Highway WA 168, 172
Heathlands Ranger Base Qld 288, 290, 294
Heathlands Reserve Qld 263, 287, 290, 292
Heathlands station Qld 287
Hebel Qld 351 H8
Helen Hill WA 136
Helena Spring WA 139, 145, 146, 147
Helenvale Qld 360 F5
Hells Gate Qld 305, 306, 310

Hells Gate Roadhouse campground Qld 306, 311
Hells Gate Roadhouse Qld 355 L1, 357 L6, 360 A7, 304, 311
Henwood Road Qld 269
Hermannsburg NT 355 I6, 96, 99
Herne Spur Vic. 235
Herne Spur Track Vic. 235
Hervey Bay Qld 351 L6
Hewart Downs NSW 244, 248
Heywood Vic. 348 D7
High Country Vic. 212–39
Hillston NSW 349 G4
Hippos Yawn WA 159
Hi-Way Inn Roadhouse NT 357 I5
Hobart Tas. 361 E7
Hodgson River NT 357 I5, 314, 320
Holbrook NSW 349 G6
Holland, John 156, 158, 161, 162, 163, 165
Holland Track WA 156–65
Home Hill Qld 351 H1
Home Valley station camping areas WA 58, 59, 60, 61, 64
Homevale National Park Qld 351 I2
Honeymoon Bay WA 67, 69
Honeymoon Bay camping area WA 69, 72
Hooker Creek (Lajamanu) NT 355 G2, 357 G7, 54
Hope Vale Qld 360 F5, 268
Hopetoun WA 352 A7, 358 F7
Hornsby NSW 349 J4
Horse Creek NT 313
Horseshoe Lagoon camping area Qld 266, 269
Horsham Vic. 348 D6
Howard Springs NT 357 G2
Howitt Vic. 231, 238
Howitt, Alfred 18, 19, 253
Howitt Hut Vic. 230, 238
Howitt Plains Vic. 212, 230, 238
Howqua Hills Vic. 212
Howqua Hills Historic Area Vic. 213, 230
Howqua River Vic. 230, 239
Hughenden Qld 350 F2
Humbert River NT 100, 103, 107, 108, 111
Humbert River station NT 100, 110, 113
Humbert Track NT 105, 107, 110, 112
Humffray River Vic. 235
Humffray River Track Vic. 235
Hungerford Qld 350 F8

INDEX

Huonville Tas. 361 D7
Hyden WA 358 E6, 156, 157, 158, 159, 160, 162

I

Idalia National Park Qld 350 F5
Ilfracombe Qld 350 F4
Ilkurlka Roadhouse WA 188, 189, 190, 197, 198
Illily NT 96
Iluka NSW 349 K1
Imangara NT 355 J4
Imintji WA 354 C1, 356 C6, 57, 73, 80
Ingebong Hills WA 120, 127
Ingham Qld 360 F8
Injinoo Qld 360 D1, 263, 287, 288, 297
Injune Qld 351 I6
Innamincka SA 350 D7, 6, 9, 10, 11, 12, 13, 14, 15, 16, 17, 19, 240, 242, 243, 250, 251, 254, 257, 258, 259
Innamincka Crossing SA 19, 257
Innamincka Regional Reserve SA 11, 13, 14, 17, 241, 244, 245, 251
Innamincka station SA 14
Innamincka Town Common camping area SA 12, 13, 18, 242, 243, 251, 254, 255, 257
Innes National Park SA 348 A5, 353 K7
Innisfail Qld 360 F7
Inverell NSW 349 J1
Ipswich Qld 351 K7
Iron Range National Park Qld 263, 275, 276, 277, 282, 283, 284, 285
Iron Range National Park Ranger Base Qld 284
Irrapatana SA 27
Isabella Qld 263
Isabella Creek Qld 268
Isisford Qld 350 F4
Italian Flat camping area Vic. 225, 226, 229
Ivanhoe NSW 348 F3
Iwantja (Indulkana) SA 353 I1
Iwupataka NT 355 I6

J

Jabiru NT 357 H2
Jack Rileys Grave Vic. 216
Jackey Jackey 294
Jacks Waterhole WA 64
Jalmurark campground NT 314, 316, 321
Jam Tin Flat Track Vic. 221

Jandamarra 78, 82
Jane Table Hill Qld 273
Janies Waterhole WA 62
Jardine, Frank 295, 299
Jardine River Qld 287, 293, 294, 295, 296, 297
Jardine River ferry Qld 286, 297
Jardine River Ferry camping area Qld 288, 289, 296
Jardine River National Park Qld 360 D2, 262, 263, 287, 288, 292, 293
Jarra Jarra NT 355 I4
JC Hotel Qld 259
Jenkins Track WA 90, 91, 138, 142
Jericho Qld 351 G4
Jerilderie NSW 349 G5
Jerramungup WA 352 A7, 358 E7
Jeweller Shop Mine Vic. 233, 234
Jigalong WA 354 A6, 359 F5
Jilbadji Nature Reserve WA 352 A5, 157, 164
Jimmy Iversons camping area Vic. 225, 229
Jindabyne NSW 349 H6
Joes Bore WA 128
Jolly Sailor Vic. 231
Jolly Sailor Mine Vic. 233
Julia Creek Qld 350 E2
Jundah Qld 350 E5
Jundee Gold Mine WA 175
Jungle Creek Falls Vic. 231
Jupiter Well WA 90, 91, 92, 94
Jupiter Well bush camping WA 92, 94

K

Kadina SA 348 B4, 353 L6
Kajabbi Qld 350 D1
Kakadu National Park NT 357 H2
Kalamurina homestead SA 8
Kalanbie SA 208
Kalbarri WA 358 A3
Kalbarri National Park WA 358 B3
Kalgoorlie–Boulder WA 352 B4, 163, 167, 176, 177, 187
Kalka SA 354 F8
Kalkaringi NT 355 G1, 357 G6, 100, 101, 102, 106, 107, 114, 115
Kalpowar Crossing Qld 264
Kalpowar Crossing camping area Qld 266, 267, 271
Kaltukatjara (Docker River) NT 354 F7
Kalumburu WA 356 D4, 56, 57, 65, 66, 67, 69, 71, 72, 74

Kalumburu Mission camping area WA 69, 72
Kalumburu Road Junction WA 356 D5, 58, 66, 73
Kambalda WA 352 B5
Kandiwal WA 356 D4
Kangaroo Island SA 348 A6, 353 K8
Kanypi SA 355 G8
Karijini National Park WA 359 D5
Karns Creek NT 311
Karratha WA 359 C4
Karratha Roadhouse WA 359 C4
Karumba Qld 360 B7
Karunjie Track WA 58, 59, 62, 63, 64
Katanning WA 358 D7
Katherine NT 357 H4, 321, 100, 101, 104, 115
Kathleen Creek SA 29
Katoomba NSW 349 I4
Keep River National Park NT 356 F5
Kempsey NSW 349 K2
Kennedy, Edmund 294
Kennedy Bend camping area Qld 266, 267, 270
Kennedy Creek WA 126
Kennedy Range National Park WA 359 B7
Kennedy River Qld 270
Kerang Vic. 348 E6
Kew NSW 349 K3
Kiama NSW 349 J5
Kidman, Sidney 14
Kidson WA 173
Kidson Bluff WA 142
Kidson Track (WAPET Rd) WA 354 A4, 359 F3, 86
Kilanbar Bore SA 8
Killagurra Gorge WA 121, 133
Kimba SA 348 A3, 353 K6
Kimberley Downs WA 83
Kimberley Grand Tour WA 56–83
Kimberley Plateau WA 79
Kimberley Safari Camp WA 71
Kinchega National Park NSW 348 D3
King, John 10, 13, 18, 252–3, 255, 307
King Billy Saddle Vic. 238
King Edward River WA 66, 67, 68, 69, 70
King Edward River camping area WA 68, 69, 70
King Hill WA 137
King Leopold Ranges WA 73, 81
King Leopold Ranges Conservation Park WA 57, 73, 79
King River WA 56, 58, 59, 62

369

INDEX

King Rock WA 163
King Sound WA 77
Kingaroy Qld 351 K6
Kingfisher Camp Qld 310
Kingoonya SA 353 J4, 202, 203, 204, 211
Kings Canyon NT 96
Kings Marker camping site SA 12, 13, 18
Kings Plain Track Vic. 220
Kingscote SA 348 B5, 353 K8
Kingston S.E. SA 348 C6
Kintore NT 354 F6, 49, 85, 90, 91, 95
Kitchener Siding WA 183
Kiwirrkurra WA 354 E5, 94
Knolls Track SA 33, 38, 41, 42
Kokatha SA 211
Kondinin WA 358 E6, 157, 159
Kookynie WA 352 B3, 358 F3
Koolan WA 354 B1, 356 B6
Koortanyaninna Creek SA 15
Kosciuszko National Park NSW 349 H6, 213, 215, 219
Kowanyama Qld 360 C5
Krakouer Rock WA 165
Kruse, Tom 4, 7
Kulgera NT 355 I8, 30, 31, 36, 166
Kumarina Roadhouse WA 359 E6
Kunawarritji WA 354 C5, 85, 86, 90, 91, 92, 118, 119, 120, 138, 139, 142
Kunawarritji camping area WA 86, 87, 89, 91, 92
Kuncherinna 1 Oil Well SA 42
Kuncherinna Junction SA 42
Kununurra WA 356 F5, 56, 57, 58, 62, 64, 67, 100, 119
Kupungarri WA 354 D1, 356 D6, 76
Kwinana WA 358 C6
Kynuna Qld 350 E2
Kyogle NSW 351 K8

L

Lady Barron Tas. 361 F3
Lajamanu (Hooker Creek) NT 355 G2, 357 G7, 54
Lake Aerodrome WA 128
Lake Auld WA 137
Lake Blanche SA 14
Lake Callabonna SA 14
Lake Cargelligo NSW 349 G4
Lake Carnegie WA 170
Lake Disappointment WA 121, 131, 134, 135
Lake Emma camping area Qld 266, 267, 269

Lake Eyre SA 5, 20, 22, 23, 27, 39
Lake Eyre North SA 22
Lake Eyre South SA 20, 22, 26
Lake Eyre National Park SA 350 B7, 353 L2, 21, 23, 27
Lake Gairdner National Park SA 348 A2, 353 J4
Lake Grace WA 358 E6
Lake Gregory WA 140, 151
Lake Harry SA 4, 6
Lake Hill Track Vic. 221
Lake Howitt saltpan SA 4
Lake King WA 352 A6, 358 F6, 159
Lake O'Connor WA 159
Lake Poeppel salt lake SA 38
Lake Stewart NSW 244, 248, 249
Lake Surprise Bore SA 6, 9
Lake Thomas salt lake SA 38
Lake Torrens National Park SA 348 B1, 353 K4
Lake Varley WA 159
Lake Violet station WA 175
Lakefield Qld 270, 273
Lakefield National Park Qld 360 E5, 262, 263, 264, 265, 266, 268, 269, 274
Lakefield Ranger Station Qld 264, 271, 272, 273, 274
Lakeland Qld 360 E6, 274
Lakes Entrance Vic. 349 H7
Lancelin WA 358 C5
Laramba NT 355 I5
Larrimah NT 357 I5
Laterite National Park WA 57
Launceston Tas. 361 E5
Laura Qld 360 E5, 268, 270, 273, 274, 278
Laura River Qld 264, 269
Laver, Charles 199
Laverton WA 352 B3, 172, 180, 186, 187, 192, 196, 198, 199, 200, 201
Lawi Causeway NT 115
Lawley River National Park WA 70
Lawn Hill National Park Qld 310
Lawn Hill station Qld 131
Leeton NSW 349 G5
Leeuwin–Naturaliste National Park WA 358 B8
Leichhardt, Ludwig 302, 304, 312, 314
Leichhardt Falls Qld 309
Leichhardt Hole camping area Qld 266, 269
Leichhardt River Qld 309
Leichhardts Caravan Park NT 316, 320
Leigh Creek SA 348 B1, 353 L4, 6, 11
Leinster WA 352 A2, 358 F2
Len Beadell marker WA 94, 95

Len Beadell Tree WA 173
Lennard Gorge WA 73, 79, 81
Lennard River WA 73, 79, 81
Leongatha Vic. 349 G8
Leonora WA 352 A3, 358 F3
Leopold Downs WA 83
Lewis, John 39
Libral Well (Well 37, Haunted Well) WA 141, 144
Licola Vic. 238
Lightning Ridge NSW 349 H1, 351 H8
Likkaparta NT 355 J3, 357 J8
Lillimulura Police station WA 82
Limestone Creek NT 104
Limestone Creek SA 17
Limestone Creek Vic. 215
Limestone Creek Billabong NT 102, 105–6
Limestone Creek camping area Vic. 216, 217, 220
Limestone Creek Track Vic. 215, 220
Limestone Gorge NT 102, 103, 104, 105
Limestone Gorge camping area NT 103, 105
Limestone–Black Mountain Road Vic. 220, 221
Limmen Bight River NT 319
Limmen Bight River Fishing Camp NT 314, 315, 316, 317, 319
Limmen National Park NT 357 J4, 303, 314, 315, 318, 320
Lincoln National Park SA 348 A5, 353 J7
Lindsay, David 28, 39, 179, 199
Lindsay Junction SA 38
Link Track Vic. 218
Lismore NSW 349 K1, 351 K8
Litchfield National Park NT 357 G3
Lithgow NSW 349 I4
Little Bynoe River Qld 308
Little Desert National Park Vic. 348 D6
Little Sandy Desert WA 354 A7, 359 F6, 118, 120, 169
Little Topar Roadhouse NSW 348 E2
Little Towns River NT 320
Little Wearyan Creek NT 313
Livingstone Creek Vic. 224
Lizard Island Qld 360 F5
Lock SA 348 A4, 353 J6
Lockerbie homestead Qld 299
Lockerbie Scrub Qld 287
Lockhart River Qld 360 D3, 275, 276, 277, 282, 284
Logan Creek Qld 293

370

INDEX

Lomarieum Lagoon NT 314, 317, 320
Lombadina WA 354 B1, 356 B6
Lone Gum SA 32, 41
Lone Oak station SA 203
Longreach Qld 350 F4
Looma WA 354 C2, 356 C7
Loongana WA 352 E4
Loongana Mine WA 180, 183
Lorella Springs NT 315, 319
Lorne Vic. 348 E8
Louth NSW 348 F1
Lovicks Vic. 238
Low Lake Qld 273
Low Saddle Track Vic. 222, 238
Lowther Creek SA 37
Loyalty Beach campground Qld 288, 297, 298
Ltyentye Purte (Santa Teresa) NT 355 J6
Lucky Well (Well 10) WA 120, 128
Lyndhurst SA 348 B1, 353 L3, 10, 11, 12, 15, 16, 17, 19, 251, 257
Lyndhurst Roadhouse SA 12
Lynette's Bore WA 173

M

Mabel Creek SA 188, 189, 191, 192, 195
Mac Creek WA 81
Macalister River Vic. 238
Macalister Springs Vic. 230, 238
McAllister Qld 308
McArthur River NT 312, 313, 314
McCarthys camping area Vic. 216, 217, 220
McCarthys Track Vic. 215, 220
McConckey Hill WA 128
MacDonnell Creek SA 15
MacDonnell Ranges NT 48
McGowans Beach WA 67, 69
McGowans Beach camping area WA 69, 72
McIvor Valley Qld 268
Mackay Qld 351 I2
MacKenzie Gorge WA 176, 177, 178, 179, 181
McKinlay Qld 350 D2
McMillan Road Vic. 230, 234
McMillan Walking Track Vic. 227
Macs Creek Track Vic. 220
McTavish Claypan WA 88
Macumba No. 1 Oil Well SA 41
Madigan, Cecil 39
Madura WA 352 E5
Magico Qld 288

Magnetic Island Qld 351 H1
Main Range Vic. 214
Main Roads rest area WA 65
Maitland NSW 349 J4
Maitland SA 348 B4, 353 K7
Malbooma SA 202, 204
Malbooma outstation SA 210
Mallacoota Vic. 349 I7
Mallee Vic. 348 E5
Mallee Cliffs National Park NSW 348 E4
Mallowa Native Well WA 138
Manangoora NT 313
Mandurah WA 358 C6
Mangkili (Mungkilli) Claypan Nature Reserve WA 167, 168, 171, 172, 174
Maningrida NT 357 I2
Manjimup WA 358 D8
Manmoyi NT 357 I2
Mannahill SA 348 C3
Manning Gorge WA 73, 74, 78
Manning Gorge camping area WA 75, 76, 78
Manning River WA 76
Mansfield Vic. 349 G7, 212, 213, 230, 238, 239
Manton Knob WA 177, 178, 181
Manyallaluk NT 357 H4
Mapoon Qld 360 C2
Maralinga SA 195
Maranboy NT 357 H4
Marble Bar WA 359 E4, 88, 136
March Fly Glen WA 81
Mareeba Qld 360 F6
Margaret SA 26
Margaret Creek SA 26
Margaret River WA 358 C7
Maria Island National Park Tas. 361 F7
Maria Lagoon NT 319
Marion Bay SA 348 A5, 353 K7
Marla SA 353 I1, 20, 21, 22, 23, 27, 29
Marlborough Qld 351 J4
Maroochydore Qld 351 L7
Marralum NT 356 F5
Marrawah Tas. 361 B4
Marree SA 348 B1, 353 L3, 2, 3, 4, 6, 7, 9, 15, 20, 21, 22, 23, 27, 43
Marsh Road WA 63, 64
Marunbabidi WA 70
Marvel Loch WA 352 A5, 358 E5
Mary River National Park NT 357 H2
Mary River Roadhouse NT 357 H3
Maryborough Qld 351 K6
Maryborough Vic. 348 E7
Maryfarms Qld 360 F6

Massacre Inlet Qld 304
Mataranka NT 357 I4, 302, 303, 314
Mataranka Homestead Resort NT 321
Mataranka Thermal Pool NT 321
Matherson Spur Vic. 228, 229
Matherson Track Vic. 228
Matteo Rock WA 62
Maurice, Richard Thelwall 191
May River WA 73, 83
Meda WA 83
Meekatharra WA 358 D1, 359 D8, 122
Mein Telegraph station Qld 279
Melaleuca camping area Qld 266, 271
Melbourne Vic. 348 F7
Melon Creek SA 43
Melon Creek Bore SA 9
Melton Vic. 348 F7
Melton Mowbray Tas. 361 D6
Memana Tas. 361 F3
Menindee NSW 348 E3, 252, 253
Menzies WA 352 A4, 358 F4
Merimbula NSW 349 I7
Merredin WA 358 E5
Merrijig Vic. 239
Merty Merty homestead SA 10, 14, 17
Messmate Spur Track Vic. 228
Mick Fienn campsites Qld 266, 271
Middle Island Qld 351 J3
Middlemount Qld 351 I3
Middleton Qld 350 D3
Midway camping area Qld 266, 271
Miena Tas. 361 D6
Mildura Vic. 348 E4
Miles Qld 351 J6
Milikapiti NT 357 G1
Milingimbi NT 357 J2
Millicent SA 348 C7
Milparinka NSW 348 D1, 240, 242, 243, 244, 245, 247, 248
Milyakburra NT 357 K3
Mimili SA 353 H1
Minamia NT 357 J5
Mindibungu (Billiluna) WA 354 E3, 356 E8, 47, 48, 54, 55, 118, 119, 139, 140, 153
Miners Pool camping area WA 68, 69, 70
Mingal Camp WA 174
Mingela Qld 351 H1
Mingenew WA 358 B4
Minilya Roadhouse WA 359 A6
Minjilang NT 357 H1
Minkie Waterhole campsite SA 12, 13, 18
Minnipa SA 353 J5

■ 371

INDEX

Mintabie SA 353 I1
Minyerri NT 357 I4
Mirra Mitta Bore SA 4, 5, 8
Misery Trail Vic. 220
Mistake Creek NT 354 F1, 356 F6
Mistake Creek Qld 293
Mistake Creek WA 76
Mitchell Qld 351 H6
Mitchell Falls WA 57, 66, 68, 69, 71
Mitchell Falls camping area WA 68, 69, 71
Mitchell Plateau WA 56, 60, 67, 70, 71
Mitchell River National Park WA 57
Mitchell–Alice Rivers National Park Qld 360 C5
Moe Vic. 349 G7
Mokari Airstrip SA 41
Mongrel Downs NT 53, 54
Monkey Mia WA 358 A1, 359 A8
Montecollina Bore SA 10, 12, 13, 14, 16
Montecollina Bore camping area SA 12, 13, 16
Monto Qld 351 J5
Moochalabra Dam WA 62, 63
Moolawatana homestead SA 16
Mooliampah Qld 250
Moomba SA 10, 14, 15, 17, 240, 250, 251
Moongara 1 & 2 Bores SA 9, 43
Moongara Channel SA 43
Moonie Qld 351 J7
Moora WA 358 C5
Moore River National Park WA 358 C5
Moorrinya National Park Qld 351 G2
Moranbah Qld 351 I3
Morawa WA 358 C4
Moree NSW 349 I1, 351 I8
Morehead River Qld 273
Moreton Island Qld 351 L7
Moreton Island National Park Qld 351 L7
Moreton Telegraph Station Qld 275, 277, 281, 285
Mortlake Vic. 348 E7
Morton National Park NSW 349 I5
Morven Qld 351 H6
Moscow Villa hut Vic. 212, 215, 217, 221
Moscow Villa camping area Vic. 216, 217, 221
Moss Vale NSW 349 I5
Mossman Qld 360 F6
Mount Augustus National Park WA 359 C6
Mount Baldy Track Vic. 218
Mount Barker SA 348 C5, 353 L7
Mount Barker WA 358 E8

Mount Barnett WA 354 D1, 356 D6, 57, 62
Mount Barnett Roadhouse WA 73, 74, 76
Mount Beadell WA 166, 168, 171, 173
Mount Birregun Vic. 224, 228
Mount Browne goldfields NSW 242, 244, 245, 247
Mount Buller Vic. 239
Mount Coolon Qld 351 H2
Mount Curtis Creek SA 15
Mount Cynthia Vic. 234
Mount Dare SA 355 J8, 29, 30, 31, 32, 33, 34, 36, 39
Mount Dare camping area SA 34
Mount Davis WA 127
Mount Dutton SA 28
Mount Ebenezer Roadhouse NT 355 I7
Mount Eccles National Park Vic. 348 D7
Mount Elizabeth station camping area WA 75, 76, 78
Mount Elliot Ridge Track Vic. 218
Mount Ernest WA 150, 152
Mount Everard WA 168, 170, 173
Mount Ewen Track Vic. 229
Mount Field National Park Tas. 361 D7
Mount Finke SA 202, 204, 205, 206, 207, 208, 209, 210
Mount Finke campsites SA 206, 207, 209
Mount Ford WA 139, 149
Mount Frankland National Park WA 358 D8
Mount Freeling SA 15
Mount Gambier SA 348 D7
Mount Garnet Qld 360 F7
Mount Gason Wattle Project SA 8
Mount Gordon WA 170
Mount Hart WA 81
Mount Hart Track Vic. 235
Mount Hart Wilderness Lodge WA 74
Mount Henderson Qld 259
Mount Holland WA 158, 162, 163
Mount Hope SA 353 J6
Mount Hopeless SA 16, 253
Mount Hotham Vic. 224, 226, 227, 231
Mount House homestead WA 76, 77, 80
Mount Howitt Vic. 230, 238
Mount Isa Qld 350 C2
Mount Kaputar National Park NSW 349 I2
Mount Keith WA 352 A2, 358 F2, 359 F8

Mount Kosciuszko NSW 214
Mount Kosciuszko Lookout Vic. 227
Mount Liebig NT 355 H6, 95, 96
Mount Lyndhurst SA 15
Mount Lyndhurst Creek SA 15
Mount Magnet WA 358 D3
Mount Morgan Qld 351 J4
Mount North Creek WA 82
Mount Nossiter WA 174
Mount Pinnibar Vic. 212, 214, 215, 218, 219
Mount Poole NSW 244, 246, 247
Mount Romilly WA 149
Mount Samuel Junction WA 168
Mount Sanford Junction NT 112
Mount Sanford station NT 107, 108, 113, 114
Mount Sanford Track NT 115
Mount Sonder NT 97, 98
Mount Sturt NSW 248
Mount Surprise Qld 360 E7
Mount Tanami NT 48
Mount Theo Aboriginal Community Outstation NT 52
Mount Tozer Qld 276
Mount Tozer Lookout Qld 283
Mount Von Guerard Vic. 235
Mount Wedge station NT 49
Mount William Lambert WA 166, 174
Mount William National Park Tas. 361 F4
Mount Windarra mine WA 198
Mountain Creek NT 320
Moura Qld 351 J5
Muchea WA 358 C5
Mudgee NSW 349 I3
Mujingerra Cave WA 138
Mukinbudin WA 358 D5
Mulga Park NT 169
Mulgathing homestead SA 211
Mulkas Cave WA 159
Mullewa WA 358 B3
Muloorina homestead SA 23
Mundrabilla Roadhouse WA 352 F5
Mundubbera Qld 351 K6
Mungerannie SA 3, 4, 6
Mungerannie Gap SA 8
Mungerannie Roadhouse SA 350 C7, 353 L2, 4, 6, 8
Mungilli (Mangkili) Claypan Nature Reserve WA 167, 168, 171, 172, 174
Mungindi NSW 351 I8
Mungkan Kandju National Park Qld 360 D3, 263, 276
Mungkarta NT 355 I4, 357 I8

372

INDEX

Mungo National Park NSW 348 E4
Munro oil field Qld 250
Murchison WA 358 C2, 359 C8
Murgenella NT 357 H1
Murnpeowie SA 15
Murray Bridge SA 348 C5, 353 L7
Murray River Vic. 212, 214, 215, 219, 220
Murray Valley Highway Vic. 216
Murray–Sunset National Park Vic. 348 D5
Murun Murula NT 355 L2, 357 L7
Murwillumbah NSW 351 L8
Musgrave Qld 270, 271, 272, 273, 274
Musgrave Roadhouse Qld 360 D5, 262, 263, 264, 265, 266, 274, 275, 276, 278
Musgrave Roadhouse camping area Qld 266, 267, 279, 280
Muswellbrook NSW 349 J3
Mutawintji National Park NSW 348 E2
Mutee Head Qld 287
Mutee Head camping area Qld 288, 289, 297
Mutonia Sculpture Park SA 23
Muttaburra Qld 350 F3
MV *Tom Brennan* Memorial SA 7
Myall Lakes National Park NSW 349 K3
Myrtleford Vic. 238

N

Nambour Qld 351 K7
Nambung National Park WA 358 B5
Nangabbittajarra WA 138
Nangalala NT 357 J2
Nannup WA 358 C7
Nanutarra Roadhouse WA 359 B5
Napier Downs WA 73, 81
Nappa Merrie (Nappamerry) Qld 19, 251, 257, 258
Nappanerica Dune (Big Red) SA 30, 32, 33, 35, 40
Naracoopa Tas. 361 A2
Naracoorte SA 348 D6
Narembeen WA 358 E6
Nariel Creek camping area Vic. 216, 217
Nariel Creek Recreation Reserve Vic. 216
Nariel Gap Vic. 216
Narrabri NSW 349 I2
Narrandera NSW 349 G5
Narrogin WA 358 D6

Naryilco Qld 250
Nathan River ranger station NT 319
Nathan River Road (Savannah Way) NT 357 J4, 309, 310, 312, 314, 318, 320
Native Cat Flat Vic. 221
Native Cat Track Vic. 215, 221
Native Dog Flat camping area Vic. 216, 217, 221
Native Rocks WA 162
Natterannie Sandhills SA 4, 7, 8
Nauiyu NT 357 G3
Neale Junction WA 352 D2, 176, 178, 179, 181, 186, 188, 191, 198, 199, 200, 201
Neale Junction camping area WA 178, 179, 182, 190, 191, 197, 199, 200
Neale Junction Nature Reserve WA 352 D2, 177, 178, 182, 187, 188, 197, 200
Neales River SA 22, 28
Nebo Qld 351 I3
Nerang Qld 351 L8
New England NSW 349 K1
New England National Park NSW 349 K2
New Good Hope Mine Vic. 230, 234
New Laura Qld 263
New Laura Ranger station Qld 264, 270, 271
New Mapoon Qld 287, 288
New Norfolk Tas. 361 D7
Newcastle NSW 349 J4
Newcastle Waters (Marlinja) NT 355 I1, 357 I6
Newhaven station NT 49
Newman WA 359 E5, 120, 121, 136
Newmont Granites Mine NT 49, 50
Ngoollalah Creek WA 72
Nguiu NT 357 G2
Ngukurr NT 357 J4, 303
Ngunarra NT 355 K2, 357 K7
Nhulunbuy NT 357 K2
Nicholson River Qld 305, 310
Nifold Plain Qld 265, 273
Nikantyarra Waterhole NT 319
Nilpinna SA 27
Nine Mile Fettlers Quarters SA 29
Nitmiluk National Park NT 357 H3
Noccundra Qld 350 E7
Nolan Brook (Bridge Creek) Qld 293
Noonamah NT 357 G2
Noonans Flat Vic. 239
Noonans Flat camping area Vic. 231, 232, 233, 239
Noosa Heads Qld 351 L6
Normanby River Qld 264, 269, 270, 271

Normanby River campsites Qld 266, 267
Normanton Qld 360 C7, 302, 303, 304, 305, 308, 309
Norseman WA 352 B6, 159
North Alice Creek Qld 290
North Creek SA 29
North Flinders Mines NT 50
North Kennedy River Qld 264, 273
North Kennedy Seven Mile Qld 271, 272
North Pool (Water 1A) WA 124
Northam WA 358 D5
Northampton WA 358 B3
Northern Bypass Road Qld 262, 286, 287, 292, 293, 294, 296
Notabilis Hill WA 173
Nowra NSW 349 I5
Nugong Tower Vic. 221
Nullagine WA 359 E4
Nullarbor WA 176, 178
Nullarbor National Park SA 353 G5
Number 5 Yard NT 115
Numbulwar NT 357 J4
Nundroo Roadhouse SA 353 H5
Nunniong Plains Vic. 221
Nunniong Plains Track Vic. 221
Nunniong Road Vic. 215, 221, 222, 223
Nunniong State Forest Vic. 213
Nurgurga Soak WA 138
Nuriootpa SA 348 C4, 353 L7
Nyarna Lake Stretch WA 140
Nyarna Lake Stretch camping area WA 140, 151, 153
Nyirripi NT 355 G6, 52
Nymagee NSW 349 G3
Nyngan NSW 349 H2

O

Oasis Roadhouse Qld 360 E8
Oatlands Tas. 361 E6
Ocean to Alice trek SA & WA 84–99
Ochre Cliffs SA 12
Ochre Pits NT 90, 93, 98
Ockenden Creek SA 28
Oenpelli NT 357 H2
Olarinna Creek SA 29
Old Faithful Waterhole Qld 270
Old Faithful Waterhole camping area Qld 266, 270
Old Ghan railway 20, 21, 22, 23, 24, 25, 26, 27, 28, 29
Old Laura camping area Qld 266, 267, 269

373

INDEX

Old Laura homestead Qld 264, 266, 270
Old Moreton Telegraph Station Qld 277, 281, 285
Old Moreton Telegraph Station campground Qld 280, 281, 285
Old Mornington WA 73, 74, 75, 76, 77, 78, 80
Old Mornington camping area WA 74, 75, 76, 77, 78
Old Mount Browne homestead NSW 247
Old Mulka homestead SA 8
Old Peake Telegraph Station SA 28
Old Strzelecki Track SA 10, 14, 17, 18–19
Old Telegraph Line Qld 289
Old Telegraph Track Qld 294
Old Wheatfields Track Vic. 221
Old Woman Creek SA 27
Ollies Jump Up camping area Vic. 225, 226, 229
Omeo Vic. 349 H7, 212, 213, 214, 215, 216, 222, 224, 226, 229
Omicron Qld 250
One Arm Point WA 354 B1, 356 B6
Onegunyah Rockhole WA 134
Oodnadatta SA 350 A7, 353 J1, 20, 21, 22, 23, 27, 29, 30, 31, 36, 192
Oodnadatta Track SA 3, 6, 20–9
Ooranillani SA 8
Orange NSW 349 I4
Orange Plains camping area Qld 266, 273
Orbost Vic. 349 H7, 222
Oriental Claims Historic Area Vic. 213, 224, 225, 227
Orientos Qld 19, 257
Ormiston Gorge NT 90, 92, 97, 98
Ormiston Gorge camping area NT 92, 93, 98
Orrtipa–Thurra NT 350 A3, 355 K5
Otway National Park Vic. 348 E8
Ouyen Vic. 348 E5
Overland Telegraph monument SA 26, 27, 29
Overlander Roadhouse WA 358 B2, 359 B8
Oxley NSW 348 F4
Oxley Wild Rivers National Park NSW 349 J2

P

Pago WA 67, 69, 72
Pago camping area WA 69, 72

Paisley Creek SA 26
Pajinka Qld 299
Pakenham Vic. 348 F7
Palana Tas. 361 F2
Palm Creek Qld 290
Palmer River Roadhouse Qld 360 E6
Palmerston NT 357 G2
Pandie Pandie SA 6, 9, 43
Pannawonica WA 359 B4
Paperbark Yard camping area NT 108, 109, 114
Papunya NT 355 H6, 49, 85, 90, 91, 95, 96
Paraburdoo WA 359 C5
Parachilna SA 348 B2, 353 L4
Pardoo Roadhouse WA 359 E3
Parkes NSW 349 H4
Paru NT 357 G2
Pascoe River Qld 276, 282, 283, 285
Paynes Find WA 358 D4
Peake Creek SA 28
Peake Hill Copper Mine SA 28
Peake Springs SA 20
Peake Telegraph Station SA 22
Pear Tree Creek Qld 309
Pelican Creek SA 15
Penarie NSW 348 E4
Peninsula Developmental Road Qld 265, 275, 277, 278, 279, 282, 284, 285
Penneshaw SA 348 B5, 353 L8
Penong SA 353 I5, 208
Pentecost River WA 56, 58, 59, 60, 61, 62, 64
Pentland Qld 351 G2
Perth WA 358 C6
Peterborough SA 348 C3, 353 L6
Petermorra Creek SA 16
Pickerings Flat camping area Vic. 232, 233, 239
Pickertaramoor NT 357 G2
Pierre Spring (Well 6) WA 120, 127, 131
Pigeon Hole WA 165
Pijallinga Claypan WA 147
Piker Creek NT 319
Pine Creek NT 357 H3
Pine Hill NT 52
Pink Roadhouse SA 29
Pinnibar Track Vic. 218
Pioneer Racecourse Vic. 234
Pirlangimpi NT 357 G1
Plain Creek WA 70
Plain Creek rest area WA 67
Planehenge SA 23
Planet Downs outstation Qld 259
Plateau Camp WA 71

Plumridge Lakes Nature Reserve WA 352 D3, 183
Poeppel, Augustus 35, 39, 255, 256
Poeppel Corner SA 350 B6, 32, 35, 37, 38, 39, 40, 41, 42, 255
Poeppel Corner Oil Well SA 40
Point Sunday WA 201
Poison Creek NT 115
Police Creek Waterhole NT 107, 111
Policemans Waterhole campsite SA 12, 13, 18
Poochera SA 353 J5
Poole's Grave NSW 247, 248
Poolowanna Oil Well SA 42
Pooncarie NSW 348 E4
Popes Bore SA 16
Popies Waterhole WA 62
Port Arthur Tas. 361 E8
Port Augusta SA 348 B3, 353 L5, 6, 15, 23, 24, 192, 211
Port Douglas Qld 360 F6
Port Fairy Vic. 348 D8
Port Hedland WA 359 D3, 84, 85, 88
Port Lincoln SA 348 A5, 353 J7
Port Macquarie NSW 349 K3
Port Pirie SA 348 B3, 353 L6
Port Roper NT 320
Port Sorell Tas. 361 D4
Port Stewart Qld 278
Port Wakefield SA 348 B4, 353 L7
Port Warrender WA 66, 70
Port Warrender Coastal Access WA 71
Portland Roads Qld 360 D3, 276, 277, 282, 284
Prairie Qld 351 G2
Premier Downs WA 183
Prenti Downs WA 175
Priscilla Creek SA 26
Prison Boab Tree WA 61, 62, 63
Proserpine Qld 351 I2
Proston Qld 351 K6
Pungalina NT 311
Punmu WA 89
Punsand Bay Qld 298, 299
Punsand Bay camping area Qld 288, 289, 299
Purladi NT 49
Purnie Bore SA 32, 33, 34, 36, 37, 41
Purnie Bore camping area SA 34, 37
Purnululu National Park WA 151

Q

Quamby Qld 350 D1
Quartz Ridge NT 53

Queanbeyan NSW 349 I5
Queen Victoria Rock WA *see* Victoria Rock
Queen Victoria Spring WA 179
Queenscliff Vic. 348 F8
Queenstown Tas. 361 C6
Quilpie Qld 350 F6
Quorn SA 348 B3, 353 L5, 24

R

Rabbit Flat NT 47, 50, 52, 53
Rabbit Flat camping area NT 50, 51, 53
Rabbit Flat Roadhouse NT 355 G4, 357 G8, 46, 48, 50, 53
Racecourse Track Vic. 230, 234
Rainbow Beach Qld 351 L6
Rainforest campground Qld 280, 284
Ramingining NT 357 J2
Ravensthorpe WA 352 A7, 358 F7
Ravenswood Qld 351 H1
Rawlinna WA 352 D4, 176, 177, 178, 180, 188
Rawlinna camping area WA 178, 179, 183
Raymond Terrace NSW 349 J4
Razorblade Bore WA 86, 89
Razorblade Bore bush campsites WA 86, 87, 89
Red Beach Qld 360 C2
Red Lily Lagoon Qld 266, 272
Redbank NT 97
Redbank Gorge NT 90, 98
Redford, Harry 10, 17
Reid WA 352 F4
Renehans Bore bush camping NT 50, 51, 52
Renmark SA 348 D4
Renner Springs NT 355 I2, 357 I7
Richmond Qld 350 F2
Richmond Tas. 361 E7
Ridgetop Camping area NT 92, 93, 98
Rig Road SA 8, 32, 33, 37, 39, 41–3
Rileys Creek Track Vic. 238
Ritchies Hut Vic. 232
Robe SA 348 C7
Robinson River NT 355 K1, 357 K6, 313
Robinvale Vic. 348 E5
Rockhampton Qld 351 J4
Rocks Track SA 37
Rocky Bar NT 314
Rocky Bar Crossing NT 320
Rocky River SA 348 A6, 353 K8

Roebourne WA 359 C4
Roebuck Roadhouse WA 354 A2, 356 A7, 359 F1
Rokeby Ranger Station Qld 278
Rolleston Qld 351 I5
Rollingstone Qld 360 F8
Roma Qld 351 I6
Roma Flat Lockerbie Scrub Walk Qld 299
Roma Gorge NT 98
Roper Bar NT 303, 314, 315, 318, 319, 320, 321
Roper Bar Store NT 357 J4
Roper River NT 315, 317, 320, 321
Rosebery Tas. 361 C5
Rosebud Vic. 348 F8
Rosedale Qld 351 K5
Ross Tas. 361 E6
Roxby Downs SA 348 A1, 353 K4, 23
Royal National Park NSW 349 J5
Ruby Plains WA 55
Rudall River National Park WA 354 B5, 359 F4, 136
Russ Creek WA 65

S

Saddler Springs WA 80
Sailor Creek Qld 291
St Arnaud Vic. 348 E6
St George Qld 351 I7
St Helens Tas. 361 F5
St Lawrence Qld 351 J3
St Marys Tas. 361 F5
St Vidgeon station 314, 320
Sale Vic. 349 G8
Salmon Gums WA 352 B6
Saltwater Creek Qld 265, 273, 274
Saltwater Creek campsites Qld 266, 267, 273–4
Salty Well (Well 21) WA 135
Sam Creek Qld 292–3, 296
Same Creek WA 81
Sandalwood Camp WA 163
Sandalwood Rocks WA 164
Sandfire Roadhouse WA 354 A4, 359 F2, 85, 86, 87, 88
Sandstone WA 358 E2
Sandy Blight Junction NT 95
Sandy Creek Qld 270
Sangsters Bore NT 53
Santa Teresa (Ltyentye Purte) NT 355 J6
Santos Qld 251
Sarina Qld 351 I2

Savannah Way (Nathan River Road) NT 309, 310, 312, 314, 318, 320
Savory Creek WA 121, 134
Sawtell NSW 349 K2
Schultz, Charlie 110
Schusters Hut Vic. 232
Scottsdale Tas. 361 E4
Scrubby Creek Qld 292, 295
Seemore Downs WA 183
Seisia Qld 262, 263, 288, 297, 298, 299
Seisia Caravan Park Qld 288, 289, 297
Seismic Line SA 193
Separation Well WA 122, 137
Serpentine Chalet bush camping NT 92, 93, 98
Serpentine Gorge NT 90
Serpentine Lakes SA 186, 188, 190, 191, 196
Serpentine Lakes camping area SA 190, 191, 196
Settlement Creek NT 311
Seven Mile Vic. 238, 239
Seven Mile camping area Vic. 232, 233, 239
Seven Mile Creek SA 43
Seven Mile Waterhole Qld 264, 271, 272, 273
Seven Mile Waterhole camping area Qld 266, 267, 272–3
Seventeen Seventy Qld 351 K5
Seymour Vic. 348 F7
Shady Creek Upper Track Vic. 218
Shannon National Park WA 358 D8
Sheepyard Flat Vic. 230, 239
Sheepyard Flat camping area Vic. 232, 233, 239
Sheepyard Flat Track Vic. 238
Sheldon Lagoon Qld 291
Sheoak Rock WA 162
Shepparton Vic. 348 F6
Shoe NT 50
Silent Grove campground WA 78, 79, 80
Silkwood Qld 360 F7
Silver City Highway NSW 242, 245
Silverton NSW 348 D2
Simpson Desert SA & Qld 350 A5, 355 K7, 6, 23, 29, 30–43
Simpson Desert Conservation Park SA 355 L8, 31, 33
Simpson Desert National Park Qld & SA 350 B5, 355 L6, 31, 38, 40
Simpson Desert Regional Reserve SA 353 K1, 355 K8, 8, 31, 33, 37, 41, 42, 43
Simpsons Gap NT 97, 99

INDEX

Singhs Garden WA 63
Singleton NSW 349 J3
Sir John Gorge WA 75, 77
Six Mile Vic. 239
Six Mile Waterhole camping area Qld 266, 267, 270
Ski Beach camping site SA 12, 13, 18
Skylab Well WA 183
Slate Range WA 136
Sly Creek NT 319
Smithton Tas. 361 B4
Snake Creek WA 76
Snake Lagoon camping area NT 306, 312, 313
Snake Lagoon homestead NT 305, 313
Snowy River National Park Vic. 349 H7
Somerset Qld 287, 295, 299
Somerset Tas. 361 C4
Sorell Tas. 361 E7
South Alice Creek Qld 290
South Basalt Knob Vic. 234
South Bruny National Park Tas. 361 D8
South Creek SA 15
South East Forest National Park NSW 349 I7
South Escarpment Track Vic. 221
South Galway Qld 259
South Island Qld 351 J3
South Spur Track Vic. 228
Southern Bypass Road Qld 262, 286, 287, 291, 292, 294, 295
Southern Cross WA 358 E5, 159, 162
Southern Lost City NT 314, 315, 317, 319
Southesk Tablelands WA 140
Southport Tas. 361 D8
Southwest National Park Tas. 361 C7
Spear Creek Qld 294
Sprigg, Reg 39
Spring Creek NT 102, 313
Spring Creek Basin SA 36
Spring Creek Delta SA 33, 37
Spring Creek Jump-up NT 105
Spring Creek Track Vic. 228
Spring Creek Valley NT 106
Spring Creek Yard camping area NT 102, 103, 106
Springsure Qld 351 I4
Staaten River National Park Qld 360 D6
Stamford Qld 350 F2
Standley Chasm NT 97, 99
Stanthorpe Qld 351 K8

Starvation Harbour WA 122
State Barrier Fence WA 159, 164
Station Creek WA 72, 76
Station Track Vic. 234
Stawell Vic. 348 E7
Steptoes Corner WA 168
Stock Route Spur Track Vic. 224, 226, 228
Stockwell Track Vic. 218
Stokes oil field Qld 251
Stonehenge Qld 350 F4
Strahan Tas. 361 B6
Strangways Bore Historic Rail Siding SA 22, 26
Strathgordon Tas. 361 C7
Streaky Bay SA 353 I5
Strzelecki Creek SA 10, 14, 16, 17, 18
Strzelecki Crossing SA 16
Strzelecki Desert Qld & SA 350 C7, 10, 14
Strzelecki Regional Reserve SA 11, 14, 16
Strzelecki Track SA 350 C8, 10–19, 244, 250, 257
Stuart, John McDouall 20, 97, 137, 202, 206
Stuart Creek Railway Bridge SA 26
Stuart Highway SA 192, 204, 211
Stuarts Well NT 355 I7
Sturt, Charles 39, 240, 243, 244, 246
Sturt Creek WA 54, 151, 153
Sturt National Park NSW 350 D8, 240, 241, 242, 244, 245, 246, 249
Sturt Stony Desert Qld & SA 350 C7, 353 L1, 5, 240, 246
Sturt's Cairn NSW 247, 248
Sunday Well WA 132
Sunset Country Vic. 348 D4
Sunshine Coast Qld 351 L6
Surat Qld 351 I7
Surfers Paradise Qld 351 L8
Surprise Creek NT 311
Surveyors Pool WA 66, 71
Swan Hill Vic. 348 E5
Swansea Tas. 361 F6
Sweetwater camping area Qld 266, 267, 274
Swifts Creek Vic. 215, 222, 223, 229
Swindell Airfield WA 87, 89
Sydney NSW 349 J4

T

Tailem Bend SA 348 C5
Talawana Track WA 121, 135, 136

Talbotville Vic. 212, 230, 234
Talbotville camping area Vic. 233, 234
Talc Mine SA 15
Tallangatta Vic. 216
Tallaringa Conservation Park SA 353 I2, 187, 188, 189, 192, 193
Tallaringa Well SA 191, 193, 195
Tambo Qld 351 G5
Tambo River Vic. 222
Tamworth NSW 349 J2
Tanami Deseart NT 355 H4, 357 H8
Tanami Downs NT 53, 54
Tanami Mine NT 46, 54
Tanami Road NT & WA 354 E3, 46–55, 140, 153
Tanami Rockhole NT 54
Tanbar Qld 259
Tannum Sands Qld 351 K4
Tansey Qld 351 K6
Tara NT 355 I4
Tarcoola SA 353 J4, 202, 203, 205, 207, 210, 211
Tardun WA 358 C3
Taree NSW 349 K3
Taroom Qld 351 J6
Tasman National Park Tas. 361 E8
Tawallah Creek NT 318
Telegraph Track Qld 360 D3, 262, 275, 276, 286, 287, 288, 290, 291, 292, 293, 294, 295, 296
Temora NSW 349 H5
Tennant Creek NT 355 I3, 357 I8, 49, 321
Tent Hill Creek SA 15
Tenterfield NSW 349 K1, 351 K8
Terrace Hill WA 134
Thargomindah Qld 350 F7, 19, 251, 258
The Bend camping area Qld 278, 279, 280
The Granites NT 50, 53
The Granites (Well 2A) WA 124
The Grotto WA 62
The Humps WA 159
The Peake bush camping SA 24, 25, 28
The Peake homestead SA 24, 25, 27
The Poplars Vic. 215
Theda homestead WA 72
Theldarpa NSW 245, 248
Theodore Qld 351 J5
Three O'Clock Creek camping area SA 33, 34, 36
Three Springs WA 358 C4
Three Ways Roadhouse NT 355 I3, 357 I8
Thring Rock WA 121, 137, 138

INDEX

Thrushton National Park Qld 351 H7
Thursday Island Qld 360 D1, 288, 299
Thursday Rock WA 158, 165
Ti Tree NT 355 I5
Tibooburra NSW 348 E1, 350 E8, 19, 240, 241, 242, 245, 247, 248, 249, 251
Tichborne, Roger 226
Tickalara oil field Qld 250, 251
Tidal River Vic. 349 G8, 361 D1
Tier Gorge WA 62
Tieri Qld 351 I4
Tilmouth Well NT 47, 49, 50
Tilmouth Well camping area NT 49, 50, 51
Tilmouth Well Roadhouse NT 355 H5, 48, 49
Tilpa NSW 348 F2
Timber Creek NT 357 G5, 100, 101, 102, 104, 106, 107
Tindelpina Creek SA 15
Tippipilla Creek SA 6, 9, 43
Tippipilla Creek bush camping SA 4, 5, 9, 34, 35, 43
Tirranna Roadhouse Qld 360 A7, 34, 43
Tjirrkarli WA 172, 173
Tjukayirla Roadhouse WA 352 C1
Tjuntjuntjara WA 182, 188, 189
Tobermorey NT 350 B3, 355 L5
Tobin Lake WA 145
Todmorden SA 29
Tom Groggin camping area Vic. 216, 217, 219
Tom Groggin station Vic. 214, 215, 218
Tom Groggin Track Vic. 215, 218, 219
Tom Price WA 359 D5
Toolachee SA 251
Toompine Roadhouse Qld 350 F7
Toona Gate Qld 250
Toonumbar National Park NSW 351 K8
Toowoomba Qld 351 K7
Top Bore WA 77
Top Humbert Yard camping area NT 108, 109, 112
Top Springs NT 355 H1, 357 H6
Top Whiphandle camping area Qld 266, 273
Torrens Creek Qld 351 G2
Totem 1 SA 188, 193, 195
Totem 2 SA 188, 193, 195
Towns River NT 319, 320
Towns River camping area NT 316, 317, 319
Townsville Qld 351 H1
Tozers Gap Qld 277, 284

Trans Australia Railway Access Road WA 176, 183, 204
Traralgon Vic. 349 G8
Triabunna Tas. 361 E7
Tufa Dams NT 104
Tullamore NSW 349 H3
Tully Qld 360 F7
Tully Inlet Qld 304
Tumby Bay SA 348 A4, 353 K7
Tumut NSW 349 H5
Tunnel Bend Vic. 239
Tunnel Bend Flat camping area Vic. 232, 233, 239
Tunnel Creek WA 73, 78, 82, 83
Tunnel Creek National Park WA 57, 74, 82
Turkey Creek Roadhouse WA 354 E1, 356 E6
Tweed Heads NSW 351 L8
Twelve Mile Waterhole camping area Qld 266, 270
Twin Falls Qld 263, 287, 288, 292, 296
Twin Heads WA 150
Two Mile campsite NT 92, 93, 98
Two Mile Creek camping area Vic. 225, 229
Two Wells SA 348 B4, 353 L7

U

Ulladulla NSW 349 I6
Uluru–Kata Tjuṯa National Park NT 355 G8
Ulverstone Tas. 361 C4
Umagico Qld 263, 287, 297
Umagico campground Qld 288, 289, 297
Umbakumba NT 357 K3
Undara Volcanic National Park Qld 360 E7
Unnamed Conservation Park SA 353 G2, 187, 188, 189, 190, 194, 196
Upper Dargo Vic. 229, 231
Upper Jamieson Hut Vic. 230, 232
Upper Jamieson Hut camping area Vic. 232, 233, 238
Upper Wickham NT 112
Urandangi Qld 350 B2, 355 L4
Ussher Point camping area Qld 297

V

Varley WA 352 A6, 358 F6
Vaughan Springs NT 52
Victor Harbor SA 348 B5, 353 L8

Victoria Falls Historic Area Vic. 213, 224, 227
Victoria Falls Historic Area campground Vic. 225, 227
Victoria Highway NT 100, 102
Victoria River NT 100
Victoria River Downs NT 110
Victoria River Roadhouse NT 357 G5
Victoria River Track Vic. 224, 226, 227
Victoria Rock WA 158, 161, 165
Victoria Rock camping area WA 161, 165
Victoria Rock Nature Reserve WA 157, 158
Victory Downs station NT 166, 169
Vokes Hill Corner SA 188, 191, 192, 193, 194
Vokes Hill Corner bush camping SA 191, 194
Vrilya Point Qld 296
Vulkathunha–Gammon Ranges National Park SA 348 C1, 353 L3

W

WAA Line SA 37, 41, 42
Wabma Kadarbu Mound Springs Conservation Park SA 21, 22, 23, 26
Wadbilliga National Park NSW 349 I6
Wagga Wagga NSW 349 H5
Wagin WA 358 D7
Waikerie SA 348 C4
Walcha NSW 349 J2
Walgett NSW 349 H1
Walkandi Junction SA 32, 41
Walker, Frederick 304, 307
Walkers Crossing Track SA 6, 9, 43
Walkerston Qld 351 I2
Walls of Jerusalem National Park Tas. 361 C5
Walpole WA 358 D8
Walpole–Nornalup National Park WA 358 D8
Walsh Qld 360 E6
Walsh Point WA 66, 69, 70, 71
Walsh Point bush camping area WA 68, 69, 71
Wanaaring NSW 348 F1
Wandoan Qld 351 J6
Wangaratta Vic. 349 G6
Wangianna SA 23
Warakurna WA 354 F7, 167
Warakurna Roadhouse WA 354 F7
Waratah Tas. 361 C5

377

INDEX

Warburton WA 352 E1, 354 E8, 166, 167, 168, 172, 174, 176, 177, 178, 180
Warburton, Peter 39, 86, 122
Warburton crossing SA 8, 33, 43
Warburton Roadhouse WA 352 E1, 168, 171, 172, 178, 180
Warburton Roadhouse camping area WA 171, 172, 178, 179, 180
Wardabunni Rockhole (Water 38) WA 144
Warialda NSW 349 J1
Warmun (Turkey Creek) WA 354 E1, 356 E6
Waroona WA 358 C6
Warrabuda Native Well WA 146
Warracknabeal Vic. 348 E6
Warragul Vic. 349 G7
Warren Creek NT 95
Warrina SA 28
Warriner Creek SA 26, 27
Warrnambool Vic. 348 E8
Warrumbungle National Park NSW 349 H2
Warruwi NT 357 I1
Warwick Qld 351 K8
Washington steam winch Vic. 215, 217, 222, 223
Washpool National Park NSW 349 K1
Watarrka National Park NT 355 G7
Water 1A (North Pool) WA 124
Water 4A (Windich Springs) WA 120, 125, 126, 131
Water 38 (Wardabunni Rockhole) WA 144
Waterford Vic. 224, 230
Watheroo National Park WA 358 C4
Watson SA 353 H4
Wattle Rocks WA 158, 162
Wauchope NT 355 I4
Wave Rock WA 157, 158, 159, 160, 161
Wave Rock camping area WA 159, 160, 161
Wearyan River NT 313
Weipa Qld 360 C3, 262, 263, 276, 278, 284, 285
Weipa camping area Qld 280
Welcome Hole camping area Qld 266, 269
Welford National Park Qld 350 E5
Well 1 WA 124
Well 2 WA 124
Well 2A (The Granites) WA 124
Well 3 and bush camping area WA 120, 124, 125, 126, 131

Well 3A WA 124
Well 4 WA 126
Well 5 (Granite Peak) WA 120, 126–7
Well 6 (Pierre Spring) and camping area WA 120, 125, 127, 131
Well 7 WA 127
Well 8 WA 127
Well 9 WA 120, 128
Well 10 (Lucky Well) WA 120, 128
Well 11 WA 128
Well 12 WA 128, 129
Well 13 and bush camping WA 129, 130, 131
Well 14 WA 129
Well 15 WA 129
Well 16 and bush camping WA 129, 130, 131, 132
Well 18 WA 134
Well 19 WA 134
Well 20 WA 135
Well 21 (Salty Well) WA 135
Well 22 WA 135
Well 23 WA 120, 121, 136
Well 24 WA 136
Well 25 WA 136
Well 26 WA 130, 136
Well 27 WA 136
Well 28 WA 137
Well 29 WA 137, 138
Well 30 (Dunda Jinnda) and bush campsite WA 131, 138
Well 31 and bush camping area WA 131, 138
Well 32 WA 138
Well 33 and bush camping WA 91, 92, 94, 121, 139, 140, 141, 142
Well 34 WA 142
Well 35 WA 139, 142, 144
Well 36 WA 139, 142, 143, 144
Well 37 (Libral Well, Haunted Well) WA 141, 144
Well 39 WA 139, 145
Well 40 WA 145
Well 41 WA 145
Well 42 (Guli Spring) WA 147
Well 43 WA 147, 148
Well 44 WA 139, 147, 148
Well 45 WA 148, 149
Well 46 and bush camping WA 139, 140, 141, 148, 149, 150
Well 47 WA 139, 149, 150
Well 48 WA 140, 150
Well 49 WA 152
Well 50 and camping area WA 140, 151, 152

Well 51 (Weriaddo Well) WA 140, 152
Wellington NSW 349 I3
Wells, Lawrence 122, 131, 137, 170
Wenlock River Qld 276, 277, 282, 285
Weriaddo Well (Well 51) WA 140, 152
Wernadinga Qld 308, 309
Werribee Vic. 348 F7
West Claudie River Qld 284
West MacDonnell Ranges NT 84, 90, 97
West MacDonnell National Park NT 355 H6, 85, 90, 93
West Wyalong NSW 349 G4
Westbury Tas. 361 D5
Western District Vic. 348 D7
Westwood Qld 351 J4
Wheatfields Track Vic. 221
Whim Creek WA 359 C4
Whirlpool Creek NT 320
White Cliffs NSW 348 E2
White Cliffs Camel station WA 201
White Lily Lagoon Qld 266, 272
White Mountains National Park Qld 351 G1
White Well WA 124
Whitemark Tas. 361 F3
Whitsunday Islands National Park Qld 351 J2
Whyalla SA 348 B3, 353 K6
Wialki WA 358 D4
Wickham WA 359 C4
Wickham River NT 100, 107, 108, 109, 113
Wickham River bush camping NT 108, 109, 113
Wickham Track NT 107, 108, 112
Widgiemooltha WA 352 B5
Wilcannia NSW 348 E2
Wilgena SA 211
Willandra National Park NSW 348 F3
Willare Bridge Roadhouse WA 354 B2, 356 B7
William Creek SA 350 A8, 353 K2, 20, 21, 22, 23, 27, 29
William (Breakfast Time) Creek SA 27
Wills, William 10, 13, 18, 240, 244, 252–3, 255, 304, 307
Wills Memorial SA 18, 19
Wills Memorial campsite SA 12, 13, 18
Willy Willy Bore WA 127
Wilpena SA 348 B2, 353 L4
Wilsons Promontory Vic. 349 G8, 361 D1
Wilsons Promontory National Park Vic. 349 G8, 361 D1

INDEX

Wiluna WA 352 A1, 358 E1, 359 F8, 118, 119, 120, 122, 124, 125, 128, 166, 167, 168, 172, 174, 175
Wiluna Club Hotel camping area WA 170, 171, 175
Wiluna Gold Mine WA 175
Wilyalallinna Creek SA 27
Wimmera Vic. 348 D6
Windarra Heritage Trail WA 198
Windich Springs (Water 4A) and camping area WA 120, 125, 126, 131
Windidda WA 175
Windjana Gorge WA 57, 73, 74, 78, 79, 83
Windjana Gorge camping areas WA 78, 79, 82
Windjana Gorge National Park WA 82, 83
Windorah Qld 350 E5, 240, 241, 254, 259
Windy Corner WA 136, 173
Winnecke, Charles 39
Winton Qld 350 E3
Wiripirie Bore SA 6, 9, 43
Wirrulla SA 353 J5, 211
Witjira National Park SA 350 A6, 353 J1, 355 J8, 23, 29, 31, 33, 34, 37, 41
Wittenoom WA 359 D5
Wodonga Vic. 349 G6, 216
Wogyala NT 355 J2, 357 J7
Wolfe Creek Meteorite camping area 50, 55, 140, 151, 153
Wolfe Creek Meteorite Crater National Park WA 47, 48, 50, 51, 55, 119, 140, 153
Wollemi National Park NSW 349 I4
Wollogorang Roadhouse NT 355 L1, 357 L6, 304, 305, 311
Wollogorang Roadhouse campground NT 306, 311
Wollogorang station NT 304, 313, 315
Wollongong NSW 349 J5
Wombarella Creek WA 81
Wombat Range Vic. 235

Wombat Range Track Vic. 230, 231, 234, 235
Wombat Spur Track Vic. 235
Wonga Corner SA 37, 41
Wongamel station WA 170, 175
Wongawol Creek WA 168, 175
Wongungarra River Vic. 234
Wonnangatta camping area Vic. 233, 235
Wonnangatta murders 236–7
Wonnangatta River Vic. 235
Wonnangatta station Vic. 235, 236–7, 238
Wonnangatta Track Vic. 235
Wonnangatta Valley Vic. 212, 230, 233, 235
Wonthaggi Vic. 348 F8
Woodlands camping area NT 92, 93, 98
Woods Point Vic. 227
Woodstock Qld 351 H1
Woolaning NT 357 G3
Woolridge Creek SA 29
Woomera SA 348 A2, 353 K4, 304, 305, 311
Wooramel Roadhouse WA 358 A1, 359 A8
Wudinna SA 348 A3, 353 J6
Wujal Wujal Qld 360 F6
Wutunugurra NT 355 J4
Wyandra Qld 351 G7
Wycliffe Well Roadhouse NT 355 I4
Wyndham WA 356 E5, 56, 57, 58, 61, 62, 63, 64, 70, 74, 100, 103, 111
Wynyard Tas. 361 C4
Wyperfeld National Park Vic. 348 D5

Y

Yalata SA 353 H4
Yalata Roadhouse SA 353 H5
Yalgoo WA 358 C3
Yalleroi Qld 351 G4
Yamarna WA 198, 201

Yamba Roadhouse SA 348 D4
Yanchep WA 358 C6
Yandama NSW 248
Yardinna SA 29
Yarra Ranges National Park Vic. 349 G7
Yarralin NT 355 G1, 357 G5
Yarram Vic. 349 G8
Yarraman Qld 351 K7
Yass NSW 349 H5
Yates Creek WA 81
Yea Vic. 348 F7
Yellabinna Regional Reserve SA 203, 204, 205, 210
Yelma station WA 175
Yelma Tank WA 175
Yelpawaralina Track SA 6, 33, 43
Yeo Lake campsites WA 199, 201
Yeo Lake homestead WA 186, 198, 199, 200, 201
Yeo Lake Nature Reserve WA 187, 198, 200, 201
Yeppoon Qld 351 J4
Yerilina Creek SA 15
Yirrkala NT 357 K2
York WA 358 D6
Yorke Peninsula SA 348 B4, 353 K7
Yorketown SA 348 B5, 353 K7
Young NSW 349 H5
Yuelamu NT 355 H5, 49
Yuendumu NT 46, 47, 48, 49, 51, 49, 52
Yulara NT 355 G7
Yumbarra Conservation Park SA 203, 204, 205, 208
Yuna WA 358 B3
Yuraygir National Park NSW 349 K1

Z

Zanthus WA 352 C5
Zeehan Tas. 361 B5
Zeka Spur Track Vic. 212, 230, 231, 238

ACKNOWLEDGEMENTS

Authors' acknowledgements
Books such as this are the result of a great many people. To everyone who has helped out in whatever way, no matter how small, please accept our heartfelt thanks. Special thanks, too, to our sponsors, who through their generous support helped make this project a reality – as well as keeping us, and our vehicle, 'The Brick', on the road, efficiently and safely: *4WD Megastores* (Australia-wide and in particular Slav and Craig and the crew at 4WD Warehouse in Kings Park, Sydney – thanks heaps guys for your ongoing support): *Land Rover* (Karen Byron); *Tyrepower* (John Klein and all the others at the Tyrepower stores we visited, who kept 'The Brick' rolling along on Kelly Tyres); *ShippShape Tents* (Jason and Terry); *GME Electrophone* (Ian Campbell for providing our ever-reliable Garmin GPS units and EPIRB); and *Graeme Cooper Automotive* (Graeme Cooper and staff).

The crew at Explore Australia Publishing, who took a punt on sending us into the great unknown of the outback for almost a year and a half (some would believe on a holiday!) to collect the information for this book – we thoroughly enjoy working with you all: Astrid Browne, our long-suffering Publications Manager, we're still 'selling the dream', and Paul de Leur, cartographer extraordinaire, who made the great maps inside this guide – we owe you both special thanks for an enjoyable working relationship; and Kim and Bernie at Hardie Grant – we loved your interest in what we were up to whenever we rang – thanks girls.

Our wonderful editor Helen Duffy skillfully caressed our words, sentences and stories into this book. You pushed us to new heights with your skills and enthusiasm for this project – a special thank you for helping us to 'build a better mousetrap'.

Thanks also to Bruce Farrands at Rabbit Flat; the staff and artists at Warlukurlangu Artists Group in Yuendumu; Len Carter, Paul Moroney and Mal Barnes at Newmont Australia; park rangers throughout Australia; Theo at Birdsville Autos; and the staff in visitor information centres across the country, who freely gave their time to answer our questions. We also extend our special thanks to the following people, all of whom helped us out in various ways: Ryan Lewis; David Summerville; Susan, Bill, Liam, Aimee and Emma Calleja; Dave Craddy of Tyrepower in Batemans Bay; Paula Lewis; Anthony, Kerry and Loren Savage; Peter and Yvonne Chance; and Brian Sommerville of GPSOz.

Finally, to the many wonderful travellers we met on our journey – you have left a lasting impression. Thanks for your company.

Publisher's acknowledgements

Publications manager
Astrid Browne

Project manager and editor
Helen Duffy

Cartography
Paul de Leur

Additional cartography
Mike Archer, Claire Johnston and Bruce McGurty

Design
Cover design
Leonie Stott

Internal design
Adrian Saunders
desertpony

Layout
Mike Kuszla, J&M Typesetting

Index
Fay Donlevy

Pre-press
Print and Publish P/L

Map data
The maps in this publication incorporate data copyright © Commonwealth of Australia (Geoscience Australia) 2005.

Aboriginal lands and parks and reserves
The maps in this book were produced with data from the following organisations:
New South Wales National Parks and Wildlife Service
Australian Capital Territory Land Information Centre
National Parks and Wildlife South Australia, Department of Environment and Heritage
Primary Industries and Resources South Australia
Department of Conservation and Land Management Western Australia
Aboriginal Affairs Department Western Australia
Parks and Wildlife Commission Northern Territory, Strategic Planning and Development Unit
Northern Territory Department of Lands, Planning and Environment (also supplied data for Alice Springs–Darwin railway)
Environmental Protection Agency (Qld)
Queensland Department of Natural Resources
Forestry Tasmania

Explore Australia Publishing indemnifies the above government authorities, which remain custodians and retain copyright of their data used in this publication. Data on Aboriginal lands and parks and reserves is current to 2000.

Photo credits
Cover
Travelling in the Simpson Desert

Except for the images listed below, all photographs in this book were taken in the field by the author and are the copyright of Craig Lewis. Additional images are: page 39 photograph courtesy of the State Library of South Australia, *Peter Ains and Ted Colson stand with Alice Colson after their return to Blood's Creek following the successful expedition to cross the Simpson Desert. 1936* [SLSA: B9113/13]; page 110 photograph courtesy of the Schultz Collection, *Charlie Schultz on his horse at Humbert River, c. 1928*, with thanks to Darrell Lewis and the Schultz family; courtesy of the National Library of Australia, page 170 James Atkinson, 'An Exploring Party in New South Wales' in *An Account of the State of Agriculture and Grazing in New South Wales …* (1826), page 246, Charles Sturt (1795–1869), *The Depot Glen*, wash drawing 17 x 28.7 cm, page 253 Nicholas Chevalier (1828–1902), *Return of Burke and Wills to Coopers Creek*, 1868, oil on canvas 89.2 x 120 cm [PIC R3863 Scr 2 Con 1723]; page 252 Elm Grove Press Collection, *The Victorian Exploring Expedition leaves Melbourne's Royal Park*.

Explore Australia Publishing Pty Ltd
85 High Street
Prahran, Victoria 3181, Australia

Published by Explore Australia Publishing Pty Ltd, 2005

Copyright © Concept, text, maps, form, and design Explore Australia Publishing Pty Ltd, 2005
Copyright © Photographs Craig Lewis, 2005

ISBN 1 74117 068 0

10 9 8 7 6 5 4 3 2 1

All right reserved. Without limiting the rights under copyright reserved above, no part of this publication my be reproduced, stored in or introduced into a retrieval system, or transmitted in any form or by any means (electronic, mechanical, photocopying, recording or otherwise) without the prior written permission of both the copyright owner and the above publisher of this book.

Printed and bound in China by Midas Printing (Asia) Ltd

Publisher's note: Every effort has been made to ensure that the information in this book is accurate at the time of going to press. The publisher welcomes information and suggestions for correction or improvement. Write to the Publications Manager, Explore Australia Publishing, 85 High Street, Prahran 3181, Australia or email explore@hardiegrant.com.au

Disclaimer: The publisher cannot accept responsibility for any errors or omissions. The representation on the maps of any road or track is not necessarily evidence of public right of way. The publisher cannot be held responsible for any injury, loss or damage incurred during outback travel. Travellers should be aware that conditions in remote areas change; it is vital to research any proposed trip thoroughly and seek the advice of relevant state and travel organisations before you leave.

4WD MEGASTORES
Everywhere

Call in and see our friendly staff at a location near you

NEW SOUTH WALES
1/12 Garling Rd, Kings Park BLACKTOWN	02 9622 1000
56 Chard Rd, BROOKVALE	02 9905 5520
2/116, Old Bathurst Rd, EMU PLAINS	02 4735 6691
18 James St, HORNSBY	02 9477 5528
6/3 Yarmouth Pl, NARELLAN	02 4647 1277
37 Peisley St, ORANGE	02 6361 7999
44 Crescent St, TAREE	02 6551 2479

QUEENSLAND
Cnr South Pine & Kremzow Rds, BRENDALE	07 3889 8555
959 Beaudesert Rd, COOPERS PLAINS	07 3277 8255
108 Pickering St, ENOGGERA	07 3855 4444
75 Moss St, SLACKS CREEK	07 3208 7811
221 Scott St, Bungalow CAIRNS	07 4033 7933
95 Gordon St, MACKAY	07 4957 3886
100 Sugar Rd, MAROOCHYDORE	07 5451 1155
17 Simpson St, MOUNT ISA	07 4749 0650
212 Denison St, ROCKHAMPTON	07 4927 6844
55-63 Dalrymple Rd, Garbutt TOWNSVILLE	07 4775 3033

VICTORIA
683 Sydney Rd, COBURG	03 9354 1116
166 Princes Hwy, DANDENONG	03 9792 1116
422 Sutton St, BALLARAT	03 5335 9777
27-29 Baldwin Ave, NORTH GEELONG	03 5277 1444
196 Argyle St, TRARALGON	03 5176 6666

AUSTRALIAN CAPITAL TERRITORY
87 Grimwade St, MITCHELL	02 6241 8161

SOUTH AUSTRALIA
163 Main North Rd, NAILSWORTH	08 8344 6444

WESTERN AUSTRALIA
44-46 Frobisher St, OSBORNE PARK	08 9443 4848

TASMANIA
120 Campbell St, HOBART	03 6238 0380
33 Strahan St, BURNIE	03 6430 2888

NORTHERN TERRITORY
2/498 Stuart Highway, Winnellie DARWIN	08 8984 4926

www.4wdmegastores.com.au

treadlightly! Australia
Respect the Environment with your Recreation

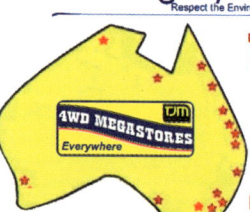

Tread lightly and look after our 4WD tracks

GROUP 4WD MEGASTORE ADMINISTRATION
02 9622 1300

MEMBERS Privilege Card

Become a member today and be eligible for "members only" specials and privileges like 5% off Driver Training Courses conducted by Great Divide Tours! It costs nothing to join!
See your local store for details

Can you spot the difference between a good and an outstanding product?
Now you can buy smarter simply by looking out for this seal of approval. Products bearing this seal are proven performers, having been field tested for toughness.

FIELD TESTED TOUGH

TJM Serious 4WD Equipment
illuminator | XGS SUSPENSION | OX RECOVERY EQUIPMENT
airtec SNORKEL | TJM CANOPIES | DBS Dual Battery System